T0145087

Communications
in Computer and Information Science 1510

More information about this series at https://link.springer.com/bookseries/7899

Vladimir Voevodin · Sergey Sobolev (Eds.)

Supercomputing

7th Russian Supercomputing Days, RuSCDays 2021
Moscow, Russia, September 27–28, 2021
Revised Selected Papers

 Springer

Editors
Vladimir Voevodin 📵
RCC MSU
Moscow, Russia

Sergey Sobolev 📵
RCC MSU
Moscow, Russia

ISSN 1865-0929   ISSN 1865-0937 (electronic)
Communications in Computer and Information Science
ISBN 978-3-030-92863-6   ISBN 978-3-030-92864-3 (eBook)
https://doi.org/10.1007/978-3-030-92864-3

This Springer imprint is published by the registered company Springer Nature Switzerland AG
The registered company address is: Gewerbestrasse 11, 6330 Cham, Switzerland

Preface

The 7th Russian Supercomputing Days Conference (RuSCDays 2021) was held during September 27–28, 2021. The conference was organized by the Supercomputing Consortium of Russian Universities and the Russian Academy of Sciences. The conference organization coordinator was the Moscow State University Research Computing Center. The conference was supported by platinum sponsors (NVIDIA, RSC, Huawei, and Intel), gold sponsors (AMD, Lenovo, and Dell Technologies in a partnership with CompTek), and silver sponsors (Hewlett Packard Enterprise and Xilinx).

Due to the COVID-19 pandemic, the conference was held in a hybrid way, combining offline and online sessions. Once again it was a challenge for the Organizing Committee to find a proper balance between online and offline parts in order to make the conference efficient and safe. Every offline session was also available online for remote attendees. The online part of the keynote session featured famous HPC specialists such as Thomas Sterling, Jack Dongarra, and many others.

RuSCDays was born in 2015 as a union of several supercomputing event series in Russia and quickly became one of the most notable Russian supercomputing international meetings. The conference caters to the interests of a wide range of representatives from science, industry, business, education, government, and academia – anyone connected to the development or the use of supercomputing technologies. The conference topics cover all aspects of supercomputing technologies: software and hardware design, solving large tasks, application of supercomputing technologies in industry, exaflops-scale computing issues, supercomputing co-design technologies, supercomputing education, and others.

All 99 papers submitted to the conference were reviewed by three referees in the first review round. During single-blind peer reviewing, the papers were evaluated according to their relevance to the conference topics, scientific contribution, presentation, approbation, and related works description. After notification of conditional acceptance, the second review round was arranged which aimed at the final polishing of papers and also at the evaluation of authors' work following revision based on the referees' comments. After the conference, the 40 best papers were carefully selected to be included in this volume.

The proceedings editors would like to thank all the conference committee members, especially the Organizing and Program Committee members as well as the referees and reviewers for their contributions. We also thank Springer for producing these high-quality proceedings of RuSCDays 2021.

October 2021

Vladimir Voevodin
Sergey Sobolev

Organization

Steering Committee

Victor A. Sadovnichiy (Chair)	Moscow State University, Russia
Vladimir B. Betelin (Co-chair)	Russian Academy of Sciences, Russia
Alexander V. Tikhonravov (Co-chair)	Moscow State University, Russia
Jack Dongarra (Co-chair)	University of Tennessee, USA
Alexey I. Borovkov	Peter the Great St. Petersburg Polytechnic University, Russia
Vladimir V. Voevodin	Moscow State University, Russia
Victor P. Gergel (Diseased)	Lobachevsky State University of Nizhni, Novgorod, Russia
Georgy S. Elizarov	NII Kvant, Russia
Vyacheslav V. Elagin	Hewlett Packard Enterprise, Russia
Elena V. Zagainova	Lobachevsky State University of Nizhni, Novgorod, Russia
Alexander K. Kim	MCST, Russia
Elena V. Kudryashova	Northern (Arctic) Federal University, Russia
Nikolay S. Mester	Intel, Russia
Eugeny I. Moiseev	Moscow State University, Russia
Alexander A. Moskovskiy	RSC Group, Russia
Vsevolod Yu. Opanasenko	T-Platforms, Russia
Gennady I. Savin	Joint Supercomputer Center, Russian, Academy of Sciences, Russia
Alexey S. Simonov	NICEVT, Russia
Victor A. Soyfer	Samara University, Russia
Leonid B. Sokolinskiy	South Ural State University, Russia
Igor A. Sokolov	Russian Academy of Sciences, Russia
Roman G. Strongin	Lobachevsky State University of Nizhni Novgorod, Russia
Alexander N. Tomilin	Institute for System Programming, Russian Academy of Sciences, Russia
Alexey R. Khokhlov	Russian Academy of Sciences, Russia
Boris N. Chetverushkin	Keldysh Institute of Applied Mathematics, Russian Academy of Sciences, Russia
Alexander L. Shestakov	South Ural State University, Russia

Program Committee

Vladimir V. Voevodin (Chair)	Moscow State University, Russia
Rashit M. Shagaliev (Co-chair)	Russian Federal Nuclear Center, Russia
Mikhail V. Yakobovskiy (Co-chair)	Keldysh Institutes of Applied Mathematics, Russian Academy of Sciences, Russia
Thomas Sterling (Co-chair)	Indiana University, USA
Sergey I. Sobolev (Scientific Secretary)	Moscow State University, Russia
Arutyun I. Avetisyan	Institute for System Programming, Russian Academy of Sciences, Russia
David Bader	Georgia Institute of Technology, USA
Pavan Balaji	Argonne National Laboratory, USA
Alexander V. Bukhanovskiy	ITMO University, Russia
Jesus Carretero	University Carlos III of Madrid, Spain
Yury V. Vasilevskiy	Keldysh Institutes of Applied Mathematics, Russian Academy of Sciences, Russia
Vasiliy E. Velikhov	National Research Center "Kurchatov Institute", Russia
Vladimir Yu. Volkonskiy	MCST, Russia
Vadim M. Volokhov	Institute of Problems of Chemical Physics, Russian Academy of Sciences, Russia
Boris M. Glinskiy	Institute of Computational Mathematics and Mathematical Geophysics, Siberian Branch of Russian Academy of Sciences, Russia
Victor M. Goloviznin	Moscow State University, Russia
Vyacheslav A. Ilyin	National Research Center "Kurchatov Institute", Russia
Vladimir P. Ilyin	Institute of Computational Mathematics and Mathematical Geophysics, Siberian Branch of Russian Academy of Sciences, Russia
Sergey I. Kabanikhin	Institute of Computational Mathematics and Mathematical Geophysics, Siberian Branch of Russian Academy of Sciences, Russia
Igor A. Kalyaev	South Federal University, Russia
Hiroaki Kobayashi	Tohoku University, Japan
Vladimir V. Korenkov	Joint Institute for Nuclear Research, Russia
Victor A. Kryukov	Keldysh Institute of Applied Mathematics, Russian Academy of Sciences, Russia
Julian Kunkel	University of Hamburg, Germany
Jesus Labarta	Barcelona Supercomputing Center, Spain
Alexey Lastovetsky	University College Dublin, Ireland
Mikhail P. Lobachev	Krylov State Research Centre, Russia

Yutong Lu — National University of Defense Technology, China

Thomas Ludwig — German Climate Computing Center, Germany

Vasili N. Lykosov (Diseased) — Institute of Numerical Mathematics, Russian, Academy of Sciences, Russia

Iosif B. Meerov — Lobachevsky State University of Nizhni Novgorod, Russia

Marek Michalewicz — University of Warsaw, Poland

Leili Mirtaheri — Kharazmi University, Iran

Alexander V. Nemukhin — Moscow State University, Russia

Happy Sithole — Centre for High Performance Computing, South Africa

Alexander V. Smirnov — Moscow State University, Russia

Hiroyuki Takizawa — Tohoku University, Japan

Michela Taufer — University of Delaware, USA

Vadim E. Turlapov — Lobachevsky State University of Nizhni Novgorod, Russia

Eugeny E. Tyrtyshnikov — Institute of Numerical Mathematics, Russian Academy of Sciences, Russia

Vladimir A. Fursov — Samara University, Russia

Thorsten Hoefler — Eidgenössische Technische Hochschule, Zürich, Switzerland

Boris M. Shabanov — Joint Supercomputer Center, Russian, Academy of Sciences, Russia

Lev N. Shchur — Higher School of Economics, Russia

Roman Wyrzykowski — Czestochowa University of Technology, Poland

Mitsuo Yokokawa — Kobe University, Japan

Industrial Committee

A. A. Aksenov (Co-chair) — Tesis, Russia

V. E. Velikhov (Co-chair) — National Research Center "Kurchatov Institute", Russia

A. V. Murashov (Co-chair) — T-Platforms, Russia

Yu. Ya. Boldyrev — Peter the Great St. Petersburg Polytechnic University, Russia

M. A. Bolshukhin — Afrikantov Experimental Design Bureau for Mechanical Engineering, Russia

R. K. Gazizov — Ufa State Aviation Technical University, Russia

M. P. Lobachev — Krylov State Research Centre, Russia

V. Ya. Modorskiy — Perm National Research Polytechnic University, Russia

A. P. Skibin — Gidropress, Russia

S. Stoyanov — T-Services, Russia

A. B. Shmelev	RSC Group, Russia
S. V. Strizhak	Hewlett-Packard, Russia

Educational Committee

V. P. Gergel (Co-chair, Diseased)	Lobachevsky State University of Nizhni Novgorod, Russia
Vl. V. Voevodin (Co-chair)	Moscow State University, Russia
L. B. Sokolinskiy (Co-chair)	South Ural State University, Russia
Yu. Ya. Boldyrev	Peter the Great St. Petersburg Polytechnic University, Russia
A. V. Bukhanovskiy	ITMO University, Russia
R. K. Gazizov	Ufa State Aviation Technical University, Russia
S. A. Ivanov	Hewlett-Packard, Russia
I. B. Meerov	Lobachevsky State University of Nizhni Novgorod, Russia
V. Ya. Modorskiy	Perm National Research Polytechnic University, Russia
S. G. Mosin	Kazan Federal University, Russia
N. N. Popova	Moscow State University, Russia
O. A. Yufryakova	Northern (Arctic) Federal University, Russia

Organizing Committee

Vl. V. Voevodin (Chair)	Moscow State University, Russia
V. P. Gergel (Co-chair, Diseased)	Lobachevsky State University of Nizhni Novgorod, Russia
B. M. Shabanov (Co-chair)	Joint Supercomputer Center, Russian Academy of Sciences, Russia
S. I. Sobolev (Scientific Secretary)	Moscow State University, Russia
A. A. Aksenov	Tesis, Russia
A. P. Antonova	Moscow State University, Russia
A. S. Antonov	Moscow State University, Russia
K. A. Barkalov	Lobachevsky State University of Nizhni Novgorod, Russia
M. R. Biktimirov	Russian Academy of Sciences, Russia
Vad. V. Voevodin	Moscow State University, Russia
T. A. Gamayunova	Moscow State University, Russia
O. A. Gorbachev	RSC Group, Russia
V. A. Grishagin	Lobachevsky State University of Nizhni Novgorod, Russia
S. A. Zhumatiy	Moscow State University, Russia
V. V. Korenkov	Joint Institute for Nuclear Research, Russia

Contents

HPC, BigData, AI: Architectures, Technologies, Tools

Distributed and Cloud Computing

Supercomputer Simulation

3D Simulation of the Reactive Transport at Pore Scale

Vadim Lisitsa$^{(\boxtimes)}$ and Tatyana Khachkova

Sobolev Institute of Mathematics SB RAS, Novosibirsk, Russia
{lisitsavv,khachkovats}@ipgg.sbras.ru

Abstract. This paper presents a numerical algorithm to simulate reactive transport at the pore scale. The aim of the research is the direct study the changes in the pore space geometry. Thus, the fluids flow and transport of chemically active components are simulated in the pore space. After that the heterogeneous reactions are used to compute the fluid-solid interaction. Evolution of the interface is implemented by the level-set methods which allows handling the changes in the pore space topology. The algorithm is based on the finite-difference method and implemented on the GP-GPU.

Keywords: Reactive transport · Digital rock physics · Porous materials · CUDA

1   Introduction

Reactive transport simulationcan can currently be used for enhanced oil recovery [9], CO_2 sequestration in carbonate reservoirs [21], biocementation [7], salt precipitation [2], injection of non-condensable gases into geothermal fields [14], etc. The main mechanism causing changes in the geometry and morphology of the pore space at the pore scale is heterogeneous reactions at the fluid-solid interface. They can lead to dissolution of the matrix or precipitation of minerals, i.e. to a change in the pore space and structure of the rock matrix at the pore scale, that ultimately affects the macroscopic properties of rocks, including porosity, hydraulic permeability [1,18,19], mechanical compliance [16], electrical resistivity [15], etc.

Predictive reactive transport modeling is currently being used to evaluate the effect of chemically active fluid filtration at the reservoir scale for CO_2 sequestration geothermal fields exploration et al. [26]. Permeability, diffusion coefficient, reaction rates and concentrations of species at the reservoir scale are determined within the grid cells and are related to porosity using some empirical relations. These relations are obtained either from the laboratory [16] or using analytical

The research was supported by the Russian Science Foundation grant no. 21-71-20003. The simulations we done using computational resources of Peter the Great Saint-Petersburg Polytechnic University Supercomputing Center (scc.spbstu.ru).

V. Voevodin and S. Sobolev (Eds.): RuSCDays 2021, CCIS 1510, pp. 3–16, 2021.
https://doi.org/10.1007/978-3-030-92864-3_1

averaging methods for relatively simple structures [6]. Typically, it is difficult to reproduce reservoir conditions (pressure, temperature, etc.) in a laboratory. In addition, experiments are time-consuming and can only be performed once for one sample. As for analytical averaging, it is applied to relatively simple models such as periodicals, and it is difficult to extend them to the structure of porous materials, and even more so to real rocks. Therefore, numerical simulation is the most appropriate choice because it combines both the flexibility of laboratory experiments and the accuracy of theoretical research. Moreover, by varying input parameters such as inlet pressure of flow rate, reaction rates, etc., it is possible to evaluate their effect on the macroscopic parameters at the reservoir scale used in reactive transport models; see [26] for an overview.

To simulate the transport of fluid flow at the pore scale, it is necessary to directly solve the Stokes or the Navier-Stokes equations. After that the solution of the convection-diffusion equation gives the distribution of active components. The most interesting stage is modeling the evolution of the fluid-solid interface [22]. There are several known approaches for this.

In methods of the first type, regular rectangular meshes are used to approximate all equations. The relative mass of the fluid is introduced for the "boundary" grid cells and changes according to an additional law, which is related to the true reaction rate [13,29]. These methods are easy to implement, but the law determining the rate of relative mass changes is empirical.

The second type, the front-tracing method, is based on an explicit interface representation. This method is usually combined with the finite-volumes with truncated cells approach [22]. However, it is quite difficult to implement if the topology and geometry of the pore space are complex, especially if the topology of the region is continuously changing.

Methods of the third type are based on implicit representations of a sharp interface, where exact boundary conditions are specified. These include methods such as the level-set [23] and the phase-field [28]. These methods make it possible to use the original relations of chemical kinetics at the pore scale. They are easy to implement even in the case of a continuous change in the topology of the pore space. Moreover, in these methods, regular rectangular grids are used to approximate the equations within the pore space, while the boundary conditions are approximated using the immersed boundary method [24,25].

In this article, we present the algorithm for modeling chemical interaction with rock based on the level-set method to account for changes in boundary position using an immersed boundary approach. The Sect. 2 is the statement of the problem and the mathematical model. The numerical algorithms used to solve the problem are presented in the 3 section. The main focus is on the approximation of boundary conditions for complex and varying pore space topology. Numerical experiments are shown in the 5 section.

2   Statement of the Problem

To simulate reactive transport at the pore scale, we assume that the interface is moving with the slowest rate, which generally determines the time scale of the problem. The fluid flow rate is also low, and it instantly stabilizes with a slight change in the geometry of the pore space. Thus, the problem can be divided into three stages: solving the Stokes equation to determine the flow in the pore space, solving the convection-diffusion equation to simulate the propagation of chemical species, and correcting the geometry of the pore space due to dissolution.

Let's consider the problem stated in a bounded domain $D \subseteq R^3$, which is a composition of the nonintersecting time-dependent subdomains $D_p(t)$ and $D_m(t)$ corresponding to the pore space and matrix, respectively. The boundary of the domain is $\partial D = S_{outlet} \cup S_{inlet} \cup S_{nf}$. Let us denote the interface between the pore space and matrix as $\bar{D}_p(t) \cap \bar{D}_m(t) = S(t)$ which is an union of the sufficiently smooth surfaces. An example of the model is shown in the Fig. 1.

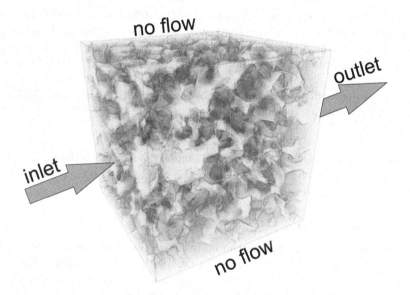

Fig. 1. The example of the model with boundary $\partial D = S_{outlet} \cup S_{inlet} \cup S_{no-flow}$.

To compute the fluid flow in the pore space $D_p(t)$ we solve the steady state Stokes equation:

$$\mu \nabla^2 \boldsymbol{u} - \nabla p = 0,$$
$$\nabla \cdot \boldsymbol{u} = 0 \tag{1}$$

with the boundary conditions:

$$\boldsymbol{u}(\boldsymbol{x}) = 0, \qquad \boldsymbol{x} \in S(t) \cup S_{nf},$$
$$p(\boldsymbol{x}) = p_{bc}(\boldsymbol{x}), \quad \boldsymbol{x} \in S_{inlet} \cup S_{outlet}, \tag{2}$$

where μ is the dynamic viscosity, $\boldsymbol{u} = (u_1, u_2, u_3)^T \in R^3$ is the velocity vector, p is the pressure, $p_{bc}(\boldsymbol{x})$ is the pressure at the inlet and outlet boundary, $\boldsymbol{x} = (x_1, x_2, x_3)^T$ is the spatial coordinates vector. We assume the slow evolution of the pore space, so that the problem can be considered in a quasi-static state; i.e., the fluid flow riches a steady-state regime for each particular pore space geometry.

Further, to simulate the propagation of chemical species in the pore space $D_p(t)$ we solve the convection-diffusion equation:

$$\frac{\partial C}{\partial t} + \nabla \cdot (\boldsymbol{u}C - D\nabla C) = 0 \tag{3}$$

with the boundary conditions:

$$\begin{array}{ll} D\frac{\partial C}{\partial n} = k_r(C - C_s), & \boldsymbol{x} \in S(t), \\ C = C_{in}, & \boldsymbol{x} \in S_{inlet}, \\ \frac{\partial C}{\partial n} = 0, & \boldsymbol{x} \in S_{outlet} \cup S_{nf}, \end{array} \tag{4}$$

where C is the reactant concentration, D is the diffusion coefficient, $\boldsymbol{n}$ is the inner (with respect to $D_p(t)$) normal vector, k_r is the reaction rate coefficient. We consider only the first order reactions, one active reactant and no reactant sources inside the computational domain; thus the right-hand side in (3) equals to zero.

Finally, to account for the evolution of the interface due to a chemical reaction, we need to satisfy the equation:

$$v_n(\boldsymbol{x},t) = \frac{K_c k}{\rho}(C - C_s), \ \boldsymbol{x} \in S(t), \tag{5}$$

where v_n is the normal component of the boundary velocity, ρ is the mass density of the matrix mineral, K_c is the stoichiometric coefficient and C_s is the reactant concentration at equilibrium.

2.1   Level-Set Method

To solve Eqs. (1) and (3) we use the finite differences, but the $S(t)$ varies and may not coincide with the grid lines. To deal with such an irregular interface geometry, we use the level-set method in which the interface $S(t)$ is implicitly defined as a constant level line of the function $\varphi(\boldsymbol{x},t)$:

$$S(t) = \{\boldsymbol{x}|\varphi(\boldsymbol{x}) = 0\}.$$

Then the subdomains D_p and D_m are defined as

$$D_p(\boldsymbol{x},t) = \{\boldsymbol{x}|\varphi(x,t) > 0\}, \ D_m(\boldsymbol{x},t) = \{\boldsymbol{x}|\varphi(x,t) < 0\}.$$

In addition, the level-set function $\varphi(\boldsymbol{x})$ is constructed as a signed distance to the interface; i.e. $\|\nabla_x \varphi(\boldsymbol{x},t)\| = 1$. This leads to a natural definition of the normal vector

$$\boldsymbol{n} = \nabla_x \varphi(\boldsymbol{x},t).$$

Using the level-set function, we can rewrite the equation for interface changes as follows [10,23]:

$$\begin{array}{l} \frac{\partial \varphi(\boldsymbol{x},t)}{\partial t} + v_n(\boldsymbol{x},t) = 0, \\ \varphi(\boldsymbol{x},0) = \varphi_0, \end{array} \tag{6}$$

where v_n is the normal velocity, defined by the Eq. (5).

3   Numerical Solution

To solve the Eqs. (1), (3) and (6) we use staggered grid finite-difference schemes. We define the grid-functions as

$$p_{i,j,k} = p(ih_1, jh_2, kh_3),$$
$$(u_1)_{i+1/2,j,k} = u_1((i + 1/2)h_1, jh_2, kh_3),$$
$$(u_2)_{i,j+1/2,k} = u_2(ih_1, (j + 1/2)h_2, kh_3),$$
$$(u_3)_{i,j,k+1/2} = u_3(ih_1, jh_2, (k + 1/2)h_3),$$
$$C_{i,j,k}^n = C(ih_1, jh_2, kh_3 n\tau),$$
$$\varphi_{i,j,k}^n = \varphi(ih_1, jh_2, kh_3, n\tau),$$

where h_1, h_2, and h_3 are the spatial steps, τ is the grid step with respect to time. The interface $S(t)$ is defined as a constant level of function φ and approximated by a piecewise linear line.

3.1   Solution of the Stokes Equation

To solve Stokes equation we consider the time-dependent problem:

$$\frac{\partial u}{\partial t} - \mu \nabla^2 u + \nabla p = 0,$$
$$\nabla \cdot u = 0 \tag{7}$$

and will seek for the stabilized solution of this problem for $t \to \infty$. This is the Navier-Stokes equation without convective term. We use the projection-type method to resolve it [5]. This approach includes the following steps:

– velocity prediction

$$\frac{[u_1]_{i+1/2,j,k}^* - [u_1]_{i+1/2,j,k}^n}{\tau} = \mu L[u_1]_{i+1/2,j,k}^n, \text{ if } \varphi_{i+1/2,j,k} > 0,$$
$$\frac{[u_2]_{i,j+1/2,k}^* - [u_2]_{i,j+1/2,k}^n}{\tau} = \mu L[u_2]_{i,j+1/2,k}^n, \text{ if } \varphi_{i,j+1/2,k} > 0, \tag{8}$$
$$\frac{[u_3]_{i,j,k+1/2}^* - [u_3]_{i,j,k+1/2}^n}{\tau} = \mu L[u_3]_{i,j,k+1/2}^n, \text{ if } \varphi_{i,j,k+1/2} > 0,$$

– pressure correction

$$\tau L[p]_{i,j,k}^{n+1} = D_1^c[u_1]_{i,j,k}^* + D_2^c[u_2]_{i,j,k}^* + D_3^c[u_3]_{i,j,k}^*, \text{ if } \varphi_{i,j,k} > 0, \tag{9}$$

– velocity correction

$$\frac{[u_1]_{i+1/2,j,k}^{n+1} - [u_1]_{i+1/2,j,k}^*}{\tau} = -D_1^c[p]_{i+1/2,j,k}^{n+1}, \text{ if } \varphi_{i+1/2,j,k} > 0,$$
$$\frac{[u_2]_{i,j+1/2,k}^{n+1} - [u_2]_{i,j+1/2,k}^*}{\tau} = -D_2^c[p]_{i,j+1/2,k}^{n+1}, \text{ if } \varphi_{i,j+1/2,k} > 0, \tag{10}$$
$$\frac{[u_3]_{i,j,k+1/2}^{n+1} - [u_3]_{i,j,k+1/2}^*}{\tau} = -D_3^c[p]_{i,j,k+1/2}^{n+1}, \text{ if } \varphi_{i,j,k+1/2} > 0,$$

where

$$L[f]_{I,J,K} = D_1^2[f]_{I,J,K} + D_2^2[f]_{I,J,K} + D_2^2[f]_{I,J,K} \tag{11}$$

is the approximation of the Laplace operator with

$$D_1^2[f]_{I,J,K} = \frac{f_{I+1,J,K} - 2f_{I,J,K} + f_{I,J,K}}{h_1^2} = \left.\frac{\partial^2 f}{\partial x_1^2}\right|_{I,J,K} + O(h_1^2), \quad (12)$$

$$D_1^c[f]_{I,J,K} = \frac{f_{I+1/1,J,K} - f_{I,J-1/2,K}}{h_1} = \left.\frac{\partial f}{\partial x_1}\right|_{I,J,K} + O(h_1^2). \quad (13)$$

In this notation, the indices I, J, K can be integer or half-integer, but i, j, k are only integers. To obtain operators that approximate derivatives with respect to another spatial direction, it is necessary to change the roles of the spatial indices. Note, that the projection methods includes solution of the Poisson equation to correct the pressure. This equation is stated with Neumann boundary conditions at the interface Γ and appropriate boundary conditions at the inlet and outlet boundary. Thus the problem is equivalent to numerical simulation of electric current in pore space, and can be efficiently solved with Krylov-type methods with suitable preconditioner [15].

Equations (1) are only valid for internal points of the domain $D_p(t)$; i.e., if all the points from a stencil belong to the pore space. Otherwise, we suggest using the immersed boundary method [12,17,20]. This approach aims to extrapolate the solution from $D_p(t)$ to the points from $D_m(t)$, which are needed for simulation. The extrapolation is based on boundary conditions set at the interface; i.e., $u = 0$ on $S(t)$; thus, the velocity vector can be considered as an odd function with respect to the interface, while p is even. Suppose we need to extrapolate the solution to the point $((x_1)_I, (x_2)_J, (x_3)_K)$. The distance from this point to the interface is determined by the level-set function $\varphi_{I,J,K}$ and the normal direction to the interface is $\boldsymbol{n} = \nabla_x \varphi(\boldsymbol{x})|_{I,J,K}$. Thus, the projection of the point onto the interface is

$$((x_1)_c, (x_2)_c, (x_3)_c) = ((x_1)_I, (x_2)_J, (x_3)_K) + \varphi_{I,J,K}\boldsymbol{n},$$

the orthogonal reflection has the coordinates

$$((x_1)_n, (x_2)_n, (x_3)_n) = 2((x_1)_I, (x_2)_J, (x_3)_K) + \varphi_{I,J,K}\boldsymbol{n},$$

and more

$$\boldsymbol{u}_{I,J,K} = -\boldsymbol{u}((x_1)_n, (x_2)_n, (x_3)_n) + O(\varphi_{I,J,K}^2).$$

The standard way to compute $\boldsymbol{u}((x_1)_n, (x_2)_n, (x_3)_n)$ is to apply bilinear interpolation using the four nearest grid points from the regular grid. However, when considering the pore space, the four nearest points do not necessarily belong to the pore space D_p. Therefore, to construct the interpolation, we use all available points. We select eight regular points belonging to the pore space, as well as a point at the interface $((x_1)_c, (x_2)_c, (x_3)_c)$. If we use no more than nine points, then we can construct an interpolation of the unknown function with the second-order of accuracy. In case there are less than four points available, we can only achieve the first order of accuracy. We use interpolation weights that are proportional to the distances from the points in question to the point $((x_1)_n, (x_2)_n, (x_3)_n)$.

3.2 Solving the Convection-Diffusion Equation

To approximate the convection-diffusion equation, the first-order scheme is used:

$$\frac{C_{i,j,k}^{n+1}-C_{i,j,k}^n}{\tau} + D_1^1[u_1C]_{i,j,k}^n + D_2^1[u_2C]_{i,j,k}^n + D_3^1[u_3C]_{i,j,k}^n - DL[C]_{i,j,k}^n = 0,$$
$$\varphi_{i,j,k} > 0,$$

(14)

where

$$D_1^1[u_1C]_{i,j,k}^n = \frac{F_{i+1/2,j,k}-F_{i_1-1/2,j,k}}{h},$$

$$F_{i+1/2,j,k} = \begin{cases} (u_1)_{i+1/2,j,k}C_{i+1,j,k}, & (u_1)_{i+1/2,j,k} < 0 \\ (u_1)_{i+1/2,j,k}C_{i,j,k}, & (u_1)_{i+1/2,j,k} > 0 \end{cases}$$

(15)

To obtain operators that approximate derivatives to another spatial direction, it's used the spatial indices' permutation. The operator $D[f]_{I,J,K}$ is introduced above in the Eq. (11). Note that the spatial discretization is governed by the pore space geometry, thus the grid steps are small and first-order upwind scheme is suitable for approximation of the convection term.

The most difficult part of the approximation is the application of boundary conditions at the interface $S(t)$. The concentration satisfies Robin boundary conditions at $S(t)$, which can be regarded as a linear combination of the Dirichlet and Neumann conditions:

$$D\nabla C \cdot n + k_r C = k_r C_s.$$

We suppose that the point $((x_1)_i, (x_2)_j, (x_2)_k) \in D_m$ belongs to a stencil centered in D_p. As before, an extrapolation is required and in our case $((x_1)_n, (x_2)_n, (x_3)_n)$ is the orthogonal reflection of the immersed point $((x_1)_i, (x_2)_j, (x_3)_k)$ over the interface. The boundary condition is approximated as

$$D\frac{C((x_1)_n, (x_2)_n, (x_3)_n) + C_{i,j,k}}{2} + k_r \frac{C((x_1)_n, (x_2)_n, (x_3)_n) - C_{i,j,k}}{2\varphi_{i,j,k}} = k_r C_s,$$

where $C((x_1)_n, (x_2)_n, (x_3)_n)$ is interpolated with using available points in the domain $D_p(t)$.

3.3 Movement of the Interface

We need to solve the Eq. (6) to simulate the movement of the interface, and we use the finite difference method:

$$\frac{\varphi_{i,j,k}^{n+1}-\varphi_{i,j,k}^n}{\tau} = -(v_n)_{i,j,k}^n,$$

(16)

where $(v_n)_{i,j,k}^n$ is the rate of the interface movement.

Equation (6) is defined everywhere in D, so its right-hand side must be defined accordingly. However, function $v_n(x)$ is only defined at S and must be continued inside the subdomains D_p and D_m. According to [23], the rate v_n can be prolongated inside the subdomains as a constant along the normal direction to the interface; i.e., it is necessary to calculate the steady-state solution of the following equation:

$$\frac{\partial q}{\partial t} + sign(\varphi) \left(\frac{\nabla \varphi}{|\nabla \varphi|} \cdot \nabla q \right) = 0,$$
$$q(\boldsymbol{x}, 0) = \tilde{v}_n(\boldsymbol{x}, t_0),$$

(17)

where $\tilde{v}_n$ are initial conditions which coincide with the velocity at the interface and are trivial elsewhere.

For approximation of the gradient of φ we use the central differences, while for approximation of the derivatives of q the upwind scheme is used [8]. Note, that an accurate solution of Eq. (17) is only needed in a vicinity of the interface; i.e., inside the strip $D_s = \{\boldsymbol{x} : |\varphi(\boldsymbol{x})| \leq 2\sqrt{h_1^2 + h_2^2 + h_3^2}\}$. Thus, to obtain an accurate solution only a few iterations are sufficient there. An additional redistancing is then applied to ensure that φ is the signed distance [27].

4   Implementation of the Algorithm

All main steps of the algorithm are executed by GPU minimizing the host-to-device and device-to-host memory transfer. The preliminary step of algorithm is implemented on CPU and it includes reading the input data and the model, provided as a segmented CT-scan of a rock sample [3,4,11], memory allocation for the level-set function, solution components, and auxiliary variables for BiCGStab and preconditionner. Construction of the level-set function, movement of the interface (16), extrapolation and redistancing the level-set (17), prediction and correction of the fluid velocity field (8), (10), and solving the convection-diffusion Eq. (14) are based on the explicit finite difference schemes. Thus, the stencil computations are used and they are easy to apply on GPU using CUDA technology.

The most complicated part of the algorithm is the solution of the Poisson equation. In particular, we suggest using the BiCGStab with preconditioning to solve it. In this, case the matrix-vector multiplication is implemented by the stencil computations. We use the solution of the Poisson equation with constant coefficients as the preconditionner. To construct it we apply FFT transform along x_2 and x_3 direction with the solution of the set of 1D Posiion equations for different spectral parameters $k_2^2 + k_3^2$. We provide the pseudo-code to solve the Poisson equation in Algorithm 1. Note that matrix-vector multiplication is implemented implicitly; i.e., the matrix is not stored in memory but implemented as a function. 2D FFT and inverse FFT are implemented using qFFT library and applied successively for all layers along x_1 direction.

Algorithm 1: Matrix-vector multiplication function

---

for *all* (i, j, k) *in parallel* **do**
    compute matrix-vector multiplication following Eq. 9
    $g(x_1, x_2, x_3) = Lp(x_1, x_2, x_3)$
end for
for *all i successively* **do**
    Apply 2D qFFT
    $\hat{g}(x_1, k_2, k_3) = \mathcal{F}_{2,3}[g(x_1, x_2, x_3)]$
end for
for *all* (k_2, k_3) *in parallel* **do**
    Solve 1D equation for homogeneous media
    $\hat{p}(x_1, k_2, k_3) = L_0^{-1}\hat{g}(x_1, k_2, k_3)$
end for
for *all i successively* **do**
    Apply 2D inverse qFFT
    $p(x_1, x_2, x_3) = \mathcal{F}_{2,3}^{-1}[\hat{p}(x_1, k_2, k_3)]$
end for
return $p(x_1, x_2, x_3)$

---

5 Numerical Experiments

The applicability of the algorithm to realistic rock models is demonstrated by the example of CT-scans of an aquifer in the Middle East carbonate samples presented in [1]. In this work, four different samples were subjected to CO_2 saturation, which led to the dissolution of the carbonate matrix. The differences between the samples were the structure of the original pore space and the saturation flow rate. During the saturation process, to follow the evolution of the pore space, ten CT-scans were acquired for each sample and provided in [1]. In our work, we use a sample called AH from the set. To simulate the reactive transport in the carbonate, we subtract a subvolume of 200^3 voxels. Since the CT-scans resolution is 5.2 μm per voxel, the size of the considered subsamples is about one mm^3.

The properties of the solid matrix and the fluid are taken from [1]. So the core matrix is calcite with mass density $\rho = 2710$ kg/m^3, and stoichiometric coefficient of the reaction equal to one; i.e., $K = 1$. The fluid is the reservoir water under the assumption that changes in the reactant concentration don't affect the physical properties of the fluid. Thus, the dynamic viscosity is fixed $\mu = 0.00028$ Pa·s. The diffusion coefficient is equal to $7.5 \cdot 10^{-9}$ m^2/s, reaction rate is $k_r = 0.08$, the pressure drop is 4 Pa. The active component is the cations H^+ with an equilibrium concentration $pH = 7$, while the acidity at the inlet is $pH = 3$ in accordance with laboratory experiments presented in [16].

In Fig. 2 we represent the pore space and the flow stream-lines at three different time instants. The main flow path is seen to form, resulting in a creation of the wormhole. To illustrate the effect of changes in the pore space on the hydrodynamical properties of the rock, we present the plots of porosity, permeability and tortuosity as the functions of model time (Fig. 3). Both porosity and permeability is increasing over time, but a relatively low increase in porosity leads to

Fig. 2. Pore space representation (left) and stream-lines (right) at different time instants for the simulation of carbonate dissolution.

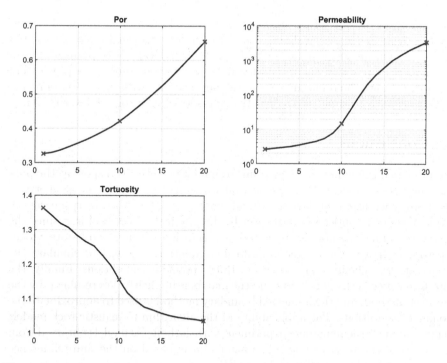

Fig. 3. Dependence of the porosity (top left), permeability (top right), and trotuosity (bottom) on the model time. Red markers correspond to instants from Fig. 2. (Color figure online)

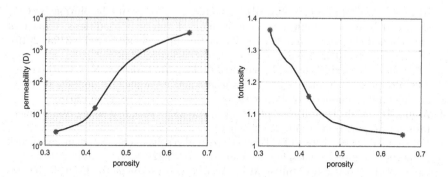

Fig. 4. Cross-plots of permeability in dependence on porosity (left) and tortuosity in dependence on porosity (right). Red markers correspond to instants from Fig. 2. (Color figure online)

the significant increase of permeability due to the formation of wormholes. And the tortuosity is decreasing slightly, since the preferred flow path already existed in the original model (top picture in Fig. 2.) The cross-plots of permeability in dependence on porosity, and tortuosity in dependence on porosity are provided in Fig. (4), it shows the rapid increase of the permeability with increasing porosity.

It took 5.3 h to simulate the reactive transport by GeForce RTX 2080 Ti.

6   Conclusions

We presented the numerical algorithm to simulate reactive transport at the pore scale in a 3D statement. We suppose that with small changes in the geometry of the pore space the fluid flow gets steady instantly. Thus, the algorithm can be implemented by splitting with respect to the physical processes. First, since the flow rate is low, the flow is simulated as a solution to the steady state Stokes equation. Further, the convection-diffusion equation is solved to simulate the propagation of chemical species using Robin boundary conditions. Finally, the interface between the pore space and the matrix is implicitly determined by the level-set method, and the immersed boundary method is used to approximate the boundary conditions. The applicability of the algorithm to realistic rock models is illustrated by the numerical experiment with carbonates models obtained from CT-scans of the rock samples. The algorithm is based on the finite-difference method and implemented on the GP-GPU.

References

1. Al-Khulaifi, Y., Lin, Q., Blunt, M.J., Bijeljic, B.: Pore-scale dissolution by CO_2 saturated brine in a multimineral carbonate at reservoir conditions: impact of physical and chemical heterogeneity. Water Resour. Res. **55**(4), 3171–3193 (2019). https://doi.org/10.5285/52b08e7f-9fba-40a1-b0b5-dda9a3c83be2
2. Alizadeh, A.H., Akbarabadi, M., Barsotti, E., Piri, M., Fishman, N., Nagarajan, N.: Salt precipitation in ultratight porous media and its impact on pore connectivity and hydraulic conductivity. Water Resour. Res. **54**(4), 2768–2780 (2018)
3. Andra, H., et al.: Digital rock physics benchmarks - part I: imaging and segmentation. Comput. Geosci. **50**, 25–32 (2013)
4. Bazaikin, Y., et al.: Effect of CT image size and resolution on the accuracy of rock property estimates. J. Geophys. Res. Solid Earth **122**(5), 3635–3647 (2017)
5. Brown, D.L., Cortez, R., Minion, M.L.: Accurate projection methods for the incompressible Navier-Stokes equations. J. Comput. Phys. **168**(2), 464–499 (2001)
6. Costa, T.B., Kennedy, K., Peszynska, M.: Hybrid three-scale model for evolving pore-scale geometries. Comput. Geosci. **22**(3), 925–950 (2018). https://doi.org/10.1007/s10596-018-9733-9
7. Dadda, A., et al.: Characterization of microstructural and physical properties changes in biocemented sand using 3D x-ray microtomography. Acta Geotechnica **12**(5), 955–970 (2017)
8. Fedkiw, R.P., Aslam, T., Merriman, B., Osher, S.: A non-oscillatory Eulerian approach to interfaces in multimaterial flows (the ghost fluid method). J. Comput. Phys. **152**(2), 457–492 (1999)

9. Ghommem, M., Zhao, W., Dyer, S., Qiu, X., Brady, D.: Carbonate acidizing: modeling, analysis, and characterization of wormhole formation and propagation. J. Petrol. Sci. Eng. **131**, 18–33 (2015)

10. Gibou, F., Fedkiw, R., Osher, S.: A review of level-set methods and some recent applications. J. Comput. Phys. **353**, 82–109 (2018)

11. Iassonov, P., Gebrenegus, T., Tuller, M.: Segmentation of x-ray computed tomography images of porous materials: a crucial step for characterization and quantitative analysis of pore structures. Water Resour. Res. **45**(9), W09415 (2009)

12. Johansen, H., Colella, P.: A cartesian grid embedded boundary method for Poisson's equation on irregular domains. J. Comput. Phys. **147**(1), 60–85 (1998)

13. Kang, Q., Chen, L., Valocchi, A.J., Viswanathan, H.S.: Pore-scale study of dissolution-induced changes in permeability and porosity of porous media. J. Hydrol. **517**, 1049–1055 (2014)

14. Kaya, E., Zarrouk, S.J.: Reinjection of greenhouse gases into geothermal reservoirs. Int. J. Greenhouse Gas Control **67**, 111–129 (2017)

15. Khachkova, T., Lisitsa, V., Reshetova, G., Tcheverda, V.: GPU-based algorithm for evaluating the electrical resistivity of digital rocks. Comput. Math. Appl. **82**, 200–211 (2021)

16. Lebedev, M., Zhang, Y., Sarmadivaleh, M., Barifcani, A., Al-Khdheeawi, E., Iglauer, S.: Carbon geosequestration in limestone: Pore-scale dissolution and geomechanical weakening. Int. J. Greenhouse Gas Control **66**, 106–119 (2017)

17. Li, X., Huang, H., Meakin, P.: Level set simulation of coupled advection-diffusion and pore structure evolution due to mineral precipitation in porous media. Water Resour. Res. **44**(12), W12407 (2008)

18. Lisitsa, V., Bazaikin, Y., Khachkova, T.: Computational topology-based characterization of pore space changes due to chemical dissolution of rocks. Appl. Math. Model. **88**, 21–37 (2020). https://doi.org/10.1016/j.apm.2020.06.037

19. Lisitsa, V., Khachkova, T.: Numerical simulation of the reactive transport at the pore scale. In: Gervasi, O., et al. (eds.) ICCSA 2020. LNCS, vol. 12249, pp. 123–134. Springer, Cham (2020). https://doi.org/10.1007/978-3-030-58799-4_9

20. Luo, K., Zhuang, Z., Fan, J., Haugen, N.E.L.: A ghost-cell immersed boundary method for simulations of heat transfer in compressible flows under different boundary conditions. Int. J. Heat Mass Transfer **92**, 708–717 (2016)

21. Miller, K., Vanorio, T., Keehm, Y.: Evolution of permeability and microstructure of tight carbonates due to numerical simulation of calcite dissolution. J. Geophys. Res. Solid Earth **122**(6), 4460–4474 (2017)

22. Molins, S., et al.: Pore-scale controls on calcite dissolution rates from flow-through laboratory and numerical experiments. Environ. Sci. Technol. **48**(13), 7453–7460 (2014)

23. Osher, S., Fedkiw, R.P.: Level set methods: an overview and some recent results. J. Comput. Phys. **169**(2), 463–502 (2001)

24. Peskin, C.S.: Flow patterns around heart valves: a numerical method. J. Comput. Phys. **10**, 252–271 (1972)

25. Sotiropoulos, F., Yang, X.: Immersed boundary methods for simulating fluid-structure interaction. Progress Aerosp. Sci. **65**, 1–21 (2014)

26. Steefel, C.I., et al.: Reactive transport codes for subsurface environmental simulation. Comput. Geosci. **19**(3), 445–478 (2014). https://doi.org/10.1007/s10596-014-9443-x

27. Sussman, M., Fatemi, E.: An efficient, interface-preserving level set redistancing algorithm and its application to interfacial incompressible fluid flow. SIAM J. Sci. Comput. **20**(4), 1165–1191 (1999)

28. Xu, Z., Meakin, P.: Phase-field modeling of solute precipitation and dissolution. J. Chem. Phys. **129**(1), 014705 (2008)
29. Yoon, H., Valocchi, A.J., Werth, C.J., Dewers, T.: Pore-scale simulation of mixing-induced calcium carbonate precipitation and dissolution in a microfluidic pore network. Water Resour. Res. **48**(2), W02524 (2012)

Application of Docking and Quantum Chemistry to the Search for Inhibitors of SARS-CoV-2 Main Protease

Anna Tashchilova[1,2], Alexey Sulimov[1,2], Ivan Ilin[1,2], Danil Kutov[1,2], and Vladimir Sulimov[1,2(✉)]

[1] Dimonta, Ltd., Moscow 117186, Russia
info@dimonta.com
[2] Research Computer Center, Lomonosov Moscow State University, Moscow 119992, Russia

Abstract. Docking and quantum-chemical molecular modeling methods have been applied to search inhibitors of the main protease of SARS-CoV-2, the coronavirus responsible for the COVID-19 pandemic. More than 14 thousand organic compounds from the commercially available Maybridge database were docked into the active site of main protease using the SOL docking program, and more than 100 ligands with the most negative SOL scores were selected for further processing. For all these top scored ligands, the enthalpy of protein-ligand binding was calculated using the PM7 semiempirical quantum-chemical method with the COSMO implicit solvent model. When calculating the enthalpy of protein-ligand binding, a best docked ligand pose was used as the initial conformation for local energy optimization by the PM7 method with varying the positions of all ligand atoms. In the optimized ligand pose, the energy of the protein-ligand complex was recalculated with the COSMO solvent for fixed positions of all atoms of the system. For further experimental testing, 18 ligands were selected with the following criteria: good SOL scores, the most negative binding enthalpies, favorable protein-ligand interactions inferred from visual inspection of the docking poses and chemical diversity of the ligands. The selected ligands are planned to be measured *in vitro* for their inhibition of the main protease SARS-CoV-2. In the case of experimental confirmation of their inhibitory activity, these compounds can be used to further optimize their chemical structure in order to obtain a lead compound – the basis for new direct-acting antiviral drugs against the SARS-CoV-2 coronavirus.

Keywords: Drug discovery · Docking · Quantum chemistry · Maybridge · Inhibitors · Mpro · SARS-CoV-2 · COVID-19 · CADD

1 Introduction

The outbreak of the COVID-19 disease pandemic caused by the SARS-CoV-2 coronavirus has led to numerous searches for direct inhibitors of key coronavirus target proteins based on structural computer modeling with the hope of a quick discovery of a direct-acting antiviral drug. Currently, there is only one direct-acting agent against

© Springer Nature Switzerland AG 2021
V. Voevodin and S. Sobolev (Eds.): RuSCDays 2021, CCIS 1510, pp. 17–28, 2021.
https://doi.org/10.1007/978-3-030-92864-3_2

SARS-CoV-2 approved by FDA, *Remdesivir*, which blocks viral polymerase [1], but its clinical efficacy is still unclear. So, the search for new medications and starting points for the development of new drugs against SARS-CoV-2 is still of great importance.

One strategy for finding an antiviral drug is repurposing drugs among existing approved drugs. This strategy has several advantages such as accelerated early drug development and simplified preclinical and clinical studies.

Docking is the most widespread method of computer modeling in the search for inhibitors [2]. There are several therapeutic target-proteins of the SARS-CoV-2 coronavirus, and the main protease is one of them [3]. Its structure was quickly determined and a computer aided structural based drug design methodology could be used to search for its inhibitors [4].

In a study [5], 2000 clinically approved drugs were virtually tested against M^{pro} using a consensus score of four docking protocols: AutoDock Vina [6], two AutoDock 4.2 and Glide [7, 8] protocols. Additional analysis was applied to the ligands with the best docking scores, including molecular dynamics simulation. The M^{pro} model was built on the basis of the Protein Data Bank complex (PDB ID: 5R82) [9]. As a result, four inhibitors with experimentally measured inhibitory activity $IC_{50} < 20$ μM were identified: *Manidipine* (hypertension), *Boceprevir* (hepatitis C), *Lercanidipine* (hypertension), and *Bedaquiline* (tuberculosis).

The results of virtual screening of all approved drugs from the ZINC database [10] were presented in [2]. Twenty compounds were selected for the experimental testing on the basis of their most negative docking scores obtained by the SOL docking program [11, 12] and most negative enthalpy of protein-ligand binding calculated by a quantum-chemical semiempirical method.

In [13], virtual screening of about 8 thousand organic compounds was carried out using the MOE platform [14], among which there were 16 antiviral drugs acting on viral proteases, and in-house database of natural and synthetic molecules. A model of the main protease SARS-CoV-2 was built on the basis of the crystal structure of this protein with a covalent inhibitor (PDB ID: 6LU7). As a result of docking, 700 best candidates were selected, and then their bound conformations were studied both visually and with using bioinformatics methods. As a result, 2 compounds from in-house chemical library and 3 approved drugs were accepted as promising candidates for inhibition of the main protease of SARS-CoV-2: *Darunavir*, *Saquinavir* and *Remdesivir*. *Darunavir* and *Saquinavir* are HIV protease inhibitors, and the *Remdesivir* metabolite, as now known, interferes with the RNA polymerase of SARS-CoV-2. However, there is no experimental *in vitro* confirmation of inhibitory activity of these compounds against the main protease (M^{pro}) of SARS-CoV-2.

In [15], a high-throughput docking study of 1 485 144 bioactive molecules (13 308 of them were medicinal compounds), taken from the ChEMBL26 database, was performed. The target was the main protease SARS-CoV-2, and its model was based on the structure with PDB ID: 6Y2G. The docking was carried out in two stages: first, 27 561 best ligands were selected using the fast rDock program [16], and then these ligands were docked more accurately using the AutoDock Vina docking program. As a result, 29 of the best compounds were selected, among which there was one approved drug (*Eszopiclone*). Experimental confirmation of the inhibition of the SARS-CoV-2 main protease by selected compounds has not been reported.

In [17], for virtual screening of two databases containing molecules of approved drugs (eDrug3D and Reaxys-marketed), three docking programs were used at once: Glide, FRED [18, 19], and AutoDock Vina. The main protease SARS-CoV-2 with PDB ID: 6LU7 was used to construct the protein model. Each of these three programs had its own threshold for assessing the energy of protein-ligand binding, from which the molecule was considered promising as an inhibitor. The molecule was selected as the putative inhibitor based on the overall scoring of these docking programs. As a result, 7 compounds were selected as promising candidates for the inhibition of the the SARS-CoV-2 main protease. *In vitro* experiments were carried out only for two of seven candidates. The tested compounds showed inhibition of the SARS-CoV-2 main protease, but it was very weak: the activity of the protein was suppressed by only a few percent at a concentration of inhibitors of 50 μM.

Virtual screening against the main protease M^{pro} (PDB ID: 6Y2F) of the ZINC and DrugBank databases in [20] made it possible to identify three compounds: cobicistat, cangrelor, and denufosol. Docking was carried out with the programs SwissDock [21, 22], PatchDock and FireDock. All of these drugs have been tested *in vitro*. *Cobicistat*, which is used to treat HIV infection, showed the best IC_{50} value of 6.7 μM. The first clinical trial of cobicistat against COVID-19 in the United States (NCT04252274) is ongoing.

Two new covalent nanomolar inhibitors of SARS-CoV-2 M^{pro} that suppress the replication of coronavirus in cell culture with an effective concentration EC_{50} of 0.53 and 0.72 μM were published in the work [23].

Currently, there are a few potent covalent inhibitors of SARS-CoV-2 M^{pro} [24]. Non-covalent inhibitors are the minority among reported agents against M^{pro}. They are originated from a plenty of repurposing research program and mostly possess weak activity. Here we consider a few examples. *Tideglusib* [25] is naphthalene-containing compound with thiadiazolidine-3,5-dione as a scaffold. *Emedastine* [26] is an anti-histamine drug consisting of a diazepane ring and benzimidazole. Compound X77 is an only non-covalent drug-like inhibitor crystallized with M^{pro}. It possesses X-like shape with imidazole, iPr-benzene, pyridine and cyclohexene as structural moieties. *Carprofen* [17] is a non-steroidal anti-inflammatory drug used now in veterinary which belongs to di-substituted carbazoles. *Celecoxib* is also a non-steroidal anti-inflammatory agent based on pyrazole scaffold substituted with methylbenzene and benzenesulfonamide. *Quercetin* [27] and *Baicalein* [28] both belong to a group of flavonoids and contain a flavone fragment substituted with a few hydroxyl groups [29]. The complex of the SARS-CoV-2 M^{pro} with *Baicalein* was recently resolved and deposited in PDB [30]. So, there is an urgent need for novel and more potent non-covalent reversible inhibitors of SARS-CoV-2 M^{pro} that can become a lead compound for new direct-acting antiviral drugs against SARS-CoV-2.

In this work, molecular modeling methods are used to identify direct inhibitors of the main protease (M^{pro} or $3CL^{pro}$) of the coronavirus SARS-CoV-2 among compounds from HitFinder chemical library from the Maybridge Screening Collection [31]. The main protease plays a key role in the replication of the virus in human cells, so blocking its work should stop the viral replication and stop the development of

COVID-19. On the basis of modeling, compounds that tightly bind to the active center of the main protease of the coronavirus and thereby block the work of its catalytic center were selected. These compounds are the most promising candidates for experimental testing of their ability to inhibit M^{pro} of the SARS-CoV-2 coronavirus. If their inhibitory activity is confirmed in experiments, they can become novel starting points for the development of a new direct-acting antiviral drug against SARS-CoV-2.

2   Materials and Methods

Virtual screening of a ligand database using docking requires some up-front work. This work includes building a complete atomistic 3D model of the protein and preparing atomistic 3D models for each ligand from the database. These are standard, but very important jobs, and the quality of the virtual screening largely depends on the correctness of the chosen techniques and software. For example, most of the protein structure in the Protein Data Bank do not contain coordinates of hydrogen atoms, because these atoms are too light and move to fast to determine their positions by X-ray structural methods. Therefore, it is necessary to correctly add several thousand hydrogen atoms to the protein structure. This cannot be done by hand, and special programs are usually used for this. The addition of hydrogen atoms must be made with regard to the pH of the environment, since some molecular groups can change their charge states depending on the pH value. The resulting model of the target protein is highly dependent on the software used to add hydrogen atoms, and in turn, the docking results may depend on the correct operation of this software [32].

2.1   Protein Model

At the beginning of this work, the Protein Data Bank contained only a few structures of the SARS-CoV-2 M^{pro}. To create a model, a high-quality structure (PDB ID: 6W63) of M^{pro} co-crystallized with a non-covalent inhibitor was taken. This structure had a good resolution <2.2 Å and did not contain missing amino acid residues and/or atoms. The non-covalent drug-like inhibitor (X77) induced the active site of the protein when binding to open an extra pocket by rotating the MET49 side chain. Some existing complexes of the SARS-CoV-2 M^{pro} contain inhibitors that are too small to cause this subpocket to open. To prepare the protein, all atoms not belonging to the protein, including ions and water molecules, were removed from the PDB-structure, then hydrogen atoms were added using the APLITE [32] program.

To test the prepared protein model, as well as the ability of the SOL docking program to reproduce the crystallized ligand position, native docking was performed. For this, the native ligand, X77, was protonated by the Avogadro program at pH = 7.4 [33]. Docking of the flexible native ligand, which contains 7 torsions, into the active site of the protein was successful with the RMSD = 1.31 Å between the docked and crystallized poses of the native ligand. The SOL score of X77 was equal to −6.27 kcal/mol. Based on this value, the threshold for selection of compounds after virtual screening by the SOL program was determined. The threshold separates inhibitors from inactive compounds.

In terms of druggability, the active site of the SARS-CoV-2 M^{pro} consists of four distinct pockets (see Fig. 1). The S1 pocket binds to Gln in the native substrate and thereby possesses affinity to bioisosteres of this residue. A hydrogen bond between the ligand acceptor and His163 is a possible interaction for this pocket. The S2 pocket consists of hydrophobic residues and engages with Leu from the native substrate. The S4 pocket has a similar hydrophobic nature. It binds to Ala from the substrate. The histidine from the catalytic dyad, His41, lies near the S1' pocket and gives it an affinity to aromatic rings which interact through pi-stacking with this residue [25].

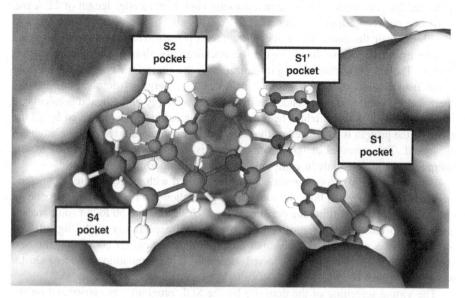

Fig. 1. The crystallized complex SARS-CoV-2 M^{pro} PDB ID 6W63 with inhibitor X77.

2.2 Preparing the Database for Virtual Screening

Compounds from the Maybridge Screening Collection [31], HitFinder library were used for virtual screening. The database was represented by 14 400 two-dimensional molecular structures corresponding to Lipinski's drug-likeness rules. In this work, the numbering of compounds corresponds to the internal numbering system present in HitFinder database. Ligands from the database were protonated at pH = 7.4 using the ChemAxon Protonation [34] module. 2D ligand structures were converted into 3D-structures by the ChemAxon Generate3D module, resulting in 30 922 different molecular structures. The increase in the number of molecular structures is mainly due to the use of several low-energy conformations of non-aromatic rings and macrocycles present in molecules. The SOL program changes the conformation of the ligand during docking varying only its internal degrees of rotation (torsions). Thus, each conformation of a non-aromatic ring or macrocycle must be docked by SOL as a separate ligand.

2.3   SOL Docking Program

The SOL [11, 12] program is based on the classical docking paradigm – the best position of the ligand must be near the global minimum of the energy of the protein-ligand complex. The SOL program uses a preliminary calculated grid of potentials describing interactions of a probe ligand atom with a rigid protein. The potentials include Coulomb and Van der Waals interactions described by the MMFF94 force field [35], and potentials of the desolvation energy, calculated within the framework of a simplified form of the Generalized Born implicit solvent model. These potentials are calculated for each node of the grid in a docking cube with an edge length of 22 Å and a distance between adjacent nodes of 0.22 Å. This size of the docking cube is large enough to cover the entire active site of the target protein with a noticeable surplus.

The ligand can move freely inside the docking cube during global optimization process. The target function during optimization is the sum of the energy of the ligand in the field created by protein atoms, including the energy of desolvation, and the internal stress energy of the ligand. The internal stress energy of the ligand is calculated using the MMFF94 force field. The energy of the ligand in the field created by all the atoms of the protein is calculated as the sum of the grid potentials over all the atoms of the ligand. The potential at the position of a given ligand atom is obtained by the interpolating the potentials in eight neighbouring grid nodes.

For global optimization, a genetic algorithm is used with the following parameters: the population size is 30 000, the number of generations is 1 000. Fifty independent runs of the genetic algorithm are performed for each ligand, and 50 found solutions are grouped into clusters. An indicator of the successful exploration of the ligand conformational space is the relatively high population of the cluster containing the best energy solution. Docking was considered successful if the population of the first cluster was not less than 10.

The virtual screening of the database by the SOL program was carried out on the Lomonosov-2 supercomputer [36] of Lomonosov Moscow State University. For high-throughput screening, thousands of computational cores were used to perform thousands of docking tasks, one ligand per one core. Depending on the size and number of ligand torsions, docking of one ligand on one core takes from one to several hours. For a given ligand, the value of the SOL scoring function depends on the target protein. The reasonable range of the scoring function is assessed based on docking results for molecules with proven activity against a given target protein. The successful application of the SOL docking program for the development of new inhibitors has been confirmed by *in vitro* experiments for various target proteins: thrombin [37], urokinase (uPA) [38, 39], and coagulation factors Xa and XIa [40–42]. In addition, SOL docking accuracy was one of the best for two of the three target proteins in the 2011–2012 CSAR docking competition, which also included other docking programs such as Gold, AutoDock, AutoDock Vina, ICMVLS, and Glide [12].

2.4   Protein-Ligand Binding Enthalpy

For the best compounds selected after docking with the SOL program, the enthalpy of protein-ligand binding was calculated using the relatively new quantum-chemical semiempirical PM7 method [43] taking into account the solvent effects within the COSMO implicit solvent model [44, 45]. The PM7 method allows one to perform quantum-chemical calculations at the level of accuracy of density functional theory (DFT) methods [46, 47] with a correct description of both dispersion interactions and the formation of hydrogen and halogen bonds, which is important for modeling protein-ligand binding. The COSMO continuum model is widely used long time in quantum-chemical calculations to describe the polar interactions of molecules with water.

MOPAC [48] implements the above-described PM7 and COSMO methods, as well as the MOZYME [49] module, which allows fast quantum-chemical calculations of proteins and protein-ligand complexes using the localized molecular orbital method. In this work, the enthalpy of binding ΔH_{bind} for the best ligands was calculated as follows:

$$\Delta H_{bind} = H(PL) - H(P) - H(L) \tag{1}$$

where $H(PL), H(P), H(L)$ – are the enthalpy of formation of the protein-ligand complex, unbound protein and unbound ligand, respectively. The more negative the value of the enthalpy of binding ΔH_{bind}, the more negative the free energy of binding and the higher the corresponding binding affinity of the ligand to the protein.

$H(PL)$ is calculated as follows: the best pose of the docked ligand in the protein-ligand complex undergoes the local optimization by the L-BFGS method implemented in MOPAC. This optimization is performed using PM7 *in vacuo* and the final enthalpy of complex formation is obtained from a single self-consistent field (1SCF) calculation with the PM7 method and the COSMO solvent model.

To find a global minimum of the unbound ligand $H(L)$, all conformations of macrocycles and non-aromatic rings were minimized in vacuo with PM7, and then their enthalpies of formation were recalculated with 1SCF and the solvent model COSMO. The best enthalpy of formation found was used for the calculation of binding enthalpy as the $H(L)$ term in formula (1). The enthalpy of formation of unbound protein $H(P)$ is calculated by the PM7+COSMO method without geometry optimization.

3   Results

Virtual screening of the prepared database revealed 100 ligands with SOL scores more negative than −6.30 kcal/mol. This SOL score for compound selection was chosen based on the score −6.27 kcal/mol of the native ligand docked into the corresponding protein of the same 6W63 complex. All selected virtual hits are subjected to quantum-chemical post-processing PM7+COSMO to calculate their binding enthalpies.

Taking into account the calculated values of the enthalpy of protein-ligand binding, the list of inhibitor candidates was narrowed. The enthalpy of binding of the native ligand was −58.46 kcal/mol, but among all 100 compounds selected after docking, there was not a single ligand with such a negative binding enthalpy. So, we selected compounds with best SOL scores and most negative values of the protein-ligand binding enthalpy. Visual inspection of ligand poses in the active site of SARS-CoV-2 M^{pro} has also been used to filter out ligands with wrong poses. We retained only those ligands that visually bind near the catalytic dyad and thereby have a potential to block its work. Some of compounds showed few interactions with protein residues and were considered as possible poor binders. Also, chemically plain (no heteroatoms) molecules and large ligands with bad complementarity to the M^{pro} active site were excluded. Some docked ligand poses exhibited wrong torsion for the arylsulfonamide group where the nitrogen lone pair or aromatic p-orbital did not lie on the bisector of the O–S–O angle as it should do according to crystallographic data and quantum-chemical calculations. Compounds with such unreliable docked conformations were also not included in the top list for experimental testing. Most ligands include in the top list formed pi-stacking interactions with catalytic histidine His41.

According to all criteria, we selected 18 best ligands as potential inhibitors of M^{pro}. The structures of the selected molecules are shown in Fig. 2, and the obtained values of the SOL scoring function and the enthalpy of protein-ligand binding are presented in Table 1. Of these, two compounds, **3155** and **13803**, contain a Michael acceptor and thus have the ability to covalently bind to M^{pro}. Besides, **13803** has rhodanine ring which is also related to molecular reactivity and the ability to covalently modify the target. It is noteworthy, that the compound **11828** contains dihydroindene-1,3-dione fragment fused with another non-aromatic cycle. Such structure presented also in one of best compounds found in virtual screening of the VGU database in the study [29]. It is assumed that the activity of the selected candidates will be tested *in vitro* for SARS-CoV-2 M^{pro}.

Table 1. SOL score and binding enthalpy of potential M^{pro} inhibitors.

Compound number	SOL score, kcal/mol	ΔH_{bind}, kcal/mol	Compound number	SOL score, kcal/mol	ΔH_{bind}, kcal/mol
1011	−6.36	−43.16	**8227**	−6.49	−42.16
1289	−7.04	−51.29	**9982**	−6.37	−38.73
1607	−6.35	−43.30	**10549**	−6.33	−46.34
3155	−6.56	−48.93	**11290**	−6.35	−43.64
4661	−6.58	−38.72	**11401**	−6.45	−40.77
5054	−6.35	−39.83	**11828**	−6.31	−43.97
6141	−6.40	−45.53	**12527**	−6.30	−44.42
6843	−6.41	−54.94	**13321**	−6.46	−40.88
7568	−6.47	−39.28	**13803**	−6.35	−39.91

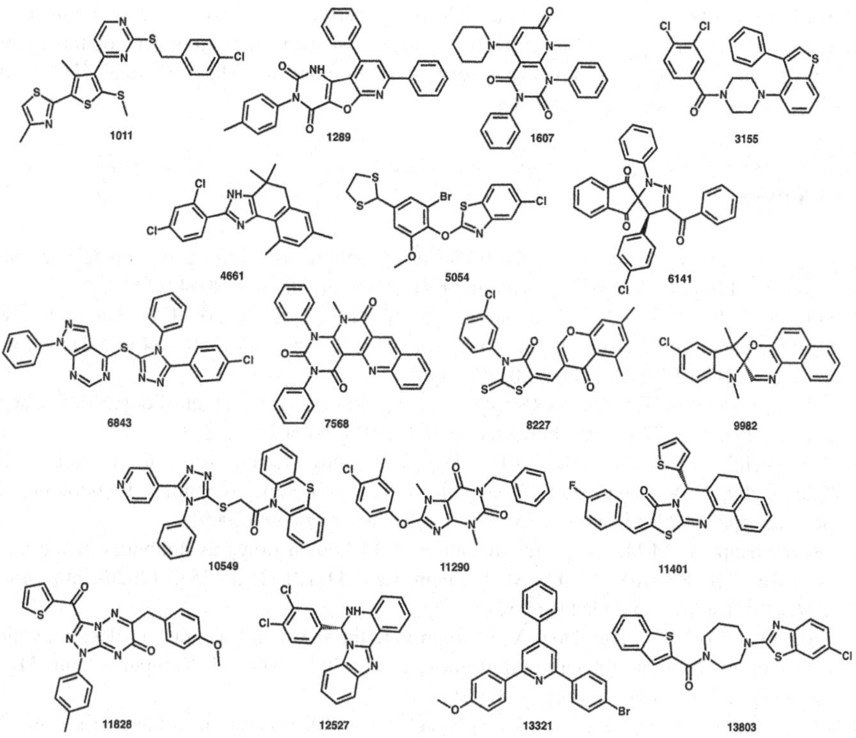

Fig. 2. Structures of the potential inhibitors of SARS-CoV-2 M^pro presented in Table 1.

4 Conclusions

In this work, a virtual screening of the HitFinder-compounds from the Maybridge Screening Collection database was carried out to search for inhibitors of the SARS-CoV-2 main protease. The search for inhibitors was made in two stages using the Lomonosov-2 supercomputer of Lomonosov Moscow State University. At the first stage, the SOL docking program was used to select 100 ligands with best SOL scores. Then, for these top 100 ligands, the enthalpy of protein-ligand binding was calculated using the PM7 quantum-chemical semiempirical method with the COSMO implicit solvent model. The corresponding values of the native inhibitor crystallized with the SARS-CoV-2 main protease in the PDB 6W63 complex were used as the threshold selection criteria.

As a result of these calculations, as well as visual analysis of the ligand docked poses and taking into account chemical diversity of the ligands, 18 compounds were selected as the best candidates for experimental *in vitro* testing their inhibitory activity against the main protease of the SARS-CoV-2 coronavirus.

Acknowledgements. The work was financially supported by the Russian Science Foundation, Agreement no. 21-71-20031. The research is carried out using the equipment of the shared research facilities of HPC computing resources at Lomonosov Moscow State University, including the Lomonosov supercomputer.

References

1. Kokic, G., et al.: Mechanism of SARS-CoV-2 polymerase stalling by remdesivir. Nat. Commun. **12**(1), 279 (2021). https://doi.org/10.1038/s41467-020-20542-0
2. Sulimov, V.B., Kutov, D.C., Taschilova, A.S., Ilin, I.S., Tyrtyshnikov, E.E., Sulimov, A.V.: Docking paradigm in Drug Design. Curr. Top. Med. Chem. **21**(6), 507–546 (2021). https://doi.org/10.2174/1568026620666201207095626
3. Ullrich, S., Nitsche, C.: The SARS-CoV-2 main protease as drug target. Bioorg. Med. Chem. Lett. **30**(17), 127377 (2020). https://doi.org/10.1016/j.bmcl.2020.127377
4. Sadovnichii, V.A., Sulimov, V.B.: Supercomputing technologies in medicine. In: Sadovnichii, V.A., Savin, G.I., Voevodin, V.V. (eds.) Supercomputing Technologies in Science, pp. 16–23. Moscow University Publishing, Moscow (2009)
5. Ghahremanpour, M.M., et al.: Identification of 14 known drugs as inhibitors of the main protease of SARS-CoV-2. ACS Med. Chem. Lett. **11**(12), 2526–2533 (2020). https://doi.org/10.1021/acsmedchemlett.0c00521
6. Trott, O., Olson, A.J.: AutoDock Vina: improving the speed and accuracy of docking with a new scoring function, efficient optimization, and multithreading. J. Comput. Chem. **31**(2), 455–461 (2010). https://doi.org/10.1002/jcc.21334
7. Friesner, R.A., et al.: Glide: a new approach for rapid, accurate docking and scoring. 1. Method and assessment of docking accuracy. J. Med. Chem. **47**(7), 1739–1749 (2004). https://doi.org/10.1021/jm0306430
8. Halgren, T.A., et al.: Glide: a new approach for rapid, accurate docking and scoring. 2. Enrichment factors in database screening. J. Med. Chem. **47**(7), 1750–1759 (2004). https://doi.org/10.1021/jm030644s
9. Berman, H.M., et al.: The Protein Data Bank. Nucleic Acids Res. **28**(1), 235–242 (2000). https://doi.org/10.1093/nar/28.1.235
10. Sterling, T., Irwin, J.J.: ZINC 15 – ligand discovery for everyone. J. Chem. Inf. Model. **55**(11), 2324–2337 (2015). https://doi.org/10.1021/acs.jcim.5b00559
11. Sulimov, V.B., Ilin, I.S., Kutov, D.C., Sulimov, A.V.: Development of docking programs for Lomonosov supercomputer. J. Turkish Chem. Soc. Sect. A Chem. **7**(1), 259–276 (2020). https://doi.org/10.18596/jotcsa.634130
12. Sulimov, A.V., Kutov, D.C., Oferkin, I.V., Katkova, E.V., Sulimov, V.B.: Application of the docking program SOL for CSAR benchmark. J. Chem. Inf. Model. **53**(8), 1946–1956 (2013). https://doi.org/10.1021/ci400094h
13. Khan, S.A., Zia, K., Ashraf, S., Uddin, R., Ul-Haq, Z.: Identification of chymotrypsin-like protease inhibitors of SARS-CoV-2 via integrated computational approach. J. Biomol. Struct. Dyn. **39**(7), 2607–2616 (2020). https://doi.org/10.1080/07391102.2020.1751298
14. Chemical Computing Group ULC: Molecular Operating Environment (MOE)
15. Tsuji, M.: Potential anti-SARS-CoV-2 drug candidates identified through virtual screening of the ChEMBL database for compounds that target the main coronavirus protease. FEBS Open Bio **10**(6), 995–1004 (2020). https://doi.org/10.1002/2211-5463.12875

16. Ruiz-Carmona, S., et al.: rDock: a fast, versatile and open source program for docking ligands to proteins and nucleic acids. PLOS Comput. Biol. **10**(4), e1003571 (2014). https://doi.org/10.1371/journal.pcbi.1003571

17. Gimeno, A., et al.: Prediction of novel inhibitors of the main protease (M-pro) of SARS-CoV-2 through consensus docking and drug reposition. Int. J. Molecul. Sci. **21**(11), 3793 (2020). https://doi.org/10.3390/ijms21113793

18. McGann, M.: FRED pose prediction and virtual screening accuracy. J. Chem. Inf. Model. **51**(3), 578–596 (2011). https://doi.org/10.1021/ci100436p

19. McGann, M.: FRED and HYBRID docking performance on standardized datasets. J. Comput. Aided Mol. Des. **26**(8), 897–906 (2012). https://doi.org/10.1007/s10822-012-9584-8

20. Gupta, A., et al.: Structure-based virtual screening and biochemical validation to discover a potential inhibitor of the SARS-CoV-2 main protease. ACS Omega **5**(51), 33151–33161 (2020). https://doi.org/10.1021/acsomega.0c04808

21. Grosdidier, A., Zoete, V., Michielin, O.: SwissDock, a protein-small molecule docking web service based on EADock DSS. Nucleic Acids Res. **39**(suppl_2), W270–W277 (2011). https://doi.org/10.1093/nar/gkr366

22. Bitencourt-Ferreira, G., de Azevedo, W.F.: Docking with SwissDock. In: de Azevedo Jr., W. F. (ed.) Docking Screens for Drug Discovery. MMB, vol. 2053, pp. 189–202. Springer, New York (2019). https://doi.org/10.1007/978-1-4939-9752-7_12

23. Dai, W., et al.: Structure-based design of antiviral drug candidates targeting the SARS-CoV-2 main protease. Science **368**(6497), 1331–1335 (2020). https://doi.org/10.1126/science.abb4489

24. Wu, Y., Li, Z., Zhao, Y.S., Huang, Y.Y., Jiang, M.Y., Luo, H.: Bin: therapeutic targets and potential agents for the treatment of COVID-19. Med. Res. Rev. **41**(3), 1775–1797 (2021). https://doi.org/10.1002/med.21776

25. Jin, Z., et al.: Structure of Mpro from SARS-CoV-2 and discovery of its inhibitors. Nature **582**(7811), 289–293 (2020). https://doi.org/10.1038/s41586-020-2223-y

26. Gao, J., et al.: Repurposing low-molecular-weight drugs against the main protease of severe acute respiratory syndrome coronavirus 2. J. Phys. Chem. Lett. **11**(17), 7267–7272 (2020). https://doi.org/10.1021/acs.jpclett.0c01894

27. Abian, O., et al.: Structural stability of SARS-CoV-2 3CLpro and identification of quercetin as an inhibitor by experimental screening. Int. J. Biol. Macromol. **164**, 1693–1703 (2020). https://doi.org/10.1016/j.ijbiomac.2020.07.235

28. Rathnayake, A.D., et al.: 3C-like protease inhibitors block coronavirus replication in vitro and improve survival in MERS-CoV–infected mice. Sci. Transl. Med. **12**(557), eabc5332 (2020). https://doi.org/10.1126/scitranslmed.abc5332

29. Sulimov, A.V., et al.: In search of non-covalent inhibitors of SARS-CoV-2 main protease: Computer aided drug design using docking and quantum chemistry. Supercomput. Front. Innov. **7**(3), 41–56 (2020). https://doi.org/10.14529/jsfi200305

30. Su, H., et al.: Anti-SARS-CoV-2 activities in vitro of Shuanghuanglian preparations and bioactive ingredients. Acta Pharmacol. Sin. **41**(9), 1167–1177 (2020). https://doi.org/10.1038/s41401-020-0483-6

31. Maybridge Screening Libraries. https://www.fishersci.com/us/en/brands/I9C8LZ5R/products.html

32. Kutov, D.C., Katkova, E.V., Kondakova, O.A., Sulimov, A.V., Sulimov, V.B.: Influence of the method of hydrogen atoms incorporation into the target protein on the protein-ligand binding energy. Bull. South Ural State Univ. Ser. Math. Model. Program. Comput. Softw. **10**(3), 94–107 (2017). https://doi.org/10.14529/mmp170308

33. Hanwell, M.D., Curtis, D.E., Lonie, D.C., Vandermeersch, T., Zurek, E., Hutchison, G.R.: Avogadro: an advanced semantic chemical editor, visualization, and analysis platform. J. Cheminform. **4**(1), 17 (2012). https://doi.org/10.1186/1758-2946-4-17

34. ChemAxon software. https://chemicalize.com

35. Halgren, T.A.: Merck molecular force field. III. Molecular geometries and vibrational frequencies for MMFF94. J. Comput. Chem. **17**(5–6), 553–586 (1996). https://doi.org/10.1002/(SICI)1096-987X(199604)17:5/6<553::AID-JCC3>3.0.CO;2-T

36. Voevodin, V.V., et al.: Supercomputer Lomonosov-2: large scale, deep monitoring and fine analytics for the user community. Supercomput. Front. Innov. **6**(2), 4–11 (2019). https://doi.org/10.14529/jsfi190201

37. Sinauridze, E.I., et al.: New synthetic thrombin inhibitors: molecular design and experimental verification. PLoS ONE **6**(5), e19969 (2011). https://doi.org/10.1371/journal.pone.0019969

38. Sulimov, V.B., et al.: Application of molecular modeling to Urokinase inhibitors development. Biomed. Res. Int. **2014**, 625176 (2014). https://doi.org/10.1155/2014/625176

39. Beloglazova, I.B., et al.: Molecular modeling as a new approach to the development of Urokinase inhibitors. Bull. Exp. Biol. Med. **158**(5), 700–704 (2015). https://doi.org/10.1007/s10517-015-2839-3

40. Sulimov, V.B., et al.: Application of molecular modeling to development of new factor Xa inhibitors. Biomed Res. Int. **2015**, 120802 (2015). https://doi.org/10.1155/2015/120802

41. Novichikhina, N., et al.: Synthesis, docking, and in vitro anticoagulant activity assay of hybrid derivatives of pyrrolo[3,2,1-ij]quinolin-2(1H)-one as new inhibitors of factor Xa and factor XIa. Molecules **25**(8), 1889 (2020). https://doi.org/10.3390/molecules25081889

42. Ilin, I.S., et al.: New factor Xa inhibitors based on 1,2,3,4-tetrahydroquinoline developed by molecular modelling. J. Mol. Graph. Model. **89**, 215–224 (2019). https://doi.org/10.1016/j.jmgm.2019.03.017

43. Stewart, J.J.: Optimization of parameters for semiempirical methods VI: more modifications to the NDDO approximations and re-optimization of parameters. J. Mol. Model. **19**(1), 1–32 (2013). https://doi.org/10.1007/s00894-012-1667-x

44. Klamt, A.: Conductor-like screening model for real solvents: a new approach to the quantitative calculation of solvation phenomena. J. Phys. Chem. **99**(7), 2224–2235 (1995). https://doi.org/10.1021/j100007a062

45. Klamt, A., Schuurmann, G.: COSMO: a new approach to dielectric screening in solvents with explicit expressions for the screening energy and its gradient. J. Chem. Soc. Perkin Trans. **2**(5), 799–805 (1993). https://doi.org/10.1039/P29930000799

46. Grimme, S.: Accurate description of van der Waals complexes by density functional theory including empirical corrections. J. Comput. Chem. **25**(12), 1463–1473 (2004). https://doi.org/10.1002/jcc.20078

47. Jurecka, P., Cerny, J., Hobza, P., Salahub, D.R.: Density functional theory augmented with an empirical dispersion term. Interaction energies and geometries of 80 noncovalent complexes compared with ab initio quantum mechanics calculations. J. Comput. Chem. **28**(2), 555–569 (2007). https://doi.org/10.1002/jcc.20570

48. Stewart, J.J.P.: Stewart Computational Chemistry. MOPAC2016. http://openmopac.net/MOPAC2016.html

49. Stewart, J.J.P.: Application of localized molecular orbitals to the solution of semiempirical self-consistent field equations. Int. J. Quantum Chem. **58**(2), 133–146 (1996). https://doi.org/10.1002/(SICI)1097-461X(1996)58:2%3c133::AID-QUA2%3e3.0.CO;2-Z

Calculation of Integral Coefficients for Correlation Magnetodynamics and Verification of the Theory

Anton Ivanov[✉], Elizaveta Zipunova, and Sergey Khilkov

Keldysh Institute of Applied Mathematics, Moscow, Russia
aiv.racs@gmail.com

Abstract. There are several ways to describe magnetic systems. The most precise is the atomistic approach, which describes the evolution of magnetization of every single atom. For practical applications, a micromagnetic approach is used. In the micromagnetic approach, the equation describes the evolution of the distribution of an average magnetization in a continuous material.

Because of the intense exchange interaction and temperature fluctuations, a correct transition from atomistic model to a micromagnetic model is a difficult problem in statistical physics. We have derived equations of correlation magnetodynamics (CMD) using the approximation of two-particles distribution function which accounts for correlations between closest magnetic moments. To estimate the level of two-particle correlations we introduce an extra equation, similar to the energy balance equation in the fluid dynamics.

To develop new theory numerical modeling was used widely. CMD equations include several coefficients, which may be obtained using numerical integration of many-particles distribution functions in a wide range of parameters. To calculate such integrals we developed specific numerical methods and parallel codes.

To verify CMD equations, a big amount of calculations in atomistic approach was processed. System of ordinary stochastic differential Landau-Lifshitz equations was solved with aid of Runge-Kutta fourth-order method with the special stochastic source of temperature fluctuations. New parallel program code was developed to model magnetic systems with various crystal lattices.

The developed system of CMD equations shows results similar to the atomistic model in a wide range of parameters for ferromagnetic with different crystal lattices.

Keywords: Correlation magnetodinamics · Landau-Lifshitz-Bloch equation · Aiwlib

V. Voevodin and S. Sobolev (Eds.): RuSCDays 2021, CCIS 1510, pp. 29–43, 2021.
https://doi.org/10.1007/978-3-030-92864-3_3

1   Introduction

Numerical simulations are commonly applied to solve engineering problems. For example, making spintronic or nanoelectronic device calls for numerous simulations based on a variety of models from quantum to macrospin. Another, less usual application of numerical simulations is providing support to a new mathematical model.

Currently atomistic model governed by the set of Landau-Lifshitz stochastic differential equations is the most accurate model of a magnetic material. It describes evolution of magnetic moments directions for singular atoms. This model allows to take into account multiple features of the material, e.g. a crystal lattice structure, defects, sophisticated variants of exchange interaction and temperature fluctuations [1]. However exceptional computational complexity of the model makes vast amount of simulations which are required to optimize a device construction unfeasible.

Thus in order to solve engineering problems [2] one has to use a low-cost model. Usually that implies micromagnetic model which describes a magnetic as a continuous medium where magnetisation is a vector field distributed over it. Nevertheless the physically correct transition from the atomistic model to a continuous model is a formidable problem. In particular an intense and short-ranged exchange interaction and presence of the temperature fluctuations make it so hard. Since its existing solutions rely on restrictive approximations, more general transition remains a fundamental problem. Nowadays commonly accepted micromagnetic model is governed by Landau-Lifshitz-Bloch equation (LLB) [3–5].

Derivation of LLB equation relied on mean field approximation which neglects correlations between magnetic moments of the nearest atoms. It introduces a number of artifacts. Among them the zero exchange energy for paramagnetic phase and underestimated relaxation time are to be mentioned [6]. Those drawbacks might restrict the simulation of spintronic and nanoelectronic devices which operate in a pulsed mode.

An approximation of the multi-particle distribution function taking correlations of the nearest neighbours into account helps to avoid those restrictions. It allows to derive LLB-like equation supplemented by the equation for two-particles correlations (exchange energy) $\langle \eta \rangle = \langle \mathbf{m}_i \cdot \mathbf{m}_j \rangle$ (where $\mathbf{m}_i$ and $\mathbf{m}_j$ are magnetic moments of adjacent atoms). It resembles the energy balance equation in fluid dynamics. The aforementioned system of equations we call correlation magnetodynamics model (CMD). Its behaviour lays in acceptable correspondence with atomistic model behaviour in cases of ferromagnetic materials with primitive, face–centred or body–centred cubic lattices.

During the CMD development numerical modeling was used in a number of ways. For one thing, the CMD system introduces coefficients obtained by multiple integration on multi-particle distribution function with respect to large number of parameters. Their estimation called for use of a computer cluster. For another thing, verification of obtained equations demanded the separate way to solve the same problem. So atomistic simulations in wide range of temperatures, external magnetic fields and anisotropy coefficients were used to verify the CMD system.

2 CMD Equations

In this section we are going to derive CMD system of equations. We are starting from atomistic model of magnetic, i.e. system of Landau-Lifshitz equations for each atom [1]. It describes evolution of N magnetic moments $\mathbf{m}_i(t)$, which are located at nodes of crystal lattice with coordinates $\mathbf{r}_i$:

$$\frac{d\mathbf{m}_i}{dt} = -\gamma[\mathbf{m}_i \times \mathbf{H}_i^{\text{eff}}] - \alpha\gamma[\mathbf{m}_i \times [\mathbf{m}_i \times (\mathbf{H}_i^{\text{eff}} + \sqrt{2\alpha\gamma T}\boldsymbol{\xi}_i(t))]]; \quad (1)$$

$$\mathbf{H}_i^{\text{eff}} = -\nabla_{\mathbf{m}_i}W = \mathbf{H}_i^{\text{ex}} + \mathbf{H}_i^{\text{an}} + \mathbf{H}_i^{\text{dip}} + \mathbf{H}^{\text{ext}};$$

$$\mathbf{H}_i^{\text{ex}} = \sum_j J_{ij}\mathbf{m}_j; \quad \mathbf{H}_i^{\text{an}} = 2Kn_K(\mathbf{n}_K \cdot \mathbf{m}_i);$$

$$\mathbf{H}_i^{\text{dip}} = \sum_j \frac{3(\mathbf{m}_j \cdot \mathbf{r}_{ij})\mathbf{r}_{ij} - \mathbf{m}_j r_{ij}^2}{r_{ij}^5}, \quad \mathbf{r}_{ij} = \mathbf{r}_i - \mathbf{r}_j.$$

Here γ is a gyromagnetic ratio, α is the damping parameter, $\mathbf{H}^{\text{eff}}$ stands for effective magnetic field, W is the full energy of the system, T is the temperature of the system measured in units of energy. Vector $\boldsymbol{\xi}(t)$ is Gaussian white noise vector, which means it composed of δ–correlated random variables with the normal distribution, zero mean and variance equals to one. Notation $\nabla_{\mathbf{m}_i}$ means the ∇ differential operator with respect to the magnetic moment $\mathbf{m}_i$, $\mathbf{H}^{\text{ex}}$ is the exchange field, J_{ij} is the exchange integral (usually nonzero only for adjacent atoms i and j). Anisotropic field $\mathbf{H}^{\text{an}}$ is described in terms of an anisotropy coefficient K and a direction of an anisotropic axis $\mathbf{n}_K$, $|\mathbf{n}_K| = 1$. The dipole–dipole interaction field (magnetostatic) is referred to as $\mathbf{H}^{\text{dip}}$. Here and farther we use the dimensionless system of units which has $|\mathbf{m}_i| = 1$, $\Delta W = J$, $\gamma = 1$ and the temperature is measured in the units of energy.

The system of Eqs. (1) allows to take into account multiple features of the system, such as temperature fluctuations and defects of the crystal lattice. However it turns out to have exceptionally high computational cost for the real devices.

The Bogolyubov hierarchy (BBGKY) helps to obtain the continuous medium model which might has a relatively low computational cost. There are different approaches to complete BBGKY hierarchy. The mean field approach $f_{ij}^{(2)} \approx \approx f_i^{(1)}f_j^{(1)}$ is one of them. It leads to LLB equation [3]

$$\langle\dot{\mathbf{m}}\rangle = -\gamma\Big[\langle\mathbf{m}\rangle \times \mathbf{H}^{\text{L}}\Big] - 2\gamma K\Big(\boldsymbol{\Phi} + \alpha\boldsymbol{\Theta}\Big)$$

$$- \alpha\gamma\widehat{\Xi} \cdot \Big(\mathbf{H}^{\text{L}} + n_b\varepsilon_G J\langle\mathbf{m}\rangle\Big) - 2\alpha\gamma T\langle\mathbf{m}\rangle, (2)$$

$$\mathbf{H}^{\text{L}} = \mathbf{H}^{\text{ext}} + a^2 J\Delta_{\mathbf{r}}\langle\mathbf{m}\rangle + \mathbf{H}^{\text{dip}}, \quad \widehat{\Xi} = \Big\langle\mathbf{m} \otimes \mathbf{m} - \widehat{I}\Big\rangle,$$

$$\boldsymbol{\Phi} = \langle \mathbf{m} \times \mathbf{n}_K (\mathbf{m} \cdot \mathbf{n}_K) \rangle, \qquad \boldsymbol{\Theta} = \langle \mathbf{m} \times [\mathbf{m} \times \mathbf{n}_K] (\mathbf{m} \cdot \mathbf{n}_K) \rangle,$$

where $\mathbf{H}^L$ contains parts of the field which does not depend on average magneti-sation $\langle \mathbf{m} \rangle$ or depend on it linearly. From physical point of view $\mathbf{H}^L$ contains the interaction terms describing interaction on the scale large than infinitesimal volume. $\widehat{I}$ denotes the identity matrix with sizes 3×3, the symbol $\otimes$ stands for the tensor product operator. The constant number of nearest neighbours n_b depends on the type of the lattice. The multiplier $\varepsilon_G < 1$ was introduced by Garanin to account for fluctuations of mean field. It also helps to achieve the correct value of the critical temperature [7]. Finally the averaging over the corresponding distribution function denoted by angular brackets.

Integral coefficients $\boldsymbol{\Phi}$, $\boldsymbol{\Theta}$, $\langle \mathbf{m} \otimes \mathbf{m} \rangle$ depend on high order moments of the one-particle distribution function. In order to estimate them we approximate it as

$$f(\mathbf{m}, \mathbf{r}, t) \approx \frac{e^{\mathbf{p} \cdot \mathbf{m}}}{\mathcal{Z}(p)}, \qquad \mathcal{Z}(p) = \int_{S_2} e^{\mathbf{p} \cdot \mathbf{m}} \, d\mathbf{m} = 4\pi \frac{\sinh p}{p}, \tag{3}$$

where approximation parameter $\mathbf{p} = \mathbf{p}(\mathbf{r}, t)$ is parallel to average magnetisation $\mathbf{p} \parallel \langle \mathbf{m} \rangle$ and obeys the equation $|\langle \mathbf{m} \rangle| = \coth p - 1/p \equiv \mathcal{L}(p)$. The function $\mathcal{L}$ is called Langevin function. Coefficients $\boldsymbol{\Phi}$, $\boldsymbol{\Theta}$, $\langle \mathbf{m} \otimes \mathbf{m} \rangle$ might be estimated numerically and analytically [8].

In order to conserve the correlations between adjacent magnetic moments we approximate two-particle distribution with

$$f_{ij}^{(2)} \approx \frac{1}{Z_{ij}^{(2)}} \left[f_i(\mathbf{m}_i, t) \, f_j(\mathbf{m}_j, t) \right]^{\rho} e^{\lambda \mathbf{m}_i \cdot \mathbf{m}_j}, \tag{4}$$

$$Z_{ij}^{(2)} = \iint_{S_2} \left[f_i(\mathbf{m}_i, t) \, f_j(\mathbf{m}_j, t) \right]^{\rho} e^{\lambda \mathbf{m}_i \cdot \mathbf{m}_j} \, d\mathbf{m}_i \, d\mathbf{m}_j,$$

where the parameter $\lambda \geq 0$ describes correlations (indirect included) between adjacent magnetic moments $\mathbf{m}_i$ and $\mathbf{m}_j$. The exponent $\frac{1}{2} \leq \rho \leq 1$ is meant to guaranty that $f_i \approx \int_{S_2} f_{ij}^{(2)} \, d\mathbf{m}_j$. However it is easier to calculate ρ from the equation $\langle \mathbf{m} \rangle = \iint_{S_2} \mathbf{m}_i \, f_{ij}^{(2)} \, d\mathbf{m}_i \, d\mathbf{m}_j$. Thus ρ may be considered as a function of λ. This approximation could be applied to every two-particle distribution function regardless of the particles relative positions. However we are using it only for adjacent particles.

Let's consider the approximation (4) asymptotic behaviour. If $\lambda \ll 1$ than $\rho \to 1$ and the approximation (4) approaches mean field approximation. If $\lambda \gg 1$ the exponent in approximation (4) becomes a lead term which essentially behaves as δ-function. This corresponds to $\rho \to \frac{1}{2}$. Despite of the exponent ρ the dimensionality of the approximation (4) always remains correct due to $Z^{(2)}$.

After that, with a number of transitions [6,9–11] it is possible to obtain the system of CMD equations. Both equations describe the evolution for the spatial distribution of a certain quantity. The first one works with the average magnetisation $\langle \mathbf{m} \rangle (\mathbf{r}, t)$, while the second one deals with two-point correlations for adjacent magnetic moments $\langle \eta \rangle (\mathbf{r}, t) = \langle \mathbf{m}_i \cdot \mathbf{m}_j \rangle$:

$$\langle \dot{\mathbf{m}} \rangle = -\gamma \left[\langle \mathbf{m} \rangle \times \mathbf{H}^{\mathbf{L}} \right] - 2\gamma K \left(\boldsymbol{\Phi} + \alpha \boldsymbol{\Theta} \right)$$
$$- \alpha \gamma \, \widehat{\boldsymbol{\Xi}} \cdot \mathbf{H}^{\mathbf{L}} - 2\alpha\gamma (T - n_b J \Upsilon) \langle \mathbf{m} \rangle, \tag{5}$$

$$\frac{\langle \dot{\eta} \rangle}{4\alpha\gamma} = \mathbf{H}^{\mathbf{L}} \cdot \langle \mathbf{m} \rangle \, \Upsilon - K \Psi - \frac{J}{2} \left[\langle \eta^2 \rangle - 1 + \sum_k Q_k \right] - T \langle \eta \rangle, \tag{6}$$

$$\Psi = \left\langle \mathbf{m}_i \cdot \left[\mathbf{m}_j \times [\mathbf{m}_j \times \mathbf{n}_K] \right] (\mathbf{m}_j \cdot \mathbf{n}_K) \right\rangle,$$

$$\Upsilon = \frac{1 - \rho}{\lambda}, \qquad Q_k = \left\langle \mathbf{m}_i \cdot \left[\mathbf{m}_j \times [\mathbf{m}_j \times \mathbf{m}_k] \right] \right\rangle,$$

where the coefficient Υ is a function of approximation parameters for two–particle distribution $f^{(2)}$. The coefficient Ψ reflects the contribution of anisotropy into the evolution of two–particles correlations $\langle \eta \rangle$. The coefficients Q_k describes the impact of three–particles correlations on the evolution of the two-particles correlations $\langle \eta \rangle$. The summation is carried out over all j which are adjacent to k except i.

The Eq. (5) is the modification of Landau-Lifshitz-Bloch equation (2) in which the exchange field inside infinitesimal volume manifests as the antidiffusion for one–particle distribution in the magnetic moment directions space with the coefficient $n_b J \Upsilon$.

The integral coefficients Υ, Ψ, $\langle \eta^2 \rangle$ and Q_k are the functions of $\langle m \rangle$ and $\langle \eta \rangle$ but their direct calculation is an intricate problem. The hardest part is to estimate the coefficients Q_k which depend on three–particle distribution functions. The approximations for three-particles distribution depend on lattice geometry and additional assumptions. In almost all cases the calculation of the integral coefficients requires the multiple integration of the multi-particle distributions over the sphere in a wide range of approximation parameters.

3   Calculation of Integral CMD Coefficients

Approximation of two-particle distribution function (4) allows to calculate values $\langle m \rangle$, $\langle \eta \rangle$ as functions of parameters ρp, λ

$$\langle \mathbf{m} \rangle = \iint\limits_{S_2} \mathbf{m}_i f^{(2)}(\mathbf{m}_i, \mathbf{m}_j) \, d\mathbf{m}_i \, d\mathbf{m}_j, \qquad \langle \eta \rangle = \iint\limits_{S_2} \mathbf{m}_i \cdot \mathbf{m}_j f^{(2)}(\mathbf{m}_i, \mathbf{m}_j) \, d\mathbf{m}_i \, d\mathbf{m}_j,$$

one has to compute three double integrals over the unit sphere to calculate them (the first integral defines the normalization factor $Z^{(2)}$). Due to symmetry, those double integrals can be reduced analytically to single integrals, so they can be calculated numerically with the low computational cost, Fig. 1. Functions $\langle m \rangle (\rho p, \lambda)$, $\langle \eta \rangle (\rho p, \lambda)$ define curvilinear coordinates and implicitly define a function

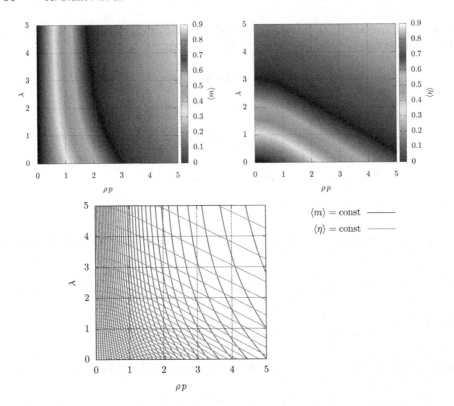

Fig. 1. Dependence of moments $\langle m \rangle$, $\langle \eta \rangle$ on parameters ρp, λ of approximation for two-particle distribution function $f^{(2)}$ and curvilinear coordinate system $\langle m \rangle = \text{const}$, $\langle \eta \rangle = \text{const}$ for calculation of integral coefficients determined by the parameters

$$\Upsilon(\langle m \rangle, \langle \eta \rangle) = \frac{1-\rho}{\lambda} = \frac{1}{\lambda}\left[1 - \frac{\rho p}{\mathcal{L}^{-1}(\langle m \rangle)}\right], \qquad \mathcal{L}(x) = \frac{1}{\tanh x} - \frac{1}{x},$$

where $\mathcal{L}^{-1}$ is inverse Langenev function, because $\langle m \rangle = \mathcal{L}(p)$. Function Υ can be calculated at nodes of uniform rectangular mesh of ρp, λ and then approximated analytically with absolute error less than 10^{-3} (Fig. 2a):

$$\Upsilon \approx \frac{1-\langle \eta \rangle}{1-\langle m \rangle^2} \cdot \frac{\langle m \rangle}{p} \cdot \left[1 + 0.3684 \cdot \langle \eta \rangle^2 + 0.1873 \cdot \langle \eta \rangle^3\right.$$
$$\left. - 0.3236 \cdot \langle \eta \rangle \langle m \rangle^2 - 0.2523 \cdot \langle \eta \rangle^2 \langle m \rangle^2\right].$$

Curveature $\langle \eta \rangle = \langle m \rangle^2$ correspondes to mean field approximation. In area $\langle \eta \rangle < \langle m \rangle^2$ parameter $\lambda < 0$, which doesn't describe ferromagnetic physically correct. No integral coefficients were calculated for this area.

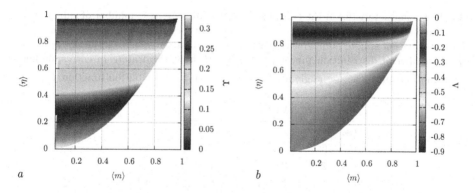

Fig. 2. Functions Υ and Λ, estimated numerically

As will be shown later, the parameter

$$\Lambda = \frac{1-2\rho}{\rho}\left(1 - \langle\eta^2\rangle\right) - 2\frac{1-\rho}{\rho\lambda}\langle\eta\rangle, \qquad \lim_{\langle m\rangle\to 0}\Lambda = \langle\eta^2\rangle - 1,$$

is more convenient than $\langle\eta^2\rangle$. Λ can be calculated and approximated the same way, Fig. 2b.

$$\Lambda \approx \frac{1-\langle\eta\rangle}{1-\langle m\rangle^2}\Big[-0.6639 - 0.7617\cdot\langle\eta\rangle + 0.2718\cdot\langle\eta\rangle^2$$
$$- 1.367\cdot\langle\eta\rangle^3 + 0.5078\cdot\langle\eta\rangle^4 + 0.2689\cdot\langle\eta\rangle\langle m\rangle$$
$$+ 0.3472\cdot\langle\eta\rangle\langle m\rangle^2 - 0.418\cdot\langle\eta\rangle^2\langle m\rangle + 1.833\cdot\langle\eta\rangle^2\langle m\rangle^2\Big].$$

Same approach was used to calculate integral coefficients Ψ and Q_k, but this calculations have much higher computational complexity.

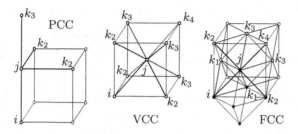

Fig. 3. Primitive, VCC and FCC latices and examples of three-particle distribution function $f_{ijk}^{(3)}$. Indices $k_{1...4}$ represent the coordination sphere to which the third atom belongs

To calculate integral coefficients Q_k one needs three-particle distribution functions $f_{ijk}^{(3)}$ which depend on the crystal latice. We considered ferromagnet-

Table 1. Characteristics of the considered crystal lattices: n_{sc}—number of sublattices, n_b—number of nearest neighbours, $n_{f.t.}$—number of types of distribution functions $f_{ijk}^{(3)}$, k—coordination sphere numbers, R_k—radii of coordination spheres in lattice periods, n_{fk}—number of distribution functions $f_{ijk}^{(3)}$, which have third atom in corresponding coordination sphere, $\angle_{ijk}$—angle at the second atom for distribution function $f_{ijk}^{(3)}$

c.l	PCC		VCC			FCC			
n_{sc}	1		2			4			
n_b	6		8			12			
$n_{f.t.}$	**2**		**3**			**4**			
k	2	3	2	3	4	1	2	3	4
R_k	$\sqrt{2}$	2	1	$\sqrt{2}$	$\sqrt{3}$	$\dfrac{\sqrt{2}}{2}$	1	$\sqrt{\dfrac{3}{2}}$	$\sqrt{2}$
$\angle_{ijk}$	$\dfrac{\pi}{2}$	π	$\dfrac{2\pi}{5}$	$\dfrac{\pi}{2}$	π	$\dfrac{\pi}{3}$	$\dfrac{\pi}{2}$	$\dfrac{2\pi}{3}$	π
n_{fk}	**4**	**1**	**3**	**3**	**1**	**4**	**2**	**4**	**1**

ics with primitive cubic crystal (PCC), body centered crystal (VCC) and face centered crystal (FCC) lattices see Table 1 and Fig. 3.

Let's denote three-particle distribution functions for $\mathcal{X}$CC lattice with k atom located on the coordination sphere s by $f_{k=s}^{\mathcal{X}\text{CC}}$. Consider $f_{ijk}^{(3)}$, which has all three atoms located on one line: $f_{k=3}^{\text{PCC}}$, $f_{k=4}^{\text{VCC}}$ and $f_{k=3}^{\text{FCC}}$. If we neglect indirect correlations between atoms i and k, than such distribution function can be written as $f_{\angle}^{(3)} \approx f_{ij}^{(2)} f_{jk}^{(2)} / f_j$, which is extension of mean-field approximation on three-particle distribution function. Corresponding coefficient $Q_{\angle}$ takes the form:

$$Q_{\angle} = \frac{1-\rho}{\rho}\left[1 - \frac{2}{\lambda}\langle\eta\rangle - \langle\eta^2\rangle\right].$$

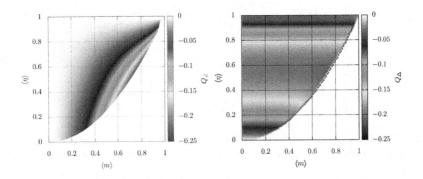

Fig. 4. Dependence of coefficients $Q_{\angle}$ and $Q_{\triangle}$ on parameters $\langle m \rangle$, $\langle \eta \rangle$

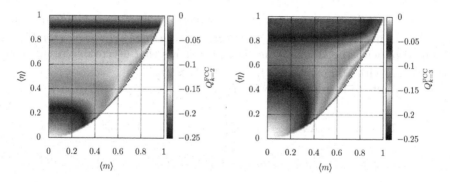

Fig. 5. Dependence of coefficients $Q^{\text{FCC}}_{k=2}$ and $Q^{\text{FCC}}_{k=3}$ on parameters $\langle m \rangle$, $\langle \eta \rangle$

Another extreme case is fully symmetrical distribution function

$$f^{\text{FCC}}_{k=1} \equiv f^{(3)}_{\triangle} \approx \frac{1}{Z^{(3)}} \exp\left[\sigma \mathbf{p} \cdot \left(\mathbf{m}_i + \mathbf{m}_j + \mathbf{m}_k\right) + \varsigma\left(\mathbf{m}_i \cdot \mathbf{m}_j + \mathbf{m}_j \cdot \mathbf{m}_k + \mathbf{m}_k \cdot \mathbf{m}_i\right)\right],$$

were parameters σ, ς can be defined as

$$\iiint\limits_{S_2} \mathbf{m}_i f^{(3)}_{\triangle} \, d\mathbf{m}_{i,j,k} = \langle m \rangle, \qquad \iiint\limits_{S_2} \eta f^{(3)}_{\triangle} \, d\mathbf{m}_{i,j,k} = \langle \eta \rangle.$$

Likewise, $f^{\text{FCC}}_{k=2}$ can be calculated by integration symmetrical six-particle distribution function, corresponding to correct octahedron (Fig. 3, the vertices of the octahedron are highlighted in black), if one neglects indirect correlations between opposite vertices of the octahedron. Mean field approximation for $f^{\text{FCC}}_{k=3}$ gives

$$f^{\text{FCC}}_{k=3} \approx \int\limits_{S_2} \frac{f^{(3)}_{\triangle ijl} f^{(3)}_{\triangle jkl}}{f^{(2)}_{jl}} \, d\mathbf{m}_l.$$

Let's consider symmetrical function

$$\begin{aligned}
f^{(4)}_{ijkl} \sim \exp\Big[&\sigma \mathbf{p} \cdot \left(\mathbf{m}_i + \mathbf{m}_j + \mathbf{m}_k + \mathbf{m}_l\right) \\
&+ \varsigma\left(\mathbf{m}_i \cdot \mathbf{m}_j + \mathbf{m}_j \cdot \mathbf{m}_k + \mathbf{m}_k \cdot \mathbf{m}_l + \mathbf{m}_l \cdot \mathbf{m}_i\right) \\
&+ \epsilon\varsigma\left(\mathbf{m}_i \cdot \mathbf{m}_k + \mathbf{m}_j \cdot \mathbf{m}_l\right)\Big], \quad \epsilon < 1,
\end{aligned}$$

with its help we can obtain three–particle function

$$f^{\text{PCC}}_{k=2} \equiv f^{(3)}_{\boxtimes} = \int\limits_{S_2} f^{(4)}_{ijkl} \, d\mathbf{m}_l.$$

There are three independent parameters and two conditions, following from expression for $\langle m \rangle$, $\langle \eta \rangle$. To gain thurd condition we assume that bonds determined by indirect correlations $\epsilon\varsigma$ which lie on diagonals in $f^{(4)}_{ijkl}$ differ from bonds ς on outer ribs by J/T, $\epsilon = 1 - J/T\varsigma$.

Functions $f^{\text{VCC}}_{k=2,3}$ provide most of the troubles. Atoms of those functions lie at nodes of the irregular octahedron, so we can't use the same approach as for $f^{\text{FCC}}_{k=2}$. Comparison with the atomistic modeling (1) shows that acceptable results can be obtained with approximation $f^{\text{VCC}}_{k=2} + f^{\text{VCC}}_{k=3} \approx 2f^{(3)}_{\boxtimes}$.

As a result (6) takes the following form

$$\frac{\langle \dot{\eta} \rangle}{4\alpha\gamma} = \mathbf{H}^{\text{L}} \cdot \langle \mathbf{m} \rangle \Upsilon - K\Psi - \frac{J}{2}\big[\Lambda + \mathcal{Q}\big] - T\langle\eta\rangle, \qquad \Lambda = \langle\eta^2\rangle - 1 + Q_\angle, \quad (7)$$

$$\mathcal{Q}_{\text{PCC}} = 4Q_{\boxtimes}, \qquad \mathcal{Q}_{\text{FCC}} = 4Q_\triangle + 2Q^{\text{FCC}}_{k=2} + 4Q^{\text{FCC}}_{k=3}, \qquad \mathcal{Q}_{\text{VCC}} = 6Q_{\boxtimes}.$$

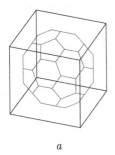 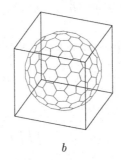 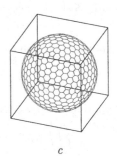

a b c

Fig. 6. Spherical mesh which consists of pentagons and hexagons. It is dual to the mesh obtained as a result of recursive subdivision of pentakis dodecahedron faces: without subdivision (a), one step (b), two steps (c)

To calculate integrals we used spherical mesh which consists of pentagons and hexagons. It is dual to the mesh obtained as a result of recursive subdivision of the pentakis dodecahedron faces, Fig. 6. It is implemented using C++ language as a part of the aiwlib [12] library. In comparison with uniform spherical mesh in traditional spherical coordinates, this mesh takes one and a half times fewer nodes with the same calculation accuracy and doesn't have singularities on poles. For example using the mesh for integrating the four-particle distribution function is roughly five times faster.

Each coefficient Q was calculated by the individual program written in C++. With help of Symmetries of the coefficients, some parts of the integrals were calculated analytically. The rest of the integrals were written as nested loops over spherical mesh cells. To parallelize the external loop OpenMP was used.

Parameter $\langle m \rangle' \in [0, 0.95]$ was taken from uniform mesh with step size 0.025 or 0.05, $20 \div 40$ nodes in total. This mesh was transformed into non-uniform mesh by the formula $\sigma p = \mathcal{L}^{-1}(\langle m \rangle')$. Parameter $\lambda \in [0, 4]$ was also taken from uniform mesh with step size $0.04 \div 0.3$, and for larger values $\lambda \in [4, 20]$ the logarithmic mesh with step size $1.1 \div 1.15$ was used. The rank of the spherical mesh subdivision in calculations was either 2 (482 cells) or 3 (1922 cells). Numerical calculations of coefficients were processed on cluster K60 of the Institute of Applied Mathematics. M.V. Keldysh RAS, which consists of dual-processor nodes based on Intel Xeon E5-2690 v4. Normally the calculation of a single coefficient took 12 h on the single node (28 cores, 56 threads). The total calculations time for $Q_\boxtimes(\langle m \rangle, \langle \eta \rangle, T)$ coefficients of the VCC lattice come up to 128 node-hours. The temperature T in our calculations was taken from the interval $[0.1, 15]$. We used the logarithmic mesh with fifty nodes and multiplicative step ~ 1.1.

Calculation of integral coefficients for ferromagnetics demanded the calculation of multiple integrals in mesh nodes for two-three dimensional space of model parameters. Extension of CMD on anti- and ferrimagnetic case demands calculations in four-six dimensional space of model parameters. The development of supercomputers makes it possible to solve such problems, but nevertheless their computational complexity turns out to be extremely high. It seems promising to expand the function under integral into various series using the methods of computer algebra and to use analytical integration afterwards.

4   CMD Equations Verification

To verify the derived system of CMD equations stochastic differential Landau-Lifshitz equations, written for magnetization of each atom, were numerically integrated.

For the purpose, Runge-Kutta fourth-order method was implemented on C++ using aiwlib library. Developed code allows modeling magnetic materials with primitive, body-centered, and face-centered cubic crystal lattices. A cubic sample with periodic boundaries was modeled. To improve data locality we used Morton Z-curve [13] which was implemented in aiwlib library as Zcube container. Each container's cell contained several (by the number of sublattices) three-component aiwlib vectors made of four-byte floating-point numbers. Four equal size containers was used—$\mathbf{m}^0$, $\mathbf{m}^1$, $\mathbf{m}^2$ and $\delta\mathbf{m}$. Values of all magnetisations at the beginning of time step were saved to $\mathbf{m}^0$. Here is the numerical scheme at one time step:

$$\mathbf{H}^{\text{eff}} := \mathbf{H}^{\text{exch}}_{i,0} + \mathbf{H}^{\text{ext}} + 2\,K(\mathbf{n}_K \cdot \mathbf{m}^0_i)\mathbf{n}_K, \tag{8}$$

$$\dot{\mathbf{m}} := -\gamma\Big[\mathbf{m}^0_i \times \big(\mathbf{H}^{\text{eff}} + \alpha\mathbf{m}^0_i \times \mathbf{H}^{\text{eff}}\big)\Big], \quad \mathbf{m}^1_i := \mathbf{m}^0_i + \frac{\delta t}{2}\dot{\mathbf{m}}, \quad \delta\mathbf{m}_i := \dot{\mathbf{m}};$$

$$\mathbf{H}^{\text{eff}} := \mathbf{H}^{\text{exch}}_{i,1} + \mathbf{H}^{\text{ext}} + 2\,K(\mathbf{n}_K \cdot \mathbf{m}^1_i)\mathbf{n}_K, \tag{9}$$

$$\dot{\mathbf{m}} := -\gamma\Big[\mathbf{m}^1_i \times \big(\mathbf{H}^{\text{eff}} + \alpha\mathbf{m}^1_i \times \mathbf{H}^{\text{eff}}\big)\Big], \quad \mathbf{m}^2_i := \mathbf{m}^0_i + \frac{\delta t}{2}\dot{\mathbf{m}}, \quad \delta\mathbf{m}_i \mathrel{+}= \dot{\mathbf{m}};$$

$$\mathbf{H}^{\text{eff}} := \mathbf{H}^{\text{exch}}_{i,2} + \mathbf{H}^{\text{ext}} + 2\,K(\mathbf{n}_K \cdot \mathbf{m}^2_i)\mathbf{n}_K, \tag{10}$$

$$\dot{\mathbf{m}} := -\gamma\Big[\mathbf{m}^2_i \times \big(\mathbf{H}^{\text{eff}} + \alpha\mathbf{m}^2_i \times \mathbf{H}^{\text{eff}}\big)\Big], \quad \mathbf{m}^1_i := \mathbf{m}^0_i + \delta t\dot{\mathbf{m}}, \quad \delta\mathbf{m}_i \mathrel{+}= \dot{\mathbf{m}};$$

$$\mathbf{H}^{\text{eff}} := \mathbf{H}_{i,1}^{\text{exch}} + \mathbf{H}^{\text{ext}} + 2\,K(\mathbf{n}_K \cdot \mathbf{m}_i^1)\mathbf{n}_K, \tag{11}$$

$$\dot{\mathbf{m}} := -\gamma\Big[\mathbf{m}_i^1 \times (\mathbf{H}^{\text{eff}} + \alpha\mathbf{m}_i^1 \times \mathbf{H}^{\text{eff}})\Big], \quad \mathbf{m}_i^0 +\!= \frac{\delta t}{3}\left(\delta\mathbf{m}_i + \frac{1}{2}\dot{\mathbf{m}}\right),$$

$$\mathbf{m}_i^0 := \frac{\mathbf{m}_i^0}{|\mathbf{m}_i^0|} \circlearrowleft \left[2\sqrt{\delta t \alpha \gamma T}\,\xi_i\,\frac{\mathbf{k} \times \mathbf{m}_i^0}{|\mathbf{k} \times \mathbf{m}_i^0|} \circlearrowleft 2\pi\beta_i\mathbf{m}_i^0\right], \tag{12}$$

where δt is time step, $\mathbf{H}^{\text{eff}}$, $\dot{\mathbf{m}}$ are temporary variables, $:=$ is the assignment operation, ξ_i is a random number with normal distribution $N(0,1)$, β_i is a random number with even distribution on the interval $[0,1]$, $\mathbf{k}$ is the unit vector corresponding to the minimum vector component $\mathbf{m}_i^0$, $\mathbf{a} \circlearrowleft \mathbf{b}$ is the operation of rotation $\mathbf{a}$ around $\mathbf{b}$ on angle b

$$\mathbf{a} \circlearrowleft \mathbf{b} = \mathbf{a}\cos b - \mathbf{a} \times \mathbf{b}\frac{\sin b}{b} + \mathbf{b}(\mathbf{a}\cdot\mathbf{b})\frac{1 - \cos b}{b^2}.$$

Each stage from (8–11) was performed in a separate parallel container cycle. OpenMP was used for parallelization, for 28 cores it was $70 \div 80\%$ efficient. Operations with the random source of temperature fluctuations (12) were processed at the end of the fourth stage (11). The random source provides diffusion in space of magnetic moments with the intensity equals to $2\sqrt{\delta t \alpha \gamma T}$ [14].

In the calculation process, average magnetisation, full energy, one-particle distribution function, and two-particle correlations for different coordination spheres were calculated and saved.

To define a crystal lattice one needs to define the number of sublattices and bonds between atoms. Since the lattice is spatially uniform defining the bonds for each atom in elementary cell is enough. Bond is defined by a shift to adjacent cell and number of sublattice in this cell, so the table of bonds for VCC lattice is shown down below:

```
const Link nb_pos[2][8] =
{{ Link(0,0,0, 1), Link(-1,0,0, 1), Link(0,-1,0, 1), Link(0,0,-1, 1),
   Link(0,-1,-1, 1), Link(-1,0,-1, 1), Link(-1,-1,0, 1), Link(-1,-1,-1, 1)
   },
 { Link(0,0,0, 0), Link(1,0,0, 0), Link(0,1,0, 0), Link(0,0,1, 0),
   Link(0,1,1, 0), Link(1,0,1, 0), Link(1,1,0, 0), Link(1,1,1, 0)
   }
};
```

First three arguments of the constructor of a structure `Link` define shifts. The last argument defines the numbers of sublattices. Similar tables were used to calculate correlations. In order to generate all the tables Python code, analyzing the disposition of atoms in space, was used.

The uniform magnetisation was taken as initial condition. Each calculation contained two stages, relaxation to stationary state and collecting statistics in a stationary state. At the second stage the average magnetisation also was averaged in time.

Calculations were managed and systematized with aid of RACS (Results and Algorithms Control System) which is a part of the aiwlib library [12,15]. RACS

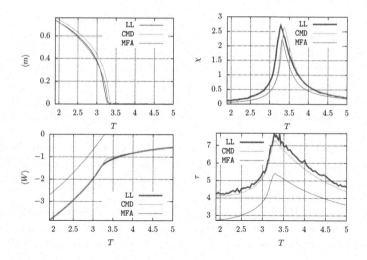

Fig. 7. Face-centered crystal lattice, $H^{\text{ext}} = 0$, $K = 0$

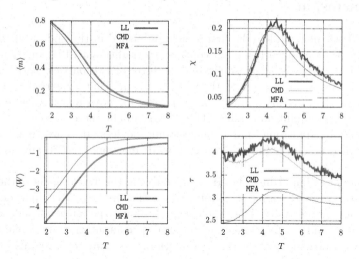

Fig. 8. Face-centered crystal lattice, $H^{\text{ext}} = 1$, $K = 0$

stores calculation results in non-relational database specifically designed for numerical modeling. It helps to start batch jobs on cluster and stores the metadata for every job in the unique directory. RACS also provides the interface for multiparametric queries and helps to analyze results.

The sample size in calculations equals 64^3 cells. Calculations were preformed for different crystal lattices in a wide range of temperatures, external fields, and anisotropy values. The final series producing coefficients estimations were processed at K60 and count up to four thousands of calculations. It adds up in calculation time exceeding 1300 node-hours. This estimation doesn't account for improving a setup. With it taken into account total calculation time becomes greater than 4000 node-hours.

Figures 7, 8 show the dependences of the equilibrium magnetization $\langle m \rangle$, energy $\langle W \rangle$, susceptibility χ, and relaxation time τ on temperature T, obtained in different approximations (atomistic—LL, correlation magnetodynamics—CMD and mean-field approximation—MFA) for face-centered lattice at various parameters. More complete information on the simulation results can be found in [11].

Graphics for equilibrium magnetization and susceptibility are similar for different approximations. Without external field the CMD approximation shifts the phase transition point due to the imperfection of assumptions about the form of the three-particle distribution function.

Dependencies of the energy and the relaxation time in CMD match results of atomistic modeling much better than a mean-field approximation. In some cases relaxation time error in mean-field approximation can reach 50%, Fig. 7, 8.

5   Conclusion

The CMD is a new model (the first article published in the end of 2019) which only starts to come into being. In contrast to traditional LLB equation, CMD operates in the extended phase space. The level of two-particle correlations is taken into account in addition to the magnetisation. That leads to a wider range of processes that the model describes correctly for both quasi–static processes and highly non-equilibrium once. Thus CMD might increase the accuracy of simulations for spintronic and nonoelectronic devices. It is worth mentioning that obtained system is fully self–consistent. It does not contain any adjustable parameters.

The numerical modeling played a crucial role in the development of the CMD. At the moment the estimation of integral coefficients for CMD equations could be done only numerically. The problem of obtaining the integral coefficients for ferrimagnetic and antiferromagnetic materials is computationally demanding. It also requires development of the new methods to compute integrals of multiparticle distribution functions.

The atomistic simulations were required for verification of the model. Currently only the spatially uniform case was tested since testing of the spatially nonuniform case calls for dramatically larger number of atomistic simulations.

References

1. Evans, R.F.L., Fan, W.J., Chureemart, P., Ostler, T.A., Ellis, M.O.A., Chantrell, R.W.: Atomistic spin model simulations of magnetic nanomaterials. J. Phys. Condens. Matter **26**(10), 103202 (2014)
2. Knizhnik, A.A., et al.: A software package for computer-aided design of spintronic nanodevices. Nanotechnol. Russ. **12**, 208–217 (2017). https://doi.org/10.1134/S1995078017020082

3. Garanin, D.A.: Fokker-Planck and Landau-Lifshitz-Bloch equations for classical ferromagnets. Phys. Rev. B **55**, 3050 (1997). https://arxiv.org/abs/cond-mat/9805054v2

4. Atxitia, U., Hinzke, D., Nowak, U.: Fundamentals and applications of the Landau-Lifshitz-Bloch equation. J. Phys. D Appl. Phys. **50**, 033003 (2016)

5. Chubykalo-Fesenko, O., Nieves, P.: Landau-Lifshitz-Bloch approach for magnetization dynamics close to phase transition. In: Andreoni, W., Yip, S. (eds.) Handbook of Materials Modeling. Springer, Cham (2018). https://doi.org/10.1007/978-3-319-42913-7_72-1

6. Ivanov, A., Khilkov, S., Zipunova, E.: Approximation of multiparticle distribution function in micromagnetic modeling. J. Phys. Conf. Ser. **1740**, 012025 (2021). https://doi.org/10.1088/1742-6596/1740/1/012025

7. Garanin, D.A.: Self-consistent Gaussian approximation for classical spin systems: thermodynamics. Phys. Rev. B **53**, 11593 (1996). https://arxiv.org/abs/cond-mat/9804040

8. Ivanov, A.: Approximating Landau-Lifshitz-Bloch coefficients in micromagnetic simulation. Keldysh Inst. Prepr. **105**, 16 (2019). https://doi.org/10.20948/prepr-2019-105-e

9. Ivanov, A.: The account for correlations between nearest neighbors in micromagnetic modeling. Keldysh Inst. Prepr. **118**, 30 (2019). https://doi.org/10.20948/prepr-2019-118

10. Ivanov, A., Zipunova, E.: Micromagnetic modeling with account for the correlations between closest neighbors. AIP Conf. Proc. **2300**(1), 020050 (2020). https://doi.org/10.1063/5.0032075

11. Ivanov, A.: Approximation of many-particle distribution functions for ferromagnetics with different crystal lattices. Keldysh Inst. Prepr. **11**, 22 (2021). https://doi.org/10.20948/prepr-2021-11

12. Ivanov, A., Khilkov, S.: Aiwlib library as the instrument for creating numerical modeling applications. Sci. Vis. **10**(1), 110–127 (2018). https://doi.org/10.26583/sv.10.1.09

13. Morton, G.M.: A computer oriented geodetic data base and a new technique in file sequencing (1966)

14. Ivanov, A.: Kinetic modeling of magnetic's dynamic. Math. Models Comput. Simul. **19**(10), 89–104 (2007). http://www.mathnet.ru/links/82020fa1add2512759e063c1cb0a7ebf/mm1204.pdf

15. Ivanov, A.: Using the library aiwlib on the example of numerical modeling of stochastic resonance. Keldysh Inst. Prepr. **89**, 30 (2018). https://doi.org/10.20948/prepr-2018-89

Clumps and Filaments Generated by Collisions Between Rotating and Non-rotating Molecular Clouds

Boris Rybakin[1]([⊠]) and Valery Goryachev[2]

[1] Department of Gas and Wave Dynamics, Moscow State University,
Moscow, Russia
rybakin@vip.niisi.ru
[2] Department of Mathematics, Tver State Technical University, Tver, Russia

Abstract. Numerical modeling of direct and shear collisions for two molecular clouds is carried out. The simulation was performed using the author's computational code with parallelization. Various scenarios of the impact of non-rotating clouds and mutual penetration of swirling clouds according to different schemes have been investigated. A numerical experiment was carried out with a change in the number of nodes of the computational mesh from 256^3 to 1024^3. The influence of variable swirling regimes of colliding clouds on the change in the shape of the lenticular compression zones in the region of the main impact is analyzed. Rotation in clouds with spiral transfer before stagnation zone leads to radial redistribution of compressed gas in the collision core and accelerates flexural corrugation of core before destruction. Modeling has shown that ring wave disturbances of matter in a compressed core can be caused by the Kelvin-Helmholtz instability, and non-linear thin-shell instability, leading to local density disturbances in the formed clumps and filaments.

Keywords: Parallel computing · Instability · Molecular cloud-cloud collision

1 Introduction

Studying the dynamics of molecular clouds (MCs) - immense accumulations of gas in the interstellar medium (ISM) is important for the explanation of changes in the Universe, primarily for understanding the star formation processes accompanying collision, mutual penetrations and the confluence of these giant formations. Modeling of such processes plays an important role in the study of the evolution of galaxies and the diversity of nebulae accompanied by dissipative interplay between turbulent, thermal and magnetic fields of interstellar matter under conditions of gravitational collapse in deep space observed.

Molecular Cloud-Cloud Collisions (CCC) within ISM are widespread events. Among recent studies, one can reference [1] with a review of the recent astrophysical discoveries and the numerical modeling of MCs collisions [2] and articles that describe a nebulae collisions with compressed clumps and filaments origination that serve a trigger of pre-stellar areas formation in the cluster NGC 3603 [3].

V. Voevodin and S. Sobolev (Eds.): RuSCDays 2021, CCIS 1510, pp. 44–57, 2021.
https://doi.org/10.1007/978-3-030-92864-3_4

Among the various scenarios of emergent pre-stellar zones as a result of collisions, one can single out the main gravitational-turbulent model of mutual MCs penetration with compressed clumps and filaments morphing accompanied by aftershock destruction of them. Modeling of these processes was carried out at different times in a one-dimensional approximation, with two and three-dimensional descriptions for counter gas flows. Most simulations have started with the pioneering work on two-dimensional MCs collision modeling performed in [4] and CCC scenario with rotation of colliding clouds in-plane orthogonal the view line of observation [5]. They showed how compressed cores are formed in thin areas of superficial contact layers and how the process of clumps formation from disturbed clouds fragments begins. Among the modern numerical approaches of gas dynamics, SPH simulations taking into account the effects of gravity, turbulence and magnetic interplay of contrary moved streams and jets, the works [6–8] can be noted. In the last reference numerical study of the formation of giant dense cloud complexes and of stars within them uses SPH approach for simulations of gas inflowing collisions is presented and done some recommendations to find and imitate star clusters in modeling practice. The preface in [8] gives a fairly complete description of the development modeling methods performed with a large number of cited publications used in our study too.

The influence of emerging hydrodynamic instabilities, such as Rayleigh-Taylor (RT), Kelvin-Helmholtz instability (KHI) in head-on superficial layers of counter streams and their consequences for clouds reformatting structure have been noted in many studies. In particular, Nonlinear Instability of Thin Shells (NTSI) from [9, 10] was used for describing oscillations with growing amplitude of shock layers on velocity discontinues surfaces of contrary streams [11]. Such instabilities are caused by shock front, behind which gas matter cools faster than the dynamical velocities front moves, which has in many astrophysical transients, including supernova remnants interacting ISM matter and radiation transfer cases in a collision of star wind streams. Compressed layers here are susceptible to thin-shell instabilities, creating a 'corrugated' shock interface [10–12]. In the last report, these results confirm the suggestion that hot stellar dense outflows from Wolf-Rayet stars can initiate such radiative and adiabatic regimes of instability. As a consequence after relatively long mutual penetration of molecular clouds, turbulization of new formation over compressed core becomes more voluminous and intense.

The rotation of colliding MCs sometimes can be additional drivers of star formation activity in pre-stellar areas. Against the general background of publications on topic of cloud-cloud collision and other interplay, the number of studies taking into account the angular momentum of clouds rotation is relatively small. The importance of rotation in cloud evolution has been recognized but remains poorly-formalized. One can note the role of rotation in the change in the kinematic structure of the spiral-shaped molecular cloud G052.24 + 00.74, which was analyzed in [13]. The spiral-shaped morphology of the cloud suggests that the cloud is rotating. The study showed how cloud fragmentation is regulated through the interaction of rotation and gravity, and partially revealed some of the details of this case using modern astrophysical observation techniques. It was noted that the cloud rotates with some acceleration and was found that cloud is unstable against gravitational collapse. One of the first 3D numerical simulations of collisions between rotating MCs was presented in above mentioned paper [5]. The results show that rotation can significantly extend the evolution time of residual clumps structure compared to cases without rotation. The growth of angular velocity leads to some expansion of the clouds, but the redistribution of translational energy in the collision produces a flattened structure of new formation. Among simulations of mutual shock penetration of swirling nebulae, one can note [14, 15], wherein the axes of MCs co-rotation were supposed in perpendicular to the direction of their collision by scheme: "bullet" cloud penetrates into "target" cloud. It has shown that collision favor fragmentation in clouds cores is a very important one, because each of the dense clumps formed along the filament in the center of the colliding layer, could eventually form a proto-star. The influence of rotation on this process is not noted in articles in detail.

The authors' studies of the collision of MCs and the interaction of nebulae, whose axes of rotation coincide with the line of nebulae collision, is carried out for the first time, as far as the authors know.

2   Modeling and Parallel Code Realization

The presented study of the MCs collision is a continuation of the numerical calculation of gas-dynamic astrophysics processes, starting with work [16]. We use Euler's definition and finite difference method to numerically simulate cloud-cloud collisions using different scenarios of their mutual collision and penetration, with and without additional cloud rotation. Simulation is performed with an emphasis on taking into account, first of all, the force impact and turbulent perturbations during a collision, to analyze mainly this effect.

The problems being solved consider supersonic compressible gas flows using the nonsteady definition of equations for conservation laws of mass, momentum, and energy that are described by a set of equations:

$$\frac{\partial \rho}{\partial t} + \nabla \cdot (\rho \mathbf{u}) = 0 \,, \tag{1}$$

$$\frac{\partial \rho \mathbf{u}}{\partial t} + \nabla \cdot (\rho \mathbf{u}\mathbf{u}) + \nabla P = 0 \,, \tag{2}$$

$$\frac{\partial \rho E}{\partial t} + \nabla \cdot [(E+P)\mathbf{u}] = 0 \,. \tag{3}$$

In these equations: $E = \rho(e + \mathbf{u}^2/2)$ is the total gas energy, e – the internal energy, ρ is the gas density, $\mathbf{u} = (u, v, w)$ – velocity vector. The total energy E and gas pressure P are related through the ideal gas closure $P = (\gamma - 1)\rho\, e$, where adiabatic index γ is equal to 5/3. The boundary conditions are set as open.

The numerical realization was done using in-house software developed for multi-processor computers. The calculation algorithm was based on the application of the method of splitting calculations by physical coordinates. From a five-dimensional array of conservative variables, a one-dimensional section of the original array was cut out for each spatial variable and distributed between the processors. At each time step of integration, the values determined at the centers of the grid cells were calculated, and then the fluxes through the boundaries for pressure waves moving to the right and waves moving to the left were calculated. Equations are solved on high refinement mesh with number of nodes reached a level 1024^3 with adaptive Roe solver using the schemes of TVD type [17, 18].

Calculation tuning with Intel VTune Amplifier XE is carried out for Xeon E2630 and Xeon E5 2650 Ivy Bridge processors. To the realization of parallel computations, OpenMP technologies for CPU and CUDA - for graphics processors units with calculation acceleration were employed. Intel VTune Amplifier XE toolkit allows profiling applications directly on the nodes of the cluster computing system. To determine the quality of parallelization of CPU, Light Weight Hotspots test [19] was used. Some routines used in numerical code were calculated on graphics processing units. To check acceleration of calculation Client Utilities & Framework (CUF) core technology [20] was used. The numerical practice revealed that for not very large mesh nodes sizes (up to $1024 \times 512 \times 512$ nodes) parallelization on the GPU gave greater acceleration of operations than parallelization using OpenMP. As the grid size increases, data does not fit in the GPU memory. Therefore, performance is slowed down due to data transfer on the relatively slow PSI-E bus. The quality of computing performance improvement was analyzed when solving test problems with the goal of debugging the calculation technique. Acceleration was checked in the variants with the largest calculation time. It can be seen from the results that, for a small computational grid, the use of OpenMP technology does not give any acceleration, but rather slows down the computation. However, the small size of the grid cells does not have a significant negative effect inherent in graphic cards when working with small amounts of data. With an increase in the number of computing nodes on the GPU, there is a significant acceleration of calculation - more than 25 times, compared with a work on a single core of the central processor used. Comparison conducted on a single server node with two Intel® XEON® CPU E5-2630 2.0 GHz processors and two Tesla K40 GPUs.

Parallel realization of in-house code is discussed in [20]. A set of solver utilities and postprocessing system HDVIS using new parallelization options to create animations of generated scenes were used to analyze a very large output of numerical results.

3   Results and Discussion

The main goal of modeling performed is to study the morphological changes of colliding clouds and study matter compression dynamics in the reshaping MC's core under various conditions of mutual penetration of one cloud into another taking into account different realizations of their rotation schemes.

It was assumed that oppositely moving clouds collide with each other with relative colliding velocity of 5.32 km/s. The speed of sound in the ISM: $c_s = 11.772$ km·s^{-1} was taken as a unit of speed. The angular velocity of rotation of the clouds was taken equal to $\Omega = 2.5969 \times 10^{-15}$ s^{-1}. The computing area used is a box of $10 \times 10 \times 10$ pc dimensions. The diameter and mass of the initially spherical clouds were taken to be equal respectively: for first cloud MC_1 – 3.36 pc and 10.85 $M_\odot$; for second cloud MC_2

– 3.44 pc and 10.54 $M_\odot$. The distribution of matter density inside the clouds plays an essential role in the impulse action of clouds mass in a collision and density pertur-bation. Initial density for overlapping gas layers in transitional zone were regulated by parameters of its radial profile distribution taken from [21, 22]. Initial density contrast $\chi = \rho_{cl}/\rho_{ism}$, designated for values between MC's centers and ISM are taken equal to 500. The ambient gas density in ISM is taken as $\rho_{ism} = 1 \times 10^{-25}$ g·cm^{-3}.

The simulation of the idealized colliding was carried out according to various CCC scenarios with head-on or displaced clouds impact, taking into account the effects of possible rotation around the central axis.

Four interaction options were used in calculations: a) head-on collision without clouds rotation; b) the impact of the non-rotated cloud with a rotating one; c) case of clouds colliding with rotation in the same direction; d) case of clouds mutual pene-tration with a counter swirling. Modeling was repeated for situations when a shift was set between the clouds interaction lines. The axes of the rotation of clouds coincided with the impact direction (Fig. 1).

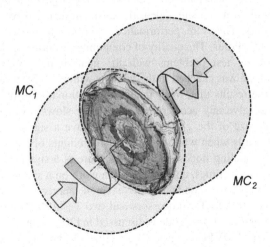

Fig. 1. Molecular clouds collision with counter-rotating.

It was revealed that during mutual penetration clouds can be going three main stages: monotonic increase of density in the compressed lens-like core, the initiation of unstable deformation inside concentric layers of compression core, and a rapid increase in the number of nucleated clumps and filaments observed both in front of and behind the compressed core.

Spatial reshaping of two colliding MCs with mutual penetration is illustrated in Fig. 2 where originated clump formations and filament embryos are shown during the collision follow two scenarios of non-rotated clouds (a) and clouds swirling in a contrary direction (d). In the lower part of the figure, two views of a compressed core formation are shown for the variant of cloud collision without rotation. Viewpoints are in the line of sight from opposite sides of core. The screenshot shows the isodensity layers on a level of $\chi = 18000$ during MCs interaction at the beginning of the third phase of the collision, at t = 304. Wisps of clumps from colliding streams are fragmented and redistributed across the rings around the impact axis. Gas streams move from the zone of the central stagnation spot (two-sided formation) to the periphery with the repetition of the spatial density of the substance in the ring-shaped formations.

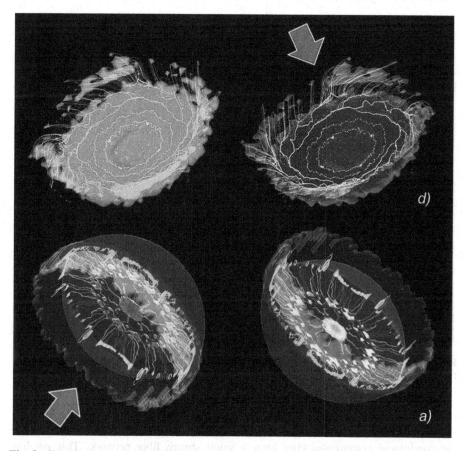

Fig. 2. Fragmentation and reshaping of compressed core and clumps in MCs interaction zone happen according to two schemas: the clouds collision without rotation (a) and collision of clouds with the opposite direction of rotation (d).

Another distribution of matter in a collision according to the scheme of interaction of a cloud with opposite rotation - case (d), which occurred at the same time, is shown in the upper part of Fig. 2. One can see a network of spiral particle trajectories formed in a swirling velocity field over isodensity surface (density contrast $\chi = 18000$). Flow particles move spirally towards the core center from points of spatial curl field, the vortex flocks (depicted as translucent) of which shown in front of the isodensity surface. The local velocity of flow varies greatly in the braking area in a head-on collision. A rapid change in the tending to zero gas flow swirl on inner stagnation layers leads to the appearance of gas density fluctuations and periodic excitation of them near outer boundaries with a large curvature on the disk-like surface periphery. This leads to a local spatial density perturbation originated by Kelvin-Helmholtz instability and unstable growth of "finger" structures repeating in the azimuthal direction and curved according to tangential gas acceleration. This is illustrated in Fig. 3.

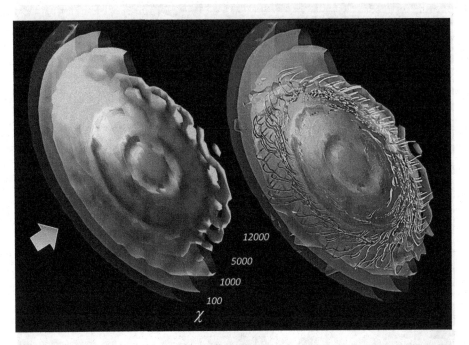

Fig. 3. Isodensities layers for case (b) - impact of the non-rotated cloud with rotating one. Unstable growth of "finger" structures for inner density layers with $\chi = 12000$.

The processing of modeling velocities fields during a collision of clouds, rotating in various combinations, showed that the resulting flows of gas in their final movement to the conditional compressed core form a spiral stream fiber network. This net has merging streams and concentrically distributed waved channels, where gas particles from the external environment are attracted to the core (Fig. 4). There are many confluent streamlets tending to the curves of attraction, towards and away from the axis of rotation of the clouds. This description fits both the frontal impact of the clouds and the situation with a shift in the direction of their impact, an example of this scene is shown in the right part of the figure. With the oncoming movement of clouds according to the last scenario, the forming core takes a sigmoid shape with transverse thickenings. The trajectories of moving fluid particles partially repeat this relief. The spiral motion is more diverse here. The formation is similar to the Cat's Eye Nebula in general features.

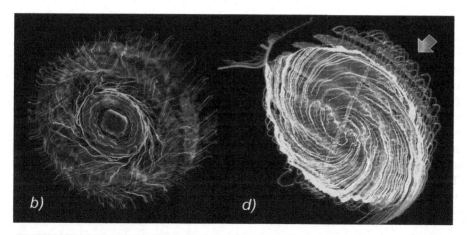

Fig. 4. The multi-arm spiral structure of gas streams over colliding clouds core. Left: collision of rotated cloud with non-rotated one (b). Right: the collision of clouds shifted related to the direction of moving, with the opposite direction of move and swirl (d).

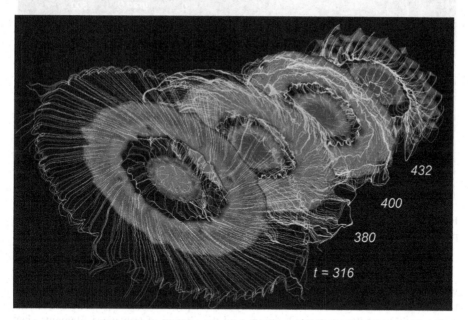

Fig. 5. Shape changing of the core in the collision of clouds rotating in the same direction.

One can see the features of the formation of ragged arm-like streams, which repeat the structure inherent in multi-armed spiral galaxies, arisen due to the spatial inhomogeneity of star clusters rotating within galaxies, whose sizes differ by orders of magnitude.

Figure 5 shows the evolution of mutual clouds swirling penetration of one into another. Time redistribution of pressure and velocity fields for counter gas flows changes the shape of a central core. Changing the density of core layers and gas confluent streams in attractive zones is accompanied by a slight decrease of clouds outer diameter and radial ring stratification. Common in the observed process of mutual penetration of clouds is a rapid change of pressure in the contact layer and spatial corrugation with redistribution of energy inside it.

As the pressure in the collision core increases, density perturbations begin to increase under influence of NTSI effects. Bending deformation spread throughout the compressed core radially and azimuthally fragmenting density inclusions into clumps. This is illustrated in Figs. 6 and 7 where twisted and splitting spiral streamlines in the velocity field crossed with gradient lines of internal energy are shown.

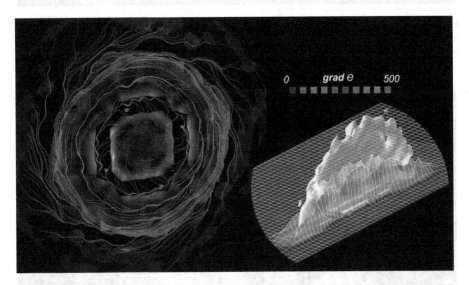

Fig. 6. Relief map of changes in the modulus of the internal energy gradient in the meridional plane of the collision region and gas pathlines, colour-coded by local value of this value.

Figure 6 represent a scene of the interplay of fluctuated values of energy magnitude with velocity field for a case (d) – a collision of clouds with contrary rotation at time t = 400. Radial changes in the core density are sharply intermittent, which is reflected in the position of the segmented clumps and the change of transverse filaments size. The high relief of the distribution of the modulus of the internal energy gradient has the form of two separated reliefs, squeezing on the sides a flattened compressed gas matter core with a density contrast value of 18000. NTSI accelerates the generation of vortices inside the clouds formation, which is reflected in corrugated forms of shock core layers with the sharp growth of compress in the core. A compressed layer stochastically changes its density and structure of spatial blobs originated above stagnation points. The kinetic energy changing accumulated between local gas jets on the contact spots is provoked by propagating of oblique shocks. Density and velocity fields here are quite intermittent. Any imbalance in the directions of a collision on either shock front direction can enhance perturbation of the stream interface and allow this instability to grow. Observable NTS instability initiates to corrugate shock front and creates a distribution of energy and density fields, shown in Fig. 6.

Figure 7 shows comparative morphological changes for three variants of collision and interpenetration of molecular clouds. All variants – collisions of clouds with rotation. The local changes in the energy transfer in layers are clearly correlating with the change of compressed blobs sizes inside the layer. In this place, the gas streamlines merge or bifurcate, or sharply bend in spirals. Comparison of changes during the evolution of colliding clouds showed that their initial rotation leads to a certain progressive decrease of the collision core diameter and increasing dispersion of decaying clumps during the transition from the case (a) to the scheme (b), (c) and (d) respectively. In the figure, internal energy gradient lines are coded by red color, pathlines of velocity field coded by white color. The close to the orthogonal intersection of the velocity vectors and temperature gradient is an indicator of the formation of zones with an increase in bending instability. One can suppose that gas incipient blobs can be concentrated along such pathlines dragging to separatrix lines, and these zones can initial for the filamentation growth here.

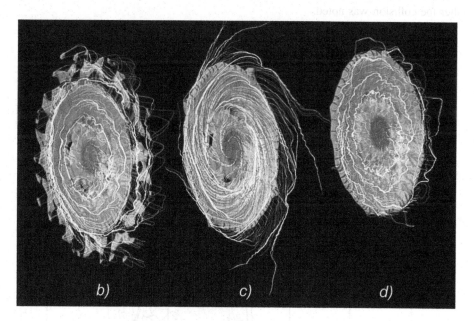

Fig. 7. The morphing of core compressed during a collision in accordance with scenarios: b) impact of the non-rotated cloud with a rotating one; c) colliding clouds rotating in the same direction; d) colliding clouds with the counter direction of swirl.

The complex dynamics of colliding streams before the stagnation zone leads to a rather unexpected spatial distribution of gas clumps on intermediate transform trajectories.

For different CCC scenarios, an analysis was carried out of the change in the mass fraction of the density in the compressed layers of clouds and clumps, which significantly change in the course of the evolution of new formations. Mass fraction distribution is shown in the graphs in Fig. 8. It was revealed that the maximum mass fraction of density decreases with the complication of the conditions for the transmission of the shock impulse - with a change in the direction of oncoming rotation or displacement of the impact. The largest mass fraction drop-down is achieved in the case of head-on penetration for oppositely swirling clouds. The distribution of denser mixture fractions has two and more local maximums that are reached before the moment of cloud envelopes breakthrough and after a sufficiently deep penetration of one cloud into another. The process of compression of the gas matter is most active in the evolution time range 270–350. At the end of the destruction of clumps, the oscillation amplitude of local density in evanescent remnants can reach 20–30% from the average value in this period.

Calculations did not reveal a radical effect of cloud rotation on the integral increase or decrease in the density of formations inside the compressed core. When the direction of rotation is changed, an increase in the variance of the density values in the residuals after the collision was noted.

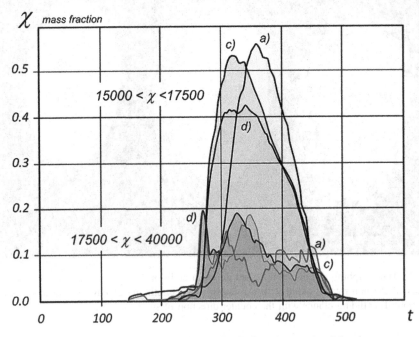

Fig. 8. Changes in mass fraction of reshaping clouds for two ranges of density contrast over time.

A similar picture of the change in the fractional composition of clouds is repeated during the collision of molecular clouds, displaced in the direction of motion and swirling in various combinations. As an important addition, a large increase in the range of gas density values of ablating residues at the final stage, after reaching the maximum values of the gas density, can be noted. The largest spread in density was observed in case (b) - impact non-rotated cloud collides with a rotating one shifted in a moving direction.

Some new calculations with a change in the mass scale of colliding clouds by orders of magnitude, to the generally accepted scale of giant molecular clouds, showed that the reshaping and destruction of remnants after their collisions remains qualitatively the same, but the dispersion of the formed clumps increases significantly. The post-shock stage of mutual penetration of molecular clouds with a diameter of about 13 pc colliding with a relative velocity of about 5 km/s is shown in Fig. 9. The figure shows the distribution of clumps at the third stage of evolution when they have already formed in clusters.

After mutual penetration of one cloud through another the gas density in clumps that appeared outside can reach the highest density values compared with the values observed throughout the entire period of clouds interplay. Density contrast in transformation zone can be thousand-fold higher than the initial average values.

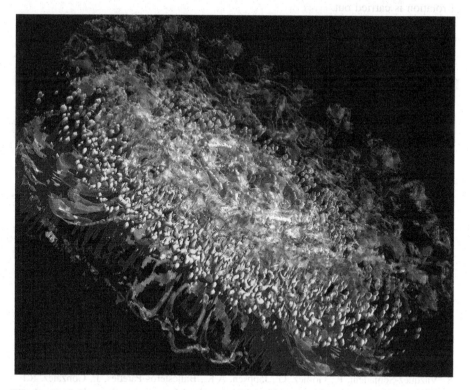

Fig. 9. Spatial vortex streams at the moment of complete mutual passage of clouds, piercing separated clumps formations (density contrast is over 30000) with concentric distribution and ring clustering possible pre-stellar zones for a head-on collision of giant molecular clouds.

The numerical experiments revealed that the density of originated clumps can be vary in the range of 10^{-21}–10^{-19} g·cm^{-3}, which corresponds to the generally accepted values for the pre-stellar conglomeration.

4 Conclusion

The influence of angular momentum on the structure of gas flows in the zone of deceleration of counter flows in different schemes of molecular clouds colliding is studied. Using the parallel modeling code, new studies of MC's collisions, the axes of rotation of which coincide with the collision line of the nebulae, have been carried out. It was revealed how the shock interplay between colliding clouds is provoked and magnified via Kelvin-Helmholtz and Nonlinear Thin Shell Instability in clouds layers in bent corrugated core. NTSI effects revealed in spiral-arm clouds transformation modeling can be expanded by data obtained in the presented simulation with revealing their influence onto originated perturbation in reshaping compressed layers in MCs collision. The analysis of the influence of swirling matter distribution in collisions of molecular clouds on the wave redistribution of density with the transfer of maximum values to the periphery of the new formation and increased turbulization along the axis of rotation is carried out.

Acknowledgements. This work has been supported by RFBR Grant 19-29-09070 mk.

References

1. Dobbs, C.L., et al.: Formation of molecular clouds and global conditions for star formation. In: Beuther, H., Klessen, R., Dullemont, C., Henning, Th. (eds.). Protostars and Planets VI. University of Arizona Press, pp. 3–26 (2014)
2. Special Issue: Star Formation Triggering by Cloud-Cloud Collision. Publication of the Astronomical Society of Japan – PASJ, 70 (SP2) (2018)
3. Fukui, Y., Ohama, A., Hanaoka, N., et al.: Molecular clouds toward the super star cluster NGC 3603. Possible evidence for a cloud-cloud collision in triggering the cluster formation. Astrophys. J. **780**(36), 13 (2014)
4. Habe, A., Ohta, K.: Gravitational instability induced by a cloud-cloud collision: the case of head-on collision between clouds with different sizes and densities. Publ. Astron. Soc. Japan **44**, 203–226 (1992)
5. Lattanzio, J.C., Monaghan, J.J., Pongracic, H., Schwarz, M.P.: Interstellar cloud collisions. MNRAS **215**(2), 125–147 (1985)
6. Parkin, E.R., Pittard, J.M.: Numerical heat conduction in hydrodynamical models of colliding hypersonic flows. MNRAS **406**, 2373–2385 (2010)
7. Vazquez-Semadeni, E., Ryu, D., Passot, T., Gonzalez, R.F., Gazol, A.: Molecular cloud evolution. I. Molecular cloud and thin cold neutral medium shift formation. Astrophys. J. **643**, 245–259 (2006)
8. Vazquez-Semadeni, E., Gomez, G., Jappsen, A.K., Ballesteros-Paredes, J., Gonzalez, R.F., Klessen, R.: Molecular cloud evolution. II. From cloud formation to the early stages of star formation in decaying conditions. Astrophys. J. **657**, 870–883 (2007)

9. Vishniac, E.T.: Nonlinear instabilities in shock-bounded slabs. Astrophys. J. **428**, 186–208 (1994)
10. Folini, D., Walder, R.: Supersonic turbulence in shock-bound interaction zones. I. Symmetric settings. A&A **459**, 1–19 (2006)
11. McLeod, A.D., Whitworth, A.P.: Simulations of the non-linear thin shell instability. MNRAS **431**, 710–721 (2013)
12. Calderón, D., Cuadra, J., Schartmann, M., Burkert, A., Prieto, J., Russell, C.: Three-dimensional simulations of clump formation in stellar wind collision. MNRAS **493**, 447–467 (2020)
13. Li, G.-X., Wyrowski, F., Menten, K.: Revealing a spiral-shaped molecular cloud in our galaxy: cloud fragmentation under rotation and gravity. A&A **598**(A96), 1–15 (2017)
14. Arreaga-García, G., Saucedo-Morales, J.: Physical properties of a molecular cloud after a penetrating collision. Open Astron. J. **8**, 18–37 (2015)
15. Arreaga-García, G., Klapp, J.: Accretion centers induced in a molecular cloud core after a penetrating collision. In: Klapp, J., Chavarría, G.R., Ovando, A.M., Villa, A.L., Sigalotti, L. G. (eds.) Selected Topics of Computational and Experimental Fluid Mechanics. ESE, pp. 505–513. Springer, Cham (2015). https://doi.org/10.1007/978-3-319-11487-3_41
16. Rybakin, B., Goryachev, V.: Parallel algorithms for astrophysics problems. Lobachevski J. Math. **39**(4), 562–570 (2018)
17. Rider, W.J.: An adaptive Riemann solver using a two-shock approximation. Comput. Fluids **28**(6), 741–777 (1999)
18. De Zeeuw, D., Powell, K.G.: An adaptively refined Cartesian Mesh solver for the Euler equations. J. Comput. Phys. **104**(1), 56–68 (1993)
19. Intel® VTune™ Profiler User Guide. Intel Corporation (2018)
20. CUF (Client Utilities and Framework). Utility libraries and an application-level framework for building GUI applications. https://sourceforge.net/projects/cuf/
21. Nakamura, F., McKee, C., Klein, R.I., Fisher, R.T.: On the hydrodynamic interaction of shock waves with interstellar clouds. II. The effect of smooth cloud boundaries on cloud destruction and cloud turbulence. Astrophys. J. **164**, 477–505 (2006)
22. Pittard, J.M., Falle, S.A.E.G., Hartquist, T.W., Dyson, J.E.: The turbulent destruction of clouds. MNRAS **394**, 1351–1378 (2009)

Exploiting Structural Constraints of Proteolytic Catalytic Triads for Fast Supercomputer Scaffold Probing in Enzyme Design Studies

Alexander Zlobin[1,2,3(✉)], Alexander-Pavel Ermidis[3],
Valentina Maslova[2,3], Julia Belyaeva[2,3], and Andrey Golovin[1,2,3(✉)]

[1] Shemyakin–Ovchinnikov Institute of Bioorganic Chemistry, Russian Academy
of Sciences, 117997 Moscow, Russian Federation
`zlobin.as@talantiuspeh.ru`, `golovin@belozersky.msu.ru`
[2] Sirius University of Science and Technology, 354340 Sochi,
Russian Federation
[3] Faculty of Bioengineering and Bioinformatics, Lomonosov Moscow State
University, 119991 Moscow, Russian Federation
`{alexandrpavele,val_ma,belyaevajuly}@fbb.msu.ru`

Abstract. Evolutionary constraints on the effectiveness of enzymatic function result in well-defined architectures of active sites. In this study we show that these constraints are fully pronounced even at the backbone level. We explore the possibility of defining catalytic triads in proteases just by their relative backbone orientations to dramatically speed up the scaffold search problem of *de novo* enzyme design. An order of magnitude speed-up achieved this way paves a way to a routine scanning of the whole structural proteome including modeled structures.

Keywords: Enzyme design · Structural bioinformatics · Structural similarity · Protease

1 Introduction

Proteases comprise a group of structurally and functionally diverse enzymes that have the common ability to catalyze the hydrolysis of peptide bonds [1]. This ability is facilitated by active sites of varying composition that give different classes of proteolytic enzymes their respective names. This way there are serine, cysteine, threonine, aspartyl, glutamyl proteases and metalloproteases. Among these groups, serine and cysteine proteases are the most studied and act under the widest condition ranges. Most serine proteases employ a catalytic triad consisting of Ser, His and Asp residues as an active site. Three residues must be positioned in a specific way to facilitate Ser deprotonation in order to perform a nucleophilic attack on a substrate (Fig. 1). Ser must be hydrogen bonded to His, which in turn has a second hydrogen bond to Asp that positions His correctly and shifts its pKa. More generally and according to the

V. Voevodin and S. Sobolev (Eds.): RuSCDays 2021, CCIS 1510, pp. 58–72, 2021.
https://doi.org/10.1007/978-3-030-92864-3_5

performed function these three residues are called a nucleophile, a base and an acid (or an activator). A base formed by histidine is a widespread scenario. In turn, a nucleophile and an activator may be different from the most common Ser and Asp residues [2]. Thereby exist classes of triad-harbouring cysteine proteases [3]. In general, this evolutionary successful arrangement of three residues is exploited for other hydrolytic functions. Despite the pronounced need for a specific hydrogen bonding of triad residues, it can be achieved by more than one spatial arrangement. Comparisons of single representative enzymes showed that, for example, inside the class of serine triad-harbouring proteases, chymotrypsin and subtilisin implement different triad architectures. On the other hand, cysteine TEV protease is remarkably similar to serine protease trypsin in terms of active site spatial arrangement. Systematic investigation into the space of all triad architectures was not performed to date.

Animal, plant, and, especially, microbial proteases represent the largest and most important segment of an industrial enzyme market where they are used in detergents, food processing or leather industry, as biocatalysts in organic synthesis, and as therapeutics. The list of potential practical applications of proteases can be greatly expanded, especially for therapeutic applications, once their catalytic activities can be engineered for specific uses [1]. This can be done with the help of state-of-the-art computational techniques. A combination of structural analysis, reaction modelling and rational design can be used to modify specificity, stability or other properties of existing enzymes, including proteases [4–7]. Among the examples of sound success stories in protease design is Kuma062, a kumamolisin variant repurposed to process gluten [8]. To face humanity's demand for applied proteolytic functions, modification of existing enzymes alone is, however, not sufficient. The computational methods of *de novo* introduction of enzymatic function into previously non-catalytic protein folds are regarded as a major step forward in addressing the needs of industry and medicine [9]. These efforts are, however, limited to the approach implemented in Rosetta3 enzyme design protocol [10]. This method was previously successfully used for transfer of existing active sites into manually generated folds and for computational design of previously non-existent enzymatic functions such as retro-aldolase or Diels-Alder reaction catalysts [11–14].

The underlying computational procedure starts from the definition of a theozyme – a set of atoms at their respective coordinates mimicking the crucial step of the enzymatic process, e.g. transition state. Most commonly a theozyme is constructed from the substrate moiety and the sidechains of active site residues. After theozyme is constructed, a suitable backbone scaffold to harbour its residues needs to be obtained either by searching the space of known structures or by constructing it from scratch. One can focus only on backbone scaffolds because there is only a limited set of them, and they are highly degenerate in terms of underlying sequences; thus it is unnecessary to perform placement search in all individual proteins with known structure. The searching algorithm implemented in the Rosetta Match application is rather slow as it scans through rotameric libraries of the desired active site residues' sidechains. The sampling takes even longer if the geometry constraints tolerate fluctuations in the theozyme structure. The further design is based on preservation and additional stabilisation of some interactions between the active site sidechains and the transitional state of the reaction [10].

Such technique does not require the similarity between the active site backbone conformations in the newly constructed enzyme and in the initial source of theozyme, and relies on idealized backbone-dependent rotamer libraries for sidechains. However, in some enzymes the backbone of the active site residues plays a key role in the oxyanion hole formation. For example, both in serine and cysteine proteases the catalytic Ser/Cys backbone N forms a hydrogen bond with the carbonyl O of the substrate. Such interaction is crucial for the catalysis [15, 16]. Moreover, it was shown that the residues directly involved in the catalytic act more often are rotameric outliers [17, 18].

Conformations of protease catalytic residues are highly specific being the result of evolutionary selection. Since rotamer distributions are inherently backbone conformation-dependent, and since backbone is likely to itself participate in the reaction, we suggest that relative backbone geometries of catalytic residues are themselves highly specific. What is more, we hypothesize that by knowing the relative geometries of the triad's backbones one can derive the triad's full structure. It makes it possible to make theozyme placement search task completely sidechain-agnostic. In this work we provide justification for this idea. We propose a description of the catalytic site using the involved residues' backbone orientation. We demonstrate a distinguishable difference between triads in active sites found in available serine and cysteine proteases and other non-catalytic combinations of the same residues. Once the hypothesis is proven, we show that the natural consequence of it is the possibility to drastically speed up the scaffold searching. We present a computational protocol for theozyme placement based on scaffold backbone orientation analysis. When applied to the search for trypsin catalytic triad placement, our backbone-based approach outperforms Rosetta Match in speed by at least 30 times while retaining the accuracy. Low computational cost of the presented solution allows one to run over about 180 000 structures (a full PDB) placement search for one active site in a matter of minutes when using supercomputer resources.

2   Materials and Methods

2.1   Backbone-Based Vectorization of Triads

We define triad as a triplet of unique protein residues with known position of their backbone atoms N, CA, C. For each residue we introduce a virtual point in space called BB placed at the geometric center between its N and C atoms. For a pair of residues i and j, a number of terms is computed. Term α_{ij} is defined as an angle between atoms i_C–i_{BB}–j_{BB}. Term θ_{ij} is defined as a torsion angle constructed for atoms i_C–i_{BB}–j_{BB}–j_C. Term η_{ij} is defined as a torsion angle constructed for atoms i_{CA}–i_C–i_{BB}–j_{BB}. Triad vector V for residues i, j, k is then constructed from these terms as follows:

$$V_{ijk} = \left\{ \alpha_{ij}, \alpha_{ji}, \theta_{ij}, \eta_{ij}, \alpha_{jk}, \alpha_{kj}, \theta_{jk}, \eta_{jk}, \alpha_{ki}, \alpha_{ik}, \theta_{ki}, \eta_{ki} \right\} \tag{1}$$

Throughout the paper all angular terms are expressed in degrees.

2.2   Protease Triads Dataset Construction

For this work, a collection of PDB IDs matching EC codes 3.4.21 (Serine endopeptidases) and 3.4.22 (Cysteine endopeptidases) with resolution under 3 Å and R-free under 0.4 was obtained. To ensure non-redundancy the dataset was culled at the 90% sequence similarity level using Pisces [19]. The resulting PDB IDs dataset comprised 811 entries.

   We then searched for catalytic-like triads in the structures of these proteins. Search and analysis was performed with the help of ProDy [20]. First, all histidine residues were selected. We then analyzed the surroundings of both its sidechain N_δ and N_ε nitrogen atoms. Catalytic-like triad was identified as a triplet of residues Nuc-His-Act, where Nuc (nucleophile) is either Ser or Cys and Act (activator) is either Asp, Glu, Asn or Gln, if there was simultaneously $O\gamma$ or $S\gamma$ atom of Nuc closer then 3.5 Å to any one nitrogen atom of His and one of the sidechain oxygens of Act closer then 3.5 Å to another nitrogen of His. If the analyzed structure comprised several copies of the same subunit the triad from only one of them was retained for subsequent studies.

   For each catalytic-like triad obtained this way a triad vector was computed as described above. The resulting triad dataset comprised 312 entries.

2.3   Clusterization of Triad Vectors

We chose to compose our vector only from angular and torsional terms to avoid normalization problems since all the values are expressed in the same units and lie in the same range. However, half of vector values represent torsions which are naturally periodic. Because of this, straightforward implementation of distance-based clusterization is incorrect since commonly used distance metrics are not periodic. We thus precompute the distance matrix manually. For two triad vectors V_{ijk} and V_{abc}, the distance D between them is the Euclidean norm of a vector ΔV:

$$D = \|\Delta V\|_2 = \left\| \{ \Delta\alpha_{ij,ab}, \Delta\alpha_{ji,ba}, \Delta\theta_{ij,ab}, \Delta\eta_{ij,ab}, \Delta\alpha_{jk,bc}, \Delta\alpha_{kj,cb}, \right.$$
$$\left. \Delta\theta_{jk,bc}, \Delta\eta_{jk,bc}, \Delta\alpha_{ki,ca}, \Delta\alpha_{ik,ac}, \Delta\theta_{ki,ca}, \Delta\eta_{ki,ca} \} \right\|_2 \tag{2}$$

Where

$$\Delta\alpha_{ij,ab} = \alpha_{ij} - \alpha_{ab} \tag{3}$$

$$\Delta\theta_{ij,ab} = min\left(\left| \theta_{ij} - \theta_{ab} \right|, 360 - \left| \theta_{ij} - \theta_{ab} \right| \right) \tag{4}$$

$$\Delta\eta_{ij,ab} = min\left(\left| \eta_{ij} - \eta_{ab} \right|, 360 - \left| \eta_{ij} - \eta_{ab} \right| \right) \tag{5}$$

and similar for all other instances of α, θ and η.

   Precomputed distance matrix was utilized to perform density-based clusterization. DBScan from the sklearn Python package was utilized for the task [21]. The epsilon parameter, specifying the maximum distance between two samples for one to be considered as in the neighborhood of the other, was set to 50. The number of samples in a neighborhood for a point to be considered as a core point was set to 10. 4 clusters were identified, with 86 points not being in any of them.

2.4   Visualization of Clusterization Results

Informative visualization of clusterization results of data represented as a 12-dimensional vector naturally calls for a dimensionality reduction. UMAP technique was selected for the task, implemented in the umap-learn Python package [22]. All parameters were set to default except for the metric which in our case was set to "precomputed" since we used an already built distance matrix as an input.

Protein structures with triads from the same clusters were superposed with the help of pair_fit functionality in PyMol, which was also used for molecular visualization throughout the paper [23].

2.5   Scaffold Preprocessing and Placement Search Procedure

For a given protein scaffold query and a triad vector template the placement search procedure is intended to produce a ranked list of triples of scaffold residues most closely matching the relative backbone orientation of the template. To enforce reusability, a protein scaffold is first preprocessed. Protein structure is transformed into a graph with its residues represented as nodes in this graph. The edge between two nodes i and j is drawn if the distance between CA atoms of two respective residues (d_{CA}) lies between 4 and 13 Å and the distance between their CB atoms (d_{CB}) does not exceed d_{CA} by more then 1 Å. The edge is assigned a data container comprised of two vectors $\{\alpha_{ij}, \alpha_{ji}, \theta_{ij}, \eta_{ij}\}$ and $\{\alpha_{ji}, \alpha_{ij}, \theta_{ji}, \eta_{ji}\}$. The list of all triads is then obtained by performing a clique search and selecting all the cliques of length 3. An additional filter is imposed on a triad ijk so that the area of the triangle with vertices CA_i, CA_j and CA_k does not exceed 35 Å^2. As discussed earlier, the construction of a final triad vector relies on specifying the sequence of its constitutive residues. For all selected cliques all permutations of its vertices are constructed and assigned a triad vector by combining the respective components of a data stored on the graph's edges. The final list of all triad vectors and respective residue indices in each sequential order is saved as a Python pickle for further use. All graph manipulations are performed with the help of the networkx Python package [24].

For a placement search for a specified template and a scaffold a list of stored triad vectors is further reduced by considering that only half of the six permutations of triad indices are relevant for each single search task. For the input template triad ijk it is calculated whether the triple of vectors $\underline{N_iC_i}$, $\underline{N_jC_j}$, $\underline{N_kC_k}$ is right-handed or otherwise, and only matching triples from the scaffold are retained for search. Finally, distance between each scaffold triad vector and template vector is calculated as described earlier, and scaffold positions are reported if such distance is below the threshold.

2.6   Scaffold Library Construction

CATH non-redundant S40 collection of domains was obtained as PDB files totaling 31879 scaffolds [25]. Since the position of CB atoms is a prerequisite for one of the filter stages in a placement search, all positions in all scaffolds were turned into alanines without moving altering backbone coordinates with Rosetta3 fixbb protocol [26]. Each structure then was preprocessed as was described earlier.

Preprocessing and scaffold searching was carried out using the equipment of the shared research facilities of HPC computing resources at the Lomonosov Moscow State University ("Lomonosov-2" supercomputer) [27]. Preprocessing stage took 30 min 22 s on 64 cores with average preprocessing time for one scaffold of 3.66 s. Scaffold searching stage took 5 min 43 s on 64 cores with average search time for one scaffold of 0.69 s.

2.7   Rosetta Match Assessment

Structure of Porcine Pancreatic Trypsin (PDB ID 4DOQ) was used to assess the computational time of Rosetta Match application [10]. The theozyme included the catalytic triad Ser-His-Asp and a water molecule as a dummy substrate. The search was performed into the whole protein structure (221 residues). The -consolidate_matches flag was used to prevent massive and time-consuming output of nearly identical structures.

Rosetta Match was tested with -packing:ex1 and -packing:ex2 levels set to either default 1 or 3 for more precise rotamer sampling.

3   Results and Discussion

3.1   Backbone-Based Vectorization of Triads

We start by hypothesizing that for a scaffold searching task a theozyme for enzyme design may be in principle reduced to just the relative organization of backbones of crucial residues. Similar reduction was previously shown to be beneficial to the design of small-molecule binding sites [28]. Rationale for such reduction was given in the introduction section of the manuscript.

Another aspect that would benefit a scaffold searching problem is an ability to directly compare different backbone organizations by having a distance metric defined for such an object type. This notion requires a vectorization procedure as well. Trivial way to perform such vectorization is by expressing each triad as a vector of each of its atoms' coordinates. Once this is done, root mean square deviation of atomic positions (RMSD) is a natural measure of similarity between two such objects. However, such comparison requires an optimal superposition performed firsthand; what is more, such a description is redundant since it explicitly differentiates between translated and rotated copies of the same triad. It is possible to construct a more concise vectorization that would be translation- and rotation-invariant and thus would not require preemptive superposition.

Backbone orientation of each residue may be represented as an oriented triangle with vertices N-CA-C (Fig. 1A). All measures of these triangles are fixed since the length of N-CA and CA-C bonds and the angle between them may be safely considered a constant for all protein structures. The vectorization task therefore is reduced to the problem of encoding the relative orientations of three such triangles. Taking rotational and translational invariance into account, only 12 degrees of freedom are left. For a pair of residues 6 values are sufficient to describe the relative orientations of their backbone: 5 angles defined in the Fig. 1B and the distance between any pair of their atoms. It is possible to construct an asymmetric triad vector by choosing a pivot residue and constructing two sets of 6 values each to explicitly encode the positions of two remaining residues. However, we decided to choose a different formalization in which each pair of residues forming a triad contributes 4 degrees of freedom, all expressed in angular or torsional form. Such vectorization is thus symmetric and uniform in data ranges and units which is useful for the calculation of distance between two such vectors without need for normalization (see Materials and Methods).

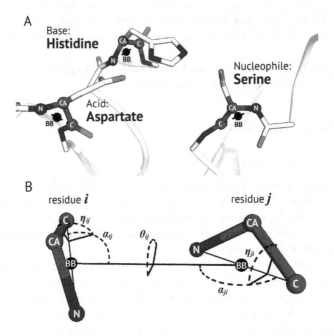

Fig. 1. Catalytic triad typical organization and vectorization. A. Architecture of the trypsin's catalytic triad. Backbone atom names are labeled and highlighted in gray. B. Vectorization introduced in current work.

3.2   Space of Architectures of Proteases' Catalytic Triads

We intended to investigate whether our simplistic approach is useful to describe the space of active site architectures. In this work we focused on catalytic triads of serine and cysteine endopeptidases. We found that clusterization based on our 12-dimensional vectorization produces highly informative insights, clearly distinguishing between different classes of proteolytic triads and non-catalytic triads (Fig. 2). The following clusters were formed: subtilisin-like architectures (Fig. 3A), trypsin-like architectures (Fig. 3B), papain-like architectures (Fig. 3C), caseinolytic protease-like (CLP-like), Backbone-based superposition to the cluster centers revealed that, indeed, backbone-only representation is sufficient to discriminate between various architectures more often described in terms of their sidechain relative orientations (Fig. 3). Our method was also sensitive enough to correctly assign a cluster label to the PDB entries harbouring substitutions in their active sites and ones covalently or noncovalently inhibited, even if sidechain geometry in these cases was distorted.

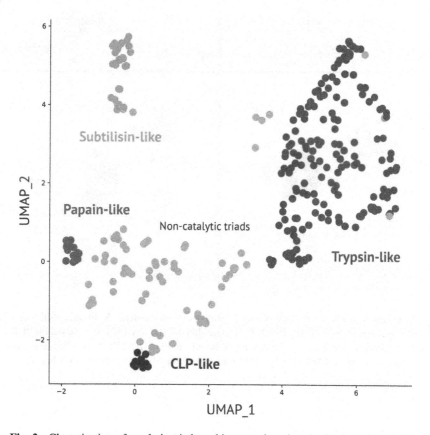

Fig. 2. Clusterization of catalytic triads architectures based on backbone vectorization.

Thus, a backbone-based approach was proven to not only be applicable to scaffold searching, but also to be a powerful tool to study the space of catalytic site architectures. Further generalization of the approach on different enzyme classes may produce new insight into the intricacies and evolutionary constraints of biocatalytic machineries.

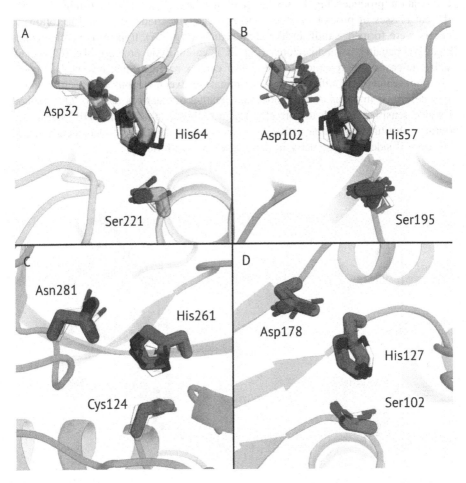

Fig. 3. Catalytic triad architecture of representatives of all clusters. A. Subtilisin-like cluster. Numbering is based on PDB ID 3BX1. B. Trypsin-like cluster. Numbering is based on PDB ID 1AVW. C. Papain-like cluster. Numbering is based on PDB ID 5Z5O. D. CLP-like cluster. Numbering is based on PDB ID 6NAH. Carbon coloration is in accordance with Fig. 2.

3.3 Scaffold Searching

We utilized our study of proteases to devise a distance threshold to be used to distinguish between adequate and inadequate placements, as well as some filters to reduce the number of scaffold triads to search through. We found that distributions of average distances to other cluster mates vary between triad architectures (Fig. 4), however always lying much lower than those of non-catalytic ones (minimal average distance of 224°). For the placement search for exact architecture type it is thus preferable to use a relevant threshold that we define as 90th percentile in the mean distances distribution within the cluster. However, due to the dramatic difference between catalytic and non-catalytic architectures, a milder threshold may be used, e.g. the maximum of the thresholds (in our case 47°, for trypsin-like triads).

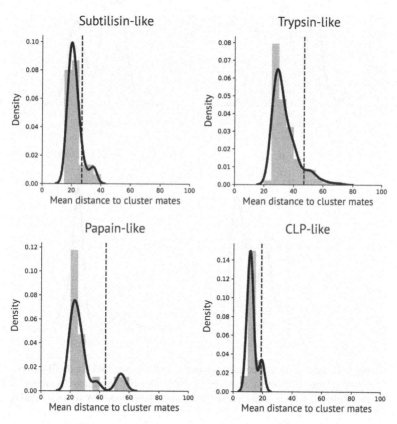

Fig. 4. Distributions of mean distances between each point in a cluster and every other point inside the same cluster. Upper-left: subtilisin-like triads, upper-right: trypsin-like triads, lower-left: papain-like triads, lower-right: CLP-like triads. Black dash represents the 90th percentile.

We further demonstrate our scaffold searching procedure on two examples: trypsin- and papain-templated search against a TEV protease scaffold, and trypsin-templated search against the whole CATH S40 non-redundant domains datased.

Prior to performing scaffold search we preprocessed each structure by converting it into a set of vectorized triads. To reduce the number of triads we applied several filters derived from the distributions studied for natural catalytic triads in proteases (Fig. 5).

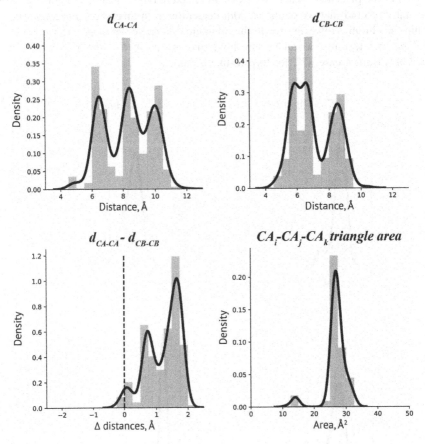

Fig. 5. Distributions of various auxiliary metrics useful for scaffold triads filtration prior to placement search. Upper-left: inter-CA-atomic distance, upper-right: inter-CB-atomic distance, lower-left: their difference, lower-right: area of the triangle built upon CA atoms of triad residues.

TEV protease is known to harbour a triad very much resembling that of trypsin despite being a cysteine protease [29]. On the other hand, it does not share much in common with papain-like architectures. Trypsin-templated search was able to easily identify the correct placement of TEV protease catalytic triad with the distance to it of 41.83° separated from all others by a significant margin (Table 1). On the other hand, papain-templated search did not find any promising placements at all since all the best ones had a distance significantly higher than 47° from the reference vector (Table 2).

Table 1. Best 5 placements from trypsin-templated search against TEV protease scaffold.

Rank	Distance	Composition according to 1LVM chain A
1	*41.83°*	*Cys151, His46, Asp81 (catalytic triad)*
2	86.46°	Val112, Thr17, Ile14
3	87.50°	Leu190, Leu98, Phe37
4	96.64°	Phe37, Leu189, Phe186
5	97.71°	Leu190, Phe94, Phe37

Both these searches were performed under 2 s on a single core. We decided to compare the computational effectiveness of our approach with those of Rosetta Match on a trivial case of trypsin-templated search against trypsin scaffold. Naturally, both methods succeeded in correctly identifying an ideal placement. However, it took Rosetta Match 42 s to perform the task with a standard level of rotamer sampling and 1 m 10 s with sampling extended to 3σ. Extending the number of samples per constraint skyrockets the computational time beyond 1 day. Our backbone-vectorization based approach took just 1.29 s. This comparison clearly shows the strength and practical applicability of our approach.

As an example of a near real-world application we performed a search against the whole CATH S40 non-redundant domains datased. It took on average 0.69 s to scan through all the possible placements inside a scaffold. In total, 16 placements with distance below 47° were found (Table 3).

Table 2. Best 5 placements from papain-templated search against TEV protease scaffold.

Rank	Distance	Composition according to 1LVM chain A
1	82.65°	Gly152, Tyr33, Ser15
2	94.64°	Ile144, Cys110, Val125
3	97.70°	Gly152, Try33, Ile18
4	101.90°	Ile84, Leu189, Ile42
5	111.13°	Gly152, Tyr33, Thr113

Unsurprisingly, the top of the table is occupied by other proteases. Starting from the 8th hit, 1AUK with a distance of 39.72°, is a transition towards non-proteolytic folds. Whether they can in fact be successfully engineered into proteases utilizing the recommendations from the scaffold search is a matter of further study. If so, the recommended threshold at 90th percentile is indeed a reasonable assumption. We note however that a protein designer may want to search for looser matches if one has means of computational backbone reengineering at a disposal. The used dataset is also only

Table 3. Hits (distance <47°) from trypsin-templated search against CATH S40 domains dataset.

Rank	Distance	PDB ID	Positions	Comment
1	16.96°	3OTP	Ala210, His105, Asp135	Protease, S > A mutant
2	18.73°	1WXR	Ser207, His73, Asp101	Protease
3	25.98°	4BXS	Ser362, His211, Asp265	Protease
4	29.60°	2F83	Ser557, His413, Asp462	Protease
5	36.18°	3H09	Ser288, His100, Asp164	Protease
6	37.94°	3SZE	Ala263, His127, Asp156	Protease, S > A mutant
7	38.87°	4B6E	Ser139, His57, Asp81	Protease
8	*39.72°*	*1AUK*	*Gly292, Glu285, Asp30*	*Not a protease*
9	39.81°	4M9F	Ser1135, His1051, Asp1075	Protease
10	*40.52°*	*4AKF*	*Ala72, Gly289, Ser268*	*Not a protease*
11	42.67°	2WV9	Ser135, His51, Asp75	Protease
12	*42.68°*	*1WKB*	*Thr319, Pro226, Trp263*	*Not a protease*
13	*42.79°*	*1NFV*	*Leu37, Leu45, Ile157*	*Not a protease*
14	*44.00°*	*3H75*	*Ala285, Phe273, Pro267*	*Not a protease*
15	*44.67°*	*3TGH*	*Gln115, Thr101, Trp144*	*Not a protease*
16	*46.42°*	*3QZ0*	*Val56, Lys78, Arg95*	*Not a protease*

partially reflecting real-world enzyme design studies since more specific, potentially *de novo* modeled scaffolds may be of better use to scan for. Concreticising use-cases as well as fine-tuning the filters and adding new ones is certainly needed in order to turn the presented approach into a tool or a web-service that can be accessed by a global community.

4   Conclusions

In the presented study a simplistic approach to the scaffold search problem of *de novo* enzyme design is proposed and validated. We show that by reducing the problem to the level of relative backbone orientations we can achieve a dramatic speed-up compared to existing approaches while producing meaningful results. Our solution makes it possible to routinely scan the whole structural proteome for promising placements of catalytic architectures on a working station or a small cluster. What is more, proposed vectorization allows to uncover hidden patterns in the organization of enzymes that may lead to new fundamental discoveries in the field of structural enzymology.

Acknowledgements. This work was supported by Russian Science Foundation Grant 21-74-20113. This research has been conducted in frame of the Interdisciplinary Scientific and Educational School of Moscow State University "Molecular Technologies of the Living Systems and Synthetic Biology".

References

1. López-Otín, C., Bond, J.S.: Proteases: multifunctional enzymes in life and disease. J. Biol. Chem. **283**, 30433–30437 (2008)
2. Di Cera, E.: Serine proteases. IUBMB Life **61**, 510–515 (2009)
3. Brömme, D.: Papain-like cysteine proteases. Curr. Protoc. Protein Sci. **Chapter 21**, Unit 21.2 (2001)
4. Leis, J.P., Cameron, C.E.: Engineering proteases with altered specificity. Curr. Opin. Biotechnol. **5**, 403–408 (1994)
5. Lau, Y.-T.K., et al.: Discovery and engineering of enhanced SUMO protease enzymes. J. Biol. Chem. **293**, 13224–13233 (2018)
6. Chowdhury, R., Maranas, C.D.: From directed evolution to computational enzyme engineering—a review. AIChE J. **66** (2020)
7. Vaissier Welborn, V., Head-Gordon, T.: Computational design of synthetic enzymes. Chem. Rev. **119**, 6613–6630 (2019)
8. Pultz, I.S., et al.: Gluten degradation, pharmacokinetics, safety, and tolerability of TAK-062, an engineered enzyme to treat celiac disease. Gastroenterology (2021)
9. Mokrushina, Y.A., et al.: Multiscale computation delivers organophosphorus reactivity and stereoselectivity to immunoglobulin scavengers. Proc. Natl. Acad. Sci. U. S. A. **117**, 22841–22848 (2020)
10. Richter, F., Leaver-Fay, A., Khare, S.D., Bjelic, S., Baker, D.: De novo enzyme design using Rosetta3. PLoS ONE **6**, e19230 (2011)
11. Linder, M.: Computational enzyme design: advances, hurdles and possible ways forward. Comput. Struct. Biotechnol. J. **2**, e201209009 (2012)
12. Siegel, J.B., et al.: Computational design of an enzyme catalyst for a stereoselective bimolecular Diels-Alder reaction. Science **329**, 309–313 (2010)
13. Jiang, L., et al.: De novo computational design of retro-aldol enzymes. Science **319**, 1387–1391 (2008)
14. Zanghellini, A.: de novo computational enzyme design. Curr. Opin. Biotechnol. **29**, 132–138 (2014)
15. Freiberger, M.I., Guzovsky, A.B., Wolynes, P.G., Parra, R.G., Ferreiro, D.U.: Local frustration around enzyme active sites. Proc. Natl. Acad. Sci. U. S. A. **116**, 4037–4043 (2019)
16. Ferreiro, D.U., Komives, E.A., Wolynes, P.G.: Frustration in biomolecules. Q. Rev. Biophys. **47**, 285–363 (2014)
17. Whiting, A.K., Peticolas, W.L.: Details of the acyl-enzyme intermediate and the oxyanion hole in serine protease catalysis. Biochemistry **33**, 552–561 (1994)
18. Ménard, R., Storer, A.C.: Oxyanion hole interactions in serine and cysteine proteases. Biol. Chem. Hoppe Seyler. **373**, 393–400 (1992)
19. Wang, G., Dunbrack, R.L., Jr.: PISCES: a protein sequence culling server. Bioinformatics **19**, 1589–1591 (2003)
20. Bakan, A., et al.: Evol and ProDy for bridging protein sequence evolution and structural dynamics. Bioinformatics **30**, 2681–2683 (2014)
21. Garreta, R., Moncecchi, G.: Learning Scikit-Learn: Machine Learning in Python. Packt Publishing Ltd. (2013)
22. McInnes, L., Healy, J., Saul, N., Großberger, L.: UMAP: uniform manifold approximation and projection. J. Open Sour. Softw. **3**(29), 861 (2018)
23. The PyMOL Molecular Graphics System, Version 2.0 Schrödinger, LLC

24. Hagberg, A., Schult, D., Swart, P.: Exploring network structure, dynamics, and function using Networkx. In: Varoquaux, G., Vaught, T., Millman, J. (eds.). Proceedings of the 7th Python in Science Conference 2008, Pasadena, CA USA, pp. 11–15 (2008)
25. Sillitoe, I., et al.: CATH: comprehensive structural and functional annotations for genome sequences. Nucleic Acids Res. **43**, D376–D381 (2015)
26. Leaver-Fay, A., et al.: ROSETTA3: an object-oriented software suite for the simulation and design of macromolecules. Methods Enzymol. **487**, 545–574 (2011)
27. Supercomputer lomonosov-2: large scale, deep monitoring and fine analytics for the user community. Supercomput. Front. Innov. **6** (2019)
28. Polizzi, N.F., DeGrado, W.F.: A defined structural unit enables de novo design of small-molecule-binding proteins. Science **369**, 1227–1233 (2020)
29. Phan, J., et al.: Structural basis for the substrate specificity of tobacco etch virus protease. J. Biol. Chem. **277**, 50564–50572 (2002)

Fast Computation of Electromagnetic Field in the Far Field Zone Based on Spherical Coordinates Splitting

Anton Ivanov[1(✉)], Ilya Valuev[2], Sergey Khilkov[1,2], Anastasia Perepelkina[1,2], and Sergei Belousov[2,3]

[1] Keldysh Institute of Applied Mathematics, Moscow, Russia
mogmi@ya.ru
[2] Kintech Lab Ltd., Moscow, Russia
{valuev,belousov}@kintechlab.com
[3] National Research Center 'Kurchatov Institute', Moscow, Russia

Abstract. We present a new algorithm of the fast calculation of electromagnetic field in the far field zone based on the spherical coordinates splitting. By splitting the Huygens surface into tiles, introducing intermediate spherical coordinate meshes, and grouping of the far field directions, we reduce the computational complexity and hence the calculation time of the near-to-far field transform.

Keywords: Computational electromagnetics · Near to far field transform · HIPERCONE code · LRnLA · Aiwlib

1 Introduction

Near-to-far field transform (NTFF transform) is one of the typical problems in the electromagnetic modeling [1]. Usually, the Maxwell equations are solved in the near field zone with the finite difference time domain method [2]. Then the Kirchhoff integral over the Huygens surface located near the computational domain boundaries is calculated to obtain the far field, which can be done either directly [3,4], or employing a spherical multipole expansion of the fields on the surface [5].

NTFF transform is required in a wide range of physical problems, from the fundamental Mie scattering [6], to the design of angular emission patterns for organic light-emitting diodes [7,8], ultra wideband terahertz technology [9], efficient antennae for 5G Internet of Things applications [10], and many others.

One of the key ingredients to success in the engineering design applications lies in a fast and computationally efficient modeling tools [11]. In particular, locally recursive non-locally asynchronous algorithms have helped to boost the performance of the finite-difference time-domain (FDTD) method by at least an order of magnitude [12–14]. As a result, a NTFF transform, with its inefficient brute force calculation of the Kirchhoff integral either in the time domain or the

ⓒ Springer Nature Switzerland AG 2021
V. Voevodin and S. Sobolev (Eds.): RuSCDays 2021, CCIS 1510, pp. 73–86, 2021.
https://doi.org/10.1007/978-3-030-92864-3_6

frequency domain for a large number of frequencies, potentially becomes much longer than the FDTD simulation itself.

Here we present a new algorithm for a fast and efficient calculation of electromagnetic fields in the far field zone, based on the spherical coordinates splitting. The Huygens surface is split in into quadratic tiles. In each tile, its own spherical coordinate system is used, with the polar angle relative to the tile normal. All far field directions are then grouped by the azimuthal angle φ. A 1D mesh with its axis belonging to the surface of the tile is introduced for each group. The data from the tile are transferred onto this mesh and subsequently to the directions in the current group. Such approach allows decreasing the computational complexity of the NTFF transform in the time domain by an order of magnitude and boosting the computation efficiency.

If the NTFF transform in the frequency domain with a large number of frequencies is required, it is more favorable to first compute the far field in the time domain and then apply the fast Fourier transform to obtain the frequency spectra. As a result, the developed technique boosts the efficiency of the NTFF transform in the frequency domain as well.

2   Method Theory

Spatial components of the electromagnetic field in the far zone can be calculated based on the Kirchhoff integral for $u = E_{x,y,z}, H_{x,y,z}$:

$$u(\mathbf{r}, t) = -\frac{1}{4\pi} \oint_G \left[\frac{\nabla_{\mathbf{r}'} u(\mathbf{r}', \tau)}{|\mathbf{r} - \mathbf{r}'|} - \frac{\mathbf{r} - \mathbf{r}'}{|\mathbf{r} - \mathbf{r}'|^3} u(\mathbf{r}', \tau) - \frac{\mathbf{r} - \mathbf{r}'}{c(\mathbf{r} - \mathbf{r}')^2} \frac{\partial u(\mathbf{r}', \tau)}{\partial \tau} \right] \cdot \mathbf{n}_G \, d\mathbf{r}',$$

where G is the surface of integration (Huygens surface), $\mathbf{n}_G$ is the integration surface normal, $\mathbf{r}$ is an observation point in the far zone beyond the integration surface, τ is the signal delay time, $\tau = t - |\mathbf{r} - \mathbf{r}'|/c$. The second item can be neglected in the far zone, $\mathbf{r} - \mathbf{r}' \approx \mathbf{r}$, so

$$u(\mathbf{n}, t) \approx -\frac{1}{4\pi} \oint_G \left[\nabla_{\mathbf{r}'} u(\mathbf{r}', \tau) - \frac{\mathbf{n}}{c} \frac{\partial u(\mathbf{r}', \tau)}{\partial \tau} \right] \cdot \mathbf{n}_G \, d\mathbf{r}', \tag{1}$$

where $\mathbf{n} = \mathbf{r}/r$ is the direction to the observation point, and $\tau \approx t + \mathbf{n} \cdot \mathbf{r}'/c$.

Thus for the electric field in the time domain we have

$$\mathbf{E}(\mathbf{r}, t) \approx -\frac{1}{4\pi} \oint_G \left[\frac{(\mathbf{n}_G \cdot \nabla_{\mathbf{r}'})}{r} \mathbf{E}(\mathbf{r}', \tau) - \frac{(\mathbf{n}_G \cdot \mathbf{r})}{cr^2} \frac{\partial \mathbf{E}(\mathbf{r}', \tau)}{\partial \tau} \right] d\mathbf{r}', \tag{2}$$

and in the frequency domain

$$\mathbf{E}(\mathbf{r}, \omega) \approx -\frac{1}{4\pi} \oint_G \left[\frac{(\mathbf{n}_G \cdot \nabla_{\mathbf{r}'})}{r} \mathbf{E}(\mathbf{r}', \omega) - i\omega \frac{(\mathbf{n}_G \cdot \mathbf{r})}{cr^2} \mathbf{E}(\mathbf{r}', \omega) \right] e^{-i\omega \mathbf{n} \cdot \mathbf{r}'/c} \, d\mathbf{r}'. \tag{3}$$

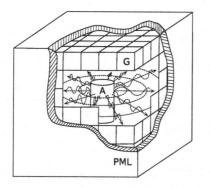
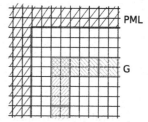

Fig. 1. A simulated device (A) is surrounded by the Huygens surface (G) split by square tiles. The Huygens surface is surrounded by the absorbing layer (PML). The thickness of the Huygens surface is two Yee cells, at the edges and vertices the same Yee cell belongs to two different surface tiles.

Magnetic field in vacuum can be recovered from the known electric field and the direction of propagation.

The Kirchhoff integral is calculated on the Huygens surface, Fig. 1. The Huygens surface is located in a vacuum and completely surrounds the simulated volume. In turn, the Huygens surface is at some distance surrounded by a PML (Perfectly Matched Layer) that absorbs the outgoing electromagnetic radiation [15]. The Huygens surface is divided into square fragments (tiles) with the sizes of $T \times T$ cells each. Since Eqs. (2), (3) contain derivatives along the normal to the Huygens surface, the Huygens surface has a thickness of two cells. At the edges and vertices, the same cell belongs to several tiles.

The components of the electric field in the Yee cells are located at different spatial points (at the centers of the cell faces). This is taken into account when calculating the far field by the regular offsets for various components, converted to time delays or phase shifts.

3   Far Field Calculation Algorithms

The use of LRnLA algorithms imposes a number of restrictions. Most of them are related to the asynchronous nature of the FDTD mesh update in LRnLA: the mesh is synchronous in time only at special time moments (algorithmic checkpoints) called synchronization times. Depending on the type and rank of the LRnLA update, the synchronization time may vary from 8 to 256 simulation time steps.

A special buffer is allocated to store the fields on the Huygens surface between synchronization times. In progress of FDTD calculation, between the moments of synchronization, the field components are accumulated in the buffer. Then, at times of synchronization, the accumulated data is processed (summed up). After the completion of the whole calculation, the final data processing is performed.

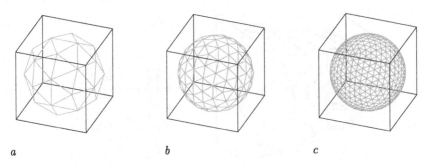

a b c

Fig. 2. A spherical grid of triangles based on a recursive tiling of a pentakisdodecahedron: no partitioning (a), single partitioning (b), double partitioning (c).

Table 1. Spherical grid characteristics for different ranks of R. Distortion means the
ratio of the maximum and minimum edges in a cell.

Rank of grid	Number of cells	Number of nodes	Average distortion	Maximum distortion	Average grid spacing
0	60	32	1.1186	1.1186	38.855°
1	240	122	1.12675	1.16177	19.8642°
2	960	482	1.12705	1.17215	9.98804°
3	3840	1922	1.1269	1.17472	5.00105°
4	15360	7682	1.12683	1.17536	2.50141°
5	61440	30722	1.12682	1.17552	1.25081°
6	245760	122882	1.12681	1.17556	0.62542°
7	983040	491522	1.12681	1.17557	0.312712°
8	3932160	1966082	1.12681	1.17557	0.156356°

The directions for calculating the far field correspond to the nodes of a
grid obtained by the recursive partition of the pentakisdodecahedron, Fig. 2 and
Table 1. Compared to the traditional uniform grid in spherical coordinates, such
a grid at a given accuracy (maximum cell size) requires one and a half times
fewer nodes and has no strong singularities at the poles [16]. It also provides the
ability to calculate the far field for only some fragments of the sphere.

In the following we compare traditional far field algorithms calculation for
asynchronous mesh update for both time and frequency domains with the fast
ones proposed in the current work.

3.1   Traditional Algorithms

The traditional algorithm for calculating the far field in the time domain in
asynchronous mesh update is as follows.

1. A buffer is created for the Huygens surface with the size of $N_G \times (N_s + 1)$ cells, where N_G is the number of cells on the Huygens surface, N_s is the number of steps between synchronization times.
2. A buffer is created to store the far field with the size of $N_t \times N_d$ cells, where N_t is the number of time steps and N_d is the number of directions **n**.
3. FDTD calculation is performed in a time-based loop, with:
   (a) between synchronization times, data from the Huygens surface is accumulated in the buffer;
   (b) at the time of synchronization, in a sequential loop over the tiles of the Huygens surface:
      i. in a parallel loop in directions (parallelization is carried out by means of OpenMP), traversal of all cells of the tile for all time steps between the moments of synchronization, these cells are summed up to the far field in a given direction;
      ii. Tile data corresponding to the last moment in time between synchronization steps is copied to the place of the tile data corresponding to the "before the first" moment in time between the synchronization stages, which allows calculating the time derivatives present in (2).
4. The calculated far field is written to disk, post-processing is carried out if necessary which may include calculation of radiation patterns, Fourier transform, etc.

In the case of parallel calculation on several compute nodes (for example, MPI parallelization), each node stores its own fragment of the Huygens surface and its own buffer for the far field. Each node independently calculates its contribution to the total far-field; in the final stage, far-fields from different nodes are summed up.

With this algorithm, the introduction of tiles makes it possible to increase the locality of the processed data in the computer memory.

The traditional algorithm for calculating the far-field in the frequency domain is as follows.

1. A buffer is created for the Huygens surface with the size of $N_G \times N_s$ cells.
2. A buffer is created for the Huygens surface with the size of $N_\omega \times N_G$ cells, where N_ω is the number of frequencies.
3. FDTD calculation is performed in a time-based loop, with:
   (a) between synchronization times, data from the Huygens surface is accumulated in the buffer;
   (b) at the time of synchronization, in a parallel loop over the cells of the Huygens surface (parallelization is carried out by means of OpenMP), all data entries corresponding to times between synchronization steps are traversed and the Fourier transform is performed on the fly.
4. A buffer is created to store the far field with the size of $N_\omega \times N_d$ cells.
5. In a sequential loop over the tiles of the Huygens surface:
   (a) in a parallel loop in directions (parallelization is carried out by means of OpenMP), all cells of the Fourier tile of the image are traversed for all frequencies, these cells are summed up to the far field in a given direction;

6. The calculated far field is written to disk, post-processing is performed if necessary.

Let a simulated volume have the shape of a cube with an edge of N cells, then the area of the Huygens surface is $\sim 6N^2$ cells. The computational complexity of FDTD is $C_{\text{FDTD}} \sim N_t N^3$, computational complexity of traditional algorithms for calculating far-field is then

$$C_{\text{NTFF}}^{t,\text{trad.}} \sim 6N^2 N_t N_d, \qquad C_{\text{NTFF}}^{\omega,\text{trad.}} \sim 6N^2 N_t N_\omega + 6N^2 N_\omega N_d = 6N^2 N_\omega \left(N_t + N_d\right).$$

It is easily seen that

$$\frac{C_{\text{NTFF}}^{t,\text{trad.}}}{C_{\text{FDTD}}} \sim \frac{6 N_d}{N}, \qquad \frac{C_{\text{NTFF}}^{\omega,\text{trad.}}}{C_{\text{FDTD}}} \sim \frac{6 N_\omega}{N N_t}\left(N_t + N_d\right).$$

For $N_d \sim N$, the computational complexity of the traditional far field computation in the time domain can significantly exceed the complexity of the underlying FDTD calculation itself. For small N_ω computational complexity of traditional far-field computation in the frequency domain has acceptable values, however, as N_ω grows, the situation starts to deteriorate. A good solution would be to use the fast Fourier transform, but this requires a ready-made far field result in the time domain.

The implementation of the fast Fourier transform together with the calculation of the FDTD encounters some algorithmic difficulties, moreover, it does not decrease the complexity of the final stage of direct calculation of the far field in the frequency domain.

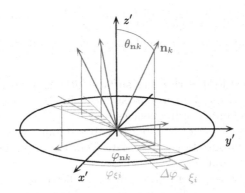

Fig. 3. For each tile, a local Cartesian coordinate system x', y', z' is introduced. In this coordinate system, a set of axes $\boldsymbol{\xi}_i$ is introduced, located at different angles $\varphi_{\xi i}$ with a step $\Delta\varphi$. All directions $\mathbf{n}_k$, in which the far field is considered, are divided into groups with angles close to φ.

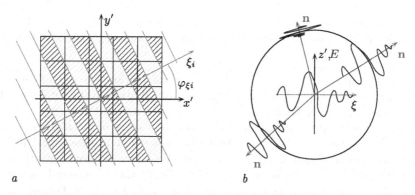

Fig. 4. A one-dimensional regular grid is introduced along each of the ξ_i axes, the data from the tile cells are recalculated to the grids by ξ_i (fig. a). Then the data from each grid ξ_i is recalculated to the directions **n** corresponding to group ξ_i.

3.2 Spherical Coordinates Splitting Algorithms

To speed up the calculation of the far field, we propose a new algorithm based on splitting in spherical coordinates, Fig. 3, 4.

1. Buffers are created for the Huygens surface with sizes of $N_G \times (N_s + 1)$ cells and for storing the far field with sizes of $N_t \times N_d$ cells.
2. Tables of weights of the transition from the cells of the Huygens surface to the grids ξ_i are calculated, Fig. 4a.
3. N_φ buffers of size N_ξ are created, where N_φ is the number of ξ_i axes, N_ξ is the number of cells along the ξ axis.
4. FDTD calculation is performed in a time-based loop, with:
   (a) between synchronization times, data from the Huygens surface is accumulated in the buffer;
   (b) at the time of synchronization, in a sequential loop over the tiles of the Huygens surface:
      i. in a sequential cycle through time steps:
         A. in a parallel loop in the corners $\varphi_{\xi i}$ (parallelization is carried out by means of **OpenMP**), all the cells of the tile are traversed, the cell data are summed up into the buffer corresponding to the ξ_i axis, Fig. 4a;
         B. in a parallel loop in directions (parallelization is carried out by means of **OpenMP**), defines the ξ_i axis to which the direction belongs, and data from the temporary buffer are summed up to the direction data, Fig. 4b. At this stage, interpolation is possible between adjacent axes ξ.
      ii. Tile data corresponding to the last point in time between synchronization steps is copied to the place of the tile data corresponding to the before the firstmoment in time between the synchronization stages, which allows calculating the time derivatives present in (2).

5. The calculated far field is written to disk, post-processing is carried out if necessary, for example, calculation of radiation patterns, Fourier transform, etc.

As for the traditional algorithm, in the case of calculations on several compute nodes, each node independently calculates its contribution to the total far-field; in the final stage, far fields from different nodes are summed up.

A similar algorithm can be applied at the final stage of calculating the far field in the frequency domain, but that does not result in substantial performance gain. For a small number of frequencies N_ω, the traditional algorithm has sufficient performance. For large values of $N_\omega \sim N_t$, the constructed algorithm cannot reduce the computational complexity associated with the Fourier transform on the fly. In this case, it is necessary to calculate the far field in the time domain and then apply the FFT to it.

The computational complexity of the new algorithm can be estimated as

$$C_{\text{NTFF}}^{t,\text{fast}} \sim N_t \frac{6\,N^2}{T^2} \left[N_\varphi T^2 + N_\xi N_d \right].$$

The smaller the values of N_φ and N_ξ are, the lower is the computational complexity, but also the lower is the accuracy of the far field calculation. From general considerations, with a rather complex structure of the electromagnetic field on the Huygens surface, the minimum permissible values are $N_\varphi \sim T$, $N_\xi \sim T$, from where follows

$$C_{\text{NTFF}}^{t,\text{fast}} \sim 6\,N^2 N_t \left[T + \frac{N_d}{T} \right], \tag{4}$$

with the minimum of this function at $T \sim \sqrt{N_d}$.

4   Calculation Results

The proposed method was implemented in the C++ language within the EMTL [17] code, the implementation also uses aiwlib [16] library.

As a test case, we considered the Mie problem on the scattering of plane polarized light on a spherical particle. An electromagnetic wave with polarization $(1,0,0)$ propagates in the direction $(0,0,1)$ and falls on a sphere with a radius of 10 microns with a refractive index $n = 3$. The sphere is located in the center of the computational domain of 64^3 microns in size. The wave is generated in the TFSF region of 30^3 microns in size. The time dependence of the signal is chosen as

$$E_x(t) = A \exp\left[-\frac{(t - t_0)^2}{\tau^2} \right] \sin\left[\frac{2\pi c(t - t_0)}{\lambda} \right],$$

with parameters $\tau = 30$ microns/c, $\lambda = 10$ microns, where c is the speed of light. Courant parameter was 0.4. We considered two variants of grid resolution: $N = 256$ cells (4 cells per micron) and $N = 512$ cells (8 cells per micron).

Since long-lived resonance modes appear in a spherical particle (Fig. 5), the simulation time was longer than 130 λ/c or 12800 $\div$ 25600 time steps.

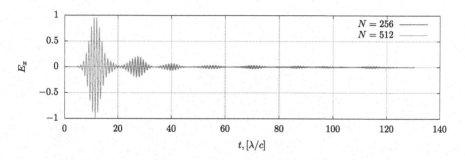

Fig. 5. Dependence of the signal $E_x(t)$ in the far zone in the direction $\mathbf{n} = (0, 0, 1)$.

The radiation patterns are shown in Fig. 6.

First of all the size of the tile T needs to be determined. We used a grid of directions of the second rank of 482 nodes, which corresponds to a grid step of $10°$, Fig. 2c. According to the estimate (4), the optimal tile size from the point of view of performance should be $T \approx \sqrt{482} \approx 22$. Let us introduce the parameter α as the ratio of the net time of calculating the far field stages to the time of calculating the basic FDTD inside the region. It should be noted that simply saving data from the Huygens surface to the buffer slows down the FDTD calculation by about 30%, and we include this time in the basic FDTD calculation time.

The $\alpha(T)$ dependency is shown in Fig. 7. It can be seen that the optimal tile size is 32 cells for problems with a computational domain size of 256^3 and 512^3 cells, the deviation from the estimate (4) is explained by the fact that different stages of the algorithm have different weights. As expected, the efficiency of calculating the far field for a larger problem turns out to be higher, since the ratio of the Huygens surface to the volume of the computational domain is smaller. In the following, all calculations were carried out with the tile size $T = 32$.

We used a web-based Mie-calculator from OMLC [18] to obtain the analytical solution. We should note at this point, that the numerical errors arising in the FDTD calculation of the Mie scattering problem are due to several factors, including the staircasing effect in the approximation of the sphere on a rectangular mesh, finite number of time iterations in the simulation, numerical integration over the Huygens surface, as well as interpolations between adjacent far field directions etc. In this work we are interested in an additional error arising from our NTFF algorithm. Apart from the size of the tile, the algorithm has the following two parameters: the size of the mesh N_φ and the characteristic ratio of the mesh step ξ to the FDTD mesh step, $\xi_{\text{scale}} \sim N_\xi^{-1}$. Increasing N_φ, N_ξ increases the accuracy as well as the computational complexity of the far field calculation.

From general considerations, at $N_\varphi = 3/2T$ and $\xi_{\text{scale}} = 1$ the accuracy of the far field calculation with the fast algorithm becomes equal to the accuracy of the traditional brute force algorithm. Comparison of the analytical solution to the FDTD results for this case is shown in Fig. 8. The mean error in the $L1$

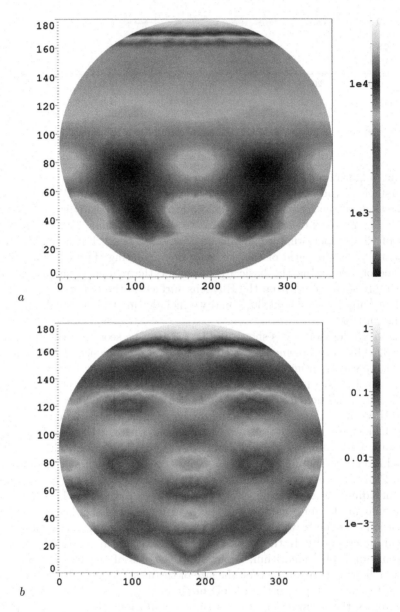

Fig. 6. Radiation patterns: general (integral over time, a) and at wavelength $\lambda = 10$ microns (b).

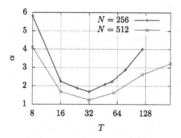

Fig. 7. Dependence of the efficiency of the far field calculation $\alpha(T)$.

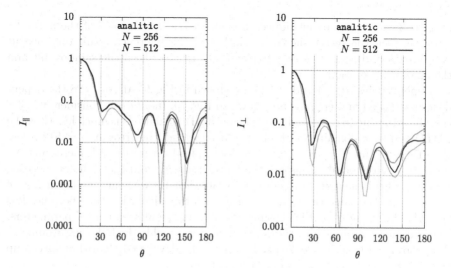

Fig. 8. Comparison of the analytical solution to the simulation results for $N_\varphi = 3/2T$, $\xi_{\text{scale}} = 1$.

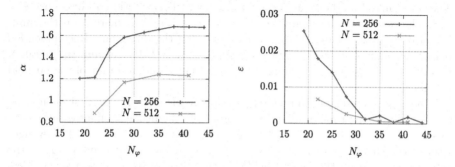

Fig. 9. Dependencies $\alpha(N_\varphi)$ and $\varepsilon(N_\varphi)$ at $\xi_{\text{scale}} = 1$.

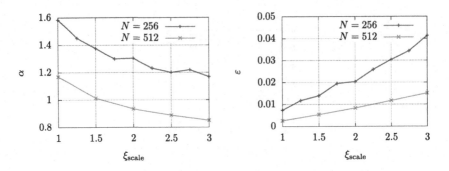

Fig. 10. Dependencies $\alpha(\xi_{\text{scale}})$ and $\varepsilon(\xi_{\text{scale}})$ at $N_\varphi = 28$.

norm is $3 \cdot 10^{-2}$. Let us introduce an error metric ε as a ratio of the norm $L1$ error between the result shown in Fig. 8 and the reference result obtained at $N_\varphi = 3/2T$ and $\xi_{\text{scale}} = 1$, to the norm $L1$ error between the same result and the analytical solution.

Dependencies $\alpha(N_\varphi)$ and $\varepsilon(N_\varphi)$ are shown in Fig. 9. At $N_\varphi = 28$ the dependencies $\alpha(\xi_{\text{scale}})$ and $\varepsilon(\xi_{\text{scale}})$ are shown in Fig. 10. In all cases considered $\varepsilon \ll 1$ (i.e. the error due to the speed up of the far field calculation) is much less than the FDTD and time domain NTFF errors. As expected, the error at $N = 512$ is less than the error at $N = 256$. The error does indeed saturates with increasing N_φ up to $\approx T$. In general, adjusting the parameters N_φ and ξ_{scale} allows speeding up the far field calculation roughly by a factor of 1.5 without significant loss of accuracy. At the same time, the NTFF transform calculation time becomes less than the duration of the FDTD simulation. Using similar numerical parameters, the brute force approach to the NTFF transform yields the following results: at $N = 256$ $\alpha \approx 14$, at $N = 512$ $\alpha \approx 10$. Thus, the developed algorithm speeds up the NTFF transform by an order of magnitude.

5   Conclusion

The constructed method has three parameters: tile size, grid size in φ, grid size in ξ. The size of the tile should be chosen as $T \approx 1.5\sqrt{N_d}$, where N_d is the number of directions, assuming a uniform grid along the directions. Recommended parameter values are $N_\varphi \approx T \div 1.5T$, $\xi_{\text{scale}} \approx 1 \div 2$. By varying the parameters N_φ and ξ_{scale}, one can change the performance and accuracy of the far field calculation.

The constructed method makes it possible to increase the speed of calculating the far field in the time domain by an order of magnitude without a significant loss of accuracy. For the HIPERCONE code, built on the basis of LRnLA algorithms, the time for calculating the far field turns out to be comparable to the time for calculating the basic FDTD update, that is, the far field slows down the overall calculation by no more than two times. For less efficient FDTD codes this ratio should be much better.

The constructed method can be used for calculating the far field in the frequency domain, while the main problem here is the implementation of the fast Fourier transform on the Huygens surface. If this calculation is not efficiently implemented, then for a large number of required frequencies it turns out that it is more efficient to compute the far field in the time domain and then apply FFT to the results. The constructed method for near-to-far field transform calculation is independent from the numerical method used to compute the near fields. In particular, it can be applied to computing the NTFF together with any frequency domain method.

References

1. Bondeson, A., Rylander, T., Ingelström, P.: Computational Electromagnetics. Springer, New York (2012). https://doi.org/10.1007/978-1-4614-5351-2
2. Taflove, A., Hagness, S.C.: Computational Electrodynamics: The Finite-difference Time-domain Method. Artech House, London (2005)
3. Luebbers, R.J., Kunz, K.S., Schneider, M., Hunsberger, F.: A finite-difference time-domain near zone to far zone transformation (electromagnetic scattering). IEEE Trans. Antennas Propag. **39**(4), 429–433 (1991)
4. Martin, T.: An improved near-to far-zone transformation for the finite-difference time-domain method. IEEE Transa. Antennas Propag. **46**(9), 1263–1271 (1998)
5. Oetting, C.C., Klinkenbusch, L.: Near-to-far-field transformation by a time-domain spherical-multipole analysis. IEEE Trans. Antennas Propag. **53**(6), 2054–2063 (2005)
6. Wriedt, T.: Mie theory: a review. In: Hergert, W., Wriedt, T. (eds.) The Mie Theory. SSOS, vol. 169. Springer, Heidelberg. https://doi.org/10.1007/978-3-642-28738-1_2
7. Belousov, S., Bogdanova, M., Teslyuk, A.: Outcoupling efficiency of OLEDs with 2D periodical corrugation at the cathode. J. Phys. D Appl. Phys. **49**(8), 085102 (2016)
8. Zakirov, A., Belousov, S., Valuev, I., Levchenko, V., Perepelkina, A., Zempo, Y.: Using memory-efficient algorithm for large-scale time-domain modeling of surface plasmon polaritons propagation in organic light emitting diodes. J. Phys. Conf. Ser. **905**, 012030 (2017)
9. Russer, J.A., Haider, M., Russer, P.: Time-domain modeling of noisy electromagnetic field propagation. IEEE Trans. Microwave Theor. Tech. **66**(12), 5415–5428 (2018)
10. Costanzo, A., Masotti, D.: Energizing 5G: near-and far-field wireless energy and data trantransfer as an enabling technology for the 5G IoT. IEEE Microwave Mag. **18**(3), 125–136 (2017)
11. Sumithra, P., Thiripurasundari, D.: Review on computational electromagnetics. Adv. Electromagn. **6**(1), 42–55 (2017)
12. Levchenko, V., Perepelkina, A.: Locally recursive non-locally asynchronous algorithms for stencil computation. Lobachevskii J. Math. **39**(4), 552–561 (2018)
13. Zakirov, A., Levchenko, V., Perepelkina, A., Zempo, Y.: High performance FDTD algorithm for GPGPU supercomputers. J. Phys. Conf. Ser. **759**, 012100 (2016)
14. Belousov, S., Khilkov, S., Levchenko, V., Perepelkina, A., Valuev, I.: Hipercone FDTD: vectorized highly scalable full-wave electromagnetic solver. In: 2018 International Applied Computational Electromagnetics Society Symposium (ACES), pp. 1–2. IEEE (2018)

15. Berenger, J.P.: Three-dimensional perfectly matched layer for the absorption of electromagnetic waves. J. Comput. Phys. **127**(2), 363–379 (1996)
16. Ivanov, A., Khilkov, S.: Aiwlib library as the instrument for creating numerical modeling applications. Sci. Vis. **10**(1), 110–127 (2018). https://doi.org/10.26583/sv.10.1.09
17. Electromagnetic template library (EMTL), February 2014. http://fdtd.kintechlab.com/en/start
18. Prahl, S.: Mie scattering calculator. https://omlc.org/calc/mie_calc.html

Greedy Dissection Method for Shared Parallelism in Incomplete Factorization Within INMOST Platform

Kirill Terekhov[1,2]([⊠])

[1] Marchuk Institute of Numerical Mathematics, RAS, Moscow 119333, Russia
terekhov@inm.ras.ru
[2] Moscow Institute of Physics and Technology, Moscow 141701, Russia

Abstract. In this work, we augment the parallel preconditioner based on multi-level inverse-based second-order Crout incomplete factorization with the greedy dissection method to unlock the shared parallelism. The greedy heuristics is used to find the smallest separator in the graph and symmetrically reorder the system to doubly-bordered block-diagonal form. In parallel each independent diagonal block is rescaled to the I-dominant matrix, reordered for fill-in reduction and factorized with a delayed-pivoting strategy. For the next factorization level, the Schur complement is formed by the block corresponding to the separator augmented with the delayed pivots. Besides, unsymmetric preordering is used on each level system to place the maximum transversal onto the diagonal.

Keywords: Linear solver · Preconditioner · Nested dissection · Hypergraph · Maximum transversal

1 Introduction

In the previous work [1], we considered a domain-decomposition linear solver with multi-level Crout incomplete factorization preconditioner on sub-domains. The feature of the solver is the monitoring of the growth of inverse factors and factorization postponement upon the growth beyond the prescribed norm, motivated by [2]. The postponed part of the system is reordered and forms the Schur complement for the next level system as in [3]. On each level, the system is preordered by placing maximum transversal onto diagonal and rescaled into I-dominant matrix [4,5] and then ordered by a weighted version of reverse Cuthill-Mckee algorithm [6]. The quality of both, the factorization and the Schur complement computation are enhanced using second-order dropping strategy [7].

The drawback of the restricted additive Schwarz domain-decomposition method is the deterioration of the performance with the growth of the number of domains and reduction of the local problem size. Overcoming the issue includes increasing matrix overlap and construction of the problem coarse space [8,9]. A more straightforward approach is to reduce the number of blocks by exploiting hybrid parallelism which we consider in the present work.

© Springer Nature Switzerland AG 2021
V. Voevodin and S. Sobolev (Eds.): RuSCDays 2021, CCIS 1510, pp. 87–101, 2021.
https://doi.org/10.1007/978-3-030-92864-3_7

In the considered sub-domain preconditioner the most time-consuming Crout factorization and elimination steps remain to be strictly sequential whereas the Schur complement computation can be easily parallelized. To factorize the problem in parallel the matrix is reordered into bordered block-diagonal form [10,11]. In this form, the matrix contains several independent diagonal blocks and wide border blocks.

The unsymmetric reordering results in singly-bordered block-diagonal form with rectangular diagonal blocks having more columns than rows. In this version, the individual blocks may miss the diagonal and are unsuitable for the factorization as is. To this end, the maximum transversal is found independently in each block and permuted to the diagonal as suggested in [12]. This variant has drawbacks discussed further in Sect. 4. We use symmetric reordering that results in doubly-bordered block diagonal form.

The reordering is based on a node dissection graph partitioning algorithm that aims to find the smallest graph separator. The smallest separator problem can be solved by finding the Fiedler vector of graph Laplacian [13]. Alternative heuristic approaches are Kernighan-Lin [14,15] or Fiduccia-Mattheyses [16] methods. There are many open-source implementations available such as Metis [17,18], Patoh [19], Mondrean [20], Zoltan [21], Chaco [22]. For the present work, we implement a simple greedy dissection algorithm [23,24]. The resulting greedy algorithm is sequential.

This work was motivated by implementations in [12] and [25]. The solver discussed here is available open-source as a part of INMOST platform [26–30].

Section 2 specify the INMOST platform functional. Section 3 describes the greedy dissection algorithm. In Sect. 4, the integration into solver is considered. Section 5 contains the results of numerical experiments. The final section summarizes the findings.

2   INMOST Linear Solvers

The linear solvers implemented in INMOST parallel platform are based on the combination of the following components:

- *Iterative method.* Preconditioned Krylov solver for non-symmetric matrices.
- *Parallelization.* Domain decomposition.
- *Preconditioning.* Incomplete LU-factorization.

The iterative solver is the preconditioned biconjugate gradient stabilized method BiCGStab(ℓ) [31]. Parallelization of the BiCGStab(ℓ) is straightforward as it only requires to accumulate sums of scalar products computed on each processor and synchronize vector elements after matrix-vector multiplication.

Distributed implementation of the preconditioner is based on the combination of an incomplete LU factorization and the restricted additive Schwartz domain-decomposition with user-specified overlapping parameter. Overlapping of a local matrix and a local vector requires their extension by data from adjacent processors. To construct the overlap, the sparsity pattern is analyzed for the global column indices that lay outside of the local processor and the local matrix is augmented with the rows from remote processors as illustrated in Fig. 1. The procedure of matrix extension is repeated as specified by the user. No overlap corresponds to the block Jacobi method. Reducing overlap leads to the iteration count growth and performance deterioration with larger number of domains. Increased overlap improves convergence of domain-decomposition method but introduces additional penalty due to increasing communication time that may become prohibitively large.

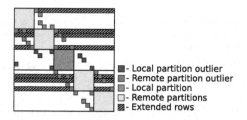

**- Local partition outlier
**- Remote partition outlier
**- Local partition
**- Remote partitions
**- Extended rows

Fig. 1. Sparse matrix extension procedure from [1].

In the former version from [1], each core performed sequential incomplete LU factorization on the local extended matrix. In the present work the matrix has to be distributed among processors and multiple cores of the same processor perform factorization. Due to high core count in modern processors such strategy allows to drastically reduce the number of domains.

There are several choices for incomplete LU factorization algorithm within INMOST platform. Further, the multilevel method is discussed. The multilevel incomplete LU factorization is based on the following components:

- *Factorization.* Crout LU factorization with adaptive dropping.
- *Preprocessing.*
  - Non-symmetric maximum transversal permutation.
  - Symmetric reordering to doubly-bordered block diagonal form.
  - Symmetric fill-in reduction permutation.
  - Matrix rescaling into I-dominant form.
- *Pivoting.* Deferred multi-level factorization.

INMOST contains interfaces to solvers from PETSc [33], Trilinos [32] and Super-LU [34].

3   Greedy Dissection

The general graph bisection problem as well as it's good approximate solution are NP-hard problems [35]. Therefore, the partitioning problems are solved in acceptable computing time with heuristics. We use a greedy approach inspired by [23].

For a linear system $Ax = b$ with $A = \{a_{ij}\} \in \mathbb{R}^{n \times n}$, the graph $G = (V, E)$ is formed by vertices $V = \{1, \ldots, n\}$ and edges $E = \{G_i = \{j | a_{ij} \neq 0\} | \forall i \in V\}$. CSR-format is used to store the graph G in ia, ja arrays, identical to those of the original matrix A.

Algorithm 1. Greedy dissection.

1: **function** GREEDYDISSECTION(A, $parts$)
2:     Let $G = (V, E)$, where   ▷ Graph induced by matrix
3:         $V = \{1, \ldots, n\}$,   ▷ Vertex set
4:         $G_i = \{j | a_{ij} \neq 0\}$.   ▷ Edge set
5:     Let $H = G^T G$.   ▷ Graph product
6:     Let $\omega_B = \{\omega_B^i = \|G_i\| | \forall i \in V\}$.   ▷ Weights for block growth
7:     Let $\omega_H = \{\omega_H^i = \|H_i\| | \forall i \in V\}$.   ▷ Weights for separator growth
8:     Let $B_i = \{\emptyset\}, \forall i \in \{1, \ldots, parts\}$.   ▷ Blocks
9:     Let $S = \emptyset$.   ▷ Separator
10:     Let $R = C = V$.   ▷ Candidate row and column sets
11:     Let $P_i = Q_i = 0, \forall i \in \{1, \ldots, n\}$.   ▷ Rows and columns reordering matrices
12:     $r = c = q = 1$.   ▷ Row and column index and current block
13:     **while** $R \neq \emptyset$ **do**
14:         $i = \arg\min\limits_{j \in R} \left(\omega_B^j + \omega_H^j \right)$,   ▷ Minimal growth of both the block and separator
15:         $R = R \setminus \{i\}$,   ▷ Remove from the candidate set
16:         $P_i = r$,
17:         $r = r + 1$,   ▷ Enumerate row
18:         $B_q = B_q \cup \{i\}$,   ▷ Augment current block
19:         **if** $i \in S$ **then** $S = S \setminus \{i\}$.
20:         **for** $m \in H_i \cap R$ **do**
21:             $\omega_H^m = \omega_H^m - 1$.   ▷ Update weights for separator growth
22:         **end for**
23:         **for** $j \in G_i \cap C$ **do**
24:             $C = C \setminus \{j\}$,
25:             $Q_j = c$,
26:             $c = c + 1$.   ▷ Enumerate column
27:             **for** $k \in G_j^T$ **do**
28:                 $\omega_B^k = \omega_B^k - 1$.   ▷ Update weights for block growth
29:                 **if** $k \notin S$ **then**
30:                     $S = S \cup \{k\}$,
31:                     $\omega_H^k = \omega_H^k - 1$.   ▷ Add row to separator
32:                     **for** $m \in H_k \cap R$ **do**
33:                         $\omega_H^m = \omega_H^m - 1$.   ▷ Update weights for separator growth
34:                     **end for**
35:                 **end if**
36:             **end for**
37:         **end for**
38:         **if** $\|B_q\| \geq \|R\| / parts$ **then**
39:             $R = R \setminus S$,   ▷ Remove current separator from candidate set
40:             $q = q + 1$.   ▷ Consider next block
41:         **end if**
42:     **end while**
43:     **for all** $i \in S$ **do**
44:         $P_i = r$,
45:         $r = r + 1$.
46:     **end for**
47:     $Q = P$.   ▷ Match row and column indices.
48:     **return** [P,Q,B,S]
49: **end function**

Algorithm 1 outlines the greedy dissection method. Here, in addition to G we also compute it's transpose G^T and graph product $H = G^T G$. Using H for a given edge we can traverse all the edges that depend on it. If we put an edge into current block B_q, all the dependent edges are to be placed into separator S. Further, either candidate edges or separator edges may be selected to augment the block. On each step of the method we pick the edge G_i from the candidate row set R of the graph that leads to minimal growth of both the current block B_q and the separator S by maintaining and updating the weights ω_B and ω_H. To perform the choice the weights and edge indices are stored in priority heap. Upon the selection of suitable edge all the weights are recomputed using the graphs G^T and H. The drawback of the Algorithm 1 is it's sequential nature.

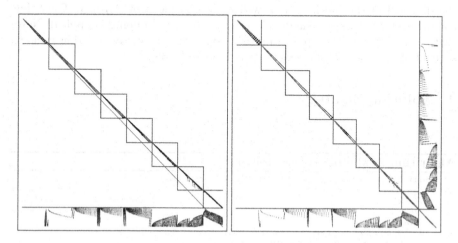

Fig. 2. Unsymmetric (left) and symmetric (right) results of greedy dissection algorithm with 8 blocks on $50 \times 50 \times 50$ Poisson problem matrix. The nonzeroes are magnified for visibility. Green and red colors correspond to dominant and non-dominant diagonal entries, respectively. (Color figure online)

Originally, the method produces unsymmetric dissection with rectangular blocks as in Fig. 2 (left). The unsymmetric reordering results in singly-bordered block-diagonal form with rectangular diagonal blocks having more columns than rows. The singly-bordered A_{SBBD} and doubly-bordered A_{DBBD} block-diagonal forms has the following patterns:

$$A_{SBBD} = \begin{pmatrix} A_{11} & & & \\ & A_{22} & & \\ & & A_{33} & \\ B_{41} & B_{42} & B_{43} & B_{44} \end{pmatrix}, \quad A_{DBBD} = \begin{pmatrix} A_{11} & & & B_{14} \\ & A_{22} & & B_{24} \\ & & A_{33} & B_{34} \\ B_{41} & B_{42} & B_{43} & C_{44} \end{pmatrix}. \quad (1)$$

In A_{SBBD} version, the individual blocks may miss the diagonal and are unsuitable for the factorization as is. To this end, the maximum transversal is found independently in each block A_{ii} and permuted to the diagonal as suggested in [12]. The shortcoming of this approach is that the maximum transversal problem in each block is over-determined. As a result, there are multiple suitable alternative paths for the transversal. The algorithm still produces an I-matrix in the block but good pivots may appear in the border and their reappearance in the next level is very sensitive to the quality of the Schur complement computation. Often in practice, the Schur complement becomes singular if dropping strategy is applied. It also increases deferring of pivots during factorization and increases Schur size for the next level.

By assigning the row indices to column indices the result can be symmetrized as in Fig. 2 (right) and A_{DBBD} form is obtained. Due to symmetry a good pivoting sequence found with the maximum transversal ordering is retained on the diagonal of the blocks A_{ii} as well as in C_{44} block of A_{DBBD}. The Schur complement remains non-singular even if aggressive dropping is applied. Note, that in this version the application of maximum transversal ordering remains sequential, but parallel implementation is possible [38].

4   Solution Strategy

Algorithm 2. Multi-level factorization.

1: **function** MULTILEVELINCOMPLETECROUTLDU2($A, \tau_1, \tau_2, \kappa, parts$)
2:    $l = 1$ ▷ Level number
3:    $P = Q = I$ ▷ Reordering of rows and columns
4:    $D_L = D_R = I$ ▷ Rescaling of rows and columns
5:    **repeat**
6:       $[Q, D_L, D_R]$ = MAXIMUMTRANSVERSAL(A)
7:       $[P, Q, B, S]$ = GREEDYDISSECTION(AQ)
8:       $d_i = 0 \quad \forall i \in \{1, \ldots, n_l\},$ ▷ Deferring
9:       **for** $i \in S$ **do**
10:          $d_i = 1.$ ▷ Defer factorization of the border
11:       **end for**
12:       **for** $B^q \in B$ **in parallel do**
13:          $A^q = \{D_L P A Q D_R\}_{ij}, \quad \forall i, j \in B_q$
14:          $[P^q, Q^q]$ = WEIGHTEDREVERSECUTHILLMCKEE(A^q)
15:          $[D_L^q, D_R^q]$ = IMPROVEDOMINANCE($P^q A^q Q^q$)
16:          $[L^q, L^{2,q}, D^q, U^q, U^{2,q}, d^q]$ = INCOMPLETECROUTLDU2($D_L^q P^q A^q Q^q D_R^q, \tau_1, \tau_2, \kappa, d^q$)
17:       **end for**
18:       **if** $\sum_{k \in \{1, n_l\}} d_i \neq 0$ **then**
19:          [P,Q] = DEFERPIVOTING(d)   ▷ Place deferred part to the end
20:          $[E, F, C]$ =BLOCKS($LPAQR$)
21:          $A = C - E(U + U^2)^{-1} D^{-1} (L + L^2)^{-1} F$
22:          Store unscaled matrices L, D, U, E, F
23:          Advance level $l = l + 1$
24:       **else**
25:          Store unscaled matrices L, D, U
26:       **end if**
27:    **until** $s \neq 0$
28:    **return** $[L_k, D_k, U_k, \forall k \in [1, l], E_k, F_k, B_k \forall k \in [1, l-1], P, Q, l]$
29: **end function**

The second-order Crout incomplete factorization method with estimation of inverse factors norms was detailed in [1]. The details on the implementation can be found in the reference. Here in the Algorithm 2 we augment the pseudo-code with the greedy dissection method from Sect. 3. In the algorithm the P and

Q are the accumulated reordering matrices and D_L and D_R are scaling matrices. The superscript q here and further denotes that all the operations are performed on the independent block B^q of the matrix. The algorithm restores the scaling at the end but the ordering is retained.

In addition we shall detail on dropping strategy for the Schur complement. The deferring reordering leads to the block structure

$$PAQ = \begin{bmatrix} B & F \\ E & C \end{bmatrix}, \tag{2}$$

where $B \approx (L + L^2)D(U + U^2)$ is the factorized part of the matrix and $\nu_L \approx \|(L + L^2)^{-1}\|$ and $\nu_U \approx \|(U + U^2)^{-1}\|$ are estimated norms of inverse factors. The Schur complement is approximated by

$$S \approx C - E(U + U^2)^{-1}D^{-1}(L + L^2)^{-1}F. \tag{3}$$

Expression (3) is computed in three steps. First, we compute $E_{UD} = E(U + U^2)^{-1}D^{-1}$. Second, we compute $F_{LD} = D^{-1}(L + L^2)^{-1}F$. At last we find the sparse matrix multiplication $E_{UD}DF_{LD}$ and subtract it from C. All the operations are efficiently implemented using ordered dense linked-lists. The structure was detailed in [1].

Computation of E_{UD} requires the solution of the system $x_i^T D(U + U^2) = e_i^T$, where x_i^T is a sparse row of E_{UD} and e_i^T is a sparse row of E, see Fig. 3. To this end, the rows of E_{UD} can be computed in parallel. Similarly, the solution to $(L + L^2)Dy_i = f_i$ with a sparse column f_i of F is required to obtain column y_i of F_{LD}. It is convenient to store E and E_{UD} in compressed row format and F and F_{LD} in compressed column format.

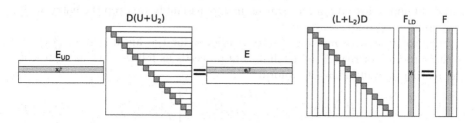

Fig. 3. Computation of a row of E_{UD} and a column of F_{LD} matrices.

For $x_i^T = (x_{i1}, x_{i2}, \ldots, x_{in})$ the solution can be outlined as follows:

$$x_{i1} = e_{i1}/u_{11},\ x_{i2} = (e_{i2} - u_{21}x_{i1})/u_{22}, \ldots, x_{in} = \left(e_{in} - \sum_{k=1}^{n} u_{nk}x_{ik} \right)/u_{nn}, \tag{4}$$

where $u_{ij}, \forall i \le j \le n$ are components of upper triangular matrix $(U + U^2)D$. As a result the sparse vector x_i^T should be always ordered. Whence x_{ij} is known it gets eliminated from all subsequent $x_{ik}, k > j, u_{kj} \neq 0$. During elimination a new nonzero $x_{ik} = -u_{kj}x_{ij}/u_{kk}$ may be introduced. To reduce the fill-in we introduce new nonzero only if $x_{ik}d_k \geq \tau_E$, where $\tau_E = \min(\tau_1^2, \tau_2)\|e_i^T\|_2/\nu_U$. The reasoning for F_{LD} is identical.

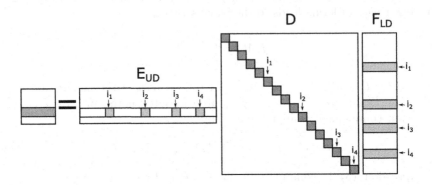

Fig. 4. Multiplication of E_{UD}, D and F_{LD} matrices.

Once E_{UD} and F_{LD} are obtained it remains to compute their product. For the product, we reassemble F_{LD} matrix in row-major format. Then it suffices to compute the sum of sparse rows of F_{LD} corresponding and multiplied by nonzero entries of E_{UD} as illustrated in Fig. 4 and subtract the result from sparse row of C. This operation can be done independently in parallel for each row of the Schur complement.

To reduce the fill-in of the Schur complement we first perform the multiplication without matrix assembly. During this step the maximum values over rows r and columns c are computed. During matrix assembly we drop the entry s_{ij} if $s_{ij} < \min(r_i, c_j) \min(\tau_1^2, \tau_2)/(\nu_L\nu_U)$.

The solution with multi-level preconditioner for the linear system $Ax = b$ with reordering of rows P and columns Q proceeds as follows. Let us represent the reorder system in the block form

$$(PAQ)(Q^Tx) = \begin{bmatrix} B & F \\ E & C \end{bmatrix}\begin{bmatrix} u \\ y \end{bmatrix} = \begin{bmatrix} f \\ g \end{bmatrix} = Pb. \qquad (5)$$

Then the problem for u, y is solved with the steps

$$h = B^{-1}f, \quad t = g - Eh, \quad y = S^{-1}t, \quad u = h - B^{-1}Fy, \qquad (6)$$

where $S = C - EB^{-1}F$ is the Schur complement. These steps are summarized in Algorithm 3. During the solve phase we also use the matrix decomposition to perform eliminations with independent blocks in parallel.

5   Numerical Experiment

To obtain the results we use a single node of INM RAS cluster [39].

Algorithm 3. Multi-level elimination.

```
 1: function SOLVE(b, x, m)
 2:     if m < l then
 3:        [f, g]^T = Pb
 4:        for B^q ∈ B in parallel do
 5:           h^q = (L_l^q)^{-1} f^q                              ▷ Forward substitution
 6:           h^q = (D_l^q)^{-1} h^q
 7:           h^q = (U_l^q)^{-1} h^q                              ▷ Backward substitution
 8:        end for
 9:        t = g - E_l h
10:        SOLVE(t, y, m + 1)
11:        z = F_l y
12:        for B_q ∈ B in parallel do
13:           z^q = (L_l^q)^{-1} z^q                              ▷ Forward substitution
14:           z^q = (D_l^q)^{-1} z^q
15:           z^q = (U_l^q)^{-1} z^q                              ▷ Backward substitution
16:        end for
17:        u = h - z
18:        x = Q[u, y]^T
19:     else                                                    ▷ Last level
20:        x = L_l^{-1} b                                        ▷ Forward substitution
21:        x = D_l^{-1} x
22:        x = U_l^{-1} x                                        ▷ Backward substitution
23:     end if
24: end function
```

5.1 Poisson Problem Matrix

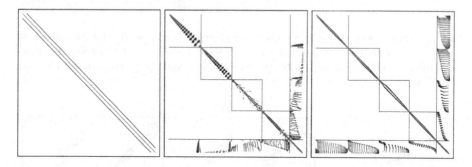

Fig. 5. Initial matrix of 3D Poisson problem (left) symmetrically reordered with greedy dissection (middle) and diagonal blocks reordered with reverse Cuthill-McKee algorithm.

We first consider a matrix obtained from discretization of a 3D Poisson problem on a Cartesian $n \times n \times n$ grid. The reordering steps on the initial matrix with $n = 45$ are illustrated in Fig. 5. Further application of the reordering steps to the next level Schur complement are illustrated in Fig. 6. In Fig. 7 and Fig. 8 we demonstrate the application of alternative approach with unsymmetric greedy dissection.

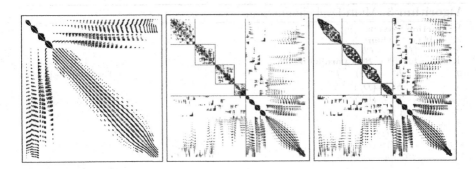

Fig. 6. Second level Schur complement (left) symmetrically reordered with greedy dissection (middle) and diagonal blocks reordered with reverse Cuthill-McKee algorithm.

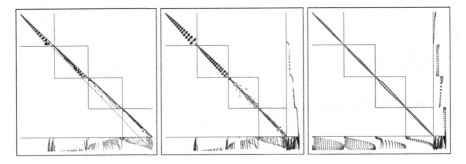

Fig. 7. Matrix reordered with unsymmetric greedy dissection (left) with maximum transversal reordering in diagonal blocks (middle) and reverse Cuthill-McKee algorithm reordering in diagonal blocks. Note, that the Schur complement structure for the next level is destroyed.

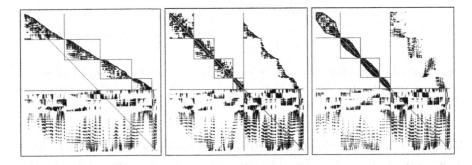

Fig. 8. Next level Schur complement reordered with unsymmetric greedy dissection (left) with maximum transversal reordering in diagonal blocks (middle) and reverse Cuthill-McKee algorithm reordering in diagonal blocks. Note, that the Schur complement structure for the next level is destroyed.

In Table 1 we report the solver runtime for $n = 100$ with $\tau_1 = 5 \times 10^{-2}$, $\tau_2 = \tau_1^2 = 2.5 \times 10^{-3}$, $\kappa = 5$. The notation in the table is the following:

- T_{tot} - total solution time in seconds,
- iters - number of linear iterations in BiCGStab method,
- T_{iter} - total time in seconds spend in linear iterations,
- levels - number of levels in multi-level method,
- pivots - total number of differed pivots during factorization,
- T_{prec} - total time in seconds for preconditioner construction,
- $T_{ord} = T_{mpt} + T_{snd} + T_{rcm}$ - total time in seconds for matrix reordering,
- T_{mpt} - time for finding maximum transversal,
- T_{snd} - time for greedy dissection algorithm,
- T_{rcm} - time for weighted reverse Cuthill-Mckee ordering,
- T_{sc} - time for 8 rescaling iterations to improve matrix I-dominance,
- T_{fact} - time spent in factorization,
- T_{schur} - time for Schur complement computation.

Additional unreported time is spent in reassembling the matrix and rescaling the results.

Table 1. Results on a matrix of a 3D Poisson problem on $100 \times 100 \times 100$ grid. The first column corresponds to single-level method.

Threads	1	1	2	4	8	16
T_{tot}	42.7	47	29.2 (1.6x)	20.2 (2.3x)	13.4 (3.5x)	10.8 (4.3x)
Iters	17	23	27	25	27	29
T_{iter}	6	7.8	4.77 (1.6x)	3.2 (2.4x)	2 (3.9x)	1.64 (4.8x)
Levels	1	2	5	6	7	7
Pivots	0	40564	63588	85689	109995	142988
T_{prec}	36.2	38.7	23.9 (1.6x)	16.5 (2.3x)	10.8 (3.6x)	8.6 (4.5x)
T_{ord}	0.5 (1.4%)	0.7 (2%)	2.6 (11%)	2.4 (15%)	2.3 (21%)	2.55 (29%)
T_{mpt}	0.3 (0.8%)	0.4 (1%)	0.4 (1.6%)	0.4 (2.4%)	0.41 (3.7%)	0.44 (5%)
T_{snd}	– (–%)	– (–%)	1.9 (8%)	1.9 (11%)	1.8 (16.6%)	2.04 (24%)
T_{rcm}	0.2 (0.6%)	0.4 (1%)	0.3 (1.3%)	0.17 (1%)	0.1 (0.9%)	0.06 (0.8%)
T_{sc}	0.9 (2.5%)	1 (2.7%)	0.5 (2.1%)	0.33 (2%)	0.2 (1.9%)	0.17 (1.9%)
T_{fact}	34.2 (95%)	12.7 (23%)	6.3 (26.4%)	4 (24%)	2.48 (23%)	1.32 (15%)
T_{schur}	– (–%)	23.7 (71%)	13.9 (58.2%)	9.2 (55%)	5.35 (49%)	4.04 (47%)

For the reference we add the results with a single-level method without deferred pivoting in the first column of Table 1. It appears that the multilevel algorithm is slightly less efficient for this matrix.

The factorization step scales efficiently with larger core count. However, with the increasing core count the number of levels and deferred pivots increases. As a result the Schur complement computation time is less scalable and dominates the solution time. The Schur complement is bigger with the larger core count due to bigger separator sizes.

In addition the time for the greedy dissection algorithm rises to almost 30%. Sequential greedy dissection algorithm limits the method scalability due to Amdahl's law. It should be noted that the time for computing graphs for greedy dissection algorithm is negligible (10x smaller) in comparison with the time used for the greedy dissection algorithm itself.

5.2 Black-Oil Problem Matrix

Second, we consider the three-phase black-oil problem [40] with the permeability and porosity from the SPE10 dataset [41] that has $60 \times 220 \times 85 = 1\,122\,000$ property entries in a domain with $240\,\text{m} \times 440\,\text{m} \times 320\,\text{m}$ dimensions. The media permeability property is given by a diagonal tensor $\text{diag}(k_x, k_y, k_z)$ with $k_x = k_y$. The anisotropy ratio in the individual cells data is 10458.2 and between adjacent cells is 3.85×10^{10}. The grid is additionally vertically distorted by a randomly generated surface map. The permeability tensor is rotated to follow the grid stratigraphy. The detailed definition of the problem can be found in [42]. The grid generator is available at [43].

The considered matrix corresponds to a few days of the simulation. It's size is $3\,366\,001 \times 3\,366\,001$ with $53\,513\,144$ nonzeroes. In contrast to the matrix from Sect. 5.1, here we consider a larger real-world problem matrix. We report the results in Table 2 with the parameters $\tau_1 = 5 \times 10^{-2}$, $\tau_2 = \tau_1^2 = 2.5 \times 10^{-3}$ and $\kappa = 2.5$.

Table 2. Results on a black-oil problem matrix. The first column corresponds to single-level method.

Threads	1	1	2	4	8	16
T_{tot}	46.3	56.6	44.7 (1.3x)	37.2 (1.5x)	30.5 (1.9x)	29.4 (1.9x)
Iters	19	30	30	32	29	35
T_{iter}	11.3	25	14.2 (1.8x)	10.7 (2.3x)	6.3 (4x)	6.1 (4.1x)
Levels	1	5	6	8	9	10
Pivots	0	167799	201296	278060	355152	458293
T_{prec}	33.7	30.2	29.1 (1x)	25.2 (1.2x)	22.9 (1.3x)	22 (1.4x)
T_{ord}	5.4 (16%)	5.5 (18%)	13.1 (45%)	13.3 (53%)	12.3 (54%)	11.5 (52%)
T_{mpt}	2.9 (9%)	2.8 (9%)	2.4 (8%)	2.4 (9%)	2.3 (10%)	2.4 (11%)
T_{snd}	– (–%)	– (–%)	7.9 (27%)	8 (32%)	7.8 (34%)	7.8 (36%)
T_{rcm}	2.5 (7%)	2.7 (9%)	2.8 (10%)	2.9 (11%)	2.3 (10%)	1.2 (5.5%)
T_{sc}	4.4 (13%)	4.6 (15%)	2.6 (9%)	1.7 (7%)	1 (4%)	0.8 (4%)
T_{fact}	20.3 (60%)	9.4 (31%)	5.2 (18%)	3 (12%)	3.1 (13%)	2.4 (11%)
T_{schur}	– (–%)	7.1 (23%)	5.2 (18%)	4.8 (19%)	4.3 (19%)	5.2 (24%)

According to the results the reordering and rescaling takes much time even for a single thread. Single-level algorithm is also faster due to smaller iteration count. This may be caused by the dropping strategy from the Schur complement. Even with two threads the reordering takes almost half of the preconditioner time with the sequential greedy dissection and maximum transversal algorithms taking together 35% of time. As a result we shall further focus on parallel graph dissection algorithm.

6   Conclusions

In this work, we considered shared parallelism in the multilevel incomplete factorization preconditioner. It is based on matrix reordering into doubly-bordered block diagonal form allowing for simultaneous factorization of independent blocks. The remaining border is deferred to the next level thanks to the multilevel algorithm. The new strategy leads to the reduction of domain count in the domain-decomposition method.

Most of the parts except for maximum transversal and greedy dissection algorithms were parallelised using OpenMP. Considerable speedup was obtained in matrix factorization. However, Amdahl's law prohibits to obtain reasonable acceleration of overall solver with a large core count due to sequential greedy dissection algorithm. In the following, we shall consider parallelisation of the remaining algorithms as wells as focus on the block version of the factorization for greater robustness.

Acknowledgements. This work has been supported by Russian Science Foundation grant 21-71-20024.

References

1. Terekhov, K.: Parallel multilevel linear solver within INMOST platform. In: Voevodin, V., Sobolev, S. (eds.) RuSCDays 2020. CCIS, vol. 1331, pp. 297–309. Springer, Cham (2020). https://doi.org/10.1007/978-3-030-64616-5_26
2. Bollhöfer, M.: A robust ILU with pivoting based on monitoring the growth of the inverse factors. Linear Algebra Appl. **338**(1–3), 201–218 (2001)
3. Bollhöfer, M., Saad, Y.: Multilevel preconditioners constructed from inverse-based ILUs. SIAM J. Sci. Comput. **27**(5), 1627–1650 (2006)
4. Olschowka, M., Arnold, N.: A new pivoting strategy for Gaussian elimination. Linear Algebra Appl. **240**, 131–151 (1996)
5. Duff, I.S., Kaya, K., Uçar, B.: Design, implementation, and analysis of maximum transversal algorithms. ACM Trans. Math. Softw. (TOMS) **38**(2), 1–31 (2012)
6. Cuthill, E., McKee, J.: Reducing the bandwidth of sparse symmetric matrices. In: Proceedings of the 1969 24th National Conference (1969)
7. Kaporin, I.E.: High quality preconditioning of a general symmetric positive definite matrix based on its UTU+ UTR+ RTU-decomposition. Numer. Linear Algebra Appl. **5**(6), 483–509 (1998)
8. Mandel, J.: Balancing domain decomposition. Commun. Numer. Methods Eng. **9**(3), 233–241 (1993)

9. Spillane, N., Dolean, V., Hauret, P., Nataf, F., Pechstein, C., Scheichl, R.: Abstract robust coarse spaces for systems of PDEs via generalized eigenproblems in the overlaps. Numer. Math. **126**(4), 741–770 (2014)
10. Duff, I.S., Scott, J.A.: Stabilized bordered block diagonal forms for parallel sparse solvers. Parallel Comput. **31**(3–4), 275–289 (2005)
11. Hu, Y., Scott, J.: Ordering techniques for singly bordered block diagonal forms for unsymmetric parallel sparse direct solvers. Numer. Linear Algebra Appl. **12**(9), 877–894 (2005)
12. Grigori, L., Boman, E.G., Donfack, S., Davis, T.A.: Hypergraph-based unsymmetric nested dissection ordering for sparse LU factorization. SIAM J. Sci. Comput. **32**(6), 3426–3446 (2010)
13. Fiedler, M.: A property of eigenvectors of nonnegative symmetric matrices and its application to graph theory. Czechoslov. Math. J. **25**(4), 619–633 (1975)
14. Kernighan, B.W., Lin, S.: An efficient heuristic procedure for partitioning graphs. Bell Syst. Tech. J. **49**(2), 291–307 (1970)
15. Dutt, S.: New faster Kernighan-Lin-type graph-partitioning algorithms. In: Proceedings of 1993 International Conference on Computer Aided Design (ICCAD), pp. 370–377. IEEE, November 1993
16. Fiduccia, C.M., Mattheyses, R.M.: A linear-time heuristic for improving network partitions. In: 19th Design Automation Conference, pp. 175–181. IEEE, June 1982
17. Karypis, G., Kumar, V.: METIS: a software package for partitioning unstructured graphs, partitioning meshes, and computing fill-reducing orderings of sparse matrices (1997)
18. LaSalle, D., Karypis, G.: Efficient nested dissection for multicore architectures. In: Träff, J.L., Hunold, S., Versaci, F. (eds.) Euro-Par 2015. LNCS, vol. 9233, pp. 467–478. Springer, Heidelberg (2015). https://doi.org/10.1007/978-3-662-48096-0_36
19. Çatalyürek, Ü.V., Aykanat, C.: PaToH (partitioning tool for hypergraphs). In: Padua, D. (eds.) Encyclopedia of Parallel Computing, pp. 1479–1487. Springer, Boston (2011). https://doi.org/10.1007/978-0-387-09766-4
20. Mondriaan for sparse matrix partitioning. https://webspace.science.uu.nl/~bisse101/Mondriaan/. Accessed 15 Apr 2021
21. Boman, E.G., Çatalyürek, Ü.V., Chevalier, C., Devine, K.D.: The Zoltan and Isorropia parallel toolkits for combinatorial scientific computing: partitioning, ordering and coloring. Sci. Program. **20**(2), 129–150 (2012)
22. Hendrickson, B., Leland, R.: The Chaco users guide. version 1.0 (No. SAND-93-2339). Sandia National Labs., Albuquerque, NM (United States) (1993)
23. Battiti, R., Bertossi, A.A.: Greedy, prohibition, and reactive heuristics for graph partitioning. IEEE Trans. Comput. **48**(4), 361–385 (1999)
24. Jain, S., Swamy, C., Balaji, K.: Greedy algorithms for k-way graph partitioning. In: the 6th International Conference on Advanced Computing, p. 100 (1998)
25. Aliaga, J.I., Bollhöfer, M., Martín, A.F., Quintana-Ortí, E.S.: Parallelization of multilevel ILU preconditioners on distributed-memory multiprocessors. In: Jónasson, K. (ed.) PARA 2010. LNCS, vol. 7133, pp. 162–172. Springer, Heidelberg (2012). https://doi.org/10.1007/978-3-642-28151-8_16
26. INMOST: a toolkit for distributed mathematical modelling. http://www.inmost.org. Accessed 15 Apr 2021
27. Vassilevski, Yu.V., Konshin, I.N., Kopytov, G.V., Terekhov, K.M.: INMOST - Programming Platform and Graphical Environment for Development of Parallel Numerical Models on General Grids. Moscow University Press, Moscow (2013). (in Russian)

28. Vassilevski, Y., Terekhov, K., Nikitin, K., Kapyrin, I.: Parallel Finite Volume Computation on General Meshes. Springer, Cham (2020). https://doi.org/10.1007/978-3-030-47232-0

29. Danilov, A.A., Terekhov, K.M., Konshin, I.N., Vassilevski, Y.V.: INMOST parallel platform: framework for numerical modeling. Supercomput. Front. Innov. 2(4), 55–66 (2015)

30. Konshin, I., Terekhov, K.: Sparse system solution methods for complex problems. In: Proceedings of PaCT-21 Conference, Kaliningrad, pp. 1–20 (2021)

31. Sleijpen, G.L.G., Diederik, R.F.: BiCGstab (l) for linear equations involving unsymmetric matrices with complex spectrum. Electron. Trans. Numer. Anal. 1(11), 2000 (1993)

32. Trilinos - platform for the solution of large-scale, complex multi-physics engineering and scientific problems. http://trilinos.org/. Accessed 10 Mar 2019

33. PETSc - Portable Extensible Toolkit for Scientific Computation. https://www.mcs.anl.gov/petsc/. Accessed 15 Apr 2021

34. SuperLU - Supernodal LU solver for large, sparse, nonsymmetric linear systems. https://portal.nersc.gov/project/sparse/superlu/. Accessed 15 Apr 2021

35. Bui, T.N., Jones, C.: Finding good approximate vertex and edge partitions is NP-hard. Inf. Process. Lett. 42(3), 153–159 (1992)

36. Barnard, S.T., Simon, H.D.: Fast multilevel implementation of recursive spectral bisection for partitioning unstructured problems. Concurr. Pract. Exp. 6(2), 101–117 (1994)

37. Karypis, G., Kumar, V.: A fast and high quality multilevel scheme for partitioning irregular graphs. SIAM J. Sci. Comput. 20(1), 359–392 (1998)

38. Azad, A., Halappanavar, M., Dobrian, F., Pothen, A.: Computing maximum matching in parallel on bipartite graphs: worth the effort? In: Proceedings of the 1st Workshop on Irregular Applications: Architectures and Algorithms, pp. 11–14, November 2011

39. INM RAS cluster. http://cluster2.inm.ras.ru/en. Accessed 15 Apr 2021

40. Aziz, K., Settari, A.: Petroleum Reservoir Simulation, pp. 135–139. Applied Science Publishers Ltd., London (1979)

41. SPE10 dataset. https://www.spe.org/web/csp/datasets/set01.htm. Accessed 15 Apr 2021

42. Konshin, I., Terekhov, K.: Solution of large-scale black oil recovery problem in parallel using INMOST platform. In: Voevodin, V., Sobolev, S. (eds.) RuSCDays 2021. CCIS, vol. 1510, pp. 240–255. Springer, Cham (2021). https://doi.org/10.1007/978-3-030-92864-3_19

43. SPE10 distorted grid generator. https://github.com/kirill-terekhov/spe10grdecl. Accessed 15 Apr 2021

Heterogeneous Parallel Algorithm for Compressible Flow Simulations on Adaptive Mixed Meshes

Sergey Soukov[✉]

Federal Research Center Keldysh Institute of Applied Mathematics, Russian Academy of Sciences, Moscow 12504, Russia

Abstract. The paper describes a parallel heterogeneous algorithm for compressible flow simulations on adaptive mixed meshes. The numerical algorithm is based on an explicit second order accurate finite-volume method for Navier-Stokes equations with linear reconstruction of variables. Gas dynamics equations are discretized on hanging node meshes of tetrahedra, prisms, pyramids, and hexahedra. The mesh adaptation procedure consists in the recursive refinement and/or the coarsening of cells using predefined templates. Heterogeneous parallelization approach uses MPI + OpenMP + CUDA program model that provides portability across a hybrid supercomputers with multicore CPUs and Nvidia GPUs. A two-level domain decomposition scheme is used for the static load balance among computing devices. First level decomposition involves the mesh partitioning between supercomputer nodes. At the second level node subdomains are partitioned between devices. The Cuthill-McKee reordering is used to set cell local indexes in the MPI process computational domain to speed up CFD kernels for the CPU. The CUDA implementation includes a communication and computation overlap that hides the communication overhead. The heterogeneous execution scalability parameters are shown by the example of simulating a supersonic flow around a sphere on different adaptive meshes using up to 70 multicore CPUs and 105 GPUs.

Keywords: Heterogeneous computing · Unstructured mesh refinement · Parallel CFD

1 Introduction

The time and results of CFD simulations strongly depend on the type and size (number of nodes, elements, faces, etc.) of the computational mesh. Hybrid and mixed meshes [1] are most suitable for modeling flows around the complex shape bodies. Adaptive mesh refinement methods are often used to improve solution accuracy and decrease the mesh size [2]. The adaptive mesh is statically or dynamically refined directly to the flow features. Static adaptation is used for steady flow simulations. The launch of the parallel CFD program alternates with the solution analysis and mesh adaptation [3]. This approach can be used for multiple simulations with different flow parameters and the same starting coarse mesh. Dynamic adaptation techniques are applied for the simulations of unsteady flows [4, 5]. The mesh is refined during the time the solution is

V. Voevodin and S. Sobolev (Eds.): RuSCDays 2021, CCIS 1510, pp. 102–113, 2021.
https://doi.org/10.1007/978-3-030-92864-3_8

being calculated. For example, the fine cells zones are moved according to the current positions of the turbulent regions after each time integration step. In this case, the mesh adaptation routines are included directly to the main CFD code.

This paper describes a parallel algorithm for compressible flow simulations on hanging node mixed meshes. Heterogeneous parallelization approach is based on MPI + OpenMP + CUDA hybrid program model. The CUDA implementation includes a communication and computation overlap. A distinctive feature of the proposed algorithm in comparison with existing CFD codes is that it can be used both for simulations on hanging node meshes and arbitrary polyhedral meshes.

The paper is organized as follows. The mathematical model and numerical method are briefly outlined in Sect. 2. The parallel algorithm and details of the overlap mode and heterogeneous execution are described in Sect. 3. The results of the study of parallel efficiency and performance are presented in Sect. 4. And Sect. 5 contains some conclusions.

2 Mathematical Model and Numerical Method

A compressible viscous fluid is modeled by the Navier–Stokes equations:

$$\frac{\partial \boldsymbol{Q}}{\partial t} + \nabla \cdot \boldsymbol{F} = 0, \tag{1}$$

where $\boldsymbol{Q} = (\rho, \rho u, \rho u, \rho u, E)^T$ is a vector of conservative variables, $\boldsymbol{F} = \boldsymbol{F}^C + \boldsymbol{F}^D$ is a flux vector that consists of convective and diffusive fluxes, respectively.

The Eq. (1) are discretized on an hanging node mixed meshes using a explicit cell-centered finite-volume method with a polynomial reconstruction. The starting conformal mesh combines tetrahedra, prisms, pyramids, and hexahedrons. The mesh adaptation procedure consists in the recursive refinement and/or the coarsening of cells using predefined templates (Fig. 1). A subset of the mesh cells are marked for dividing or agglomeration based on the adaption function, which is created from numerical solution data. After adaptation, neighboring cells can't to differ by more than one level of refinement.

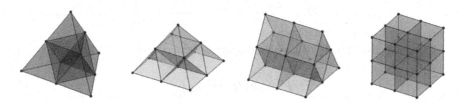

Fig. 1. Cells refinement templates.

During CFD simulations, non-conformal hanging node mesh is transformed to a conformal polyhedral mesh. If a cell is adjacent to four cells along a face, then this face is divided into four parts (Fig. 2).

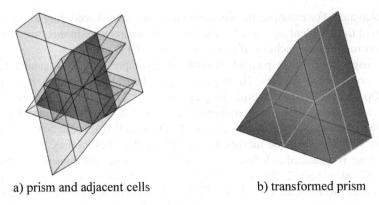

a) prism and adjacent cells   b) transformed prism

Fig. 2. Example of transforming a prism to a polyhedron.

Each polyhedral cell C_i has a volume $|C_i|$ and surface ∂C_i. In accordance with the finite volume method, a balancing relation is written for cells as:

$$\frac{\partial}{\partial t}\int_{C_i} Q d\Omega + \oint_{\partial C_i} F dS = 0. \tag{2}$$

The discrete values of the mesh function Q_i are defined at the cell-centroid r_i as integral average

$$Q_i = \frac{1}{|C_i|}\int_{C_i} Q d\Omega. \tag{3}$$

Surface ∂C_i of an internal cell consists of flat faces ∂C_{ij}. The geometry of the face ∂C_{ij} between cells C_i and C_j is set by the unit normal n_{ij}, the face-midpoint r_{ij} and its square S_{ij}.

The discrete variant of (2) has the form

$$\frac{\partial Q_i}{\partial t} + \sum_{j\in I_i}\left(F_{ij}^C + F_{ij}^D\right)S_{ij} = 0, \tag{4}$$

where I_i is the set of C_i neighbors.

The convective flux F_{ij}^C is computed using a Riemann solver

$$F_{ij}^C = \Phi\left(Q_{ij}^L, Q_{ij}^R, n_{ij}\right), \tag{5}$$

where Q_{ij}^L and Q_{ij}^R are the values from the left and right states evaluated at the interface ∂C_{ij}. The implemented set of Riemann solvers [6, 7] Φ includes CUSP, Roe, Roe–Pike for subsonic flows; HLL, HLLE, HLLC, Rusanov and AUSMDV for supersonic flows.

It is assumed that the solution is piecewise linearly distributed over the control volume. In this case, the left and right states can be found from the relations

$$Q_{ij}^{L/R} = Q_{i/j} + \Psi_{i/j}(\nabla Q_{i/j} \cdot (r_{ij} - r_{i/j})), \qquad (6)$$

where $\nabla Q_i = (\partial Q/\partial x, \partial Q/\partial y, \partial Q/\partial z)$ is the gradient of Q at the i-th cell center and Ψ denotes a limiter function [8, 9].

The algorithm for gradient calculation is based on the Green-Gauss approach. For the original mesh cells, the linear reconstruction coefficients are calculated as

$$\nabla Q_i = \frac{1}{|C_i|} \sum_{j \in I_i} \left(g_{ij}^i Q_i + g_{ij}^j Q_j \right) n_{ij} S_{ij}. \qquad (7)$$

Geometrical coefficients g_{ij}^i and g_{ij}^j are inversely to the distances from the cell-centroids to the face plane and satisfy $g_{ij}^i + g_{ij}^j = 1$.

For reconstruction over transformed polyhedra, dummy control volumes are used. Dummy cell C_i' vertices are placed at the points of intersection between ∂C_{ij} planes and lines connecting the polyhedra centroid r_i and adjacent cells centroids r_j. The volume of C_i' is bounded by triangulation of the convex hull of its vertices. The values of variables at the vertices and faces midpoints are computed by linear interpolation on segments and triangles. Figure 3 shows reconstruction control volume for transformed prism (Fig. 2). The dummy control volume approach can also be used to calculate gradients in the conformal mesh cells.

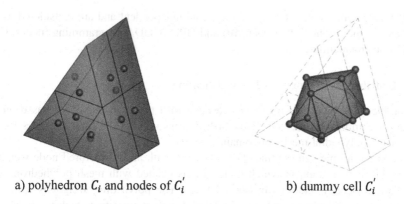

a) polyhedron C_i and nodes of C_i' b) dummy cell C_i'

Fig. 3. Dummy control volume for transformed prism.

In order to evaluate the diffusive fluxes F_{ij}^D first derivatives of the velocity components and temperature at face-midpoints are computed as the combination of the averaged gradients $\overline{\nabla Q}_{ij}$ and the directional derivatives:

$$\overline{\nabla Q}_{ij} = \frac{\nabla Q_i + \nabla Q_j}{2}, \tag{8}$$

$$\nabla Q_{ij} = \overline{\nabla Q}_{ij} - \left[\overline{\nabla Q}_{ij} \mathbf{t}_{ij} - \frac{Q_j - Q_i}{l_{ij}}\right] \mathbf{t}_{ij}. \tag{9}$$

Here $l_{ij} = |r_j - r_i|$ represents the distance between the cell-centroids, and $\mathbf{t}_{ij} = (r_j - r_i)/l_{ij}$ is the unit vector along the line connecting them.

The boundary conditions are specified by setting the appropriate flow variables $Q_{i\Gamma}^R$ or fluxes $F_{i\Gamma}$ at the midpoints of the faces $\partial C_{i\Gamma}$ at the computational domain boundary Γ.

Finally, explicit multi-stage Runge–Kutta (RK) time integration schemes are used.

3   Parallel Algorithm and Implementation

3.1   Sequential Time Integration Step Algorithm

Each explicit RK step include multiple execution of the following operations:

- Reconstruction kernel – to get gradients at the cell centers, a loop over the cells;
- Fluxes kernel – calculation of convective and diffusive fluxes through inner and boundary faces, a loop over the faces;
- Update kernel – summation of fluxes along adjacent faces and calculation of the flow variables at a new RK scheme stage or time step, a loop over the cells.

The statement blocks of the loops are data independent and are considered as the parallelism units in the CPU (OpenMP) and GPU (CUDA programming model) CFD kernel implementations.

3.2   Distributed-Memory MPI Parallelization

The problem of static load balancing between MPI processes is solved based on the domain decomposition method. Each MPI process updates the flow variables for the cells of the polyhedral mesh subdomain (Fig. 4).

Graph partitioning subroutines [10, 11] work with an unstructured node-weighted dual graph. It is a graph in which nodes are associated with mesh polyhedrons, and edges are adjacency relations by shared faces. The polyhedron weight is set as the integer equal to the number of faces. As a result of decomposition, each mesh cell gets the rank of the MPI process, the subdomain of which it belongs to, and each process gets a list of its own cells.

The set of own cells is divided into subsets of inner and interface cells. The interface cells spatial scheme stencil includes cells from neighbouring subdomains or halo cells. Thus, the local computational domain of the MPI process joins up its own and halo cells. The interface cells of one subdomain are halo cells for one or more neighboring subdomains.

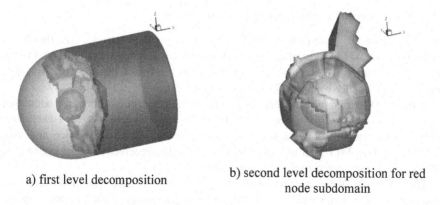

a) first level decomposition

b) second level decomposition for red node subdomain

Fig. 4. Two-level decomposition.

The local indexes of the computational domain cells are ordered according to their type: inner, interface, halo. In addition, Cuthill-McKee reordering [12] is used to set indexes within inner and interface cell groups. This approach optimizes the data location in RAM and improves the CFD kernels performance. The halo cell indexes are ordered by the MPI process ranks. Figure 5 shows the distribution of cells by type for the computational domain, built around the 8×8 cells subdomain of a structured grid.

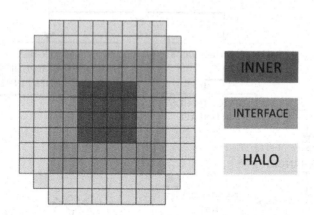

Fig. 5. Computational domain structure in 2D.

Parallel execution of the RK stage starts with asynchronous MPI exchanges. The data transfer includes only the flow variables. Halo cells gradients and interface/halo face fluxes computations are duplicated. Persistent requests for messages are created before the simulation starts by the subroutines MPI_Send_Init and MPI_Recv_Init. At the synchronization point, the MPI process packs the interface data to the send buffers, starts collecting requests (MPI_Startall routine) and then waits for all given requests to complete (MPI_Waitall routine). Halo data is received directly to the calculation data arrays without intermediate bufferization.

3.3   Heterogeneous Execution and Overlap Mode

Each MPI process is bound either to fixed CPU cores number or to one core (host) and one GPU (device). The sizes of the local computational domains are proportional to the device performance. The relative performance ratio between CPU and GPU is determined experimentally by the CFD kernels execution time.

If the CFD kernels are running on a GPU, parallel execution includes additional device-to-host and host-to-device data transfers before and after the MPI exchange. Interface flow variables are packed to intermediate buffers on the device and then copied to the host MPI send messages buffers. Halo data received to intermediate host buffers, which are copied to device data arrays.

The execution of the kernels on the GPU allows to overlap communication and computation. The inner cells are computed simultaneously with the halo update operation, then the interface cells are computed using the updated halo. In this case, host intermediate buffers are allocated in page-locked (or pinned) memory. Two asynchronous CUDA streams are created on the device. First stream used as a queue for halo update procedures execution. CFD kernels are placed to the second stream. The algorithm for executing the RK stage on the GPU in overlap mode is shown in Fig. 6.

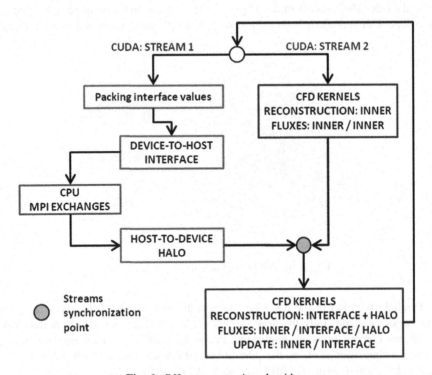

Fig. 6. RK stage execution algorithm.

4   Parallel Efficiency and Scalability

The study of the parallelization efficiency, the overlap mode and the heterogeneous execution performance was carried out during numerical simulation of the supersonic flow around a sphere at Mach number 2 and Reynolds number 300. The mesh adaptation algorithm and the numerical simulation results discussed in [13]. The computational mesh is refined at the detached shock wave position, near the isosurface with a local Mach number ($M = 1$) and near the recirculation region boundary (Fig. 7a). Figure 7b illustrates the flow structure.

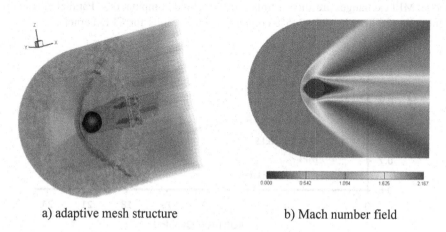

a) adaptive mesh structure   b) Mach number field

Fig. 7. Flow around a sphere.

Coarse and fine adaptive hanging node meshes were used for testing (Table 1). Both meshes contain cells of the first and second refinement levels.

Table 1. Computational meshes parameters.

Parameter	Coarse mesh	Fine mesh
Number of nodes	452288	3486628
Number of tetrahedral	224696	1588900
Number of hexahedrons	306713	2463616
Number of prisms	99622	881851
Number of pyramids	9741	54911
Total number of cells	640772	4989278

The parallel program was run on a heterogeneous supercomputer K-100 with asymmetric nodes. Two Intel Xeon X5670 CPUs and three NVIDIA 2050 GPUs are available on one node to run the program.

4.1   MPI Parallelization and Overlap Mode

Figure 8 shows parallel efficiency graphs for a coarse mesh in the GPU mode (3 MPI processes per node). Blue line - results of pure computations without MPI exchange. The minimum parameter value (24 GPU and about 25000 mesh cells per device) is 87%. Here, the CFD kernels execution time increases due to domain decomposition imbalance and duplication of calculations at halo cells. Explicit MPI exchanges (red line) visibly increase the program execution time. For a group of 24 devices, communications are comparable to the computation time. Parallel efficiency drops to 64% and the speedup turns out to be 1.6 times lower than the expected value. In overlap mode, MPI exchanges are successfully hidden behind computations. Parallel efficiency (green line) differs by only 2–5% compared to the results for CFD kernels.

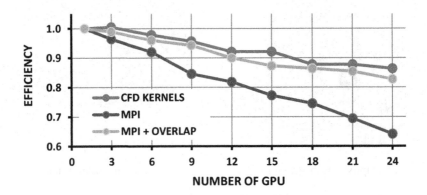

Fig. 8. Parallel efficiency. (Color figure online)

4.2   Heterogeneous Execution

To measure the efficiency of a heterogeneous mode, the values of absolute and relative performance are used. The absolute performance P_N^{mode} on N nodes for specific mode (CPU only, GPU only, heterogeneous CPU + GPU) is equal to the number of RK time integration steps per second. The relative performance R_N^{mode} is calculated as

$$R_N^{mode} = \frac{P_N^{mode}}{P_N^{CPU} + P_N^{GPU}}. \qquad (10)$$

In CPU only mode, each MPI process occupies 3 cores to run OpenMP threads (4 MPI processes per supercomputer node). The configuration for running 6 processes per node in a heterogeneous mode is shown in Fig. 9. Here, MPI processes and OpenMP threads get strong affinity to CPU cores.

Figure 10 shows a graph of relative performance for a coarse mesh. The ratio of values practically does not change for a different number of nodes. The relative heterogeneous performance is about 83%. The difference between R_N^{HET} and $R_N^{CPU} + R_N^{GPU} = 1$ is partly due to the fact that 3 cores are used to control the execution of CFD kernels

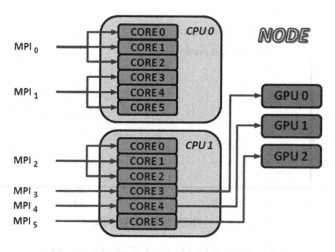

Fig. 9. Program launch configuration.

on devices. In this case, the ideal value is $R_N^{HET} = 0.75R_N^{CPU} + R_N^{GPU} \approx 0.91$. Thus, the real R_N^{HET} differs from the theoretical maximum value by only 8%.

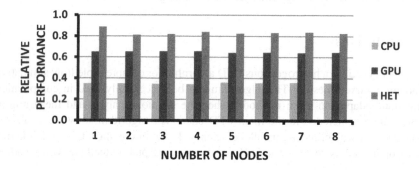

Fig. 10. Relative performance.

4.3   Parallel Program Scaling

The study of the program scaling was carried out for a fine 5 million cells mesh. Figure 11 shows a speedup graph for heterogeneous parallelization (green line). For comparison, there is a graph of ideal linear speedup (red dashed line). The performance ratio of the CPU and the GPU has a fixed value of 1:1.6. The low current efficiency of the CFD algorithm implementation for the GPU is explained by the use of the same parallelism units.

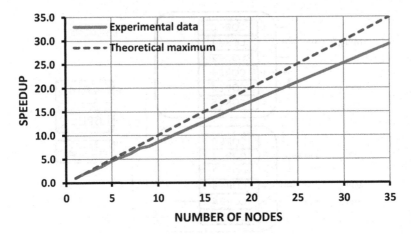

Fig. 11. Speedup for fine mesh. (Color figure online)

The speedup for 35 nodes (70 CPUs, 105 GPUs, 210 processes MPI group size) is 29.3 times, which corresponds to a parallel efficiency of 84%. The absolute performance is $P_N^{HET} \approx 56$ steps per second. That is, it takes 0.0179 s for one time integration step or 0.0045 s for RK stage (include MPI exchange).

5   Conclusions

This paper describes a heterogeneous CFD algorithm for compressible flow simulations on adaptive mixed meshes. This algorithm can be successfully used in computations using static adaptation mesh methods, when the solution analysis and mesh refining routines are not included in the main CFD code. The algorithm software implementation has high scalability and parallel efficiency. In the future, the CUDA CFD kernels will be optimized as described in [14] and dynamic adaptation methods will be added.

Acknowledgments. The work has been funded by the Russian Science Foundation, project 19-11-00299. The results were obtained using the equipment of Shared Resource Center of KIAM RAS (http://ckp.kiam.ru).

References

1. Liou, M.-S., Kao, K.-H.: Progress in grid generation: from chimera to DRAGON grids. In: NASA Technical Reports, 19970031503, pp. 1–32, National Aeronautics and Space Administration (1994)
2. Powell, K., Roe, P., Quirk, J.: Adaptive-mesh algorithms for computational fluid dynamics. In: Hussaini, M.Y., Kumar, A., Salas, M.D. (eds.). Algorithmic Trends in Computational Fluid Dynamics. ICASE/NASA LaRC Series. Springer, New York (1993). https://doi.org/10.1007/978-1-4612-2708-3_18
3. https://www.ansys.com/products/fluids/ansys-fluent

4. Antepara, O., Lehmkuhl, O., Chiva, J., Borrell, R.: Parallel adaptive mesh refinement simulation of the flow around a square cylinder at Re = 22000. Procedia Eng. **61**, 246–250 (2013). https://doi.org/10.1016/j.proeng.2013.08.011

5. Schwing, A., Nompelis, I., Candler, G.: Parallelization of unsteady adaptive mesh refinement for unstructured Navier-Stokes solvers. In: AIAA AVIATION 2014 -7th AIAA Theoretical Fluid Mechanics Conference. American Institute of Aeronautics and Astronautics Inc. (2014). https://doi.org/10.2514/6.2014-3080

6. Toro, E.F.: Riemann Solvers and Numerical Methods for Fluid Dynamics. Springer, Heidelberg (2009). https://doi.org/10.1007/b79761

7. Wada, Y., Liou, M.-S.: A flux splitting scheme with high resolution and robustness for discontinuities. In: AIAA Paper 94-0083

8. Barth, T.J.: Numerical aspects of computing high-Reynolds number flows on unstructured meshes. In: AIAA Paper 91-0721 (1991)

9. Kim, S., Caraeni, D., Makarov, B.: A multidimensional linear reconstruction scheme for arbitrary unstructured grids. In: Technical report. AIAA 16th Computational Fluid Dynamics Conference, Orlando, Florida. American Institute of Aeronautics and Astronautics (2003)

10. Golovchenko, E.N., Kornilina, M.A., Yakobovskiy, M.V.: Algorithms in the parallel partitioning tool GridSpiderPar for large mesh decomposition. In: Proceedings of the 3rd International Conference on Exascale Applications and Software (EASC 2015), pp. 120–125. University of Edinburgh (2015)

11. Schloegel, K., Karypis, G., Kumar, V.: Parallel multilevel algorithms for multi-constraint graph partitioning. In: Bode, A., Ludwig, T., Karl, W., Wismüller, R. (eds.) Euro-Par 2000 Parallel Processing: 6th International Euro-Par Conference Munich, Germany, August 29 – September 1, 2000 Proceedings, pp. 296–310. Springer, Heidelberg (2000). https://doi.org/10.1007/3-540-44520-X_39

12. Cuthill, E., McKee, J.: Reducing the bandwidth of sparse symmetric matrices. In: Proceedings of the ACM 24th National Conference, pp. 157–172 (1969)

13. Soukov, S.A.: Adaptive mesh refinement simulations of gas dynamic flows on hybrid meshes. Dokl. Math. **102**, 409–411 (2020). https://doi.org/10.1134/S1064562420050427

14. Gorobets, A., Soukov, S., Bogdanov, P.: Multilevel parallelization for simulating turbulent flows on most kinds of hybrid supercomputers. Comput. Fluids **173**, 171–177 (2018). https://doi.org/10.1016/j.compfluid.2018.03.011

High-Performance Atomistic Modeling of Evaporation of Thin Films Under Intense Laser Irradiation

Fedor Grigoriev[(✉)], Vladimir Sulimov, and Alexander Tikhonravov

Research Computing Center, M.V. Lomonosov Moscow State University,
Leninskie Gory, Moscow 119234, Russia
vs@dimonta.com, tikh@srcc.msu.ru

Abstract. This paper presents the results of high-performance atomistic modeling of heating and the initial stage of evaporation of thin silicon dioxide films under the action of high-power laser radiation. Both dense isotropic films obtained by normal deposition and highly porous anisotropic silicon dioxide films obtained by deposition at a large angle to the substrate are investigated. The dependence of the initial stage of film evaporation on its structural properties is analyzed.

Keyword: Atomistic modeling · Silicon dioxide films · High-performance simulations · Laser irradiation

1 Introduction

Thin film optical coatings are important elements of high intensity laser installations, among which the most impressive examples are petawatt laser systems used in nuclear fusion plants [1–3]. The main limiting factor preventing a further increase in lasers power is the laser induced damage in thin films of optical coatings [4–6]. The issue of increasing the laser radiation resistance of optical thin films has been on the agenda for more than three decades. To date, experimental methods for studying the laser induced damage in thin films are well developed and described by international standards [7]. At the same time, the general theoretical understanding of the physical mechanism of laser induced damage is still very far from what is desired. But such an understanding is vital for further progress in many critical areas requiring the use of powerful lasers.

Recently, molecular dynamics methods have been actively used to study the interaction of laser irradiation with various materials [8–11], including their heating and subsequent evaporation. These processes play an important role in laser damage [12]. For optical coatings, one of the most important thin film materials is silicon dioxide. The study of heating SiO_2 films under intense laser irradiation was begun in Ref. [13]. This article presents the latest results in this direction.

© Springer Nature Switzerland AG 2021
V. Voevodin and S. Sobolev (Eds.): RuSCDays 2021, CCIS 1510, pp. 114–124, 2021.
https://doi.org/10.1007/978-3-030-92864-3_9

2 Method

Following [14–16] we assume that the absorption of the high-energy laser irradiation occurs due to nonlinear processes such as multiphoton absorption. The process of the interaction of electron subsystem with laser irradiation is not considered explicitly within the framework of this paper, but is taken into account trough the simulation parameters. The transfer of energy from the electronic sub-system of to the nuclei is a short-time process. In our simulations, this transfer is considered as a rapid, almost instantaneous increase in the nuclei kinetic energy. After this moment, the further nuclei moving are considered using the classical molecular dynamics (MD). The energy of interatomic interactions is calculated in the frame of the DESIL force field [17]:

$$U = q_i q_j / r_{ij} + A_{ij} / r_{ij}^{12} - B_{ij} / r_{ij}^{6} \tag{1}$$

where $q_{i(j)}$ is the charge of the $i(j)$-th atom, $q_O = -0.5 q_{Si} = -0.65e$, A_{ij} and B_{ij}, are parameters of the Lennard-Jones potential for the van der Waals interaction, r_{ij} is the interatomic distance, $A_{SiO} = 4.6 \cdot 10^{-8}$ kJ·(nm)^{12}/mol, $A_{SiSi} = A_{OO} = 1.5 \cdot 10^{-6}$ kJ·(nm)^{12}/mol, $B_{SiO} = 4.2 \cdot 10^{-3}$ kJ·(nm)^{6}/mol, $B_{SiSi} = B_{OO} = 5 \cdot 10^{-5}$ kJ·(nm)^{6}/mol.

The atomistic clusters, representing the thin film, were obtained in our previous works [18, 19] using the step-by-step procedure. At each step, silicon and oxygen atoms with stoichiometric proportion of 1:2 are inserted randomly at the top of the simulation box. The initial values of the silicon and oxygen atoms kinetic energies are $E(Si) = 10$ eV and $E(O) = 0,1$ eV, which corresponds to the high-energy deposition processes. The initial velocities of the oxygen and silicon atoms are directed to the substrate at the deposition angle α (Fig. 1) The NVT (constant number of particles, volume and temperature) ensemble is used at every injection step. The vertical dimension of the simulation box is increased by 0.01 nm after each injection step in order to compensate for the growth of film thickness. The duration of one injection step is 10 ps and the time step of MD modeling is 0.5 fs.

The atomistic clusters were deposited at two different deposition angles $\alpha = 0$ and $70°$. Deposition at $\alpha = 0$ leads to the formation of dense and homogeneous films, while deposition at large values of α leads to the formation of porous and anisotropic structures (Fig. 1). In this work, we investigate the differences in the heating and evaporation processes for these cases.

The MD simulation of the film heating is organized as described in [13]. At the initial moment, the atoms of the films acquire additional kinetic energy, which corresponds to the following exponentially decreasing temperature distribution over the cluster thickness:

$$T(x) = \frac{T_m}{e-1} \left(e^{\left(\frac{2x}{L}-1\right)} - 1 \right) + T_0 \text{ if } L/2 < x \leq L$$
$$T(x) = T_0, \text{ if } 0 \leq x \leq L/2. \tag{2}$$

Here $T_0 = 300$ K is the film and substrate temperature before the laser radiation absorption, L is the film thickness, T_m is the maximum temperature at the upper edge of

Simulation of the thin films deposition

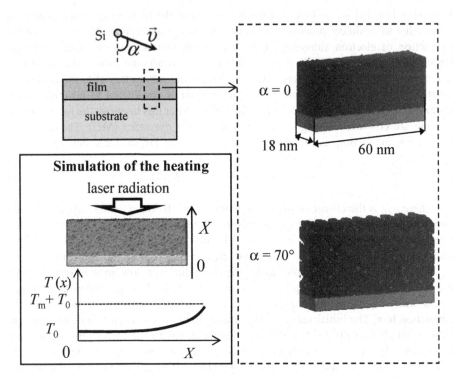

Fig. 1. Scheme of the molecular dynamic simulation of the thin film deposition and heating of the film.

the film. This temperature distribution is schematically shown in Fig. 1. In the present work the T_m value varies from $3 \cdot 10^3$ K to $1.2 \cdot 10^4$ K. At such temperatures, activation of the evaporation process can be expected, since the boiling point for quartz is about of $3 \cdot 10^3$ K [20]. The T_0 value is equal to room temperature, 300 K. The substrate temperature is maintained at T_0 during heating and evaporation using the Berendsen thermostat [21]. The simulations are carried out in the *NVT* ensemble, periodic boundary conditions are applied in all directions. The evaporated atoms can move in the empty volume above the cluster surface.

The duration of the simulation trajectories is about of several tens of picoseconds. This duration is enough to describe the initial stage of the evaporation process.

MD simulations are performed using the GROMACS program [22].

3   Results and Discussion

Films deposited at large angles of incidence α are characterized by the formation of specific structures like slanted columns [23, 24]. These columns are shown in Fig. 1. Since the horizontal dimension of columns exceeds several nanometers, the clusters having at least one dimension equal to several tens of nanometers are needed for the simulation. Therefore, in this work the horizontal dimensions of the substrate are 18 nm and 60 nm (see Fig. 1).

At the end of the simulation of the deposition process, the total number of atoms in the clusters is about of $2.5 \cdot 10^6$. The effective simulation with such number of atoms can be carried out only using parallel calculations. In this work, all simulations are carried out on the supercomputer "Lomonosov-2" of HPC computing resources at Lomonosov Moscow State University [25]. The calculations efficiency is investigated for two main queues available for users: «compute» and «pascal». The processors with following characteristics are used: Intel Haswell-EP E5-2697v3, 2.6 GHz, 14 cores with graphics accelerator NVidia Tesla K40M («compute») and Intel Xeon Gold 6126, 2.6 GHz, 12 cores with graphics accelerator 2 x Nvidia P100, 3584 cuda cores, 16 GB («pascal»), for the further details see [26]. The effectiveness is investigated for the MD trajectory with duration 10 ps, number of atom is about of $2.5 \cdot 10^6$.

The results of the simulation are presented in Fig. 2a,b. As can be seen from Fig. 2a, the simulation time at $N = 64$ is about ten minutes, which makes it possible to systematically investigate the evaporation process. The calculations are performed faster using the «pascal» queue.

The effectiveness of parallel calculation is calculated as follows:

$$a(N) = Nt_8/(8t_N) \qquad (3)$$

where N is the number of cores, t_8 and t_N are the simulation time using 8 and N cores, respectively. As can be seen from Fig. 2b, the values of the effectiveness for both queues are almost identical. The decrease in efficiency with an increase in the number of cores can be caused by an increase in the relative computational cost of non-paralleled processes, such as reading of initial geometry, etc.

The simulation results for heating and evaporation are shown in Figs. 3, 4 and Tables 1, 2 and 3.

The time evolution of the temperature distribution over the film volume after absorption of laser radiation is shown in Fig. 3a,b. The cluster is deposited at an angle $\alpha = 70°$. The value of the maximum temperature T_m at the moment $t = 0$ is 4200 K for the plots in Fig. 3a. At this temperature, the evaporation process has not yet been observed. As can be seen from plots in Fig. 3a, the temperature of the upper edge of the films rapidly decreases from T_m value to approximately 1500 K. This effect is associated with the transfer of a part of the additional kinetic energy to the potential energy [13]. This leads to cooling of the film. After that, the temperature distribution changes insignificantly for several tens of picoseconds. This is due to the fact that the characteristic time τ of thermal energy transfer from hot to cold layers of the cluster is much longer than a picosecond. Indeed, the value of τ can be estimated from the heat

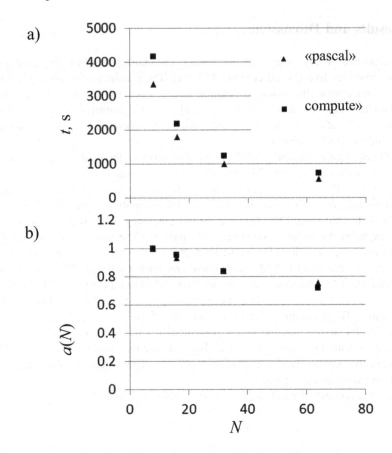

Fig. 2. Dependence of the simulation time t on the number of cores N for queues «compute» and «pascal».

equation as $\tau \sim c\rho L^2/\chi$, where the values of the specific heat capacity, mass density, and heat conductivity are equal to $c = 10^3$ J/(kg·K), $\rho = 2.2 \cdot 10^3$ kg/m^3, and $\chi = 2.0$ W/(m·K) [27]. Since the characteristic cluster thickness L is about 40 nm, we obtain $\tau \sim 1$ ns. In this work, we focused on the investigation of the evaporation process, that occurs in the first few tens of picoseconds (see below). Therefore, we did not study the nanoseconds evolution of temperature profiles.

Temperature distributions at $T_m = 8400$ K are shown in Fig. 3b. As in the case of $T_m = 4200$ K, the temperature rapidly decreases during the firsts picoseconds after the absorption of laser energy. But in this case this decrease is more significant. In addition, a fluctuation of the temperature distribution is observed near the upper edge of the film cluster. These differences are associated with the beginning of the evaporation process. Indeed, the energy of a cluster decreases when evaporated atoms leave it. This can be illustrated using the data shown in Table 1. In this table, the averaged kinetic energy of the evaporated atoms situated in a layer with a lower coordinate x and a thickness of

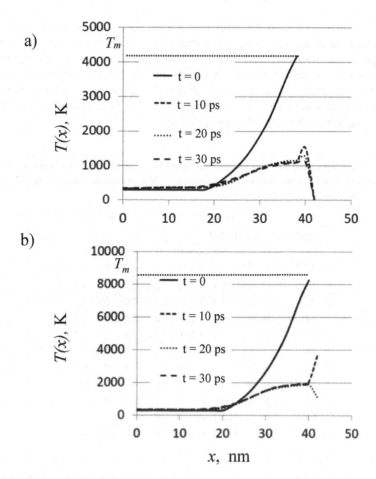

Fig. 3. Temperature distribution $T(x)$ over the cluster thickness for different times t after the absorption of laser radiation. a) $T_m = 4200$ K, b) $T_m = 8400$ K. The upper edge of the film corresponds to $x = 43$–44 nm.

2 nm is calculated and converted to temperature $T(x,t)$. The values of $T(x,t)$ are calculated for the MD frame at the moment t. Then the evaporated atoms are removed from the simulation cluster and the MD simulation continues. This means, for example, that at time $t = 12$ ps, $T(x,t)$ is calculated only for the atoms that have evaporated during the time period from $t = 10$ ps to $t = 12$ ps. Zero values in Table 1 mean that there are no evaporated atoms in the corresponding layer. The coordinate of the upper film edge is approximately 44 nm.

As can be seen from Table 1, the temperature can reach 10^5 K, which corresponds to a kinetic energy of about 10 eV. Since the maximum value of the temperature at the initial moment is less than 1 eV, this means that the evaporated atoms receive energy from collisions with other atoms of the clusters. The release of high-energy atoms from the film leads to its cooling, which is more significant than in the absence of evaporation. This explains the differences of the temperature distributions shown in Fig. 3a, b.

Evaporated atoms heated to a temperature of about $10^{4 \div 5}$ K can form regions with plasma, which can significantly affect the absorption of laser radiation. It is worth mentioning here that it was previously assumed that the laser-induced damage of transparent crystals and films can be associated with the formation of a locally plasma region as a result of the matter heating [28–30].

Table 1. The temperature $T(x,t)$ of atoms evaporated from the film, x is the vertical coordinate, t is the time counted from the moment of absorption of laser radiation. Large values of $T(x,t)$ are highlighted in bold.

t, ps →	2	4	6	8	10	12	14	16	18
x,nm	$T(x,t)$, K·10^4								
46	0	1.8	3.9	3.6	0	0	0	0	0
48	0	3.5	3.1	4.2	1.6	2.7	6.3	5.1	4.3
50	0	2.5	6.9	3.3	0	2.2	0	0	4.5
52	0	2.3	5.9	3.5	0	1.6	4.6	5.8	3.7
54	0	0	8.9	5.9	0	0	3.6	5.4	3.4
56	0	0	7.9	4.9	0	4.2	3.4	4.7	4.5
58	0	0	8.0	5.8	0	0	7.3	6.6	0
60	0	0	7.3	0	0	0	7.1	0	6.4
62	0	0	**10.6**	0	0	0	0	**10.8**	0
64	0	0	0	0	0	0	0	9.8	0
66	0	0	**12.1**	0	0	0	0	0	0
68	0	0	**13.4**	0	0	0	0	0	0

The time dependence of the number of evaporated atoms after the absorption of laser energy is presented in Table 2. The $N(t)$ values are calculated as $N(t) = N_{at}$ $(t + \Delta t) - N_{at}(t)$, where $N_{at}(t + \Delta t)$ and $N_{at}(t)$ are the number of atoms in the cluster at the moments t and Δt respectively, $\Delta t = 2$ ps. Every 2 ps, the evaporated atoms are removed from the simulation area to prevent their possible return to the cluster.

As can be seen from Table 2, evaporation begins within the first few picoseconds after absorption of laser energy and lasts about twenty picoseconds. At $T_m = 4200$ K, the number of the evaporated atoms is negligible for both values of the deposition angle. In the case of $\alpha = 70°$, the evaporation process is more intense than in the case of $\alpha = 0°$. We assume that this is due to differences in the structure of the films.

The dependence of the total number of evaporated atoms on the maximum initial temperature of the clusters is presented in Table 3. The fraction of evaporated atoms does not exceed several percent even for the highest T_m values. This is explained as follows. The cohesion energy of silica is about 20 eV per one SiO_2 group [31], while the maximum additional kinetic energy of an atom at $T_m = 12400$ K is about 1 eV. So only a small part of atoms can receive enough energy to leave the atomistic cluster.

Table 2. The dependence of the number of evaporated atoms $N(t)$ on the simulation time t, α is the deposition angle, T_m is the maximum initial temperature of the cluster, see Eq. 2.

α	0°		70°	
T_m, K	4200	8400	4200	8400
t, ps	$N(t)$			
0	0	1	0	0
2	1	1	0	1
4	0	1	0	4827
6	2	1630	1	54369
8	1	1280	0	29961
10	0	95	0	9511
12	0	22	1	1361
14	1	30	0	375
16	0	215	0	213
18	1	822	1	41
20	0	128	0	16
22	0	13	0	8
24	0	2	0	0
26	0	0	0	3
28	0	0	0	0
30	0	0	0	6

Table 3. The dependence of the total number of evaporated atoms N_{tot} on the maximum initial temperature T_m for films deposited at different values of the deposition angle α, $f(\%)$ is the ratio of N_{tot} to the initial number of atoms in clusters.

α	0°		70°	
T_m, K	N_{tot}	$f(\%)$	N_{tot}	$f(\%)$
4200	6	0.0	3	0.0
5500	2	0.0	5	0.0
6900	20	0.0	3	0.0
8400	4240	0.17	5	0.0
9600	11570	0.46	100692	4.03
11000	26265	1.05	145543	5.82
12400	48415	1.94	162670	6.51

As expected, the number of evaporated atoms grows with increasing T_m. The dynamic of this growth substantially depends on the deposition angle α. At an angle $\alpha = 70°$, the evaporation process starts more rapidly than at $\alpha = 0°$. This is accompanied by a difference in the evolution of the structure with increasing T_m (Fig. 4). Visual analysis shows that the structure of the film deposited at $\alpha = 0°$ practically does not changes. Whereas in the case of $\alpha = 70°$, an increase in T_m leads to noticeable changes of the structure. At $T_m = 4200$ K, the shape of slanted columns changes, and a deep depression is observed in the central part of the cluster. We assume that these differences in the evolution of the structure affect the intensity and rate of the evaporation process in films deposited at $\alpha = 0°$ and $\alpha = 70°$.

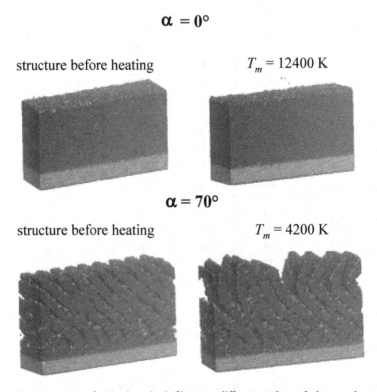

$$\alpha = 0°$$

structure before heating $T_m = 12400$ K

$$\alpha = 70°$$

structure before heating $T_m = 4200$ K

Fig. 4. The structures of the deposited films at different value of the maximum initial temperature T_m.

4   Conclusions

In this work we perform the molecular dynamic simulation of heating and the initial stage of evaporation of silicon dioxide films. The films are deposited at angles $\alpha = 0$ and $\alpha = 70°$ and an energy of incident atoms of 10 eV. Heating is performed by short and intensive laser radiation, which is simulated by the addition of the kinetic energy to atoms at the initial moment. The maximum initial temperature T_m in the top cluster layers vary from $4.2 \cdot 10^3$ K to $1.2 \cdot 10^4$ K.

It was found that the evaporation process begins approximately 2–4 ps after the absorption of laser radiation and lasts approximately 20 ps. The intensive evaporation process begins when T_m exceeds $8 \cdot 10^3$ K. The evaporation process is more intense at $\alpha = 70°$ and is accompanied by a significant change in the film structure.

The work was supported by the Russian Science Foundation (Grant No. 19-11-00053).

References

1. Danson, C., Hillier, D., Hopps, N., Neely, D.: High Power Laser Sci. Eng. **3**, 1–14 (2015)
2. Danson, C.N., et al.: High Power Laser Sci. Eng. **7**(54), (2019)
3. Lawrence Livermore National Laboratory: https://lasers.llnl.gov/
4. Kozlowski, M.R., Chow, R.: Role of defects in laser damage of multilayer coatings. In: SPIE Proceedings Volume 2114, Laser-Induced Damage in Optical Materials: 1993 (1994) https://doi.org/10.1117/12.180876
5. Stolz, C., et al.: Optical Interference Coating, Banff, Canada, (2001)
6. Natoli, J.-Y., Gallais, L., Akhouayri, H., Amra, C.: Appl. Opt. **41**, 3156–3166 (2002)
7. ISO 21254-1, Laser and laser-related equipment - Test methods for laser-induced damage threshold (2011)
8. Jeschke, H.O., Diakhate, M.S., Garcia, M.E.: Appl. Phys. A **96**(1), 33–42 (2009)
9. Wu, C.: Lasers in Materials Science, vol.191/ed. Z.L. Castillejo M., Ossi P. – Springer, 67–100 (2014) https://doi.org/10.1007/978-3-319-02898-9
10. Bai, Q.S.: Molecular simulation and ablation property on the laser-induced metal surface. In: Bai, Q.S. et al. Proc.SPIE. vol. 11063 (2019)
11. Klein, D., Eisfeld, E., Roth, J.: J. Phys. D: Appl. Phys. **54**, 015103 (2021)
12. Yu, J., et al.: Advances in condensed matter physics, 2014, 364627 (2014)
13. Grigoriev, F.V., Zhupanov, V.P., Chesnokov, D.A., Sulimov, V.B., Tikhonravov, A.V.: Lobachevskii Journal of Mathematics **42**(7), 1514–1520 (2021)
14. Keldysh, L.V.: Sov. Phys. JETP **20**, 1307 (1965)
15. Mero, M., Liu, J., Rudolph, W., Ristau, D., Starke, K.: Phys. Rev. B **71**(115109), 1–7 (2005)
16. Jasapara, J., Nampoothiri, A.V.V., Rudolph, W., Ristau, D., Starke, K.: Phys. Rev. B **63** (045117), 1–5 (2001)
17. Grigoriev, F., Sulimov, V., Tikhonravov, A.: J. Non-Cryst. Solids **512**, 98–102 (2019)
18. Grigoriev, F., Sulimov, V., Tikhonravov, A.: Coatings **9**, 568 (2019)
19. Grigoriev, F.V., Sulimov, A.V., Kochikov, I.V., Kondakova, O.A., Sulimov, V.B., Tikhonravov, A.V.: Supercomputer modeling of the ion beam sputtering process: full-atomistic level. In: Proceedings of the Optical Systems Design 2015: Advances in Optical Thin Films V, International Society for Optics and Photonics, Bellingham, WA, USA, 7–10 September 2015, vol. 9627, p. 962708 (2015)
20. Perry, D.L.: Handbook of Inorganic Compounds. CRC Press (2016). https://doi.org/10.1201/b10908
21. Berendsen, H.J.C., Postma, J.P.M., Van Gunsteren, W.F., DiNola, A., Haak, J.R.: J. Chem. Phys. **81**, 3684–3690 (1984)
22. Abraham, M.J., et al.: SoftwareX **1**, 19–25 (2015)
23. Robbie, K., Brett, M.J., Lakhtakia, A.: Nature **384**, 616 (1996)
24. Hawkeye, M.M., Brett, M.J.: J. Vac. Sci. Technol. **25**, 1317 (2007)
25. Voevodin, V.V., et al.: Supercomput. Front. Innov. **6**(2), 4–11 (2019)
26. https://parallel.ru/cluster/lomonosov2.html

27. Leko, V.K., Mazurin, O.V.: Properties of Quartz Glass. Nauka, Leningrad (1985).[in Russian]
28. Carr, C.W., Radousky, H.B., Rubenchik, A.M., Feit, M.D., Demos, S.G.: Phys. Rev. Lett. **92** (8), 087401 (2004)
29. Carr, C. W., Radousky, H. B., Demos, S. G.: Phys. Rev. Lett. **91**, 127402 (2003)
30. Chen, M., Ding, W., Cheng, J., Yang, H., Liu, Q.: Crystal. Appl. Sci. **10**, 6642 (2020)
31. Demuth, T., Jeanvoine, Y., Hafner, J., Angyan, J.G.: J. Phys.: Condens. Mat. **11**, 3833 (1999)

High-Performance Implementation of 3D Seismic Target-Oriented Imaging

Maxim Protasov[✉]

Institute of Petroleum Geology and Geophysics, Novosibirsk, Russia
protasovmi@ipgg.sbras.ru

Abstract. The paper presents the high-performance implementation of the target-oriented 3D seismic imaging procedure. The migration algorithm uses individual Gaussian beams for focusing seismic energy inside every target image point with the best resolution, and the imaging operator provides data transformation in the angle domain coordinates. The parallel implementation of the imaging procedure can process large volumes of 3D seismic data in production mode. The paper provides test results for a representative set of synthetic and real data.

Keywords: 3D seismic imaging · Beams · Target-oriented · Parallelization

1 Introduction

At present, in seismic data processing, prestack depth migration is one of the most computationally expensive procedures. In terms of image quality, target-oriented reservoir imaging is more attractive than conventional full-volume migration. Target-oriented methods require more resources than standard migration for the same data and image area from the computational perspective. For 2D problems, the difference of required computational resources is not crucial, and target-oriented imaging operates as a high-quality full volume migration in production mode within reasonable timelines. However, for large-scale 3D seismic data, such migration algorithms need optimization and effective parallelization.

Gaussian beam imaging is one of the most robust depth migration approaches. Gaussian beams are waves, which are concentrated within the exponentially vanishing vicinity of a ray. They keep the ray method's advantages. They form a full base that a superposition of these beams can provide any solution of elastic wave equation [2]. Hill introduces Gaussian beam migration by using Gaussian beam representation of Green's function in the Kirchhoff integral [6, 7]. The prestack migration procedure presented in [7] operates on common-offset gathers. It is highly efficient because it uses data beam decomposition in the mid-point domain only with equal beams at the acquisition surface. This migration has become the industry standard and operates as a full volume beam migration [7].

Along with the correct recovery of geological objects' spatial position, it is essential to construct their true-amplitude images representing variations of some physical parameters. The true-amplitude Gaussian beam prestack depth migration operates in

V. Voevodin and S. Sobolev (Eds.): RuSCDays 2021, CCIS 1510, pp. 125–136, 2021.
https://doi.org/10.1007/978-3-030-92864-3_10

the same way as proposed in [7] and uses the wavefield decomposition into Gaussian beams [1]. However, these migrations provide images of regular data in the midpoint domain for each offset in acoustic media. The further development of the approach gives the 3D anisotropic migration algorithm that handles irregular data with any acquisition topography [12].

The described above Gaussian beam migrations utilize beam data decomposition and ray tracing from beam center location to subsurface, allowing algorithm optimizations and effective parallelization. In this paper, similarly to the two-dimensional predecessor [10], the algorithm is implemented by ray tracing from the subsurface image points to the observation system and using individual Gaussian beams instead of decomposing the wavefield into Gaussian beams. Shooting from the target area leads to the imaging operator handling the angle domain coordinates. The algorithm provides high resolution of a subsurface image via focusing seismic energy by individual Gaussian beams. Ray tracing from the image point controls the structural angles (the angle domain coordinates). Hence one can easily compute so-called selective images (which are images for the fixed structural angels). Selective images are significant for the detection of diffractions produced by small-scale objects [11]. The approach helps achieve a better subsurface illumination in complex structures and provides an efficient parallel implementation for target-oriented imaging. One of the algorithmic optimizations consists of dividing migration into two parts: the ray tracing (or beam attribute computation) part and the process of summing data with beam weights. Each of these two parts is effectively implemented using MPI and Open-MP technologies [8]. Beam data summation utilizes MPI parallelism of seismic data decomposition. In general, this approach made it possible to create a technological version of target-oriented migration providing superior quality comparing to conventional beam imaging, especially in terms of the diffraction imaging results. However, the method is not as efficient as the conventional Gaussian beam migration for full subsurface imaging. Synthetic and field data examples demonstrate the validity and capability of the developed parallel implementation of target-oriented beam-based imaging.

2   Target-Oriented Imaging Operator

The migration algorithm starts with the tracing of two rays from every image point $\bar{p}_i = (x_i, y_i, z_i)$ within the macro-velocity anisotropic model defined by the elastic parameters $c^0_{ijkl}(\bar{p})$, and density $\rho_0(\bar{p})$. The initial ray directions and hence the rays are parameterized by structural angles: structural dip γ, structural azimuth θ, ray opening angle β, and the azimuth of the ray opening az [12]. Anisotropic elastic Gaussian beams are constructed along with these rays [5, 9], and they are denoted by $\overrightarrow{u}^{gbr}(\bar{p}_r; \bar{p}_i; \gamma, \theta, \beta, az; \omega)$, and $\overrightarrow{u}^{gbs}(\bar{p}_s; \bar{p}_i; \gamma, \theta, \beta, az; \omega)$. Here $\bar{p}_r = (x_r, y_r, z_r)$ is the receiver coordinate, $\bar{p}_s = (x_s, y_s, z_s)$ is the source coordinate, ω is the frequency. Then on the acquisition surface, integration beam weights are computed: one is the normal derivative of the Gaussian beam at the receivers, another one is the normal derivative of the scalar part of the corresponding beam in the sources:

$$\vec{T}^{gbr}(\bar{p}_r; \bar{p}_i; \gamma, \theta, \beta, az; \omega), T^{gbs}(\bar{p}_s; \bar{p}_i; \gamma, \theta, \beta, az; \omega). \tag{1}$$

Suppose the Born integral [4] describes seismic data $\vec{u}^{obs}(\bar{p}_r; \bar{p}_s; \omega)$:

$$\vec{u}^{obs}(\bar{p}_r; \bar{p}_s; \omega) = \int G(\bar{p}_r; \bar{p}; \omega) \cdot L_1 \vec{u}^0(\bar{p}; \bar{p}_s; \omega) d\bar{p}. \tag{2}$$

Here $\vec{u}^0$ is the incident wavefield propagating in the macro-velocity model from a point source, G – Green's matrix for the smooth background and operator L_1 introducing by the true-amplitude image target that is rough perturbations $c^1_{ijkl}(\bar{p})$ and $\rho_1(\bar{p})$:

$$(L_1 \langle \vec{u}^0 \rangle)_j = -\sum_{i,l,l=1}^{3} \frac{\partial}{\partial x_i} \left(c^1_{ijkl} \frac{\partial u^0_l}{\partial x_k} \right) - \rho_1 \omega^2 u^0_j; (x_1, x_2, x_3) \equiv (\bar{p}). \tag{3}$$

Both sides of Born integral (2) are multiplied by the constructed weights (1) and integrated with respect to the source and receiver coordinates. Using saddle point technique for every beam weight (details described in the papers [10, 12]), one can come to the following identity:

$$\int T^{gbs}(\bar{p}_s; \bar{p}_i; \gamma, \theta, \beta, az; \omega) \vec{T}^{gbr}(\bar{p}_r; \bar{p}_i; \gamma, \theta, \beta, az; \omega) \vec{u}^{obs}(\bar{p}_r; \bar{p}_s; \omega) d\bar{p}_r d\bar{p}_s$$
$$= \int \vec{u}^{gbr}(\bar{p}_r; \bar{p}_i; \gamma, \theta, \beta, az; \omega) \cdot L_1 \vec{u}^{gbs}(\bar{p}_s; \bar{p}_i; \gamma, \theta, \beta, az; \omega) d\bar{p}. \tag{4}$$

Computations of beam derivatives (operator L_1) retaining terms up to the first order only, together with the microlocal analysis (details described in the papers [10, 12]) of the right-hand side of (4) gives the following:

$$\int T^{gbs}(\bar{p}_s; \bar{p}_i; \gamma, \theta, \beta, az; \omega) \vec{T}^{gbr}(\bar{p}_r; \bar{p}_i; \gamma, \theta, \beta, az; \omega) \vec{u}^{obs}(\bar{p}_r; \bar{p}_s; \omega) d\bar{p}_r d\bar{p}_s$$
$$= \omega^2 \int \exp\{i\omega(\nabla \tau_s + \nabla \tau_r) \cdot (\bar{p}_i - \bar{p})\} f(\bar{p}; \gamma, \theta, \beta, az) d\bar{p} \tag{5}$$

Here τ_s, τ_r are travel times from the image point $\bar{p}_i$ to the corresponding acquisition point, f is a linearized reflection coefficient. Then the change of variables (γ, θ, ω) (k_x, k_y, k_z) in the right-hand side of (5) is used:

$$\bar{k} = (k_x, k_y, k_z) = \omega(\nabla \tau_s(\bar{p}_i; \gamma, \theta, \beta, az) + \nabla \tau_r(\bar{p}_i; \gamma, \theta, \beta, az)). \tag{6}$$

Multiplication by the normalized Jacobian $J(\bar{p}_i; \gamma, \theta, \beta, az)$ having the explicit form (analog of Beylkin's determinant [3]), and integration of both parts of the identity (5) with respect to γ, θ, ω gives the final asymptotic inversion result (details described in the papers [10, 12]):

$$f(\bar{p}_i; \beta, az) = \int J(\bar{p}_i; \gamma, \theta, \beta, az) \cdot T^{gbs}(\bar{p}_s; \bar{p}_i; \gamma, \theta, \beta, az; \omega)$$
$$\cdot \vec{T}^{gbr}(\bar{p}_r; \bar{p}_i; \gamma, \theta, \beta, az; \omega) \vec{u}^{obs}(\bar{p}_r; \bar{p}_s; \omega) d\bar{p}_r d\bar{p}_s d\gamma d\theta d\omega. \tag{7}$$

The formula (7) is called imaging condition in structural angles. The last means the imaging condition provides handling angle domain coordinates. The integral operator (7) uses structural dip and azimuth angles (γ, θ) in the inversion process, and the final image depends on the ray opening angle and the azimuth of the ray opening (β, az). Note, in the standard industrial technology of seismic processing, the data is usually processed in common midpoint and offset domains. In this case, the inversion is done with respect to midpoints, while the final image is got with respect to offsets.

As already mentioned, tracing from the image point allows one to control the structural angles. Therefore, in the practical implementation of the imaging condition (7), the integrals with respect to these angles are computed directly. Also, it becomes possible to construct selective or partial images and scattering indicatrix with respect to structural angles in true amplitudes:

$$
\begin{aligned}
f_{sel}(\overline{p}_i; \gamma, \theta, \beta, az) = \int J(\overline{p}_i; \gamma, \theta, \beta, az) \cdot T^{gbs}(\overline{p}_s; \overline{p}_i; \gamma, \theta, \beta, az; \omega) \\
\cdot \vec{T}^{gbr}(\overline{p}_r; \overline{p}_i; \gamma, \theta, \beta, az; \omega) \vec{u}^{obs}(\overline{p}_r; \overline{p}_s; \omega) d\overline{p}_r d\overline{p}_s d\omega.
\end{aligned} \tag{8}
$$

The 3D image $f_{sel}(\overline{p}_i; \gamma, \theta, \beta, az)$ is a selective image obtained for fixed structural angles and all image points. In this case, the diffraction imaging possibilities arise. The specific option of three dimensions is the construction of the scattering indicatrix. For its recovery, one should calculate the integral (8) with respect to the structural azimuth and fixed image point and fixed angles. This option is crucial for determining the diffraction type (3D point or 3D edge) and, consequently, determining the properties of diffraction objects, such as fracture orientation.

3 Implementation of Imaging Operator

The software implementation utilizes the division of the whole imaging procedures by two blocks (Fig. 1). The first one computes beam attributes and stores them on the disk. The second one provides weighted data summation where weights are Gaussian beams calculated during summation via attributes usage. The division into two parts makes it possible to implement angle domain imaging conditions (7) and (8) effectively. This way provides an opportunity to compute beam attributes once and then use all the attributes for any part of seismic data independently. Therefore, attributes avoid repeated calculations, and consequently, such decomposition saves computational resources.

Since the attribute's computation block operates separately from the migration itself, the parallelization works independently for each block. Scheme for the attributes computation utilizes two-level parallelism. The first level uses MPI parallelization done independently for every set of image points. Every node loads the full migration model and computes beam attributes for the corresponding image point (Fig. 2). On every computational node, the second parallelization level provides OpenMP realization with respect to the number of structural angles. In this case, every CPU core provides tracing a couple of rays and calculation of beam attributes for every fixed value of structural angles from the corresponding set of angles (Fig. 2).

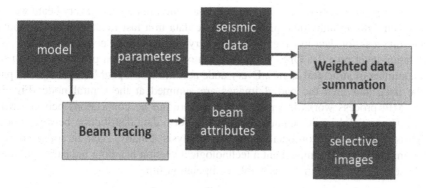

Fig. 1. General upper-level diagram for the realization of the target-oriented imaging algorithm.

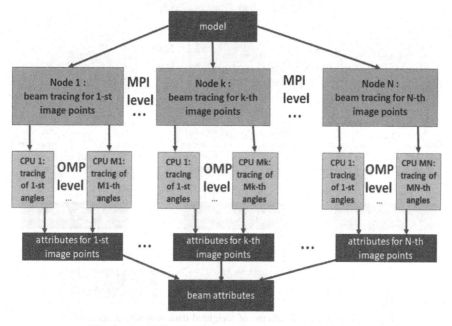

Fig. 2. Parallelization scheme of beam tracing procedure.

After the beam attributes computation procedure finishes, the weighted data summation block starts processing. Its realization also utilizes MPI and OpenMP technologies. As mentioned above, the MPI realization uses data decomposition (Fig. 3). The motivation for such an approach lies in the two facts: usual 3D seismic data needs a huge amount of memory; every beam weight uses a specific individual piece of seismic data, and the required pieces intersect with each other. Therefore, one needs to get the particular part of data from the huge data set as fast as possible in a parallel mode. This issue is resolved efficiently so that every computational node loads the corresponding part of data from the hard disk to the memory. Then the whole summation process is provided for the loaded part only. In this case, every beam weight is summed with an individual piece of seismic data in a fast mode without computational time loss for data loading. Then on every computational node, the second parallelization level provides OpenMP realization of the summation process with respect to the number of structural angles. Every node accumulates OpenMP results for its part of the data, and then the partial images are summed at the central node (Fig. 3). Every MPI process works independently, so there are no connections between MPI nodes. The optimal implementation requires uniform data distribution between nodes which is realized based on data coordinates analysis. Finally, such an approach provides an opportunity to implement a technological version handling industrial volumes of 3D seismic data within a reasonable computation time.

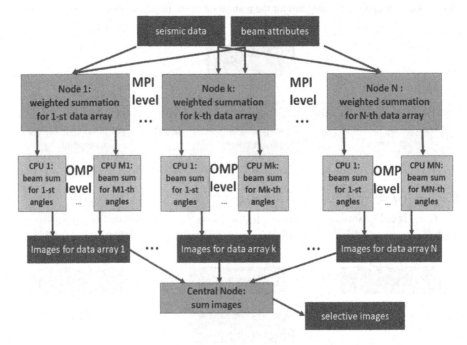

Fig. 3. Parallelization scheme of weighted data summation procedure.

4   Numerical Examples

4.1   Angle Domain Imaging vs. Acquisition Domain Migration

As mentioned above, target-oriented beam migration provides high-quality images, which is possible due to the control of the beam width at the image point. Therefore, the beam width controls the image resolution, and the optimal width value is approximately one dominant wavelength [10]. In the acquisition domain realization of beam migration, this option is absent due to equal beams at the acquisition system. Therefore spatial image resolution is not perfect. Figure 4 shows selective images and the full images obtained with target-oriented beam migration and midpoint-offset domain full volume migration. The best resolution is observed on the images (especially on the selective images) obtained with target-oriented beam migration.

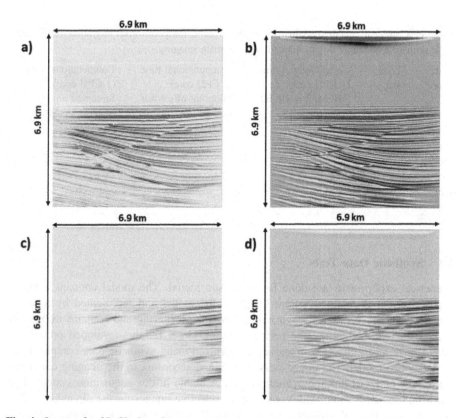

Fig. 4. Images for 2D Sigsbee data set: a) image stack by angle domain migration; b) image stack by midpoint-offset full volume migration; c) selective image by angle domain migration; c) selective image by midpoint-offset domain full volume migration.

However, the imaging condition in midpoint-offset coordinates makes it possible to implement a technological version of full volume migration [12]. In contrast, the full volume migration algorithm based on the imaging condition (7) in structural angles requires more computational resources. Conducted specific calculations for these implementations on identical data and equipment show that the computational time difference reaches two orders of magnitude (Table 1). This difference leads to the fact that structural angle realization is acceptable only for a relatively small image area. One has to use it as a target-oriented migration procedure. Comparing the last and the technological full volume migration for the identical data and equipment, but using typical target image areas for angle domain variant, one can observe the same order of computational times and even less (Table 1). The results mean that developed target-oriented imaging allows handling large enough data set within reasonable computational resources, and therefore it is suitable for industrial processing for typical target objects.

Table 1. Computational time comparison for full volume midpoint-offset migration, full volume angle domain realization, target-oriented angle domain imaging.

Data type	Data size	Computational time (1 CPU core) Structural angle full volume	Computational time (1 CPU core) Midpoint-offset full volume	Computational time (1 CPU core) Structural angle target-oriented
2D data set	2 GB	40 h	1 h	2 h
3D data set	26 GB	4000 h	37 h	58 h

4.2 Synthetic Data Tests

Numerical experiments are done for a realistic model. The model contains a target object distributed along the entire length of the model and represented by a set of channels. Such a geological environment provides scattering and contains diffraction objects; therefore, they are the perfect imaging target for the developed procedure. Image stack and diffraction image are constructed using synthetic data computed for the described model. The image stack is obtained according to the imaging condition (7) for the range of dip and azimuth angles available in this acquisition system. The diffraction image is calculated by the sum of selective images for the dip angle of 30° and all 360° range of azimuths. In this case, all available reflective elements remain outside the reconstructed domain. Therefore, the resulting image mainly represents objects of scattering and diffraction. Figure 5a shows the image stack at the level of buried channels. Figure 5b provides the selective diffraction image obtained at the same level, respectively. In this case, the image stack's quality and the quality of the selective diffraction image allow interpreting most of the channels well enough. However, the diffraction image gives a more evident geometry of the channels themselves, shows better channel details, and provides low contrast channels invisible on the image stack.

4.3 Real Data Tests

The next example is presented for real land 3D seismic data. The standard wide azimuth land seismic acquisition is used. The experiments use the part of the data within the 85 km² area. The data passes through the standard preprocessing workflow. The interpretation of the standard seismic section got for the data allows the detection

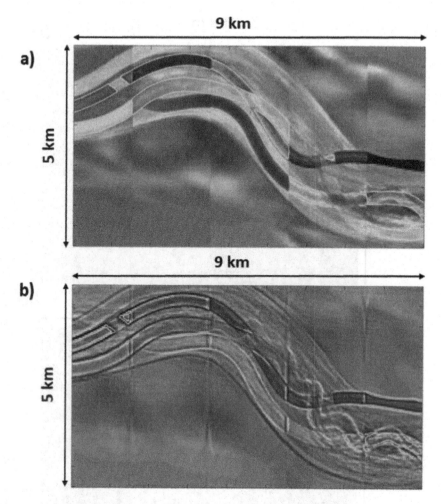

Fig. 5. 2D horizontal sections of 3D images at the level of buried channels: a) image stack; b) selective diffraction image.

of two strong faults. The developed technology provides selective diffraction images where these main faults are perfectly distinguished (Fig. 6). But as one can see in Fig. 6, other diffraction objects are identified between the two strong faults. Note these objects are not visible. At one level, one can observe contrast image events corresponding to reefs. At another level, there are lineaments interpreted as smaller scale faults and other singular objects requiring additional interpretation.

Table 2 shows the computational times and resources required for the target-oriented imaging of typical geological objects described in the paper. One can observe that the developed parallel implementation of target-oriented beam-based imaging can handle large enough data sets. Simultaneously, it produces images of the required size using reasonable computational resources within production data processing timelines.

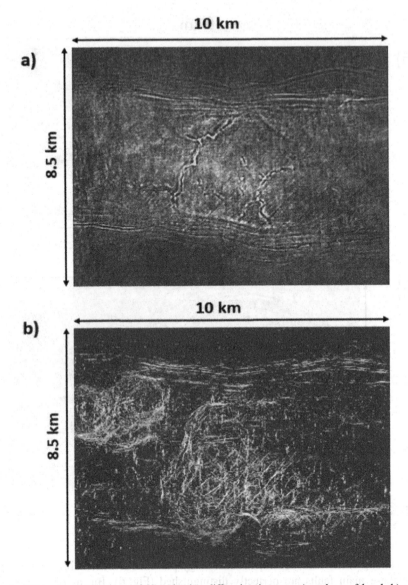

Fig. 6. 2D horizontal sections of 3D selective diffraction images: a) at the reef level; b) at the level of small-scale faults.

Table 2. Computational times for the developed target-oriented beam migration.

Image size nx × ny × nz × na	Data size	Computational resources	Computational time
450 × 400 × 2 × 8	23 GB	2 Nodes × 24 CPU cores	≈2.3 h
200 × 1 × 125 × 24	44 GB	4 Nodes × 24 CPU cores	≈0.6 h
270 × 250 × 1 × 24	44 GB	4 Nodes × 24 CPU cores	≈1.2 h

5 Conclusions

The paper presents the parallel implementation of the 3D seismic target-oriented imaging algorithm. Angle domain realization and usage of individual Gaussian beams focusing seismic energy inside every target image point with the best resolution provides the possibility to construct high-quality object-oriented images, including diffraction images. The implementation of beam imaging utilizes MPI and OpenMP technologies, effectively providing two-level parallelization with division into beam attribute computation block and data summation block based on data decomposition. Create a technological version of target-oriented migration providing superior quality comparing to conventional beam imaging, especially in terms of the diffraction imaging results. Synthetic and field data examples demonstrate that the developed parallel implementation of target-oriented beam-based imaging can process large enough volumes of 3D seismic data in production mode.

Acknowledgments. The work is supported by RSF grant 21-71-20002. The numerical results of the work were obtained using computational resources of Peter the Great Saint-Petersburg Polytechnic University Supercomputing Center (scc.spbstu.ru).

References

1. Albertin, U., Yingst, D., Kitchenside, P., Tcheverda, V.: True-amplitude beam migration. SEG Expanded Abstracts, 398–401 (2004)
2. Babich, V.M., Popov, M.M.: Gaussian beam summation (review). Izv. Vyssh. Uchebn. Zaved Radiofiz. **32**, 1447–1466 (1989)
3. Beylkin, G.: Imaging of discontinuous in the inverse scattering problem by inversion of causual generalized Radon transform. J. Math. Phys. **26**(1), 99–108 (1985)
4. Devaney, A.J.: Geophysical diffraction tomography. IEEE Trans. Geosci. Remote Sens. **22**, 3–13 (1984)
5. Nomofilov, V.E.: Asymptotic solutions of a system of equations of the second order which are concentrated in a neighborhood of a ray. Zap. Nauch. Sem. LOMI **104**, 170–179 (1981)
6. Hill, N.R.: Gaussian beam migration. Geophysics **55**, 1416–1428 (1990)
7. Hill, N.R.: Prestack Gaussian-beam depth migration. Geophysics **66**, 1240–1250 (2001)
8. Parallel data processing homepage, https://parallel.ru/vvv/. Accessed 3 Mar. 2021
9. Popov, M.M.: Ray theory and Gaussian beam for geophysicists. EDUFBA, SALVADOR-BAHIA (2002)
10. Protasov, M.I.: 2-D Gaussian beam imaging of multicomponent seismic data in anisotropic media. Geophys. J. Int. **203**, 2021–2031 (2015)

11. Protasov, M.I., Gadylshin, K.G., Tcheverda, V.A., Pravduhin, A.P.: 3D diffraction imaging of fault and fracture zones via image spectral decomposition of partial images. Geophys. Prospect. **67**, 1256–1270 (2019)
12. Protasov, M.: Parallel implementation of 3D seismic beam imaging. In: Gervasi, O., et al. (eds.) ICCSA 2021. LNCS, vol. 12949, pp. 611–621. Springer, Cham (2021). https://doi.org/10.1007/978-3-030-86653-2_44

Implementation of Elliptic Solvers Within ParCS Parallel Framework

Gordey Goyman[1,2,3(✉)] and Vladimir Shashkin[1,2,3]

[1] G.I. Marchuk Institute of Numerical Mathematics, RAS, Moscow, Russia
[2] Hydrometeorological center of Russia, Moscow, Russia
[3] Moscow Institute of Physics and Technology,
Dolgoprudny, Moscow Regions, Russia
v.shashkin@inm.ras.ru

Abstract. One of the most important aspects that determine the efficiency of an atmospheric dynamics numerical model is the time integration scheme. It is common to apply semi-implicit integrators, which allow
to use larger time steps, but requires solution of a linear elliptic equation
at the every time step of a model. We present implementation of linear solvers (geometric multigrid and BICGstab) within ParCS parallel
framework, which is used for development of the new non-hydrostatic
global atmospheric model at INM RAS and Hydrometcentre of Russia. The efficiency and parallel scalability of the implemented algorithms
have been tested for the elliptic problem typical for numerical weather
prediction models using semi-implicit discretization at the cubed sphere
grid.

Keywords: Solvers · Multigrid · BiCGstab · Numerical weather
prediction · Scalability · Parallel efficiency · Cubed sphere

1 Introduction

The grid dimension of a modern operational numerical weather prediction
(NWP) models tends to 10^{10}, moreover there is a tight operational timescales
for a forecast to be delivered. Therefore, it is critical for such models to exploit
numerically efficient and highly scalable algorithms, allowing to use about
10^4–10^6 CPU cores.

The atmospheric hydro-thermodynamics is a typical stiff system describing a
wide spectrum of phenomena with time scales ranging from seconds to months.
This makes it attractive to use semi-implicit [11] time integrators for global
atmospheric models. The main idea of the semi-implicit method is implicit integration of linear terms of equations that describe the propagation of fast acoustic
and gravity waves and explicit approximation for non-linear terms. This allows
to use much larger time step size than those determined by CFL stability criterion for fast waves at the cost of solution of linear system with sparse matrix at
the every time step. The expediency of applying the semi-implicit approach is
thus determined by the numerical efficiency and parallel scalability of the matrix

V. Voevodin and S. Sobolev (Eds.): RuSCDays 2021, CCIS 1510, pp. 137–147, 2021.
https://doi.org/10.1007/978-3-030-92864-3_11

inversion procedure used. At the same time, in order to achieve maximum performance of these solvers, it is important not only to choose the optimal algorithm, but also to take as much as possible the specifics of the problem into account during its implementation [9]. That is why it is common in NWP models to use own implementations of algorithms [2, 4, 8, 9] even if there are generic library analogues.

At the moment, the next generation global atmospheric model is under development at INM RAS and Hydrometcentre of Russia. We consider semi-implicit time stepping method as a promising option for the time integration scheme. Therefore, the model must be equipped with effective methods for solving linear systems of equations arising from the application of a semi-implicit integrator. Along with the development of the model, we also work on our own software infrastructure, which provides key components for the model development and maintenance (data structures, parallel communication routines, model I/O and diagnostics, etc.). One of the components of such infrastructure is a parallel framework called ParCS (Parallel Cubed Sphere) [14]. ParCS is an object-oriented parallel infrastructure library written in Fortran 2008 programming language that provides algorithms and structures for the domain decomposition, parallel exchanges and data storage at the paneled logically-rectangular computational grids. The purpose of this work is to implement efficient and scalable algorithms for solving linear equations typical for models using semi-implicit time discretization within ParCS library.

2   Model Elliptic Equation

The idea of semi-implicit discretization can be illustrated by the example of one-dimensional linear shallow water equations:

$$\frac{\partial u}{\partial t} + c_{adv}\frac{\partial u}{\partial x} = -g\frac{\partial h}{\partial x}, \tag{1}$$

$$\frac{\partial h}{\partial t} + c_{adv}\frac{\partial h}{\partial x} = -H\frac{\partial u}{\partial x}. \tag{2}$$

This system describes advection with the speed c_{adv} and propagation of gravitational waves with the phase speed of $\sqrt{gH}$. If we assume that $c_{adv} \ll \sqrt{gH}$, then stability of explicit time discretization are determined by the speed of gravitational waves. This situation actually takes place in the real atmosphere, where $C_{adv} \sim 100\ m/s$ and phase speed of gravitational waves $\sim 350\ m/s$. Therefore, following the logic of semi-implicit time method, we should use implicit discretization for terms describing waves propagation and explicit approximation for the advection terms. Here is the example of such a semi-discrete scheme:

$$\frac{u^{n+1} - u^{n-1}}{2\Delta t} + c_{adv}\frac{\partial u^n}{\partial x} = -\frac{g}{2}\left(\frac{\partial h}{\partial x}^{n+1} + \frac{\partial h}{\partial x}^{n-1}\right), \tag{3}$$

$$\frac{h^{n+1} - h^{n-1}}{2\Delta t} + c_{adv}\frac{\partial h^n}{\partial x} = -\frac{H}{2}\left(\frac{\partial u}{\partial x}^{n+1} + \frac{\partial u}{\partial x}^{n-1}\right). \tag{4}$$

For simplicity, leapfrog time stepping is used here. Differentiating the first equation with respect to x and putting the expression for $\frac{\partial u}{\partial x}^{n+1}$ to the second equation leads to the Helmholtz type elliptic problem:

$$\left(I - gH\Delta t\frac{\partial^2}{\partial x^2}\right)h^{n+1} = \tilde{R}_h. \tag{5}$$

An analogous equation is obtained as a result of the semi-implicit discretization of 3D atmospheric equations.

In order to test implemented algorithms we consider the following model elliptic equation

$$\left(\frac{1}{\gamma_k^2} - \nabla \cdot \nabla\right)\psi_k = f_k, k = 1..N_z, \tag{6}$$

where ∇ and $\nabla\cdot$ are the horizontal spherical gradient and divergence operators respectively, γ_k^2 is the vertical level dependent constant and N_z is the number of vertical levels. Equations of this form result from the semi-implicit time discretization and have to be solved at the every time step of the model.

We use the equiangular gnomonic cubed sphere grid [10,12] obtained by the central projection of the grid on the cubes faces to the inscribed sphere for the spatial discretization. The grid points on the cube's faces are determined by the angular coordinates α, β, such that

$$x = \tan\alpha, \; y = \tan\beta, \; \alpha, \beta \in [-\pi/4, \pi/4]. \tag{7}$$

The covariant components of horizontal gradient operator are given by

$$\nabla f = \left(\frac{\partial f}{\partial \alpha}, \frac{\partial f}{\partial \beta}\right). \tag{8}$$

The horizontal divergence operator using contravariant components $\tilde{u}$, $\tilde{v}$ of vector $\mathbf{v}$ can be written as

$$\nabla \cdot \mathbf{v} = \frac{1}{G}\left(\frac{\partial G\tilde{u}}{\partial \alpha} + \frac{\partial G\tilde{v}}{\partial \beta}\right), \tag{9}$$

where G is a square root of metric tensor determinant. We use Arakawa C-type variables staggering [1] with the scalar quantity located at the grid points of a cube panel with coordinates (α_i, β_j), where

$$\alpha_i = -\pi/4 + (i - 1/2)h, \; \beta_j = -\pi/4 + (j - 1/2)h, \; h = \pi/(2n) \tag{10}$$

and n is the number of points along panel edge. In the interior of cube panels, operators ∇, $\nabla\cdot$ in Eq. (6) are discretized using standard C-grid second order formulae. We use halo interpolation procedure, described in [15], near panels egdes. We use bilinear interpolation to transform between the covariant and contravariant horizontal vector components.

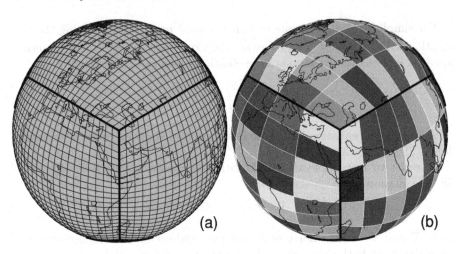

Fig. 1. (a) Cubed sphere grid with 24 cells along the cubes edge (C24). (b) Partition of cubed-sphere grid between 192 MPI-processes (the colors can repeat).

After discretizing the operators in space, we obtain the system of linear equations

$$\left(\frac{1}{\gamma_k^2}I - L\right)x = b, k = 1..N_z.   (11)$$

It can be shown [6,7], that condition number of this system is determined by the maximum value of the $\frac{\gamma_k^2}{\Delta x^2}$ which can be estimated as $(\frac{c_s \Delta t}{4 \max \Delta x})^2$, where Δx is the horizontal grid step in physical length units, Δt is the time step of the model and c_s is the maximum velocity of the horizontal waves. If we define the wave Courant number as CFL $= \frac{c_s \Delta t}{\max \Delta x}$, then the linear system conditioning is determined by the $\frac{4}{\text{CFL}^2}$ ratio, i.e. for large values of CFL, the system is close to the ill-conditioned discrete Poisson equation. Typical values of CFL for atmospheric models using semi-implicit time integration are about 4–10.

3   Solvers Description

In the following, we describe algorithms and details of their implementation within ParCS parallel framework.

3.1   BICGstab

BICGstab algorithm [18] is a Krylov subspace method, which iteratively construct the approximate solution of a linear system $Ax = b$ in a m-dimensional Krylov subspace

$$K_m = \text{span}\{b, Ab, A^2b, ..., A^{m-1}b\}.   (12)$$

This method allows to solve equations with non-symmetric matrices and does not require storing the whole basis of the solution search space. This method is completely matrix-free, i.e. there is no need to explicitly know the entries of a matrix, and only result of the matrix-vector product operations are needed.

One of the main disadvantage of this method is the need to perform global communications in order to calculate dot products and vector norms at each iteration of the method. This potentialy limits scalability and efficiency of this method at massively-parallel systems.

The following operations have to be carried out at each iteration of the BICGstab algorithm:

- 2 matrix-vector products $y = Ax$;

- 4 **axpy** type operations, e.g. $y = ax + y$;

- 4 dot products (x, y) or (x, x).

3.2 Geometric Multigrid

Multigrid methods [5,17] are one of the most efficient algorithms suitable for solution of elliptic problems, including those arising in global atmospheric models [2,8,9,13,16,19,21]. The main components of the multigrid method are defined as follows.

Coarse Grids Construction. The sequence of coarse grids at each panel are defined as

$$\alpha_i^l = -\pi/4 + (i - 1/2)h2^{l-1}, \ i = 1..2^{-l+1}N, \ l = 2..L, \tag{13}$$

where L is the number of levels used in the multigrid algorithm. Here the coarse grid points are not a subset of the fine grid points, that is so-called cell-centered coarse grid construction method.

Intergrid Transfer Operators. We use 4-point cell average to transfer residual to coarse grids. In stencil notation [17], this corresponds to

$$\frac{1}{4G_{i,j}^{2h}} \begin{bmatrix} G_{2i-1,2j-1}^h & G_{2i,2j-1}^h \\ G_{2i-1,2j}^h & G_{2i,2j}^h \end{bmatrix}. \tag{14}$$

Here $G_{i,j}^h$, $G_{i,j}^{2h}$ are a square root of metric tensor determinant at the points of a fine and coarse grid respectively. The bilinear interpolation is used as prolongation operator to transfer solution correction from coarse to finer grid, which in stencil notation [17] corresponds to

$$\frac{1}{16} \begin{bmatrix} 1 & 3 & 3 & 1 \\ 3 & 9 & 9 & 3 \\ 3 & 9 & 9 & 3 \\ 1 & 3 & 3 & 1 \end{bmatrix}. \tag{15}$$

Coarse Grid Matrices. The coarse grid matrices are constructed using discretization of the initial operator, which is more efficient than Galerkin product [17] construction approach.

Smoothing. One of the main components of the multigrid method is the smoothing procedure, i.e. approximate matrix inversion algorithm allowing to effectively eliminate high frequency components of the solution error. In general, the efficiency of the smoothing procedure can strongly depend on the specific problem being solved. The fixed point iteration method of the form

$$x^{k+1} = x^k + P^{-1}(b - Ax^k) = x^k + P^{-1}r^k \tag{16}$$

can be used as a smoother, for a fairly wide class of problems. Here, x^k is the approximate solution at the k-th iteration and P is the preconditioning matrix, which is determined by the specific type of the fixed iteration method. In this work we use the weighted Jacobi method ($P = cD(A)$). This type of smoother requires only explicit knowledge of matrix diagonal entries, which facilitates the use of matrix-free approach.

Coarse Grid Solver. At the coarsest level, it is sufficient to use several iterations of smoothing procedure for approximate matrix inversion, since the Δx is huge and the Helmholtz operator matrix is well-conditioned at this grid.

3.3   Implementation

ParCS parallel framework is used for the implementation of the algorithms (domain decomposition, halo exchanges, distributed data storage). The basic description of ParCS package is presented in [14]. Briefly, the computational domain is decomposed into the set of tiles (rectangular section of the grid) distributed among MPI-processes, and each MPI-process can handle different number of tiles. Halo zones (overlap regions between tiles) are used to enable calculations requiring data outside the tile. At this point, pure MPI parallel implementation is used.

The following basic abstractions have been defined in ParCS package for implementation of the linear solvers:

- `matrix_t` – object which implements matrix-vector product operation.
- `solver_t` – object which implements approximate solution of the system $Ax = b$.

`matrix_t` operates on instances of a `grid_function_t` type, which implements distributed storage of a given field quantities and basic linear algebra operations.

For the BICGstab algorithm, user need to pass an instance of `matrix_t` as an input argument.

In the multigrid code, smoothing procedure implemented as an instance of the `solver_t`. To initialize a multigrid method, user need to pass as an input argument `matrix_factory_t` and `solver_factory_t` type instances, which implement creation of `matrix_t` and `solver_t` type instances respectively at the every multigrid level. All other components of the multigrid algorithm are independent of the specific matrix to be inverted.

4   Performance and Scalability

In the following we present scalability test results of the solvers described above. We consider solution of the model elliptic system presented in Sect. 2. The right-hand-sides are chosen by multiplying a random solution vector by the matrix to be inversed, and the test results are averaged over 100 solves. In all runs, the first guess is initialized with zero, and the stopping criterion is a decrease in the relative norm of the residual by a factor of 10^{-5}. Scalability tests are carried out for problems at three grids: C216L30, C432L30, C1080L30, where numbers after C and L denote the number of grid points along edge of the cubed sphere panel and the number of vertical levels correspondingly. The total number of degrees of freedom and horizontal resolution is 8.39×10^6, 46 km for C216L30, 3.36×10^7, 23 km for C432L30 and 2.1×10^8, 9 km for C1080L30. The maximum value of CFL equals 7.5, so as the number of horizontal grid points increases, we scale the maximum value of γ_k to keep the CFL constant. The number of levels in the multigrid algorithm is $L = 4$. In general, the number of levels can be chosen as $\log_2$ CFL.

All tests were run on the Cray XC40 supercomputer system installed at Roshydromet's Main Computing Center. This system uses the Cray ARIES interconnect, each node is comprised of dual socket, Intel Xeon E2697v4 18-core CPUs, i.e. 36 CPU cores per node. The code was compiled with the Intel Fortran compiler.

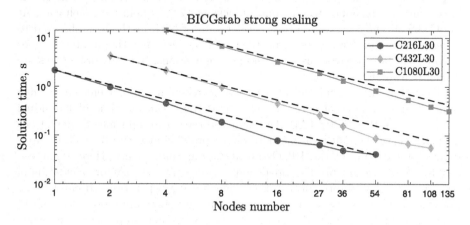

Fig. 2. Strong scaling of the BICGstab algorithm for problems with different size. The black dashed lines show ideal parallel acceleration. Each node has 36 processor cores.

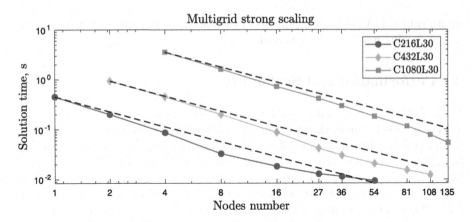

Fig. 3. Strong scaling of the multigrid algorithm for problems with different size. The black dashed lines show ideal parallel acceleration. Each node has 36 CPU cores.

Figures 2 and 3 show time per matrix solve in seconds for different problem sizes for the BICGstab and geometric multigrid algorithms respectively. For both methods, superlinear acceleration is observed, which seems to be caused by the better cache use efficiency with the smaller number of grid points per CPU core. It is seen from the figures, that for all grids and nodes number configurations, the multigrid method is approximately 4–5 times faster than the BICGstab algorithm. For the smallest problem with C216L30 grid, both methods show approximately the same strong scalability, although, as will be shown below, the drop in parallel efficiency at the large number of cores is due to different reasons. The maximum number of cores at which acceleration is observed for this grid is 1944, which corresponds to horizontal blocks of 12×12 points on each core. At the C432L30 and C1080L30 grids, acceleration of both methods is observed to at least 3888 and 4860 cores respectively. We believe that the greater number of cores can be effectively used in these configurations, but only 4860 cores are currently available for tests.

To better understand the reasons for decrease in parallel efficiency when using a large number of cores, we measured the execution time of individual components of the BICGSTAB algorithm and the execution time of calculations at each level of the multigrid method for the problem at C216L30 grid. Figure 4 shows elapsed time of the BICGstab algorithm components. Here, "matvec" denotes matrix-vector product operations, "collectives" stands for calculation of dot products and vectors norm, "other" denotes `axpy` operations. It can be seen from the figure that the matrix-vector product and `axpy` operations scale up to 1944 cores, while the elapsed time of collective operations stops decreasing when using more than 576 cores, which leads to the loss of parallel efficiency of the entire algorithm. The situation can be improved by using a modified version [3,20] of this algorithm, where collective operations are grouped in such a way that the number of global communication phases is reduced. Another option is

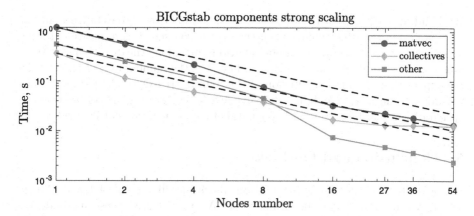

Fig. 4. Strong scaling of the BICGstab algorithm components for C216L30 grid. "matvec" denotes matrix-vector products, "collectives" – calculation of dot products and norms, "other" – axpy operations. The black dashed lines show ideal parallel acceleration. Each node has 36 CPU cores.

to use preconditioners (several iterations of the Jacobi method, for example), which will reduce the number of iterations, but at the same time will increase the number of matrix-vector products per iteration.

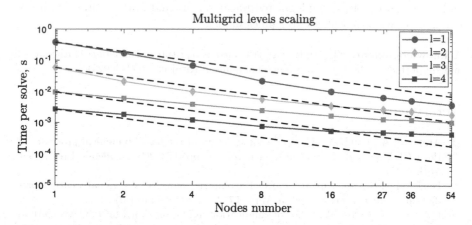

Fig. 5. Scaling of computatations elapsed time at different multigrid levels at C216L30 grid. The black dashed lines show ideal parallel acceleration. Each node has 36 CPU cores.

Figure 5 shows elapsed time at each level of the multigrid method for the problem at C216L30 grid. It can be seen from the figure that execution time at first two levels scales up to 1944 cores, while the last two levels time accelerates only until 972 cores. The decrease in parallel efficiency on coarse grids, on the one hand, is associated with a decrease in the number of degrees of freedom per CPU core. On the other hand, when the grid is coarsened, computational work imbalance occurs if the initial number of grid points along the direction at a MPI-process is not evenly divisible to 2^{L-1}, where L is the number of multigrid levels. We expect that the implementation of the hybrid MPI-OpenMP parallelization will allow to improve scalability at coarse levels, and we are also considering the option of using reduced precision for parallel communications at coarse levels.

5   Conclusion and Outlook

We presented details of implementation and scalability tests of linear elliptic solvers within ParCS parallel framework. We have tested these methods for inversion of matrices resulting from the discretization of Helmholtz problem at the cubed sphere grid. Strong scaling tests have been carried out for grids with horizontal resolution varying from 43 to 9 km. The considered algorithms show reasonable scalability and scales efficiently at least up to 4860 CPU cores at the grid with 9 km resolution. The use of the multigrid method allows us to speed up the matrix inversion by 3–5 times in comparison with the BICGstab algorithm. The scalability of the BICGstab algorithm are mostly constrained by the collective communications, while for the multigrid algorithm bottleneck is a computations at the coarse levels.

We consider results of this article as a good starting point for further testing and optimization of the implemented linear solvers and ParCS library within a non-hydrostatic atmospheric dynamics model.

Acknowledgement. The study was performed at Institute of Numerical Mathematics and supported by the Russian Science Foundation (project 21-71-30023).

References

1. Arakawa, A., Lamb, V.: Computational design of the basic dynamical processes of the UCLA general circulation model, vol. 17, pp. 173–265. Academic Press, New York (1977)
2. Buckeridge, S., Scheichl, R.: Parallel geometric multigrid for global weather prediction. Numer. Linear Algebra Appl. **17**(2–3), 325–342 (2010)
3. Cools, S., Vanroose, W.: The communication-hiding pipelined biCGSTAB method for the parallel solution of large unsymmetric linear systems. Parallel Comput. **65**, 1–20 (2017)
4. Deconinck, W., et al.: Atlas?: a library for numerical weather prediction and climate modelling. Comput. Phys. Commun. **220**, 188–204 (2017). https://doi.org/10.1016/j.cpc.2017.07.006
5. Fedorenko, R.P.: A relaxation method for solving elliptic difference equations. Zhurnal Vychislitel'noi Matematiki i Matematicheskoi Fiziki **1**(5), 922–927 (1961)
6. Hess, R., Joppich, W.: A comparison of parallel multigrid and a fast fourier transform algorithm for the solution of the helmholtz equation in numerical weather prediction. Parallel Comput. **22**(11), 1503–1512 (1997)

7. Leslie, L.M., McAVANEY, B.J.: Comparative test of direct and iterative methods for solving helmholtz-type equations. Mon. Weather Rev. **101**(3), 235–239 (1973)
8. Maynard, C., Melvin, T., Müller, E.H.: Multigrid preconditioners for the mixed finite element dynamical core of the lfric atmospheric model. Q. J. R. Meteorol. Soc. **146**(733), 3917–3936 (2020)
9. Müller, E.H., Scheichl, R.: Massively parallel solvers for elliptic partial differential equations in numerical weather and climate prediction. Q. J. R. Meteorol. Soc. **140**(685), 2608–2624 (2014)
10. Rančić, M., Purser, R., Mesinger, F.: A global shallow-water model using an expanded spherical cube: gnomonic versus conformal coordinates. Q. J. R. Meteorol. Soc. **122**(532), 959–982 (1996)
11. Robert, A., Yee, T., Ritchie, H.: A semi-lagrangian and semi-implicit numerical integration scheme for multilevel atmospheric models. Mon. Weather Rev. **113**, 388–394 (1985). https://doi.org/10.1175/1520-0493
12. Sadourny, R.: Conservative finite-difference approximations of the primitive equations on quasi-uniform spherical grids. Mon. Weather Rev. **100**(2), 136–144 (1972). https://doi.org/10.1175/1520-0493
13. Sandbach, S., Thuburn, J., Vassilev, D., Duda, M.G.: A semi-implicit version of the MPAS-atmosphere dynamical core. Mon. Weather Rev. **143**(9), 3838–3855 (2015)
14. Shashkin, V., Goyman, G.: Parallel efficiency of time-integration strategies for the next generation global weather prediction model. In: Voevodin, V., Sobolev, S. (eds.) Supercomputing, pp. 285–296. Springer International Publishing, Cham (2020)
15. Shashkin, V.V., Goyman, G.S.: Semi-lagrangian exponential time-integration method for the shallow water equations on the cubed sphere grid. Russ. J. Numer. Anal. Math. Model. **35**(6), 355–366 (2020)
16. Tolstykh, M., Goyman, G., Fadeev, R., Shashkin, V.: Structure and algorithms of SL-AV atmosphere model parallel program complex. Lobachevskii J. Math. **39**(4), 587–595 (2018)
17. Trottenberg, U., Oosterlee, C.W., Schuller, A.: Multigrid. Elsevier, Amsterdam (2000)
18. Van der Vorst, H.A.: Bi-CGSTAB: a fast and smoothly converging variant of bi-cg for the solution of nonsymmetric linear systems. SIAM J. sci. Stat. Comput. **13**(2), 631–644 (1992)
19. Yang, C., Xue, W., Fu, H., You, H., Wang, X., Ao, Y., Liu, F., Gan, L., Xu, P., Wang, L., et al.: 10m-core scalable fully-implicit solver for nonhydrostatic atmospheric dynamics. In: SC 2016: Proceedings of the International Conference for High Performance Computing, Networking, Storage and Analysis, pp. 57–68. IEEE (2016)
20. Yang, L.T., Brent, R.P.: The improved bicgstab method for large and sparse unsymmetric linear systems on parallel distributed memory architectures. In: Fifth International Conference on Algorithms and Architectures for Parallel Processing, pp. 324–328. IEEE (2002)
21. Yi, T.H.: Time integration of unsteady nonhydrostatic equations with dual time stepping and multigrid methods. J. Comput. Phys. **374**, 873–892 (2018)

JAD-Based SpMV Kernels Using Multiple-Precision Libraries for GPUs

Konstantin Isupov$^{(\boxtimes)}$ⓘ and Ivan Babeshkoⓘ

Vyatka State University, Kirov, Russia
{ks_isupov,stud120279}@vyatsu.ru

Abstract. Sparse matrix computations often arise in real-world applications, and sparse matrix-vector multiplication (SpMV) is one of the key operations in linear algebra. At the same time, single and double precision arithmetic, which is the most common in scientific computing and natively supported by hardware and programming languages, introduces round-off errors that may affect the SpMV results and in some cases cause serious problems. In this paper we implement SpMV kernels for graphics processing units using available software libraries that support multiple-precision computation. We use the Jagged Diagonal (JAD) sparse matrix storage format, which is very close to CSR in terms of memory consumption, but provides efficient accesses to nonzero matrix entries. We evaluate the implemented kernels on NVIDIA RTX 2080 for various sparse matrices from the SuiteSparse Matrix Collection.

Keywords: Sparse matrices · SpMV · GPU programming · Multiple-precision computation

1 Introduction

Sparse matrix vector multiplication (SpMV), which computes the product of a sparse matrix by a dense vector ($y = Ax$), occupies an important place in scientific applications and network analytics. While a serial implementation of SpMV is trivial, its efficient implementation on massively parallel architectures such as the graphics processing unit (GPU) architecture is complicated by irregular memory references [2]. For this reason, there is a great deal of research aimed at optimizing SpMV for parallel GPU architectures.

On the other hand, single and double precision floating-point arithmetic, which is widely used in scientific computing, introduces rounding errors that affect numerical results. For some applications, such as machine learning, rounding errors are not critical, but for other applications they can cause problems. In particular, iterative Krylov methods [13] are known for their sensitivity to rounding errors and, being convergent in theory, they may converge poorly or not at all when using finite-precision floating-point arithmetic [14]. Consequently, accurate methods that minimize the effect of rounding errors on numerical results

V. Voevodin and S. Sobolev (Eds.): RuSCDays 2021, CCIS 1510, pp. 148–161, 2021.
https://doi.org/10.1007/978-3-030-92864-3_12

are of particular importance. Today, the demand for such techniques is growing as the scale of high performance computing becomes enormous.

There are various approaches to fully or partially eliminate the effects of rounding errors. The papers [3,5,10,14] offer highly accurate versions of SpMV and some other computational kernels using double-double (DD) arithmetic that represents numbers by two double precision floating-point numbers to emulate quadruple precision [4]. Well-known implementations of DD arithmetic are the QD [4] and GQD [9] libraries for CPU and GPU, respectively. There are also multiple-precision GPU libraries such as CUMP, MPRES-BLAS and CAMPARY, which provide not only DD/quadruple precision, but also (almost) arbitrary precision. In this paper, we use these libraries to implement multiple-precision sparse matrix-vector multiplication kernels.

It is well known that the sparse matrix format has a significant impact on the performance of SpMV computation. There are several well-known formats such as Coordinate (COO), Compressed Sparse Row (CSR) and ELLPACK. The CSR format is the most popular choice in iterative solvers. However, the scalar CSR kernel has drawbacks in that it does not provide coalesced memory access for nonzero matrix coefficients. In turn, the vector CSR kernel provides only a partially coalesced memory access [2]. We therefore use the Jagged Diagonal (JAD) sparse matrix format [1,8] for our multiple-precision implementation. This format is more complex than CSR as it requires some preprocessing of the matrix. On the other hand, it does not suffer from the drawbacks of CSR.

The rest of the paper is structured as follows. In Sect. 2, the background on multiple-precision CUDA libraries and JAD matrix storage format is described. Section 3 provides the implementation details of multiple-precision SpMV kernels. Section 4 gives performance and memory evaluation of the kernels, and also presents a vector JAD implementation with multiple threads per row. Conclusions are provided in Sect. 5.

2   Background

2.1   Multiple-Precision GPU Libraries

Although most of the well-known multiple precision libraries are designed for central processors, there are libraries that target the GPU architecture:

1. CUMP[1] [11] is a library for arbitrary precision floating-point arithmetic on CUDA based on the well-known GNU MP Library (GMP). In CUMP, each multiple precision number is represented as a sequence of integers (limbs) with a single exponent. To deliver high performance, the library applies some optimization techniques, such as register blocking, little-endian word order, and using 64-bit full words as the basic arithmetic type.
2. MPRES-BLAS[2] [6] is a library of multiple-precision linear algebra operations that can also be thought of as a general purpose arithmetic library as it

---

[1] https://github.com/skystar0227/CUMP.
[2] https://github.com/kisupov/mpres-blas.

provides basic multiple-precision arithmetic operations for CPUs and NVIDIA GPUs. MPRES-BLAS differs from the above libraries in that it uses a residue number system (RNS) rather than weighted number systems to provide multiple precision capabilities. The RNS is interesting, in particular, because it provides efficient addition, subtraction and multiplication of large integers. These operations work on residues independently, i.e., without carry propagation between them, instead of directly with the complete number [12]. MPRES-BLAS currently provides several dense linear algebra operations, like the BLAS (Basic Linear Algebra Subprograms) routines, as well as several SpMV implementations in various sparse matrix formats.

3. CAMPARY[3] [7] uses floating-point expansions and provides flexible CPU and GPU implementations of high precision operations. Both binary64 and binary32 formats can be used as basic blocks for the floating-point expansion, and the precision is specified as a template parameter. The library contains "certified" algorithms with rigorous error bounds, as well as "quick-and-dirty" algorithms that perform well for the average case, but do not consider the corner cases. CAMPARY is better suited for moderate precision, up to a few hundred bits.

2.2 Jagged Diagonal Format

Like the CSR format, the JAD format only stores nonzero matrix entries without any additional entries for padding. Accordingly, it provides the same good memory footprint as CSR, plus one integer array of size M (the number of matrix rows) is required to store row permutations.

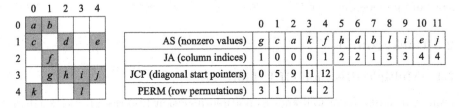

Fig. 1. The JAD format of a sparse matrix.

Figure 1 shows an example of a sparse matrix representation using the JAD storage format. This format consists of the following arrays:

- AS is a floating-point array storing nonzero entries of a sparse matrix;
- JA is an integer array storing the column index of each nonzero;
- JCP is an integer array storing the first index of the entries of each diagonal;
- $PERM$ is an integer array storing permutations of matrix rows.

---

[3] https://homepages.laas.fr/mmjoldes/campary.

The JAD representation for a given sparse matrix is constructed as follows:

1. The rows of the matrix are compressed by eliminating all zero entries.
2. The compressed rows are sorted by nonincreasing order of the number of nonzeros within each row; row permutations are stored in the *PERM* array.
3. The result of the previous steps is a compressed and sorted matrix whose columns are called "jagged diagonals". These diagonals are stored contiguously in the *AS* array, while the original column indices are stored in the *JA* array. The array *JCP* holds the first index of the entries of each diagonal within *AS* and *JA* arrays.

In respect to work distribution, a typical JAD implementation is very similar to the scalar CSR kernel, since one thread processes each row of the matrix to exploit fine-grained parallelism [8]. However, the manner in which parallel threads access the *AS* and *JA* arrays is significantly different:

1. In the case of scalar CSR, the nonzero values and column indices for a given row are stored contiguously but are accessed sequentially (Fig. 2a). Thus, memory accesses from consecutive threads are serialized, which has a bad performance impact.
2. In the case of JAD, the nonzero values and column indices for adjacent rows are stored contiguously and are accessed simultaneously (Fig. 2b). Thus, consecutive threads can access contiguous memory addresses, which can improve the memory bandwidth by coalescing memory transactions [8].

On the other hand, it is possible to implement a vector kernel in which the jagged diagonals are computed in parallel using multiple CUDA threads. Although this approach does not provide memory coalescing, it can give performance improvements for matrices with a small number of rows. We evaluate this approach in Sect. 4.

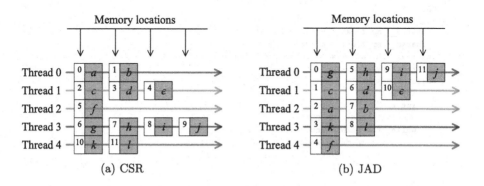

Fig. 2. Memory access pattern of SpMV kernels.

3   JAD Kernels Using Multiple-Precision Libraries

In this section, we present GPU-accelerated JAD kernels based on the multiple-precision arithmetic libraries MPRES-BLAS, CAMPARY, and CUMP.

MPRES-BLAS. This library uses a residue number system and therefore, for the desired precision, the appropriate set of RNS moduli $\{m_1, m_2, \ldots, m_n\}$ must be specified. The moduli must be pairwise relatively prime integers. Let M be the product of all the m_i's. Then the precision in bits is $p = \lfloor \log_2 \sqrt{M} \rfloor - 1$. For example, for the precision of 106 bits (two times higher than double precision), the moduli set

$$\{m_1, m_2, \ldots, m_8\} = \{113812103, 113812105, 113812107, 113812109,$$
$$113812111, 113812117, 113812121, 113812123\}$$

is an appropriate choice. There are several predefined sets of moduli providing different levels of precision. To represent a multiple-precision floating-point number, MPRES-BLAS defines the C data type `mp_float_t`. Variables of this type can be declared and defined both on the host side and directly from the device code. The exchange of multiple-precision data between the host and the device is performed by calling the standard CUDA API functions.

A multiple-precision JAD kernel using MPRES-BLAS is shown in Fig. 3. Since MPRES-BLAS allows one to compute the product of a multiple-precision number by a standard double-precision number (the routine `mp_mul_d`), the matrix remains in double precision and only the input and output vectors are composed of multiple-precision numbers. This greatly reduces memory consumption and time required to build the JAD structure. We use a shared memory

```
Input:
    int M, int MAXNZR, double *AS, int *JA, int *JCP, int *PERM, mp_float_t *X
Output:
    mp_float_t *Y
Computation:
    __shared__ mp_float_t sums[nThreads]
    __shared__ mp_float_t prods[nThreads]
    int row = threadIdx.x + blockIdx.x * blockDim.x
    int k = threadIdx.x
    while (row < M) {
        int i = row
        int t = 0
        sums[k] = cuda::MP_ZERO
        while (t < MAXNZR and i < JCP[t + 1]) {
            cuda::mp_mul_d(prods[k], X[JA[i]], AS[i])
            cuda::mp_add(sums[k], sums[k], prods[k])
            i = row + JCP[++t]
        }
        cuda::mp_set(Y[PERM[row]], sums[k])
        row += gridDim.x * blockDim.x
    }
```

Fig. 3. JAD kernel pseudocode using MPRES-BLAS.

cache to optimize accesses to intermediate multiple-precision results, and we evaluate the performance gains provided by caching in Sect. 4.

Note that besides the data type `mp_float_t`, MPRES-BLAS also defines two vector types, `mp_array_t` and `mp_collection_t`, which are designed for efficient computations with arrays of multiple-precision numbers on the GPU. The `mp_array_t` stores a multiple-precision array in a decomposed form, i.e., as a set of arrays representing separate parts of multiple-precision numbers. In turn, `mp_collection_t` can be thought of as a lightweight version of `mp_array_t`. However, these vector types are well suited for dense linear algebra kernels with their regular patterns of memory accesses. In turn, the JAD kernel assumes indirect and irregular access to the input and output vectors, so using special vector data types in this case does not provide significant advantages.

CAMPARY. This library uses n-term floating-point expansions (generalization of the DD format to an arbitrary number of terms) to provide multiple (extended) precision arithmetic capabilities. Like the DD format, the precision is extended by representing real numbers as the unevaluated sum of several standard floating-point numbers, and CAMPARY defines the data type `multi_prec<prec>`, where the template parameter `prec` specifies the precision in terms of "doubles". Specifically,

- `multi_prec<2>` corresponds to 2-double format (106 bits of precision),
- `multi_prec<4>` corresponds to 4-double format (212 bits of precision),
- `multi_prec<6>` corresponds to 6-double format (318 bits of precision), etc.

A multiple-precision JAD kernel using CAMPARY is shown in Fig. 4. The library provides overloaded operators and also allows one to compute the product

```
Input:
    int M, int MAXNZR, double *AS, int *JA, int *JCP, int *PERM, multi_prec<prec> *X
Output:
    multi_prec<prec> *Y
Computation:
    __shared__ multi_prec<prec> sums[nThreads]
    __shared__ multi_prec<prec> prods[nThreads]
    int row = threadIdx.x + blockIdx.x * blockDim.x
    int k = threadIdx.x
    while (row < M) {
        int i = row
        int j = 0
        sums[k] = 0
        while (t < MAXNZR and i < JCP[t + 1]) {
            prods[k] = AS[i] * X[JA[i]]
            sums[k] += prods[k]
            i = row + JCP[++t]
        }
        Y[PERM[row]] = sums[k]
        row += gridDim.x * blockDim.x
    }
```

Fig. 4. JAD kernel pseudocode using CAMPARY.

of a multiple-precision variable by a double precision variable, so the matrix is also represented in double precision, not in multiple precision.

CUMP. This library contains two kinds of multiple-precision data types and two kinds of functions:

- data types and functions for host code;
- data types and functions for device code.

The host data types are `cumpf_t` and `cumpf_array_t`, which represent a single multiple-precision variable and an array of multiple-precision variables, respectively. In turn, the multiple-precision device data types are `cump::mpf_t` and `cump::mpf_array_t`. In CUMP, the initialization of multiple-precision arrays and their copying to the GPU are performed using special functions. A multiple-precision JAD kernel using CUMP is shown in Fig. 5.

```
Input:
    int M, int MAXNZR, mpf_array_t AS, int *JA, int *JCP, int *PERM, mpf_array_t X,
    mpf_array_t BUF
Output:
    mpf_array_t Y
Computation:
    using namespace cump
    int row = threadIdx.x + blockIdx.x * blockDim.x
    while (row < M) {
        int i = row
        int t = 0
        while (t < MAXNZR and i < JCP[t + 1]) {
            j = PERM[row]
            mpf_mul(BUF[j], X[JA[i]], AS[i])
            mpf_add(Y[j], Y[j], BUF[j])
            i = row + JCP[++t]
        }
        row += gridDim.x * blockDim.x
    }
```

Fig. 5. JAD kernel pseudocode using CUMP.

Unlike the above two libraries, arithmetic operations between scalar arguments (`cump::mpf_t`) and arrays (`cump::mpf_array_t`) are not available in CUMP. For this reason, the CUMP kernel uses an auxiliary global memory buffer `BUF` to store intermediate multiple-precision products. The summation of partial products is also performed in global memory, i.e., directly in the output vector. Moreover, CUMP does not support mixed "double precision plus multiple-precision" operations, so nonzero matrix values are represented in multiple-precision format. This limitation seems rather restrictive, since the memory requirements of the CUMP implementation can be unacceptably large, regardless of the matrix sparsity.

4 Performance and Memory Evaluation

The experiments were performed on a system with an NVIDIA RTX 2080 GPU (46 streaming multiprocessors, 8 GB of GDDR6 memory, compute capability version 7.5), an Intel Core i5 7500 processor and 16 GB of DDR4 RAM, running Ubuntu 20.04.1 LTS. We used CUDA Toolkit version 11.1.105 and NVIDIA driver version 455.32.00. The source code was compiled with the -*O3* option.

We evaluated the performance and memory consumption of the presented SpMV kernels on sparse matrices taken from the SuiteSparse Matrix Collection (https://sparse.tamu.edu). An overview of the matrices used in the experiments is presented in Table 1, while Fig. 6 illustrates the distribution of nonzero entries for each test matrix. The corresponding input vector was composed of randomly generated floating-point numbers in the range of −1 to 1.

Table 1. Matrices for experiments.

Name	Rows	Nonzeros (NNZ)	Avg. NNZ per row	Description
t3dl	20,360	509,866	25.04	Micropyros thruster
rma10	46,835	2,329,092	50.69	3D CFD of Charleston harbor
consph	83,334	6,010,480	72.12	FEM concentric spheres
crankseg_1	52,804	10,614,210	201.01	Linear static analysis of a crankshaft detail
pwtk	217,918	11,524,432	53.39	Pressurized wind tunnel
af_shell2	504,855	17,562,051	34.84	Sheet metal forming
F1	343,791	26,837,113	78.06	Engine crankshaft stiffness simulation
inline_1	503,712	36,816,170	73.09	Inline skater

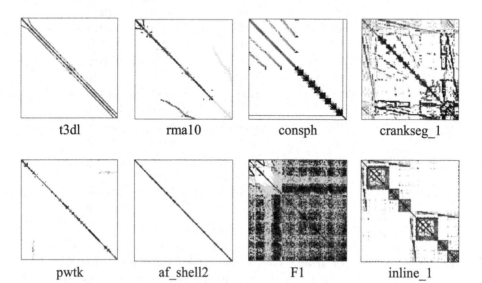

t3dl   rma10   consph   crankseg_1

pwtk   af_shell2   F1   inline_1

Fig. 6. Distribution of nonzero entries in test matrices.

We ran the benchmarks with 106, 212, 318, and 424 bits of precision. The measured execution times versus precision are shown in Table 2. Measurements do not include the time taken to build the JAD structures and transfer data between the CPU and GPU.

Table 2. Execution time in ms of JAD kernels on NVIDIA RTX 2080.

Matrix	Precision in bits	MPRES-BLAS	CAMPARY	CUMP
t3dl	106	0.73	0.09	2.58
	212	0.47	0.75	3.24
	318	0.55	1.46	3.66
	424	0.87	2.37	4.68
rma10	106	1.96	0.39	14.03
	212	1.81	3.33	22.27
	318	2.42	6.59	27.85
	424	3.80	10.70	37.40
consph	106	2.89	0.94	21.40
	212	4.42	8.53	36.28
	318	5.80	16.51	45.01
	424	9.00	26.87	63.79
crankseg_1	106	19.30	3.39	59.12
	212	14.07	22.12	93.89
	318	18.31	41.37	114.67
	424	26.60	68.36	146.59
pwtk	106	15.12	1.70	29.30
	212	8.39	16.00	51.88
	318	11.21	31.68	67.45
	424	18.06	50.99	92.76
af_shell2	106	46.25	1.98	32.55
	212	12.66	19.37	61.43
	318	17.08	37.40	78.08
	424	27.43	61.19	108.29
F1	106	17.98	3.81	164.96
	212	22.13	28.90	253.76
	318	28.80	57.10	294.28
	424	42.49	93.44	380.78
inline_1	106	45.76	4.86	249.96
	212	30.16	39.62	384.36
	318	39.89	78.18	444.35
	424	60.32	129.03	570.26

We also calculated the performance of SpMV kernels in *billions of multiple-precision operations per second, Gop/s*. The performance is calculated as $P = 2 \times NNZ / (1000 \times T)$, where T is the measured execution time in ms. Note that each multiple-precision operation consists of several standard operations. The performance in *Gop/s* is reported in Fig. 7.

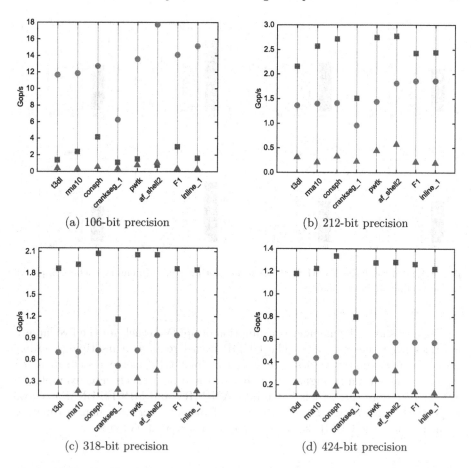

(a) 106-bit precision (b) 212-bit precision

(c) 318-bit precision (d) 424-bit precision

Fig. 7. Performance of multiple-precision JAD kernels: ■ MPRES-BLAS, ● CAM-PARY, and ▲ CUMP.

The results show that implementations using different multiple-precision libraries exhibit different behavior. The CAMPARY kernel is fastest for 106-bit precision (2-fold the double precision) because CAMPARY provides optimized algorithms for DD arithmetic. However for other precision levels, the MPRES-BLAS kernel has better performance. The CUMP kernel performs slower than the other two implementations because of high memory bandwidth requirements. We also see that on some test matrices, the MPRES-BLAS implementation performance for 106-bit precision is lower than for 212-bit precision. This is because there are too many roundings when using 106-bit precision. The optimized rounding algorithm should be an important improvement for MPRES-BLAS.

We also evaluated the performance impact of accessing intermediate results through a shared memory cache. Figure 8 shows the speedup of the MPRES-BLAS kernel with caching enabled (cf. Fig. 3) compared to the version without caching. We see that caching generally provides significant performance improvements.

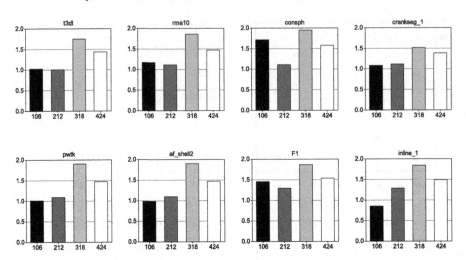

Fig. 8. Speedup of the MPRES-BLAS kernel with a shared memory cache compared to the version without caching.

Figure 9 shows the memory consumption of SpMV kernels for the five largest matrices from the test suite. The CUMP kernel requires a multiple-precision array of nonzero matrix values to be stored in global GPU memory, so its memory requirements are much higher than that of the other kernels. For example, at 424-bit precision, the kernels based on CAMPARY and MPRES-BLAS occupy, respectively, on average 15 and 19 bytes of memory per each nonzero matrix element, while the CUMP kernel occupies an average of 98 bytes.

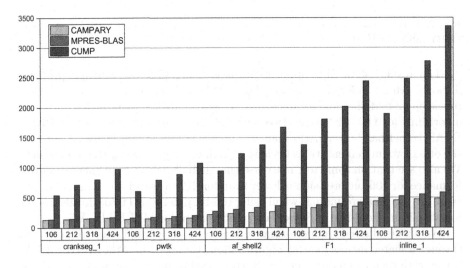

Fig. 9. Memory consumption of multiple-precision JAD kernels (in MB).

For the remainder of our evaluation, we implemented a vector JAD kernel using the MPRES-BLAS library. In this implementation, multiple CUDA threads simultaneously process different jagged diagonals for the same matrix row. Accordingly, shared memory is used not as a managed cache, but as a buffer for communication between parallel threads. The pseudocode is given in Fig. 10.

While the general design is similar to the vector CSR kernel from [2], it is possible to assign a variable number of threads per row by changing the template parameter *TPR*, which allows the kernel to adapt to different sparse matrices.

```
Input:
    int M, int MAXNZR, double *AS, int *JA, int *JCP, int *PERM, mp_float_t *X
Output:
    mp_float_t *Y
Computation:
    __shared__ mp_float_t sums[nThreads]
    __shared__ mp_float_t prods[nThreads]
    int lane = (threadIdx.x + blockIdx.x * blockDim.x) & (TPR - 1)
    int row = (threadIdx.x + blockIdx.x * blockDim.x) / TPR
    int k = threadIdx.x
    while (row < m) {
        sums[k] = cuda::MP_ZERO
        for (int t = lane; t < MAXNZR; t += TPR) {
            int i = row + JCP[t]
            if (i < JCP[t + 1]) {
                cuda::mp_mul_d(prods[k], X[JA[i]], AS[i])
                cuda::mp_add(sums[k], sums[k], prods[k])
            }
        }
        if (TPR >= 32 and lane < 16) cuda::mp_add(sums[k], sums[k], sums[k + 16])
        if (TPR >= 16 and lane < 8)  cuda::mp_add(sums[k], sums[k], sums[k + 8])
        if (TPR >= 8 and lane < 4)   cuda::mp_add(sums[k], sums[k], sums[k + 4])
        if (TPR >= 4 and lane < 2)   cuda::mp_add(sums[k], sums[k], sums[k + 2])
        if (TPR >= 2 and lane < 1)   cuda::mp_add(sums[k], sums[k], sums[k + 1])
        if (lane == 0) cuda::mp_set(Y[PERM[row]], sums[k])
        row += gridDim.x * blockDim.x / TPR
    }
```

Fig. 10. JAD (vector) kernel pseudocode using MPRES-BLAS.

We evaluated the performance of the vector method on three sparse matrices that differ in the average number of nonzero elements per row, namely, af_shell2 (34.84 nonzero per row), inline_1 (73.09 nonzeros per row), and crankseg_1 (201.01 nonzeros per row). The results are reported in Table 3.

Comparing these results with Table 2, it can be seen that the vector kernel provides some benefits for matrices with a small number of long rows. In particular, for the crankseg_1 matrix, the kernel with four threads assigned to each row provides a speedup of 1.5× to 1.9× over the kernel in Fig. 3. However, to obtain good performance, the *TPR* parameter must be carefully tuned.

Table 3. Execution time in ms of the vector MPRES-BLAS-based JAD kernel on NVIDIA RTX 2080.

Matrix	Precision in bits	Threads per row (TPR)				
		2	4	8	16	32
af_shell2	106	48.32	57.85	77.80	112.60	191.57
	212	13.30	15.41	21.66	33.36	56.11
	318	18.06	22.16	30.55	46.41	70.32
	424	30.12	35.81	49.28	71.15	82.64
inline_1	106	37.53	41.75	52.59	75.83	114.37
	212	28.50	28.97	37.04	48.24	66.15
	318	41.63	44.41	46.62	56.84	83.26
	424	52.14	68.35	78.78	105.44	136.16
crankseg_1	106	13.67	10.08	8.18	8.74	11.53
	212	8.73	9.20	10.99	13.42	16.80
	318	11.46	11.95	13.69	16.90	21.15
	424	17.60	18.05	19.51	21.81	28.70

5   Conclusions

As multiple-precision computations become more and more in demand, in this paper we implemented and evaluated the SpMV kernels for GPUs using CUDA-enabled multiple-precision arithmetic libraries. The kernels based on CAMPARY and MPRES-BLAS can be used for large problems, since they have good performance and do not lead to unacceptably high memory consumption. In general, CAMPARY is the optimal choice for 106-bit precision, while MPRES-BLAS performs better for other precision levels. The CUMP library implements optimized arithmetic routines, but has limited functionality due to which the SpMV kernel using CUMP shows poor performance and wastes a lot of memory. We have also proposed the vector JAD kernel using MPRES-BLAS and have shown that it can offer performance improvements provided that matrix rows contain a large enough number of nonzero elements. In the future, we plan to implement GPU-accelerated multiple-precision iterative solvers using the MPRES-BLAS library.

Acknowledgements. This work was funded by the Russian Science Foundation grant number 20-71-00046.

References

1. Ahmed, N., Mateev, N., Pingali, K., Stodghill, P.: A framework for sparse matrix code synthesis from high-level specifications. In: SC 2000: Proceedings of the 2000 ACM/IEEE Conference on Supercomputing, pp. 58–58 (2000). https://doi.org/10.1109/SC.2000.10033

2. Bell, N., Garland, M.: Implementing sparse matrix-vector multiplication on throughput-oriented processors. In: Proceedings of the Conference on High Performance Computing Networking, Storage and Analysis, Portland, OR, USA, pp. 1–11, November 2009. https://doi.org/10.1145/1654059.1654078

3. Furuichi, M., May, D.A., Tackley, P.J.: Development of a stokes flow solver robust to large viscosity jumps using a Schur complement approach with mixed precision arithmetic. J. Comput. Phys. **230**(24), 8835–8851 (2011). https://doi.org/10.1016/j.jcp.2011.09.007

4. Hida, Y., Li, X.S., Bailey, D.H.: Algorithms for quad-double precision floating point arithmetic. In: Proceedings of the 15th IEEE Symposium on Computer Arithmetic, Vail, CO, USA, pp. 155–162, June 2001. https://doi.org/10.1109/ARITH.2001.930115

5. Hishinuma, T., Hasegawa, H., Tanaka, T.: SIMD parallel sparse matrix-vector and transposed-matrix-vector multiplication in DD precision. In: Dutra, I., Camacho, R., Barbosa, J., Marques, O. (eds.) VECPAR 2016. LNCS, vol. 10150, pp. 21–34. Springer, Cham (2017). https://doi.org/10.1007/978-3-319-61982-8_4

6. Isupov, K., Knyazkov, V.: Multiple-precision BLAS library for graphics processing units. In: Voevodin, V., Sobolev, S. (eds.) RuSCDays 2020. CCIS, vol. 1331, pp. 37–49. Springer, Cham (2020). https://doi.org/10.1007/978-3-030-64616-5_4

7. Joldes, M., Muller, J.-M., Popescu, V., Tucker, W.: CAMPARY: Cuda multiple precision arithmetic library and applications. In: Greuel, G.-M., Koch, T., Paule, P., Sommese, A. (eds.) ICMS 2016. LNCS, vol. 9725, pp. 232–240. Springer, Cham (2016). https://doi.org/10.1007/978-3-319-42432-3_29

8. Li, R., Saad, Y.: GPU-accelerated preconditioned iterative linear solvers. J. Supercomput. **63**(2), 443–466 (2013). https://doi.org/10.1007/s11227-012-0825-3

9. Lu, M., He, B., Luo, Q.: Supporting extended precision on graphics processors. In: Sixth International Workshop on Data Management on New Hardware (DaMoN 2010), Indianapolis, Indiana, USA, pp. 19–26, June 2010. https://doi.org/10.1145/1869389.1869392

10. Masui, K., Ogino, M., Liu, L.: Multiple-precision iterative methods for solving complex symmetric electromagnetic systems. In: van Brummelen, H., Corsini, A., Perotto, S., Rozza, G. (eds.) Numerical Methods for Flows. LNCSE, vol. 132, pp. 321–329. Springer, Cham (2020). https://doi.org/10.1007/978-3-030-30705-9_28

11. Nakayama, T., Takahashi, D.: Implementation of multiple-precision floating-point arithmetic library for GPU computing. In: Proceedings of the 23rd IASTED International Conference on Parallel and Distributed Computing and Systems (PDCS 2011), Dallas, USA, pp. 343–349, December 2011. https://doi.org/10.2316/P.2011.757-041

12. Omondi, A., Premkumar, B.: Residue Number Systems: Theory and Implementation. Imperial College Press, London (2007)

13. Saad, Y.: Iterative Methods for Sparse Linear Systems, 2nd edn. SIAM, Philadelphia (2003)

14. Saito, T., Ishiwata, E., Hasegawa, H.: Analysis of the GCR method with mixed precision arithmetic using QuPAT. J. Comput. Sci. **3**(3), 87–91 (2012)

Modeling the Process of Mixing Water in the Estuarine Area in the Presence of a Density Gradient of the Aquatic Environment Using Hybrid MPI/OpenMP Technology

Alexander Sukhinov[1], Asya Atayan[1], Inna Kuznetsova[2], Vasilii Dolgov[1], Alexander Chistyakov[1(✉)], and Alla Nikitina[2]

[1] Don State Technical University, Rostov-on-Don, Russia
[2] Southern Federal University, Rostov-on-Don, Russia
`ikuznecova@sfedu.ru`

Abstract. The paper investigates a mathematical model of the hydrophysics of the estuarine area, taking into account the following factors: movement of the aquatic environment; variable density depending on salinity; complex geometry of the computational domain in the presence of a significant density gradient of the aquatic environment. Distinctive features of the developed model are: taking into account the density stratification and the presence of zones with low microturbulent exchange in the vertical direction, taking into account surging phenomena, dynamically reconstructed bottom geometry, and rejection of the hydrostatic approximation. An increase in the accuracy of calculations by the model is achieved through using a function of partial filling of the computational cells, vortex-resolving difference schemes that are stable in the case of large grid Peclet numbers, as well as the absence of non-conservative dissipative terms and nonphysical field sources arising as a result of finite-difference approximations. Parallel algorithms for solving the problem on a multiprocessor computer system using hybrid MPI/OpenMP technology have been developed. Numerical experiments were carried out to simulate the process of mixing of waters in the estuary area.

Keywords: Mathematical modeling · Estuarine areas · Density gradient of the aquatic environment · Parallel algorithm · MPI · OpenMP

1 Introduction

In the Russian Federation, scientific research on the creation of mathematical models of complex marine systems has more than half a century history. G.G. Matishov and V.G. Ilyichev were actively involved in the study of the issue of optimal exploitation of water resources, the development of models for the

V. Voevodin and S. Sobolev (Eds.): RuSCDays 2021, CCIS 1510, pp. 162–173, 2021.
https://doi.org/10.1007/978-3-030-92864-3_13

transport of pollutants in water bodies and the study of assessing their impact on the biological resources of a water body [1]. M.E. Berland carried out great theoretical work in this direction [2]. He investigated and developed the basic models of the spread of pollutants from point, linear and area sources of both continuous and instantaneous action.

In [3], the method of smoothed incompressible particle hydrodynamics (SPH) together with the large eddy simulation (LES) approach is used to simulate coastal solitary wave mechanics. The equations of incompressible Navier-Stokes fluid in Lagrangian form are solved by a two-step fractional method. Article [4] is devoted to the description of the numerical model of the wave run-up on uneven inclined surfaces. The hydrodynamics of incompressible smoothed particles (ISPH) is described, which makes it possible to effectively track the deformation of the free surface in the Lagrangian coordinate system.

However, despite a significant number of publications, many effects that are significant for improving the accuracy and reliability of forecasts of natural and technogenic hazards associated with spatial heterogeneity of the environment, interaction of populations, movement of the aquatic environment, interspecific competition, taxis, catch, gravitational subsidence, biogenic, temperature and oxygen regimes, salinity and so on were not taken into account earlier when constructing mathematical models of hydrobiological processes. Continuous and discrete models of hydrophysics, used up to the present time, are, as a rule, strongly idealized, use simplified parameterization, or are described by Cauchy problems for ordinary differential equations. They also do not take into account the spatial heterogeneity of the medium. However, the point description is fundamentally incorrect in systems with significant inhomogeneity of space, which was noted in the work of Yu.M. Svirezhev and D.O. Logofeta [5]. Analysis of the existing mathematical models of hydrobiological processes showed that many of them are focused on the use of hydrodynamic models that do not take into account the complex geometry of the coastline and the bottom, surge phenomena, friction against the bottom and wind stresses, turbulent exchange, Coriolis force, river flows, evaporation, etc., exhibiting instability at significant changes in depths typical for the coastal parts of water bodies, including shallow ones.

Russian scientists have made a tangible contribution to the creation and research of methods for solving algebraic grid equations, as well as to the theory of distributed computing [6–9]. However, when solving real problems of hydrophysics in areas of complex shape, there is a need to modernize existing methods for solving grid equations.

Only a few works are associated with the parallel numerical implementation of problems of this class [10–14]. However, with the onset of unfavorable and catastrophic phenomena in the coastal zones of water bodies, the forecast of the development of such phenomena and decision-making should be carried out in short periods of time, when it is still relevant. This requires the implementation of models of the processes under consideration on supercomputing systems; for this, it is necessary to develop efficient parallel algorithms that numerically implement the set model problems at a given time, limited by regulatory documentation. A separate problem is the need to quickly obtain input data for the developed mathematical model of hydrophysics, which can be solved by using field data obtained in expeditionary research, as well as data from remote sensing of the Earth.

2   Problem Setup

The initial equations of the hydrodynamics of shallow water bodies are [12]:

– equation of motion (Navier – Stokes):

$$u'_t + uu'_x + vu'_y + wu'_z = -\frac{1}{\rho}P'_x + \left(\mu u'_x\right)'_x + \left(\mu u'_y\right)'_y + \left(\nu u'_z\right)'_z,$$

$$v'_t + uv'_x + vv'_y + wv'_z = -\frac{1}{\rho}P'_y + \left(\mu v'_x\right)'_x + \left(\mu v'_y\right)'_y + \left(\nu v'_z\right)'_z, \qquad (1)$$

$$w'_t + uw'_x + vw'_y + ww'_z = -\frac{1}{\rho}P'_z + \left(\mu w'_x\right)'_x + \left(\mu w'_y\right)'_y + \left(\nu w'_z\right)'_z + g,$$

– continuity equation in the case of variable density:

$$\rho'_t + (\rho u)'_x + (\rho v)'_y + (\rho w)'_z = 0, \qquad (2)$$

where $V = \{u, v, w\}$ – velocity vector components [m/s]; P – pressure [Pa], ρ – density [kg/m^3], μ, ν – horizontal and vertical components of the turbulent exchange coefficient [m^2/s], g – acceleration of gravity [m/s^2].

The system of equations (1)–(2) is considered under the following boundary conditions:

– at the entrance $u = u_0$, $v = v_0$, $P'_n = 0$, $V'_n = 0$,
– the lateral boundary (bank and bottom) $\rho\mu u'_n = -\tau_x$, $\rho\mu v'_n = -\tau_y$, $V_n = 0$, $P'_n = 0$,
– upper bound $\rho\mu u'_n = -\tau_x$, $\rho\mu v'_n = -\tau_y$, $w = -\omega - P'_t/\rho g$, $P'_n = 0$, where ω – evaporation rate of liquid, τ_x, τ_y – components of the tangential stress.

The components of the tangential stress τ_x and τ_y for the free surface are $\{\tau_x, \tau_y\} = \rho_a Cd_s |w| \{w_x, w_y\}$, $Cd_s = 0.0026$, where w – vector of the wind speed relative to the water, ρ_a – density of the atmosphere, Cd_s – dimensionless coefficient of surface resistance, which depends on the wind speed, is considered in the range 0.0016–0.0032.

The components of the tangential stress for the bottom, taking into account the movement of water, can be written as follows $\{\tau_x, \tau_y\} = \rho Cd_b |V| \{u, v\}$, $Cd_b = gn^2/h^{1/3}$, where $n = 0.04$ – the group coefficient of roughness in the Manning's formula, 0.025–0.2; h – water area depth, [m].

To describe the transport of suspended particles, we use the diffusion-convection equation, which can be written in the following form [15–17]:

$$c'_t + (uc)'_x + (vc)'_y + ((w + w_s) c)'_z = (\mu c'_x)'_x + (\mu c'_y)'_y + (\nu c'_z)'_z + F, \qquad (3)$$

where c – suspension concentration [mg/l]; w_s – speed of suspension sedimentation [m/s]; F – function describing the intensity of the distribution of suspended matter sources [mg/l · s].

On the free surface, the flow in the vertical direction is zero: $c'_z = 0$.

Near the bottom surface: $D_v c'_z = w_s c$.

There is no flow on the lateral surface $c'_n = 0$, if $(V, n) \geq 0$, and the suspension goes beyond the boundary of the computational domain $D_h c'_n = V_n c$, if $(V, n) < 0$, where V_n – normal component of the velocity vector, n – normal vector directed inside the computational domain.

The density of the aquatic environment is calculated according to the formula

$$\rho = (1 - V)\rho_0 + V\rho_v, \quad c = V\rho_v, \tag{4}$$

where V – volume fraction of the suspension; ρ_0 – density of fresh water under normal conditions; ρ_v – suspension density.

3 Method for Solving Grid Equations

To solve the grid equations obtained by approximating the problem (1)–(4) we will use the modified alternately triangular method of minimal corrections for solving a system of grid equations with a non-self-adjoint operator [18].

In the class of two-layer iterative methods, one of the most successful is the alternately triangular method, proposed by A.A. Samarsky [21]. Later A.N. Konovalov developed an adaptive version of alternately triangular method [8,22]. The proposed version of the modified alternately triangular method is described by an iterative process

$$B\frac{x^{m+1} - x^m}{\tau_{m+1}} + Ax^m = f, \quad B : H \to H. \tag{5}$$

In equation (5), m – the iteration number, $\tau_{m+1} > 0$ – an iteration parameter, B – some invertible operator.

The inversion of the operator B in (5) should be much simpler than the direct inversion of the original operator A. When constructing B we will proceed from the additive representation of the operator A_0 – the symmetric part of the operator A.

$$A_0 = R_1 + R_2, \quad R_1 = R_2^*, \tag{6}$$

where R_1, R_2 – lower and upper triangular operators.

Also here and below we will use the skew-symmetric part of the operator A

$$A_1 = \frac{A - A^*}{2}.$$

By virtue of (6) $(Ay, y) = (A_0 y, y) = 2(R_1 y, y) = 2(R_2 y, y)$. Therefore, in (6) $R_1 > 0, R_2 > 0$. Suppose that in (5)

$$B = (D + \omega R_1)D^{-1}(D + \omega R_2), \quad D = D^* > 0, \quad \omega > 0, y \in H, \tag{7}$$

where D – some operator (for example, the diagonal part of the operator A).

Since $A_0 = A_0^* > 0$, together with (6) this gives $B = B^* > 0$. Relations (5)–(7) specify the modified alternating triangular method for solving the problem, if operators are defined R_1, R_2 and methods for determining the parameters τ, ω and operator D.

The algorithm for solving the system of grid equations by the modified alternating-triangular method of the variational type will be written as [18]:

$$r^m = Ax^m - f, B(\omega_m)w^m = r^m, \tilde{\omega}_m = \sqrt{\frac{(Dw^m, w^m)}{(D^{-1}R_2w^m, R_2w^m)}},$$

$$s_m^2 = 1 - \frac{(A_0w^m, w^m)^2}{(B^{-1}A_0w^m, A_0w^m)(Bw^m, w^m)}, \, k_m^2 = \frac{(B^{-1}A_1w^m, A_1w^m)}{(B^{-1}A_0w^m, A_0w^m)}, \quad (8)$$

$$\theta_m = \frac{1 - \sqrt{\frac{s_m^2 k_m^2}{(1+k_m^2)}}}{1 + k_m^2(1 - s_m^2)}, \tau_{m+1} = \theta_m \frac{(A_0w^m, w^m)}{(B^{-1}A_0w^m, A_0w^m)},$$

$$x^{m+1} = x^m - \tau_{m+1}w^m, \omega_{m+1} = \tilde{\omega}_m,$$

where r^m – the residual vector, w^m – the correction vector, the parameter s_m describes the rate of convergence of the method, k_m describes the ratio of the norm of the skew-symmetric part of the operator to the norm of the symmetric part.

The most time consuming part of the algorithm is calculating the correction vector from the equation:

$$(D + \omega R_1)D^{-1}(D + \omega R_2)w^m = r^m.$$

The solution to this problem is reduced to the solution of two SLAEs with lower triangular and upper triangular matrices:

$$(D + \omega R_1)y^m = r^m, \quad (D + \omega R_2)w^m = Dy^m.$$

4   Parallel Implementation of the Algorithm

Within the framework of this work, a parallel algorithm that implements the formulated three-dimensional problem of hydrodynamics and substance transfer (1)–(4) on a multiprocessor computer system using the hybrid MPI/OpenMP technology has been built. To increase the efficiency of parallel calculations, the computational domain was decomposed in two spatial directions. The method of dividing rectangles into p_1 along one direction and p_2 along the other was used [12,19,20]. This decomposition method allows you to reduce the amount of transmitted data. When using decomposition in one direction, the volume of transfers is $2 \times p \times N_y \times N_z$, where p – the number of processors involved.

In the case of decomposition in two directions, the volume of transfers is $2 \times (p_1 \times N_y + p_2 \times N_x) \times N_z$, where N_x, N_y, N_z – the number of calculated nodes along the directions of the Ox, Oy, Oz respectively.

Let us describe the parallel algorithm of the alternating triangular method.

1. Calling functions that return p – the number of processes inside the communicator and m – the number of the current processor in the private group of the communicator.
2. Set the values p_1 and p_2 (conventionally p_1 – the number of processors along the Ox and p_2 – along the Oy axis).
3. Calculate the number of processors along each direction (m_1 and m_2): $m_1 = m \bmod p_1$, $\ m_1 = \lfloor m/p_1 \rfloor$.
4. Calculate N_{11}, N_{22} – numbers of initial elements; N_1, N_2 – sizes of a fragment of the computational domain along Ox and Oy axes.

$$N_{11} = \lfloor m_1 (N_x - 2)/p_1 \rfloor, \quad N_1 = \lfloor (m_1 + 1)(N_x - 2)/p_1 \rfloor - N_{11} + 2,$$
$$N_{22} = \lfloor m_2 (N_y - 2)/p_2 \rfloor, \quad N_2 = \lfloor (m_2 + 1)(N_y - 2)/p_2 \rfloor - N_{22} + 2.$$

5. Fill auxiliary arrays with zeros.
6. Begin of a loop through iterations m.
7. Calculation of the residual vector (performed using OpenMP technology) from the equation: $r^m = Ax^m - f$.
8. Solution of a SLAE with a lower triangular matrix
   (a) Receiving data from nodes with lower numbers:
      – if $(m_1 > 0)$, receiving data (all elements with index $i = 0$ are received) from processor number $p - 1$;
      – if $(m_2 > 0)$, receiving data (all elements with index $j = 0$ are received) from processor number $p - p_1$.
   (b) Calculation of vector y^m (performed using OpenMP technology) from the equation: $(D + \omega R_1)y^m = r^m$.
   (c) Sending data to nodes with highest numbers:
      – if $(m_1 < p_1 - 1)$, sending data (elements with index $i = N_1 - 2$ are sent) to processor number $p + 1$;
      – if $(m_2 < p_2 - 1)$, sending data (elements with index $j = N_2 - 2$ are sent) to processor number $p + p_1$.
9. Solution of a SLAE with an upper triangular matrix.
   (a) Receiving data from nodes with large numbers:
      – if $(m_1 < p_1 - 1)$, receiving data (all elements with index $i = N_1 - 1$ are received) from processor number $p + 1$;
      – if $(m_2 < p_2 - 1)$, receiving data (all elements with index $j = N_2 - 1$ are received) from processor number $p + p_1$.
   (b) Calculation of the correction vector w^m (performed using OpenMP technology) from the equation: $(D + \omega R_2)w^m = Dy^m$.
   (c) Sending data to nodes with lower numbers:
      – if $(m_1 > 0)$, sending data (elements with index $i = 1$ are sent) to processor number $p - 1$;
      – if $(m_2 > 0)$, sending data (elements with index $j = 1$ are sent) to processor number $p - p_1$.

10. Calculation of iterative parameters τ_{m+1}, ω_{m+1} (performed using OpenMP technology).
11. Calculating vector values x^{m+1} on the next iteration $x^{m+1} = x^m - \tau_{m+1} w^m$.
12. If the norm of the residual vector is less than the specified error, then exit the loop by iterations, otherwise return to step 6.
13. Return the values of the solution.

Numerical experiments were carried out on a cluster at the Sirius University of Science and Technology. Access was provided to a cluster with 24 computing nodes (48 processors with 12 cores each) of the Intel (R) - Xeon (R) Gold 5118 CPU 2.30 GHz family, the drive type of each computer is SSD 3.84 TB. Taking into account the limited computing power, a parallel algorithm for solving the problem (1) - (4), based on the hybrid MPI/OpenMP technology, has been developed to speed up the computation time. When using only MPI technology in the algorithm, the maximum number of parallel threads was 24. To increase the number of threads, each node generated an additional 24 threads inside itself.

Table 1 shows the results of comparing the operation of the constructed parallel algorithm based on the hybrid MPI/OpenMP technology with the operation of the algorithm using only MPI technology for parallelization.

Table 1. Results of parallel algorithms operation based on MPI technology and hybrid MPI/OpenMP technology

Number of computational nodes (p)	Computational domain decomposition ($p_1 \times p_2$)	Time, Sec.		Acceleration of parallel algorithm		
		MPI	MPI/OpenMP	MPI	OpenMP	MPI/OpenMP
1	1 × 1	38.160	4.785	1.00	7.975	7.975
2	2 × 1	19.690	2.117	1.938	9.303	18.029
3	3 × 1	13.533	1.385	2.820	9.774	27.559
4	2 × 2	10.001	1.343	3.816	7.445	28.407
	4 × 1	10.210	1.062	3.737	9.613	35.928
8	4 × 2	5.219	0.709	7.312	7.360	53.817
	8 × 1	5.370	0.675	7.107	7.961	56.572
16	4 × 4	2.987	0.696	12.776	4.289	54.800
	8 × 2	3.004	0.582	12.704	5.159	65.534
	16 × 1	3.162	0.574	12.069	5.506	66.446
20	5 × 4	2.499	0.690	15.270	3.621	55.285
	10 × 2	2.548	0.650	14.979	3.919	58.704
	20 × 1	2.682	0.644	14.227	4.167	59.286
24	6 × 4	2.241	0.637	17.028	3.516	59.872
	8 × 3	2.242	0.614	17.018	3.655	62.202
	12 × 2	2.246	0.610	16.993	3.681	62.554
	24 × 1	2.509	0.590	15.208	4.256	64.720

From the acceleration values shown in Table 1, we can see that the parallel algorithm for solving problem (1) - (4) using the MPI technology showed higher acceleration values (17 times) than the algorithm with OpenMP (9.8 times). With an increase in the number of working nodes, the efficiency of parallelization into cores decreased. Relatively low acceleration values for a system with shared memory are associated with latency in exchanges with RAM. Comparison of algorithms is given for a different number of processors with a variable decomposition of the computational domain.

In Fig. 1 shows the graphs of acceleration of the developed parallel algorithms based on MPI and hybrid technology MPI/OpenMP, depending on the number of computers involved (taking into account various options for decomposition of the computational domain). The maximum number of computers used is 24, the size of the computational grid was $1000 \times 1000 \times 60$ nodes.

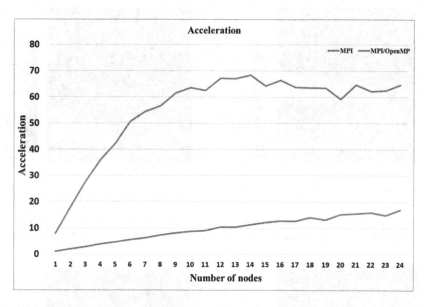

Fig. 1. Dependence of acceleration of parallel algorithms based on MPI and MPI/OpenMP technologies on the number of computers

The parallel algorithm developed on the basis of hybrid MPI/OpenMP technology, used to solve three-dimensional diffusion-convection problems, showed higher efficiency compared to the parallel algorithm based on MPI technology.

5 Results of Numerical Experiments

Let us describe the numerical implementation of a mathematical model of water movement in the estuary area in the presence of a significant density gradient of the aquatic environment on the basis of the developed software package focused on a multi-computing system. The developed software package can be used to calculate the transfer for both heavy impurities and impurities that are lighter than water, for example, such as microplastics.

The parameters of the computational domain were set as follows: length is 50 m; width is 50 m; the steps along the horizontal and vertical spatial coordinates are 0.5 m and 0.1 m, respectively; calculated interval is 5 min, time step is 0.25 s.

The initial data for modeling are: flow speed is 0.2 m/s; depth is 2 m; deposition rate is 2.042 mm/s (Stokes); fresh water density under normal conditions is 1000 kg/m^3; suspension density is 2700 kg/m^3; the volume fraction of the suspension is 1/17.

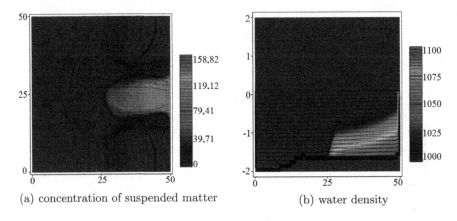

(a) concentration of suspended matter   (b) water density

Fig. 2. The movement of waters in the estuary area in the presence of a significant density gradient of the aquatic environment after 30 s from the start of calculations

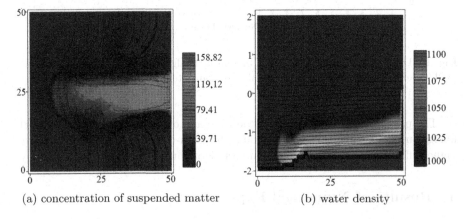

(a) concentration of suspended matter   (b) water density

Fig. 3. The movement of waters in the estuary area in the presence of a significant density gradient of the aquatic environment after 1 min from the start of calculations

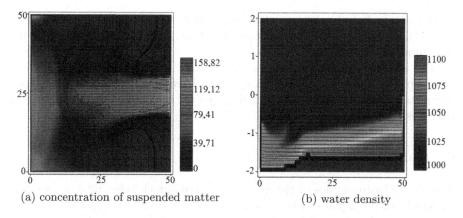

(a) concentration of suspended matter   (b) water density

Fig. 4. The movement of waters in the estuary area in the presence of a significant density gradient of the aquatic environment after 2 min from the start of calculations

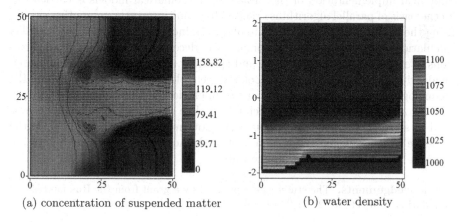

(a) concentration of suspended matter   (b) water density

Fig. 5. The movement of waters in the estuary area in the presence of a significant density gradient of the aquatic environment after 5 min from the start of calculations

Figures 2, 3, 4 and 5 show the results of modeling the process of suspension transport as a result of mixing and movement of waters in the estuary area in the presence of a significant density gradient of the aquatic environment (on the left is the average concentration of suspended matter in depth, on the right its density in the section by the plane xOz passing through the center of the computational domain ($y = 25$ m)) after 30 s, 1 min, 2 min, and 5 min after the start of calculations.

Figure 2, 3, 4 and 5 describe the movement of suspended matter in the mouth area; parts (a) of Fig. 2, 3, 4 and 5 show the change in the concentration of suspended matter in the stratified layers of the aquatic environment with changing density over time. To study the transport of suspended matter in the mouth area, a software package was developed that numerically implements the developed parallel algorithms, which made it possible to significantly reduce the calculation time, including by optimizing the decomposition process of the computational domain.

The software toolkit created on the basis of the hybrid technology made it possible to carry out computational experiments in a wide range of input parameters to simulate a complex hydrodynamic picture in the mixing zone of river fresh and sea salt waters.

6   Conclusions

A model of hydrophysics of the estuarine region, which takes into account the movement of the aquatic environment, is considered and investigated; variable density depending on salinity; complex geometry of the computational domain in the presence of a significant density gradient of the aquatic environment. The numerical implementation of the proposed mathematical models is carried out on the basis of parallel algorithms oriented to a multiprocessor computing system using the hybrid MPI/OpenMP technology. To increase the efficiency of parallel calculations, the computational domain was decomposed in two spatial directions. Comparison of running time and speeding up of parallel programs based on algorithms using hybrid MPI/OpenMP technology and algorithms using MPI technology is given. A significant increase in efficiency is shown when using parallel algorithms based on hybrid technology. The developed software package is used to solve the model problem of water movement in the estuary area in the presence of a significant density gradient of the aquatic environment due to the presence of suspended matter in the water.

Acknowledgements. The study was supported by a grant from the Russian Science Foundation (project No. 21-71-20050).

References

1. Matishov, G.G., Il'ichev, V.G.: Optimal utilization of water resources: the concept of internal prices. Doklady Earth Sci. **406**(1), 86–88 (2006)
2. Berland, M.E.: Prediction and Regulation of Air Pollution. Hydrometeoizdat, Leningrad (1985)
3. Lo, E.Y.M., Shao, S.: Simulation of near-shore solitary wave mechanics by an incompressible SPH method. Appl. Ocean Res. **24**(5), 275–286 (2002). https://doi.org/10.1016/S0141-1187(03)00002-6
4. Hejazi, K., Ghavami, A., Aslani, A.: Numerical modeling of breaking solitary wave run up in surf zone using incompressible smoothed particle hydrodinamics (ISPH). Coastal Eng. Proc. **35**, 31 (2017). https://doi.org/10.9753/icce.v35.waves.31
5. Logofet, D.O., Lesnaya, E.V.: The mathematics of Markov models: what Markov chains can really predict in forest successions. Ecol. Model. **126**, 285–298 (2000)
6. Samarskiy, A.A., Nikolaev, E.S.: Methods for Solving Grid Equations. Nauka, Moscow (1978)

7. Goloviznin, V.M., Chetverushkin, B.N.: New generation algorithms for computational fluid dynamics. Comput. Math. Math. Phys. **58**(8), 1217–1225 (2018).
   https://doi.org/10.1134/S0965542518080079
8. Konovalov, A.: The steepest descent method with an adaptive alternating-
   triangular preconditioner. Differ. Equ. **40**, 1018–1028 (2004)
9. Chetverushkin, B.N., Yakobovskiy, M.V.: Numerical algorithms and architecture
   of HPC systems. Keldysh Inst. Prepr. **52**, 12 (2018). https://doi.org/10.20948/
   prepr-2018-52
10. Milyukova, O.Y., Tishkin, V.F.: A multigrid method for a heat equation with
    discontinuous coefficients with a special choice of grids. Math. Models Comput.
    Simul. **8**(2), 118–128 (2016). https://doi.org/10.1134/S2070048216020101
11. Voevodin, V.V.: The solution of large problems in distributed computational
    media. Autom. Remote Control **68**(5), 773–786 (2007). https://doi.org/10.1134/
    S0005117907050050
12. Sukhinov, A.I., Chistyakov, A.E., Shishenya, A.V., Timofeeva, E.F.: Predictive
    modeling of coastal hydrophysical processes in multiple-processor systems based
    on explicit schemes. Math. Models Comput. Simul. **10**(5), 648–658 (2018). https://
    doi.org/10.1134/S2070048218050125
13. Gergel, V., Kozinov, E., Linev, A., Shtanyk, A.: Educational and research systems
    for evaluating the efficiency of parallel computations. In: Lecture Notes in Com-
    puter Science, vol. 10049, pp. 278–290 (2016). https://doi.org/10.1007/978-3-319-
    49956-7_22
14. Sidnev, A.A., Gergel, V.P.: Automatic selection of the fastest algorithm implemen-
    tations. Num. Methods Program. **15**(4), 579–592 (2014)
15. Sukhinov, A.I., Chistyakov, A.E., Kuznetsova, I.Y., Protsenko, E.A.: Modelling
    of suspended particles motion in channel. J. Phys. Conf. Series **1479**(1),(2020).
    https://doi.org/10.1088/1742-6596/1479/1/012082
16. Sukhinov, A.I., Chistyakov, A.E., Kuznetsova, I.Y., Protsenko, E.A., Belova, Y.V.:
    Modified upwind leapfrog difference scheme. Comput. Math. Inf. Technol. **1**(1),
    56–70 (2020). https://doi.org/10.23947/2587-8999-2020-1-1-56-70
17. Samarskii, A.A., Vabishchevich, P.N.: Numerical Methods for Solving Convection-
    diffusion Problems. URSS, Moscow (2009)
18. Sukhinov, A.I., Chistyakov, A.E.: An adaptive modified alternating triangular
    iterative method for solving difference equations with a nonselfadjoint opera-
    tor. Math. Models Comput. Simul. **4**, 398–409 (2012). https://doi.org/10.1134/
    S2070048212040084
19. Sukhinov, A.I., Chistyakov, A.E., Litvinov, V.N., Nikitina, A.V., Belova, Yu.V.,
    Filina, A.A.: Computational aspects of mathematical modeling of the shallow water
    hydrobiological processes. Num. Methods Program. **21**, 452–469 (2020). https://
    doi.org/10.26089/NumMet.v21r436
20. Sukhinov, A.I., Chistyakov, A.E., Filina, A.A., Nikitina, A.V., Litvinov, V.N.:
    Supercomputer simulation of oil spills in the Azov Sea. Bullet. South Ural State
    Univ., Series: Math. Model., Program. Comput. Softw. **12**(3), 115–129 (2019).
    https://doi.org/10.14529/mmp190310
21. Samarskii, A.A.: Difference Scheme Theory. Nauka, Moscow (2009)
22. Konovalov, A.N.: To the theory of the alternating triangular iterative method.
    Siberian Math. J. **43**(3), 552–572 (2002)

Multicomp: Software Package for Multiscale Simulations

Mikhail Akhukov[1], Daria Guseva[2], Andrey Kniznik[1],
Pavel Komarov[2,3(✉)], Vladimir Rudyak[4], Denis Shirabaykin[1],
Anton Skomorokhov[1], Sergey Trepalin[1], and Boris Potapkin[1]

[1] Kintech Lab Ltd., Moscow, Moscow, Russia
{ma.akhukov,knizhnik,wasp,antonskomorokhov,trep,
potapkin}@kintechlab.com
[2] Institute of Organoelement Compounds RAS, Moscow, Russia
guseva@polly.phys.msu.ru
[3] Tver State University, Tver, Russia
komarov.pv@tversu.ru
[4] Lomonosov Moscow State University, Moscow, Russia
rudyak@polly.phys.msu.ru

Abstract. Here, we present a computational package for collaborative distributed design of new nanocomposite materials using multi-level modeling technology by one user and a group of engineers or researchers. It contains a high-level set of integrated, versatile tools to simulate and analyze elastomeric nanocomposites, consisting of cross-linked linear/branched copolymers containing different discrete fillers. The package can also be used to study the formation and properties of nanocomposite interpenetrating polymer networks and microphase-separated organic-inorganic hybrid materials.

Keywords: Multiscale simulations · Nanotechnology · Software package · Computer design · Polymer nanocomposites

1 Introduction

Nanotechnology is an emerging field of science and technology. This concept hides a set of science-intensive technologies to obtain nanomaterials by controlling matter at the atomic and molecular levels. Currently, nanotechnology development is the solution to problems associated with improving traditional materials such as polymers. One possible way is to introduce nanosized fillers in the form of inorganic nanoparticles (NPs) into polymers, i.e., objects having at least one direction the size lying in the nanometer range. Polymer nanocomposites (PNCs) obtained in this way are widely used in industry due to the possibility of fine adjustment of mechanical, electrical and optical, and other properties [1] of traditional polymers. In this case, as a rule, the mass fraction of the added filler reaches small values of (1–3% [2]), which makes PNCs relatively light compared to metals and ceramics.

It is challenging to experimentally study polymer nanocomposites' structures and control their synthesis parameters [3]. Therefore, until now, the optimal way to obtain

© Springer Nature Switzerland AG 2021
V. Voevodin and S. Sobolev (Eds.): RuSCDays 2021, CCIS 1510, pp. 174–185, 2021.
https://doi.org/10.1007/978-3-030-92864-3_14

PNCs has been selected in many respects empirically. In addition, the experimental study of PNCs can be time-consuming and costly since PNCs often have a complex composition and their preparation process can be multi-stage and have high sensitivity to various parameters. Therefore, like in any innovation, nanotechnologies' development requires the theoretical elaboration of ideas, methods, and models. This is impossible without computer simulation and design.

Currently, there are several levels of computer modeling. The most rigorous level is provided by the methods of quantum mechanics (QM). However, it can be used to study systems of up to several thousand atoms at time intervals up to 10–100 ps. Simultaneously, these methods do not require parameterization, which can be regarded as an essential advantage. The next most accurate modeling level includes classical methods of molecular mechanics, such as atomistic molecular dynamics (MD) and Monte Carlo (MC). These methods can be viewed as microscopic theories. At present, they can be used to study the properties of systems containing up to a million atoms at time intervals of the order of a microsecond and to predict the thermophysical, mechanical, and other properties of PNCs with sufficiently high accuracy. Coarse-grained models based on the Monte Carlo method, Langevin, Brownian, and Dissipative Particle Dynamics (DPD) are used to model molecular systems at intermediate spatial scales (20–100 nm) and time intervals (1–1000 μs). This can be achieved by neglecting the precise detailing of the chemical structure through collective variables. The so-called "coarse-grained" valence force fields (VFF) variants describe interactions between mesoparticles. They can be reconstructed based on statistical processing of the results obtained in atomistic simulations or by calculating the energy characteristics of the interaction of groups of atoms by QM methods. Coarse-grained models can be used to study relatively slow structure formation processes in polymer systems, which are difficult to study within MD modeling. Macroscopic scale systems are modeled using the methods of continuum mechanics, hydrodynamics, and finite elements (FEM). In particular, calculations using continuous medium models are based on generalizing atomistic and mesoscopic modeling data in equations of state, mechanical characteristics, kinetic constitutive relations for describing plasticity and fracture.

The methods of molecular mechanics, mesoscale modeling, and finite elements require preliminary parameterization of both the force constants that determine the interaction of the structural elements of the used models and information on the structure of the filler's distribution in the bulk of the material. This information can be taken from the results of experimental studies. However, in the case of new materials, this is not always possible. The difficulties of computer model parameterization can be solved within the framework of complex computational schemes based on the concept of multiscale modeling (MM) [4–12].

MM is currently the most consistent approach to study practically any molecular system based on its chemical structure, quantitative ratio of components, and physical conditions. In essence, it means identifying the critical degrees of freedom that determine the system's properties under study at different spatial and temporal scales. At the same time, each group of variables should be described by its modeling method. Moving from one scale level to another one implies the sequential parameterization of the involved modeling levels. For example, QM calculations make it possible to determine the interaction of individual atoms and different groups of atoms, which is essential for MD simulation. Within the framework of molecular mechanics methods, it is possible to parameterize the interaction of mesoscale particles and calculate the properties of the polymer matrix, nanoparticles, and the polymer/NP interface. The latter is essential for the parameterization of the finite element method.

On the other hand, the mesoscale methods allow studying the distribution of NPs in a polymer matrix. It is also crucial for the parameterization of the model within the framework of the finite element method. Thus, the MM-scheme represents a sequence of models interconnected through the exchange of information, implementing a hierarchical consideration of the relationship "structure" → "property".

At the moment, there are several software packages designed for atomistic and multi-level modeling of material properties, including PNC. Thus, Materials Design develops an integrated environment MedeA [13] for atomistic modeling of material properties and offers a set of modules for generating structures of polymer matrices. BIOVIA offers a more comprehensive solution, the software package Materials Studio [14], for atomistic and mesoscopic modeling of materials properties, including polymers. However, these products do not provide multi-level integration to the macroscale since they have no models for calculating polymers and composites' properties. On the other hand, specialized software packages for modeling composites' properties at the macro level, such as the DIGIMAT package from MSC Software [15] or the Ultasim package from BASF [16], do not consider the atomistic structures of PNC. Now, there is no such problem-oriented domestic software on the Russian market.

During the last decade, our challenge was to develop a simulation methodology that allows the generation of polymer matrices with embedded nanoparticles, emphasizing the dispersion state of the nanoparticles and predicting the basic properties of the composite material under study. This article presents a description of our hierarchical multiscale simulation package, which we named Multicomp. It is based on well-proven modeling techniques, molecular dynamics, reactive dissipative particle dynamics, and finite element methods [17–21] and our developments [22–27]. Multicomp provides a high-level set of versatile integrated tools to design, simulate and predict the morphology, thermal, mechanical, and other nanoparticle-filled polymers properties. It demonstrates that nanocomposites can be simulated at different spatial resolution levels by transferring the data between the resolution levels in the chain "atomistic simulations ⟷ mesoscopic simulations → finite element method".

2 Multicomp Package

In our integrated Multicomp package, we have combined several computational strategies, including mapping/reverse mapping of coarse-grained and atomistic structures, mesoscale chemistry for creating copolymers with desired functionalities, topological analysis of polymer network, fully atomistic and finite element methods.

The Multicomp package architecture consists of client and server parts. The client part (graphical shell) of Multicomp can be installed on personal workstations running Windows and Linux operating systems. The functionality of the graphical shell is based on the Scientific Workflow concept. It includes a set of interconnected modules, which allows the creation of flexible modeling schemes. Each module has input and output ports for different types of automated data exchange with other modules. The output port of one module can be connected to another module's input port, provided that the data types in the ports are matched (see Fig. 1). This mechanism makes available high flexibility of calculation scenarios and reuses the results of the module calculations. The obtained results in the calculation script become available when the module is selected in Workflow.

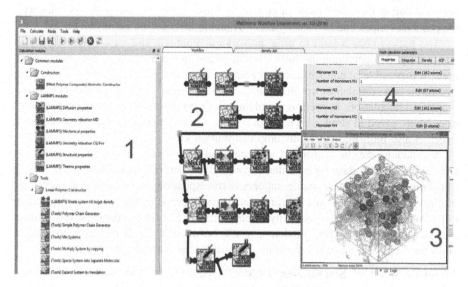

Fig. 1. The figure shows an example of a user's project for constructing a model of a photoactive layer for plastic solar cells on the base of P3HT and $PC_{61}BM$. The user can specify the sequence of starting the computational modules represented as tiles (1), determine the data transfer between the modules connected by the arrows (2), select the number of processors, and execute them all together or separately. Each module allows calling up graphical (3) and text editors to enter and change module parameters (4), control the progress of calculations, import/export calculation results, view calculation results, and log files.

The server (calculation) part of the package can be installed (and automatically configured) on the same machine as the client. In addition, it is possible to install the server part on remote Linux workstations or supercomputer systems with different architectures to perform remote calculations. The run manager, which controls the server-side operation, allows functional parallelism to calculate several modules (where possible) simultaneously. The server part of the package supports different job scheduling systems for high-performance systems, such as Slurm and PBS. User experience design of working with high-performance servers is implemented without any low-level interactions, and all routines concerning data exchange with remote computers are entirely automated. Supercomputer calculations allow achieving high parallelism within calculations in one computational module. It makes studying large systems and performing calculations over long simulation times (using MPI or hybrid MPI/OpenMP parallelization). For different modules in a single calculation procedure, different calculation servers may be used simultaneously.

The main window of the graphical user interface is divided horizontally into three parts (see Fig. 1). In the left part, in the tree structure, the available computational modules are presented. In the central part, there is a constructor of the simulation script from these modules. It is possible to set the operational parameters for the module selected from the procedure in the upper-right part. Upon completing the calculations, the results appear in the bottom part (including the final structure and the results obtained during the calculation, in graphic and text form). In case of errors, files with the program output and run logs present available information about the errors.

The package has a built-in program to view atomistic and mesoscopic structures (for input ports containing atomistic structures and not connected to any other output ports, it is possible to edit structures in addition to viewing). It is also possible to view structures and simulation results (surface and volume mesh obtained before the properties calculation, as well as a volume mesh with a solution after the properties calculation, saved in similar VTK format) at the macro level in the Paraview program, which is also built into the Multicomp distribution kit.

Simulations can be performed at three levels: *atomistic, mesoscale, macroscale*, and module ports' data types differ accordingly. There are additional ports for the calculation results (matrix with components corresponding to the diffusion coefficient in different directions; elastic tensor; matrix with thermal conductivity coefficients in different directions; scalar viscosity coefficient). The software package has built-in mechanisms for transferring modeling results between levels. It makes it possible to build hierarchical multi-level modeling procedures, as is shown in Fig. 1.

Atomistic Level of Simulations. LAMMPS package is built into the Multicomp software package to simulate PNCs at the atomistic level [17]. The user can parameterize interactions using four options for the VFF: PCFF [28], CVFF [29], COMPASS [30], and ClayFF [20]. The latter field is included to describe fillers in the form of layered silicates. Multicomp has built-in modules that perform typing procedures for atomistic systems in an automated mode. It is possible to build systems consisting of their structures, parameterized by different force fields. The methods of atomistic modeling in various thermodynamic ensembles (including isotropic and anisotropic isobaric-isothermal (NPT), canonical ensemble (NVT), and microcanonical (NVE) can be used.

In atomistic simulations, a great difficulty arises at constructing molecular structures, building initial configurations of the system, and bringing them to an equilibrium state. The Multicomp package includes an advanced toolkit for building polymers: a module for building simple polymer molecules and constructing block copolymer chains with complex structure and various utility modules for working with polymer systems.

For convenient preparation of nanocomposites, the Multicomp package includes three special constructors. They provide rich opportunities to generate composite structures and matrices with a complex composition and morphology. They are also a constructor of cross-linked polymer matrices and composites based on them, a constructor of non-crosslinked polymer matrices and composites based on them, as well as a constructor of layered structures, which can correspondingly use the results of the work of the first two constructors in addition to elementary atomistic structures for input data. The molecular systems prepared can be brought to an equilibrium state using modules running calculations using the MC and MD methods.

The set of modules included in the Multicomp package, which are designed to evaluate physical properties at the atomistic level, includes the modules for calculating the diffusion coefficient, mechanical properties, structural properties (radial distribution function, XRD, SAED, porosity, trajectories during simulation), thermal conductivity coefficient and viscosity.

Mesoscale Level of Simulations. The LAMMPS package and our developments of a reactive version of dissipative particle dynamics [27] are used to simulate PNCs at the mesoscale level. Preparation of initial configurations for mesoscale modeling is performed using a special constructor. The construction process is implemented as follows. In the beginning, a single filler particle is generated in the form of a generalized ellipsoid. The entire filler phase is built based on the particle by randomly arranging a number of copies of the resulting filler particle in a cell (translation and rotation) with a given volume concentration.

Macroscale Level of Simulations. At this modeling level, the effective material properties are calculated using the finite element method. The grid for solving the system of equations is built based on mesoscale modeling of the filler distribution in the polymer matrix using our implementation of the universal algorithm for constructing the Marching Cubes surface [19], which serves as the basis for constructing a three-dimensional grid using TetGen [21]. The resulting meshes (both before and after solving the system) are saved in the VTK format to be viewed in the Paraview program (viewing is possible from the Multicomp graphical shell since Paraview is included in the distribution kit). Calculations are performed by code based on the libMesh library [31].

The package includes modules for uploading and saving atomistic and mesoscopic structures obtained during the calculations. Import and export of atomistic, meso- and macrostructures are also possible.

3   Examples of Simulations Performed in Multicomp and Productivity Evaluation

This section presents three examples of calculations performed in the Multicomp package for solving problems of multi-level modeling of the structure and physical properties of polymer matrices and nanocomposites based on them. The procedures are shown, including different levels of modeling, and the possibilities of transferring data between the levels are demonstrated.

Highly Cross-Linked Polymer. To study the dependence of the properties of the cross-linked polymer matrix on the degree of cross-linking, we built material samples based on the epoxy monomer 3,4-epoxy cyclohexyl methyl (ECC) and the cross-linking agent (hardener) hexahydrophthalic anhydride (MHHPA). We change the duration of the stage of simulating chemical reactions to prepare samples with different levels of conversions. As a result, the obtained atomistic structures of cross-linked matrices differed in the degree of cross-linking.

For the prepared structures, the elastic moduli were obtained using the MD method. The results show that the elastic modulus of the epoxy matrix depends on the degree of matrix cross-linking. For a degree of cross-linking of 0.593, the elastic modulus was 5.10 GPa. For a degree of cross-linking of 0.754, the elastic modulus was 5.63 GPa. Thus, with a change in the degree of cross-linking from 0.593 to 0.754, an increase in the Young modulus by 10% was observed. These results are in agreement with the data presented in the literature [32].

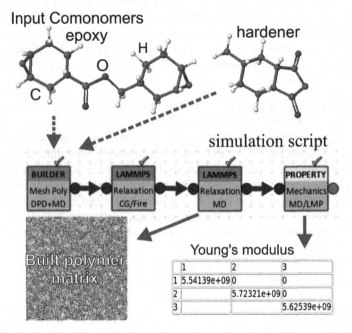

Fig. 2. An example of evaluation of mechanical properties of a high cross-linked matrix on the base3,4-epoxy cyclohexyl methyl (epoxy) and hexahydrophthalic anhydride (hardener).

Figure 2 shows the calculation script used to obtain the described results. The calculation scenario consists of four modules. The first module builds a cross-linked polymer matrix in the course of a multi-level procedure. The second and third modules provide the relaxation of the obtained atomistic structure using the conjugate gradient and MD simulations. Two relaxation stages make it possible to perform a quick rough relaxed structure to perform a further productive run. The fourth module is used to evaluate the mechanical properties.

Modeling of Layered Silicates. An essential problem in the preparation of PNCs based on polyamide-6/montmorillonite is to adjust the interaction of the components to ensure the most effective separation of the filler. For this purpose, organo-modification of montmorillonite, i.e., intercalation of organic ions, can be used. Because of electrostatic interactions, the ions are attracted to the charged surface of the filler. Also, due to a long organic tail, they have negative energy of interaction with the polymer.

As a result of modeling at the atomistic level using molecular dynamics, it was shown that the polymer matrix structure near the filler particles changes significantly. Namely, a layered polymer chain organization is observed, which is confirmed by analyzing the density and orientation parameters. A significant decrease in the mobility of polymer chains was noted near the clay surface. The filled matrix's elastic modulus is twice higher the elastic modulus of the unfilled polymer. Such results can be due to polymer chains' ordering on the clay surface and the atomistic mobility decrease. We published the described results in more detail in the paper [24].

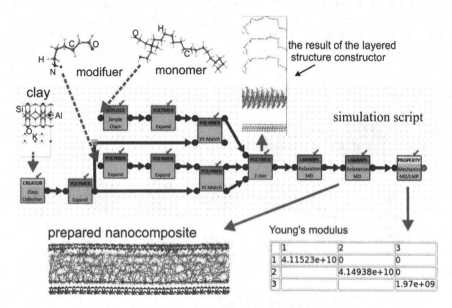

Fig. 3. An example of evaluation of mechanical properties of nanocomposite on base layered silicate.

To model nanocomposites based on layered silicates, the Multicomp package includes a layered structure designer for building periodic systems that can also include individual molecules. The script to build a layered structure (shown in Fig. 3) consists of six modules. The first module is a library of layered silicates (structures were created following the original work [20] and can be typed using the ClayFF parameterization, from which the atomistic structure of the desired clay was selected). Then the clay is multiplied (by replicating the cell in planar directions using the replication module), and cells containing the polymer and the modifier are multiplied in parallel. The resulting structure is highly nonequilibrium and requires prolonged relaxation since the polymer chains' mobility and the modifier is significantly reduced due to the filler's interaction. The layered structures designer module performs the final stage of aligning structures with the exact planar dimensions. The resulting layered structure was relaxed, and then its mechanical properties were calculated.

Macro-Level Simulations. For PNCs containing many filler particles, an important property is an elastic modulus, which can be calculated using the FEM. It is a characteristic averaged over the orientation and arrangement of filler particles, i.e., it is a macroscopic characteristic of a material.

In the example presented (see Fig. 4), for a system with an equilibrium filler distribution obtained using DPD simulation (similar to the previously presented example with a filler distribution), a volume mesh was built to calculate the effective mechanical properties using FEM. This example shows that the macroscopic mechanical properties depend on the distribution of the filler in the polymer matrix. For a uniform distribution of spherical filler particles (with an elastic modulus of 100 GPa) in the polymer matrix (with an elastic modulus of 1 GPa), the elastic modulus is 4.2 GPa, in the case of percolation in the direction x, the elastic modulus in the corresponding direction is 11 GPa.

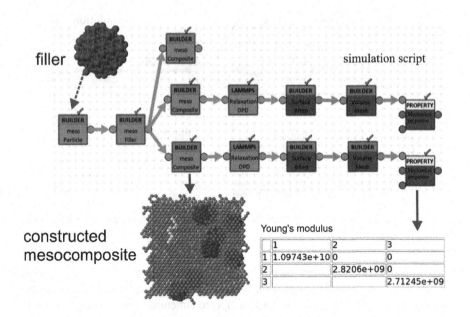

Fig. 4. An example of calculating macroscopic properties.

Performance Evaluations. Based on the simulation described above, we evaluated a normalized performance of the Multicomp. For molecular dynamics simulations, normalized performance is equal to 20000 (step × atom)/(core × second). It means that the simulation of length 1 million steps (which corresponds to 1 ns when using time step equal to 1 femtosecond) for the structure having 100000 atoms takes less than one day on 100 cores, and due to linear scalability of molecular dynamics performance, calculation times or computational resources for larger systems studying can be estimated. For dissipative particle dynamics simulation, normalized performance is 155000 (step $\times$ bead)/(core $\times$ second), which is considerably higher than the molecular dynamics because of the absence of long-range interactions in the dissipative particle dynamics method. FEM calculations of the systems containing 100000 elements (in Multicomp, it is a typical size of the meshes derived from the conversion of structures occurring during dissipative particle dynamics simulation) took times of the order of minutes.

4 Summary

During the last decade, our challenge was to develop a simulation methodology that allows the generation of polymer matrices with embedded nanoparticles, emphasizing the nanoparticles' dispersion state and predicting the basic properties of the composite material under study. To that end, we have combined several computational strategies, including methods for mapping/reverse mapping of coarse-grained and atomistic structures, mesoscale chemistry for creating copolymers with desired functionalities, topological analysis of polymer network, and fully atomistic models and methods.

Our multiscale approach allows the simulation of polymerization processes for, in principle, arbitrary monomers. In the course of chemical reactions, it is possible to incorporate various types of unmodified and surface-functionalized nanofillers, such as single-wall and multi-wall nanotubes, graphite, graphene, mica, clays, carbon black, amorphous, and crystalline silica. All these developments constitute a basis for our multiscale simulation strategy.

The main methodology used in Multicomp is based on the fact that nanomaterials have a hierarchical structure, i.e., the lower level structure is a part of the most complicated structure of a higher level. The direct simulations for considerable time and space scales (which are impossible with current computer resources) are replaced by simulations on each scale level with the end-to-end transfer of the calculation results (structure and properties) from the structure's bottom scale to a higher level. The significant advantage of Multicomp is the ability to generate different structures of nanocomposites and simulate them starting from chemical formulas and the composition of a material. The previous level results are used as input parameters at each subsequent level, and the simulation uses physical models and methods specifically designed for the corresponding space and time scales. All parameters are automatically transferred between simulation levels, which is also an essential feature of Multicomp because it is not implemented in other packages and usually requires direct user involvement. The functionality of the Multicomp package allows the creation of flexible calculation scenarios using high-performance computing resources.

Scientists from different areas, such as academic researchers and industrial developers, can use Multicomp. It provides the technical ability to simulate the filled polymer systems containing up to several millions of atoms using fully atomistic molecular dynamics to simulate coarse-grained nanocomposite models on length scales up to 10 μm on time scales up to 100 μs.

An essential advantage of the Multicomp package is calculating the macroscopic properties of polymeric materials. The construction begins at the atomistic level and ends at the macroscopic level. The package enables predictive calculations of the properties of polymer matrix nanocomposites based on multi-level simulations, including the determination of the composite structure, the distribution of the filler in the matrix, and the determination of the effective macroscopic properties of the entire composite. This can be used to build full-scale virtual prototyping of systems covering the whole design process of new materials.

Multicomp can also be used both for the practical development of new materials and for teaching students computational materials science methods since it has a simple interface and allows automation of engineering work.

In addition, it should be pointed that the Multicomp package is an open platform that implements the Scientific Workflow concept and allows users to create their calculation scenarios and add new calculation modules without developers' participation.

Acknowledgments. This work was supported by the Russian Foundation for Basic Research (project 19-53-52004) and was carried out using high-performance computing resources of the Federal center for collective usage at NRC "Kurchatov Institute" (http://computing.kiae.ru/). P.K. and D.G. also acknowledge access to electronic scientific resources was provided by INEOS RAS with the support from the Ministry of Science and Higher Education of the Russian Federation.

References

1. Fedullo, N., et al.: Polymer-based nanocomposites: overview, applications and perspectives. Prog. Org. Coat. **58**(2–3), 87–95 (2007)
2. Wang, Y., et al.: Identifying interphase properties in polymer nanocomposites using adaptive optimization. Compos. Sci. Technol. **162**, 146–155 (2018)
3. Zeng, Q.H., Yu, A.B., Lu, G.Q.: Multiscale modeling and simulation of polymer nanocomposites. Prog. Polym. Sci. **33**(2), 191–269 (2008)
4. Zhong, Y., Godwin, P., Jin, Y., Xiao, H.: Biodegradable polymers and green-based antimicrobial packaging materials: a mini-review. Adv. Ind. Eng. Poly. Res. **3**(1), 27–35 (2020)
5. Wu, C., Xu, W.: Atomistic molecular modelling of cross-linked epoxy resin. Polymer **47**(16), 6004–6009 (2006)
6. Li, C., Strachan, A.: Molecular dynamics predictions of thermal and mechanical properties of thermoset polymer EPON862/DETDA. Polymer **52**(13), 2920–2928 (2011)
7. Abbott, L.J., Colina, C.M.: Atomistic structure generation and gas adsorption simulations of microporous polymer networks. Macromolecules **44**(11), 4511–4519 (2011)
8. Nouri, N., Ziaei-Rad, S.: A molecular dynamics investigation on mechanical properties of cross-linked polymer networks. Macromolecules **44**(13), 5481–5489 (2011)
9. Shenogina, N.B., et al.: Molecular modeling approach to prediction of thermo-mechanical behavior of thermoset polymer networks. Macromolecules **45**(12), 5307–5315 (2012)
10. Khare, K.S., Khabaz, F., Khare, R.: Effect of carbon nanotube functionalization on mechanical and thermal properties of cross-linked epoxy–carbon nanotube nanocomposites: role of strengthening the interfacial interactions. ACS Appl. Mater. Interfaces **6**(9), 6098–6110 (2014)

11. Masoumi, S., Arab, B., Valipour, H.: A study of thermo-mechanical properties of the cross-linked epoxy: an atomistic simulation. Polymer **70**, 351–360 (2015)
12. Hadden, C.M., et al.: Mechanical properties of graphene nanoplatelet/carbon fiber/epoxy hybrid composites: multiscale modeling and experiments. Carbon **95**, 100–112 (2015)
13. Materials Exploration and Design Analysis, Materials Design, Inc., https://www.koreascience.or.kr. Accessed 12 Apr 2021
14. BIOVIA Materials Studio. https://www.3ds.com/products-services/biovia/products/. Accessed 12 Apr 2021
15. DIGIMAT package from MSC Software. https://www.dynamore.de. Accessed 12 Apr 2021
16. Ultasim package from BASF. https://plastics-rubber.basf.com/global/en/performance_polymers/services/service_ultrasim.html. Accessed 12 Apr 2021
17. Plimpton, S.: Fast parallel algorithms for short-range molecular dynamics. J. Comput. Phys. **117**(1), 1–19 (1995)
18. Groot, R.D., Warren, P.B.: Dissipative particle dynamics: bridging the gap between atomistic and mesoscopic simulation. J. Chem. Phys. **107**(11), 4423–4435 (1997)
19. Lorensen, W.E., Cline, H.E.: Marching cubes: a high resolution 3D surface construction algorithm. ACM Siggraph Comput. Graph. **21**(4), 163–169 (1987)
20. Cygan, R.T., Liang, J.J., Kalinichev, A.G.: Molecular models of hydroxide, oxyhydroxide, and clay phases and the development of a general force field. J. Phys. Chem. B **108**(4), 1255–1266 (2004)
21. Si, H.: TetGen, a delaunay-based quality tetrahedral mesh generator. ACM Trans. Math. Softw. (TOMS). **41**(2), 1–36 (2015)
22. Komarov, P.V., Chiu, Y.-T., Chen, S.-M., Khalatur, P.G., Reineker, P.: Highly cross-linked epoxy resins: an atomistic molecular dynamics simulation combined with a mapping/reverse mapping procedure. Macromolecules **40**(22), 8104–8113 (2007)
23. Gavrilov, A.A., Komarov, P.V., Khalatur, P.G.: Thermal properties and topology of epoxy networks: a multiscale simulation methodology. Macromolecules **48**(1), 206–212 (2015)
24. Skomorokhov, A.S., Knizhnik, A.A., Potapkin, B.V.: Molecular dynamics study of ternary montmorillonite–MT2EtOH–Polyamide-6 nanocomposite: structural, dynamical, and mechanical properties of the interfacial region. J. Phys. Chem. B **123**(12), 2710–2718 (2019)
25. Komarov, P.V., Guseva, D.V., Rudyak, V., Chertovich, A.V.: Multiscale simulations approach: crosslinked polymer matrices. Supercomput. Front. Innovat. **5**(3), 55–59 (2018)
26. Komarov, P.V., Guseva, D.V., Khalatur, P.G.: Silicone-urea copolymer as a basis for self-organized multiphase nanomaterials. Polymer **143**, 200–211 (2018)
27. DPD_chem, a software package for simulation of polymers and liquids using dissipative particle dynamics. https://www.researchgate.net/project/DPDChem-Software. Accessed May 2021
28. Sun, H., et al.: An ab initio CFF93 all-atom force field for polycarbonates. J. Am. Chem. Soc. **116**(7), 2978–2987 (1994)
29. Dauber-Osguthorpe, P., Roberts, V.A., Osguthorpe, D.J., Wolff, J., Genest, M., Hagler, A.T.: Structure and energetics of ligand binding to proteins: Escherichia coli dihydrofolate reductase-trimethoprim, a drug-receptor system. Prot. Struct. Funct. Genet. **4**(1), 31–47 (1988)
30. Sun, H.: COMPASS: an ab initio force-field optimized for condensed-phase applications overview with details on alkane and benzene compounds. J. Phys. Chem. B **102**(38), 7338–7364 (1998)
31. Kirk, B.S., et al.: libMesh: a C++ library for parallel adaptive mesh refinement/coarsening simulations. Eng. Comput. **22**(3–4), 237–254 (2006)
32. Li, C., Strachan, A.: Molecular scale simulations on thermoset polymers: a review. J. Polym. Sci., Part B: Polym. Phys. **53**(2), 103–122 (2015)

Parallel Algorithm for Calculating the Radius of Stability in Multicriteria Optimization Conditions for Catalytic Reforming of Gasoline

Kamila Koledina[1,2]([✉]) [iD], Sergey Koledin[2] [iD],
and Irek Gubaydullin[1,2] [iD]

[1] Institute of Petrochemistry and Catalysis of RAS, Ufa, Russia
[2] Ufa State Petroleum Technological University, Ufa, Russia

Abstract. In the work the problem of multicriteria optimization for reaction conditions of the catalytic reforming of gasoline was solved based on a kinetic model. The criteria of the process optimality are considered, such as minimization of the aromatic hydrocarbons content in the final reformate in accordance with environmental requirements and; maximizing the octane number of the reformate. The problem of analyzing the stability of the Pareto set is formulated. A parallel algorithm for calculating the radius of stability for the solution of the problem of multicriteria optimization with the decomposition of the Pareto set into subsets according to the number of processors is developed. The radius of stability of the optimum temperature values at the reactor inlet was calculated for the catalytic reforming of gasoline. Evaluation of the efficiency of parallel program execution is carried out.

Keywords: Multicriteria optimization · Catalytic reforming of gasoline · Radius of stability · Parallel algorithm for calculating the stability radius

1 Introduction

In the study of chemical kinetics, it is necessary to consider the factors that affect the solution accuracy such as inaccuracy of initial data, inadequacy of models of real processes, error of numerical methods, rounding errors, etc. [1–3]. The problem of chemical reaction conditions optimization is based on a kinetic model. It is impossible to correctly formulate and correctly solve an arbitrary optimization problem without examining it for stability. Complex multistage chemical processes require the determination of the permissible ranges of parameter values that ensure stability of the calculated solution with an acceptable error.

Papers [4, 5] are devoted to assessing the stability of optimal solutions in optimization problems. Stochastic stability which is based on Lyapunov stability was studied. Extreme level of initial perturbation data, under which the solution is Pareto optimal, is possible [6].

In [1], the general formulation and solution of the stability problem for multicriteria trajectory problems is investigated. The type of stability in the problem of independent perturbations in the input data, for which new effective solutions do not appear, is

© Springer Nature Switzerland AG 2021
V. Voevodin and S. Sobolev (Eds.): RuSCDays 2021, CCIS 1510, pp. 186–197, 2021.
https://doi.org/10.1007/978-3-030-92864-3_15

investigated and also formula for calculating the radius of stability of the problem is determined, necessary and sufficient conditions for stability are indicated [1]. For problems of chemical kinetics, it is necessary to determine the radius of stability for each parameter in order to possibly change the calculated values with an area of a given error while analyzing the stability of multicriteria optimization (MCO). A solution to the problem of multicriteria optimization is the Pareto-set of unimprovable solutions with a sufficiently large power to determine the smoothest solution possible. That is, solutions are determined with no discontinuity and the presence of the maximum number of points. Determining the radius of stability requires solving direct kinetic problems for each solution from the entire Pareto set. Mathematical models of complex, especially industrial processes, have a large dimension and are computationally complex. It is relevant to use parallel algorithms to solve the problem of analyzing the stability of the Pareto set.

The industrial process of catalytic reforming of gasoline is the when analyzing the stability of multicriteria optimization (MCO). The main problems of the catalytic reforming of gasoline are restrictions on the content of benzene and the amount of aromatic hydrocarbons in the final reformate. As a result, a restriction is imposed on the process product in terms of the content of these components. However, the main purpose of the catalytic reforming process is to increase the octane number (ON) of gasoline. Therefore, along with environmental criteria, the octane number of the mixture is the necessary criterion, which value depends on the composition of the product [7]. Therefore, it is relevant to solve the problem of multicriteria optimization of the process conditions.

In this paper, the application of methods for analyzing the stability of multicriteria optimization problems for research industrial catalytic reforming of gasoline with parallelization calculations will be shown.

2 Multicriteria Optimization in Catalytic Reforming of Gasoline Based on a Kinetic Model

The reactor unit of a catalytic reforming process consists of three adiabatic reactors, each of which is supplied with mixture which is heated to the desired temperature. The variable parameters are operating conditions: temperatures at the inlet to the reactor T_j, $j = 1, 2, 3$. Vector variable parameters $X = (x_1, x_2, x_3)$, where $x_1 = T_1$; $x_2 = T_2$; $x_3 = T_3$.

The complex industrial process of catalytic reforming of gasoline is characterized by the following optimality criteria [8]:

1) The main criterion of optimality for the catalytic reforming of gasoline is an increase in the octane number (ON_i) of the reformate. In the calculations, octane number additivity of the mixture components is allowed. Then

$$f_1(X) = \sum_{i=1}^{I} y_i(T_1, T_2, T_3) \cdot ON_i \rightarrow \max, \tag{1}$$

where ON_i – octane number of the i-th component according to the research method, y_i – group concentration of catalytic reforming of gasoline components.

2) Increasing the octane number of gasoline in reforming is achieved due to the complete conversion of naphthenic (cyclic) hydrocarbons into arenes (aromatic hydrocarbons) with a high octane number, and also due to the partial conversion of paraffins into naphthenic hydrocarbons, which in turn are converted into arenes. However, according to environmental requirements in commercial gasoline (Technical Regulation № 609 «On requirements to emissions of motor vehicles manufactured in circulation in the territory of the Russian Federation, harmful (polluting) substances», from January 1, 2016) the content of aromatic hydrocarbons and benzene in particular is limited to 35 and 1% vol. respectively. Therefore, it is necessary to set the criteria for the optimality of the benzene proportion (A_6) and the amount of aromatic hydrocarbons (A_i) in the reformate. Environmental restrictions apply to commercial gasoline and not directly to reformate. But they determine the proportion of reformate in the composition of commercial gasoline. Therefore, for catalytic reforming, this criterion value should be kept to a minimum.

$$f_2(X) = \sum_{i=6}^{11} y_{A_i}(T_1, T_2, T_3) \rightarrow \min, \qquad (2)$$

$$f_3(X) = y_{A_6}(T_1, T_2, T_3) \rightarrow \min. \qquad (3)$$

A decrease content of aromatic hydrocarbons and benzene in the composition in the reformate will entail a decrease in the octane number. Then, the optimality criteria (1) and (2), (3) are contradictory and can be studied in the MCO problem.

3) The criterion for the optimality of the catalytic reforming of gasoline is the yield of the target product – reformate. It is the product of the process minus the cracking gases. Thus, the optimality criterion is:

$$f_4(X) = 1 - \sum_{i=1}^{5} y_i(T_1, T_2, T_3) - \Delta y_{H_2}(T_1, T_2, T_3) \rightarrow \max, \qquad (4)$$

where Δy_{H_2} – change the proportion of hydrogen in the product. Shares can be: mass, molar, volumetric.

Based on the above optimality criteria, variable parameters and a kinetic model, the formulation of the MCO problem of conditions for catalytic reforming of gasoline based on the kinetic model is [9]:

- Vector variable parameters $X = (x_1, x_2, x_3) = (T_1, T_2, T_3)$. Where T_1, T_2, T_3 – the inlet temperature of the first, second and third reactor, respectively.
- Vector function optimality criteria $F(X) = (f_1(X), f_2(X), f_3(X), f_4(X))$. As optimality criteria for catalytic reforming considered: f_1 – RON (research octane number) (1), f_2 - content of total aromatic hydrocarbons (2), f_3 - benzene content (3), f_4 - target product reformate yield (4).

– $F(X)$ with values in target space $\{F\} = R^{(F)} = R^4$ defined in the area $D_X \subset \{X\} = R^{|X|} = R^3$: $T_1 \in [T_1^-; T_1^+]$, $T_2 \in [T_2^-; T_2^+]$, $T_3 \in [T_3^-; T_3^+]$.

Then it is necessary to maximize the optimality criteria in the D_X domain.

The mathematical model of catalytic reforming is a system of ordinary nonlinear differential equations with initial data [10].

$$\frac{dy_i}{d\tau} = \sum_{j=1}^{J} v_{ij}(k_j^0 \exp(-\frac{E_j^+}{RT}) \cdot \prod_{i=1}^{I} (\frac{y_i}{Q})^{|\alpha_{ij}|} - k_{-j} \cdot \prod_{i=1}^{I} (\frac{y_i}{Q})^{\beta_{ij}}); \tag{5}$$

$$\frac{dT}{d\tau} = -\frac{\sum_{i=1}^{I} \frac{dy_i}{d\tau} \cdot \Delta H_i(T)}{\sum_{i=1}^{I} y_i \cdot C_{pi}(T)}; \tag{6}$$

$$\frac{dQ}{d\tau} = \sum_{i=1}^{I} \frac{dy_i}{d\tau}; \tag{7}$$

$$\tau \in [0, \tau_1] \cup [\tau_1, \tau_2] \cup [\tau_2, \tau_3]; \tag{8}$$

$$\tau = 0 : y_i(0) = y_i^0; Q(0) = Q^0; \tag{9}$$

$$T(0) = T_1; \ T(\tau_1) = T_2; \ T(\tau_1) = T_3; \ i - 1, \ldots I; \tag{10}$$

$$\Delta H_i(T) = \Delta H_i(298) + \int_{298}^{T} C_{pi}(T)dT; \quad C_{pi}(T) = a_i + b_i T + c_i T^2 + d_i T^3 + e_i T^4; \tag{11}$$

where y_i – group concentration of reactants in reaction, mol frac.; τ – conditional contact time, kg*min/mol; J – number of stages; I – number of substances; v_{ij} – stoichiometric matrix coefficients; w_j – rate j-th stage, 1/min; k_j, k_{-j} – rate constants of forward and reverse reaction, 1/min; α_{ij} – negative matrix elements v_{ij}, β_{ij} – positive elements v_{ij}, k_j^0, k_{-j}^0 – pre-exponential factors, 1/min; E_j^+, E_j^- – activation energies of the forward and reverse reactions, kcal/mol; R – universal gas constant, kcal/mol*K); T – temperature, K, $\Delta H_i(T)$ – formation enthalpy of i-th component at a temperature T, J/mol; $C_{pi}(T)$ – specific heat capacity of the i-th component at temperature T, J/(-mol*K); a_i, b_i, c_i, d_i, e_i – coefficients of the heat capacity temperature dependence i-th component; Q – molar flow rate, mol/min.

Solution (5)–(11) is a direct kinetic problem. Solution of the problem is performed by MCO algorithm Pareto approximation NSGA-II [11–13] in Matlab.

On Fig. 1 the solution to the two-criterion problem of optimizing the temperature regime in the catalytic reforming of gasoline is shown. The solution is the values of the three temperatures at the inlet of the three reactors and the corresponding values of the optimization criteria. All determined values are optimal. The choice of a specific

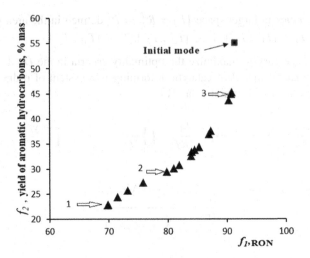

Fig. 1. Approximation of the Pareto front in MCO problem of catalytic reforming of gasoline for optimality criteria: RON, the yield of aromatic hydrocarbons.

Table 1. Approximation value set and Pareto front MCO problem for catalytic reforming of gasoline

№	$x_1 - T_1$	$x_2 - T_2$	$x_3 - T_3$	f_1 - RON	f_2 - Aromatic hydrocarbons, % mass
1	400,0	400,0	400,0	69,8	22,8
2	499,6	426,2	440,0	81,9	30,8
3	425,6	488,0	494,7	90,7	45,0

temperature regime depends on the person making the decision. In Fig. 1, some points are marked, designated as 1, 2, 3, for which Table 1 shows the values of the varied parameters and optimality criteria. Non-improved combinations of aromatic content and RON presented in the graph in Fig. 1 represent the boundary of the range of values of possible combinations of optimality criteria (Pareto front). The physical meaning of each point is that at the current value of RON, the lowest possible aromatic content and, conversely, at the current value of aromatic, the maximum possible RON. As a result, it is possible to distinguish a mode providing a decrease in the content of the sum of aromatic hydrocarbon by 10% with a loss of RON by 2 points (point 3).

At the next stage of solving the MCO-problem for catalytic reforming of gasoline, minimization of the benzene content in the product was investigated without a significant decrease in the RON and the maximum yield of reformate (Fig. 2, Table 2).

Some highlighted points of optimal temperature regimes and the corresponding values of RON, benzene yield and reformate yield when solving the MCO problem are given in Table 2 (points 1, 2, 3 in Fig. 2). That is, each point determines three temperatures of the reaction mixture at the inlet to the reactor, providing:

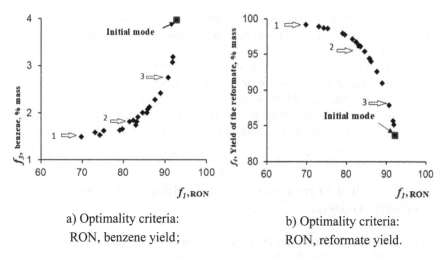

a) Optimality criteria:
RON, benzene yield;

b) Optimality criteria:
RON, reformate yield.

Fig. 2. Pareto front approximation of the MCO-problem for catalytic reforming of gasoline

- minimum benzene content and maximum reformate yield at the current RON,
- maximum RON value and reformate yield at the current benzene yield,
- minimum benzene and maximum RON at the current reformate yield.

It defines the physical meaning of each point on the graph of Fig. 2. The marker indicates the initial industrial mode of the process (benzene 4%; RON 92.7; reformate yield 84.3%).

Table 2. Optimal values of variable parameters and optimality criteria for the catalytic reforming of gasoline when solving MCO problem: RON, benzene yield, reformate yield

№	$x_1 - T_1$	$x_2 - T_2$	$x_3 - T_3$	$f_1 - RON$	f_3 – yield of the benzene, % mass	f_4 – yield of the reformate, % mass
4	400,0	400,0	400,0	69,8	1,49	99,2
5	499,0	440,5	443,1	83,0	1,74	96,3
6	479,8	486,3	484,4	90,8	2,75	87,9

As a result, a mode was determined, in which a decrease in the content of benzene amount from 4 to 3% of the mass is achieved with a loss of RON by 1 point and an increase in the yield of reformate by 1.5% of the mass (Table 2, line 3). It is possible to distinguish the temperature regime (Table 2, line 3), at which a decrease in the benzene content from 4 to 3% of the mass is achieved, while the RON decreased from 92.7 to 91.8 points. Temperature regime No. 3 (Table 2) provides a decrease in the benzene content in the reformate by 23% with the minimum possible decrease in RON relative to the initial regime.

It should be noted that, along with the product of catalytic reforming, commercial gasoline also contains products of the catalytic cracking of vacuum gas oil and low-temperature catalytic isomerization of the pentane-hexane fraction. Therefore, a slight decrease in RON reformate can be compensated for by the products of such processes. And the main share of aromatics and benzene in commercial gasoline belongs to the catalytic reforming reformate.

Solution of MCO problem made it possible to determine the temperature regime in reactor block, which makes it possible to reduce the benzene yield without a significant loss of octane number and with an increase in the reformate yield.

The found Pareto set is unimprovable, but in order to apply it in practice, it is necessary to study the stability of the regimes and possible areas of failure in optimal solution.

3   Mathematical Formulation of the Problem of Pareto Set Stability Analysis

Solution of the MCO problem of the conditions for carrying out the catalytic reaction (5)–(11) in the form of the Pareto frontier is denoted as $F_s^n(X)$, where X – matrix of optimal values of varied parameters $X = (x_{ij}) \in R^{s \times m}$; m – number of variable parameters, n – number of optimality criteria, s – cardinality of the set solutions to the MCO problem. Then it is necessary to analyze the stability of the Pareto frontier in the optimal conditions for carrying out catalytic processes $F_s^n(X)$ to small perturbations in the parameters based on the kinetic model.

The stable state of equilibrium of the system according to Lyapunov means that with a sufficiently small deviation from the equilibrium position, the system will never go far from the singular point [14]. Pareto frontier $F_s^n(X)$ is stable in the case when, for small independent perturbations of the matrix elements X set values s - effective trajectories deviate from the initial state by some small values.

By analogy with [14], the definition of the stability of the Pareto frontier $F_s^n(X)$: if $B = (b_i) \in R^m$– disturbance vector to X, can always find a vector $\Delta = (\delta_j) \in R^n$.

$$\forall b_i > 0 \ \exists \ \Delta : \left| F_s^j(X) - F_s^j(X+B) \right| \leq \delta_j, \tag{12}$$

where i = 1,...,m; j = 1,...,n.

Then the radius of stability of the Pareto frontier defined as

$$\rho_s^j(X) = \begin{cases} \sup P_j(X), & \text{if } P(X) \neq \emptyset \\ 0, & \text{if } P(X) = \emptyset \end{cases}, \tag{13}$$

where $P_j(X) = \{B > 0 | \left| T_s^j(X) - T_s^j(X+B) \right| \leq \delta_j \}$.

The Pareto frontier of the problem $F_s^n(X)$ is stable if and only if $\rho_s^j(X) > 0, j = 1, ...,n$ [1]. Moreover, depending on the set of permissible deviations Δ, different radius of stability is determined by variable parameters.

Thus, it is proposed to evaluate the influence of the disturbance of optimal values of all investigated variable parameters on the values of optimality criteria.

4   Parallel Algorithm for Analyzing the Stability of the Pareto Frontier

According to the definition of stability Pareto frontier for the conditions for carrying out catalytic reactions based on the kinetic model (1)–(11), an algorithm for calculating the radius of stability of the problem is developed in this work (Fig. 3).

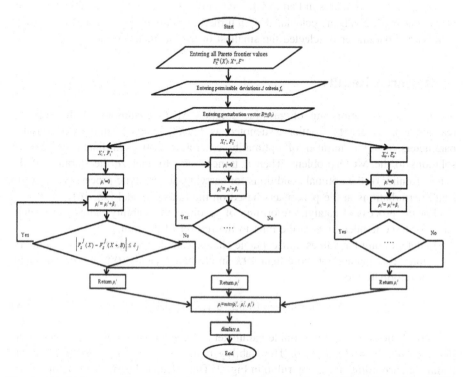

Fig. 3. Block diagram of a parallel algorithm for calculating the stability radius of the MCO solution

Input data are: calculated values of the Pareto frontier $F_s^n(X)$– matrix of optimal values for varied parameters X^*, values optimality criteria F^*, values of permissible deviations Δ optimality criteria f_j, disturbance vector B for each optimality criterion. The stability radius is determined for each variable parameter based on the definition of the stability of the Pareto frontier (12).

According to Fig. 2 the parallelization is realized by elements of the Pareto sets X^*, F^*. Depending on the number of available processors P sets X^*, F^* are divided into P subsets.

$$X* = \bigcup_{p=1}^{P} X_p*,$$

$$F* = \bigcup_{p=1}^{P} F_p*.$$

On subsets of elements in Pareto set, the stability radius of each variable parameter is calculated ρ_i^p. Next, the calculated ρ_i^p returned to the main process and for each of them varied parameter is selected the smallest of the calculated values.

5   Research Results

For the catalytic reforming of gasoline solution MCO conditions of the catalytic reaction (1), (2) Pareto frontier is denoted as $F_s^n(X)$. $m = 3$ – number of variable parameters, $n = 4$ – number of optimality criteria, $s = 50$ – cardinality of the set solutions to the MCO problem. Then it is necessary to analyze the stability of the Pareto frontier of the optimal conditions for carrying out catalytic processes $F_{50}^4(X)$ to small perturbations in the parameters based on the kinetic model [15, 16].

For the process of catalytic reforming of gasoline, the stability radius were calculated for three temperatures at the inlet to the reactor of the unit.

In determining the values of acceptable change calculated trajectories Δ assume no more than 2% octane. Not more than 10% in aromatics yield, 10% in benzene yield, 10% in reformate yield.

$$\Delta = (\delta_1, \ \delta_2) = (0.02, \ 0.1, \ 0.1, \ 0.1, \ 0.1). \tag{14}$$

Perturbations are set for variable parameters - three temperatures at the inlet to the block reactor: $B = (b_1, \ b_2, \ b_3)$. The stability radius is determined for each variable parameter, according to the algorithm in Fig. 2. The calculated permissible temperature change at the inlet to the reactor blocks corresponding to the permissible changes in the values of the optimality criteria (14) is 22 °C.

Consecutive calculation for all elements of the Pareto set takes considerable time, due to the complexity of solving the direct kinetic problem (5) - (11). Therefore, the parallelization of the computational process was implemented by the elements of the calculated Pareto set, according to the algorithm in Fig. 2.

The computational experiment time depending on the number of processors is shown in Fig. 3. For the calculation, use a 4-core PC Intel Core i7-8550U CPU, RAM 16GB, OS Windows10, Software system: Matlab (MATrix LABoratore).

To assess parallelization acceleration and efficiency was defined (Fig. 4). For the selected algorithm parallelizing of computational process stability radius calculation for catalytic reforming solutions MCO problem gasoline efficiency is 74% (Fig. 5).

Perhaps the use of more processors will make it possible to conduct a computational experiment more efficiently. What will be implemented in further research.

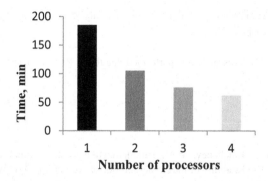

Fig. 4. Computing experiment time depending on the number of processors

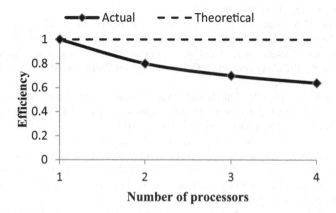

Fig. 5. Efficiency of the parallel program for calculating the stability radius of the MCO problem solution

6   Conclusion

The multicriteria optimization for the conditions for multistage chemical reactions based on the kinetic model is relevant for both laboratory and industrial processes. Complex multistage chemical processes require the determination of the permissible ranges for parameter values that ensure the stability of the calculated solution with an acceptable error, for the application of the obtained solutions in practice. In the catalytic reforming of gasoline MCO conditions solved the problem based on a kinetic model and calculated optimal radius resistance values of the inlet temperature to the reactor. Calculated allowable change in temperature at the inlet of reactor blocks corresponding to changes in allowable values optimality criteria (12) is 22 °C. A parallel algorithm for solving the problem of analyzing the stability of the Pareto set is developed and the efficiency of parallel program execution is estimated. The defined efficiency of the developed parallelization algorithm for calculating the stability radius of the solution to the MCO problem was 74%. The developed parallel algorithm for calculating the stability of the Pareto frontier will be used to analyze other catalytic industrial and laboratory processes [17, 18].

Acknowledgement. This research was performed due to the Russian Science Foundation grant (project No. 21-71-20047).

References

1. Bukhtoyarov, S.E., Emelichev, V.A.: Parametrization of the optimality principle ("from Pareto to Slater") and stability of multicriteria trajectory problems. Disc. Anal. Oper. Res. **10** (2), 3–18 (2003)
2. Akhmadiev, F.G., Gizzyatov, R.F., Nazipov, I.T.: Mathematical modeling of kinetics and optimization of grain material separation processes on sieve classifiers. Lobachevskii J. Math. **41**(7), 1155–1161 (2020)
3. Gubaidullin, D.A., Snigerev, B.A.: Mathematical modelling of gas flow with heavy solid particles based on eulerian approach. Lobachevskii J. Math. **40**(11), 1944–1949 (2019)
4. Podgaets, A.R.; Ockels, W.J.: Stability of optimal solutions: multi- and single-objective approaches. In: IEEE Symposium on Computational Intelligence in Multi-Criteria Decision-Making, pp. 395–402 (2007)
5. Gitman, M.B., Trusov, P.V., Yakubovich, M.B.: Stability of contracted beam with stochastic distribution of initial parameters. In: Proceedings of XIII School on Simulations in Continuous Medium Mechanics, pp. 152–159 (1999)
6. Emelichev, V., Kuz'min, K., Nikulin, Y.: Stability analysis of the Pareto optimal solutions for some vector boolean optimization problem. Optimization **54**(6), 545–561 (2005)
7. Zagoruiko, A.N., Noskov, A.S., Belyi, A.S., Smolikov, M.D.: Unsteady-state kinetic simulation of naphtha reforming and coke combustion processes in the fixed and moving catalyst beds. Catal. Today **220**, 168–177 (2014)
8. Zainullin, R.Z., Zagoruiko, A.N., Koledina, K.F., Gubaidullin, I.M., Faskhutdinova, R.I.: Multi-criterion optimization of a catalytic reforming reactor unit using a genetic algorithm. Catal. Ind. **12**(2), 133–140 (2020). https://doi.org/10.1134/S2070050420020129
9. Koledina, K.F., Koledin, S.N., Karpenko, A.P., Gubaydullin, I.M., Vovdenko, M.K.: Multi-objective optimization of chemical reaction conditions based on a kinetic model. J. Math. Chem. **57**(2), 484–493 (2018). https://doi.org/10.1007/s10910-018-0960-z
10. Zainullin, R.Z., Koledina, K.F., Akhmetov, A.F., Gubaidullin, I.M.: Kinetics of the catalytic reforming of gasoline. Kinet. Catal. **58**(3), 279–289 (2017)
11. Deb, K., Mohan, M., Mishra, S.: Towards a quick computation of well-spread Pareto-optimal solutions. In: Fonseca, C.M., Fleming, P.J., Zitzler, E., Thiele, L., Deb, K. (eds.) EMO 2003. LNCS, vol. 2632, pp. 222–236. Springer, Heidelberg (2003). https://doi.org/10.1007/3-540-36970-8_16
12. Srinivas, N., Deb, K.: Muiltiobjective optimization using nondominated sorting in genetic algorithms. Evol. Comput. **2**(3), 221–248 (1994)
13. Munoz, M.A., Kirley, M., Halgamuge, S.K.: Exploratory landscape analysis of continuous space optimization problems using information content. IEEE Trans. Evol. Comput. **19**(1), 74–87 (2015)
14. Emelichev, V.A., Girlich, E., Nikulin, Y., Podkopaev, D.P.: Stability and regularization of vector problems of integer linear programming. Optimization **51**(4), 645–676 (2002)

15. Koledina, K.F., Koledin, S.N., Nurislamova, L.F., Gubaydullin, I.M.: Internal parallelism of multi-objective optimization and optimal control based on a compact kinetic model for the catalytic reaction of dimethyl carbonate with alcohols. In: Sokolinsky, L., Zymbler, M. (eds.) PCT 2019. CCIS, vol. 1063, pp. 242–255. Springer, Cham (2019). https://doi.org/10.1007/978-3-030-28163-2_17

16. Lotov, A.V., Ryabikov, A.I.: Launch pad method in multiextremal problems of multicriteria optimization. J. Comput. Math. Math. Phys. **59**(12), 2111–2128 (2019)

17. Vovdenko, M.K., Gabitov, S.A., Koledina, K.F., Ahmerov, E.A., Sannikov, A.D.: Mathematical modeling of isopropylbenzene oxidation reaction and oxidation reactor. IOP Conf. Ser. J. Phys. Conf. Ser. **1096**, 012189 (2019)

18. Koledina, K.F., Gubaidullin, I.M., Koledin, S.N., Baiguzina, A.R., Gallyamova, L.I., Khusnutdinov, R.I.: Kinetics and mechanism of the synthesis of benzylbutyl ether in the presence of copper-containing catalysts. Russ. J. Phys. Chem. A **93**(11), 2146–2151 (2019). https://doi.org/10.1134/S0036024419110141

Parallel Global Search Algorithm for Optimization of the Kinetic Parameters of Chemical Reactions

Irek Gubaydullin[1,2], Leniza Enikeeva[2,3](ID), Konstantin Barkalov[4(✉)](ID), and Ilya Lebedev[4](ID)

[1] Institute of Petrochemistry and Catalysis - Subdivision of the Ufa Federal Research Centre of RAS, Ufa, Russia
[2] Ufa State Petroleum Technological University, Ufa, Russia
[3] Novosibirsk State University, Novosibirsk, Russia
[4] Lobachevsky State University of Nizhny Novgorod, Nizhny Novgorod, Russia
{konstantin.barkalov,ilya.lebedev}@itmm.unn.ru

Abstract. The paper considers the application of parallel computing technology to the simulation of a catalytic chemical reaction, which is widely used in the modern chemical industry to produce synthesis gas. As a chemical reaction, the process of pre-reforming propane on a Ni catalyst is assumed. To simulate a chemical process, it is necessary to develop a kinetic model of the process, that is, to determine the kinetic parameters. To do this, the inverse problem of chemical kinetics is solved, which predicts the values of kinetic parameters based on laboratory data. From a mathematical point of view, the inverse problem of chemical kinetics is a global optimization problem. A parallel information-statistical global search algorithm was used to solve it. The use of the parallel algorithm has significantly reduced the search time to find the optimum. The found optimal parameters of the model made it possible to adequately simulate the process of pre-reforming propane on a Ni-catalyst.

Keywords: Global optimization · Multiextremal functions · Parallel computing · Chemical kinetics · Inverse problems

1 Introduction

One of the areas of the Laboratory of Mathematical Chemistry of the Institute of Petrochemistry and Catalysis of the UFIC RAS is the study of chemical reactions by mathematical modeling methods [11,30,31]. At the moment, a large number of complex chemical processes have been studied, among them, the reaction of cycloalumination of alkenes with triethylaluminium into alumacyclopentanes, the reaction of hydroalumination of olefins with organoaluminum compounds, the reaction of alcohols with dimethyl carbonate, etc. The mathematical description of chemical reactions is necessary for the development the mathematical models of chemical kinetics, which are called kinetic models [14].

© Springer Nature Switzerland AG 2021
V. Voevodin and S. Sobolev (Eds.): RuSCDays 2021, CCIS 1510, pp. 198–211, 2021.
https://doi.org/10.1007/978-3-030-92864-3_16

The kinetic model is the basis for mathematical modeling of chemical reactions and the initial level for mathematical modeling of chemical reactors. When developing a kinetic model of a multi-stage chemical reaction, the inverse problem of chemical kinetics (CK) is solved. The inverse problem of CK is generally called the process of selecting the mechanism of a complex process and determining its quantitative characteristics – the rate constants of reactions based on experimental data about the dynamics of the process. From a mathematical point of view, the inverse problem of chemical kinetics is a global optimization problem, so the problem of choosing an optimization method is relevant [6,7].

A method for solving the optimization problems of such type should account for the following aspects. First, the objective function of the problem is a "black box" since it is defined not by a formula but in the form of some algorithm for computing its values. Second, computing even a single value of the objective function is time-consuming operation since it requires numerical modeling [16]. The aspects listed above don't allow employing the multistart methods based on the ideas of multiple gradient descents for solving the inverse problems. On one hand, computing the gradients would be too expensive operation in this case. On the other hand, the multistart methods are hardly applicable for the essentially multiextremal problems, which the inverse problems of chemical kinetics belong to.

The features of inverse problems of chemical kinetics listed above were taken into account in the parallel global search algorithm developed in University of Nizhni Novgorod. The information-statistical approach described in [25] in details makes a theoretical basis for this algorithm. The developed algorithm is based on a reduction of the initial multidimensional problem to an equivalent one-dimensional problem followed by solving the latter by efficient optimization methods for the functions of single variable. The issues of the parallelization of the algorithm on various architectures were considered in [1,2,24]. In the present paper, the results obtained with the use of the parallel global search algorithm for solving the inverse problem of chemical kinetics are presented.

2   Mathematical Model

The process under study is propane pre-reforming into methane-rich gas over Ni catalyst, which is an industrially important chemical process [27,28]. Pre-reforming of propane was studied over industrial nickel-chromium catalyst at pressure of 1 and 5 bar in the temperature range of 220–380 °C and at flow rates of 4000 and 12000 h^{-1}. The experimental data on propane pre-reforming was acquired from our previous work [27]. The reaction scheme consists of two reactions: propane steam conversion and CO_2 methanation [26]:

$$C_3H_8 + 6H_2O \rightarrow 10H_2 + 3CO_2 \tag{1}$$
$$CO_2 + 4H_2 \rightleftharpoons CH_4 + 2H_2O, \tag{2}$$

where the rates of reactions (1)–(2) are expressed according to the Langmuir-Hinshelwood model [28]:

$$W_{ref} = \frac{k_{ref}^0 \cdot \exp\left(-\dfrac{E_{ref}}{RT}\right)}{(1 + B \cdot C_{C3H8})^m},$$

$$W_{met} = k_{met}^0 \cdot \exp\left(-\frac{E_{met}}{RT}\right) \cdot C_{H2} \cdot \left[1 - \frac{P_{CH4}P_{H2O}^2}{K_{eq}P_{CO2}P_{H2}^4}\right],$$

where W_{ref} and W_{met} are the reaction rates; E_{ref} and E_{met} are the observed activation energies, J/mol; k_{ref}^0 and k_{met}^0 are the pre-exponential multipliers; B is the constant parameter, T is the temperature, K; R is the universal gas constant, J/(K $\cdot$ mol). The "ref" and "met" indexes refer to pre-reforming and methanation reactions, respectively. C_{C3H8} and C_{H2} are concentrations of propane and hydrogen, mol/m^3; m is order of the denominator, which varied from 0 to 2; K_{eq} is the equilibrium constant of CO_2 methanation; P_{CH4}, P_{H2O}, P_{CO2}, P_{H2} are partial pressures of the corresponding substances, bar. The mathematical model is a system of equations of material balance:

$$\begin{cases} G\dfrac{dy_i}{dl} = \left(\nu_i^{ref}W_{ref} + \nu_i^{met}W_{met}\right)m_i, \\ 0 \le l \le, i \in \{C_3H_8, CH_4, H_2O, H_2, CO_2\}, \\ l = 0, y_i = y_{i0}, \end{cases} \qquad (3)$$

where G is a mass flow of the mixture, kg/(m^2· sec); y_i is a mass fraction of the i-th component; ν_i is a stoichiometric coefficient of the i-th component; m_i is a molar mass of the i-th component, kg/mol; l is coordinate along the catalytic layer, m; L is a length of the catalytic layer, m. The length of the catalytic layer is 0.008 m. The mathematical model of chemical kinetics problems is a system of differential equations that describes the variations in substance concentrations over time according to the rates of reaction stages. The system of differential equations is a Cauchy problem containing the initial data [3,5]. The numerical solving of such a system of equations is a direct problem of chemical kinetics.

Systems of ordinary differential equations (ODES) describing chemical processes are often stiff due to the presence of fast-flowing and slow-flowing reactions. Therefore, the RADAU-IIA method was chosen as a method for solving the ODE system, which is suitable for solving stiff ODE systems. Let us consider in the general case the Cauchy problem of the form:

$$\frac{dx}{dt} = f(\mathbf{x}, y), \mathbf{x}(0) = \mathbf{x}_0, 0 \le t \le T, \qquad (4)$$

where x is the vector of concentrations of reaction substances with dimension of 5 (the substances are C_3H_8, CH_4, H_2O, H_2, CO_2), and f is the right-hand side of the Eq. (3). Then the s-stage Runge-Kutta method for solving the (4) system is written as follows:

$$\begin{cases} X_i = x_n + h \sum_{j=1}^{s} a_{ij} f(X_j, t_n + c_j h), 1 \leq i \leq s, \\ x_{n+1} = x_n + h \sum_{i=1}^{s} b_i f(X_i, t_n + c_i h), \end{cases} \quad (5)$$

where x_n, x_{n+1}, X_i are approximate solutions of the system (4) at time points t_n, $t_{n+1} = t_n + h$, $t_n + c_i h$. The coefficients of the Runge-Kutta methods are usually written in the form of a Butcher tableau:

$$\begin{array}{c|cccc} c_1 & a_{11} & a_{12} & \dots & a_{1s} \\ c_2 & a_{21} & a_{22} & \dots & a_{2s} \\ \dots & \dots & \dots & \dots & \dots \\ c_s & a_{s1} & a_{s2} & \dots & a_{ss} \\ \hline & b_1 & b_2 & \dots & b_s \end{array} \quad (6)$$

The Butcher tableau contains the vectors b and c, consisting of the coefficients b_i and c_i, respectively, and the matrix A of dimension $s \times s$, including the coefficients a_{ij}. The coefficients of fifth-order Rado-IIA method (Radau 5) are presented below:

$$\begin{array}{c|ccc} \dfrac{4-\sqrt{6}}{10} & \dfrac{88-7\sqrt{6}}{360} & \dfrac{296-169\sqrt{6}}{1800} & \dfrac{-2+3\sqrt{6}}{225} \\ \dfrac{4+\sqrt{6}}{10} & \dfrac{296+169\sqrt{6}}{1800} & \dfrac{88+7\sqrt{6}}{360} & \dfrac{-2-3\sqrt{6}}{225} \\ 1 & \dfrac{16-\sqrt{6}}{36} & \dfrac{16+\sqrt{6}}{36} & \dfrac{1}{9} \\ \hline & \dfrac{16-\sqrt{6}}{36} & \dfrac{16+\sqrt{6}}{36} & \dfrac{1}{9} \end{array} \quad (7)$$

The solution of the system of ordinary differential equations is a vector of the calculated concentrations of the reaction components, which are then compared with the experimental data. Determining the kinetic parameters of reaction stages by comparing calculated values of substance concentrations and experimental results is an inverse problem of chemical kinetics. The mathematical problem is to minimize the functional of the deviation between calculated and experimental values. The objective function determined as the sum of absolute deviations between calculated and experimental concentrations:

$$F = \sum_{i=1}^{M} \sum_{j=1}^{N} |x_{ij}^{calc} - x_{ij}^{exp}| \to \min, \quad (8)$$

where x_{ij}^{calc} and x_{ij}^{exp} are calculated and experimental values of component concentrations; M is the number of measuring points; N is the number of substances involved in the reaction.

3   Parallel Global Search Algorithm

Let us consider global optimization problem of the form

$$\varphi(y^*) = \min\{\varphi(y) : y \in D\}, \tag{9}$$

$$D = \{y \in R^N : a_i \leq y_i \leq b_i, \ a_i, b_i \in R, \ 1 \leq i \leq N\}, \tag{10}$$

where the objective function is a black-box function and it is assumed to satisfy the Lipschitz condition

$$|\varphi(y_1) - \varphi(y_2)| \leq L \|y_1 - y_2\|, \ y_1, y_2 \in D,$$

with the constant L, $L < \infty$, unknown a priori.

The assumption of the objective function to be Lipschitzian is typical of many approaches to the development of the deterministic global optimization algorithms. The first methods of Lipschitz optimization were proposed in the early 1970s [19,23]. Since that time, this line of research has continued to develop actively [8,13,17,18].

Currently, nature-inspired algorithms are widely used for solving optimization problems with the black-box objective functions; for example, see [4,9,29]. Such algorithms, in one way or another, employ the ideas of random search. Due to simple implementation and use, they have become very popular. However, these algorithms are inferior to the deterministic counterparts in terms of quality [15,21] (e.g., measured by the number of correctly solved problems from a certain set).

One of the efficient deterministic methods for solving multiextremal optimization problems is *the information-statistical global search algorithm* [25]. This method initially proposed for solving unconstrained optimization problems was successfully generalized to the classes of optimization problems with non-convex constraints and multicriteria optimization problems. For different versions of the algorithm, parallelization methods taking into account the architecture of modern computing systems were also suggested [1,10,24].

Many state-of-the-art global optimization algorithms use the idea of reducing the dimensionality for solving multidimensional problems; see, for example, the diagonal partitions method [20] or the simplicial partitions method [32]. The parallel global search algorithm described in this section uses the Peano curves [22,25], which continuously and unambiguously map the unit interval $[0, 1]$ onto the N-dimensional cube D from (10). By using this kind of mapping, it is possible to reduce the multidimensional problem (9) to a univariate problem

$$\varphi(y^*) = \varphi(y(x^*)) = \min\{\varphi(y(x)) : x \in [0, 1]\},$$

where the function $\varphi(y(x))$ will satisfy a uniform Hölder condition

$$|\varphi(y(x_1)) - \varphi(y(x_2))| \leq H |x_1 - x_2|^{1/N}$$

with the Hölder constant H linked to the Lipschitz constant L by the relation $H = 2L\sqrt{N+3}$ and $y(x)$ is a Peano curve from $[0, 1]$ onto D.

Note that theoretically the Peano curve $y(x)$ is defined as a limit object. Therefore, in practical implementation, only some approximation to the true space-filling curve can be constructed. Some methods for constructing this type of approximations (called *evolvents*) are considered in [22,25]. In this case, the accuracy of the approximation to the true curve $y(x)$ depends on the density of the evolvent m (which is a parameter for constructing the evolvent) and is of the order of 2^{-m} for each coordinate. Examples of evolvents with different values of m for the dimensionality $N = 3$ are shown in Fig. 1.

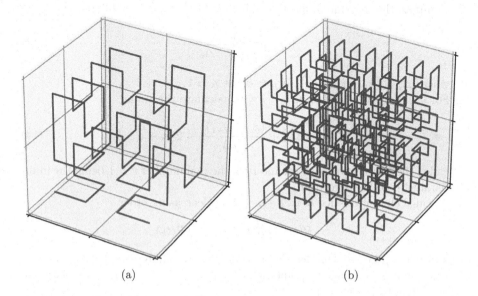

(a)   (b)

Fig. 1. Evolvents in three dimensions with (a) $M = 3$ and (b) $M = 4$

Let us call the process of computing a function value (including the construction of the image $y = y(x)$) as a *trial*, and the pair $\{x, z = \varphi(y(x))\}$ as the outcome of the trial. When describing a parallel algorithm, we will use the term *iteration* to denote the simultaneous (parallel) execution of several trials (each trial is executed by a separate processor). The number of trials during the n-th iteration we will denote as p, and the total number of trials executed during all n iterations as $k(n)$. In other words, we assume that we have p processors at our disposal while executing the n-th iteration.

The parallel global search algorithm used in this research (according to [25]) can be formulated as follows. The first p trials are executed at the points $x^0 = 0$, $x^1 = 1$ and at the arbitrary internal points $x^2, ..., x^{p-1}$ of the interval $(0,1)$. Let us assume $n \geq 1$ iterations of the method to be completed, in the course of which the trials in $k = k(n)$ points $x^i, 0 \leq i \leq k$, have been executed. Then, the points $x^{k+1}, ..., x^{k+p}$ of the search trials for the next $(n+1)$-th iteration are determined according to the following rules.

1. Renumber the inverse images of all the points from the trials already performed

$$y^0 = y(x^0), y^1 = y(x^1), ..., y^k = y(x^k) \tag{11}$$

by subscripts in the increasing order of their coordinates, i.e.

$$0 = x_0 < x_1 < \cdots < x_k = 1, \tag{12}$$

and associate these with the values $z_i = \varphi(y(x_i)), 0 \le i \le k$, computed at these points.

2. Compute the maximum absolute value of the first divided differences

$$\mu = \max_{1 \le i \le k} \frac{|z_i - z_{i-1}|}{\Delta_i}, \tag{13}$$

where $\Delta_i = (x_i - x_{i-1})^{1/N}$. If $\mu = 0$, set $\mu = 1$.

3. For each interval (x_{i-1}, x_i), $1 \le i \le k$, calculate the value

$$R(i) = r\mu\Delta_i + \frac{(z_i - z_{i-1})^2}{r\mu\Delta_i} - 2(z_i + z_{i-1}) \tag{14}$$

called the *characteristic* of the interval; the real number $r > 1$ being the input parameter of the algorithm.

4. Arrange characteristics $R(i), 1 \le i \le k$, in decreasing order

$$R(t_1) \ge R(t_2) \ge \cdots \ge R(t_k) \tag{15}$$

and select p largest characteristics with interval numbers $t_j, 1 \le j \le p$.

5. Carry out new trials at points $x^{k+j} \in (x_{t_j-1}, x_{t_j}), 1 \le j \le p$, computed according to the formula

$$x^{k+j} = \frac{x_{t_j} + x_{t_j-1}}{2} - \text{sign}(z_{t_j} - z_{t_j-1})\frac{1}{2r}\left[\frac{|z_{t_j} - z_{t_j-1}|}{\mu}\right]^N.$$

The algorithm stops if condition $\Delta_{t_j} < \epsilon$ is satisfied for at least one index $t_j, 1 \le j \le p$; here $\epsilon > 0$ is the predefined accuracy. Also, the algorithm stops if the maximum allowed number of trials K_{max} preset prior to running is exhausted.

The considered variant of the parallelization is *synchronous*, when the transition to the next iteration is performed after full termination of the current one, i.e., after completing the last trial of the current iteration. Particular implementation of this parallelization scheme will depend on the computer system architecture as well as on the requirements to the software necessary for computing the objective function values. In the present study, the conducting of trials required solving a stiff ODE system (for solving this one, Radau IIA method was used). Therefore, the parallelization was organized on CPU using MPI technology. The global search algorithm was run on a single (master) processor. The rest (slave) processors conducted parallel trials within the Step 5 of the algorithm. The amount of data transferred between the processes was small: it was only required to send out the coordinates of trial points and then to collect the computed values of the objective function at these points. At the same time, the time of conducting a single trial was not less 1 sec that considerably exceeded the time of data transfer between the processes. This way, the overhead costs for the data transfer didn't essentially affect the parallelization efficiency.

4 Numerical Experiments

Thus, as a result of solving the inverse problem of chemical kinetics by the parallel global search method, the kinetic parameters of the propane pre-reforming process on a Ni catalyst were calculated (Table 1). To interpret the results obtained, the solution of the direct problem of chemical kinetics was carried out, namely, the concentrations of the reaction components were calculated and compared with the experimental data. Figure 2 shows a comparison of the calculated concentrations with the experimental ones under different conditions: (a) GHSV = $4000\,h^{-1}$, (b) GHSV = $12000\,h^{-1}$. The results of the calculations are qualitatively consistent with the experiment.

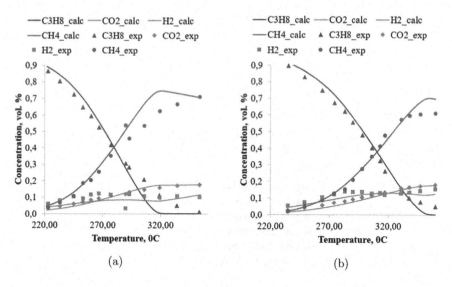

Fig. 2. Temperature dependences of the output concentrations of propane C3H8, methane CH4, hydrogen H2 and CO2 in the process of propane pre-reforming. Experimental conditions: 220–380 °C, (a) GHSV = $4000\,h^{-1}$, (b) GHSV = $12000\,h^{-1}$, 1 bar pressure. Concentrations of the gas components on the figure are given on the dry basis. Points are experimental concentrations ("exp"-index), lines are simulated concentrations ("calc"-index).

Table 1. Calculated kinetic parameters

E_{ref}, kJ/mol	E_{met}, kJ/mol	k_{ref}, (mole $\cdot$ m^{-3})m $\cdot$ s^{-1}	k_{met}, s^{-1}	m	B
99.23	37.08	$2.4 \cdot 10^{10}$	$1.93 \cdot 10^5$	0.82	4.8

For comparison with the previous calculations, an Arrhenis plot was constructed (Fig. 3), which shows the dependence of the decimal logarithm on the reaction rate constants (1) and (2) on the inverse temperature. The designations "GA", "GSA" and "PGSA" mean solutions obtained by various optimization algorithms, the genetic algorithm, the gravity search algorithm, and the parallel global search algorithm, respectively. The blue lines refer to the pre-reforming reaction (1), and the yellow lines refer to the methanation reaction (2). Note that the lines of the same color are parallel to each other, which means that the activation energies of the reaction calculated by different methods have approximately the same values, which indicates the adequacy of the calculations.

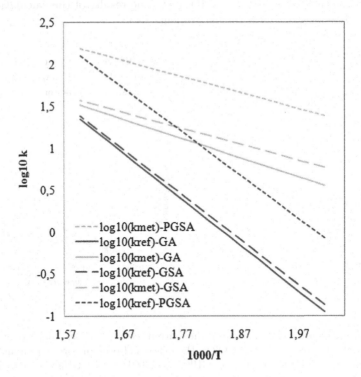

Fig. 3. Comparison of the obtained solution with the other algorithms found on the Arrhenius plot (Color figure online)

Numerical experiments were performed on the Lobachevsky supercomputer of the University of Nizhni Novgorod (operating system – CentOS 7.2, control system – SLURM). One supercomputer node has 2 Intel Sandy Bridge E5-2660 2.2 GHz processors, 64 Gb RAM. The CPU is 8-core (i.e. a total of 16 CPU cores are available on the node). The numerical experiments were performed using the Globalizer system [10]. To build the system for running on the Lobachevsky supercomputer, the GCC 5.5.0 compiler and Intel MPI 2017 were used. To solve the stiff system of equations arising in computing the objective function values, Radau method from SciPy library from Python 3.9 was used.

Global search algorithm was run with the following parameters: the reliability parameter $r = 5$, the search precision $\epsilon = 0.01$, the evolvent density $m = 10$, the maximum allowed number of trials $K_{max} = 5000$. Upon completing the execution of the algorithm, the solution found was refined with a local search using Hooke–Jeeves method [12]. The local search precision was $\epsilon = 0.001$. To evaluate the parallelization efficiency, the global search algorithm was run in the sequential regime and in the parallel one, the maximum number of computer nodes employed was 20. Correspondingly, the maximum number of processors employed was 40. In Fig. 4 and Fig. 5 the plots reflecting the running time and the speedup of the parallel algorithm *vs* the number of processors employed, respectively are presented (the time is in hours).

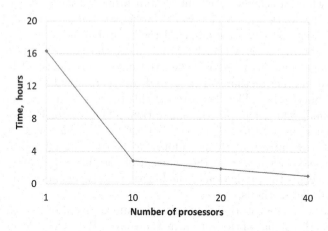

Fig. 4. The parallel algorithm running time

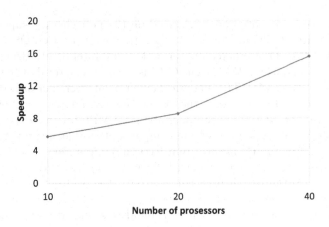

Fig. 5. Speedup of the parallel algorithm

5   Conclusions and Future Work

In the future, it is planned to simulate other chemical processes, namely, the first task is to simulate the process of sulfuric acid alkylation of isobutane with olefins, for which a scheme of chemical transformations has been compiled, a literature review of the process has been conducted, and experimental data have been found. The mathematical model of the reaction of sulfuric acid alkylation of isobutane by olefins is a Cauchy problem, at the moment the direct problem of chemical kinetics is solved, then the inverse problem will be solved by the proposed parallel methods. The second task is to simulate the synthesis of methyl-tert-butyl ether. The chemistry of this process is known, and the problem has a small dimension, but the simulation of the reactor is time-consuming and represents the solution of a second-order partial differential equation. At the moment, the difference scheme is formed, the run-through method is implemented, the next stage will be the solution of the direct problem of chemical kinetics, as well as the prediction of the kinetic parameters of the process by the proposed parallel methods.

The plans of further work include also the improvement of the parallelization efficiency for the global optimization method used. Relatively low indicators of speedup in the solving of the present problem can be explained by two factors. First, a synchronous parallelization scheme was applied in the implementation of the parallel algorithm. The master process (which the optimization method worked in) was waiting for the finish of execution of all trials performed by the slave processes when executing Step 5 of the algorithm. However, the time of executing a single trial in the problem considered varied from 1 up to 40 s subject to particular values of parameters (as it was found experimentally). The implementation of the asynchronous scheme of executing the trials at Step 5 of the algorithm seems to be a promising way of improving the parallelization efficiency. In this case, the trial results obtained by a slave process may be sent to the master process for processing immediately without waiting for the competing of other trials. Afterwards, the slave process receives a new point of the next trial form the master one. Theoretically, the asynchronous parallelization scheme can provide a full load of the computer resources employed even if the trial execution times are different at different points of the search domain.

Second, the local search, which is performed to refine the solution after completing the global search phase becomes a "bottleneck" at large-scale parallelization. The local search requires insufficient number of trials (as compared to the global one), but these trials should be performed sequentially. And at the parallel run this insufficient number of sequential trials becomes comparable to the number of the parallel global search iterations. In future, we plan to use the parallel implementation of the local search method in the final stage of the work that can improve the overall parallelization efficiency.

Acknowledgments. This study was supported by the Russian Science Foundation, project No. 21-11-00204 and by RFBR, project No. 19-37-60014.

References

1. Barkalov, K., Lebedev, I.: Solving multidimensional global optimization problems using graphics accelerators. In: Voevodin, V., Sobolev, S. (eds.) RuSCDays 2016. CCIS, vol. 687, pp. 224–235. Springer, Cham (2016). https://doi.org/10.1007/978-3-319-55669-7_18
2. Barkalov, K., Lebedev, I.: Adaptive global optimization based on nested dimensionality reduction. Adv. Intel. Syst. Comput. **991**, 48–57 (2020)
3. Chainikova, E., et al.: Interplay of conformational and chemical transformations of ortho-substituted aromatic nitroso oxides: experimental and theoretical study. J. Org. Chem. **82**(15), 7750–7763 (2017)
4. Eiben, A., Smith, J.: Introduction to Evolutionary Computing. Springer, Heidelberg (2015). https://doi.org/10.1007/978-3-662-44874-8_17
5. Enikeev, M., et al.: Analysis of corrosion processes kinetics on the surface of metals. Chem. Eng. J. **383**, 123,131 (2020)
6. Enikeeva, L., Marchenko, M., Smirnov, D., Gubaydullin, I.: Parallel gravitational search algorithm in solving the inverse problem of chemical kinetics. In: Voevodin, V., Sobolev, S. (eds.) RuSCDays 2020. CCIS, vol. 1331, pp. 98–109. Springer, Cham (2020). https://doi.org/10.1007/978-3-030-64616-5_9
7. Enikeeva, L.V., Potemkin, D.I., Uskov, S.I., Snytnikov, P.V., Enikeev, M.R., Gubaydullin, I.M.: Gravitational search algorithm for determining the optimal kinetic parameters of propane pre-reforming reaction. React. Kinet. Mech. Catal. **132**(1), 111–122 (2021). https://doi.org/10.1007/s11144-021-01927-8
8. Evtushenko, Y., Posypkin, M.: A deterministic approach to global box-constrained optimization. Optim. Lett. **7**, 819–829 (2013)
9. Gendreau, M., Potvin, J.Y.: Handbook of Metaheuristics. Springer, Boston (2010). https://doi.org/10.1007/978-1-4419-1665-5
10. Gergel, V., Barkalov, K., Sysoyev, A.: A novel supercomputer software system for solving time-consuming global optimization problems. Numer. Algebra Control Optim. **8**(1), 47–62 (2018)

11. Gubaidullin, I., Koledina, K., Sayfullina, L.: Mathematical modeling of induction period of the olefins hydroalumination reaction by diisobutylaluminiumchloride catalyzed with Cp2ZrCl2. Eng. J. **18**(1), 13–24 (2014)
12. Hooke, R., Jeeves, T.: "Direct search" solution of numerical and statistical problems. J. ACM **8**(2), 212–229 (1961)
13. Jones, D.R.: The DIRECT global optimization algorithm. In: Floudas, C.A., Pardalos, P.M. (eds.) The Encyclopedia of Optimization, pp. 725–735. Springer, Heidelberg (2009). https://doi.org/10.1007/978-0-387-74759-0
14. Koledina, K., Gubaidullin, I., Koledin, S., Baiguzina, A., Gallyamova, L., Khusnutdinov, R.: Kinetics and mechanism of the synthesis of benzylbutyl ether in the presence of copper-containing catalysts. Russ. J. Phys. Chem. A **93**, 2146–2151 (2019)
15. Kvasov, D., Mukhametzhanov, M.: Metaheuristic vs. deterministic global optimization algorithms: the univariate case. Appl. Math. Comput. **318**, 245–259 (2018)
16. Modorskii, V., Gaynutdinova, D., Gergel, V., Barkalov, K.: Optimization in design of scientific products for purposes of cavitation problems. In: AIP Conference Proceedings, vol. 1738 (2016). https://doi.org/10.1063/1.4952201
17. Paulavičius, R., Žilinskas, J., Grothey, A.: Investigation of selection strategies in branch and bound algorithm with simplicial partitions and combination of Lipschitz bounds. Optim. Lett. **4**(2), 173–183 (2010)
18. Pinter, J.: Global Optimization in Action (Continuous and Lipschitz Optimization: Algorithms, Implementations and Applications). Kluwer Academic Publishers, Dordrecht (1996)
19. Piyavskii, S.: An algorithm for finding the absolute extremum of a function. Comp. Math. Math. Phys. **12**(4), 57–67 (1972)
20. Sergeyev, Y., Kvasov, D.: Global search based on efficient diagonal partitions and a set of Lipschitz constants. SIAM J. Optim. **16**(3), 910–937 (2006)
21. Sergeyev, Y., Kvasov, D., Mukhametzhanov, M.: On the efficiency of nature-inspired metaheuristics in expensive global optimization with limited budget. Sci. Rep. **8**(1), 435 (2018)
22. Sergeyev, Y.D., Strongin, R.G., Lera, D.: Introduction to Global Optimization Exploiting Space-Filling Curves. SpringerBriefs in Optimization, Springer, New York (2013). https://doi.org/10.1007/978-1-4614-8042-6
23. Shubert, B.: A sequential method seeking the global maximum of a function. SIAM J. Numer. Anal. **9**, 379–388 (1972)
24. Strongin, R., Gergel, V., Barkalov, K., Sysoyev, A.: Generalized parallel computational schemes for time-consuming global optimization. Lobachevskii J. Math. **39**(4), 576–586 (2018)
25. Strongin, R.G., Sergeyev, Y.D.: Global Optimization with Non-convex Constraints. Sequential and Parallel Algorithms. Kluwer Academic Publishers, Dordrecht (2000)
26. Uskov, S., et al.: Kinetics of low-temperature steam reforming of propane in a methane excess on a Ni-based catalyst. Catal. Ind. **9**, 104–109 (2017)
27. Uskov, S., Potemkin, D., Enikeeva, L., Snytnikov, P., Gubaidullin, I., Sobyanin, V.: Propane pre-reforming into methane-rich gas over Ni catalyst: experiment and kinetics elucidation via genetic algorithm. Energies **13**(13), 3393 (2020)
28. Uskov, S., et al.: Fibrous alumina-based Ni-MOx (M = Mg, Cr, Ce) catalysts for propane pre-reforming. Mater. Lett. **257**, 126,741 (2019)
29. Yang, X.S.: Nature-Inspired Metaheuristic Algorithms. Luniver Press, Frome (2008)

30. Zainullin, R., Zagoruiko, A., Koledina, K., Gubaidullin, I., Faskhutdinova, R.: Multicriteria optimization of the catalytic reforming reactor unit using the genetic algorithm. Kataliz v promyshlennosti **19**, 465–473 (2019)
31. Zaynullin, R., Koledina, K., Gubaydullin, I., Akhmetov, A., Koledin, S.: Kinetic model of catalytic gasoline reforming with consideration for changes in the reaction volume and thermodynamic parameters. Kinet. Catal. **61**, 613–622 (2020)
32. Žilinskas, J.: Branch and bound with simplicial partitions for global optimization. Math. Model. Anal. **13**(1), 145–159 (2008)

Parameters Optimization of Linear and Nonlinear Solvers in GeRa Code

Igor Konshin[1,2,3,4,5], Vasily Kramarenko[1,2,4]([✉]), Georgiy Neuvazhaev[2],
and Konstantin Novikov[1]

[1] Marchuk Institute of Numerical Mathematics of RAS, Moscow 119333, Russia
{konshin,kramarenko,novikov}@dodo.inm.ras.ru
[2] Nuclear Safety Institute of RAS, Moscow 115191, Russia
neyvazhaev@ibrae.ac.ru
[3] Dorodnicyn Computing Centre, FRC CSC RAS, Moscow 119333, Russia
[4] Sechenov University, Moscow 119991, Russia
[5] Moscow Institute of Physics and Technology (State University),
Dolgoprudny 141701, Moscow Region, Russia

Abstract. Modeling of underground water flow processes in GeRa code is considered. The main attention is paid to the study of the parallel efficiency of various linear solvers as the most time-consuming stage of the solution. Eleven different solvers are considered and their properties are discussed in solving both model and real-life problems with complex geological structures. The optimization of the relaxation parameter to accelerate the convergence of Newton's method is also investigated. Numerical experiments were performed on the INM RAS cluster using from 1 to 384 computational cores.

Keywords: Subsurface flow and transport · Radioactive waste · Linear solver · Parallel efficiency · Speedup

1 Introduction

Modeling groundwater flow is an important task to ensure the safety of radioactive waste disposal [1,2]. It is required to make calculations for several years with a relatively small time step of several days. To guarantee the required accuracy of calculations, it is necessary to use a detailed distributed unstructured computational grid together with the use of parallel computations [3–6].

In this paper, the computational code GeRa (Geomigration of Radionuclides), developed at IBRAE and INM RAS, is considered to solve the problems of radioactive waste disposal safety assessment. This computational code uses the INMOST software platform [7–9] for operations with distributed grids, assembling and solving linear systems. Parallelization is based on the use of MPI technology.

Most of the calculation time is the solution of linear systems of equations, therefore, the greatest attention in the paper is paid to this particular issue. The INMOST software platform for solving linear systems allows one to use a

V. Voevodin and S. Sobolev (Eds.): RuSCDays 2021, CCIS 1510, pp. 212–226, 2021.
https://doi.org/10.1007/978-3-030-92864-3_17

large number of both internal linear solvers and linear solvers from other popular packages such as PETSc [10] and Trilinos [11]. In previous papers [1–6], only a very limited set of linear solvers available in the INMOST software platform was considered; in this paper, we tried to analyze the properties of a much larger number of available linear solvers.

The relevance of the problems under consideration is described in detail in previous works on the GeRa code (see [1,2]). In this paper, we focused on the parallel solution of linear systems, dynamic optimization of some parameters of linear solvers, as well as accelerating the convergence of Newton's method by tuning the relaxation coefficient.

Section 2 describes the models under study, including a model with a real geological structure. Section 3 contains the results of numerical experiments, including experiments on calculating scalability. Section 4 describes a technique for optimizing the parameters of linear solvers directly in the simulation process, and also presents the results of experiments on dynamically tuning the parameters of linear solvers. Section 5 examines the convergence acceleration for the Newton's method by tuning the relaxation coefficient. The final Sect. 6 provides a short summary.

2   Description of Models

The first test case was taken from the 2nd verification test of the GeRa code. This test is a classic in simulating groundwater flow problems and comparing solutions from different packages. Hereinafter, this model is referred to as the V2 model. A computational grid of more than 4 million cells was constructed. Figure 1 shows a comparison of the water head solution with the widely used MODFLOW package [12] on the V2 model. White isolines show MODFLOW solutions, while color filling shows the solution obtained using the GeRa code.

Figure 2 shows a real three-dimensional geological model, which we will further denote as model H3. The computational domain of the model has dimensions: 34×25 km along the surface, the depth is 300 m. When creating a model and taking into account hydrogeological conditions, 14 geological layers were identified (see Fig. 3). Due to the complex geological structure, the model has pinch-outs of layers, while the difference in permeability coefficients between layers is 10^5, and the anisotropy within one layer reaches 100. The computational grid takes into account the peculiarities of the geometry of the geological model. The model consists of more than 1 million cells with a step of about 100 m. During the modeling, a triangular-prismatic computational grid was used, taking into account the boundaries of the computational domain and the features of the geometry of the geological model.

When determining the external boundaries of the groundwater flow model, local and regional drains were taken into account, which is important from the point of view of understanding the location of the area and the nature of groundwater discharge. The upper boundary of the model is the day surface, on which the infiltration supply is set, the value of which was selected during the calibration process and was taken as 10^{-4} m/day. Groundwater flow was simulated in

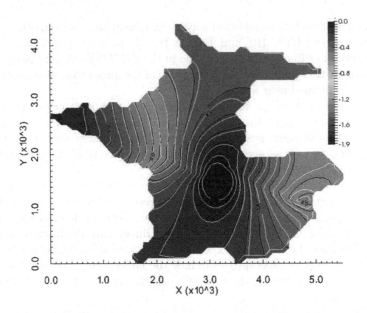

Fig. 1. Comparison of water head solution with MODFLOW for model V2.

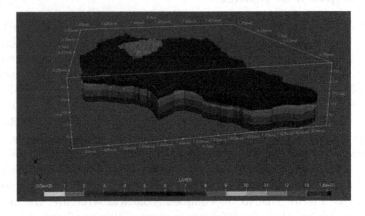

Fig. 2. 3D geological model H3.

a confined–unconfined stationary setting. Figure 4 shows an example of solving a groundwater flow problem.

3   Numerical Experiments for Different Linear Solvers

We consider the different types of linear solvers available through the INMOST software platform. We note right away, that all internal INMOST solvers use the approximate second-order factorization ILU2(τ) [13], where τ is the filtering

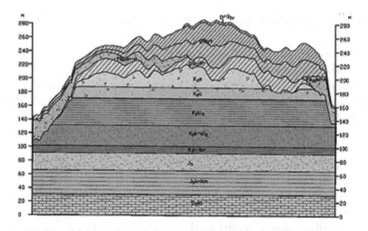

Fig. 3. Vertical cross-section of the H3 model with pinch-outs of geological layers.

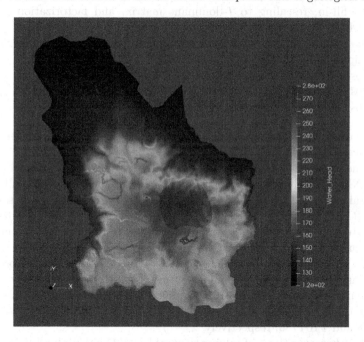

Fig. 4. An example of solving the groundwater flow problem for the H3 model.

threshold of the triangular factorization. Below is a complete list of eleven used linear solvers.

– fcbiilu2: preconditioning based on the decomposition BIILU2(τ, q) [14,15], which is a combination of the decompositions ILU2(τ) and BIILU(q), where q is the overlap size parameter for subdomains associated to each process;

- k3biilu2: similar preconditioning BIILU2(τ, q) with some additional parameter settings;
- inner_ilu2: matrix is rescaled using norm equilibration and factorized by the row-wise ILU2(τ) method;
- inner_ddpqiluc2: the matrix is scaled using norm balancing and factorized using estimates of the norms of inverse triangular factors and adaptive use of τ in the ILU2(τ) method;
- inner_mptilu2: matrix is permuted to maximize transversal product and rescaled to equilibrate row and column norms and factorized with the row-wise ILU2(τ) method;
- inner_mptiluc: matrix is permuted to maximize transversal product, symmetrically permuted to reduce fill-in, rescaled to equilibrate row and column norms and factorized with the Crout-ILU2(τ) method;
- inner_mlmptiluc: nested multi-level factorization strategy is adopted with permutation to maximize transversal product, symmetrical permutation to reduce fill-in, rescaling to I-dominant matrix, and factorization with the Crout-ILU2(τ) method with delayed pivoting;
- petsc: traditional ILU(k) factorization with restricted Additive Schwartz decomposition AS(q);
- trilinos_aztec: ILUT($k = 2$) with AS($q = 2$);
- trilinos_ifpack: ILU($k = 5$) with AS($q = 3$);
- trilinos_ml: multilevel version of the linear solver.

It is worth noting that of the 11 different linear solvers considered now, only two of them were used in previous works [1–6]: 'fcbiilu2' and 'petsc'.

For the numerical experiments, we used the x12core computational segment of the INM RAS cluster [16]. 16 compute nodes Arbyte Alkazar R1Tw50SM G5 contained two 12-core Intel Xeon Silver 4214@2.20 GHz processors with 128 GB RAM running the SUSE Linux Enterprise Server 15 SP2 (x86_64) operating system. All 384 available computational cores were involved in numerical experiments.

When solving the stationary problem V2, it is necessary to solve one linear system, and when solving the nonlinear problem H3, it is necessary to solve 60 different linear systems. The total number of computational cells (as well as the dimensions of the linear systems being solved) for problems V2 and H3 are 4 161 488 and 1 104 789, respectively.

Table 1 shows the times of solving the problem V2 by the solvers 'fcbiilu2' and 'k3biilu2' using from 1 to 384 computational cores. In what follows, the following notations are used: p is the number of computational cores used, T_{solve}, T_{total}, and $T_{rest} \equiv T_{total} - T_{solve}$ denote the linear systems solution time, the total solution time, and additional time spent on the discretization of the problem and the linear systems assembling, respectively, with all times given in seconds, while S_{solve}, S_{total}, and S_{rest} are the respective speedups calculated relative to the solution time on 1 computing core. All parallel computations show reasonable speedup, which is especially noticeable if the speedup for solving linear systems is calculated relative to the computation time on one 24-core computational node, S_{24}. If we compare the solution times for 'fcbiilu2' and 'k3biilu2' with each other, it can be noted that both implementations of the same BIILU2(τ, q) algorithm do not differ very much. The behavior of the time 'rest' is very stable in all experiments, so in what follows we omit the data on the columns 'total' and 'rest', focusing our attention on the parallel solution of linear systems.

Table 1. Times of solving problem V2 by the solvers 'fcbiilu2' and 'k3biilu2' using from 1 to 384 computational cores.

Solver	p	T_{solve}	S_{solve}	S_{24}	T_{total}	S_{total}	T_{rest}	S_{rest}
fcbiilu2	1	318.84	1.00	–	494.44	1.00	175.60	1.00
	2	161.03	1.97	–	257.29	1.92	96.26	1.82
	3	115.00	2.77	–	174.54	2.83	59.54	2.94
	6	63.74	5.00	–	99.34	4.97	35.60	4.93
	12	36.74	8.67	–	55.67	8.88	18.93	9.27
	24	40.48	7.87	1.00	52.52	9.41	12.04	14.58
	48	20.54	15.52	1.97	27.36	18.07	6.82	25.75
	96	10.56	30.19	3.83	14.62	33.82	4.06	43.25
	192	5.51	57.85	7.34	8.29	59.66	2.78	63.26
	384	3.98	80.02	10.17	6.24	79.18	2.26	77.70
k3biilu2	1	165.35	1.00	–	339.56	1.00	174.20	1.00
	2	102.72	1.60	–	198.29	1.71	95.57	1.82
	3	65.22	2.53	–	124.30	2.73	59.09	2.94
	6	40.75	4.05	–	76.45	4.44	35.71	4.87
	12	26.20	6.31	–	45.00	7.54	18.80	9.26
	24	18.50	8.93	1.00	29.93	11.34	11.43	15.23
	48	9.73	16.99	1.90	16.18	20.98	6.45	27.00
	96	5.37	30.81	3.44	9.25	36.68	3.89	44.78
	192	2.90	56.93	6.37	5.48	61.91	2.58	67.53
	384	1.94	85.16	9.53	4.01	84.72	2.07	84.31

Table 2 contains the times of solving linear systems for problem H3 by various internal INMOST solvers using from 1 to 384 computational cores. Note that the scalability of the computations is very good, even if we ignore the cases of super-linear speedup. The latter is probably due to the fact that with fewer processes a much more reliable preconditioner is constructed, which requires additional time. The difference in time of solving various solvers among themselves is also due to the fact that for each of the implemented algorithms its own method of obtaining a reliable solution is used.

Table 3 shows the times for solving problem H3 using external packages 'petsc' and 'trilinos' when using from 1 to 384 computational cores. All external linear solvers performed well and showed over 150 speedup for 384 cores.

Table 2. Times of solving problem H3 by the INMOST inner solvers for $p = 1, ..., 384$.

p	inner_ilu2		inner_ddpqiluc2		inner_mptilu2		inner_mptiluc		inner_mlmptiluc	
	T_{solve}	S_{solve}	T_{solve}	S_{solve}	T_{solve}	S_{solve}	T_{solve}	S_{solve}	T_{solve}	S_{solve}
1	27043.45	1.00	382.50	1.00	6211.47	1.00	2837.41	1.00	3551.79	1.00
2	13005.17	2.07	211.70	1.80	3443.78	1.80	1455.65	1.94	1842.66	1.92
3	8253.01	3.27	136.59	2.80	2410.97	2.57	987.98	2.87	1271.88	2.79
6	3752.37	7.20	79.98	4.78	1399.36	4.43	475.75	5.96	612.87	5.79
12	1875.16	14.42	49.12	7.78	705.38	8.80	226.61	12.52	281.15	12.63
24	949.29	28.48	30.66	12.47	390.01	15.92	112.35	25.25	145.79	24.36
48	312.01	86.67	16.16	23.67	178.48	34.80	39.32	72.16	48.60	73.07
96	95.72	282.51	8.37	45.68	77.53	80.11	22.17	127.99	28.17	126.06
192	31.12	869.11	5.35	71.44	44.06	140.96	10.81	262.57	13.56	261.88
384	10.94	2473.00	2.44	156.55	19.52	318.14	4.84	586.01	5.85	607.27

Table 3. Times of solving problem H3 by petsc and several trilinos solvers for $p = 1, ..., 384$.

p	petsc		trilinos_aztec		trilinos_ifpack		trilinos_ml	
	T_{solve}	S_{solve}	T_{solve}	S_{solve}	T_{solve}	S_{solve}	T_{solve}	S_{solve}
1	380.96	1.00	298.10	1.00	376.38	1.00	41107.97	1.00
2	211.15	1.80	168.90	1.76	218.45	1.72	14828.03	2.77
3	136.70	2.78	108.86	2.73	154.00	2.44	14665.59	2.80
6	80.54	4.72	63.64	4.68	83.51	4.50	5578.35	7.36
12	47.93	7.94	34.25	8.70	49.88	7.54	4243.03	9.68
24	30.35	12.55	19.44	15.33	28.88	13.03	2418.69	16.99
48	15.89	23.97	10.06	29.64	14.85	25.34	1294.63	31.75
96	8.40	45.35	4.90	60.81	8.03	46.89	722.79	56.87
192	5.47	69.59	2.47	120.77	4.58	82.13	374.53	109.76
384	2.50	152.25	1.49	200.02	2.33	161.52	269.62	152.46

However, the 'trilinos_ml' was unable to solve several linear systems, as a result of which the time step was fragmented during the simulation, which led to the solution of additional linear systems and to a significant increase in the total solution time.

Table 4 summarises the comparison of the time of solving problems V2 and H3 on 384 computational cores for all types of linear solvers considered. Among external solvers, the 'trilinos_aztec' has the best solution time. The 'trilinos_ifpack' could not solve the V2 problem. On the other hand, the 'trilinos_ml' showed the absolute best time for the V2 problem, but at the same moment, its solution time for the H3 problem turned out to be the worst. Fairly good results have been obtained for most of INMOST's internal solvers, especially for problem H3. On the whole, the 'k3biilu2' performed better than others, solving the V2 problem in less than 2 s.

4   Run-Time Parameters Optimization

To reduce the running time of a parallel application, it is necessary to correctly select the parameters for solving auxiliary problems. The task, which takes up to 90% of the time of the entire modeling process, is to solve linear systems arising during discretization. However, the use of traditional optimization methods to find the optimal parameters of linear solvers is difficult due to the unknown previously optimized function, as well as the fact that it can change during the simulation. Moreover, additional calculation of the optimized function (i.e., repeated solution of the same linear system with different parameters) would be highly undesirable. For such a class of solving non-stationary problems, automatic optimization algorithms may be suitable, which make it possible to additionally analyze the behavior of the function to be minimized (the time of solving a linear system) during the modeling process and make runtime assumptions about its properties.

Table 4. Comparison of the solving times T_{solve} for problems V2 and H3 on 384 computational cores for all types of linear solvers.

Solver	V2	H3
fcbiilu2	3.98	49.78
k3biilu2	1.94	3.63
inner_ilu2	6.86	10.94
inner_ddpqiluc2	4.30	2.44
inner_mptilu2	–	19.52
inner_mptiluc	12.05	4.84
inner_mlmptiluc	13.35	5.85
petsc	4.44	2.50
trilinos_aztec	2.19	1.49
trilinos_ifpack	–	2.33
trilinos_ml	0.90	269.62

To carry out automatic optimization of the parameters of linear solvers, the INM RAS has developed an additional module TTSP [2,17] for the INMOST software platform [7–9]. It allows directly in the process of modeling to analyze the progress of solving the problem and, without additional solutions of linear systems, to select more optimal parameters of linear solvers, thereby reducing the total time for solving the non-stationary problem.

In this paper, using the H3 model as an example, the operation of one of the automatic optimization methods '*Alternating*' is analyzed. The main idea of this algorithm for optimizing the parameters of a linear solver for a non-stationary problem is to study the area near the current local minimum. The algorithm will remain near the local minimum if it does not move very quickly during the simulation, and by studying the nearby region it can find more and more optimal values up to the global minimum.

When carrying out numerical experiments for the H3 model considered in Sect. 2, several linear solvers were chosen based on the approximate second-order factorization [13]. The second-order factorization ILU2 (τ) is used due to its higher reliability and efficiency in comparison with the structural factorization of ILU(k) or with the traditional threshold factorization ILU(τ). The 'fcbiilu2' and 'k3biilu2' solvers use the factorization BIILU2(τ, q) [14, 15], which is a combination of the factorizations ILU2(τ) and BIILU(q). Here q is the parameter of the size of the overlap of subdomains for each of the processors, and τ is the filtering threshold of the triangular factorization for each of these subdomains. The 'inner_ilu2', 'inner_mptilu2', 'inner_mptiluc', and 'inner_mlmptiluc' solvers, together with the second-order factorizations ILU2(τ), use the traditional AS(q) overlapping Schwartz parallelization scheme (Additive Schwartz).

Table 5 shows the results of experiments without and with optimization of the drop tolerance threshold parameter τ for small elements in the triangular factors. The rest of the parameters were selected by default values. For the experiments, $p = 24$ computational cores were used. The notation τ_3 and τ_2 indicate that the initial parameter τ was chosen to be 10^{-3} and 10^{-2}, respectively. There is no data for the solver 'fcbiilu2' with τ_3 due to the memory limitation for decomposition with such a low threshold, but we note that there is enough memory for τ_2. The results labeled 'std' and 'opt' indicate that parameter optimization has not been used here and has been used, respectively. The differences in the obtained optimal values of the drop tolerance threshold τ_{opt} express the differences in the specific implementations of these algorithms.

Table 5. Computation time and speedup when using optimization of the parameter τ.

Solver	$\tau_{3,std}$	$\tau_{3,opt}$	std/opt	$\tau_{2,std}$	$\tau_{2,opt}$	std/opt	τ_{opt}
fcbiilu2	–	–	–	50.93	15.90	3.20	0.025
k3biilu2	51.99	31.11	1.67	24.53	20.45	1.19	0.025
inner_ilu2	923.02	795.31	1.16	334.97	103.69	3.23	0.063
inner_mptilu2	324.26	203.55	1.59	145.49	141.86	1.02	0.025
inner_mptiluc	118.01	83.49	1.41	72.84	52.50	1.38	0.079
inner_mlmptiluc	126.99	92.87	1.36	82.78	61.03	1.35	0.079

Figure 5 shows how the τ parameter changes during the simulation for the entire set of linear solvers considered. The parameter was changed from some fixed value $\tau = 10^{-2}$ to some optimal and solver-dependent value τ_{opt}. For the 'inner_mptiluc' and 'inner_mlmptiluc' solvers, changing τ_{opt} is the same due to the same nature of both solvers. However, the multilevel solver 'inner_mlmptiluc' is usually used to solve the most complex linear systems.

The experimental results given in Table 5 show that due to the dynamic selection of the parameter τ in all considered cases it was possible to reduce the solution time and in some cases more than 3 times.

5   Adaptive Relaxation for Newton's Method

Both good initial guess and continuous differentiability of the residual in the vicinity of the solution are necessary for the convergence of Newton's method. In practice one may have bad initial guess, no residual derivatives at some point, or the values of the derivatives may be sensitive to small changes in the unknowns. It leads to the lack of convergence of Newton's method.

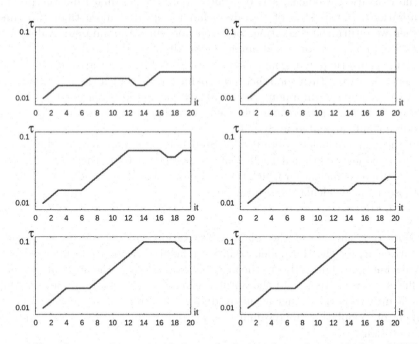

Fig. 5. Changing parameter τ during simulation for solvers fcbiilu2, k3biilu2, inner_ilu2, inner_mptilu2, inner_mptiluc, inner_mlmptiluc.

The convergence region may be increased by smoothing the residual or using relaxed Newton's method, in which the change in the vector of unknowns at each iteration is multiplied by some constant. The GeRa code implements the adaptive relaxation for Newton's method, in which the relaxation coefficient is selected at each iteration in order to minimize the Euclidean norm of the residual.

The adaptive relaxation for Newton's method in GeRa is based on fitting the Euclidean norm of the residual as a function of the relaxation coefficient by a quadratic polynomial and choosing the relaxation coefficient that minimizes the value of this polynomial. In more detail, the algorithm of the function for calculating the relaxation coefficient may be described as follows:

1. If the iteration number is less than 5, return the coefficient equal to 1.
2. If the norm of the residual obtained using the relaxation coefficient equal to 1 falls relative to the norm of the residual at the previous iteration by at least half, return the coefficient equal to 1.
3. If the norm of the residual obtained using the relaxation coefficient equal to 0.5 falls relative to the norm of the residual at the previous iteration by at least half, return the coefficient equal to 0.5.
4. We find the least squares quadratic regression for the residual norm using all the previously calculated values of the residual norms, including the values for the relaxation coefficients 1, 0.5, and 0 (i.e., the residual from the previous iteration). If this step of the algorithm is repeated more than two times, then we return the relaxation coefficient for which the minimum value of the residual norm was obtained among those already calculated.
5. If the quadratic polynomial calculated in Step 4 has a negative leading coefficient, then we return the relaxation coefficient for which the minimum value of the residual norm among those already calculated is obtained.
6. We calculate a new relaxation coefficient that minimizes the value of the polynomial calculated in Step 4.
7. If the new coefficient obtained in Step 6 is less than zero or differs from the previously obtained coefficients by less than 0.01, then we return the relaxation coefficient for which the minimum value of the residual norm among those already calculated is obtained.
8. Go to Step 4.

Note that the use of the adaptive relaxation will not always be justified. In particular, for the H3 model, adaptive relaxation leads to an increase in the calculation time. This is due to the fact that in most cases the optimal relaxation coefficient is close to 1, and the optimal change in the residual does not differ significantly from the change in the residual without relaxation. In this case, time is spent on calculating the residual at trial points, which leads to a slowdown in computations.

To illustrate the work of Newton's method with adaptive relaxation, a model of coupled processes of groundwater flow, 2D surface runoff, and surface runoff in rivers defined by a one-dimensional domains is used. Fluid dynamics is modeled using the Richards equation for the subsurface region and a diffusive wave approximation for shallow water equations for surface waters. A feature of this model is the use of discontinuous flow functions between the 3D subsurface layer, the 2D surface water layer, and the 1D river domain. This feature leads to slow convergence of Newton's method and the need for multiple decreases in the time step. The reservoir of the Borden military base is used as an object of modeling. Field study simulation for this reservoir is a traditional benchmark for models able to simulate coupled surface-subsurface flow [18–21]. The experimental site is approximately 18 by 90 m; an artificial channel of about 60 cm wide with an average slope of less than 1° has been created on the site. The channel is located about 1.2 m below the surrounding terrain, surrounded by banks with a slope of 5 to 9°. The geometry of the computational domain and an example of the results of calculating the water saturation for a given reservoir are shown in Fig. 6.

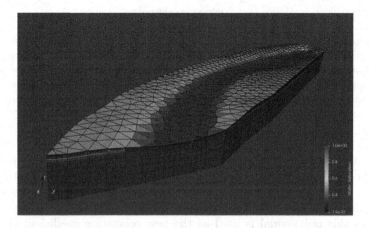

Fig. 6. Computational domain geometry and numerical water saturation results for Borden benchmark.

Table 6. Comparison of the computation time when using different relaxation approaches.

Relaxation coefficient	Number of iterations	Computation time (s)
Adaptive	13493	6646
1.0	27590	9172
0.9	32119	9891

The calculations for this test were carried out using three relaxation approaches: no relaxation (i.e., the coefficient is 1), a constant coefficient equal to 0.9, and also the adaptive relaxation coefficient, the fitting method for which is described in this section. An example of the algorithm for finding the optimal relaxation coefficient is shown in Fig. 7. First, the values of the Euclidean norm of the residual are calculated for the relaxation coefficients of 0 (i.e., for

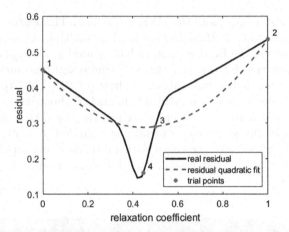

Fig. 7. Illustration of the algorithm for finding the optimal relaxation coefficient: the real residual function (blue line) is approximated by a quadratic polynomial (red line), sample points are shown in yellow, the order of calculating the residual at these points is written next to the points themselves. As a result of the search, a relaxation coefficient of 0.447 was obtained, for which the residual is more than three times lower than for a unit relaxation coefficient. (Color figure online)

the residual from the previous iteration), 1, and 0.5. For these coefficients, the fall of the residual after the current iteration is considered unsatisfactory (i.e., the norm does not fall 2 or more times), the calculated values of the residual are approximated by a quadratic polynomial. The value of the argument that minimizes this polynomial is used as the new relaxation coefficient since this coefficient provides a sufficient reduction of the residual.

Comparison of the computation time and the number of iterations for different relaxation approaches is given in Table 6. As can be seen from this table, the use of adaptive relaxation can reduce the calculation time by 27.5% and the total number of iterations of Newton's method by 51.1% relative to calculations without relaxation. In this case, the use of a constant coefficient of relaxation coefficient equal to 0.9 does not improve the convergence of Newton's method and accelerate the calculation.

6   Conclusion

The paper discusses ways to accelerate hydrogeological calculations in the GeRa code. Using a complex realistic model as an example, the parallel efficiency of various linear solvers using up to 384 computational cores is investigated. It is shown that most of the considered linear solvers provide sufficiently high speedup, often more than 150, sometimes more than 200. The method is used to reduce the cost of multiple solutions of linear systems by dynamically tuning a drop tolerance threshold when constructing a preconditioner for linear solvers. When solving nonlinear problems, a method is proposed for choosing the relaxation coefficient to accelerate the convergence of Newton's method.

References

1. Kapyrin, I.V., Konshin, I.N., Kopytov, G.V., Nikitin, K.D., Vassilevski, Yu.V.: Hydrogeological modeling in problems of safety substantiation of radioactive waste burials using the GeRa code. In: Supercomputer Days in Russia: Proceedings of the International Conference, Moscow, 28–29 September 2015, pp. 122–132. Publishing House of Moscow State University, Moscow (2015). (in Russian)
2. Kapyrin, I., Konshin, I., Kramarenko, V., Grigoriev, F.: Modeling groundwater flow in unconfined conditions of variable density solutions in dual-porosity media using the GeRa code. In: Voevodin, V., Sobolev, S. (eds.) RuSCDays 2018. CCIS, vol. 965, pp. 266–278. Springer, Cham (2019). https://doi.org/10.1007/978-3-030-05807-4_23
3. Konshin, I., Kapyrin, I.: Scalable computations of GeRa code on the base of software platform INMOST. In: Malyshkin, V. (ed.) PaCT 2017. LNCS, vol. 10421, pp. 433–445. Springer, Cham (2017). https://doi.org/10.1007/978-3-319-62932-2_42
4. Anuprienko, D.V., Kapyrin, I.V.: Modeling groundwater flow in unconfined conditions: numerical model and solvers' efficiency. Lobachevskii J. Math. **39**(7), 867–873 (2018). https://doi.org/10.1134/S1995080218070053
5. Kapyrin, I.V., Konshin, I.N., Kopytov, G.V., Kramarenko, V.K.: Parallel computations in the hydrogeological computational code GeRa: organization and efficiency. Numer. Methods Program. **19**(4), 356–367 (2018). (in Russian)
6. Bagaev, D., Grigoriev, F., Kapyrin, I., Konshin, I., Kramarenko, V., Plenkin, A.: Improving parallel efficiency of a complex hydrogeological problem simulation in GeRa. In: Voevodin, V., Sobolev, S. (eds.) RuSCDays 2019. CCIS, vol. 1129, pp. 265–277. Springer, Cham (2019). https://doi.org/10.1007/978-3-030-36592-9_22
7. Vassilevski, Yu., Konshin, I., Kopytov, G., Terekhov, K.: INMOST - A Software Platform and Graphical Environment for Development of Parallel Numerical Models on General Meshes, 144 p. Lomonosov Moscow State University Publications, Moscow (2013). (in Russian)
8. Vassilevski, Y., Terekhov, K., Nikitin, K., Kapyrin, I.: Parallel Finite Volume Computation on General Meshes. Springer, Cham (2020). https://doi.org/10.1007/978-3-030-47232-0
9. INMOST - a toolkit for distributed mathematical modeling. http://www.inmost.org/. Accessed 15 Apr 2021
10. PETSc - Portable, Extensible Toolkit for Scientific Computation. https://www.mcs.anl.gov/petsc. Accessed 15 Apr 2021
11. Trilinos - platform for the solution of large-scale, complex multi-physics engineering and scientific problems. http://trilinos.org/. Accessed 15 Apr 2021
12. Panday, S., Langevin, C.D., Niswonger, R.G., Ibaraki, M., Hughes, J.D.: MODFLOW-USG version 1.4.00: an unstructured grid version of MODFLOW for simulating groundwater flow and tightly coupled processes using a control volume finite-difference formulation. U.S. Geological Survey Software Release (2017)
13. Kaporin, I.E.: High quality preconditioning of a general symmetric positive definite matrix based on its $U^T U + U^T R + R^T U$-decomposition. Numer. Linear Algebra Appl. **5**(6), 483–509 (1998)

14. Kaporin, I.E., Konshin, I.N.: Parallel solution of large sparse SPD linear systems based on overlapping domain decomposition. In: Malyshkin, V. (ed.) PaCT 1999. LNCS, vol. 1662, pp. 436–446. Springer, Heidelberg (1999). https://doi.org/10.1007/3-540-48387-X_45

15. Kaporin, I.E., Konshin, I.N.: A parallel block overlap preconditioning with inexact submatrix inversion for linear elasticity problems. Numer. Linear Algebra Appl. **9**(2), 141–162 (2002)

16. INM RAS cluster. http://cluster2.inm.ras.ru/en/. Accessed 15 Apr 2021

17. Bagaev, D., Konshin, I., Nikitin, K.: Dynamic optimization of linear solver parameters in mathematical modelling of unsteady processes. In: Voevodin, V., Sobolev, S. (eds.) RuSCDays 2017. CCIS, vol. 793, pp. 54–66. Springer, Cham (2017). https://doi.org/10.1007/978-3-319-71255-0_5

18. Abdul, A.: Experimental and numerical studies of the effect of the capillary fringe on stream flow generation. Ph.D. thesis, University of Waterloo, Waterloo, Ontario, Canada (1985)

19. Kollet, S., et al.: The integrated hydrologic model intercomparison project, IH-MIP2: a second set of benchmark results to diagnose integrated hydrology and feedbacks. Water Resour. Res. **53**(1), 867–890 (2016)

20. Novikov, K., Kapyrin, I.: Coupled surface-subsurface flow modelling using the GeRa software. Lobachevskii J. Math. **41**, 538–551 (2020). https://doi.org/10.1134/S1995080220040162

21. Kramarenko, V., Novikov, K.: Surface runoff model in GeRa software: parallel implementation and surface-subsurface coupling. Math. Montisnigri **49**, 70–86 (2020)

Quantum-Chemical Calculations of the Structure and Thermochemical Properties of 3,6-bis(2,2,2-trinitroethylnitramino)-1,2,4,5-tetrazine

Vadim Volokhov[iD], Elena Amosova[✉][iD], Alexander Volokhov[iD],
David Lempert[iD], and Anatoly Korepin

Institute of Problems of Chemical Physics of RAS,
Chernogolovka, Russian Federation
{vvm,aes,vav,lempert,agkor}@icp.ac.ru

Abstract. The work addresses to the study of the structure and thermochemical properties of a new high-enthalpy compound 3,6-bis(2,2,2-trinitroethylnitramino)-1,2,4,5-tetrazine (NBTAT), first obtained in the IPCP RAS in 2020. The enthalpy of formation of NBTAT, IR absorption spectra and molecule structure were calculated by various ab initio quantum-chemical methods using Gaussian 09.

Keywords: Enthalpy of formation · Energetic ability ·
Quantum-chemical calculations · High-enthalpy compounds · 3, 6-bis(2, 2, 2-trinitroethylnitramino-1, 2, 4, 5-tetrazine)

1 Introduction

In the last two or three decades, computer methods of studying physical and chemical properties of the existing and, more importantly, new not yet synthesized compounds have been developing very actively [1–3]. In the classical work [4], it was demonstrated for 454 substances consisting of atoms of the first and second periods of the periodic table that the calculation accuracy by the G4 method is no worse than 1 kcal/mol, which puts such calculations of the enthalpy of formation on a par with the experiment in terms of the reliability [4–6]. Large-scale studies in the various countries have shown that tetrazine is a promising initial structure for computer design of new high-enthalpy compounds. There are many energy-intensive compounds created on one or more tetrazine cycles [7–15]. Recently [16], a new representative of the class of nitrosubstituted 1,2,4,5-tetrazine namely 3,6-bis(2,2,2-trinitroethylnitramino)-1,2,4,5-tetrazine (NBTAT, $C_6H_4N_{14}O_{16}$; $\alpha = 1.14$; Fig. 1) has been synthesized based on 3,6-bis(2,2,2,-trinitroethylamino)-1,2,4,5-tetrazine (BTAT, Fig. 2) described in [15] nitrated with a mixture of nitric acid and trifluoroacetic anhydride [16]. In this work, parameters of the NBTAT molecule in the gas phase and its physicochemical properties have been determined by quantum-chemical calculations. Values of enthalpy of formation have been calculated by methods of different complexity and compared.

© Springer Nature Switzerland AG 2021
V. Voevodin and S. Sobolev (Eds.): RuSCDays 2021, CCIS 1510, pp. 227–239, 2021.
https://doi.org/10.1007/978-3-030-92864-3_18

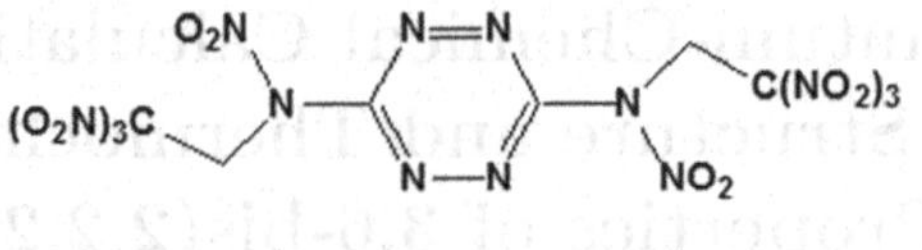

Fig. 1. NBTAT.

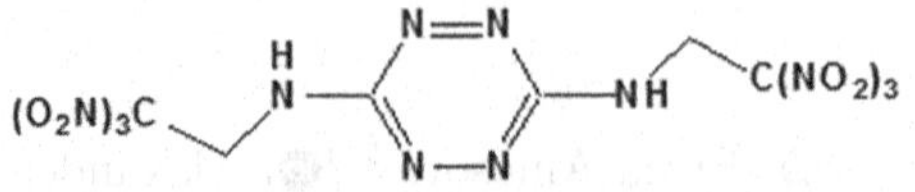

Fig. 2. BTAT.

2 Methods

Physicochemical properties of the newly synthesized compound NBTAT have been studied by complex quantum-chemical calculations using the quantum-chemical package Gaussian 09 [17]. The enthalpy of formation was calculated by the atomization method as was described in our previous works [18–22]. The main steps of the calculation by the atomization method of the enthalpy of formation of compounds with the common formula $C_w H_x N_y O_z$ are listed below:

1. Calculation of the atomization energy in the nonrelativistic approximation.

$$\sum D_0 = w E_0(C) + x E_0(H) + y E_0(N) + z E_0(O) - E_0(C_w H_x N_y O_z), \quad (1)$$

where $E_0(C), E_0(H), E_0(N), E_0(O)$ are calculated total energies of atoms. Total energy of the molecule $E_0(C_w H_x N_y O_z)$ is calculated by the formula $E_0(C_w H_x N_y O_z) = \varepsilon_0 + ZPE$, where ε_0 is a total electronic energy of the molecule, and ZPE is a sum of zero-point energies of all vibrational modes of the molecule.

2. Calculation of the enthalpy of formation at $0K$

$$\begin{aligned} \Delta H_f^\circ(C_w H_x N_y O_z, 0K) = {} & w\Delta H_f^\circ(C, 0K) + x\Delta H_f^\circ(H, 0K) \\ & + y\Delta H_f^\circ(N, 0K) + z\Delta H_f^\circ(O, 0K) - \sum D_0, \end{aligned} \quad (2)$$

where the first four summands are the enthalpies of formation of gaseous atomic components known from experiment.

3. Calculation of the enthalpy of formation at $298.15K$

$$\begin{aligned} \Delta H_f^\circ(C_w H_x N_y O_z, 298K) = {} & \Delta H_f^\circ(C_w H_x N_y O_z, 0K) \\ & + (H^0(C_w H_x N_y O_z, 298K) - H^0(C_w H_x N_y O_z F_p, 0K)) \\ & - w(H^0(C, 298K) - H^0(C, 0K)) \\ & - x(H^0(H, 298K) - H^0(h, 0K)) \\ & - y(H^0(N, 298K) - H^0(N, 0K)) \\ & - z(H^0(O, 298K) - H^0(O, 0K)), \end{aligned} \quad (3)$$

where the second summand is obtained from the calculation of the molecule, the third to sixth summands are known from experiment (or calculated from experimental molecular constants). The values of the enthalpy of formation of gaseous atoms and thermal corrections can be taken from various reference books or literature sources, for example [6, 23–26].

In this work, we used the experimental atomic enthalpies of formation from the NIST-JANAF thermochemical tables [23]. Since the theoretical calculation systematically overestimates the values of the zero-point frequencies, the frequencies are corrected using empirically selected coefficients. To obtain more accurate frequencies, it is necessary to correct the vibration frequencies when calculating the ZPE corrections and corrections $(H^0(C_wH_xN_yO_z, 298K)$ - $H^0(C_wH_xN_yO_z, 0K))$. The values of the scaling factors are used for this, which are recommended in the literature for various calculation methods and various basis sets [6].

3   Results and Discussion

3.1   Structure

Results of quantum-chemical ab initio calculations have shown that NBTAT can exist in the gas phase as two isomers (Fig. 3 and 4) As follows from Fig. 4 for the trans-isomer, the structure of the molecule practically does not differ from that of BTAT (Fig. 5) except for the $>NH$ groups being replaced by the $>NNO_2$ groups.

3.2   Enthalpy of Formation

Cis- and trans-isomers have very close values of the enthalpy of formation in the gas phase $(\Delta H_f^\circ(g))$ (622 and 618 kJ/mol, accordingly).

Table 1 and Fig. 6 show enthalpies of formation of NBTAT calculated at different levels: B3LYP, CBS-4M and G4(MP2). Though in most cases the replacement of hydrogen atoms by the nitro group (i.e. the transition from R_1-NH-R_2 to $R_1-N(NO_2)-R_2$) leads to a decrease in the enthalpy of formation (per mole), NBTAT, the nitrated derivative of BTAT, is characterized by the increased value of the enthalpy of formation, which is due to a significant stress in the NBTAT molecule because of the substitution of two hydrogen atoms in BTAT by the nitro groups.

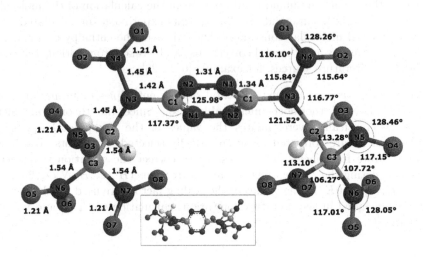

Fig. 3. Molecular structure of NBTAT in the gas phase (cis-isomer) with indicated angles and bond lengths.

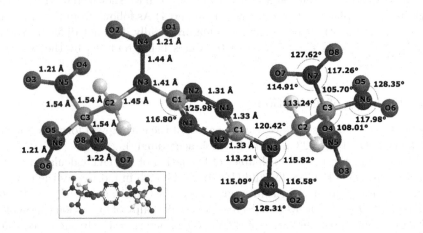

Fig. 4. Molecular structure of NBTAT in the gas phase (trans-isomer) with indicated angles and bond lengths.

Table 1. Calculated values of enthalpy of formation of NBTAT and BTAT.

Compound		$\Delta H_f^o(g)$, kJ/mol		
		B3LYP/6-311+G(2d,p)	CBS-4M	G4(MP2)
NBTAT	Cis-isomer	947	622	685
	Trans-isomer	946	618	683
BTAT		691	424, 422 [15]	478

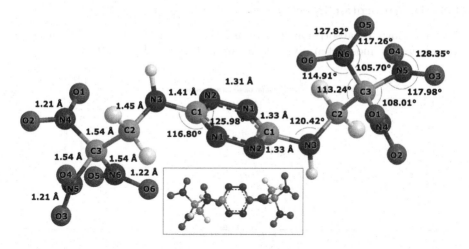

Fig. 5. Molecular structure of BTAT in the gas phase with indicated angles and bond lengths.

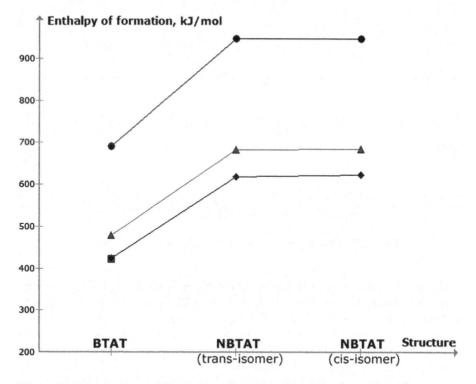

Fig. 6. Enthalpies of formation of the calculated structures (B3LYP - dark blue rounds, G4 (MP2) - violet triangles, CBS-4M - green diamonds and value from [15] - red square). (Color figure online)

3.3   IR Absorption Spectra

Figure 7 shows IR absorption spectra of NBTAT and BTAT. The displacement vectors for the most intense vibrations are pictured on Figs. 8, 9, 10.

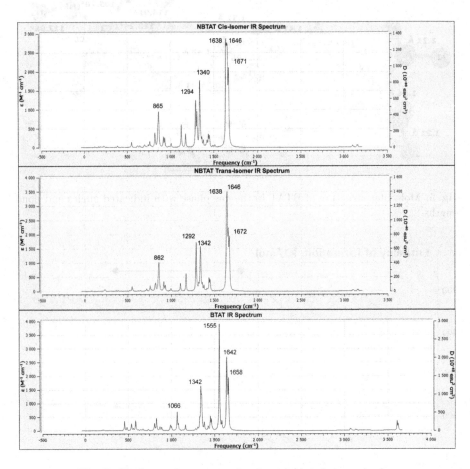

Fig. 7. IR absorption spectra for the calculated compounds.

Figures 7, 8, 9 show that the highest frequencies ($1638\,\mathrm{cm^{-1}}$–$1672\,\mathrm{cm^{-1}}$) with noticeable intensities are observed in both NBTAT isomers in the NO_2 groups and correspond to the vibrations of nitrogen atoms along the N-O bonds. Vibrations of the nitrogen atoms in the NO_2 groups along the N-C bond are characterized by frequencies ($1337\,\mathrm{cm^{-1}}$–$1345\,\mathrm{cm^{-1}}$) with lower intensities. Frequencies ($1292\,\mathrm{cm^{-1}}$–$1294\,\mathrm{cm^{-1}}$) corresponding to the vibrations of N3 atoms along the C-N bond are also characterized by noticeable intensities. Vibrations of N4 atoms along the N-N bond are characterized by frequencies with lower intensity: $865\,\mathrm{cm^{-1}}$ for cis-isomer and $862\,\mathrm{cm^{-1}}$ for trans-isomer. Figures 7 and 10 show that frequencies ($1555\,\mathrm{cm^{-1}}$) with the highest intensity correspond to vibrations of nitrogen atoms along the N3-C1 bond. Vibrations of nitrogen atoms along the N-O bonds are characterized by frequencies ($1637\,cm^{-1}$–$1658\,cm^{-1}$) with lower intensities. Frequency $1342\,cm^{-1}$ with high intensity corresponds to vibrations of nitrogen atoms in the NO_2 groups along the N-C bond. Vibrations of the nitrogen atoms in the ring are also characterized by frequencies ($1066\,cm^{-1}$) with noticeable intensity. The highest-frequency vibration of nitrogen atoms in the NO2 groups along the N-O bonds in BTAT and NBTAT ($1638\,cm^{-1}$–$1672\,cm^{-1}$) makes a significant contribution to the enthalpy of formation of both compounds. The fact that there are six such groups in BTAT and eight in NBTAT explains why the enthalpy of formation of NBTAT is approximately 200 kJ/mol higher than that of BTAT.

4   Computational Details

Calculations were performed at the computational node Lomonosov-2 with the following configuration: Intel(R) Xeon(R) Gold 6140 CPU @ 2.30 GHz, RAM 259 Gb, 20 Tb disk space. The authors did not intend to elaborate upon the parallelization degree of the performed calculations (despite the fact that the Gaussian package usually uses its own Linda parallelization software). However, steady acceleration on pools up to 8 cores was observed, but further this effect reduced (Fig. 11), so our calculations used 8 cores per task. It should be noted that the processors' support of the avx2 and sse42 instructions is also critical to the speed of calculations, especially the former one that can benefit by 8–10 times on some tasks using processors with a close clock rate [27]. It is highly desirable to perform calculations on SSD disks or high-speed SAS disks with a large amount of allocated disk memory, since the package creates giant intermediate files up to 2TB during the calculations. It can take up to 35–50 min to record them on an SSD disk and, of course, significantly longer on SATA arrays. The different publications report that the speed of calculations is greatly influenced by the availability of the latest versions of the Gaussian package, which makes maximum use of the hardware capabilities provided by the new series of processors, accelerating calculations for most of the used bases by up to 7–8 times. Calculation time for NBTAT by G4 (MP2) method by given conditions reached 19000 core-hours (more than three months).

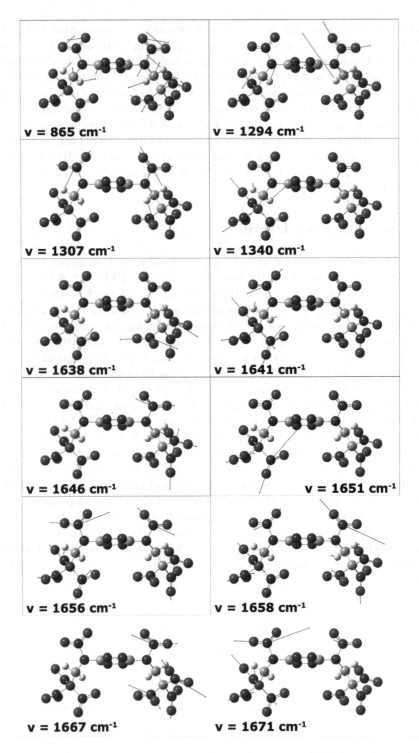

Fig. 8. Displacement vectors for the indicated frequencies (NBTAT cis-isomer).

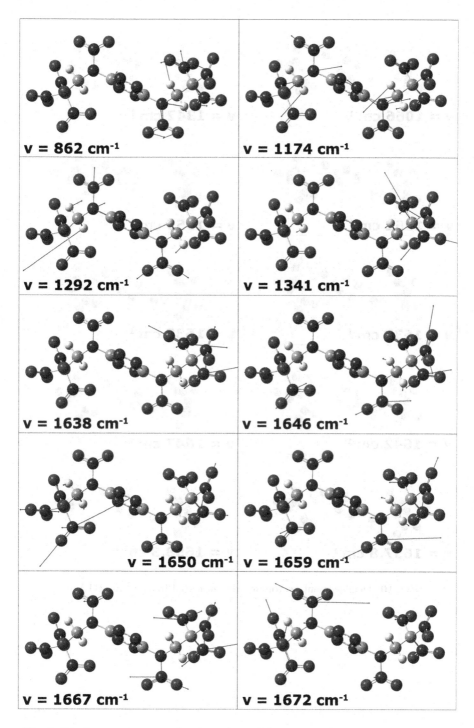

v = 862 cm⁻¹

v = 1174 cm⁻¹

v = 1292 cm⁻¹

v = 1341 cm⁻¹

v = 1638 cm⁻¹

v = 1646 cm⁻¹

v = 1650 cm⁻¹

v = 1659 cm⁻¹

v = 1667 cm⁻¹

v = 1672 cm⁻¹

Fig. 9. Displacement vectors for the indicated frequencies (NBTAT trans-isomer).

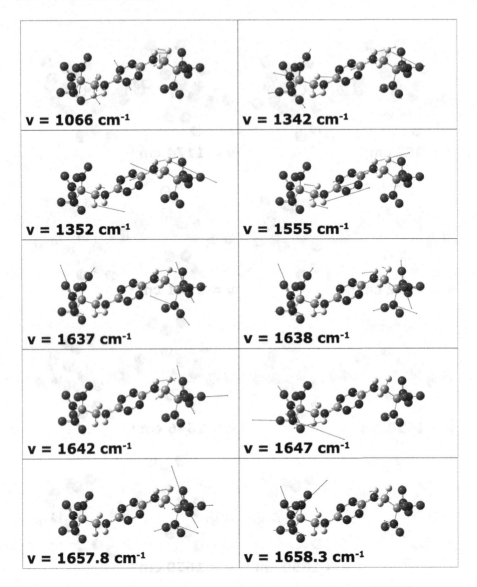

Fig. 10. Displacement vectors for the indicated frequencies (BTAT).

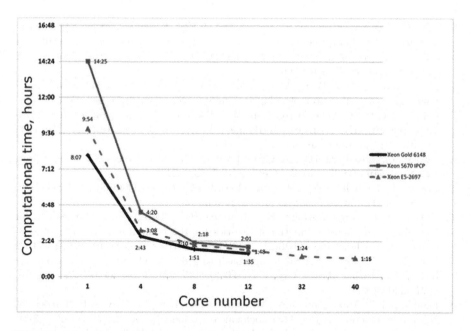

Fig. 11. Comparison of the computational time for the standard task in the Gaussian package on various computational configurations.

5 Conclusions

Parameters of the NBTAT molecule in the gas phase have been determined for the first time by quantum-chemical ab initio methods within Gaussian 09. There are two isomers (cis- and trans-), with the enthalpy of formation of the trans-isomer being 4 kJ/mol lower than that of the cis isomer. These values of enthalpies of formation are significantly higher than those of BTAT, from which NBTAT was obtained by nitration. The calculations were performed by methods of different complexity. Calculation time for NBTAT by G4 (MP2) method reached three and a half months.

Acknowledgements. The work was performed using the equipment of the Center for Collective Use of Super High-Performance Computing Resources of the Lomonosov Moscow State University [28–30] (projects Enthalpy-2065 and Enthalpy-2219). This work was carried out with the support of the RFBR grant No. 20-07-00319 and according to the state task No. AAAA-A19-119120690042-9.

References

1. Hosseini, S.G., Moeini, K., Abdelbaky, M.S.M., Garcia-Granda, S.: Synthesis, characterization, crystal structure, and thermal behavior of a new triazolium salt along with docking studies. J. Struct. Chem. **61**(3), 389–399 (2020). https://doi.org/10.26902/JSC_id52850

2. Abdulov, Kh.Sh., Mulloev, N.U., Tabarov, S.Kh., Khodiyev, M.Kh.: Quantum-chemical determinations of the molecular structure of 1,2,4-triazole and calculation of its IR spectrum. J. Struct. Chem. **61**(4), 540–544 (2020). https://doi.org/10.26902/JSC_id53992 [in Russian]

3. Lv, G., Zhang, D.-L., Wang, D, Pan, L., Liu, Y.: Synthesis, crystal structure, antibone cancer activity and molecular docking investigations of the heterocyclic compound 1-((2S,3S)-2-(benzyloxy)pentan-3-yl)-4-(4-(4-(4-hydroxyphenyl)piperazin-1-yl) phenyl)-1H-1,2,4-triazol-5(4H)-one. J. Struct. Chem. **60**(7), 1219–1225 (2019). https://doi.org/10.26902/JSC_id43057

4. Curtiss, L.A., Redfern, P.C., Raghavachari, K.: Gaussian-4 theory. J. Chem. Phys. **126**(8), 084108 (2007). https://doi.org/10.1063/1.2436888

5. Curtiss, L.A., Redfern, P.C., Raghavachari, K.: Gn theory. Comput. Mol. Sci. **1**(5), 810–825 (2011). https://doi.org/10.1002/wcms.59

6. Curtiss, L.A., Raghavachari, K., Redfern, P.C., Pople, J.A.: Assessment of Gaussian-2 and density functional theories for the computation of enthalpies of formation. J. Chem. Phys. **106**(3), 1063 (1997). https://doi.org/10.1063/1.473182

7. Palysaeva, N.V., et al.: A direct approach to a 6-Hetarylamino[1,2,4]triazolo[4,3-b][1,2,4,5]tetrazine library. Org. Lett. **16**(2), 406–409 (2014). https://doi.org/10.1021/ol403308h

8. Konkova, T.S., Matyushin, Y.N., Miroshnichenko, E.A., Vorobev, A.B., Palysaeva, N.V., Sheremetev, A.B.: Thermochemical properties of [1,2,4]Triazolo[4,3-b]-[1,2,4,5]tetrazine derivatives. Russ. J. Phys. Chem. B **14**(1), 69–72 (2020). https://doi.org/10.1134/S1990793120010042

9. Wang, G., Fu, Z., Yin, H., Chen, F.-X.: Synthesis and properties [1,2,4]Triazolo[4,3-b][1,2,4,5]Tetrazine N-Oxide explosives. Prop. Explos. Pyrotech. **44**(8), 1010–1014 (2019). https://doi.org/10.1002/prep.201900014

10. Yao, Y.-R., et al.: Synthesis, crystal structure and thermodynamic properties of 3-(3,5-dimethylpyrazol-1-yl)-6-(benzylmethylene) hydrazone-s-tetrazine. J. Chem. Thermodyn. **104**, 67–72 (2017). https://doi.org/10.1016/j.jct.2016.09.020

11. Hammerl, A., Klapötke, T.M., Rocha, R.: Azide-tetrazole ring-chain isomerism in polyazido-1,3,5-triazines, triazido-s-heptazine, and diazidotetrazines. Eur. J. Inorg. Chem. **2006**(11), 2210–2228 (2006). https://doi.org/10.1002/ejic.200600100

12. Klapötke, T.M., Piercey, D.G., Stierstorfer, J., Weyrauther, M.: The synthesis and energetic properties of 5,7-dinitrobenzo-1,2,3,4-tetrazine-1,3-dioxide (DNBTDO). Prop. Explos. Pyrotech. **37**(5), 527–535 (2012). https://doi.org/10.1002/prep.201100151

13. Hu, L., et al.: Conjugated energetic salts based on fused rings: insensitive and highly dense materials. J. Am. Chem. Soc. **140**(44), 15001–15007 (2018). https://doi.org/10.1021/jacs.8b09519

14. Tang, Y., Kumar, D., Shreeve, J.M.: Balancing excellent performance and high thermal stability in a dinitropyrazole fused 1,2,3,4-tetrazine. J. Am. Chem. Soc. **139**(39), 13684–13687 (2017). https://doi.org/10.1021/jacs.7b08789

15. Göbel, M., Klapötke, T.: Development and testing of energetic materials: the concept of high densities based on the trinitroethyl functionality. Adv. Funct. Mater. **19**(3), 347–365 (2009). https://doi.org/10.1002/adfm.200801389

16. Lempert, D.B., et al.: Synthesis of 3,6-bis(2,2,2-trinitroethylnitramino)-1,2,4,5-tetrazine. In: XV All-Russian Symposium on Combustion and Explosion Proceedings, vol. 2, pp. 161–162 (2020). (in Russian)

17. Frisch, M.J., Trucks, G.W., Schlegel, H.B., et al.: Gaussian 09, Revision B.01. Gaussian Inc., Wallingford (2010)

18. Volokhov, V.M., et al.: Computer design of hydrocarbon compounds with high enthalpy of formation. In: Sokolinsky, L., Zymbler, M. (eds.) PCT 2020. CCIS, vol. 1263, pp. 291–304. Springer, Cham (2020). https://doi.org/10.1007/978-3-030-55326-5_21

19. Volokhov, V., et al.: Predictive quantum-chemical design of molecules of high-energy heterocyclic compounds. In: Voevodin, V., Sobolev, S. (eds.) RuSCDays 2020. CCIS, vol. 1331, pp. 310–319. Springer, Cham (2020). https://doi.org/10.1007/978-3-030-64616-5_27

20. Volokhov, V.M., et al.: Quantum chemical simulation of hydrocarbon compounds with high enthalpy of formation. Russ. J. Phys. Chem. B Focus Phys. 15(1), 12–24 (2021). https://doi.org/10.1134/S1990793121010127

21. Volokhov, V.M., et al.: Predictive modeling of molecules of high-energy heterocyclic compounds. Russ. J. Inorg. Chem. 66(1), 78–88 (2021). https://doi.org/10.1134/S0036023621010113

22. Volokhov, V.M., et al.: Computer design of structure of molecules of high-energy tetrazines. Calculation of thermochemical properties. Supercomput. Front. Innov. 7(4), 68–79 (2020). https://doi.org/10.14529/jsfi200406

23. NIST-JANAF Thermochemical tables. https://janaf.nist.gov/. Accessed 30 Mar 2021

24. Computational Chemistry Comparison and Benchmark DataBase. https://cccbdb.nist.gov/hf0k.asp. Accessed 30 Mar 2021

25. Efimov, A.I., Belorukova, L.P., Vasilkova, I.V., et al.: Properties of Inorganic Compounds. Reference Book. Khimiya, Leningrad (1983). (in Russian)

26. Gurvich, L.V.: Bond Dissociation Energies. Nauka, Moscow (1974).[in Russian]

27. Grigorenko, B., Mironov, V., Polyakov, I., Nemukhin, A.: Benchmarking quantum chemistry methods in calculations of electronic excitations. Supercomput. Front. Innov. 5(4), 62–66 (2019). https://doi.org/10.14529/jsfi180405

28. Voevodin, Vl.V., Antonov, A.S., Nikitenko, D.A., et al.: Supercomputer Lomonosov-2: largescale, deep monitoring and fine analytics for the user community. Supercomput. Front. Innov. 6(2), 4–11 (2019). https://doi.org/10.14529/jsfi190201

29. Voevodin, V.V., Zhumatiy, S.A., Sobolev, S.I., et al.: Practice of "Lomonosov" supercomputer. Open Syst. 7, 36–39 (2012). (in Russian)

30. Nikitenko, D.A., Voevodin, V.V., Zhumatiy, S.A.: Deep analysis of job state statistics on "Lomonosov-2" supercomputer. Supercomput. Front. Innov. 5(2), 4–10 (2019). https://doi.org/10.14529/jsfi180201

Solution of Large-Scale Black Oil Recovery Problem in Parallel Using INMOST Platform

Igor Konshin[1,2,3,4] and Kirill Terekhov[1,2(✉)]

[1] Marchuk Institute of Numerical Mathematics, RAS, Moscow 119333, Russia
`terekhov@inm.ras.ru`
[2] Moscow Institute of Physics and Technology, Moscow 141701, Russia
[3] Dorodnicyn Computing Centre of FRC CSC, RAS, Moscow 119333, Russia
[4] Sechenov University, Moscow 119991, Russia

Abstract. We consider the parallel solution of large-scale black oil recovery problem using INMOST software platform. The primary purpose of this work is to test the limit in the ability to process large-scale meshes and solve large-scale systems using mesh data tools, partitioners and solvers provided by the INMOST platform. The black oil problem is of particular industrial interest and the solution of large-scale problems is required to address challenges posed by hard-to-recover reservoirs with contrast heterogeneous media properties. Typical reservoir scale is measured in kilometers. Geological scale properties at several meters may be available with heterogeneities consisting of thin high permeability features. Upscaling of the model with such properties results in the loss of the ability to properly capture the pressure depletion. In this paper, we deform and refine the SPE10 data up to 200 million cells with up to half a million cells per core.

Keywords: Distributed mesh · Parallel linear solvers · Black oil problem

1 Introduction

Black-oil reservoir simulation is one of the most important industrial problems. Most of the largest oil companies are involved in reservoir simulation. Oil companies are developing their own simulation software capable of solving such problems. For the most adequate modeling, it is required to solve large-scale problems of several hundred million cells in the presence of several thousand injection and production wells.

There are several publicly available systems to help formulate and solve subsurface flow simulation problems. For example, BOAST [1], Dune [2], DuMu^x [3], MRST [4], OPM [5], Trilinos [6,7], FreeFEM [8], INMOST [9] systems, and some others. Commercial oil companies usually develop their own software tools and build their own oil simulators.

© Springer Nature Switzerland AG 2021
V. Voevodin and S. Sobolev (Eds.): RuSCDays 2021, CCIS 1510, pp. 240–255, 2021.
https://doi.org/10.1007/978-3-030-92864-3_19

If one considers the solution of modeling problems for several decades of three-phase flows with dimensions of 10^9 cells using from 300 to 3000 wells, the following examples can be given. Saudi Aramco (GigaPowers) such results were obtained in 4 days of calculations [10], while several years later, similar results were obtained on 5640 computational cores in 21 h of calculations [11]. At Total/Schlumberger (Intersect), an analogous simulation on 576 cores took 10.5 h [12]. In 2017 ExxonMobil was able to solve almost the same problem using 716,800 computing cores of Cray XE6 "Blue Waters" petascale system [13]. In the same year StoneRidge (Echelon) calculates with 120 Nvidia Tesla P100 GPU accelerators in just 92 min [14].

In the present paper, we investigated the possibility of solving large-scale problems using the INMOST software platform. Of course, we do not have the ability to perform simulations on such powerful supercomputers as the largest oil companies, but we would like to demonstrate the competence to solve large-scale problems. The classical SPE10 problem [15] was considered, the formulation of which was refined to 200 million cells.

Section 2 specify the INMOST platform functional. Section 3 describes the black oil recovery problem setting. In Sect. 4, the use of the INMOST parallel sets to operate with wells is considered. Section 5 contains the results of numerical experiments. The final section summarizes the findings.

2   INMOST Functionality

To implement the model, we use the INMOST mathematical modeling toolkit [9,16–18]. INMOST provides a vast functionality that covers:

- distributed mesh and data input-output, migration and balancing of a mesh with an arbitrary number of overlapping layers, parallel organization of elements into hierarchy of sets, and dynamic mesh modification [19,20] in parallel;
- mesh partitioners including built-in K-means and reverse Cuthill–McKee (RCM) ordering based partitioners as well as external packages Metis [21], ParMetis [22], and Zoltan [23];
- automatic differentiation including management of unknowns on the mesh, along with evaluation, storage, and communication of expression calculation result with the derivatives, as well as operations on the residual vector with an automatic assembly of Jacobian matrix [17];
- linear system solution using built-in advanced incomplete factorization methods [24,25] or external solvers such as PETSc [26], Trilinos [6] or SuperLU-dist [27];
- and finally, management of complex coupled models and visualization tools.

The particular functionality that we use in the present paper is the mesh input–output, mesh overlapping and data communication, automatic differentiation with the management of unknowns, evaluation of expressions, automatic Jacobian assembly, and linear system solver.

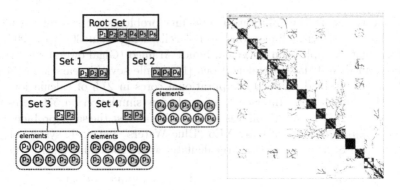

Fig. 1. Example of a distributed hierarchy of sets (left) and a distributed linear system (right).

Since we consider large mesh files, a stand-alone mesh partitioner has been developed to avoids loading the entire mesh file into memory [28]. The tool prepares a distributed mesh that is later used in calculations. It does not account for wells that may cross multiple partitions. We represent the wells as parallel sets containing all the cells penetrated by the well. The ability to synchronize set connections and set data between processors turns out to be very handy in representing distributed wells. The wells are discussed in detail later in Sect. 4.

Due to support of dynamic mesh modification in INMOST, memory is fragmented into chunks of a fixed size. When adding new elements, a new memory chunk is allocated when the existing memory is exhausted. As a result of such organization, we avoid memory invalidation due to reallocation and ensure continuous in-memory data access during mesh modification. Data can be moved between the chunks of memory for compaction, and unused chunks are released.

Such data organization leads to non-contiguous data representation and complicates message passing. Moreover, the transfer of data of a different nature is required. Such data includes values of computed expressions with derivatives or names of the sets, along with information on the set hierarchy (Fig. 1). In INMOST, data is first packaged into an intermediate binary buffer using MPI_Pack and then recovered with MPI_Unpack. The buffers are transferred via non-blocking MPI_Isend and MPI_Irecv communications, where the buffer size may be communicated a priori unless it can be predicted. Writing a file to intrinsic binary mesh format .pmf has a similar pattern. For files, the buffer information is augmented with the byte order and datatype size to ensure compatibility of binary files written by different architectures.

Conventional MPI implementations use the int datatype to represent the size in a buffer. This limits the raw binary data size corresponding to MPI_BYTE intrinsic datatype to 2 GB. The limitations affect almost all functionality, such as message passing, buffer packing, collective operations, and parallel file writing. A typical recommendation to circumvent this issue is to specify a larger intrinsic datatype, which is not suitable for raw binary data we are using. BigMPI [29] library is being developed to overcome the issue. Large buffer size is mandatory during mesh migration and large file writing. We address this issue by splitting all calls to MPI functions into multiple calls that are limited by INT_MAX buffer size. Several collective operations, including file writing procedures, have been replaced with non-collective algorithms.

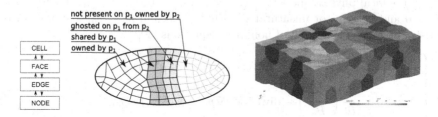

Fig. 2. Diagram of adjacency connections in INMOST (left), illustration for ghost layers (middle), and partitioned mesh (right).

Internally, INMOST uses several predefined datatypes for mesh data storage:

- INMOST_DATA_REAL_TYPE – double, 64-bit floating point,
- INMOST_DATA_ENUM_TYPE – unsigned 32-bit unsigned integer,
- INMOST_DATA_INTEGER_TYPE – int, 32-bit signed integer.

This choice may lead to a limitation of upto 2 billion active unknowns in the system. To support extra-large problem sizes, we added a compile-time option to choose a larger datatype and adopted the code accordingly. Such an option is not used in the present paper.

Additional improvements have been made to memory consumption. In the linear solver [24], we refactored and localized the memory usage to particular procedures. For the mesh, we have provided the functionality to partially delete and later restore the information on adjacency between elements (Fig. 2). This is possible since mutual connections form two adjacency graphs transposed to each other. In addition to that, the mutual adjacency connections between cells and nodes were completely eliminated, and the algorithms for their retrieval were changed accordingly. In the black-oil model implementation [17] we also removed all the unnecessary intermediate data.

3   Problem Setting

In the present section, we formulate the classical problem of isothermal secondary oil recovery control. In this problem a water is injected under pressure into the porous rock reservoir filled with water, oil, and gas of kilometer scale to recover the oil. The filtration problem governed by Darcy law for fluids and gas is solved with no-flow boundary conditions imposed at the reservoir boundaries. A feature of the problem is the complexity of physical processes, the difficulty of solving the arising linear systems, modeling for a long period. A separate requirement of real industrial applications is the solution of large-scale problems up to several hundred thousand computational cells, which is required to ensure the accuracy of modeling.

We solve for primary scalar unknowns corresponding to oil pressure p_o, water saturation S_w, and either gas saturation S_g or bubble-point pressure p_b, depending on the local physical model state. The physical state is either saturated with $S_g > 0$ and $p_b = p_o$ or unsaturated with $S_g = 0$ and $p_b < p_o$. The unknowns satisfy the following system of nonlinear equations [30]:

$$\begin{cases} \dfrac{\partial}{\partial t}\left(\dfrac{\phi S_w}{B_w}\right) - \operatorname{div}\left(\lambda_w \mathbb{K}\left(\nabla p_w - \rho_w g \nabla z\right)\right) = q_w, \\[2ex] \dfrac{\partial}{\partial t}\left(\dfrac{\phi S_o}{B_o}\right) - \operatorname{div}\left(\lambda_o \mathbb{K}\left(\nabla p_o - \rho_o g \nabla z\right)\right) = q_o, \\[2ex] \dfrac{\partial}{\partial t}\left(\phi \dfrac{S_g}{B_g} + \phi R_s \dfrac{S_o}{B_o}\right) - \operatorname{div}\left(\lambda_g \mathbb{K}\left(\nabla p_g - \rho_g g \nabla z\right)\right) \\[2ex] \qquad\qquad - \operatorname{div}\left(R_s \lambda_o \mathbb{K}\left(\nabla p_o - \rho_o g \nabla z\right)\right) = q_g + R_s q_o, \end{cases} \quad \text{in } \Omega. \tag{1}$$

System (1) is typically supplemented with the no-flow boundary conditions. In (1), the quantities are:

- ϕ^0 and $\mathbb{K}$ are piecewise-constant media properties, corresponding to the rock porosity representing the fracture of the void space in porous media and permeability tensor relating pressure gradient to the filtration velocity in the Darcy law $-\mathbb{K}\nabla p = \mathbf{u}$;
- g is the gravity constant;
- the porosity as a function of pressure is

$$\phi(p_o) = \phi^0 \left(1 + C_R(p_o - p^0)\right), \tag{2}$$

where C_R is the rock compressibility parameter and p^0 is the reference pressure;
- the water and gas pressures are

$$p_w = p_o - P_{cow}(S_w), \quad p_g = p_o + P_{cog}(S_g), \tag{3}$$

where P_{cow} and P_{cog} are oil-water and oil-gas capillary pressures dependent on water and gas saturations;
- the oil saturation is obtained from the relation

$$S_w + S_o + S_g = 1, \tag{4}$$

which indicates that the phases fill all voids;
- $R_s(p_b)$ denotes the gas solubility at given bubble-point pressure;
- $B_w(p_o)$, $B_g(p_o)$, and $B_o(p_o, p_b)$ are the water, gas, and oil formation volume factors as a function of oil pressure p_o and bubble-point pressure p_b, the factors denote the ratio between volume, occupied by the phase at surface conditions to the volume at a given pressure;
- $B_w(p_o)$ is usually parameterized by

$$B_w(p_o) = B_w^0 / \left(1 + C_{B_w}(p_o - p^0) + C_{B_w}^2(p_o - p^0)^2/2\right), \tag{5}$$

where B_w^0 is the formation volume factor at reference pressure p^0 and C_{B_w} is water compressibility;
– the oil formation volume factor is extrapolated by

$$B_o(p_o, p_b) = B_o^u(p_s + p_o - p_b) + B_o^s(p_b) - B_o^u(p_s), \tag{6}$$

where $B_o^u(p)$ and $B_o^s(p)$ are the oil formation volume factor data for unsaturated and saturated states, respectively, and p_s corresponds to minimum pressure in unsaturated state datum;
– densities are defined as

$$\rho_w(p_o) = \frac{\rho_w^s}{B_w(p_o)}, \quad \rho_g = \frac{\rho_g^s}{B_g(p_o)}, \quad \rho_o = \frac{\rho_o^s + R_s(p_b)\rho_g^s}{B_o(p_o, p_b)}, \tag{7}$$

where ρ_o^s, ρ_w^s, and ρ_g^s are the constant oil, water, and gas-phase densities at surface condition, while oil density includes dissolved gas;
– mobilities are defined by

$$\lambda_w(S_w, p_o) = \frac{k_{rw}(S_w)}{B_w(p_o)\mu_w(p_o)},$$

$$\lambda_g(S_g, p_o) = \frac{k_{rg}(S_g)}{B_g(p_o)\mu_g(p_o)}, \tag{8}$$

$$\lambda_o(S_w, S_g, p_o, p_b) = \frac{k_{ro}(S_w, S_g)}{B_o(p_o, p_b)\mu_o(p_o, p_b)},$$

where
– $\mu_w(p_o)$, $\mu_g(p_o)$, and $\mu_o(p_o, p_b)$ are the water, gas, and oil viscosity parameters;
– $\mu_w(p_o)$ is usually parameterized by

$$\mu_w(p_o) = \mu_w^0 / \left(1 - C_{\mu_w}(p_o - p^0) + C_{\mu_w}^2(p_o - p^0)^2/2\right), \tag{9}$$

where μ_w^0 is the water viscosity at reference pressure p^0 and C_μ is called water "viscosibility";
– $\mu_o(p_o, p_b)$ is defined similar to (6) by

$$\mu_o(p_o, p_b) = \mu_o^u(p_s + p_o - p_b) + \mu_o^s(p_b) - \mu_o^u(p_s), \tag{10}$$

where $\mu_o^u(p)$ and $\mu_o^s(p)$ are viscosity data for unsaturated and saturated states, respectively, and p_s corresponds to minimum pressure in unsaturated state datum;
– $k_{rw}(S_w)$, $k_{rg}(S_g)$, and $k_{ro}(S_w, S_g)$ are relative permeabilities of water in the water-oil flow, gas in the gas-oil flow, and oil in the water-oil-gas flow;
– the oil relative permeability in water-oil-gas flow is given by the second Stone's model [31]:

$$k_{ro} = \max\left(k_{rc}\left(k_{row}/k_{rc} + k_{rw}\right)\left(k_{rog}/k_{rc} + k_{rg}\right) - \left(k_{rw} + k_{rg}\right), 0\right), \quad (11)$$

where $k_{row}(S_w)$ and $k_{rog}(S_g)$ are oil relative permeability in oil-water and oil-gas flows, respectively, and $k_{rc} = \max(k_{row}) = \max(k_{rog})$;
- q_w, q_o, and q_g are source-sink terms for water, oil, and gas, respectively, which will be described in Sect. 4.

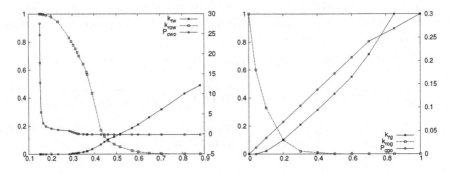

Fig. 3. Relative permeability data for oil-water (left) and oil-gas (right) flows with respect to phase saturation and corresponding capillary pressures. The scales for relative permeability and capillary pressure (in bar) are given on the left and right sides of the graph, respectively.

Formula (6) extrapolates the unsaturated state data at a given bubble point pressure. Typically at a saturated state, the oil phase volume expands at pressure growth due to the expansion of dissolved gas.

In the unsaturated state, the volume shrinks with pressure increasing, see [32] for more details. The relative permeability curves are displayed in Fig. 3. The properties of the oil and gas fluid are given in Fig. 4. Parameters for reference pressure, rock compressibility, water formation volume factor and viscosity, as well as surface density for the phases, are given in Table 1.

Table 1. Media properties.

p_0, bar	C_R	B_w^0	C_{B_w}	μ_w^0	C_{μ_w}	ρ_w^s	ρ_o^s	ρ_g^s	g
248.2113	1.450377×10^{-5}	1.0034	C_R	0.96	0	720	1000	1.124496	9.80665×10^{-5}

The phase change is performed as follows. The saturated state ($S_g > 0$, $p_b = p_o$) is changed to the unsaturated state if the gas saturation is negative after the solution update. This effect corresponds to the dissolution of gas in the oil. To physically motivate the solution update in the cell, we take into account the ratio between gas and oil accumulation terms:

$$\frac{Rs(p_b)S_o/B_o(p_b)}{S_o/B_o(p_b)} = \frac{S_g/B_g(p_o) + Rs(p_o)S_o/B_o(p_o)}{S_o/B_o(p_o)}, \tag{12}$$

where on the left is the unsaturated state, and on the right is the saturated state. The expression reduces to

$$Rs(p_b) = Rs(p_o) + \frac{S_g/B_g(p_o)}{S_o/B_o(p_o)} < Rs(p_o), \tag{13}$$

where p_o, S_g, and S_o are updated oil pressure, negative gas, and positive oil saturations, while bubble point pressure p_b is the unknown. Solution to the nonlinear problem yields the bubble point pressure for the unsaturated state $(S_g = 0, p_b < p_o)$ due to $p_b < p_o$ for $Rs(p_b) < Rs(p_o)$. Upon gas emission due to $p_b > p_o$ after update in the unsaturated state, we also take into account (12). This yields the gas concentration expression

$$S_g = \frac{S_o}{B_o(p_o)}B_g(p_o)\left(Rs(p_b) - Rs(p_o)\right) > 0, \tag{14}$$

due to $Rs(p_b) > Rs(p_o)$ for $p_b > p_o$ for unsaturated state and we switch to the saturated state $(S_g > 0, p_b = p_o)$.

The complete linear system corresponding to (1) is assembled and solved in a fully implicit fashion. To improve the performance of the linear solver, we apply Constrained Pressure Residual (CPR) scaling method [33,34] to the assembled linear system. This scaling is usually used along with multi-stage linear system solution methods where the pressure block is solved by a multigrid method. In [35], the scaling was found to significantly improve the performance of the incomplete factorization method applied to the full system as well.

The CPR procedure is performed as follows. Let $\mathcal{R}_w^i$, $\mathcal{R}_o^i$, and $\mathcal{R}_g^i$ correspond to water, oil, and gas residuals at i-th cell, respectively. Then, for each i-th cell, we compute and store two coefficients:

$$\gamma_g^i = -\frac{\partial \mathcal{R}_o^i}{\partial Y} \bigg/ \frac{\partial \mathcal{R}_g^i}{\partial Y}, \qquad \gamma_w^i = -\left(\frac{\partial \mathcal{R}_o^i}{\partial S_w} + \gamma_g \frac{\partial \mathcal{R}_g^i}{\partial S_w}\right) \bigg/ \frac{\partial \mathcal{R}_w^i}{\partial S_w}, \tag{15}$$

where Y is either S_g or p_b depending on the state in the i-th cell. It is assumed that $\partial \mathcal{R}_w^i / \partial Y = 0$. The oil residual for each i-th cell is modified as follows:

$$\mathcal{R}_o^i = \mathcal{R}_o^i + \gamma_w^i \mathcal{R}_w^i + \gamma_g^i \mathcal{R}_g^i, \tag{16}$$

which partially decouples the oil pressure unknown.

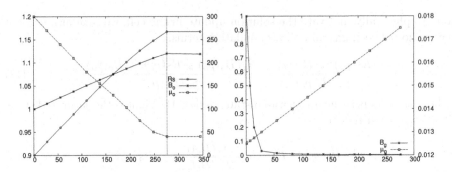

Fig. 4. The properties of the phase fluid for oil (left) and gas (right) with respect to pressure. In the left figure, the scales for oil formation volume factor and viscosity are given on the left side and solubility to the right side. In the right figure, on the left and right, the scales for the gas formation volume factor and viscosity are shown, respectively. Oil properties correspond to saturated and unsaturated states to the left and right of the vertical dashed line, respectively.

Coefficients (15) can be computed after assembling the accumulation term or the whole system to obtain true-IMPES or quasi-IMPES CPR scaling.

In the present paper, for simplicity, we use the two-point flux approximation method to calculate fluxes on interfaces of the mesh [36]. The mobilities are taken upstream based on the sign of the phase pressure head. Prior to this, the density ρ_α in the pressure head is taken upstream based on the gravity vector direction.

4   Wells

The source term for the phase α at the cell with center $\mathbf{x}_0$ is calculated by the Peaceman formula [37]:

$$q_\alpha = \lambda_\alpha WI \left(p_{bh} - p_o - \rho_\alpha g(z_{bh} - z) \right) \delta(\mathbf{x} - \mathbf{x}_0), \tag{17}$$

where q_α is the well rate, λ_α is the upstream mobility, p_{bh} is the bottom hole pressure, z_{bh} is the bottom hole depth. For a vertical source in a cubic cell with dimensions (h_x, h_y, h_z) and a diagonal permeability tensor $\mathbb{K} = \text{diag}(k_x, k_y, k_z)$, the well index WI is defined by the well bore radius r_w and skin factor s:

$$WI = \frac{2\pi h_z \sqrt{k_x k_y}}{\log\left(\frac{0.28}{r_w} \frac{\sqrt{h_x^2 (k_y/k_x)^{1/2} + h_y^2 (k_x/k_y)^{1/2}}}{(k_y/k_x)^{1/4} + (k_x/k_y)^{1/4}}\right) + s}. \tag{18}$$

Usually, the mobility λ_α upstream is taken based on the type of the well. For an injection well, the well injection stream and well pressure are used to calculate the mobility, for a production well reservoir saturations and oil pressure are used. This approach may cause problems due to cross-flow.

For a water injection well, we take

$$\lambda_\alpha^{inj} = \begin{cases} \lambda_\alpha(1, 0, p_{bh}, p_{bh}), & \text{if } p_{bh} - p_o - \rho_\alpha g(z_{bh} - z) > 0, \\ \lambda_\alpha(S_w, S_g, p_o, p_b), & \text{if } p_{bh} - p_o - \rho_\alpha g(z_{bh} - z) < 0. \end{cases} \tag{19}$$

For a production well, we take

$$\lambda_\alpha^{prod} = \begin{cases} \lambda_\alpha(S_w^n, S_g^n, p_{bh}, p_{bh}), & \text{if } p_{bh} - p_o - \rho_\alpha g(z_{bh} - z) > 0, \\ \lambda_\alpha(S_w, S_g, p_o, p_b), & \text{if } p_{bh} - p_o - \rho_\alpha g(z_{bh} - z) < 0, \end{cases} \tag{20}$$

where S_w^n and S_g^n are water and gas reservoir saturations on the previous time step. Here we assume that the production well injects back to the reservoir the same mixture that was earlier present in the reservoir. By doing so we avoid the negative diagonal in the Jacobian due to cross-flow. Note, that the density ρ_α in the phase pressure head is taken upstream using either reservoir pressure or well pressure based on the sign of $z_{bh} - z$.

The well may be controlled either by bottom hole pressure or by the total rate. In the first case, the bottom hole pressure p_{bh} is known. In the latter case, the bottom hole pressure p_{bh} is an unknown in the system. The corresponding equation is added to the system. For a well with N completions, it results in the additional equation of the form:

$$\sum_{\alpha \in \{o,w,g\}} \sum_{i=1}^N q_\alpha^i = \sum_{\alpha \in \{o,w,g\}} \sum_{i=1}^N \lambda_\alpha^i WI^i \left(p_{bh} - p_o^i - \rho_\alpha^i g(z_{bh} - z^i)\right) = q_{tot}, \tag{21}$$

where q_{tot} is the prescribed total well rate, and superscript i denotes the completed cell.

The additional equation poses a problem if the rate-controlled well crosses multiple partitions in parallel simulation. It introduces a dense row and column that couple the partitions as in Fig. 5. Usually, to circumvent the issue, the mesh partitioner is usually adopted to not cut the well [38]. We use K-means algorithm to partition the mesh due to its efficiency on extra-large meshes, but it does not currently account for the presence of wells.

An additional issue arises in the additive Schwarz parallelization of the linear solver. Wells may cause very rapid growth in the dimension of the overlapped matrix. Due to this fact, we use the block Jacobi method.

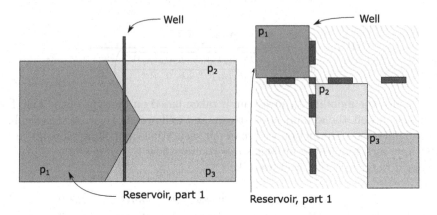

Fig. 5. Well crosses multiple partitions of the reservoir (left) and results in an additional equation in the distributed matrix (right).

Wells are implemented using the INMOST functionality of the parallel sets. The unknown well pressure is associated with the root set that resides on the lowest-ranked processor. All the cells, corresponding to the well completions, are ghosted on that processor to assemble the well equation and calculate the total production rate.

5   Numerical Experiment

Fig. 6. Several layers of porosity from the SPE10 dataset with vertical grid distortion.

We consider the permeability and porosity from the SPE10 dataset [15] that is originally has $60 \times 220 \times 85 = 1\,122\,000$ entries. The permeability is a diagonal tensor $\mathrm{diag}(k_x, k_y, k_z)$ with $k_x = k_y$. The anisotropy ratio in the individual cells data is 10458.2. The anisotropy ratio between adjacent cells is 3.85×10^{10}. We define the initial domain as a box with $240\,\text{m} \times 440\,\text{m} \times 320\,\text{m}$ dimensions in Ox, Oy, and Oz directions, respectively. To generate a finer mesh, we refine each cell by $n \times m \times k$ times in each direction. The mesh is additionally vertically distorted by a randomly generated surface map by $\tilde{z} = z + f(x, y)$. The example of vertically distorted grid colored with ten vertical layers of SPE10 porosity data is displayed in Fig. 6. The permeability tensor is rotated to follow the grid stratigraphy

$$\mathbb{K} = Q \operatorname{diag}(k_x, k_y, k_z) Q^T, \tag{22}$$

where Q is defined by the shortest arc rotation from the vertical vector $\mathbf{a} = (0, 0, 1)^T$ to vector

$$\mathbf{b} = \frac{(\partial f(x, y)/\partial x, \partial f(x, y)/\partial y, 1)^T}{\sqrt{1 + (\partial f(x, y)/\partial x)^2 + (\partial f(x, y)/\partial y)^2}}.$$

The shortest arc rotation matrix Q from vector $\mathbf{a}$ to vector $\mathbf{b}$ is defined as follows. Let $\mathbf{c} = -\mathbf{a} \times \mathbf{b}$ and $\omega = \sqrt{(\mathbf{a}^T \mathbf{a}) (\mathbf{b}^T \mathbf{b})} + \mathbf{a}^T \mathbf{b}$. Then

$$Q = \left(\mathbf{I} \left(1 - 2\mathbf{c}^T \mathbf{c} \right) + 2\mathbf{c}\mathbf{c}^T + 2\omega \operatorname{cross}(\mathbf{c}) \right) / \left(\mathbf{c}^T \mathbf{c} + \omega^2 \right), \tag{23}$$

where $\operatorname{cross}(\mathbf{x})$ is the matrix representing the cross-product with the vector $\mathbf{x} = (x, y, z)^T$:

$$\operatorname{cross}(\mathbf{x}) = \begin{bmatrix} & -z & y \\ z & & -x \\ -y & x & \end{bmatrix}. \tag{24}$$

The generator is available at [39] and is able to generate .grdecl, .vtu, and .vtk mesh files. We generate two variants of the grid from full SPE10 dataset. The variants are spe10_100M and spe10_200M with each cell refined by $3 \times 3 \times 10$ and $3 \times 3 \times 20$ that results in $100\,980\,000$ and $201\,960\,000$ cells, respectively. After grid generation, we partition the mesh for 320 cores with [28] and run the black oil problem simulation.

For simplicity, the initial conditions are uniform, oil pressure $p_o = 230\,\text{bar}$, water saturation $S_w = 0.266$, and gas saturation $S_g = 10^{-13}$. Initially all cells are in saturated state.

We introduce five vertical wells into the model. Four production wells with bottom hole pressure control are located in the corners of the mesh and one injection well with total rate control is located in the middle of the mesh. The data for the wells is given in Table 2. The well bore radius for all wells is $r_w = 5 \times 10^{-3}$ and skin factor is zero $s = 0$. A set of well completions is defined by the intersection of a segment (x, y, z)-top to (x, y, z)-bottom with the reservoir cells. For all wells $z_{bh} = 0$. The well index is computed using Peaceman formula (18) with the dimensions of a bounding box of the cell and diagonal part of the permeability tensor $\operatorname{diag}(\mathbb{K})$.

Table 2. The injection and production wells data.

Name	Control	(x, y, z)-bottom	(x, y, z)-top
INJ1	$q_{tot} = 50000$	$(118, 219, 0)$	$(118, 219, 400)$
PROD1	$p_{bh} = 175\,\mathrm{bar}$	$(1, 1, 0)$	$(1, 1, 400)$
PROD2	$p_{bh} = 175\,\mathrm{bar}$	$(1, 439, 0)$	$(1, 439, 400)$
PROD3	$p_{bh} = 175\,\mathrm{bar}$	$(239, 1, 0)$	$(239, 1, 400)$
PROD4	$p_{bh} = 175\,\mathrm{bar}$	$(239, 439, 0)$	$(239, 439, 400)$

To solve arising linear systems, we use INNER_MLMPTILUC linear solver that corresponds to BiCGStab and additive Schwartz domain decomposition method with multi-level inverse-based second-order Crout incomplete factorization preconditioner in subdomains [24]. The parameters for the preconditioner are the following: block Jacobi method with zero overlapping layers $L = 0$, dropping tolerances $\tau_1 = 10^{-2}$ and $\tau_2 = 10^{-3}$, pivoting on the growth of inverse factors norms over $\varkappa = 2.5$. The tolerances are additionally adapted during factorization according to the inverse factor norms. The maximum number of iterations is $N_l = 5000$. The convergence tolerances for the linear problem are $\tau_{l,rel} = 10^{-6}$ and $\tau_{l,abs} = 10^{-3}$.

The nonlinear problem tolerances for simplicity are $\tau_{n,rel} = 10^{-5}$ and $\tau_{n,abs} = 10^{-2}$. The maximal number of nonlinear iterations is $N_n = 15$. The Newton update is constrained by multiplying it by the parameter α. It is determined from the limit on maximum change of $0 - \varepsilon \leqslant S_w + \alpha \Delta S_w \leqslant 1 + \varepsilon$, with tolerated saturation over- and undershoot $\varepsilon = 10^{-2}$, $-\theta - \varepsilon \leqslant S_g + \alpha \Delta S_g \leqslant 1 + \varepsilon$ for saturated state with $\theta = 0.25$ and $p_b + \alpha \Delta p_b < p_o + \alpha \Delta p_o + w$ for the unsaturated state with $w = 20\,\mathrm{bar}$.

The initial time step is $\Delta t_0 = 10^{-4}$ days, maximal time step is $\Delta t = 1$ day and total simulation time is $T = 10$ days. On success, the current time step is multiplied by 1.2 until Δt is reached, on failure it is multiplied by 0.5. In total 40 time steps are performed.

The computations were performed on INM RAS cluster [40]. We have used eight compute Node Arbyte Alkazar R2Q50 G5 with 40 cores (two 20-core processors Intel Xeon Gold 6230@2.10 GHz) and 384 GB RAM.

The performance results for two large-scale problems are presented in Table 3. We have used the following notation:

- T_{mat} – linear system assembly time in seconds;
- T_{prec} – preconditioner construction time in seconds;
- T_{iter} – time in seconds for BiCGStab linear iterations;
- T_{upd} – time in seconds for the solution update along with constraints and phase switch;
- N_n – average number of nonlinear iterations;
- N_l – average number of linear iterations.

Memory usage is an important metric for large-scale problem simulation. We present this data in Table 4, where the following notation is used:

Table 3. Performance data average over Newton steps.

Case	T_{mat}	T_{prec}	T_{iter}	T_{sol}	T_{upd}	N_n	N_l
SPE10_100M	14	18.5	55.4	78.6	0.2	402	3.5
SPE10_200M	29.6	34.7	64.1	107.5	0.38	428	3.96

– M_{grid} – the average memory in MB per core for the grid and data storage;
– M_{mat} – the average memory in MB per core for the linear system;
– M_{prec} – the average memory in MB per core for the preconditioner;
– M_{tot} – the maximum peak memory in MB over all cores.

Table 4. Memory usage data.

Case	M_{grid}	M_{mat}	M_{prec}	M_{tot}
SPE10_100M	856.7	165.6	558.4	1943.6
SPE10_200M	1624	346.5	1054.3	4365.6

6   Conclusions

In the present paper, we studied the applicability of the INMOST mathematical modeling toolkit to very large problem sizes. We successfully applied the toolkit functionality to the solution of a black-oil problem with up to 200 million cells on 320 cores. Peculiarity of this work consists in modification of the open-source software INMOST to enable its application to large scale industrial problem with linear system size of more than half billion unknowns.

In the future work we shall consider even larger problem size and study the parallel efficiency as well as apply different discretization schemes. This may require code adaptation for even less memory consumption. Another direction is to consider hybrid MPI+OpenMP parallelism that requires a suitable parallel linear solver.

Acknowledgements. This work has been supported by Russian Science Foundation grant 21-71-20024.

References

1. Fanchi, J.R., Harpole, K.J., Bujnowski, S.W.: BOAST: a three-dimensional, three-phase black oil applied simulation tool (version 1.1). Volume II. Program User's Manual. US Department of Energy, Tulsa-Bartlesville, Oklahoma (1982)
2. DUNE, the Distributed and Unified Numerics Environment is a modular toolbox for solving partial differential equations (PDEs) with grid-based methods. https://dune-project.org/. Accessed 15 Apr 2021

3. DuMu^x - DUNE for multi-phase, component, scale, physics flow and transport in porous media. https://dumux.org/. Accessed 15 Apr 2021

4. The MATLAB Reservoir Simulation Toolbox (MRST). http://www.sintef.no/MRST/. Accessed 15 Apr 2021

5. The Open Porous Media (OPM) initiative. https://opm-project.org/. Accessed 15 Apr 2021

6. Trilinos - platform for the solution of large-scale, complex multi-physics engineering and scientific problems. http://trilinos.org/. Accessed 15 Apr 2021

7. Maliassov, S., Beckner, B., Dyadechko, V.: Parallel reservoir simulation using a specific software framework. In: SPE Reservoir Simulation Symposium, The Woodlands, Texas, USA, February 2013. Paper number: SPE-163653-MS

8. FreeFEM - a high level multiphysics finite element software. https://freefem.org/. Accessed 15 Apr 2021

9. INMOST: a toolkit for distributed mathematical modelling. http://www.inmost.org. Accessed 15 Apr 2021

10. Dogru, A.H., Fung, L.S.K., Middya, U., et al.: A next generation parallel reservoir simulator for giant reservoirs. In: Proceedings of the SPE Reservoir Simulation Symposium, The Woodlands, Texas, February 2009. Paper number: SPE-119272-MS

11. Dogru, A.H., Fung, L.S.K., Middya, U., et al.: New frontiers in large scale reservoir simulation. In: Proceedings of the SPE Reservoir Simulation Symposium, The Woodlands, Texas, February 2011. Paper number: SPE-142297-MS

12. Obi, E., Eberle, N., Fil, A., Cao, H.: Giga cell compositional simulation. In: IPTC 2014: International Petroleum Technology Conference (2014). Paper number: IPTC-17648-MS

13. ExxonMobil sets record in high-performance oil and gas reservoir computing. https://corporate.exxonmobil.com/Operations/Energy-technologies/Exploration-technology/ExxonMobil-sets-record-in-high-performance-oil-and-gas-reservoir-computing. Accessed 15 Apr 2021

14. Echelon 2.0: the fastest reservoir simulation software in the world. https://www.stoneridgetechnology.com/echelon-reservoir-simulation-software/. Accessed 15 Apr 2021

15. SPE10 dataset. https://www.spe.org/web/csp/datasets/set01.htm. Accessed 15 Apr 2021

16. Vassilevski, Y.V., Konshin, I.N., Kopytov, G.V., Terekhov, K.M.: INMOST - Programming Platform and Graphical Environment for Development of Parallel Numerical Models on General Grids. Moscow University Press, Moscow (2013). (in Russian)

17. Vassilevski, Y., Terekhov, K., Nikitin, K., Kapyrin, I.: Parallel Finite Volume Computation on General Meshes. Springer, Cham (2020). https://doi.org/10.1007/978-3-030-47232-0

18. Danilov, A.A., Terekhov, K.M., Konshin, I.N., Vassilevski, Y.V.: INMOST parallel platform: framework for numerical modeling. Supercomput. Front. Innov. **2**(4), 55–66 (2015)

19. Terekhov, K.: Parallel dynamic mesh adaptation within INMOST platform. In: Voevodin, V., Sobolev, S. (eds.) RuSCDays 2019. CCIS, vol. 1129, pp. 313–326. Springer, Cham (2019). https://doi.org/10.1007/978-3-030-36592-9_26

20. Terekhov, K., Vassilevski, Y.: Mesh modification and adaptation within INMOST programming platform. In: Garanzha, V.A., Kamenski, L., Si, H. (eds.) Numerical Geometry, Grid Generation and Scientific Computing. LNCSE, vol. 131, pp. 243–255. Springer, Cham (2019). https://doi.org/10.1007/978-3-030-23436-2_18

21. METIS - Serial graph partitioning and fill-reducing matrix ordering. http://glaros. dtc.umn.edu/gkhome/metis/metis/overview. Accessed 15 Apr 2021
22. ParMETIS - parallel graph partitioning and fill-reducing matrix ordering. http:// glaros.dtc.umn.edu/gkhome/metis/parmetis/overview. Accessed 15 Apr 2021
23. Zoltan - a toolkit of parallel services for dynamic, unstructured, and/or adaptive simulations. https://trilinos.github.io/zoltan.html. Accessed 15 Apr 2021
24. Terekhov, K.: Parallel multilevel linear solver within INMOST platform. In: Voevodin, V., Sobolev, S. (eds.) RuSCDays 2020. CCIS, vol. 1331, pp. 297–309. Springer, Cham (2020). https://doi.org/10.1007/978-3-030-64616-5_26
25. Kaporin, I.E., Konshin, I.N.: A parallel block overlap preconditioning with inexact submatrix inversion for linear elasticity problems. Numer. Linear Algebra Appl. 9(2), 141–162 (2002)
26. PETSc - Portable Extensible Toolkit for Scientific Computation. https://www. mcs.anl.gov/petsc/. Accessed 15 Apr 2021
27. SuperLU - Supernodal LU solver for large, sparse, nonsymmetric linear systems. https://portal.nersc.gov/project/sparse/superlu/. Accessed 15 Apr 2021
28. VTU mesh partitioner. https://github.com/kirill-terekhov/vtu2pvtu. Accessed 15 Apr 2021
29. Hammond, J.R., Schafer, A., Latham, R.: To INT_MAX... and beyond! Exploring large-count support in MPI. In: Proceedings of the 2014 Workshop on Exascale MPI, pp. 1–8. IEEE Press (2014)
30. Aziz, K., Settari, A.: Petroleum Reservoir Simulation, pp. 135–139. Applied Science Publishers Ltd., London (1979)
31. Stone, H.L.: Estimation of three-phase relative permeability and residual oil data. J. Can. Petrol. Technol. 12(04), 53–61 (1973). Paper number: PETSOC-73-04-06. https://doi.org/10.2118/73-04-06
32. Al-Marhoun, M.A.: The oil compressibility below bubble point pressure revisited-formulations and estimations. In: SPE Middle East Oil and Gas Show and Conference, Manama, Bahrain (2009). Paper number: SPE-120047-MS
33. Wallis, J.R., Kendall, R.P., Little, T.E., Nolen, J.S.: Constrained residual acceleration of conjugate residual methods. In: SPE Reservoir Simulation Symposium. Society of Petroleum Engineers (1985). Paper number: SPE-13536-MS
34. Lacroix, S., Vassilevski, Y., Wheeler, J., Wheeler, M.: Iterative solution methods for modeling multiphase flow in porous media fully implicitly. SIAM J. Sci. Comput. 25(3), 905–926 (2003)
35. Konshin, I., Terekhov, K.: Sparse system solution methods for complex problems. In: Malyshkin, V. (ed.) PaCT 2021. LNCS, vol. 12942, pp. 53–73. Springer, Cham (2021). https://doi.org/10.1007/978-3-030-86359-3_5
36. Eymard, R., Gallouët, T., Guichard, C., Herbin, R., Masson, R.: TP or not TP, that is the question. Comput. Geosci. 18(3), 285–296 (2014). https://doi.org/10.1007/s10596-013-9392-9
37. Peaceman, D.W.: Interpretation of well-block pressures in numerical reservoir simulation (includes associated paper 6988). Soc. Petrol. Eng. J. 18(03), 183–194 (1978)
38. Usadi, A.K., Mishev, I.: Parallel adaptive data partitioning on a reservoir simulation using an unstructured grid. US patent WO 2009/075945 A1, 18 June 2009
39. SPE10 distorted grid generator. https://github.com/kirill-terekhov/spe10grdecl. Accessed 15 Apr 2021
40. INM RAS cluster. http://cluster2.inm.ras.ru/en. Accessed 15 Apr 2021

Supercomputer Simulation of Turbulent Flow Around Isolated UAV Rotor and Associated Acoustic Fields

Vladimir Bobkov[1]([✉]), Andrey Gorobets[1], Tatiana Kozubskaya[1], Xin Zhang[2,3], and Siyang Zhong[2]

[1] Keldysh Institute of Applied Mathematics of RAS, Moscow, Russia
{vbobkov,gorobets,tkozubskaya}@keldysh.ru
[2] Department of Mechanical and Aerospace Engineering, The Hong Kong University of Science and Technology, Kowloon, Clear Water Bay, Hong Kong SAR, China
{aexzhang,zhongsy}@ust.hk
[3] HKUST-Shenzhen Research Institute, Shenzhen, Nanshan District, China

Abstract. The paper presents the results of supercomputer simulations of turbulent flow around a rotor of a small-scale unmanned aerial vehicle. Rotor aerodynamics and near-field acoustics are modeled using both RANS and scale-resolving hybrid RANS-LES approaches. The underlying numerical method uses an edge-based reconstruction scheme for higher-accuracy discretization on unstructured mixed-element meshes. The far-field acoustics are evaluated using the integral Ffowcs-Williams and Hawkings method. The numerical results are compared with the available experimental data. The simulations were carried out on a hybrid supercomputer using several dozen GPUs. The parallel efficiency of the simulation code and comparison of performance on different types of computing devices are also presented.

Keywords: UAV rotor · Supercomputer simulation · Turbulent flow · Computational aerodynamics · Computational aeroacoustics · GPU computing

1 Introduction

The interest in Unmanned Aerial Vehicles (UAVs) is growing rapidly, especially nowadays, since small UAVs are widely intruding in our everyday life and in civil applications. The unique ability of vertical-lift vehicles to hover has great potential for passenger and cargo transportation, delivery systems, inspection and surveillance missions, and disaster relief. Modern low-fidelity conceptual design and sizing tools previously developed for the developments of large helicopters can also be used for the design of small-scaled aircrafts. At the same time,

V. Bobkov—Dedicated to my father passed away in 2021 - the Engineer and the Dreamer who has always expired.

© Springer Nature Switzerland AG 2021
V. Voevodin and S. Sobolev (Eds.): RuSCDays 2021, CCIS 1510, pp. 256–269, 2021.
https://doi.org/10.1007/978-3-030-92864-3_20

an accurate prediction of rotorcraft performance continues to be challenging. The inherent turbulent flows are essentially unsteady, nonlinear and complex. Moreover, the civil orientation of UAVs poses rather stringent requirements on the noise generated by them, and especially on the noise heard on the ground. High-fidelity Computational Fluid Dynamics (CFD) methods have a definite advantage over low-fidelity tools for the investigations of unsteady turbulent aerodynamics with multiple interactions (for instance, in case of multi-rotor vehicles) and aeroacoustics of UAVs. However, these methods usually require highly refined meshes and long computation times. Only modern supercomputers are able to perform such computations and thus make them available to UAV engineers and designers. Nowadays, CFD methods are widely used not only for simulating the aerodynamics and acoustics of isolated UAVs propellers [1], but also for modeling fully assembled UAVs including multiple rotors, airframe and landing gears [2,3]. The objective of the present work is to compare a high-fidelity scale-resolving approach with a low-fidelity method based on solving the Reynolds-Averaged Navier–Stokes (RANS) equations as applied to simulating aerodynamics and acoustics of the isolated UAV rotor in hover. As a scale-resolving approach, we use the Improved Delayed Detached Eddy Simulation (IDDES) method.

2 Mathematical Model and Numerical Method

The flow around a rotor rotating at an angular velocity ω is calculated using the system of Reynolds-averaged Navier–Stokes equations closed by the Spalart–Allmaras turbulence model. The system of equations is considered in a noninertial rotating reference frame. The coordinate axes rotate around the fixed rotor axis at a constant angular velocity equal to that of blade rotation. This means that the rotor blades in a flow are fixed, while the upstream flow direction changes depending on the azimuth angle ψ.

As shown in [4], in the absence of turbulence the system of Navier–Stokes equations for a compressible gas written in a noninertial rotating reference frame for the absolute velocity vector takes the form

$$\frac{\partial \rho}{\partial t} + \mathrm{div}\,\rho\,(\mathbf{u} - \mathbf{V}) = 0$$
$$\frac{\partial \rho \mathbf{u}}{\partial t} + \mathrm{div}\,\rho\,(\mathbf{u} - \mathbf{V}) \otimes \mathbf{u} + \nabla p = \mathrm{Div}\mathbf{S} - \rho\,(\omega \times \mathbf{u}) \qquad (1)$$
$$\frac{\partial E}{\partial t} + \mathrm{div}\,(\mathbf{u} - \mathbf{V})\,E + \mathrm{div}\mathbf{u}p = \mathrm{div}\mathbf{q} + \mathrm{div}\mathbf{S}\mathbf{u}$$

where ρ is the density, $\mathbf{u}$ is the absolute velocity vector in the fixed reference frame, p is the pressure with respect to the equation of state $p = \rho\varepsilon(\gamma - 1)$, ε is the internal energy, γ is the specific ratio, $E = \rho\mathbf{u}^2/2 + \rho\varepsilon$ is the total energy, $\mathbf{S}$ is the viscous stress tensor, $\mathbf{q}$ is the heat flux and $\mathbf{V} = \omega \times \mathbf{r}$ is the vector of the linear velocity of rotation determined by the angular velocity vector ω. From the standpoint of an observer in the fixed reference frame the system of Eq. (1) governs the variation in the conservative variables due to the

following three reasons: the transport in the medium rotating at the velocity
V, the pressure gradient and the vector velocity rotation through the azimuthal
angle $\psi(t) = -|\boldsymbol{\omega}|t$.

In this study, the technique of the RANS-based modeling of turbulent flow
needs the introduction of the turbulent viscosity. To determine it, the RANS
system is supplemented with the Spalart–Allmaras (SA) transport equation

$$\frac{\partial \rho \tilde{\nu}}{\partial t} + \mathrm{div}\rho\tilde{\nu}\left(\mathbf{u} - \mathbf{V}\right) = D_\nu + G_\nu - Y_\nu. \tag{2}$$

The definition of terms D_ν, G_ν and Y_ν describing, respectively, the diffusion,
generation and dissipation of turbulence can be found, for example, in [5]. The
value $\tilde{\nu}$ is used to calculate the turbulent viscosity coefficient μ_T as

$$\mu_T = \rho\tilde{\nu}\frac{\chi^3}{\chi^3 + 357.911}, \quad \chi = \frac{\rho\tilde{\nu}}{\mu},$$

where μ is the molecular viscosity coefficient.

The recent formulation of the hybrid RANS-LES approach IDDES [6] based
on the SA turbulence model [5] is used for scale-resolving simulations. It is
advanced by using special adapting subgrid scale [7,8] that facilitates faster
RANS-to-LES transition in shear layers.

In this work, the integral formulation "1A" of the Ffowcs-Williams and Hawkings (FWH) method proposed by Farassat [12] is used for estimating the acoustic
characteristics of the rotor. The "1A" formulation supposes the use of a control
surface of an arbitrary shape so that the velocity in the control-surface points is
assumed to be subsonic. Otherwise, when passing over the speed of sound, the
integral formula contains a singularity that makes it difficult to apply the FWH
for a rotating rotor. Some solutions of this problem are proposed in [13,14]. However, their implementation is quite complicated and entails significant additional
computational costs. A rather simple and efficient way to implement the modification of "1A" formulation for a rotating rotor is proposed in [15]. The key idea
of this modification is the parameterization of control surface in the absolute reference frame associated with the helicopter fuselage and not in the non-inertial
rotating reference frame associated with the rotor. It is required that the control
surface must be a surface of revolution about the axis of the rotor. This assumption keeps the surface non-deforming under the proposed parameterization. In
addition, the use of a uniform surface mesh in spherical coordinates provides a
simple procedure of the variables interpolation and the corresponding calculation of the angular derivatives at each point laying on the control surface. As a
result, the problem reduces to calculating the surface integral with delay basing
on the necessary data on the surface moving with respect to the background
flow.

To solve the problem numerically, we use the higher-accuracy finite-volume
method implemented in the NOISEtte code [17]. It is based on the EBR (Edge-
Based Reconstruction) scheme for unstructured meshes [9], the higher accuracy
of which is ensured by the quasi-1D reconstructions of variables on the extended

edge-oriented stencils to calculate the numerical flux. The method is built for the vertex-centered formulation meaning that the variables are defined in the mesh nodes while the fluxes – in the midpoints of mesh edges. The techniques are developed for mixed-element unstructured meshes consisting of tetrahedrons, hexahedrons, triangular prisms and pyramids. To apply the finite-volume app-roach, around the mesh vertices we construct cells of the dual mesh and approxi-mate the Navier – Stokes equations (1) by writing the conservation laws for these cells.

Let us $Q = (\rho, \rho\mathbf{u}, E, \rho\tilde{\nu})$ is the vector of conservative variables. Than the conservation law for the system of Eqs. (1)–(2) for the cell K_i (Fig. 1, left) built around the node i can be written in the following integral form:

$$\int_{K_i} \frac{dQ}{dt} dV + \int_{\partial K_i} \left(\mathcal{F}^C (Q) \cdot n - (V \cdot n) Q \right) dS = \int_{\partial K_i} \mathcal{F}^V (Q, \nabla Q) \cdot n \, dS$$

$$+ \int_{K_i} S(Q, \nabla Q) \, dV,$$

where $\mathcal{F}^C (Q)$ and $\mathcal{F}^V (Q, \nabla Q)$ are the convective and viscous fluxes, respec-tively, $S(Q, \nabla Q)$ is the source term (right hand side of the Eq. (2)), ∂K_i is the boundary of cell K_i, n is the external unit normal to the boundary ∂K_i.

The numerical scheme is built as

$$\frac{dQ_i}{dt} = -\frac{1}{|K_i|} \sum_{j \in N_1(i)} h_{ij} + S(Q_i, (\nabla Q)_i), \quad h_{ij} = h_{ij}^C + h_{ij}^V,$$

where $|K_i|$ is the volume of the cell K_i, $N_1(i)$ is the set of mesh nodes neighboring to the vertex i, h_{ij} is the numerical flux approximating the physical flux at the boundary face between the cells K_i and K_j. Note that the numerical flux h_{ij} consists of two parts: h_{ij}^C and h_{ij}^V corresponding to the approximate convective and viscous fluxes respectively.

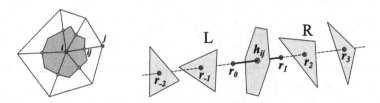

Fig. 1. Median control volume (left) and spatial EBR5 scheme stencil (right) (Color figure online)

The approximation of convective flux h_{ij}^C is governed by an approximate Riemann solver. Here we use the Roe method allowing to represent the flux as the weighted sum of central-difference and upwind approximations. The upwind summand is responsible for the scheme dissipation and can be controlled by the weight coefficient.

$$h_{ij}^C (t) = \underbrace{\frac{\mathcal{F}^C (\boldsymbol{Q}_i) + \mathcal{F}^C (\boldsymbol{Q}_j)}{2} \cdot \boldsymbol{n}_{ij} - V_{ij} \frac{\boldsymbol{Q}_i + \boldsymbol{Q}_j}{2}}_{transport}$$

$$\underbrace{- \frac{\delta}{2} \boldsymbol{T} \, |\boldsymbol{\Lambda}_{ij} - V_{ij} \boldsymbol{I}| \, \boldsymbol{T}^{-1} (\boldsymbol{Q}_j - \boldsymbol{Q}_i)}_{diffusion} , \tag{3}$$

$$\boldsymbol{n}_{ij} = \int\limits_{\partial K_i(t) \cap K_j(t)} \boldsymbol{n} dS , \quad V_{ij} = \int\limits_{\partial K_i \cap K_j} \boldsymbol{V} \cdot \boldsymbol{n} dS , \quad \boldsymbol{A}_{ij} = \frac{d\mathcal{F}^C}{d\boldsymbol{Q}} (\boldsymbol{Q}_{ij}) = \boldsymbol{T}_{ij} \boldsymbol{\Lambda}_{ij} \boldsymbol{T}_{ij}^{-1} ,$$

where $\boldsymbol{A}_{ij}$ is the Jacobi matrix for the conservative variables $\boldsymbol{Q}_{ij}$ defined in the edge ij midpoints, $\boldsymbol{\Lambda}_{ij}$ is the diagonal matrix consisting of the eigenvalues of the Jacobian $\boldsymbol{A}_{ij}$, $\boldsymbol{n}_{ij}$ is the oriented square of the face ij, δ the weight coefficient controlling the numerical dissipation.

To improve the accuracy of convective-flux h_{ij}^C approximation (3) we use the quasi-1D reconstruction on the extended edge-oriented stencil [10]. To do this, we replace the values $\boldsymbol{Q}_i$ and $\boldsymbol{Q}_j$ in (3) by their values $\boldsymbol{Q}_{ij}^L$ and $\boldsymbol{Q}_{ij}^R$ reconstructed from the both sides (denote them as left (L) and right (R) ones) from the face separated the cells K_i and K_j, and keep the same matrices $\boldsymbol{S}$ and $\boldsymbol{\Lambda}$. For the EBR5 scheme, the reconstructed $\boldsymbol{Q}_{ij}^L$ and $\boldsymbol{Q}_{ij}^R$ are calculated using the stencil with the corresponding notations (Fig. 1, right). It consists of six points (three marked in red and three marked in blue in Fig. 1). The reconstruction operators $\mathbb{R}_{ij}^{EBR5,L}$ and $\mathbb{R}_{ij}^{EBR5,R}$ as applied to an arbitrary mesh function $\{Y_k\}$ can be written in terms of finite differences $\Delta Y_{k+1/2} = \dfrac{(Y_{k+1} - Y_k)}{\Delta r_{k+1/2}}$, where $\Delta r_{k+1/2} = |\boldsymbol{r}_{k+1} - \boldsymbol{r}_k|$, in the following form

$$\mathbb{R}_{ij}^{EBR5,L} (\{Y\}) = Y_i + \frac{\Delta r_{7/2}}{2} \left(-\frac{1}{15} \Delta Y_{-\frac{3}{2}} + \frac{11}{30} \Delta Y_{-\frac{1}{2}} + \frac{4}{5} \Delta Y_{\frac{1}{2}} - \frac{1}{10} \Delta Y_{\frac{3}{2}} \right) ,$$

$$\mathbb{R}_{ij}^{EBR5,R} (\{Y\}) = Y_j - \frac{\Delta r_{7/2}}{2} \left(-\frac{1}{15} \Delta Y_{\frac{5}{2}} + \frac{11}{30} \Delta Y_{\frac{3}{2}} + \frac{4}{5} \Delta Y_{\frac{1}{2}} - \frac{1}{10} \Delta Y_{-\frac{1}{2}} \right) .$$

The numerical viscous flux h_{ij}^V evaluated using Galerkin's finite element method based on piecewise linear approximation.

It should be noted that on translationally-invariant meshes (i.e. on the meshes invariant with respect to the transfer on each edge-vector) in the linear case with a smooth solution, the EBR5 scheme reduces to the finite-difference scheme of the 5th order of accuracy. As a finite-volume method on an arbitrary unstructured mesh, the EBR5 scheme (as all the schemes of EBR family) provides the accuracy order not higher than second. However, the EBR schemes usually give much lower error in practical applications compared to the traditional Godunov-type methods (comparative tests can be found, for instance, in [9]).

For the temporal integration, we use the second-order implicit BDF2 scheme with the Newton linearization of the space-discretized equations. At each Newton iteration, the corresponding system of linear algebraic equations is solved by the preconditioned BiCGSTAB method [11].

3 Parallel Implementation

The scale-resolving CFD simulations shown here are typically rather resource-intensive. As always, supercomputer resources are scarce, and a long queue forms around them in a big spiral. Therefore, being able to efficiently use whatever supercomputer equipment that is miraculously available at the moment is of critical importance. In order to compute on everything our parallel implementation is highly portable. It is based on a multilevel MPI+OpenMP+OpenCL parallelization.

Distributed-memory MPI parallelization works at the upper level. It is well suited for large supercomputers with thousands of compute nodes. Let us briefly summarize here its key features:

- two-level decomposition, first between cluster nodes, then between MPI processes inside nodes to reduce network traffic;
- reordering of nodes of MPI subdomains into inner and interface sets to simplify management of communications;
- overlap of communications and computations to hide data transfer overhead;
- multithreaded packing and unpacking of MPI messages to speedup updates of mesh functions in the interface zones between subdomains;

Then, shared-memory OpenMP parallelization takes care of manycore CPUs and accelerators (such as the Intel Xeon Phi), occupying them with dozens and hundreds of parallel threads needed to saturate their simultaneously-multithreaded cores. The OpenMP algorithm is mainly based on multi-level partitioning of the mesh graph rather than loop parallelism. Its key features are:

- decomposition-based shared memory parallelization to improve data locality;
- binding of threads to cores to prevent migration between NUMA nodes;
- reordering of nodes by subdomains of threads to improve data locality;
- Cuthill–McKee reordering [16] to improve memory access efficiency.

More detailed information about our MPI+OpenMP parallelization and its parallel efficiency in simulations can be found in [17].

Finally, to compute on GPUs and other kinds of massively-parallel accelerators, we use the OpenCL standard, which allows us to exploit GPUs of various vendors, including NVIDIA, AMD, Intel, as well as other supporting devices and CPUs. Again, some highlights of this parallel level:

- heterogeneous execution on both CPUs and GPUs using two-level partitioning with load balancing to use computing power of both kinds of devices;

- maximum similarity of the "CPU" (C++) and OpenCL versions and identical data format to ease modifiability and maintenance;
- since so called kernel code that runs on GPUs is generated at runtime of the CPU program, preprocessor directives are extensively used to avoid if-else and switch statements, which introduce notable overhead;
- automated consistency checks for OpenCL vs CPU versions to ensure that CPUs and GPUs are doing the same computational algorithm;
- overlap of communications and computations to hide data exchange costs, which are significantly higher than in the CPU computing.
- minimization of work-item tasks to increase occupancy of compute units;
- mixed single and double floating point precision (single precision in some heavy arrays of discrete operator coefficients and in the linear solver) to reduce memory consumption and memory traffic, of course without affecting the accuracy of the results [18];
- reordering of mesh objects (block Cuthill–McKee, lexicographical sorting) to improve memory access locality;
- new numerical algorithms with reduced memory consumption [18,19].

Further details on improvements of the numerical algorithm and software implementation towards heterogeneous computing can be found in [18,20].

To outline the parallel performance, several tests have been performed in the most relevant numerical configuration: the EBR5 scheme [9] on an unstructured mixed-element mesh is space, the BDF2 implicit scheme in time, and the IDDES hybrid RANS-LES approach [6] for turbulence modeling.

Heterogeneous performance is tested on the Lomonosov-2 supercomputer [21] (one 14-core Intel Xeon E5-2697 v3 CPU and and one NVIDIA K40 GPU per node). Figure 2 shows comparison of performance of the CPU-only, GPU-only and heterogeneous CPU+GPU modes on a mesh of 12.5 million nodes. The plot shows acceleration relative to the CPU-only performance on 5 nodes (minimum to fit in memory). The performance ratio can be seen along with the linearity of the speedup. The lowest parallel efficiency is in the CPU+GPU mode, which is 88% on 30 nodes. The gain from the heterogeneous mode compared to the GPU-only mode is about 25–30%.

GPU performance is tested on the K60-GPU cluster, which has newer models of compute devices (two 16-core Intel Xeon Gold 6142 CPUs and four NVIDIA V100 GPUs per node). The parallel speedup is measured starting from 3 cluster nodes (minimum for memory requirements) on a finer mesh of 80 million nodes. The parallel efficiency in the GPU mode remains rather high, 87% on 36 GPUs. The computing time per time step is about 0.7 s and 0.27 s on 12 and 36 GPUs, respectively. The GPU to CPU performance ratio appeared to be about 8:1, which agrees well with the memory bandwidth ratio about 7:1. In this practical test, we have obtained the equivalent of at least 4500 CPU cores from 36 GPUs. The gain from the overlap of communications and computations was measured on 8 nodes using 32 GPUs. The communication-hiding asynchronous mode is 11% faster than the synchronous one. The OpenMP speedup has also been measured: on these 16-core CPUs (Hyper-Threading on), it is about 13× compared to the sequential execution.

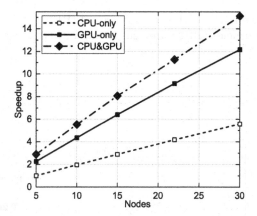

Fig. 2. Parallel speedup starting from 5 hybrid nodes of Lomonosov-2 (1 14-core CPU +1 GPU NVIDIA K40 per node) on a mesh of 12.5 million nodes relative to the CPU-only performance of 5 nodes.

4   Problem Setup

The small scaled UAV rigid rotor in hover is studied. The geometry of the rotor is based on a benchmark propeller designed and measured at the Hong Kong University of Science and Technology (HKUST). The two-bladed highly-twisted propeller shape is based on the NACA4412 airfoil profile and is 24 cm in diameter (see Fig. 3).

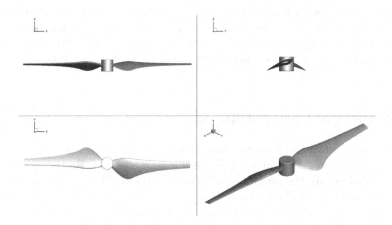

Fig. 3. UAV rotor geometry

The propeller hub is represented by 17 mm diameter cylinder with the rounded edges. In the experiment, both aerodynamics and acoustics were studied for a wide range of rotational speeds. In this study, the propeller rotational

speeds are 60, 90 and 120 revolutions per second (RPS), and the corresponding
blade passage frequencies (BPF) are 120, 180 and 240 Hz, respectively.

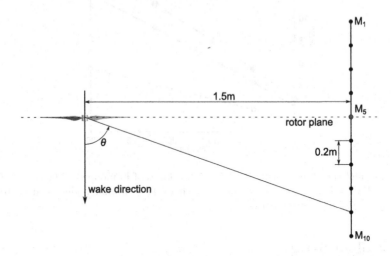

Fig. 4. Microphones array setup

The acoustics field near the rotating propeller was measured inside an ane-
choic chamber at the HKUST. The linear microphones array was placed at 1.5
meters away from the propeller parallel to the propeller axis of rotation. The
array line included 10 microphones M_1–M_{10} positioned with 0.2 m distance along
the line, so that microphone M_5 lays in the rotor plane at 1.5 m from the axis of
rotation. The elevation angle θ is the polar angle between the microphone and
the downstream direction, such that $\theta < 90°$ and $\theta > 90°$ refer to the region
that is downstream and upstream of the propeller disk plane, respectively (see
Fig. 4).

5   Numerical Case Setup

For the whole rotational velocity range, the same RANS mesh was used. Due to
rotor symmetry, as shown in [4], it is possible to model a single 180° sector with
a single blade using the periodic boundary conditions. The height of near-wall
prismatic elements is chosen to provide $y^+ < 1$ for the maximum rotational
velocity $120\,RPS$. The mesh is refined downstream the tip vortex region (see
Fig. 5, left). The RANS mesh for a single blade consists of 4.5 million nodes and
23 million elements.

The mesh for IDDES simulation is build in the same way (see Fig. 5, right) for
the whole two-blade propeller. The surface mesh on the rotor surface is refined
at the blade tip. From the preliminary RANS simulation, downstream the tip
vortex region is known and the structured mesh block is build there (Fig. 5, left)

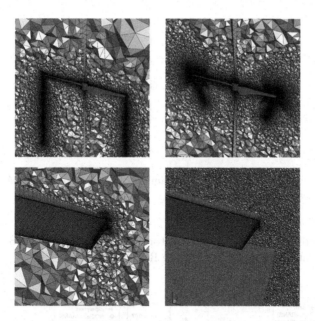

Fig. 5. Computational meshs for RANS (left) and IDDES (right) simulations

to provide a higher accuracy in this region. The DES mesh for the whole rotor consists of 60 million nodes and 200 million elements.

In all presented simulations, the boundary conditions setup is the same except for the periodic planes used only in the RANS cases. At the outer boundaries, the non-reflecting boundary conditions are set. On the rotor surface, the no-slip boundary conditions are used taking into account the surface rotational velocity within rotating frame of reference.

The Reynolds number is calculated by the maximum blade chord b = 0.32 m, the reference density $\rho_0 = 1.2046 \, \text{kg/m}^3$, the dynamic viscosity $\mu_0 = 1.815 \times 10^{-5} \, Pa \cdot s$ and the blade tip velocity V_{tip} as $Re = \rho_0 V_{tip} b / \mu_0$. The Reynolds number values corresponding to rotational speed 60, 90 and 120 RPS are 9.54×10^5, 14.22×10^5 and 19.03×10^5, respectively.

6   Results

Four computational experiments are performed: the RANS-based simulations for rotational speeds 60, 90 and 120 RPS and the scale-resolving IDDES simulation for 120 RPS. The typical flow field picture is shown in Fig. 6.

The maximum 20 m/s flow velocity induced by the rotor is observed below the rotor blade tips. The direction of streamlines above the rotor points to the low pressure zone, and a jet-like flow is observed below the rotor rotation plane.

The rotor aerodynamics are predicted well enough. The comparative analysis of thrust and torque against the experimental data shows a good agreement.

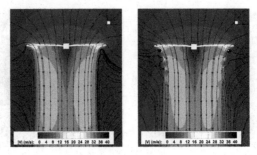

Fig. 6. Velocity magnitude field and streamlines in xOy section for RANS (left) and IDDES (right) at rotation speed 120 RPS

It is remarkable that both thrust and torque predicted by IDDES are closer to the experiment in comparison with the RANS prediction.

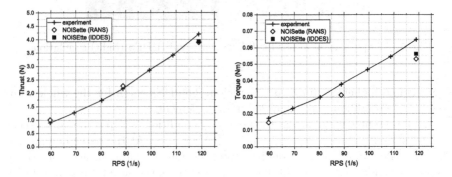

Fig. 7. Comparison of thrust (left) and torque (right) with the experimental data

The propeller acoustics predicted by RANS catches only first few blade-passing frequencies (BPF) (see Fig. 8, 9 and 10). With increasing the rotational velocity the RANS computations provides a higher accuracy of the first BPF prediction: the average error is -1.7 dB for 60 RPS, -1.6 dB for 90 RPS and $+1.5$ dB for 120 RPS. The acoustics predicted by IDDES as evaluated for 120 RPS is closer to the experiment than the RANS data: the average error is $-0.34\,dB$ for the first BPF amplitude.

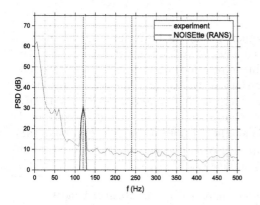
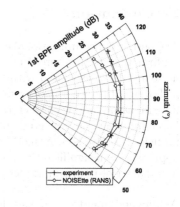

Fig. 8. Power spectral density (left) and first BPF directivity diagram, 60 *RPS*

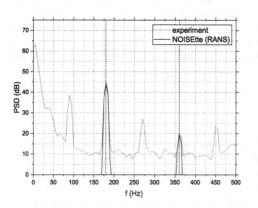
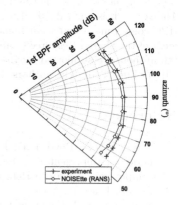

Fig. 9. Power spectral density (left) and first BPF directivity diagram, 90 *RPS*

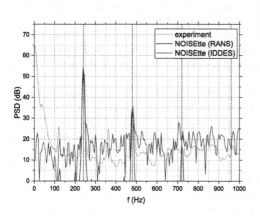
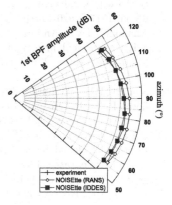

Fig. 10. Power spectral density (left) and first BPF directivity diagram, 120 *RPS*

7   Conclusion

The performed computational experiments using the RANS and IDDES methods confirm that both approaches are capable to predict aerodynamics and tonal noise at BPF (associated with the blade rotation) of an isolated UAV propeller in hover with acceptable accuracy. Both methods show reasonable results for integral aerodynamic characteristics of a rotor. As for aeroacoustics, the IDDES-based approach, as expected, allows to get more accurate sound pressure in the far field. It is also shown that the efficient heterogeneous implementation of these approaches can significantly speed up the predictions and allows to obtain results in a matter of hours on modern hybrid clusters.

Acknowledgments. The work has been supported by the Russian Fund for Basic Research (Project 19-51-80001 with acronym SONG within the BRICS STI Framework Programme). The development of the baseline OpenCL parallelization for GPU computing has been funded by the Russian Science Foundation, project 19-11-00299. The research is carried out using the equipment of the shared research facilities of HPC computing resources at Lomonosov Moscow State University [21] and the equipment of the Shared Resource Center of KIAM RAS (http://ckp.kiam.ru). The 4th and 5th authors are supported by the National Key R&D Program of China (Grant No. 2018YFE0183800). The authors thankfully acknowledge these institutions.

References

1. Zawodny, N.S., Boyd, D.D, Jr., Burley, C.L.: Acoustic Characterization and Prediction of Representative, Small-Scale Rotary-Wing Unmanned Aircraft System Components. American Helicopter Society (AHS) Annual Forum (2016)
2. Ventura Diaz, P., Yoon, S.: High-fidelity computational aerodynamics of multirotor unmanned aerial vehicles. In: 2018 AIAA Aerospace Sciences Meeting (2018). https://doi.org/10.2514/6.2018-1266
3. Zawodny, N.S., Boyd, D.D.: Investigation of Rotor-airframe interaction noise associated with small-scale rotary-wing unmanned aircraft systems. J. Am. Helic. Soc. **65**(1), 1–17 (2020). https://doi.org/10.4050/jahs.65.012007
4. Abalakin, I.V., Anikin, V.A., Bakhvalov, P.A., Bobkov, V.G., Kozubskaya, T.K.: Numerical investigation of the aerodynamic and acoustical properties of a shrouded rotor. Fluid Dyn. **51**(3), 419–433 (2016). https://doi.org/10.1134/S0015462816030145
5. Spalart, P.R., Allmaras, S.R.: A one-equation turbulence model for aerodynamic flows. In: 30th Aerospace Sciences Meeting and Exhibit, Aerospace Sciences Meetings. AIAA Paper 1992–0439 (1992). https://doi.org/10.2514/6.1992-439
6. Guseva, E.K., Garbaruk, A.V., Strelets, M.K.: Assessment of Delayed DES and Improved Delayed DES Combined with a Shear-Layer-Adapted Subgrid Length-Scale in Separated Flows. Flow, Turbulence and Combustion **98**(2), 481–502 (2017). https://doi.org/10.1007/s10494-016-9769-7
7. Duben, A.P., Kozubskaya, T.K.: Evaluation of quasi-one-dimensional unstructured method for jet noise prediction. AIAA J. **57**(7), 1–14 (2019). https://doi.org/10.2514/1.J058162

8. Pont-Vilchez, A., Duben, A., Gorobets, A., Revell, A., Oliva, A., Trias, F.X.: New strategies for mitigating the gray area in delayed-detached eddy simulation models. AIAA J. **59**, 1–15 (2021). https://doi.org/10.2514/1.J059666

9. Abalakin, I., Bakhvalov, P., Kozubskaya, T.: Edge-based reconstruction schemes for unstructured tetrahedral meshes. Int. J. Numer. Methods Fluids. **81**(6), 331–356 (2015). https://doi.org/10.1002/fld.4187

10. Bakhvalov, P.A., Kozubskaya, T.K.: Construction of edge-based 1-exact schemes for solving the Euler equations on hybrid unstructured meshes. Comput. Math. Math. Phys. **57**(4), 680–697 (2017). https://doi.org/10.1134/s0965542517040030

11. Van der Vorst, H.A.: Bi-CGSTAB: a fast and smoothly converging variant of Bi-CG for the solution of nonsymmetric linear systems. SIAM J. Sci. Stat. Comput. **13**, 631–644 (1992)

12. Farassat, F.: Derivation of formulations 1 and 1A of Farassat. NASA Technical Memorandum 2007–214853, NASA, Langley Research Center, Hampton (2007)

13. Farassat, F., Myers, M.K.: The Kirchhoff formula for a supersonically moving surface. In: First CEAS/AIAA Aeroacoustics Conference (16th AIAA Aeroacoustics Conference), Munich, Germany, June 12–15, AIAA Paper 95-062 (1995)

14. Farassat, F., Brentner, K., Dunn, M.: A study of supersonic surface sources the Ffowcs Williams-Hawkings equation and the Kirchhoff formula. In: 4th AIAA/CEAS Aeroacoustics Conference, Toulouse, France, June 2–4, AIAA Paper 98-2375 (1998)

15. Bakhvalov, P.A., Bobkov, V.G., Kozubskaya, T.K.: Technology to predict acoustic far field disturbances in the case of calculations in a rotating reference frame. Math. Models Comput. Simul. **9**(6), 717–727 (2017). https://doi.org/10.1134/S2070048217060035

16. Cuthill, E., McKee, J.: Reducing the bandwidth of sparse symmetric matrices. In: ACM '69: Proceedings of the 1969 24-th National Conference, pp. 157–172 (1969). https://doi.org/10.1145/800195.805928

17. Gorobets, A., Bakhvalov, P.: Heterogeneous CPU+GPU parallelization for high-accuracy scale-resolving simulations of compressible turbulent flows on hybrid supercomputers. Comput. Phys. Commun. **271**, 108231 (2022). https://doi.org/10.1016/j.cpc.2021.108231

18. Gorobets, A.V., Bakhvalov, P.A., Duben, A.P., Rodionov, P.V.: Acceleration of NOISEtte code for scale-resolving supercomputer simulations of turbulent flows. Lobachevskii J. Math. **41**(8), 1463–1474 (2020). https://doi.org/10.1134/S1995080220080077

19. Bakhvalov, P.A., Surnachev, M.D.: Method of averaged element splittings for diffusion terms discretization in vertex-centered framework. J. Comput. Phys., 110819 (2021). https://doi.org/10.1016/j.jcp.2021.110819

20. Gorobets, A., Bakhvalov, P.: Improving reliability of supercomputer CFD codes on unstructured meshes. Supercomput. Front. Innov. **6**(4), 44–56 (2020). https://doi.org/10.14529/jsfi190403

21. Voevodin, V.l., et al.: Supercomputer Lomonosov-2: large scale, deep monitoring and fine analytics for the user community. Supercomput. Front. Innov. **6**, 4–11 (2019). https://doi.org/10.14529/jsfi190201

Using 16-th Order Multioperators-Based Scheme for Supercomputer Simulation of the Initial Stage of Laminar-Turbulent Transitions

Andrei I. Tolstykh$^{(\boxtimes)}$ and Dmitrii A. Shirobokov

Dorodnicyn Computing Center, Federal Research Center "Computer Science and Control" of Russian Academy of Sciences, Moscow, Russian Federation
tol@ccas.ru

Abstract. The paper deals with the parallel implementation of a 16-order multioperators-based scheme for high fidelity numerical calculations of unstable solutions of fluid dynamics equations. Parallelization principle and estimates of parallel efficiency are given. As examples of the application of the developed code, some results describing the occurrence and development of unstable modes in two-dimensional and three-dimensional subsonic boundary layers without artificial exciters are presented.

Keywords: Multoperators approximations · 16th-order scheme · Parallel efficiency · Navier-Stokes equation · Boundary layer instability · Tollmien-Schlichting waves

1 Introduction

Currently, there are various classes of problems that require particularly high accuracy of the numerical methods used. Usually, high accuracy is provided by high orders of approximations of the governing equations. However, high orders do not necessarily mean high efficiency of the method. This can occur due to two reasons.

First, high-order schemes, when using a reasonable number of grid nodes, may not accurately describe the small-scale details of solutions. To partially overcome this problem, it is sometimes possible to optimize schemes by using free parameters. The goal of optimization is to reduce the deviations in the Fourier space of the images of approximating operators from the images of the "exact" operators in the domain of the shortest waves supported by the meshes.

Second, computer codes for high-order schemes can be poorly parallelized, which reduces their efficiency when using high-performance computing systems.

The use of multioperator approximations (see, for example, [1]) allows not only to obtain very high orders, but also to optimize the schemes by using the available free parameters. Thus, it remains to solve the second important task

© Springer Nature Switzerland AG 2021
V. Voevodin and S. Sobolev (Eds.): RuSCDays 2021, CCIS 1510, pp. 270–282, 2021.
https://doi.org/10.1007/978-3-030-92864-3_21

- to develop codes adapted to supercomputers. Generally, the problem is not trivial since multioperators are linear combinations of the operators of compact approximations which are superpositions of two grid operators, one of them being the inverse of some narrow stenciled operator. Hence, the Gauss eliminations are usually needed to calculate the multioperators' actions. Since such procedures are known for poor parallelism, solving this problem creates some challenge.

Th present study concerns with solving this problem for a class of multioperators-based schemes for the Euler and Navier-Stokes equations. The schemes have an important property - they use only two-point operators to be inverted. It creates the potential for efficient parallelization of the elaborated codes. Presently, the 16th and 32nd order schemes of that type are documented (see [2,3]). In the present study, the MPI parallelization procedure is described. It was applied to the 16th-order scheme from [2].

The work on the creation of such codes was carried out in the context of research in an important area from a theoretical and applied point of view-the transition of a laminar boundary layer to a turbulent one. Along with the existing classical linear theory of boundary layer instability [4], there is a huge amount of both experimental studies (see, for example, [5–8]) and results of numerical simulation of the transition process. Comprehensive numerical studies can be found in the later literature (see [9–15] and the references therein). Most publications relate to incompressible flows. Among the studies of the instability of the boundary layers of a compressible gas, we note the work [16] in which the case of hypersonic flow is considered.

The main approach in numerical studies of this phenomenon was to excite the instability of stationary solutions by introducing certain artificial exciters into equations or boundary condition.

When using high-order multi-operator schemes for direct numerical simulation of unstable flows in subsonic jets [18], underexpanded supersonic jets [17] as well as in the case of isolated vortices [19], it was observed that looking during large time intervals as steady state, numerical solutions to the Navier-Stokes or Euler equations suddenly went into unsteady quasi-periodic regimes. This led to the idea that small differences between the numerical solutions and the exact ones can be the causative agents of instability in the case of unstable flows. The crucial point here is if the accuracy and the resolution properties of a scheme with reasonable meshes are sufficient to support initiation and time evolution of unstable modes coming from the scheme-generated "background".

That idea was used in our studies of the transition process. Part of the numerical calculations of two-dimensional flows about flat plates without the introduction of exciters was published in [20]. The paper describes how very small perturbations in the form of well-organized wave packets in the vicinity of the leading edge propagate downstream, increasing their amplitudes. The contents of these packages corresponded to all the signs of Tollmien-Schlichting waves.

In the present paper, the operation properties of the parallel code for the scheme under consideration are illustrated by novel examples illustrating the details of subsonic boundary layer instability in the 2D and 3D cases.

2 Computational Details

2.1 Problem Formulation

The compressible subsonic flows described by unsteady Navier-Stokes equations in the two-dimensional (2D) and the three-dimensional (3D) boxes were considered. Assuming the oncoming flow in the x- direction, they were defined in the Cartesian coordinates (x, y, z) as

$$0 \leq x \leq 20, \, 0 \leq y \leq 0.2$$

in the 2D case and

$$0 \leq x \leq 20, \, -0.3 \leq y \leq 0.3, \, 0 \leq z \leq 0.2$$

in the 3D case. The coordinates of the solid walls were $0.25 \leq x \leq 20$ with the normal to wall coordinate y in the first case and $0.25 \leq x \leq 20$, $-0.3 \leq y \leq 0.3$ with the normal to wall coordinate z in the second case.

The unit length L was chosen to be that for which the Reynolds number is equal to 5×10^5. The one-dimensional characteristic boundary conditions were used at the upper boundary. The undisturbed Mach number 0.5 flow was assumed at the $x = 0$ boundary while the extrapolated flow parameters were set at the inflow and the outflow boundaries respectively. The surface temperature was set to the stagnation one. The flow variables were normalized using length L, the ambient density, the ambient speed of sound c_∞. The time variable t was normalized with the reference value L/c_∞.

The mesh size in the x-direction was constant up to some value $x = x_{max}$ characterizing the "working area". It smoothly increased in the region $x > x_{max}$ to form a sponge zone where flow oscillations were strongly damped due to large mesh sizes. The same type of meshing was used for the y-coordinate in the 3D case, the sponge zones being placed near the $y = \pm 0.3$ planes. In the normal to the wall direction, the mesh was non-uniform with condensing grid points in the boundary layer region as the result of a smooth coordinate transformation.

The undisturbed flow with the no-slip condition at the plate was used as the initial data. It corresponds to instantaneous insertion of the flat plate into a uniform flow.

Several numerical experiments were carried out searching for unsteady regimes of the boundary layer. It was found that the stable steady state Blasius like solution with about 10^{-8} tolerance was established when using 1500×50 mesh in the 2D case. The non stationary regime in the 2D case occurred when using 3000×100 mesh, the nodes distribution along the x-coordinate being uniform up to $x_{max} = 14.5$ with mesh size $h = 5 \times 10^{-3}$. In the 3D case, the same mesh size was used in the y-direction up to $|y| \leq y_{max}$ with $y_{max} = 0.29$.

2.2   Multioperators-Based Scheme

The scheme used in the present calculations is based on the arbitrary high-order multioperators approximations to the spatial derivatives in the hyperbolic part of the compressible Navier-Stokes equations written in the conservative form. To outline the idea, consider a uniform mesh ω_h with the mesh size h. Generally, the multioperator approximated the first derivative (say, the x-derivative) in the case of a uniform mesh looks as

$$\frac{\partial}{\partial x} \approx L_M(c_1, c_2, \ldots, c_M) = \sum_{i=1}^{M} \gamma_i l(c_i), \quad \sum_{i=1}^{M} \gamma_i = 1 \qquad (1)$$

where the basis operators $l(c_i)$ are generated by one-parameter family $l(c)$ of compact approximation to the derivative for mesh ω_h by fixing M values of parameter c. Once the parameter's values are specified, γ_i coefficients can be uniquely defined to kill $M-1$ terms in the Taylor expansion series for the multioperators truncation errors in terms of h. It gives the growth of the approximation orders proportional to either M or $2M$.

The multioperators in the present scheme belong to the recent family of $2M$th-order approximations in which $l(c)$ are half sums of two-point "left" and "right" compact approximations containing two-point operators only (see [2]). Using the uniform mesh $\omega_h : (x_j = jh, j = 0, \pm 1, \pm 2, \ldots), \quad h = const$, they look as

$$L_l(c) = \frac{1}{h} R_l(c)^{-1} \Delta_-, \quad L_r(c) = \frac{1}{h} R_r(c)^{-1} \Delta_+. \qquad (2)$$

where Δ_- and Δ_+ are the two-point left and right differences while $R_l(c)$ and $R_r(c)$ are given by

$$R_l(c) = I + c\Delta_-, \quad R_r(c) = I - c\Delta_+. \qquad (3)$$

"Left" and "right" operators $L_l(c)$ and $L_r(c)$ approximates the first derivatives with the truncation orders $O(h)$.

Assuming the Hilbert space of bounded grid functions with the inner product defined by the summation over grid points, they have the same skew-symmetric component and the self-adjoint components with opposite signs. It follows from the Eq. (2) that very simple two-diagonal inversions of the operators from Eq. (3) are needed to calculate the actions of operators L_l and L_r on known grid functions.

The one-parameter family of skew-symmetric operators $l(c)$ in Eq. (1) used in the present study is defined as $l(c) = (L_l(c) + L_r(c))/2$ providing the $O(h^{16})$ truncation error when setting $M = 8$. The difference $d(c) = (L_l(c) + L_r(c))/2$ is the one-parameter family of self-adjoint operators. When divided by h, they approximate with the second order the second derivatives. It was used to construct another multioperator serving as the necessary for computational fluid dynamics dissipation mechanism.

Using another set of the parameter's values $\bar{c}_1, \bar{c}_2, \ldots \bar{c}_M$, the multioperator looks as

$$D_M(\bar{c}_1, \bar{c}_2, \ldots, \bar{c}_M) = \sum_{i=1}^{M} \hat{\gamma}_i d(\bar{c}_i), \quad \sum_{i=1}^{M} \hat{\gamma}_i = 1. \tag{4}$$

Its action on a sufficiently smooth function $u(x)$ projected into mesh ω_h is estimated as $O(h^{2M-1})$, the values $\bar{c}_i$ being specified to guarantee its positivity.

The search for the parameters providing the desirable properties of the multioperators was carried out under the assumption that they are of uniformly distributed between their minimal and maximal values c_{min}, $\bar{c}_{min}$ and c_{max}, $\bar{c}_{max}$. In this way, their images in the Fourier space look as complex-varied functions of dimensionless wave numbers kh with two free parameters. Thus the task was reduced to the search for the points in the two dimensional space of the parameters which uniquely define multioperators with desired properties.

Considering the model equation $u_t + f(u)_x = 0$, the semi-discretized scheme with multioperators (1) and (4) in the index-free form reads

$$u_t + L_M f(u) + C\, D_M u = 0, \quad C = const \geq 0 \tag{5}$$

The second term in Eq. (5) contains operator $L_M(c_{min}, c_{max})$ with the stiffly fixed pair of the optimal parameters. They are the results of minimizations of the dispersion errors in the domain of large wave numbers supported by meshes in the case of the above model equation with $f(u) = au, a = const$. The estimates of the resulting phase errors are presented in [2]. Numerical tests for $M = 8$ and $M = 16$ have shown that the optimized scheme allows to preserve wave packets of high wave numbers harmonics during extremely long time of calculations. The present scheme is the particular case of (5) with $M = 8$.

The third term in (5) with operator $D_M(\bar{c}_{min}, \bar{c}_{max})$ and constant C can be viewed as an optional one introducing $O(h^{15})$ truncation errors. In the case of stable solutions, its role is to prevent numerical instabilities caused in particular by non monotone properties of high-order schemes with minimal influence on physically relevant solutions components.

Parameters $(\bar{c}_{min}, \bar{c}_{max})$ are the free parameters of the scheme. Using them, it is possible to control the spectral content of the dissipations introduced by operator $D_M(\bar{c}_{min}, \bar{c}_{max})$ with constant C .

In the context of the present problem, the dissipation mechanism plays a dual role. First, it tends to damp short-wave components of numerical solutions. The "ideal" option can be achieved when choosing free parameters providing damping only shortest-wave Fourier harmonics which occur as saw-type oscillations typical for high-order schemes. This choice is given in [2].

Second, the dissipative term can be viewed as an additional source term that generates small perturbations of a certain spectral composition. These perturbations can be considered as some background that creates initial data for the development of unstable modes. In this study, the values of free parameters were used at which a background with a sufficiently broad-band spectrum and small amplitudes is created (see [20]).

In the case of the Navier-Stokes equations, multioperators in Eq. (5) were used for dicretization of the y- and z-derivatives. The discretization of the terms with viscosity was carried out using the fourth-order compact approximations of the 4th order. Numerical experiments have shown that the truncation errors estimated as $O(h^4)/\text{Re}$ were too small to significantly affect the accuracy of the calculations. The fourth-order Runge-Kutta procedure with the chosen time steps was found to be sufficiently accurate to provide time steps undependable solutions.

Visualizations of the Solutions.
To describe the occurrence and development of instability, the analysis of pulsations of the stream-wise velocity component $u(x, y)$ at the bottom of the boundary layer which is generally accepted in experimental and numerical studies, was used. In the present study, it is $U(x) = u(x, y_*)$ with $y = 0.000129$ in the 2D case.

The pulsations of $U(x)$ in the form of wave packets can be particularly noticeable at the late stages of instability development downstream from the leading edge of the plate against the background of a slow change in $U(x)$ along the x coordinate. Then the direct visualization based on the displaying $U(t, x)$ at fixed time t is possible. It allows to track the dominant disturbances in the downstream region.

However, in the vicinity of the leading edge, these pulsations have very small amplitudes which makes them invisible against the background of rapidly decreasing $U(x)$. To detect them, the following procedure was used. Spatial intervals ("windows") were specified where the pulsations of interest are approximately located. Based on the grid functions values inside the windows, fitting functions were constructed approximating U in the m.r.s sense. They were chosen as the generalized polynomials with the Chebyshev basis functions. Then the differences δU between the grid functions and their approximations serve as estimates of the velocity pulsations. In this way, the pulsations with very small amplitudes can be detected allowing to calculate their spectra.

3   Parallel Implementation

According to Eq. (2), the calculations of the actions of operators L_l and L_r on known grid functions, that is calculations of the discretized derivatives in the governing equations at each node covering the x-axis, reduce to the inverting two-point operators given in Eq. (3). The inversion procedures can be carried out using very simple left and right sweeps. For example, the general form of the left sweep for calculating $v_j = R_l^{-1} f_j$, $j = 1, 2, \ldots N$ for known f_j, $j = 0, 1, \ldots N$ and N grid points looks as

$$v_j = (c_k v_{j-1} + f_j)/(1 + c_k), \; j = 1, 2, \ldots, N \tag{6}$$

where c_k, $k = 1, 2, \ldots M$ are the parameters of the multioperator (in our case $M = 8$). As seen, the operation count per node is very small.

In the case of the three-dimensional Euler equations, it is necessary to differentiate 6 functions (5 derivatives in the convective terms and pressure). For each of these six functions and $M = 8$, one needs to invert eight two-point left operators (R_l). Thus, a single x line of the mesh requires 48 left sweeps and 48 right sweeps. Assuming $Nx \times Ny$ and $Nx \times Ny \times Nz$ internal grid ponts in two-and three-dimensional cases, the above numbers should be multiplied by Ny and $NyNz$ respectively.

To parallelize the calculations described above, the domain decomposition principle was used. If the grid is Cartesian, it can be divided into blocks by drawing planes perpendicular to the coordinate axes. The particular case of 27 processors is illustrated in Fig. 1.

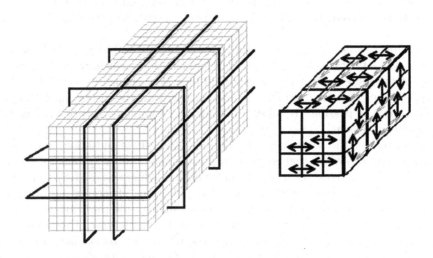

Fig. 1. Blocks of nodes and assigned processors.

Nodes located in the same block belong to the same processor, the values of the grid functions in these nodes being stored in its memory.

To explain which processors communicate with each other, let's imagine each processor as a rectangular parallelepiped. Then the set of processors forms a large parallelepiped, as shown in Fig. 1. In our case, the planes divide the calculated grid into 27 blocks (3 in each direction). Accordingly, 27 processors will be used in the calculation. When implementing the algorithm under consideration, processors exchange data with neighboring processors (two processors are neighboring if they share a common face). In the figure, the double arrows are connected to the processors that exchange with each other. Such exchanges are used when calculating the multioperator derivatives in the direction parallel to the arrows. In the two-dimensional case, the processor can be considered a square, and the set of processors a rectangle. Processors can exchange with neighboring processors, their corresponding squares have a common edge.

Next, we will consider the differentiation in x. The differentiation in the other directions is carried out in the same way. Moving along the coordinate lines according procedure Eq. (6), one can calculate the values of v_j at all points of the block, including on its right boundary. After that, the values on the right boundary must be passed to the right neighbor processor, for which they will be the initial values set on the left boundary. Thus, one can define a function $Move1(n, k)$ that inverts a two-point operator within a single processor block, where n is the number of the differentiated function and k is the number of the operator's parameter c_k. One can also define a function $Send1(n, k)$ that passes the values of the operator on the right boundary to the right processor. Redefine these functions so that they depend on only single number $m, m = 1, ..., 48$ where $m = (n - 1) * 8 + k$:

$$Move(m) := Move1([(m + 7)/8], m - 8[(m - 1)/8]),$$

$$Send(m) := Send1([(m + 7)/8], m - 8[(m - 1)/8]).$$

Here, the square brackets mean the integer parts of the numbers. Such notation will allow us to describe the invocation of these functions in a multiprocessor implementation. If, for example, we have 4 processors on the x-axis, the call graph for the left sweeps is described by the following table (the right sweeps can be organized in the same manner).

Table 1. Organizing parallel calculations for 4 processors

Processors	1	2	3	4	
Stage 1	Move(1)Send(1)				
Stage 2	Move(2)Send(2)	Move(1)Send(1)			
Stage 3	Move(3)Send(3)	Move(2)Send(2) 2	Move(1)Send(1)		
Stage 4	Move(4)Send(4)	Move(3)Send(3) 2	Move(2)Send(2)	Move(1)	
...	...	...	...	...	
Stage m	Move(m)Send(m)	Move(m-1)Send(m-1)	Move(m-2)Send(m-2)	Move(m-3)	
...	...	...	...	...	...
Stage 48	Move(48)Send(48)	Move(47)Send(47)	Move(46)Send(46)	Move(45)	
Stage 49		Move(48)Send(48)	Move(47)Send(47)	Move(46)	
Stage 50			Move(48) Send(48)	Move(47)	
Stage 51				Move(48)	

As seen, though there are idle processors, their number is rather small as compared with working ones due to the large number of sweeps.

In the 3D case, the Navier-Stokes calculations described below were carried out using different numbers of cores. The resulting speedup results are shown in Fig. 2.

It should be noted that the described approach is quite general. It can be used in the case of other multioperator schemes which use inversions of two-point operators. This is, for example, the case of the 32-th order scheme [3].

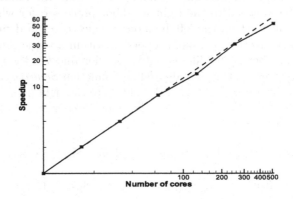

Fig. 2. Speedup estimates. The dashed line depicts the linear speedup.

4   Examples of Numerical Solutions

A large number of calculations were made in solving the initial boundary value problem formulated above. All of them used the above described MPI parallelization when implemented on the workstation and supercomputers. Some of the results were published in the [20].

Two-Dimensional Flow.
According to [20], the general scenario of the onset and development of the instability is as follows.

When using half the number of nodes as indicated above, the time integration procedure resulted in stationary solution with about 10^{-9} residuals. It looked close to the Blasius solution for incompressible flows. However, when the number of nodes doubled, a steady flow of this type was established only in a small neighborhood of the leading edge, where fluctuations of very small amplitudes along the x axis were observed. This is consistent with the linear instability theory [4], according to which the boundary layer is stable for small values of the Reynolds numbers calculated for the current coordinate x. In the rest of the computational domain, over time, the formation of a boundary layer -like structure was observed. Against its background, stationary small oscillations near the leading edge passed into wave packets travelling downstream increasing their amplitudes and enriching their contents. When entering the sponge zone at $x > 15$, the packets damped and disappeared.

The initial amplitudes of the packets varied over time forming "strong" and "weak" packets. Accordingly, either strong perturbations leading to flow separation or rather weak perturbations were observed downstream. In some cases, the latter could be observed only in the form of deviations from the root-mean-square approximations described above.

The calculated spatial spectra of the packets showed that their contents form Tollmien-Schlichting waves. It was found that the variation of these waves in time and space correlates well with the instability diagram for incompressible flows [4].

Examples illustrating the occurrence and development of instability are shown in Figs. 3,4 and 5. They complement the results described in [20]. Figure 3 shows the initial structure of the travelling downstream wave packets in the form of the deviations δU of the near-surface stream-wise velocity U from its r.m.s. values at time $t = 36$. In the left part of the Figure, one can see the formation of a wave packet of oscillations with very small amplitudes (let's call it packet 2). In the right part, the neighbor downstream interval of x is shown with a previously formed packet with significantly increased amplitudes (let's call it packet 1).

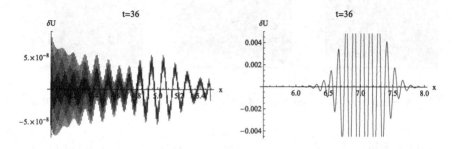

Fig. 3. Initial wave packets generated near leading edge.

The downstream locations of the travelling packets 1 and 2 are shown in Fig. 4 for successive times, the actual velocity $U(x)$ being presented. As seen, packet 1 is moving downstream with more or less constant group velocity with increasing amplitudes. At $t > 50$, negative values of U are seen which means local flow separations. The packet reaches the sponge zone at $t = 78$ and disappears in it at $t > 86$. Packet 2 which is seen first time at $t = 78$ repeats the evolution of its predecessor.

Figure 5 shows the snapshots of the stream-wise velocity $u(x, y)$ at three time instants. Considerable flow disturbances with backward flows near the surface caused by the moving wave packets are clearly seen in the Figure.

Calculations for Finite Width Flat Plate.
In the spatial case, according to the above described problem formulation, the instantaneous inclusion of a plate of finite width into an undisturbed flow was simulated. The calculations carried out for this case allowed us to estimate the parallel efficiency of the spatial code and obtain the first results describing the occurrence of instability without the introduction of artificial exciters. The obtained data allowed us to observe the formation and development of unstable span-wise modes at the early stage of the instability. Figure 6 shows in the 3D

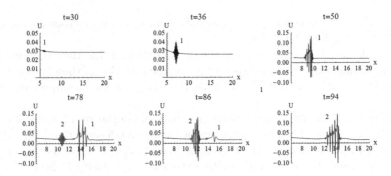

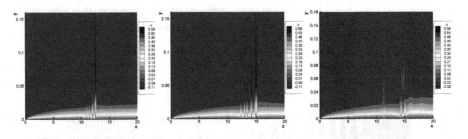

Fig. 4. Temporal evolution of instability: packets at different times t.

Fig. 5. Snapshots of stream-wise velocity field at successive times $t = 60, 70, 80$

format the field of the velocity component v (note that the z axis is normal to the surface in the 3D case). Judging from the Figure, the maximal absolute values of the velocities increased by an order of magnitude when comparing successive time instances.

5   Conclusions

The paper describes the general idea of MPI-parallelization of computer codes that implement multioperators-based schemes with the inversion of two-point operators. The high parallel efficiency of such codes was demonstrated in the case of a highly accurate 16-order scheme. The scheme was used for direct numerical simulation of the processes of occurrence and development of instability in boundary layers. The peculiarity of the problem statement in solving the Navier-Stokes equations of compressible gas was the inclusion in the flow complete flat plates with their leading edges (rather than their individual parts) and the absence of any artificial exciters usually used in well-known publications. Consequently, a novel scenario of the instability was obtained. The presented examples show that the high accuracy of the scheme allows to discern very fine details of unstable modes when using a reasonable number of nodes in the computational domain.

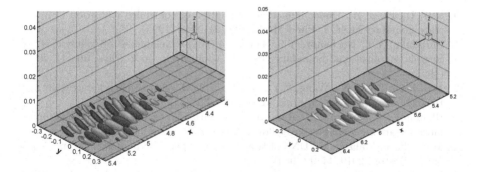

Fig. 6. Spatial fields of v- velocity; left and right pictures correspond to $t = 25$ and $t = 30$ with maximal absolute values 10^{-8} and $2 * 10^{-7}$ respectively.

Acknowledgment. The present 3D calculations were carried out using supercomputers of Joint SuperComputer Center of the Russian Academy of Sciences Branch of Federal State Institution Scientific Research Institute for System Analysis of the Russian Academy of Sciences.

Calculations related to the development of the multioperators technique were partly carried out using Lomonosov supercomputer of the Moscow State University.

References

1. Tolstykh, A.I.: Multioperators technique for constructing arbitrary high-order approximations and schemes: main ideas and applications to fluid dynamics equations. In: Petrov, I.B., Favorskaya, A.V., Favorskaya, M.N., Simakov, S.S., Jain, L.C. (eds.) GCM50 2018. SIST, vol. 133, pp. 17–31. Springer, Cham (2019). https://doi.org/10.1007/978-3-030-06228-6_3
2. Tolstykh, A.I.: 16th and 32nd multioperators based schemes for smooth and discontinuous solutions. Commun. Comput. Phys. **45**, 3–45 (2017)
3. Tolstykh, A.I.: On 32nd-order multioperators-based schemes for fluid dynamics. In: Favorskaya, M.N., Favorskaya, A.V., Petrov, I.B., Jain, L.C. (eds.) Smart Modelling for Engineering Systems. Smart Innovation, Systems and Technologies, vol. 21, Springer, Singapore (2021). https://doi.org/10.1007/978-3-030-06228-6
4. Schlichting, H.: Grenzschicht-Theorie. Verlag G. Brown, Carlsruhe (1935)
5. Schubauer, G.B., Scramstad, H.K.: Laminar-boundary-layer oscillations and transition on a flat plate. NACA Rep. 909. NACA, Langley Field (1948)
6. Klebanoff, P.S., Tidstrom, K.D., Sargent, L.M.: Numerical simulation of transition in wall-bounded shear flows. Ann. Rev. Fluid Mech. **23**, 495–537 (1962)
7. Gaster, M., Grant, I.: An experimental investigation of the formation and development of a Wavepacket in a laminar boundary layer. Proc. R. Soc. Lond. A **347**, 253–269 (1975)
8. Kachanov, Y.S., Kozlov, V.V. Levchenko, V.Y.: Nonlinear development of a wave in a boundary layer. Izv. Akad. Nauk SSSR Mekh. Zhidk. Gaza. **3**, 49–53 (1977) (Transl. (1978) Fluid Dynamics 12: 383–390.). (in Russian)
9. Fasel, H.F., Rist, U., Konzelmann, U.: Numerical investigation of the three-dimensional development in boundary-layer transition. AIAA J. **28**, 29–37 (1990)

10. Rist, U., Fasel, H.: Direct numerical simulation of controlled transition in a flat-plate boundary layer. J. Fluid Mech. **298**, 211–248 (1995)
11. Borodulin, V.I., Kachanov, Y.S.: Formation and development of coherent structures in a transitional boundary layer. J. Appl. Mech. Tech. Phys. **36** (4), 60–97 (1995)
12. Yeo, K.C., Zhao, X., Wang, Z.Y., Ng, K.C.: DNS of Wavepacket evolution in a Blasius boundary layer. J. Fluid Mech. **652**, 333–372 (2010)
13. Bhaumik, S., Sengupta, T.: Receptivity to harmonic excitation following Nonimpulsive start for boundary-layer flows. AIAA J. **55**, 3233–3238 (2017)
14. Muppidi, S., Mahesh, K.: DNS of transition in supersonic boundary layers. AIAA paper, Reston, 2010–4440 (2004)
15. Liu, C., Lu, P.: DNS Study on Physics of Late Boundary Layer Transition. AIAA paper, 2012–0083 (2012)
16. Egorov, I.V., Novikov, A.V.: Direct numerical simulation of laminarturbulent flow over a flat plate at hypersonic flow speeds. Comput. Math. Math. Phys. **56**(6), 10481064 (2016)
17. Tolstykh, A.I., Shirobokov, D.A.: Fast calculations of screech using highly accurate multioperators-based schemes. J. Appl. Acoust. **74**, 102–109 (2013)
18. Tolstykh, A.I., Lipavskii, M.V., Shirobokov, D.A.: High-order multioperators-based schemes: developments and application. Math. Comput. Simul. **139**, 67–80 (2017)
19. Tolstykh, A.I., Lipavskii, M.V.: Instability and acoustic fields of the Rankine vortex as seen from long-term calculations with the tenth-order multioperators-based scheme. Math. Comput. Simul. **147**, 301–320 (2018)
20. Tolstykh, A.I., Shirobokov, D.A.: Observing production and growth of Tollmien-Schlichting waves in subsonic flat plate boundary layer via exciters free high fidelity numerical simulation. J. Turbulence **21**, 632–649 (2020). https://doi.org/10.1080/14685248.2020.1824072

Wave Spectrum of Flowing Drops

Maria Guskova[1,2] and Lev Shchur[1,2(✉)]

[1] Landau Institute for Theoretical Physics, Chernogolovka, Russia
{mguskova,lshchur}@hse.ru, lev@landau.ac.ru
[2] HSE University, Moscow, Russia

Abstract. We simulate the drop-chain movement in the two-dimensional channel using the lattice Boltzmann method coupled with the Immersed Boundary approach. We choose the asymmetric initial state of the drop chain to generate drop oscillations and calculate the wave spectrum. The numerical results coincide qualitatively with the experimental results obtained in the quasi-two-dimensional microfluidic device.

Keywords: Lattice Boltzmann method · Immersed boundary method · Supercomputing · Computer simulations · Drop oscillations

1 Introduction

Microfluidic devices are subject to interdisciplinary studies [5], and investigation of the fluid dynamics under microfluidic conditions is a challenging problem. The restricted geometry and inhomogeneity of the complex flow compounds need careful analysis of the parameter influence on the flow details.

In the paper, we investigate the movement of the chain drop inside the channel of finite width filled with the liquid. We consider a Poiseuille flow of liquid in the channel. We use lattice Boltzmann method (LBM) coupled with immersed boundary (IB) method in simulations. We compare the results of our simulations with the results of the physics experiment in which the behavior of water droplets in oil in a quasi-two-dimensional flow was studied [2]. In the experiment, the speed of water droplets due to friction against the upper and lower walls of the channel is approximately five times less than the average flow speed. In the experiment with a chain of drops, drops oscillate, and longitudinal and transverse waves appeared. The emergence of waves was explained by the long-range hydrodynamic interaction of drops with each other. We have to note that the Reynolds number is very small and equal approximately 10^{-4}.

In some works [8,14,16,21], computer simulation of the one-dimensional chain of particles or drops motion was carried out.

The work [14] presents the results of numerical integration of the equations of droplet motion obtained in [2]. They found some difference with the experimental results. Unlike the oscillation spectra of a physical experiment, there is no straight line in the spectrum since it arises from defects in the channel.

© Springer Nature Switzerland AG 2021
V. Voevodin and S. Sobolev (Eds.): RuSCDays 2021, CCIS 1510, pp. 283–294, 2021.
https://doi.org/10.1007/978-3-030-92864-3_22

In the work [8], a computer simulation of the motion of a chain of three-dimensional drops between two parallel planes is performed. The authors used the HYDROMULTIPOLE algorithm to expand the flow field into the lateral Fourier modes in the planes parallel to the walls [1]. They investigated the influence of deformability of bodies. In contrast with the physical experiment, drops are not confined but sphere-shaped.

The authors of [21] have found new patterns of collective behavior of particles in a quasi-two-dimensional problem. The work did not consider the motion of a one-dimensional chain but used the method of the lattice Boltzmann equation. The D2Q9 model was used, moving hard disks were simulated via transfer of momentum in the "bounce-back" boundary condition, using a first-order boundary interpolation method.

In [16] a computer simulation of a chain of drops in a two-dimensional narrow channel was performed. The droplets are represented as hard disks, and the liquid is represented by idealized point particles with masses of m. At short distances, the multi-particle collision dynamics method does not resolve hydrodynamics, and the WCA potential was used to simulate the interaction of particles with each other and with the walls. A friction force was applied to the disks in order to change the two-dimensional formulation to a quasi-two-dimensional one. The initial coordinates in the chain were set as follows: alternating the y-coordinate (above the axis/below the axis) and alternating the distances between the centers of the particles along the X axis. The right particle in a pair moves faster than the left one; it catches up with the next pair and becomes left. The different distances along the X axis cause the pairs to re-form, which leads to longitudinal oscillations. The spectra of the obtained oscillations along the X and Y axes are similar to the results of [2].

This paper investigates the applicability of the immersed boundary method combined with the lattice Boltzmann method [6] for simulationof the longitudinal and transverse oscillations arising in a one-dimensional chain of drops. Unlike other discussed above works [8,14,16], we avoid the introduction of the effective interaction potentials between particles. The reason is that we would like to check the natural appearance of the wave spectrum reported in [2] without any assumptions. The second difference from the above-mentioned works is in the more realistic boundary conditions along the channel, and the Poiseuille profile is specified along the channel width. We model drops as solid disks, and the interaction between different drops and between drops and walls is wholly resolved through the liquid, which is simulated by the lattice Boltzmann method. Another significant difference is a purely two-dimensional case and the absence of a friction force acting on the discs from the side of the upper and lower walls. Because of this, the particles have a speed close to the flow. The spectrum of the simulated oscillations is compared with the experimental [2] spectrum.

2   Model and Methods

In this section, we give essentials of the lattice Boltzmann method and immersed boundary method and the derivation of the forces acting in two-dimension on the immersed boundary.

2.1   Lattice Boltzmann Method

Discretizing the Boltzmann equation in the space of velocities, coordinates and time, we obtain the lattice Boltzmann equation [11]:

$$f_i(\vec{x} + \vec{c}_i \Delta t, t + \Delta t) = f_i(\vec{x}, t) + \Omega_i(\vec{x}, t).$$

According to this expression, (pseudo-) particles $f_i(\vec{x}, t)$ move with the speed $\vec{c}_i$ to the neighboring point $\vec{x} + \vec{c}_i \Delta t$ in time Δt. At the same time, the particles are affected by the collision operator Ω_i. In this work the collision operator BGK (Bhatnagar-Gross-Krook) is used:

$$\Omega_i(f) = -\frac{f_i - f_i^{eq}}{\tau} \Delta t.$$

The set of velocities and the dimension of the problem determine the model [11], for example, D2Q9 (Fig. 1a) corresponds to a two-dimensional problem, where the velocity can be directed from a node to 4 corners of a square, to 4 midpoints of the sides square, and one does not go out of the node. Model D3Q19 (Fig. 1b) corresponds to a three-dimensional problem, and the velocities are set in 19 directions: to 12 midpoints of the edges of the cube, to 6 midpoints of faces, and one does not leave the node.

The density functions relax to the equilibrium state f_i^{eq} at a rate determined by the relaxation time τ. The equilibrium state is defined as:

$$f_i^{eq}(\vec{x}, t) = w_i \rho \left(1 + \frac{\vec{u} \cdot \vec{c}_i}{c_s^2} + \frac{(\vec{u} \cdot \vec{c}_i)^2}{c_s^2} - \frac{\vec{u} \cdot \vec{u}}{2c_s^2} \right), \tag{1}$$

where the weights w_i correspond to a set of velocities. The equilibrium state is such that its moments are equal to the moments f_i, i.e. $\Sigma_i f_i^{eq} = \Sigma_i f_i = \rho$ and $\Sigma_i \vec{c}_i f_i^{eq} = \rho \vec{u}$. This state f_i^{eq} depends only on the local density ρ and the flow rate $\vec{u}$. Calculation formulas: $\rho(\vec{x}, t) = \sum_i f_i(\vec{x}, t)$, $\rho \vec{u}(\vec{x}, t) = \sum_i \vec{c}_i f_i(\vec{x}, t)$.

The BGK lattice equation (fully discretized Boltzmann equation with BGK collision operator) can be written as

$$f_i(x + c_i \Delta t, t + \Delta t) = f_i(x, t) - \frac{\Delta t}{\tau} (f_i(x, t) - f_i^{eq}(x, t)).$$

This equation consists of two separate steps:

1. Collision step

$$f_i^\star(x, t) = f_i(x, t) - \frac{\Delta t}{\tau} (f_i(x, t) - f_i^{eq}(x, t)),$$

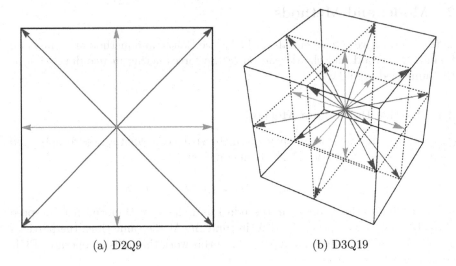

(a) D2Q9   (b) D3Q19

Fig. 1. Models

Where $f_i^\star$ represents the density function after collision and f_i^{eq} can be found from f_i by the formula (1). A collision can be effectively implemented in the form:

$$f_i^\star(x,t) = f_i(x,t)\left(1 - \frac{\Delta t}{\tau}\right) + f_i^{eq}(x,t)\frac{\Delta t}{\tau}.$$

2. Streaming step

$$f_i(\vec{x} + \vec{c}_i\Delta t, t + \Delta t) = f_i^\star(\vec{x}, t).$$

Collision is just local algebraic operations. First, the density ρ and the macroscopic velocity $\vec{u}$ are calculated in order to find the equilibrium density functions f_i^{eq} by the formula (1) and the post-collision density function $f_i^\star$. After the collision, the resulting density function f_i^{eq} propagates to neighboring nodes. After both stages are done, the one-time step has passed, the operations are repeated.

2.2   Immersed Boundary Method

The immersed boundary method is used to simulate moving boundaries, such as blood cells, bubble dynamics, and many others. Peskin first proposed the method to simulate blood flow in 1972. Since that time, the method has been utilizes many times to simulate suspensions: in conjunction with differential schemes of the Navier-Stokes equation [12,17,20] and with the lattice Boltzmann method [3,7,10,15,19,22]. We use IB-LBM as it allows to simulate moving solid bodies and IB-LBM for 3D case is already implemented in Palabos library, in this work 3D case was adapted to 2D problem.

The main idea of the immersed boundary method is to represent the boundary of a body as a set of Lagrangian points, which in the general case do not coincide with the Euler lattice sites. The combined IB-LBM approach is an iterative method. At each iteration, the body force value for the Lagrangian points is calculated – the velocities from the nodes of the Euler grid are interpolated to points on the boundary. Then the body force acting from the drop on the liquid is calculated at the lattice nodes. The calculated force is used to compute the velocity at the points of the lattice. Finally, the velocities are interpolated to the droplet boundary point, and the force acting on the droplet is corrected.

If there is an external body force $\vec{g}(\vec{x}, t)$, then the lattice equation for the particle distribution functions $f_i(\vec{x}, t)$ can be solved in two steps [7]

1. $f_i(\vec{x}, t)$ update, without taking into account the body force

$$f_i^*(\vec{x} + \vec{c}_i \Delta x, t + \Delta t) = f_i(\vec{x}, t) - \frac{1}{\tau} \left[f_i(\vec{x}, t) - f_i^{eq}(\vec{x}, t) \right]. \tag{2}$$

2. f_i^* corrected by body force

$$f_i(\vec{x}, t) = f_i^*(\vec{x}, t + \Delta t) + 3\Delta x E_i \vec{c}_i \cdot \vec{g}(\vec{x}, t + \Delta t). \tag{3}$$

The IB method assumes that an incompressible viscous fluid is inside and outside the boundary. Then the body force is applied to the lattice nodes near the boundary to satisfy the non-slip condition. The methods for determining the body force differ between different IBM versions. In paper [7] authors use the multi-direct forcing method proposed in [22]. The advantage of this method over the others is that the non-slip condition can be satisfied accurately [18].

Assuming $f_i(\vec{x}, t), \vec{u}(\vec{x}, t)$ and $p(\vec{x}, t)$ are known, intermediate values of $f_i^*(\vec{x}, t + \Delta t)$ and $u_i^*(\vec{x}, t)$ can be computed from

$$\vec{u} = \sum_{i=1}^{b} f_i \vec{c}_i, \text{ where } b = 9 \text{ for D2Q9 and } b = 19 \text{ for D3Q19} \tag{4}$$

and

$$p = \frac{1}{3} \sum_{i=1}^{b} f_i, \text{ where } b = 9 \text{ for D2Q9 and } b = 19 \text{ for D3Q19.} \tag{5}$$

Let $\vec{X}_k(t + \Delta t)$ are Lagrangian points on the moving boundary and $\vec{U}_k(t + \Delta t)$, $(k = 1, \ldots, N)$ are velocities at those points. Then the temporal velocities $\vec{u}^*(\vec{X}_k, t + \Delta t)$ at the Lagrangian boundary points $\vec{X}_k$ can be interpolate

$$\vec{u}^*(\vec{X}_k, t + \Delta t) = \sum_{x} \vec{u}^*(\vec{x}, t + \Delta t) W(\vec{x} - \vec{X}_k)(\Delta x)^d, \tag{6}$$

where $\sum_x$ is the sum over all lattice nodes $\vec{x}$, W is the weight function proposed by Peskin [12] and d is the dimension. The weighting function W is given by

$$W(x, y, z) = \frac{1}{\Delta x} w \left(\frac{x}{\Delta x} \right) \cdot \left(\frac{1}{\Delta x} \right) w \left(\frac{y}{\Delta x} \right) \cdot \left(\frac{1}{\Delta x} \right) w \left(\frac{z}{\Delta x} \right), \tag{7}$$

$$w(r) = \begin{cases} 1/8\left(3 - 2|r| + \sqrt{1 + 4|r| - 4r^2}\right), & |r| \le 1, \\ 1/8\left(5 - 2|r| - \sqrt{-7 + 12|r| - 4r^2}\right), & 1 \le |r| \le 2, \\ 0, & \text{otherwise.} \end{cases} \tag{8}$$

In the three-dimensional case, the weight function is the product of three one-dimensional weight functions; in the two-dimensional case, of two.

The body force $\vec{g}(\vec{x}, t + \Delta t)$ is determined by the following iterative procedure:

0. Calculate the initial value of the body force at the Lagrangian boundary points

$$\vec{g_0}(\vec{X_k}, t + \Delta t) = Sh\frac{\vec{U_k} - \vec{u}^*(\vec{X_k}, t + \Delta t)}{\Delta t}, \tag{9}$$

where $Sh/\Delta t = 1/\Delta x$.

1. Calculate the body force at the nodes of the Euler mesh at the l-th iteration

$$\vec{g_l}(\vec{x}, t + \Delta t) = \sum_{k=1}^{N} \vec{g_l}(\vec{X_k}, t + \Delta t)W(\vec{x} - \vec{X_k})\Delta V, \tag{10}$$

where the body force is applied not to one Lagrangian boundary point, but to a small volume element ΔV. In this method, ΔV is selected as $S/N \times \Delta x$, where $S-$ is the surface area of the body and S/N must be of the order $(\Delta x)^{d-1}$.

2. Adjust the velocities at the nodes of the Euler grid

$$\vec{u_l}(\vec{x}, t + \Delta t) = \vec{u}^*(\vec{x}, t + \Delta t) + \frac{\Delta t}{Sh}\vec{g_l}(\vec{x}, t + \Delta t). \tag{11}$$

3. Interpolate velocity at Lagrangian boundary points

$$\vec{u_l}(\vec{X_k}, t + \Delta t) = \sum_{x} \vec{u_l}(\vec{x}, t + \Delta t)W(\vec{x} - \vec{X_k})(\Delta x)^d. \tag{12}$$

4. Update the body force

$$\vec{g}_{l+1}(\vec{X_k}, t + \Delta t) = \vec{g_l}(\vec{X_k}, t + \Delta t) + Sh\frac{\vec{U_k} - \vec{u_l}(\vec{X_k}, t + \Delta t)}{\Delta t}. \tag{13}$$

It is known that the choice $l = 5$, $\vec{g}_{l=5}(\vec{x}, t + \Delta t)$ is sufficient to satisfy the non-slip condition [18].

2.3   Combined IB-LBM Algorithm

Therefore, the short protocol of the combined IB-LBM algorithm consists of the following significant steps

0. Let initial values are $f_i(\vec{x}, 0)$, calculate $\vec{u}(\vec{x}, 0)$ and $p(\vec{x}, 0)$ from Eqs. (4) and (5),

1. Calculate $\vec{X}_k(t + \Delta t)$ and $\vec{U}_k(t + \Delta t)$ from equations of body motion,
2. Compute $f_i^*(\vec{x}, t + \Delta t)$ from Eq. (2) and $\vec{u^*}(\vec{x}, t + \Delta t)$ from Eq. (4), then evaluate $\vec{u^*}(\vec{X}_k, t + \Delta t)$ from Eq. (6),
3. Compute $\vec{g}(\vec{x}, t + \Delta t)$ Eqs. (9–13),
4. Calculate $f_i(\vec{x}, t + \Delta t)$, $\vec{u}(\vec{x}, t + \Delta t)$ and $p(\vec{x}, t + \Delta x)$ by Eq. (5), Eq. (4),
5. Go to the next time step and return to 1.

2.4   Drop Motion

The drop is represented by a set of evenly distributed points on the boundary of a rigid disk. The drop motion is defined by classical mechanics laws

$$M \frac{d\vec{U}(t)}{dt} = \vec{F}(t), \tag{14}$$

$$\vec{I} \frac{\vec{\Omega}(t)}{dt} + \vec{\Omega}(t) \times [\vec{I}\,\vec{\Omega}(t)] = \vec{T}(t), \tag{15}$$

where $M = \pi R^2 \rho$ is the droplet mass, $\vec{U}(t)$ is the linear velocity, $\vec{F}(t) = -\sum \vec{g}(t)$ the net force acting on the drop, calculated by the immersed boundary method, $\vec{I}$ is the tensor of inertia, and for a hard disk it is described by the formulas: $I_z = \frac{1}{2}MR^2$, $I_x = I_y = \frac{1}{4}MR^2$, $\vec{\Omega}$ angular velocity, $\vec{T} = -\sum \vec{r} \times \vec{g}$ moment of forces, acting on a drop.

The velocity at the boundary points $\vec{u}_b$ can be calculated as

$$\vec{u}_b = \vec{U} + \vec{\Omega} \times (\vec{r}_b - \vec{X}), \tag{16}$$

Where $\vec{r}_b$ are coordinates of the boundary points and $\vec{X}$ is the center of mass.

In the two-dimensional case, the moment of forces has one nonzero component and $\vec{\Omega} = \{0, 0, \omega\}^T$, thus the Eq. (15) is simplified:

$$\frac{1}{2}MR^2 \frac{d\omega}{dt} = T_z. \tag{17}$$

We integrate Eqs. (14–17) using the explicit Euler method.

3   Simulation

3.1   Simulation Setup

Boundary conditions above and below are walls (bounce-back), on the left and on the right, the Poiseuille profile is set with an average velocity $u_{av} = 0.015$. The channel width is $80\Delta x$, the channel length is 250 times longer. Particle radius $R = 5\Delta x$. A particle in the IB-LBM method is represented by 100 points uniformly distributed around a circle. The number of IBM iterations is 4. Reynolds number $Re = 0.25$, which is three orders of magnitude higher than the Reynolds number in the [2] experiment, but it allows to run computations in a reasonable time. After the flow is fully developed, the particles are inserted on the central axis of the channel with the distance between the centers of the particles $a = 4R$. The middle drop is shifted $R/2$ above the axis in order to excite oscillations. The scheme for 12 particles is shown in Fig. 2. The density of the drop is greater than the density of the surrounding liquid $\rho_{drop} = 1000/840 \approx 1.19$, which corresponds to the ratio of the density of water to the density of oil. The density of the fluid is $\rho_{fluid} = 1$. The model is a two-dimensional D2Q9 [11].

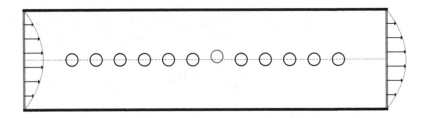

Fig. 2. Computational setup.

3.2   Details of Simulation

For the IB-LBM simulation, the open-source software Palabos [13] was used, and some modifications described in the preceding section incorporated in the code. Palabos is a library written in C++ that uses MPI for parallelization. Palabos partitions lattice into smaller regions that are distributed over the nodes or cores of a parallel machine. Other data types which require a small amount of storage space are duplicated on every node. Chain of particles processing is done as a data processor (already implemented in Palabos), which is parallelized. The current problem has been computed on one node, but it will be transformed into 3d problem, and more threads and more nodes are proposed to use in the future.

The experiments were carried out on a high-performance computing cluster "cHARISMa". The parallel implementation uses MPI with the library OpenMPI version 3.1.4. The simulation was run with 22 threads on a node with an Intel Xeon Gold 6152 2.1 GHz processor with DDR4 2.666 GHz 768 GB memory.

Computational domain is $80\Delta x \times 20000\Delta x$, $\Delta t = 0.0015$, $1.5 \cdot 10^6$ iterations were done until the flow is fully developed. 50,000 LBM iterations were performed on average in 4 min in 22 threads. 50,000 IB-LBM iterations for a chain of length 12 were performed on average in 16 min in 22 threads (with drop coordinates savings in every iteration).

3.3   Spectrum Calculation

The drop chain oscillations' spectrum was calculated similarly to Ref. [2]. The crystal oscillation spectrum was calculated from the coordinates $[x(n, t), y(n, t)]$ of all particles $n = 1 \ldots N_d$ at the time moments $t = 1 \ldots N_f$. To apply the discrete Fourier transform, it is necessary to calculate the deviations of the particles from their positions in the crystal. In the direction of the Y axis, the deviation will be the difference between the $y-$ coordinates of the center of the particle and the center of the channel. To calculate longitudinal oscillations, a new coordinate ξ is introduced, which is the difference between neighboring particles along the X axis:

$$\xi(n,t) = \begin{cases} 0, & n = 1 \\ x(n,t) - x(n-1,t), & n > 1. \end{cases} \tag{18}$$

Next, the discrete Fourier transform in space and time was calculated using the NumPy library (Python [4]):

$$X(k,\omega) = \sum_{n=1}^{N_d} \sum_{t=1}^{N_f} \xi(n,t) e^{-(2\pi i/N_d)(k-1)(n-1)} e^{-(2\pi i/N_f)(\omega-1)(t-1)} \tag{19}$$

and

$$Y(k,\omega) = \sum_{n=1}^{N_d} \sum_{t=1}^{N_f} y(n,t) e^{-(2\pi i/N_d)(k-1)(n-1)} e^{-(2\pi i/N_f)(\omega-1)(t-1)} \tag{20}$$

where k, ω, n and t are indices. The wave numbers and frequencies can be calculated as $2\pi k/L$ and $2\pi\omega/T$, respectively, where $L-$ is the length of the particle chain and $T-$ is the simulation period. Further, for each k, the maximum of the spectrum was determined modulo for $|X(k,\omega)|^2$ and $|Y(k,\omega)|^2$, disregarding the values on the line $\omega = 0$. These maxima are marked in the figures with blue dots. For symmetry, values for negative k indices have been shown, although they do not provide new information.

4   Results

In order to determine the required number of particles in a chain to obtain oscillations similar to a physical experiment, chains of different lengths were simulated using the IB-LBM. For chains with 3, 4, 5, and 6 drops, the spectrum of longitudinal and transverse oscillations is not similar to the results of the experiment shown in the Figs. 1e,f of Ref. [2]. Beginning with a chain length of 10 drops, the spectrum of transverse oscillations approaches the experimental one. We do not obtain similarity of the longitudinal spectrum with one reported in Ref. [2].

Figure 3 shows the coordinates $\xi(t)$ and $y(t)$ for a chain of 12 particles - we will use this coordinates for the calculation of the spectrum. One can see from the figure that there are no longitudinal oscillations for the chain of 12 particles. The transverse spectrum coincide well with those reported in [2]. Figures (4a, 5b) show colormap for the logarithms of $|X(k,\omega)|^2$ and $|Y(k,\omega)|^2$.

After the initial Poisuielle flow in the channel is fully developed, the drops were placed on the channel axis, while one drop in the middle of the chain shifted from the axis for the quarter drops radius R. Because of the Poiseuille profile, the velocity vanishes on the walls, and it takes maximum value at the channel center. This imposes the force acting on the shifted drop towards the channel axis. The transverse drop movement induces waves in the liquids, which act on the other drops directly as well as indirectly through the reflection from the channel walls. This is our explanation of the drop chain collective oscillations leading to the spectrum shown in the Fig. 3.

We found that the narrower the channel, the more pronounced the transverse oscillations are.

The peculiarity of the IB-LBM can explain the absence of longitudinal oscillations – the drops in this work have a velocity very close to the flow velocity.

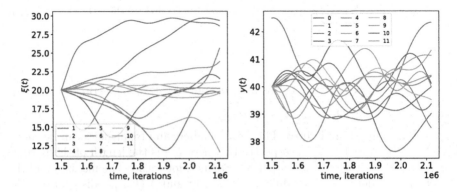

Fig. 3. Coordinates $\xi(t)$ and $y(t)$ for the chain of 12 drops.

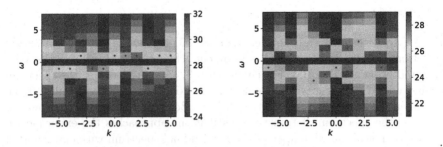

(a) Colormap for logarithm of $|X(k,\omega)|^2$ (b) Colormap for logarithm of $|Y(k,\omega)|^2$

Fig. 4. Spectrum for the chain of 12 drops

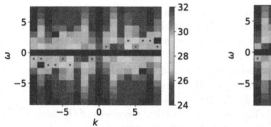 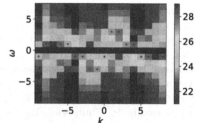

(a) Colormap for logarithm of $|X(k,\omega)|^2$ (b) Colormap for logarithm of $|Y(k,\omega)|^2$

Fig. 5. Spectrum for the chain of 18 drops

5   Conclusion

The paper presents some results of studying the possibility of the drops' long-range hydrodynamic interaction simulation in a flow by the immersed boundary method coupled with the lattice Boltzmann method. A series of computational experiments were carried out for chains of particles of different lengths. The spectra of longitudinal and transverse oscillations in the crystal were constructed. We found excellent agreement of the transverse drop oscillation spectrum with the experimental one for the drop chain length starting from 10. We propose the main effect of the particular spectrum is due to the cross-influence of the drop oscillations via the generated waves in liquid, which acts on other drops directly and after reflection from the channel walls.

Acknowledgment. This research was supported in part through computational resources of HPC facilities at HSE University [9].

Research supported by Russian Science Foundation grant 19-11-00286. MG is partially supported by the Russian Foundation for Basic Research grant 20-37-90086.

References

1. Baron, M., Bławzdziewicz, J., Wajnryb, E.: Hydrodynamic crystals: collective dynamics of regular arrays of spherical particles in a parallel-wall channel. Phys. Rev. Lett. **100**(17), 174502 (2008)
2. Beatus, T., Tlusty, T., Bar-Ziv, R.: Phonons in a one-dimensional microfluidic crystal. Nat. Phys. **2**(11), 743–748 (2006)
3. Feng, Z.G., Michaelides, E.E.: The immersed boundary-lattice Boltzmann method for solving fluid-particles interaction problems. J. Comput. Phys. **195**(2), 602–628 (2004)
4. Harris, C.R., et al.: Array programming with NumPy. Nature **585**(7825), 357–362 (2020). https://doi.org/10.1038/s41586-020-2649-2
5. Ibrahim, M., Chakrabarty, K., Zeng, J.: Biocybig: a cyberphysical system for integrative microfluidics-driven analysis of genomic association studies. IEEE Trans. Big Data **6**(4), 609–623 (2020). https://doi.org/10.1109/TBDATA.2016.2643683

6. Inamuro, T.: Lattice Boltzmann methods for moving boundary flows. Fluid Dyn. Res. **44**(2) (2012). https://doi.org/10.1088/0169-5983/44/2/024001

7. Inamuro, T.: Lattice Boltzmann methods for moving boundary flows. Fluid Dyn. Res. **44**(2), 024001 (2012)

8. Janssen, P.J., Baron, M.D., Anderson, P.D., Blawzdziewicz, J., Loewenberg, M., Wajnryb, E.: Collective dynamics of confined rigid spheres and deformable drops. Soft Matter **8**(28), 7495–7506 (2012). https://doi.org/10.1039/c2sm25812a

9. Kostenetskiy, P., Chulkevich, R., Kozyrev, V.: HPC resources of the higher school of economics. J. Phys. Conf. Ser. **1740**(1), 012050 (2021)

10. Krüger, T., Gross, M., Raabe, D., Varnik, F.: Crossover from tumbling to tank-treading-like motion in dense simulated suspensions of red blood cells. Soft Matter **9**(37), 9008–9015 (2013)

11. Krüger, T., Kusumaatmaja, H., Kuzmin, A., Shardt, O., Silva, G., Viggen, E.M.: The Lattice Boltzmann Method, vol. 10, pp. 978–973, 4–15. Springer, Cham (2017). https://doi.org/10.1007/978-3-319-44649-3

12. Lai, M.C., Peskin, C.S.: An immersed boundary method with formal second-order accuracy and reduced numerical viscosity. J. Comput. Phys. **160**(2), 705–719 (2000)

13. Latt, J., et al.: Palabos: parallel lattice Boltzmann solver. Comput. Math. Appl. **81**, 334–350 (2020)

14. Liu, B., Goree, J., Feng, Y.: Waves and instability in a one-dimensional microfluidic array. Phys. Rev. E **86**(4), 046309 (2012)

15. Mountrakis, L., Lorenz, E., Malaspinas, O., Alowayyed, S., Chopard, B., Hoekstra, A.G.: Parallel performance of an IB-LBM suspension simulation framework. J. Comput. Sci. **9**, 45–50 (2015)

16. Schiller, U.D., Fleury, J.B., Seemann, R., Gompper, G.: Collective waves in dense and confined microfluidic droplet arrays. Soft Matter **11**(29), 5850–5861 (2015)

17. Silva, A.L.E., Silveira-Neto, A., Damasceno, J.: Numerical simulation of two-dimensional flows over a circular cylinder using the immersed boundary method. J. Comput. Phys. **189**(2), 351–370 (2003)

18. Suzuki, K., Inamuro, T.: Effect of internal mass in the simulation of a moving body by the immersed boundary method. Comput. Fluids **49**(1), 173–187 (2011)

19. Thorimbert, Y., Marson, F., Parmigiani, A., Chopard, B., Lätt, J.: Lattice Boltzmann simulation of dense rigid spherical particle suspensions using immersed boundary method. Comput. Fluids **166**, 286–294 (2018)

20. Uhlmann, M.: An immersed boundary method with direct forcing for the simulation of particulate flows. J. Comput. Phys. **209**(2), 448–476 (2005)

21. Uspal, W.E., Doyle, P.S.: Collective dynamics of small clusters of particles flowing in a quasi-two-dimensional microchannel. Soft Matter **8**(41), 10676–10686 (2012)

22. Wang, Z., Fan, J., Luo, K.: Combined multi-direct forcing and immersed boundary method for simulating flows with moving particles. Int. J. Multiph. Flow **34**(3), 283–302 (2008)

HPC, BigData, AI: Architectures, Technologies, Tools

Advanced Genetic Algorithm in the Problem of Linear Solver Parameters Optimization

Andrey Petrushov[1,2] and Boris Krasnopolsky[1(✉)] ⓘ

[1] Institute of Mechanics, Lomonosov Moscow State University, Moscow, Russia
petrushov.aa18@physics.msu.ru, krasnopolsky@imec.msu.ru
[2] Physics Faculty of Lomonosov Moscow State University, Moscow, Russia

Abstract. In several areas in computational fluid dynamics, there is a need to solve differential equations of elliptic type. After discretization on a computational grid, the problem is reduced to solving a system of linear algebraic equations (SLAE). The numerical methods widely used for high-fidelity simulations of incompressible turbulent flows require solving a sequence of SLAEs with a constant matrix and changing the right-hand side. A practically important issue is the choice of the parameters of linear solvers, which can have a tangible impact on the SLAE solution time. The paper presents an algorithm for automatic parameters selection for SLAE solving methods. The proposed algorithm finds appropriate parameters for the specified configuration of numerical methods. An approach is based on a genetic algorithm in conjunction with a neural network model. The last one is trained to predict the SLAE solution time with specific parameters. Thus the neural network model acts as a source of knowledge about the influence of each parameter on the linear solver performance. It is shown that optimal parameters set for large SLAE solving can be obtained using solution statistics for smaller SLAEs, which is an important practical aspect. The performance of the algorithm is investigated for both the model SLAEs for the Poisson equation and the SLAEs from the fluid dynamics simulations. The algorithm allows to determine the corresponding optimized parameters of the linear solver and significantly reduce the overall calculations time. The corresponding speedup can reach up to 30% compared to the manually optimized solver parameters.

Keywords: Linear solver · Genetic algorithm · Neural network

1 Introduction

Many problems of mathematical physics include typical stage - solving a system of linear algebraic equations (SLAE). The wide range of applications produces the SLAEs with various properties and consequently lots of different approaches to solve these systems and solution algorithms. Using direct methods is the simplest way to solve a system. The direct methods have a small set of tuning

ⓒ Springer Nature Switzerland AG 2021
V. Voevodin and S. Sobolev (Eds.): RuSCDays 2021, CCIS 1510, pp. 297–309, 2021.
https://doi.org/10.1007/978-3-030-92864-3_23

parameters and they can be adjusted in a simple way, which makes them attractive for the researchers. However, in general these methods are resource-intensive and the algorithm complexity is $O(N^3)$, where N is the matrix size. And only in several specific cases, the fast direct methods, like fast Fourier transform [4] or Swarztrauber method [10], can be applied.

Another way is to use the linear solvers based on iterative methods. In the majority of cases, the iterative methods with appropriate preconditioners can provide the solution in a much shorter time than the direct methods. However, the choice of this optimal method and preconditioner combination can be a complex problem. These methods have much more adjustable parameters which need to be tuned by the user. In practice those adjustable parameters. which can be counted by several tens or even more, are selected from default settings or with a small perturbation of them. Therefore in many cases, the solver performance is far from its peak and can be tangibly increased after choosing an optimal parameters set.

Solving the differential equations of elliptic type is among the widespread problems in mathematical physics applications. Such problems are encountered, for example, in structural mechanics, computational fluid dynamics (CFD), electrodynamics, and others. In a number of CFD applications related to high-fidelity modeling of incompressible turbulent flows, the need for solving the elliptic equations occurs at each time step. The matrix typically remains constant and the right-hand side varies in time. The SLAE solution procedure in the corresponding simulations takes about 90–95% of the overall calculation time [6]. Therefore selection an optimal parameters set for a solver to accelerate the SLAE solution step has a significant impact on the total simulation time.

Various automated tuning strategies have been proposed to optimize the SLAE solution time. These include both tuning the code implementation details, e.g. [12], and the numerical method configurations [2,3,9]. In [12] (and in many other publications as well) the authors used the automated tuning approach based on deep learning technologies for determining the best matrix storage format to maximize the performance of sparse matrix-vector multiplication. The work [3] presents a system for adapting solution methods to specific SLAEs. Considering the properties of the matrix, adaptive system selects a method and the corresponding parameters configuration from those suggested by the user.

The several papers are devoted to suitable parameters selection for the SLAE solution process. Optimization approach described in [9] is based on a genetic algorithm as a way to find the best parameters for the solver. The authors considered the linear solver as a "black box" without a priori information about the impact of each parameter on the resulting SLAE solution time. A genetic algorithm is a flexible scheme, and it is successfully applied in many multiobjective optimization problems. But with an increase in the number of parameters their relationship becomes more and more important. And even a flexible genetic algorithm can be time-consuming to optimize target function. In [2] the authors proposed an optimization method based on the simulated annealing algorithm. This is one of the varieties of the Monte Carlo method. With a large number of parameters, it becomes more and more difficult to find the optimal configuration, as the number of combinations increases. Therefore knowledge about the approximate effect of each parameter can reduce the search area and simplify the process of finding their optimal set.

The methods discussed above are not applicable for the target problem of optimizing the solver parameters for modeling turbulent flows, as they will require solution of lots of test SLAEs to find the optimal parameters set for the specific problem of interest. The current paper proposes the combined algorithm, where the genetic algorithm is used to find the optimal parameters set, but additionally, the neural network is used as a preliminary filter to increase the convergence speed. The details of the proposed algorithm and results of the numerical experiments are presented below.

2 Optimization Approach

2.1 Genetic Algorithm

Genetic algorithm is a heuristic search scheme which is analogous to the theory of natural selection. For definiteness, we will call a set of the selected SLAE solver parameters a vector. The algorithm operates with the concepts of "generation" and "mutation". And in our problem, a generation is a group of vectors at a particular step of the algorithm. In the course of the algorithm, the vectors change from generation to generation until the convergence criterion is met, meaning the optimal (in some sense) parameters vector has been found. As a rule, the algorithm starts the search from randomly determined values from the definition range.

To determine "good" and "bad" vectors, the algorithm solves the SLAE with each parameter vector from the current generation. Parameter sets with the lowest solution time are saved and form the basis for building the next generation. Also, a certain number of random vectors is included in the next generation – this is an element of a random search. The structure of the genetic algorithm for our specific problem of interest is shown in Fig. 1. For each generation, the algorithm forms a set of vectors and with each of them, the target SLAE is solved. Then the convergence criterion is checked (for example, the solution time has not changed over the last 5 generations). If the criterion is not met, then a new generation of vectors is constructed and a direct calculation is performed again.

If we want to optimize k parameters with n_i possible discrete values for each of them, then the total number of all possible combinations will be:

$$N_{comb} = n_1 \cdot n_2 \cdot n_3 \cdot \cdots \cdot n_k. \tag{1}$$

The algorithm is able to cover only a small part of the possible combinations since the SLAE solution time is finite. And even in this small part, there may be a large number of completely ineffective vectors added randomly. It turns out that we are wasting computational time on such useless vectors, and it would be very useful to immediately recognize them and throw away without direct calculation. For this, it was decided to use solution statistics of small-scale SLAEs, and generalize it using a neural network.

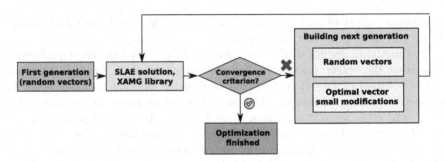

Fig. 1. Genetic algorithm structure

2.2   Introducing the Neural Network

Neural network (NN) is a widely-used predictive model which is designed to find patterns in the dataset. The structure of the NN model has several inputs and several (or one) outputs.

For the task at hand, a model of a fully connected neural network with k inputs (for each parameter) and one output was built. Fully connected models are well-known approaches in neural networks science. They are widely used in problems of predicting functions of multiple variables. Like much in the practice of machine learning, the exact architecture and the number of neurons in each layer were selected experimentally. The values of k parameters are supplied to the model input, and the output is the estimated solution time for small-scale SLAE with corresponding parameters (see Fig. 2). The model consists of one input layer, three hidden layers, and output layer.

We carried out a large number of small-scale SLAE solutions for statistics collection and compiled a dataset in the format "parameter vector → solution time". NN model was trained on that dataset and has shown useful prediction accuracy in terms of statistical data analysis (for more information on prediction efficiency, see Sect. 3).

The goal of training a model is to teach it to determine the influence of each parameter on the solver performance. Matrix properties also affect the solution time, but in this work, we will focus on the effect of parameters. Small-scale SLAEs for training the model were chosen for faster collection of statistics and for less influence of matrix properties. We assume that solver parameters will have a similar effect on performance for small and large SLAEs.

The assumptions stated above are considered acceptable, because of the main purpose of using the NN model. Due to action of preliminary filter with the genetic algorithm, the role of the NN model is to filter out notoriously "inefficient" vectors before choosing them in genetic algorithm (see Sect. 2.3 for more on vector filtering).

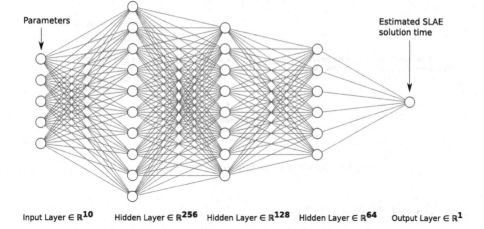

Fig. 2. Sketch of the neural network for SLAE solution time prediction (the architecture is shown, the exact number of neurons is indicated at the bottom of each layer)

2.3 Generalized Optimization Algorithm

After training the network, it became possible to integrate it into a genetic algorithm for filtering random vectors. General structure of the algorithm stays the same but there are some differences in the stage of building next generation. Instead of adding several random vectors, a large number of them are generated and passed through the neural network model. The generation includes only those vectors that showed the lowest solution time at the output of the neural network. Figure 3 shows the final version of the modified genetic algorithm.

The resulting algorithm has the following configuration:

- the number of generations is limited by 10;
- the population size is set equal to 9 vectors, of which 4 are obtained from the current optimal vector with small changes (by adding $+h_i$, $-h_i$, or 0, where h_i is a step for the i-th parameter), and 5 are random but filtered by neural network vectors;
- to add 5 filtered vectors to the generation, 12 thousand random ones are generated from the definition range and passed through the neural network; then, among them, 5 are selected with the smallest estimated SLAE solution time;
- the mutation coefficient is equal to one, that is, all parameters can change during mutation by value $+h_i$, $-h_i$, or 0 – a random choice;
- for simplicity, the crossover operator is not considered in the current version of the algorithm.

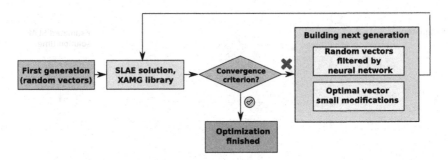

Fig. 3. Generalized optimization scheme

3 Neural Network Accuracy Evaluation

While training the NN model it is possible to observe a loss function that describes the value of prediction error on the validation data. MSE (mean squared error) was chosen as loss function, which is defined as follows (for N samples in the validation dataset):

$$MSE = \frac{1}{N} \sum_{i=1}^{N} (T_i - \hat{T}_i)^2, \tag{2}$$

where $\hat{T}_i$ is the predicted solution time and T_i is the actual one. That function is necessary for model training, however, it depends on the scale of the problem and therefore cannot be used to assess prediction quality. To evaluate the effectiveness of predictive models, the coefficient of determination is often used, which shows the proportion of the variance explained by the model. This evaluation approach is applied to neural networks for different prediction tasks (e.g. [1], [11]). Coefficient of determination can be defined in the following way:

$$R^2 = 1 - \frac{SS_{res}}{SS_{tot}}, \tag{3}$$

$$SS_{res} = \sum_{i=1}^{N} (T_i - \hat{T}_i)^2 = MSE \cdot N, \tag{4}$$

$$SS_{tot} = \sum_{i=1}^{N} (T_i - \bar{T})^2. \tag{5}$$

Thus, the effect of problem scale is minimized, since all quantities are taken in a relative sense. In the best case, the predicted values exactly match the actual values and $R^2 = 1$. A base model which always predicts $\bar{T}$ will get $R^2 = 0$ (benefit from such a model is also "zero"). R^2 can also be less than zero - the benefit from such a model is even less than the benefit from the base one.

4   Software and Numerical Methods

The development and testing of the optimization algorithm was carried out using the XAMG library [7,8]. XAMG is a newly developed library for solving sparse systems of linear algebraic equations with multiple right-hand sides. It contains the implementation of a set of Krylov subspace and algebraic multigrid iterative methods, typically used to solve the systems coming from the discretization of elliptic partial differential equations. The library provides the multilevel hierarchical parallelization with MPI+POSIX shared memory hybrid programming model and several specific code optimizations, allowing to demonstrate the superior performance compared to the well-known open-source library *hypre*.

The current paper focuses on the SLAEs obtained as a result of discretization of the Poisson equation. The XAMG library provides several internal system generators, including the ones for a cubic computational domain with a constant right-hand side on a regular grid, and the generators providing SLAEs similar to the ones in the CFD simulations when modeling turbulent flow in a channel with a matrix of wall-mounted cubes [5]. The numerical method configuration chosen comprises the BiCGStab method supplemented with the algebraic multigrid preconditioner and Chebyshev polynomial smoother. For this configuration, 10 optimization parameters were selected:

- Preconditioner
    - number of aggressive coarsening levels
    - coarse matrix size
    - number of paths for element interpolation
    - the threshold value of the bond strength of matrix elements
    - threshold value for filtering matrix elements
    - maximum number of iterations
- Smoother
    - pre-smoother polynomial order
    - pre-smoother spectrum fraction
    - post-smoother polynomial order
    - post-smoother spectrum fraction

These parameters are free and should be tuned during optimization process. A range of possible values and minimum step have been determined for each parameter. The rest of the solver, smoother, and preconditioner parameters were set by default and fixed.

The TensorFlow package was chosen as a machine learning tool. TensorFlow is one of advanced open source platforms, allowing to implement most of modern neural network architectures and learning algorithms. The entire algorithm (excluding the SLAE solver) is written in Python, and the TensorFlow module was used in the corresponding implementation for Python language.

Optimizer is integrated in the XAMG library as a separate test application. It allows to choose various numerical method configurations and specify the lists of fixed and tuned parameters as well as the optimization range for each of them. The current implementation of the optimization algorithm as a separate

test application can be used for the static parameters optimization before the
start of the main CFD calculation. In the future, the optimizer functionality will
be reorganized in the form of additional internal function of the XAMG library,
which can be directly used at the CFD calculation initialization stage.

5   Optimization Algorithm Evaluation

The calculation results presented below were obtained using two compute systems. The workstation with Intel Core-i7 8700 6-core processor was used to perform the calculations with small test matrices, and the Lomonosov-2 supercomputer was used to find the optimal parameter sets for the CFD-related SLAEs
(10 compute nodes were utilized with in total 140 computational processes).

5.1   NN Model Training

In order to obtain solution statistics for training neural network, it is necessary
to carry out a large number of SLAE solutions and here we are faced with
two opposing factors. On the one hand, the SLAE size should not be too big,
otherwise the time spent on the collection of statistics will be unacceptably large.
And on the other hand, too small SLAE scale can lead to poorly distinguishable
and highly grouped times in relation to their mean. Also on small-scale matrices,
the form of the dependence T ($parameters$) can differ greatly from the one on
large-scale matrices. In order to effectively optimize solution time for real-size
SLAE, it is better to choose a training SLAE size with a similar distribution
T ($parameters$).

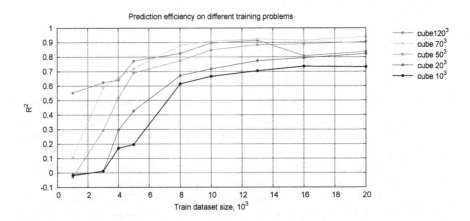

Fig. 4. Quality of prediction for the NN model for different test SLAEs and train
dataset sizes

The dependence of NN model accuracy on the dataset size is illustrated in Fig. 4. The fastest and most stable growth to its limit shows the training accuracy on the calculation statistics for 70^3 computational domain. According to these results, the matrix size of the training SLAE 70^3 was chosen for most of the following tests.

5.2   Examples of Neural Network Predictions

In terms of calculus, we are dealing with a function of time in the n-dimensional space of parameters. Solution time is the surface for which we need to find the global minimum. Also, there are local minima on that time-surface, into which the algorithm can lead us.

For clarity, consider the case with two free parameters. The rest will be fixed at their default value. Let's feed the input of the neural network with a default vector of parameters with two varying ones. Figure 5 shows the predictions of the neural network for SLAE solution time on the computational domain 70^3. The minimum time is reached at point (4; 450) for the first pair of parameters and at point (1; 450) for the second pair. Generally speaking, it is possible to fix some parameters at your discretion, and predict solution time distribution for the rest.

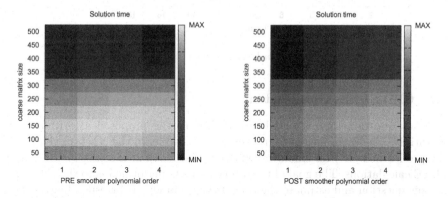

Fig. 5. Examples of neural network predictions for two pairs of varying parameters: *coarse matrix size* vs *pre-smoother polynomial order* (left) and *coarse matrix size* vs *post-smoother polynomial order* (right)

5.3   Multiple Launches: Stability Test

Stability is an important property for the optimization algorithm. Ideally, on repeated launches, the system should provide the same reduction in solution time for specified SLAE. Of course, we can set the number of generations for genetic algorithm to an extremely large one, thereby iterating over more vectors each time and increasing the chance to reach the global time minimum. But obviously, such a time investment is unacceptable in practice. Thus we have chosen a certain number of generations and fixed it at 10.

First, we carried out a series of runs of the algorithm for a model problem in the computational domain 100^3. A constant SLAE matrix with a constant right-hand side was chosen. For this SLAE, the optimization algorithm was launched 20 times using a neural network and 20 times without it. In Fig. 6, the dots mark the final solution times, which were obtained as a result of optimization procedure. All of the launches with NN model led to a greater reduction in time and the spread of optimal times has halved.

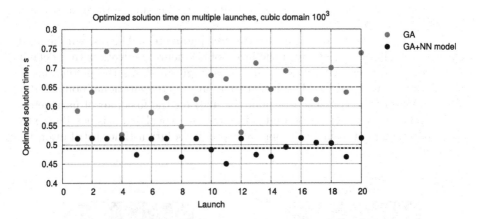

Fig. 6. Multiple algorithm launches with NN model and without it

5.4 CFD SLAEs Optimization

The key question that should be addressed to the proposed algorithm is its versatility. The main idea is to use the datasets to learn the NN (or even to use the pre-learned NN) for small test matrices, rather than the ones for the target SLAE calculations. The goal of the following tests performed is to shed the light on this question and estimate the role of the accuracy of corresponding solution time predictions on the efficiency of the proposed algorithm.

The algorithm has been tested with two SLAEs occurring when performing the direct numerical simulation (DNS) of incompressible turbulent flow in a channel with a matrix of wall-mounted cubes. The two computational grids and SLAEs of 2.32 and 9.68 million unknowns were considered (see details in [5]). The calculations were done for two algorithm configurations, assuming the use of the combined genetic algorithm with NN filtering and without it.

Figure 7 presents the obtained results for the coarser grid. Both algorithms demonstrate the tendency in decreasing the SLAE solver time with increasing the number of test SLAE solutions. However, the algorithm with NN filtering demonstrates much faster convergence, and at the scales of 40–50 solutions the solution time almost reaches the minimum. The pure GA has slower convergence

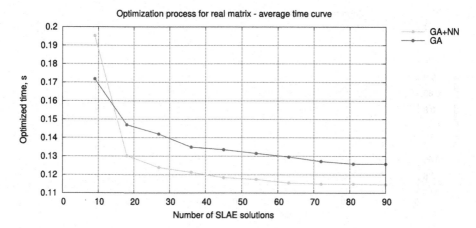

Fig. 7. Evolution of the optimal SLAE solution time with increasing the number of test SLAE solutions performed (generation number), DNS test SLAE, 2.32M unknowns

and requires multiple more SLAE solutions. For the fixed number of SLAE solutions, the GA with NN allows to additionally decrease the solution time by about 10%.

Time curves in Fig. 8 also demonstrate stable reduction in solution time and about the same 10–15% difference between typical GA launch and GA with neural network optimization. Note that all the tests performed used a neural network trained on the solution statistics for small model problem in the computational domain 70^3. This indicates that the use of solution statistics for small SLAEs is suitable for efficient parameters optimization for more complex SLAEs.

The presented results demonstrate the potential of the proposed optimization algorithm but do not allow to estimate the practical effect of these optimizations. The obtained optimized parameter sets and the corresponding calculation times were compared with the ones used in CFD calculations [5], which were optimized manually. The obtained optimized results demonstrate about 20–30% decrease in the solution time compared to manually optimized parameters. In addition, the automated tuning procedure simplifies the calculations and allows to avoid laborious manual parameters tuning process, which requires at least some basic knowledge on the characteristics of the target SLAE and the properties of the corresponding numerical methods.

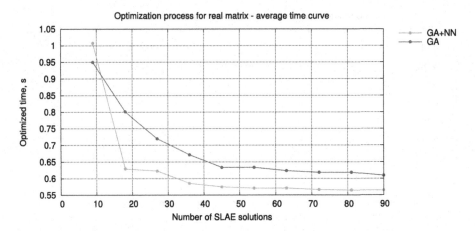

Fig. 8. Evolution of the optimal SLAE solution time with increasing the number of test SLAE solutions performed (generation number), DNS test SLAE, 9.68M unknowns

6   Conclusions

In this paper, we presented an algorithm for automatic parameters selection for the SLAE solver configuration. The proposed system is based on a genetic algorithm and an auxiliary neural network model. The system takes into account the solution statistics of small SLAEs and generalizes it to a SLAEs with greater dimension. The algorithm has been tested on two types of SLAEs arising from the discretization of the elliptic differential equations, including the Poisson equation in a cubic domain and a pressure Poisson equation on the grids used for direct numerical simulations of the turbulent flows in a channel with a matrix of wall-mounted cubes. The developed neural network model is trained to effectively predict the small SLAE solution time with a coefficient of determination $R^2 > 0.9$. It is shown that the introduction of a neural network increases the stability of the algorithm and allows to decrease the scatter of the results between different launches. Also, the use of a neural network allows to achieve a deeper time minimum in fewer SLAE solutions. A stable decrease in the target SLAE solution time is shown during the operation of the algorithm. Optimized parameters combination allows to reduce solution time by up to 30% compared to the manually optimized values. Additionally, the proposed optimization algorithm allows to automate the laborious parameters optimization procedure and simplify the modeling process.

The current paper demonstrates attractive results on the problem of automating the SLAE solver parameters optimization, which motivates the further development of this approach. The following research will be focused on extending the capabilities of the proposed algorithm, increasing the number of optimizing parameters, and detailed evaluation of this algorithm with an extended set of various test SLAEs.

Acknowledgements. The research is carried out using the equipment of the shared research facilities of HPC computing resources at Lomonosov Moscow State University and supported by the Russian Science Foundation, Grant No. 18-71-10075.

References

1. Ahangar, R.G., Yahyazadehfar, M., Pournaghshband, H.: The comparison of methods artificial neural network with linear regression using specific variables for prediction stock price in Tehran stock exchange. CoRR abs/1003.1457 (2010). http://arxiv.org/abs/1003.1457

2. Bagaev, D., Konshin, I., Nikitin, K.: Dynamic optimization of linear solver parameters in mathematical modelling of unsteady processes. In: Voevodin, V., Sobolev, S. (eds.) Supercomputing, pp. 54–66. Springer, Cham (2017). https://doi.org/10.1007/978-3-319-71255-0_5

3. Erzunov, V., Bartenev, Yu.: Solver adaptation to a SLAE flux. VANT. Ser.: Mat. Mod. Fiz. Proc. (1) (2021). http://vant.vniief.ru/ref_vant_search_en.php?ID_journal=121

4. Costa, P.: A FFT-based finite-difference solver for massively-parallel direct numerical simulations of turbulent flows. Comput. Math. Appl. **76**(8), 1853–1862 (2018). https://doi.org/10.1016/j.camwa.2018.07.034

5. Krasnopolsky, B.: An approach for accelerating incompressible turbulent flow simulations based on simultaneous modelling of multiple ensembles. Comput. Phys. Commun. **229**, 8–19 (2018). https://doi.org/10.1016/j.cpc.2018.03.023

6. Krasnopolsky, B., Medvedev, A.: Evaluating performance of mixed precision linear solvers with iterative refinement. Supercomput. Front. Innov. **8** (2021). https://doi.org/10.14529/jsfi210301

7. Krasnopolsky, B., Medvedev, A.: XAMG: a library for solving linear systems with multiple right-hand side vectors. SoftwareX **14** (2021). https://doi.org/10.1016/j.softx.2021.100695

8. Krasnopolsky, B., Medvedev, A.: XAMG: Source code repository (2021). https://gitlab.com/xamg/xamg. Accessed 10 Apr 2021

9. Mishev, I., et al.: Adaptive control for solver performance optimization in reservoir simulation. In: Proceedings of ECMOR XI - 11th European Conference on the Mathematics of Oil Recovery (2008). https://doi.org/10.3997/2214-4609.20146368

10. Swarztrauber, P.: A direct method for the discrete solution of separable elliptic equations. SIAM J. Num. Anal. **11**(6), 1136–1150 (1974). http://www.jstor.org/stable/2156231

11. Wang, Y., et al.: Prediction of tubular solar still performance by machine learning integrated with Bayesian optimization algorithm. Appl. Therm. Eng. **184** (2021). https://doi.org/10.1016/j.applthermaleng.2020.116233

12. Zhao, Y., Li, J., Liao, C., Shen, X.: Bridging the gap between deep learning and sparse matrix format selection. SIGPLAN Not. **53**(1), 94–108 (2018). https://doi.org/10.1145/3200691.3178495

Analysis of Software Package Usage Based on Methods for Identifying Similar HPC Applications

Denis Shaikhislamov[(✉)] and Vadim Voevodin

Lomonosov Moscow State University, Moscow, Russia
vadim@parallel.ru

Abstract. In the field of High Performance Computing, the task of software package detection is poorly studied, even though the information about packages used in supercomputer applications helps to better understand the peculiarities of supercomputer usage. There are several existing solutions to tackle that problem, but they are far from ideal. In this paper we show how our previously developed method for detecting similar applications can be used to solve this problem, as well as analyze results of its operation with some insights on supercomputer usage. According to the evaluation on the Lomonosov-2 supercomputer, these methods found ∼80% more jobs with package usage than the existing method.

Keywords: Supercomputers · Time-series analysis · Machine learning · Similar application detection · Package detection

1 Introduction

Modern supercomputers are extremely complex, and therefore it is necessary to constantly monitor them in order to control both correctness and efficiency of their functioning. For these purposes, supercomputer administrators collect a variety of information about the state of computing systems – the operation and state of compute nodes, resource manager, file system, communication networks, service servers, engineering infrastructure, and much, much more.

The collection of such information is carried out in different ways. To obtain data on the operation of compute nodes, various monitoring systems are most often used, such as Zabbix, Nagios, Collectd or DiMMon [12], which is used on the Lomonosov-2 supercomputer [13]. Information from the resource manager and file system can often be obtained directly. Data on the state of the engineering infrastructure is collected by a third system. Such a variety of both data sources and methods of obtaining them leads to the fact that system administrators have to deal with a huge amount of the most heterogeneous information, which is not possible to process manually.

Therefore, the problem of developing methods for "smart" analysis is becoming more and more urgent, which will allow administrators to more fully, accurately

© Springer Nature Switzerland AG 2021
V. Voevodin and S. Sobolev (Eds.): RuSCDays 2021, CCIS 1510, pp. 310–321, 2021.
https://doi.org/10.1007/978-3-030-92864-3_24

and quickly assess the supercomputer functioning as well as detect and eliminate issues leading to the utilization decrease. There are many tasks in this area that are in demand, but not yet fully implemented, such as identifying anomalies in a supercomputer's job flow or providing recommendations to users for more efficient execution of their applications.

One such task is identifying software packages used in applications running on a supercomputer. We are talking about various libraries and software tools that implement common applied tasks from different subject areas. Some of the most common packages are, for example, Gromacs, LAMMPS, NAMD, MAGMA, VASP, and so on. Such packages are very often used in HPC applications – for example, on the Lomonosov-2 supercomputer 46% of CPU-hours from the beginning till May 2021 were occupied by jobs using known packages. Therefore, it is important to be able to determine which packages are in use – this information allows more accurately understanding the structure of the supercomputer job flow, and also helps to study and compare the performance of applications in more detail.

Previously, we proposed methods based on data mining techniques that help to approach the issue of detecting software package usages from different angles. They are based on similar application detection methods, which give the estimate on how two jobs are close to each other in terms of, e.g., behavior or function names. When comparing new launched job with archived jobs using known packages, we can use the estimate to detect package usages. In this paper, it is proposed to study this topic and analyze the statistics collected using one of these methods on the Lomonosov-2 supercomputer.

The main contribution of this paper is providing ideas on how similar application detection can be used in HPC environment, what kinds of insights on supercomputer's usage can be obtained using these methods, like determining what part of the supercomputer is used to solve specific problems etc.

The paper is organized as follows. Section 2 provides the background as well as mentions existing methods in the related areas. Section 3 briefly explains our current approach for package detection and includes assessment of its accuracy in real-time operation. Section 4 looks over different ways of applying proposed method and provides interesting insights. Section 5 includes the conclusion and our plans for future work.

2   Background and Related Work

The main task of this study is to evaluate and analyze the results of software package detection methods used in supercomputer jobs. The package detection allows not only obtaining detailed information about how the supercomputer is used (e.g. what preferences are among active users), but also helping users, for example, by detecting and optimizing the most frequently used packages for a particular computing system.

Our previously proposed approach for package detection is based on two methods (static and dynamic) for finding similar jobs. In this paper, we will focus on the static method. It involves analyzing only static data that does not change during the execution of a job – namely, the executable file.

Lomonosov-2 has an existing package detection system that is based on XALT [1]. XALT replaces the linker (ld) and launcher (mpirun) commands, which allows you to get information about where all executable and linked files are located, how many executable files have been launched, how the application was compiled, etc. By searching for specific keywords in the file paths, it is possible to determine which libraries are in use. But this approach has a drawback. For example, with dynamic linking, XALT can detect the presence of certain libraries, since the names of linked files often include specific keywords, but the user can rename the executable file, and XALT will no longer be able to determine the presence of a particular software package.

There is a paper [8] that provides an overview of how software package detection is built on Ohio Supercomputer Center. They use combination of pbsacct [2] and XALT to analyze launched jobs. XALT is used the same way as in Lomonosov-2. Pbsacct is a job flow analysis system for HPC clusters that use Portable Batch System (PBS). It stores information about job scripts, which allows detecting packages used by pattern matching on job scripts. This approach is very similar to what XALT does, but in our case we can't use pbsacct because Lomonosov-2 uses Slurm instead of PBS. Also, pbsacct suffers from the same problems as XALT because it relies on keywords being present in job scripts which is not always the case.

We haven't found any works regarding more sophisticated approaches for software package detection like using machine learning methods, despite the fact that there are lots of other appliances of such methods. For example, there are many works that solve the problem of identifying abnormal behavior in jobs. In [3], the authors analyze logs using a Long-Short term memory (LSTM) model that learns from normal job behavior and alerts administrators if abnormal behavior occurs. A similar approach is used in [5], in which logs are analyzed using Markov Chain Models to highlight anomalies. In our previous papers [10,11], we also solved this problem using Random Forest and LSTM to detect supercomputer jobs with abnormal efficiency.

Another type of analysis based on machine learning techniques is prediction of different job features. In [4] authors use ML methods to predict whether submitted job was runtime underestimated or not. Runtime underestimation means that job needs more computing time than requested. In [6] authors use system logs and monitoring system data to predict HPC node failures to take proactive actions. Authors of [14] approached the task of job status prediction by training Random Forest classifier on monitoring system data to prevent the waste of resources by failed jobs.

3 Methods for Software Package Detection

3.1 Overview of Previously Developed Method

Our previous work [9] have already showed in detail how our package detection system works, so in this paper we will only briefly touch on this issue. To detect usage of packages, we use methods for similar applications detection based on static data.

Static method provides some estimate of how similar jobs are to each other. Thus, the package detection is performed as follows – a knowledge base is built using jobs in which it is already known that specific software package is used. When a new job launches, it is compared with jobs from the knowledge base. Similar jobs are detected using predefined threshold that was chosen empirically. Thus, we assume that new job uses those packages that are used in similar jobs from the knowledge base.

The static method in our case is based on the analysis of executable files. Using the UNIX nm utility, we can extract the names of the used functions and variables. We feed this list of function names to the input of the trained Doc2vec [7] model, which converts a set of words into a vector of fixed length, which can be further compared with each other. Comparison is performed using the cosine similarity function, the essence of which is to calculate the cosine of the angle between vectors, and the closer the resulting value is to 1, the closer the vectors are to each other. This estimate of distance is used in package detection. The Doc2vec model was trained on the function names of over 7000 different executables.

3.2 Assessing Real-Life Accuracy of Static Method

To test the efficiency of the packet detection, in this paper we will look over jobs that were executed on the Lomonosov-2 starting from January till May 2021. We compare the static analysis with the existing XALT-based package detection system.

The overall statistics showed that, after launching the static package detection method, the number of labelled jobs (i.e. jobs with detected package usage) doubled. But it is necessary to check if our method works correctly. We are interested in those jobs in which XALT did not detect the presence of software packages, while the static method could. The Table 1 describes on several packages how static method performed compared to XALT.

It can be seen that the static method detects an average of 40% more jobs than XALT. But, as mentioned earlier, these jobs must be checked for correctness. We can determine, what function names are commonly used by specific packages, and check whether new jobs include them. Most of the new jobs pass that test and clearly use specified package, but some use very uncommon set of function names which needed further investigation. This could mean one of two options: our method incorrectly parses the given function names and incorrectly identifies the package, or it is a variation of the package that is very different

Table 1. Number of jobs detected by XALT and static method

Package	Static + XALT	XALT	Static	Overlap (% of total)	Static excluding XALT (% of total)
LAMMPS	6066	4207	4676	46.4	30.6
NWChem	2421	1469	1164	8.8	39.3
cp2k	4860	818	4778	15.1	83.1
Amber	422	219	334	31	48.1
Gromacs	6072	4334	4828	50.9	28.6
Cabaret	318	77	282	12.9	75.8
Molpro	973	973	0	0	0
Firefly	1729	742	1636	37.5	57.1

from the average executable file of this package. After the analysis, we found that XALT detected only 1–2 jobs with these rare function names that were in the knowledge base, but later, for various reasons, could not determine the presence of certain packages. This is especially clearly seen in case of Cabaret package.

As stated earlier, XALT uses executable file paths to detect packages, and it suffers from the following problem: users often rename executable files and paths to them. This is clearly noticeable in CP2K jobs, where renaming happens often. The static method does not rely on paths and therefore can determine the similarity in such cases with ease. Partly because of this, we can conclude that XALT most often detects jobs with "popular" packages, since their executables are rarely renamed, while it does not cope that well with rarer packages such as CP2K and Cabaret.

It is also worth noting that sets of jobs detected by XALT and by static method can differ greatly. For example, in the case of NWChem, only 212 jobs were classified as the NWChem package by both XALT and the static method, making only 8.8% of the total number of detected NWChem launches. That is caused by several problems. The first problem is that often we cannot extract terms from binary files for various reasons: file modification, lack of read permissions, etc. These cases make up about 30% of all launched jobs. It should be especially noted that there are cases when users use different wrappers to launch programs. This is very relevant for packages like NAMD, where users use the Charm wrapper to run jobs, and Quantum Espresso, where users use Python. Also a special case is when we cannot get any executable files for analysis. This is especially pronounced in the molpro package, where jobs use an .exe executable file in which neither the nm nor objdump utilities could extract terms from the symbol table.

If you look at the entire supercomputer job flow, during this time period 124.4k jobs were launched, and among them we detected 26.9k jobs that use packages. This is about 21.6% of jobs. But if we consider spent resources (CPU-hours), then this ratio rise up to 45.6%. It can be concluded that the commonly used packages are demanding in terms computing power. It should also be noted that if we consider just XALT without static method, then this ratio almost halfs – 23.2%, which shows the efficiency of the static method.

Using the proposed method gives us a better picture of how the supercomputer is used, which packages should be paid more attention to, etc. This information is shown on Fig. 1, which indicates how many CPU-hours the jobs with specific package used. It can be noted that when analyzing only XALT data, we could make a false assumption that NWChem used almost 2 times less resources than Gromacs, which is actually wrong, and the difference between them is only 10%. Similar is true for Firefly and Gromacs packages – earlier we would conclude that they consume approximately the same number of resources, while in reality Firefly used 40% more resources than Gromacs.

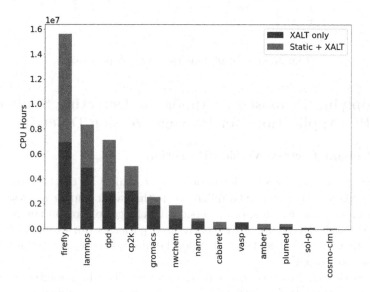

Fig. 1. Distribution of CPU-hours spent among jobs using several known packages

Similar statistics can be viewed from the perspective of determining the number of users who use packages. Figure 2 shows statistics on how many users are using a particular package. Since the launch of static method more than 50 new package users were discovered, the detailed use of whose resources we did not previously know. Considering that XALT discovered 285 users launched their jobs during the chosen time period, this is a significant increase. And, as noted earlier, the new information changes the perspective on the popularity of specific packages (for example, NWChem).

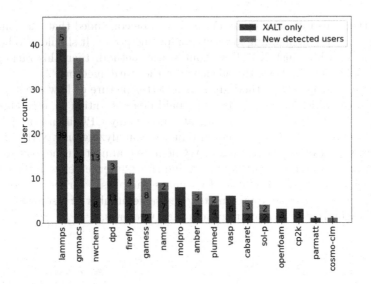

Fig. 2. Amount of users that use top packages

4   Applying Proposed Methods for Detecting Similar HPC Applications for Package Version Detection

4.1   Prebuilt Package Version Detection

The task of package version detection is very similar to the task of package detection discussed earlier. The difference is that after finding a package, you need to understand which specific version it belongs to. Lomonosov-2 includes many preinstalled versions of frequently used packages (for example, Gromacs 2020.3, 2019.4-icc, 2018-icc), and it would be interesting to know which version users use most often.

We considered two ways for solving this task. The first solution is similar to the static method for packages detection – define a knowledge base using Doc2vec, but instead of using packages as labels we use package versions. After detecting the package usage in a job, we compare this job with different versions of the packages, and if there is a similar one, we assign the version to the package.

The second solution is to use unique terms, that is, we find the names of functions and variables that are present only in this specific version of the package. Further, after finding a package in the job, we look for the unique names of functions and variables in the executable file to determine its package version. And if we find these unique names, we consider that this version of the package is used. The advantages of this method are speed and transparency – we can clearly see which function names are present and which are not. Unique terms can also tell you whether a static method will work, because in the absence of unique terms a static method will not be able to distinguish one version from another. Due to the simplicity and effectiveness it was decided to use this method.

To assess the performance of this method, we selected several of the most used packages: LAMMPS, Gromacs, NWChem, and NAMD.

With one of the packages, we immediately discovered a problem – we will not be able to identify the version of the package NAMD using the proposed methods. Users in most cases run not the executable file with the package, but the Charm wrapper. And from this wrapper it is impossible to determine which version of the package is being launched.

The situation is different with LAMMPS. More than 8 versions of this package are installed on Lomonosov-2, and unique terms of half of them stand out well, but the other half does not have unique terms, which makes it impossible to select versions. It is also worth noting that versions without unique terms are versions without GPU support. This can be explained by the fact that, despite no new functions being used, the versions have different logic that we cannot identify. The GPU versions have unique terms, as more and more new GPU functions are added with each version, which is why we can highlight only them.

We analyzed over 4700 jobs that used LAMMPS (only jobs that have executable files available to us are included). Table 2 shows how many jobs with known package versions were detected. Even though we have the 2020 version with GPU support installed on the Lomonosov-2 supercomputer, users are still using the 2018 version quite often. The reason may be the difficulty of code rewriting for a new version of the package, or the old version being more efficient in these cases (e.g. due to differences in package configuration). But even more interesting is that more than 80% of users use the CUDA version of LAMMPS, but of these we can determine the versions only for 34% of launches.

Table 2. Found versions in LAMMPS jobs

Total	CUDA (default)	30 Mar 2018 CUDA p100	22 Feb 2018 CUDA	CUDA (any version)
4743	257	861	310	3890

This leads to the question of how often users use the LAMMPS versions that are centrally installed by administrators on Lomonosov-2. And after analyzing the data, we found that out of all launches, only 25% use the preinstalled binaries, all other launches use their own LAMMPS package builds. For example, of all executable files using CUDA we cannot determine the version in 66% of cases – we can conclude that these are custom versions of packages, for which we have no information. This leaves mixed feelings, since on the one hand, users can optimize the package themselves and even most likely get a version of the package that is more suitable for their task, but on the other hand, an incorrectly built package can severely impact performance. In support of the latter statement, there is an example when a user thought that he was using a custom-built version with GPU support, but due to incorrect compilation received a CPU-only version, and for some time did not even suspect that an error had occurred.

With GROMACS, the situation is much better – out of 5000 launches, 3900 use package versions provided by system administrators of Lomonosov-2. We need to find versions for the remaining 1100. Table 3 shows total amount of detected jobs with package version along with jobs with custom builds. As you can see from the table, despite the fact that a large number of our builds are running, users who run custom builds use different, not known versions of the package.

Table 3. Found versions in GROMACS jobs

	Total	2019.4-gcc-cuda	5.1.1	2020.3-mpi-cuda	2018-icc	2018-gcc
Total	5013	18	597	337	2072	901
Only custom builds	1096	0	1	33	0	33

Nearly all custom builds' versions differ from prebuilt ones, and the reasons may vary. Maybe some are accustomed to a specific version that is not prebuilt in the system, or they seek specific functionality present only on their version of the package. Or maybe they modified parts of the package to suit their needs. Nevertheless, we should look into most popular versions, survey some of the users whether they need optimized prebuilt version and take according actions if they do.

4.2   Unknown Package Version Detection

Figure 3 shows more detailed information about what proportion of launches use centrally installed builds for some of the most popular packages. It can be seen that a significant proportion of launches are custom builds, and if we consider the amount of CPU hours each package uses, LAMMPS analysis is of most interest, because out of 8M CPU hours used only 2.4M belong to job launches of centrally installed versions. And that raises the question – can we figure out which package versions are used in other jobs using unknown custom builds? The static method provides data on how similar the executable files are to each other, so it can be used not only to find similar jobs, but to cluster the executable files. This allows us to detect new versions of executable files that are not currently installed by administrators on the supercomputer. The question arises – why is this necessary? The obvious answer is that in this way we find out which versions of the package are popular among users, which in the future will allow us to centrally install them on the supercomputer and optimize them for users' needs.

As noted earlier, LAMMPS is of most interest in terms of package version detection due to amount of resources used, that's why we tested the method on these jobs. We detected more than 10 new clusters with different versions. Table 4 updates Table 2 with top 3 of most used unknown package versions. By analysing executable files' contents of the largest cluster we detected version

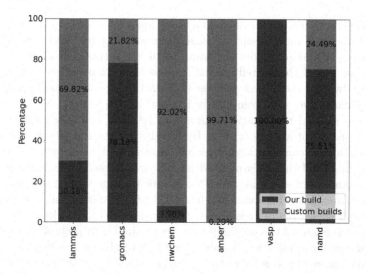

Fig. 3. Percentage of launched jobs with centrally installed vs. custom package builds

of LAMMPS dated 29 October of 2020, which is used quite often but is not centrally installed yet, meaning that it's probably a good idea to think about installing and carefully optimizing it in near future.

We could not find any version reference in two other clusters using terms. So, to determine their versions, we had to launch these executable files, and we found out that second and third most common versions are dated 31 March of 2017 and 3 March of 2020. Latter is of most interest, because Lomonosov-2 has the same centrally built version, but optimized for V100 cards. The reason why users use their custom build seems to be straightforward – they launch their application on P100 cards, and the latest centrally built version on Lomonosov-2 optimized for these cards is dated 7 August of 2019. It is most likely that users need more recent version of the package optimized for P100 cards, and we plan to address this issue in the future.

Table 4. Found versions in LAMMPS jobs with not centrally built versions (in bold)

Total	CUDA (default)	30 Mar 2018 CUDA p100	22 Feb 2018 CUDA	29 Oct 2020	31 Mar 2017	3 Mar 2020
4743	257	861	310	**660**	**445**	**349**

5 Conclusions and Future Work

In this paper, we have shown the results of real-time operation of software package detection system which is based on similar application detection method. During its evaluation we've proven its effectiveness – a number of detected software package usages has risen more than 40% compared to previous results based on XALT detection methods only. That additional information can give insights on how to achieve more accurate usage of supercomputer resources, e.g. what packages we should pay more attention to in the future. For example, in our analysis, we found that Firefly actually used more than twice as many CPU hours and dwarfed the closest package (LAMMPS) by comparison; while, based on XALT data, they were comparatively equal in this respect.

We also showed that static method can be used not only to detect what package is used, but also its version. By locating unique function names used in specific version we can detect whether new launched job uses that version or not. It should be noted that this method has its drawbacks. The main one is that we need examples of executable files for specific package version to select unique function names from. Lomonosov-2 has a list of prebuilt package versions, but during analysis we found that users, while using custom package builds, also use custom versions of the packages that are dissimilar to prebuilt ones. We can use static similar application detection method to cluster executable files with unknown package versions for further analysis. Sometimes, we can figure out the package version based on exec path used (e.g. for Gromacs), but in some cases we need to analyse binary files themselves to find package version names.

As we've shown in this paper, similar application detection methods can be used in different ways to find interesting insights on supercomputer usage. In the future we plan to study applying described similar application detection methods for solving other tasks that are of interest for administrators. One of these tasks is behaviour prediction during jobs execution that will allow us to detect anomalies in its execution in real time. Another interesting task is prediction of job's execution time based on static and dynamic data.

Acknowledgments. The results described in this paper, except of Sect. 4, were achieved at Lomonosov Moscow State University with the financial support of the Russian Science Foundation, agreement No. 21-71-30003. The results shown in Sect. 4 were achieved at Lomonosov Moscow State University with the financial support of the Russian Science Foundation, agreement No. 20-11-20194. The research is carried out using the equipment of shared research facilities of HPC computing resources at Lomonosov Moscow State University.

References

1. Agrawal, K., Fahey, M., Mclay, R., James, D.: User environment tracking and problem detection with XALT. In: 2014 First International Workshop on HPC User Support Toolspp, pp. 32–40 (2014). https://doi.org/10.1109/HUST.2014.6
2. Baer, T., Johnson, D.: Pbsacct: a workload analysis system for PBS-based HPC systems. In: Proceedings of the 2014 Annual Conference on Extreme Science and Engineering Discovery Environment, XSEDE 2014. Association for Computing Machinery, New York (2014). https://doi.org/10.1145/2616498.2616539
3. Du, M., Li, F., Zheng, G., Srikumar, V.: DeepLog: anomaly detection and diagnosis from system logs through deep learning, In: Proceedings of the 2017 ACM SIGSAC Conference on Computer and Communications Security, pp. 1285–1298. Association for Computing Machinery, New York (2017). https://doi.org/10.1145/3133956.3134015

4. Guo, J., Nomura, A., Barton, R., Zhang, H., Matsuoka, S.: Machine learning predictions for underestimation of job runtime on HPC system. In: Yokota, R., Wu, W. (eds.) SCFA 2018. LNCS, vol. 10776, pp. 179–198. Springer, Cham (2018). https://doi.org/10.1007/978-3-319-69953-0_11

5. Haque, A., DeLucia, A., Baseman, E.: Markov chain modeling for anomaly detection in high performance computing system logs. In: Proceedings of the Fourth International Workshop on HPC User Support Tools, HUST2017. Association for Computing Machinery, New York, NY (2017). https://doi.org/10.1145/3152493.3152559.

6. Klinkenberg, J., Terboven, C., Lankes, S., Müller, M.S.: Data mining-based analysis of HPC center operations. In: 2017 IEEE International Conference on Cluster Computing (CLUSTER), pp. 766–773 (2017). https://doi.org/10.1109/CLUSTER.2017.23

7. Le, Q.V., Mikolov, T.: Distributed representations of sentences and documents. CoRR abs/1405.4053 (2014)

8. Na, H., You, Z.Q., Baer, T., Oottikkal, S., Dockendorf, T., Brozell, S.: HPC software tracking strategies for a diverse workload. In: 2020 IEEE/ACM International Workshop on HPC User Support Tools (HUST) and Workshop on Programming and Performance Visualization Tools (ProTools), pp. 1–9 (2020). https://doi.org/10.1109/HUSTProtools51951.2020.00008

9. Shaikhislamov, D., Voevodin, V.: Development and practical application of methods for detecting similar supercomputer jobs. In: Sokolinsky, L., Zymbler, M. (eds.) PCT 2021. CCIS, vol. 1437, pp. 18–30. Springer, Cham (2021). https://doi.org/10.1007/978-3-030-81691-9_2

10. Shaykhislamov, D., Voevodin, V.: An approach for detecting abnormal parallel applications based on time series analysis methods. In: Wyrzykowski, R., Dongarra, J., Deelman, E., Karczewski, K. (eds.) PPAM 2017. LNCS, vol. 10777, pp. 359–369. Springer, Cham (2018). https://doi.org/10.1007/978-3-319-78024-5_32

11. Shaykhislamov, D., Voevodin, V.: An approach for dynamic detection of inefficient supercomputer applications. Procedia Comput. Sci. **136**, 35–43 (2018). https://doi.org/10.1016/j.procs.2018.08.235. https://www.sciencedirect.com/science/article/pii/S1877050918315400

12. Stefanov, K., Voevodin, V., Zhumatiy, S., Voevodin, V.: Dynamically reconfigurable distributed modular monitoring system for supercomputers (DiMMon). Procedia Comput. Sci. **66**, 625–634 (2015). https://doi.org/10.1016/j.procs.2015.11.071

13. Voevodin, V.V., et al.: Supercomputer Lomonosov-2: large scale, deep monitoring and fine analytics for the user community. Supercomput. Front. Innov **6**(2), 4–11 (2019). https://doi.org/10.14529/jsfi190201

14. Yoo, W., Sim, A., Wu, K.: Machine learning based job status prediction in scientific clusters. In: 2016 SAI Computing Conference (SAI), pp. 44–53 (2016). https://doi.org/10.1109/SAI.2016.7555961

Comparative Efficiency Analysis of MPI Blocking and Non-blocking Communications with Coarray Fortran

Galina Reshetova[1]([✉]) [ID], Vladimir Cheverda[1] [ID], and Vitaly Koinov[2]

[1] The Institute of Computational Mathematics and Mathematical Geophysics SB RAS, Novosibirsk, Russia
kgv@nmsf.sscc.ru, CheverdaVA@ipgg.sbras.ru
[2] Novosibirsk State University, Novosibirsk, Russia

Abstract. The MPI is the most widespread data exchange interface standard used in parallel programming for clusters and supercomputers with many computer platforms. The primary means of the MPI communication between processes is passing messages based on basic point-to-point blocking and non-blocking routines. The choice of the optimal implementation of exchanges is essential to minimize the idle and transmission times to achieve parallel algorithm efficiency. We used three realizations of data exchange processes based on blocking, non-blocking point-to-point MPI routines and new features of the Coarray Fortran technique to determine the most efficient parallelization strategy. For the study, the two-dimensional wave equation was used as a test problem. During the experiments, the problem size and the approaches to the data exchange for transferring data between processes were changed. For each version, we measured the computation time and the acceleration factor. The research carried out shows that the larger the problem size, the greater the benefits of delayed non-blocking routines and Coarray Fortran. The efficiency of delayed non-blocking operations is due to overlapping the data transfer in the computations background. The Coarray Fortran acceleration is achieved by using Coarray variables with shared memory. The Coarray approach starts to win with the growth of problem size.

Keywords: Acoustic wave equation · Finite difference schemes · Parallel programming · Domain decomposition method · MPI · Coarray Fortran

1 Introduction

When turning to the exascale parallel computing, there arises a serious problem of reducing communication costs. Improving the network performance is not sufficient to solve this problem, and minimizing communication latency becomes critical [1].

© Springer Nature Switzerland AG 2021
V. Voevodin and S. Sobolev (Eds.): RuSCDays 2021, CCIS 1510, pp. 322–336, 2021.
https://doi.org/10.1007/978-3-030-92864-3_25

The current scientific applications are mainly applied to the Message Passing Interface (MPI) parallel programming model based on the message-passing library interface specification. The MPI provides the fundamental concepts of communications between tasks/processes data exchange with the help of the point-to-point or the collective MPI communication routines.

Communication can be a bottleneck when implementing a parallel program. For example, in the widespread numerical seismic modeling approach based on finite difference methods with domain decomposition [2,3], the data exchange is carried out at each computational time step, and even a small reduction in communication time can lead to a significant performance improvement of parallel programs.

The cost of network communication is directly related to the programming model semantics, network topology, communication software protocols, etc. The time for communicating a message between two processes depends on preparing a message for the transmission and the time taken by a message to traverse the network to its destination. Therefore, the research into optimizing the data exchange in a parallel program is being conducted in different directions.

One of them deals with the influence of different architectures of parallel supercomputer clusters on the result of the MPI message-passing communication routines to compare and to analyze the MPI implementation performance over different interconnect technologies [4,5].

Another direction of the research is related to the non-blocking point-to-point communication, which potentially allows communication and computation to be overlapped and thus use hardware parallelism. Several studies have shown that the performance of parallel applications can be significantly enhanced with the overlapping techniques [6–8].

The highlighted research concerns the application of new programming models alternative to the MPI. The implementation of Co-Array Fortran (CAF) [9] becomes widely used in the Oil and Gas industry with data-intensive applications such as forward seismic modeling, seismic processing, reverse time migration, etc. [2,10].

The objective of this paper is to compare three strategies in the realization of communications based on the blocking (*MPI_Send, MPI_Recv*), the non-blocking (*MPI_Isend, MPI_Irecv*) point-to-point MPI routines, and the new features of the Co-Array Fortran (CAF) technique of the Fortran language. A two-dimensional wave equation describing the propagation of acoustic waves in heterogeneous media and written down as a first order hyperbolic system for the displacement velocity vector and pressure was taken as a test problem to carry out our research. We applied the finite difference method of the second order accuracy in spatial variables and time on staggered grids to numerically solve a problem. Parallelization into processes was carried out by the domain decomposition method to split the computational domain to smaller subdomains with overlapping. We have measured the computational time and acceleration coefficient by applying different communication approaches to transferring data among processes and changing the size of a problem.

2   Statement of the Problem

The investigation of a medium internal structure using wave fields is one of the primary seismic exploration tasks. The seismic observation scheme is as follows. The wavefront is excited by surface sources and propagates deep into a medium. Reflecting from the interface in the medium, it returns to the free surface, where are recording receivers. These records are used in procedures for reconstructing the velocity structure of the inner structure of the medium. This process can be mathematically described by a second order hyperbolic differential wave equation describing a change in the acoustic pressure p as a function of the coordinates x, y, z and the time t.

Let us consider the acoustic wave propagation in heterogeneous media, describing a change of the wavefield pressure $p(x, y, z, t)$ in the domain $\Omega \times (0, T)$. Suppose that a wavefield is excited by the source $f(t)$ located at the point (x_s, y_s, z_s). This process in heterogeneous media is defined by the equation

$$\rho \nabla \cdot \left(\frac{1}{\rho} \nabla p \right) - \frac{1}{c^2} \frac{\partial^2 p}{\partial t^2} = -\rho \frac{\partial^2 f}{\partial t^2}, \tag{1}$$

where c is the velocity of a wave propagating in the medium, ρ is the density, p is the acoustic pressure, and f is the volumetric-type point source.

By introducing a displacement velocity vector $\mathbf{v} = (v_x, v_y, v_z)^T$, we can represent the second order acoustic wave Eq. (1) as the first order hyperbolic system

$$\rho \frac{\partial \mathbf{v}}{\partial t} + \nabla p = 0,$$
$$\frac{1}{\kappa} \frac{\partial p}{\partial t} + \nabla \cdot \mathbf{v} = \frac{\partial f}{\partial t}, \tag{2}$$

where κ is the adiabatic compression modulus, associated with the velocity by the formula $v = \sqrt{\kappa/\rho}$. The resulting system (2) has a symmetric hyperbolic form, and this advantage we use in constructing efficient finite difference schemes on staggered grids.

By splitting the pressure $p = (p_x, p_y)^T$ to a two-dimensional case, it is also possible to rewrite (2) as a first order hyperbolic system

$$\frac{\partial v_x}{\partial t} = \frac{1}{\rho} \left(\frac{\partial p_x}{\partial x} + \frac{\partial p_y}{\partial x} \right),$$
$$\frac{\partial v_y}{\partial t} = \frac{1}{\rho} \left(\frac{\partial p_x}{\partial y} + \frac{\partial p_y}{\partial y} \right),$$
$$\frac{\partial P_x}{\partial t} = -\kappa \frac{\partial v_x}{\partial x} + F_x,$$
$$\frac{\partial P_y}{\partial t} = -\kappa \frac{\partial v_y}{\partial y} + F_y. \tag{3}$$

where F_x, F_y are the source term components in x and y directions, respectively. Proper initial and boundary conditions are assumed.

3   Numerical Approach

There are several approaches to approximate first order acoustic wave equations (3). Among the approaches used, we highlight finite element methods (FEM) [11,12], pseudospectral methods (PSM) [13,14], spectral element methods (SEM) [12,15] and the finite difference method (FDM) [16–19].

From a variety of numerical approaches, we choose the finite difference method on staggered grids. The choice of this approach results from the system structure (3): the system equations form a symmetric first order hyperbolic system of evolution equations. In this case, finite difference schemes on staggered grids appear to be the most computationally efficient approach [17,18]. We followed Virieux and developed a second order scheme accurate in space and time on a staggered grid.

To excite specific waves, we define a volumetric-type source as product of the Dirac delta function with respect to space

$$\delta(x - x_s, y - y_s) \tag{4}$$

and the Ricker wavelet with respect to time

$$f(t) = (1 - 2\pi^2 f_0^2 (t - t_0)^2) exp[-\pi^2 f_0^2 (t - t_0)^2], \tag{5}$$

where f_0 is the source central frequency and t_0 is the time wavelet delay chosen as $t_0 = 1/f_0$ s.

To simulate the wavefield propagation in an infinite medium, we assume a finite square physical domain Ω centred at the origin and surrounded by an absorbing layer to eliminate the reflections from artificial boundaries. In our simulations, we use the perfectly matched layer (PML) technique in the original split-field formulation described in [20].

For all subsequent experiments, the computational domain Ω is discretized with $N_x \times N_x$ grid points with a sampling step d_x, which amounts to approximately 20 points per wavelength for a chosen frequency f_0. The time step Δt was chosen according to the classical Courant stability criterion for the second order staggered grids with $CFL = 0.9$. The width of the absorbing PML layer was set to be equal to 15 grid points.

Figure 1 presents a typical wavefield pressure snapshot excited by the Ricker wavelet impulse.

4   Domain Decomposition

The domain decomposition method is a common approach to parallelization of a computational problem, allowing to split the original problem to several computationally smaller subproblems to be solved independent of each other or related to each other with the help of boundary conditions. This makes the domain decomposition method quite a general and convenient tool for parallel computing. In turn, the efficiency of a multiprocessor computing system is determined

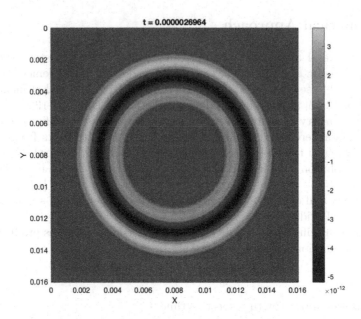

Fig. 1. A snapshot of the pressure component at the time instant $2.69 \cdot 10^{-6}$.

by how evenly the problem solution is distributed over the processes and how much transferring data between processes is minimized.

To parallelize the problem under consideration, we chose the domain decomposition method in the two directions (vertical and horizontal) to split the computational region by processes (Fig. 2). To solve the problem by the finite difference scheme on staggered grids, it is necessary to perform the data exchange at each computational time step. This raises the problem of optimizing the data exchange between processes to minimize time losses caused by slow data exchange operations.

5   Classical MPI Point-to-Point Communications

The parallel programming model MPI is based on the fact that the interaction between processes (data exchange and synchronization) occurs through message communications. The elementary MPI routines of data transferring between two processes are the point-to-point routines of sending and receiving.

The commonly used blocking routines for sending messages between two MPI processes are *MPI_Send* and *MPI_Recv*. Advantages and disadvantages of *MPI_Send* and *MPI_Recv* routines are blocking. The blocking means that the process called such a routine is suspended until the operation is complete. More specifically, the process proceeds to execute the statement following *MPI_Send* only after the data to be sent been copied to the system buffer either local or remote, depending on the MPI implementation. This blocking protects the

Domain decomposition

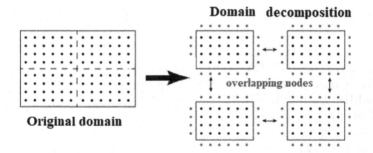

Original domain

Fig. 2. Two-dimensional domain decomposition scheme.

programmer from an error that could occur if the data have changed before sending them to another process. At the same time, it is not ensured that upon exiting a sending function, the recipient process will have time to receive a message or start receiving it. The transmission and reception of a message are called asynchronous. The *MPI_Recv* routine suspends the program execution until the process completely accepts a message and puts the data into their address space. After exiting this function, it confidently uses the receiving array, knowing that the necessary data have already been placed in it. Thus, blocking routines are good for their reliability. However, this is achieved by slightly slowing down the program.

Unlike the blocking operations, a feature of non-blocking transfers *MPI_Isend* and *MPI_Irecv* is that a call to a non-blocking transfer routine initiates but does not complete it. The execution of a routine can terminate even before a message is copied to the transfer buffer. The use of non-blocking operations improves the program performance since, in this case, overlapping (that is, concurrent execution) of computations and exchanges is allowed. The transfer of data from the buffer or their reading can occur simultaneously with the execution of other operations by the process. Completing a non-blocking exchange requires a call to an additional procedure that checks whether the data have been copied to the transfer buffer. A non-blocking exchange is performed in two stages: initializing the exchange and checking the exchange completion. Separating these steps makes it necessary to label each exchange transaction so that the completion checks can be carried out in a targeted manner.

The blocking operations are somewhat easier to use. However, the non-blocking can be used like this: call *MPI_Isend*, do some calculations, and then do *MPI_Wait*. This allows computation and communication to overlap, resulting in improved performance overall.

Using the blocking MPI routines, the program model of a parallel program looks like Listing 1.1.

Listing 1.1. A program model in the case of blocking MPI_Send and MPI_Recv

```
! Data initialization
! Preparation of the itable ()  process grid matrix
! for quick search of related processes see [24]
do while (t < T)
MPI_Send(v_x)
MPI_Recv(v_x)
MPI_Send(v_y)
MPI_Recv(v_y)
! Calculation pressure components p_x, p_y
MPI_Send(p_x)
MPI_Recv(p_x)
MPI_Send(p_y)
MPI_Recv(p_y)
! Calculation velocity displacement components v_x, v_y
end do
```

In the case of the non-blocking MPI routines, the program model is represented as Listing 1.2.

Listing 1.2. A program model in the case of the non-blocking *MPI_Isend* and *MPI_Irecv*

```
! Data initialization
! Preparation of the itable ()  process grid matrix
! for quick search of related processes see [24]
do while (t < T)
MPI_Isend(v_x)
MPI_Irecv(v_x)
MPI_Isend(v_y)
MPI_Irecv(v_y)
! Calculation pressure components p_x, p_y
! at the interior points of subdomain
MPI_Waitall ()
! Calculation pressure components p_x, p_y
! at the boundary points
MPI_Isend(p_x)
MPI_Irecv(p_x)
MPI_Isend(p_y)
MPI_Irecv(p_y)
! Calculation velocity displacement components v_x, v_y
! at the interior points of subdomain
MPI_Waitall ()
! Calculation velocity displacement components v_x, v_y
! at the boundary points
end do
```

6   Coarray Fortran

Instead of using the MPI send and receive point-to-point routines, we will take advantage of the new opportunities for exchanging data between processes provided within the Coarray Fortran approach.

The Coarray Fortran was first introduced into the Fortran 2008 standard and designed for parallel programming using the SPMD (a single program, multiple data) method. The features of the Coarray have been essentially expanded in the Fortran 2018 standard. The runtime runs several identical executables (images) of a program with Coarray, each with a unique number and a private address space. Regular variables remain private to an image, while the Coarray variables are readable and writable from any image. Communications using the Coarray Fortran have a "one-way" type. A remote call from image A to image B does not need to be accompanied by a corresponding call in image B. This feature makes programming with the Coarray Fortran much easier than with the MPI. The standard also provides internal synchronization to avoid deadlock and race conditions. Any regular variable can be converted to a scalar, array, internal, or derived Coarray variable data, pointers, and passed to the procedure. Thus, the Coarray variables are highly flexible and can be used for certain purposes. For example, a collection of the Coarray variables from all or some images can be viewed as a single large array. This is the opposite of the model partitioning logic typical of MPI programs. The Coarray can also leverage functional parallelism by delegating specific tasks to individual images or groups of images. The Coarray Fortran routines are defined in "Additional Parallel Features in Fortran" [21], which became part of the Fortran 2015 standard.

Using the Coarray Fortran routines, the programming model of a parallel program looks like Listing 1.3.

Listing 1.3. A program model in case of the Coarray Fortran

```
! Data initialization
! Ensuring that data is initialized before
! being accessed from other images
sync all
do while (t < T)
if (current_image(1) > 1)
v_x(1,:)=v_x(nx-1,:)[current_image(1)-1,current_image(2)]
if (current_image(2)>1) &
v_y(:,1)=v_y(:,ny-1)[current_image(1),current_image(2)-1]
! Guarantee that all images are loaded
sync all
! Calculation velocity displacement components v_x, v_y
if (current_image(1) < number_iprocs)
p_x(nx,:)=p_x(2,:)[current_image(1)+1,current_image(2)]
if (current_image(2) < number_jprocs)
p_y(:,ny)=p_y(:,2)[current_image(1),current_image(2)+1]
! Guarantee that all images are loaded
```

```
sync all
! Calculation pressure components p_x, p_y
end do
```

Note that in Code 1.3, the reference without [·] means local data, and the references with [·] indicate to the data defined for a corresponding image.

7   Testing and Analysis

Testing was carried out on the computers of the Siberian Branch of the Russian Academy of Sciences Siberian Supercomputer Center NKS-1P with the following specification:

– Head node (login node)
  • CPU (2 ×) Intel Xeon E5-2630v4 (2.2 GHz, 10 cores)
  • RAM 128 GB. Manufacturer: RSK (Russia)
– Cluster Interconnect Omni-Path 100 Gbps
– Intel Luster Parallel File System - 200 TB.
– (20 ×) Broadwell Compute Nodes
  • CPU (2 ×) Intel Xeon E5-2697A v4 (2.6 GHz, 16 cores)
  • RAM 128 GB. Manufacturer: RSK (Russia)
– (16 ×) Compute nodes KNL CPU
  • (1 ×) Intel Xeon Phi 7290 KNL (1.5 GHz, 72 cores, 16 GB cache MCDRAM)
  • RAM 96 GB Manufacturer: RSK (Russia).

The codes were assembled by the Intel (R) Fortran Intel (R) 64 Compiler to run applications on Intel (R) 64 (Version 19.0.3.199 Build 20190206) from the Intel Parallel Studio XE Cluster Edition for Linux (all tools) 2019 package. Calculations were performed at the Broadwell nodes. Intel Trace Analyzer and Collector were used to measure the program running time and the ratio of the running time of the serial and parallel codes.

To compare the blocking, non-blocking point-to-point routines and the Coarray Fortran, we carried out the test computations of wave fields propagation through a homogeneous medium. The size of the problem (3) depends on the size of the computational domain. We use the two-dimensional domain decomposition for parallelization and decompose the computational domain into superposition of the equal squares.

The calculation results using 32 shared memory processes on one node are presented in Table 1. We measured the computational times for problems with corresponding to 16^2, 32^2, 64^2, 128^2, 256^2, 512^2, 1024^2, 2048^2, 4096^2 elements in each subdomain.

From Table 1 one can compare the acceleration coefficients indicating the time acceleration ratio non-blocking (K_1) and the Coarray (K_2) versions of the code to the blocking one by the formula

$$K_1 = \frac{Time_{Block}}{Time_{non-Block}}, K_2 = \frac{Time_{Block}}{Time_{Coarray}}. \tag{6}$$

Table 1. The computational time comparison of the blocking, the non-blocking MPI routines and the Coarray Fortran using 32 shared memory processes on one node.

Subdomain elements	Domain elements	Time (s) MPI blocking	Time (s) MPI non-blocking	Time (s) Coarray	Acceleration K_1	Acceleration K_2
16^2	$32 \cdot 16^2$	0.7112	0.8354	1.8702	0.85133	0.38028
32^2	$32 \cdot 32^2$	0.8023	0.9521	1.5837	0.84266	0.50660
64^2	$32 \cdot 64^2$	0.9644	1.0242	1.7398	0.94161	0.55432
128^2	$32 \cdot 128^2$	1.7282	1.9274	2.9875	0.89665	0.57848
256^2	$32 \cdot 256^2$	13.4545	13.2655	15.2554	1.01425	0.88195
512^2	$32 \cdot 512^2$	58.0052	55.7663	59.4654	1.04015	0.97544
1024^2	$32 \cdot 1024^2$	235.748	231.423	229.871	1.01869	1.02557
2048^2	$32 \cdot 2048^2$	950.391	938.779	931.316	1.01237	1.02048
4096^2	$32 \cdot 4096^2$	7289.87	7224.81	7197.64	1.00901	1.01281

Table 2. The computational time comparison of the blocking, the non-blocking MPI routines and the Coarray Fortran using 81 processes on 3 nodes.

Subdomain elements	Domain elements	Time (s) MPI blocking	Time (s) MPI non-blocking	Time (s) Coarray	Acceleration K_1	Acceleration K_2
16^2	$81 \cdot 16^2$	1.9435	2.0923	15.7352	0.92888	0.12351
32^2	$81 \cdot 32^2$	1.8814	2.0553	18.9951	0.91539	0.09905
64^2	$81 \cdot 64^2$	2.3584	2.7774	26.5697	0.84914	0.08876
128^2	$81 \cdot 128^2$	4.3914	4.2807	41.3869	1.02586	0.10611
256^2	$81 \cdot 256^2$	33.6353	33.3587	78.7507	1.00829	0.42711
512^2	$81 \cdot 512^2$	147.062	139.319	203.012	1.05558	0.72440
1024^2	$81 \cdot 1024^2$	596.154	546.412	669.766	1.09103	0.89009
2048^2	$81 \cdot 2048^2$	2438.56	2268.14	3201.47	1.07514	0.76170
4096^2	$81 \cdot 4096^2$	18280.8	18191.1	19032.1	1.00493	0.96052
6144^2	$81 \cdot 6144^2$	72257.6	68475.1	70315.3	1,05523	1,02762

Up to 512^2, the values of these parameters gradually increase and begin to exceed unity. Starting from 1024^2 the acceleration coefficients decrease. We associate this to the fact that with increasing the numerical domain the computations themselves become dominant and the time for data exchange are negligible on their background.

From Table 1 we can also see that for a small number of elements in the computational domain, the Coarray is noticeably slower than the MPI routines. However, with the size of the computational domain increasing, the Coarray becomes faster in comparison with the MPI routines. The acceleration factor for the Coarray communication also tends to unity as the computational area increases.

We observe the similar results when running the program on multiple nodes. Table 2 presents the results of computations using 9×9 domain decomposition with 81 processes on 3 nodes and Table 2 shows the results using 13×13 domain decomposition with 169 processes on 6 nodes.

For convenience, we present the tabular values from Tables 1, 2 and 3 graphically (see Fig. 3, 4 and 5). For plotting, we use a double logarithmic scale since the range of values is too large.

According to the test results, we also revealed that with a small number of elements in the computational domain, the Coarray Fortran noticeably loses to the MPI communications up to 256^2 elements. However, with an increase in the computational domain, the Coarray gains efficiency comparable MPI.

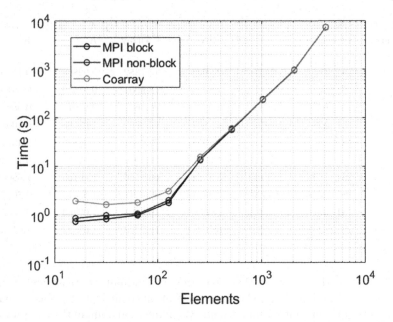

Fig. 3. The computational time comparative diagram of the blocking, the non-blocking MPI routines and the Coarray Fortran using 32 shared memory processes on one node.

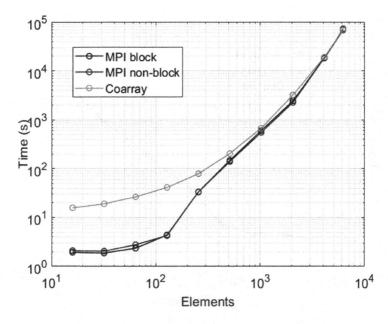

Fig. 4. The computational time comparative diagram of the blocking, the non-blocking MPI routines and the Coarray Fortran using 81 processes on 3 nodes.

Table 3. The computational time comparison of the blocking, the non-blocking MPI routines and the Coarray Fortran using 169 processes on 6 nodes.

Subdomain elements	Domain elements	Time (s) MPI blocking	Time (s) MPI non-blocking	Time (s) Coarray	Acceleration K_1	Acceleration K_2
16^2	$169 \cdot 16^2$	3.8883	4.6066	64.4715	0.84407	0.06031
32^2	$169 \cdot 32^2$	5.5972	5.0899	69.8915	1.09967	0.08008
64^2	$169 \cdot 64^2$	6.0715	5.5972	85.9082	1.08474	0.07067
128^2	$169 \cdot 128^2$	9.8369	9.6963	125.546	1.01450	0.07835
256^2	$169 \cdot 256^2$	71.9304	69.1176	225.179	1.04070	0.31944
512^2	$169 \cdot 512^2$	308.099	289.368	503.697	1.06473	0.61168
1024^2	$169 \cdot 1024^2$	1286.59	1235.63	1701.49	1.04124	0.75615
2048^2	$169 \cdot 2048^2$	5112.81	4698.08	7261.31	1.08828	0.70412
4096^2	$169 \cdot 4096^2$	39476.1	39346.7	40761.5	1.00329	0.96847
6144^2	$169 \cdot 6144^2$	146576.0	145210	148365.0	1,00941	0,987941

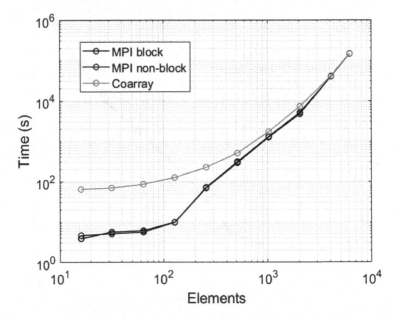

Fig. 5. The computational time comparative diagram of the blocking, the non-blocking MPI routines and the Coarray Fortran using 169 processes on 6 nodes.

8 Conclusion

We have compared various data exchanges between processes based on the blocking, the non-blocking MPI point-to-point routines, as well as the new features of the Fortran language based on the Coarray Fortran technique. For the study, a two-dimensional wave equation that describes the propagation of acoustic waves in inhomogeneous media and written down in the form of a first order hyperbolic system for the vector of displacement velocity and pressure was taken as a test problem. As a numerical solution method, the method of finite differences of the second order of accuracy in spatial variables and time on staggered grids was used to numerically solve the problem. The domain decomposition method was used for parallelization into processes to divide the computational domain into smaller subdomains with overlapping.

We change the problem sizes as well as various communication approaches to exchange data between processes. For each version, we have measured the computation time and the acceleration factor.

We have revealed the advantages of the delayed non-blocking *MPI_Isend,* *MPI_Irecv* and the Coarray Fortran when the problem size (the number of elements) increases. For the delayed non-blocking routines, the efficiency can be explained by overlapping computations against the data transfer background. In the Coarray Fortran, the speedup is achieved because the shared memory Coarray variables are read and written from any image, so there is no need to organize data transfers. The graphs show that this approach will be preferable to all others with an increase in the problem dimension.

Acknowledgements. Galina Reshetova and Vladimir Cheverda have been supported by the Russian Science Foundation, project 20-11-20112.

The research is carried out using the equipment of the shared research facilities of HPC computing resources at the Joint Supercomputer Center of RAS [22] and the Siberian Supercomputer Center [23].

References

1. Dongarra, J., et al.: The international exascale software project roadmap. Int. J. High Perform. Comput. Appl. **25**(1), 3–60 (2011)
2. Kostin, V.I., Lisitsa, V.V., Reshetova, G.V., Tcheverda, V.A.: Finite difference simulation of elastic waves propagation through 3D heterogeneous multiscale media based on locally refined grids. Siberian J. Num. Math. **16**(1), 45–55 (2013)
3. Kostin, V., Lisitsa, V., Reshetova, G., Tcheverda, V.: Parallel algorithm with modulus structure for simulation of seismic wave propagation in 3D multiscale multiphysics media. In: Malyshkin, V. (ed.) PaCT 2017. LNCS, vol. 10421, pp. 42–57. Springer, Cham (2017). https://doi.org/10.1007/978-3-319-62932-2_4
4. Asilah, N., Coddington, P.: Comparison of MPI benchmark programs on shared memory and distributed memory machines (point-to-point communication). Int. J. High Perform. Comput. Appl. **24**(4), 469–483 (2010)
5. Ismail, R., Wati Abdul Hamid, N.A., Othman, M., Latip, R., Sanwani, M.A.: Point-to-point communication on gigabit ethernet and InfiniBand networks. In: Abd Manaf, A., Sahibuddin, S., Ahmad, R., Mohd Daud, S., El-Qawasmeh, E. (eds.) ICIEIS 2011. CCIS, vol. 254, pp. 369–382. Springer, Heidelberg (2011). https://doi.org/10.1007/978-3-642-25483-3_30
6. Denis, A., Trahay, F.: MPI overlap: benchmark and analysis. In: 45th International Conference on Parallel Processing (ICPP), pp. 258–267. IEEE (2016). https://doi.org/10.1109/ICPP.2016.37
7. Kayum, N., Baddourah, A., Hajjar, O.: Methods to overlap communication with computation. In: Conference Proceedings of Third EAGE Workshop on High Performance Computing for Upstream, vol. 2017, pp. 1–10. EarthDoc (2017). https://doi.org/10.3997/2214-4609.201702326
8. Hoefler, T., Lumsdaine, A., Rehm, W.: Implementation and performance analysis of non-blocking collective operations for MPI. In: Proceedings of the ACM/IEEE Conference on High Performance Networking and Computing, SC 2007, pp. 1–10. Association for Computing Machinery, New York (2007). Article 52. https://doi.org/10.1145/1362622.1362692
9. Numrich, R.W., Reid, J.: Co-array Fortran for parallel programming. SIGPLAN Fortran Forum **17**(2), 1–31 (1998)
10. Eachempati, D., Richardson, A., Jana, S., et al.: A Coarray Fortran implementation to support data-intensive application development. Cluster Comput. **17**, 569–583 (2014). https://doi.org/10.1007/s10586-013-0302-7
11. Yoshimura, Ch., Bielak, J., et al.: Domain reduction method for three-dimensional earthquake modeling in localized regions, part II: verification and applications. Bull. Seismol. Soc. Am. **93**, 825–840 (2003)

12. Moczo, P., Kristek, J., et al.: 3-D finite-difference, finite-element, discontinuous-Galerkin and spectral-element schemes analysed for their accuracy with respect to P-wave to S-wave speed ratio. Geophys. J. Int. **187**, 1645–1667 (2011)
13. Fornberg, B.: The pseudospectral method: accurate representation of interfaces in elastic wave calculations. Geophysics **53**(5), 625–637 (1988)
14. Takenaka, H., Wang, Y.B., et al.: An efficient approach of the pseudospectral method for modelling of geometrically symmetric seismic wavefield. Earth Planets Space **51**(2), 73–79 (1999)
15. Chaljub, E., Komatitsch, D., et al.: Spectral-element analysis in seismology. Geophysics **50**(4), 705–708 (2007)
16. Moczo, P., Kristek, J., et al.: 3D fourth-order staggered-grid finite-difference schemes: stability and grid dispersion. Bull. Seismol. Soc. Am. **90**(3), 587–603 (2000)
17. Virieux, J.: P-SV wave propagation in heterogeneous media: velocity-stress finite-difference method. Geophysics **51**(1), 889–901 (1986)
18. Levander, A.R.: Fourth-order finite-difference P-W seismograms. Geophysics **53**(11), 1425–1436 (1988)
19. Tessmer, E.: Seismic finite-difference modeling with spatially varying time steps. Geophysics **65**(4), 1290–1293 (2000)
20. Collino, F., Tsogka, C.: Application of the PML absorbing layer model to the linear elastodynamic problem in anisotropic heterogeneous media. Geophysics **66**(1), 294–307 (2001)
21. TS18508: Additional Parallel Features in Fortran [Electronic resource], ISO/IEC JTC1/SC22/WG5 N 2074 (2015)
22. Joint Supercomputer Center of RAS. http://old.jscc.ru/eng/index.shtml
23. Novosibirsk Supercomputer Center of SB RAS. http://www.sscc.icmmg.nsc.ru
24. RS/6000 SP: Practical MPI Programming [Electronic resource]. http://wwwuser.gwdg.de/~applsw/Parallelrechner/sp_documentation/pe/sg245380.pdf

Investigating Performance of the XAMG Library for Solving Linear Systems with Multiple Right-Hand Sides

Boris Krasnopolsky$^{(\boxtimes)}$ and Alexey Medvedev

Institute of Mechanics, Lomonosov Moscow State University, Moscow, Russia
{krasnopolsky,a.medvedev}@imec.msu.ru

Abstract. The paper presents capabilities and implementation details for the newly developed XAMG library for solving systems of linear algebraic equations with multiple right-hand sides. The underlying code design principles and the basic data objects implemented in the library are described. Several specific optimizations providing significant speedup compared to alternative state of the art open-source libraries are highlighted. A great attention is paid to the XAMG library thorough performance investigation. The step-by-step evaluation, performed for two compute systems, compares the single right-hand side calculations against *hypre*, the performance gain due to simultaneous solution of system with multiple right-hand sides, the effect of mixed-precision calculations, and the advantages of the hierarchical MPI+POSIX shared memory hybrid programming model. The obtained results demonstrate more than twofold speedup for the XAMG library against *hypre* for the equal numerical method configurations. The solution of systems with multiple right-hand sides provides 2–2.5 times speedup compared to multiple solutions of systems with a single right-hand side.

Keywords: Systems of linear algebraic equations · Iterative methods · Multiple right-hand sides

1 Introduction

The need for solving systems of linear algebraic equations (SLAEs) with multiple right-hand sides (RHS) occurs in a variety of applications, including the structural analysis problems [7], uncertainty quantification [8], Brownian dynamics simulations [15], quantum chromodynamics [5], turbulent flow simulations [9], and others. The use of methods performing multiple solutions at once allows to significantly improve the performance of the calculations compared to the multiple solutions with single RHS due to increasing the arithmetic intensity of the corresponding methods [17]. However, the required functionality is not implemented in most of the popular open-source libraries typically used for solving large sparse SLAEs.

V. Voevodin and S. Sobolev (Eds.): RuSCDays 2021, CCIS 1510, pp. 337–351, 2021.
https://doi.org/10.1007/978-3-030-92864-3_26

The newly developed XAMG library [13,14] is among the few examples of the codes capable for solving systems with multiple RHSs. The library provides a set of Krylov subspace and algebraic multigrid iterative methods widely used to solve the systems corresponding to the elliptic differential equations. The XAMG library focuses on solution of series of systems of equations, thus reusing the *hypre* library to construct the multigrid matrix hierarchy and providing an optimized implementation for the "solve"-part of the methods only. The brief description of the XAMG library and several usage examples are presented in [13]. The current paper supplements [13], highlights some aspects of the XAMG library design and provides the thorough performance evaluation results.

The rest of the paper is organized as follows. The capabilities of the XAMG library are summarized in the first section. The second section presents some basic design features of the library developed. The third section describes some specific optimizations, implemented in the code. The fourth section presents the detailed performance evaluation results. Finally, Conclusions section summarizes the paper.

2 Capabilities of the XAMG Library

The XAMG library is a header-style template-based C++ code based on C++11 standard specification. The library implements a set of iterative methods typically used to solve large sparse systems of linear algebraic equations, corresponding to the elliptic differential equations. These include the Krylov subspace (both classical and modified formulations [6,12,16]), algebraic multigrid, Jacobi, Gauss-Seidel, and Chebyshev polynomial methods. The library provides hierarchical three-level parallelization with the hybrid MPI+POSIX shared memory parallel programming model (MPI+ShM).

The library design combining dynamic polymorphism and static template-based polymorphism opens up several opportunities compared to the popular open-source libraries like *hypre* or PETSc. Among the examples is the possibility to easily combine multiple solvers operating in different precision. The combination of this kind was used in [11] to construct the mixed-precision iterative refinement algorithm. The algorithm combines two solvers, the inner one operating with single precision, and the outer one operating with basic (double) precision. The proposed combination allows to perform most of the calculations with single precision while preserving the overall solution tolerance in double precision providing calculation speedup by a factor of 1.5–1.7.

The combination of compile-time polymorphism of matrix objects with the object-oriented style of inheritance also makes it possible to implement a sophisticated approach to data compression for different matrix elements. The matrix construction algorithms are able to detect the minimal necessary precision of integer index types for each matrix block at runtime and choose the suitable pre-compiled object template with optimal index data types. This results in a significant reduction of memory transfers.

Declaring the number of RHSs as a template parameter allows for a simple automated vectorization of main vector-vector and matrix-vector subroutines with basic C++ idioms and directives. The flexibility of the library design also introduces the capability to extend the set of matrix storage formats utilized in the library. Different storage formats can also be combined in a single matrix hierarchy. The ability to add accelerators support is also a code design feature.

3   Basic Design Features

3.1   Program Code Elements of XAMG Library

The current section provides a brief outline of the XAMG program code design principles by describing the main classes and subroutines implemented in the XAMG library. These include the vector and matrix data structures, "blas"- and "blas2"-like sparse linear algebra subroutines, solver classes, and solver parameter classes.

Vector Class. `XAMG::vector::vector` class is a simple representation of the vector type. The main integer or floating-point data type is not used in class specialization and is hidden inside via a simple type erasure technique. The vector may, in fact, represent NV vectors. The real number of vectors in this structure is not a compile-time specialization but a runtime one.

Matrix Classes. `XAMG::matrix::matrix` is an aggregation class. It holds a complex hierarchical structure of the decomposed matrix. As a result of the decomposition, the set of matrix subblocks appears, containing the actual matrix data. The matrix subblocks are implemented as classes inherited from an abstract `XAMG::matrix::backend` interface. These inherited classes represent the data structures specific to a concrete sparse matrix data storage format. The XAMG library contains implementation for two basic data storage formats, CSR and dense, and they are implemented as the `XAMG::matrix::csr_matrix` and `XAMG::matrix::dense_matrix` classes. Other matrix storage formats can be added as well. The `XAMG::matrix::matrix` class holds only references to the abstract `XAMG::matrix::backend` interface, so other matrix storage formats can be easily added. The matrix subblocks can then be stored in different matrix formats, even within a single matrix scope.

The inherited matrix classes are instantiated with a floating-point type and index types as template parameters at compile time. The runtime polymorphism of basic matrix data types is required for a more flexible design allowing *ad hoc* reduced-precision floating-point calculations and compression of indices features implementation. The special creator function is implemented for this purpose. It chooses a correct template-specialized constructor of a matrix object using a bit-encoded type fingerprint combined at runtime depending on the concrete matrix properties and decomposition. This creator function provides a runtime choice between all possible combinations of template types in matrix specializations, and it is implemented as an automatically generated if-else tree, which can be re-generated at compile time.

Basic Subroutines. Functions and procedures grouped in `XAMG::blas` and `XAMG::blas2` namespaces are designed to cover all necessary vector and matrix-vector arithmetic operations used in the main workflow of the XAMG solvers code. Most of the subroutines are specialized by a template parameter of the data type (typically, the floating-point type). Additionally, the number of RHSs, NV, is specified as an integer template parameter. This fact makes it possible for a C++ compiler to vectorize loops in the "blas" and "blas2" subroutines. The subroutines are designed to implement a loop iterating over RHS as the most nested loop. Therefore, since this loop appears to be a constant-range loop after the template instantiation, the compiler's vectorization possibilities are quite straightforward.

The matrix-vector subroutines in `XAMG::blas2` namespace are specialized by both the concrete (non-abstract) matrix class and the NV parameter. The abstract matrix class has a subset of virtual functions which work as a direct connection to the `XAMG::blas2` subroutines. This design decision makes it possible to call the `XAMG::blas2` subroutines polymorphically in runtime for any concrete matrix object via an abstract interface. This adds a necessary generalization level to a solver program code.

A special proxy-class `blas2_driver` is used to implement the "blas2" calls from an abstract matrix interface. This class adds a connection between the NV compile-time parameter, representing the number of RHSs and the concrete matrix type. This artificial connection is required because the matrix itself is not supposed to be specialized with the number of RHSs at a compile-time. The proxy-class `blas2_driver` object belongs to each matrix subblock and is created once the first "blas2" operation is started. The necessity to hold and to create these proxy-objects in runtime is a trade-off of this design.

Solver Classes. The XAMG solvers are inherited from an abstract `basic_solver_interface` class. The two main virtual functions are present: `setup()` and `solve()`. The `solve()` function encapsulates the specific solver algorithm. The `setup()` is typically an empty function, besides the algebraic multigrid solver implementation: for this solver the actions of constructing the multigrid hierarchy are placed into this function. The current multigrid solver implementation in XAMG uses the subroutines from the *hypre* library to accomplish the multigrid hierarchy construction.

Solver Parameters. A two-level parameter dictionary organizes and holds all the solver parameters. For each solver role, which can be one of the: "solver", "preconditioner", "pre_smoother", "post_smoother" and "coarse_grid_solver", the key-value directory of parameters is held. The available parameters are defined by a solver method. The key for a parameter is a string; the value type is defined individually for each parameter as a floating-point, integer, or string type. For any parameter which is not set explicitly, the appropriate default value is set by the library. The `XAMG::global_param_list` class represents the top-level dictionary, the `XAMG::param_list` is a key-value holder for each solver parameters' set. `XAMG::global_param_list::set_default()` functions must be always called after the parameters' set up to handle the default settings correctly and to perform some parameters consistency checks.

MPI+ShM Parallel Programming Model. The hierarchical three-level hybrid parallel programming model is used in vector and matrix data types representation and in basic subroutines design. The hybrid programming model implements the specific data decomposition which reflects the typical hardware structure of modern HPC systems. The hierarchy levels include cluster node level, NUMA node level within a cluster node scope, and CPU core level. Decomposition ensures better data locality on each structural level. Moreover, the POSIX shared memory is used as a storage media for all intra-node decomposition levels, which makes it possible to eliminate the message-passing parallel programming paradigm usage (MPI) on these levels and switch to shared-memory parallel programming paradigm in the subroutines design. This MPI+ShM parallel programming model helps to reach better scalability outlook compared to other sparse linear algebra libraries.

4   Code Optimizations

The XAMG library contains several specific optimizations that improve the performance of the calculations compared to other libraries. These include reduced-precision floating-point calculations, compression of indices in the matrix sub-blocks, vector status flags indicating if the whole vector is identical to zero, and others. These optimizations are discussed in detail in the current section.

4.1   Reduced-Precision Floating-Point Calculations

The use of mixed-precision calculations for preconditioning operations is a well-known way to improve the overall performance of linear solvers [3]. The reduced-precision preconditioner calculations do not affect the overall solution tolerance, but may increase the number of iterations till convergence. In most practical cases, however, the use of single-precision floating-point numbers allows to obtain the guess values without any penalty in the overall number of iterations till convergence, and, thus, can be considered as an option to speed up the calculations.

4.2   Compression of Indices

The multilevel data segmentation implemented in the XAMG library [13], leads to a multiblock representation of the matrices. Typically each block, except the diagonal one, contains only several rows and columns, and the indices range can be represented by 2-byte or even 1-byte integer numbers only. The theoretical estimates allow to predict the range of the potential speedup due to reducing the amount of memory to store the matrix by 10–20%. The corresponding speedup is expected in the calculations.

4.3   Vector Status Flags

An optimization proposed in [10] assumes the introduction of an additional boolean flag indicating if the whole vector is equal to zero or not. Simple check if the vector is zero in matrix-vector operations eliminates some trivial algorithmic steps and speeds up the calculations. The current implementation in the XAMG library extends that idea and the corresponding checks for zero vectors are used in all vector and matrix-vector operations.

4.4   Per Level Hierarchy Construction

The *hypre* library provides various coarsening and interpolation algorithms as well as lots of methods tuning parameters. Most of these algorithms and parameters can be set the same for all levels of multigrid matrix hierarchy. In practice, however, mixed combinations of coarsening and interpolation algorithms can provide a faster convergence rate or lower multigrid hierarchy matrices complexity. The optional per level matrix hierarchy construction implemented in the XAMG library allows to build the matrices level by level, and set specific algorithm parameters for every hierarchy level.

4.5   Vectorization of Basic Operations

Vectorization of the computations is an important factor in achieving the maximal performance for modern CPUs. The efficient use of long registers can provide fold calculations speedup for compute-bound applications. However, for memory-bound applications, the real performance gain is much lower. Moreover, the sparse linear algebra applications typically suffer serious difficulties in the efficient implementation of operations with sparse matrices, including SpMV, due to the use of specific data storage formats with indirect elements indexing.

The generalized sparse matrix-vector multiplication is a much better candidate for taking the benefits of CPU vector instructions. Due to the element-wise indexing of the RHS elements (m RHSs with n unknowns line up in a long vector of $m \cdot n$ elements with the element-by-element ordering, i.e. m elements with index 0, m elements with index 1, etc.), this type of operations can at least be vectorized over RHSs. The main computational kernels in the XAMG library, including the vector and matrix-vector operations, are instrumented with pragmas to maximize the vectorization effect. The list of pragmas used includes the compiler-specific data alignment and data dependency hints.

5   Performance Evaluation

The detailed evaluation procedure presented below shows the step-by-step investigation of the efficiency of the XAMG library and the impact of implemented optimization features on the overall code performance. The evaluation starts with a single-node performance analysis. This session includes (i) the comparison of execution times for identical numerical method configurations in the

XAMG and *hypre*, (ii) the performance gain for multiple RHS calculations, and (iii) the comparison of the double-precision, mixed-precision and single-precision calculations. The multi-node runs investigate (i) the XAMG library scalability compared to *hypre*, (ii) analysis of changes in the strong scalability for various numbers of RHSs, and (iii) the effect of data compression optimizations on the calculation time reduction.

5.1   Test Application

The `examples/` directory of the XAMG source code [14] contains a couple of usage examples in the form of some small and ready to use C++ and C example programs. A written in C example program can be used as a reference to the C language API of the XAMG library. Additionally, a comprehensive integration test application is provided, making it possible to easily test all the library features and make some productivity evaluations. This test code is located in the `examples/test/` directory of the library source tree. This integration test application is used to produce all evaluation results presented below. This integration test code also features:

- an internal matrix generator for two specific Poisson equation problems;
- an interface to the graph reordering library used to construct an optimal data decomposition;
- a command-line parser and YAML configuration file reader;
- some additional performance monitoring tools and profilers integration;
- a run-time debugger integration;
- a YAML output generator for a test result.

The bunch of test configurations, which are present in the `examples/test/yaml/` directory, can be used for testing purposes the way like this:

```
mpirun -np <N> ./xamg_test -load cfg.yml -result output.yml
```

The input YAML file, which name is given in the "`-load`" option here, stores all method configurations in a key-value form. A short overview of allowed solver parameters can be found in [2]. The "`-result`" key is optional and sets up the file name for the test application report output. For information on other command-line options of the integration test application, one may consult the "`-help`" option output.

5.2   Testing Methodology

The performance evaluation is performed for two groups of SLAEs. The first one corresponds to a set of model SLAEs obtained as a result of spatial discretization of the 3D Poisson equation

$$\Delta u = f$$

with the 7-point stencil in a cubic domain with the regular grid; the grid size varies from 50^3 till 300^3. The second group of test matrices corresponds to SLAEs performed in direct numerical simulation of turbulent flow in a channel with a wall-mounted cube [9]. This group includes two matrices of 2.3 mln. and 9.7 mln. unknowns with constant RHSs. The corresponding matrix generators are available with the integration test application, published in the XAMG source code repository.

The single-node runs performed in the test sessions, are calculated with native matrix ordering. The multi-node runs use graph partitioning (the PT-Scotch graph partitioning library [4] to construct optimal data decomposition) to reduce the amount and volume of inter-node communications.

Various numerical method configurations are evaluated during the tests; the specific set of the methods is indicated in the corresponding subsection. In order to avoid possible variations in the convergence rate affecting the number of iterations till convergence, all the results presented below indicate the calculation times per one iteration of the corresponding numerical method.

Comparison with the *hypre* library is performed for the most recent version 2.20.0 available to date. The library is built with Intel MKL [1] and OpenMP parallelization support.

The two compute systems, Lomonosov-2 and HPC4, are used for the performance evaluation to demonstrate the potential of the developed XAMG library. The first one consists of compute nodes with a single Intel Xeon Gold 6126 processor and InfiniBand FDR interconnect; Intel compilers 2019 with Intel MPI Library 2019 Update 9 are used to compile the code. The HPC4 system consists of compute nodes with two Intel Xeon E5-2680v3 processors and InfiniBand QDR interconnect, and GNU compilers 8.3.1 with OpenMPI 4.0.1 are used in the tests. In all the cases all available physical CPU cores per node (12 or 24 cores correspondingly) are utilized during the calculations.

5.3   Single-Node Performance Evaluation Results

Single RHS Results Comparison with *hypre*. The performance evaluation starts with the comparison of single-node calculation times for the XAMG and *hypre* libraries when solving SLAE with a single RHS. The set of test cases includes three numerical method configurations and a full set of first group test matrices. The numerical method configurations considered include the BiCGStab method used as the main solver and the classical algebraic multigrid method with V-cycle as the preconditioner. The method configurations differ in the choice of pre- and post-smoothers. The three configurations explore three popular ones, i.e. the Jacobi method, the hybrid symmetric Gauss-Seidel method, and the Chebyshev iterative method. The full method configurations can be found in the corresponding YAML configuration files stored in the project repository in `examples/test/yaml/single_node` directory.

The obtained comparison results for pure MPI execution mode demonstrate that the XAMG library in all the cases outperforms *hypre* library (Fig. 1).

The observed performance gain is about 1.2–1.4 except for the smallest test matrix, 50^3. In that case, the XAMG library demonstrates much higher performance gain, on average by a factor of 2.2 for Lomonosov-2 and by a factor of 6.5–7.5 for HPC4. Such a significant difference can in part be related to the implementation of the direct method used as a coarse grid SLAE solver. Because the solver setup phase is expected to be calculated only once for multiple SLAE solutions, XAMG multiplies the inverse matrix by the RHS instead of solving small SLAEs with the dense matrix.

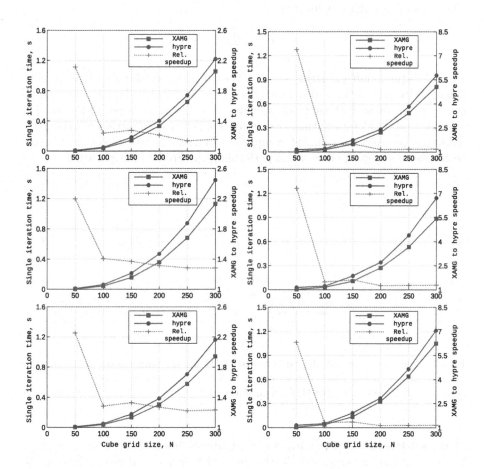

Fig. 1. Comparison of single iteration calculation times with the XAMG and *hypre* libraries, and relative calculations speedup for the single node of Lomonosov-2 (left) and HPC4 (right) supercomputers. Pure MPI execution mode; from top to bottom: Gauss-Seidel smoother, Chebyshev smoother, Jacobi smoother.

Multiple RHSs Results. The next test series focuses on the investigation of the performance gain due to the simultaneous solution of the system with multiple RHSs. The theoretical estimates, based on memory traffic reduction, predict the potential speedup by a factor of 2–2.5 [9]. The tests, performed with the SLAE from the first group with the matrix 150^3, demonstrate the behavior of the single iteration calculation time per one RHS as a function of the number of RHSs. The tests are performed for the Gauss-Seidel smoother configuration.

The obtained calculation results show a clear tendency to reduce the execution times when increasing the number of RHSs up to 32 (Fig. 2). The point of 32 RHSs becomes the global minimum for both compute systems, and the further increase of the number of RHSs leads to a slow performance gain degradation. The speedup per RHS, defined as

$$P_m = \frac{mT_1}{T_m},$$

where m is the number of RHSs and T_i is the calculation time with i RHS vectors, demonstrate the performance gain by a factor of 2.2–2.5. These values are in good agreement with theoretical estimates. The further increase in the number of RHSs leads to slow performance degradation. The role of further matrix traffic reduction becomes insignificant compared to increasing role of the matrix and vector cache sweeping effect when performing the SpMV multiplication.

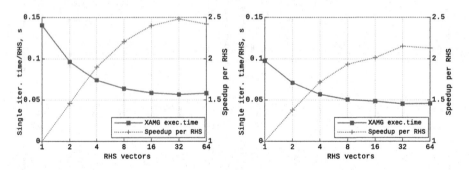

Fig. 2. Single iteration calculation times per RHS for the single node of Lomonosov-2 (left) and HPC4 (right) supercomputers. Cube test matrix 150^3, Gauss-Seidel smoother configuration, pure MPI execution mode.

Reduced-Precision Floating-Point Calculations. The third test series focuses on the investigation of the potential of reduced-precision floating-point calculations. The test series includes a comparison of double-precision calculations, double-precision calculations with multigrid preconditioner performed with single-precision, and single-precision calculations. All the scenarios can be easily realized with the XAMG library due to template-based library design. The test session uses Chebyshev smoother configuration and the first group test matrix 200^3. The use of reduced-precision for multigrid solver can be specified in the YAML configuration file by adding the parameter "mg_reduced_precision: 1" in the "preconditioner_params" section.

The single iteration calculation times presented in Fig. 3 are in agreement with the ones, presented above for the other method configuration and matrix size: the monotone decrease of the calculation time per RHS can be achieved up to 16–32 RHSs. The double-precision calculations, as expected, provide the highest calculation times among the configurations considered. The mixed-precision calculations provide speedup up to 5–10% (Fig. 4). Finally, the single-precision calculations demonstrate the speedup by a factor of 1.6–2. While the performance gain for the mixed-precision calculations remains almost constant, the single to double-precision calculation speedup shows a stable increase. The observed speedup exceeds 2 and this effect is related to the lower cache load when using single-precision floating-point numbers.

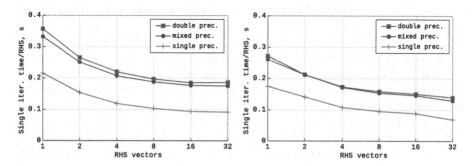

Fig. 3. Single iteration calculation times per RHS for the single node of Lomonosov-2 (left) and HPC4 (right) supercomputers with various floating-point number tolerance. Cube test matrix 200^3, Chebyshev smoother configuration, pure MPI execution mode.

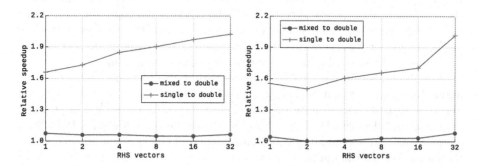

Fig. 4. Relative calculation speedup due to the use of reduced-precision floating-point data types. Results for the single node of Lomonosov-2 (left) and HPC4 (right) supercomputers. Cube test matrix 200^3, Chebyshev smoother configuration, pure MPI execution mode.

5.4   Multi-node Performance Evaluation Results

The multi-node performance is investigated for several test matrices and two numerical method configurations. The tests performed include the comparison of the XAMG library performance with *hypre* for the SLAEs with a single RHS as well as scalability results for the XAMG library with a different number of RHSs.

Single RHS Calculation Results. The first set of experiments is performed on the HPC4 compute system with two test SLAEs corresponding to cubic computational domain with 150^3 and 250^3 unknowns. The same method configuration with Gauss-Seidel smoother, as in the previous experiments, is used. The test series performed includes five different runs: the *hypre* library calculations in pure MPI and hybrid MPI+OpenMP execution modes, the XAMG library calculations with pure MPI and MPI+ShM execution modes, and the XAMG library calculations in hybrid MPI+ShM mode with data compression optimizations (compression of indices and reduced-precision floating-point calculations for multigrid hierarchy). The hybrid MPI+OpenMP and MPI+ShM modes are executed in the "2 × 12" configuration with a single communicating MPI process per each processor.

The obtained performance evaluation results are presented in Fig. 5. The data is presented in terms of the relative speedup, which is defined as a ratio of the single-node calculation time for the *hypre* library, executed in a pure MPI mode, to the calculation time with the specific number of compute nodes and execution mode:

$$S_p^i = \frac{T_1^{hypre,MPI}}{T_p^i}.$$

Results, presented in Fig. 5, show a clear advantage of hybrid programming models, and much better scalability for both the XAMG and *hypre* libraries compared to the pure MPI results. The XAMG library with MPI+ShM programming model significantly outperforms the *hypre* library. Additionally, the use of data compression allows to obtain an extra 10% calculations speedup.

The second set of experiments is performed on the Lomonosov-2 supercomputer. Here, the test matrices of the second group are used with the optimized iterative method configuration (this method configuration was used in [9] when modeling turbulent flows). The method also uses the preconditioned BiCGStab method with algebraic multigrid preconditioner and Gauss-Seidel smoother, but the parameters of the multigrid method are tuned to minimize the coarse level matrices fill in while preserving the same iterations convergence rate. The corresponding YAML configuration file is also available with XAMG source code in examples/test/yaml/multi_node/ directory.

Results, presented in Fig. 6, reproduce the same behavior for the XAMG library as above: the use of the compression techniques allow to speedup the calculations. The impact of the hybrid model (executed in the "1 × 12" configuration), however, is lower than for the HPC4 system due to twice lower the number of MPI processes per node, UMA architecture (each compute node contains a single processor only), and faster interconnect installed. Surprisingly, the *hypre* calculation times with pure MPI mode become lower than the hybrid mode ones for the considered range of compute nodes: the 1.5 times speedup is observed. Nonetheless, the XAMG library in hybrid execution mode outperforms the *hypre* library results by a factor of 1.5–1.7.

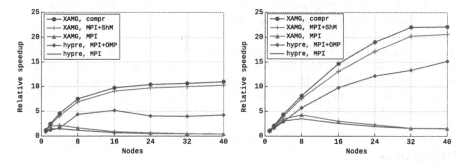

Fig. 5. Relative calculation speedup for the XAMG and *hypre* libraries in various execution modes. HPC4 supercomputer, cube test matrices with 150^3 (left) and 250^3 (right) unknowns.

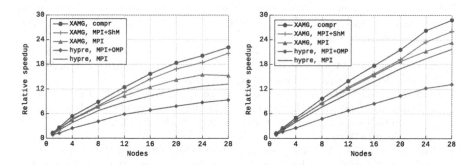

Fig. 6. Relative calculation speedup for the XAMG and *hypre* libraries in various execution modes. Lomonosov-2 supercomputer, second group test matrices with 2.3 mln. (left) and 9.7 mln. (right) unknowns.

6   Conclusions

The details of the XAMG library for solving systems of linear algebraic equations with multiple right-hand sides are presented in the paper. The XAMG library provides the implementation of a set of iterative methods typically used to solve systems of linear algebraic equations derived from elliptic differential equations. The paper highlights some fundamental library design aspects, including the basic data structures and a couple of specific optimizations implemented in the code.

The detailed performance evaluation is presented for two different compute systems with UMA and NUMA architecture. The XAMG library is compared with *hypre* for single-node and multi-node runs. The obtained results show for the single-node runs the speedup against *hypre* by a factor of 1.2–1.3, and it increases to 2 for parallel runs performed. The potential of the XAMG library for solving SLAEs with multiple RHSs is demonstrated by a series of calculations, demonstrating the performance gain due to solving system with multiple RHSs compared to multiple solutions of SLAEs with a single RHS. The corresponding results demonstrate the speedup by a factor of 2.2–2.5.

Acknowledgements. The current work is supported by the Russian Science Foundation Grant No. 18-71-10075. The research is carried out using the equipment of the shared research facilities of HPC computing resources at Lomonosov Moscow State University and computing resources of the federal collective usage center Complex for Simulation and Data Processing for Mega-science Facilities at NRC "Kurchatov Institute".

References

1. Intel Math Kernel Library (2020). https://software.intel.com/content/www/us/en/develop/tools/math-kernel-library.html. Accessed 27 Dec 2020
2. XAMG: parameters of the numerical methods (2020). https://gitlab.com/xamg/xamg/-/wikis/docs/XAMG_params_reference. Accessed 12 Apr 2021
3. Carson, E., Higham, N.: Accelerating the solution of linear systems by iterative refinement in three precisions. SIAM J. Sci. Comput. **40**, A817–A847 (2018). https://doi.org/10.1137/17M1140819
4. Chevalier, C., Pellegrini, F.: PT-Scotch: a tool for efficient parallel graph ordering. Parallel Comput. **34**(6), 318–331 (2008). https://doi.org/10.1016/j.parco.2007.12.001. Parallel Matrix Algorithms and Applications
5. Clark, M., Strelchenko, A., Vaquero, A., Wagner, M., Weinberg, E.: Pushing memory bandwidth limitations through efficient implementations of Block-Krylov space solvers on GPUs. Comput. Phys. Commun. **233**, 29–40 (2018). https://doi.org/10.1016/j.cpc.2018.06.019
6. Cools, S., Vanroose, W.: The communication-hiding pipelined BiCGstab method for the parallel solution of large unsymmetric linear systems. Parallel Comput. **65**, 1–20 (2017). https://doi.org/10.1016/j.parco.2017.04.005
7. Feng, Y., Owen, D., Perić, D.: A block conjugate gradient method applied to linear systems with multiple right-hand sides. Comput. Methods Appl. Mech. Eng. **127**(1), 203–215 (1995). https://doi.org/10.1016/0045-7825(95)00832-2
8. Kalantzis, V., Malossi, A.C.I., Bekas, C., Curioni, A., Gallopoulos, E., Saad, Y.: A scalable iterative dense linear system solver for multiple right-hand sides in data analytics. Parallel Comput. **74**, 136–153 (2018). https://doi.org/10.1016/j.parco.2017.12.005
9. Krasnopolsky, B.: An approach for accelerating incompressible turbulent flow simulations based on simultaneous modelling of multiple ensembles. Comput. Phys. Commun. **229**, 8–19 (2018). https://doi.org/10.1016/j.cpc.2018.03.023
10. Krasnopolsky, B., Medvedev, A.: Acceleration of large scale OpenFOAM simulations on distributed systems with multicore CPUs and GPUs. In: Parallel Computing: on the Road to Exascale. Advances in Parallel Computing, vol. 27, pp. 93–102 (2016). https://doi.org/10.3233/978-1-61499-621-7-93

11. Krasnopolsky, B., Medvedev, A.: Evaluating performance of mixed precision linear solvers with iterative refinement. Supercomput. Front. Innov. **8**(3), 4–16 (2021)

12. Krasnopolsky, B.: The reordered BiCGStab method for distributed memory computer systems. Procedia Comput. Sci. **1**(1), 213–218 (2010). https://doi.org/10.1016/j.procs.2010.04.024. ICCS 2010

13. Krasnopolsky, B., Medvedev, A.: XAMG: a library for solving linear systems with multiple right-hand side vectors. SoftwareX **14**, 100695 (2021). https://doi.org/10.1016/j.softx.2021.100695

14. Krasnopolsky, B., Medvedev, A.: XAMG: source code repository (2021). https://gitlab.com/xamg/xamg. Accessed 12 Apr 2021

15. Liu, X., Chow, E., Vaidyanathan, K., Smelyanskiy, M.: Improving the performance of dynamical simulations via multiple right-hand sides. In: 2012 IEEE 26th International Parallel and Distributed Processing Symposium, pp. 36–47, May 2012. https://doi.org/10.1109/IPDPS.2012.14

16. van der Vorst, H.A.: BI-CGSTAB: a fast and smoothly converging variant of BI-CG for the solution of nonsymmetric linear systems. SIAM J. Sci. Stat. Comput. **13**(2), 631–644 (1992). https://doi.org/10.1137/0913035

17. Williams, S., Waterman, A., Patterson, D.: Roofline: an insightful visual performance model for multicore architectures. Commun. ACM **52**(4), 65–76 (2009). https://doi.org/10.1145/1498765.1498785

"Mini-Benchmarking" Approach to Optimize Evolutionary Methods of Neural Architecture Search

Kamil Khamitov[✉] and Nina Popova

Lomonosov Moscow State University, Moscow, Russia
popova@cs.msu.ru

Abstract. Due to the rapid development of Artificial Neural Networks (ANN) models, the number of hyperparameters constantly grows. With such a number of parameters, it's necessary to use automatic tools for building or adapting new models for new problems. It leads to the expansion of Neural Architecture Search (NAS) methods usage, which performs hyperparameters optimisation in a vast space of model hyperparameters, so-called hyperparameters tuning. Since modern NAS techniques are widely used to optimise models in different areas or combine many models from previous experiences, it requires a lot of computational power to perform specific hyperparameters optimisation routines. Despite the highly parallel nature of many NAS methods, they still need a lot of computational time to converge and reuse information from the generations of previously synthesised models. Therefore it creates demands for parallel implementations to be available in different cluster configurations and utilise as many nodes as possible with high scalability. However, simple approaches when the NAS solving is performed without considering results from the previous launches lead to inefficient cluster utilisation. In this article, we introduce a new approach of optimisation NAS processes, limiting the search space to reduce the number of search parameters and dimensions of the search space, using information from the previous NAS launches that allow decreasing demands of computational power and improve cluster utilisation as well.

Keywords: Hyperparameters tuning · NNI · HPC · Neural Architecture Search

1 Introduction

Recent studies demonstrate a significant increase of ANN's hyperparameters of models currently used in production. The number of BERT's [4] parameters exceeds 110M. It means that even if we use computing nodes with modern Tesla GPU's (V100/A100), it is still not enough for this amount of parameters neither inference nor training. Nowadays, many researchers utilize already pre-trained ANN models as a starting point, since it allows to decrease time to

© Springer Nature Switzerland AG 2021
V. Voevodin and S. Sobolev (Eds.): RuSCDays 2021, CCIS 1510, pp. 352–364, 2021.
https://doi.org/10.1007/978-3-030-92864-3_27

production and many analytical experiments. But in the work [7] it was demonstrated that new fully-synthesized architecture may beat existing well-known analytically-created models for certain areas of tasks. In [3] authors mentioned other approaches which allow them to increase speedup convergence of such methods, but with the certain amounts of assumptions, that limits parallel efficiency. It leads us to the question about Neural Architecture Search and, in general, hyperparameters tuning. Such a task can be formulated performing optimization in vast search space of myriads of parameters, but since ANNs is not a simple graph with certain nodes, such specific of HPO optimization (that resulting graph of optimization should be a valid ANN) should be taken into consideration. It means that we require a particular set of large-scale optimization problem with certain constraints: the NAS (Neural Architecture search) problem and refining particular network topology problem. This search methodology and connecting nodes in graphs oblige us to use algorithms with prebuilt constraints to limit search space [7]. But such generic approaches can utilize a lot of computational power, although can demonstrate remarkable results [13]. In production, the range of optimizing models (during the iterative process of refining) usually are not so broad, so it leads us to the question: How we can use the information of the previously optimized generations to improve Neural Architecture Search convergence and computation power utilization?

2   Neural Architecture Search Problems

In this article we mainly focus on two formulated neural architecture search problems:

- refining existing topology by applying to new particular task,
- synthesizing new topology from scratch (Neural Architecture search).

Because of the increased resource utilization of modern DNNs, topology adaptation of neural networks has become a significant problem. In this case, the process looks like the best model development for the particular task that can be used to tune different sets of hyperparameters and then build a "distilled" model that fits the resource limitations on the particular device. In this article, we want to cover both steps of a process. The implementation of hyperparameters tuning requires a lot of computational resources, and it's significant to provide a possibility to perform such tuning on HPC clusters.

Adaptation Problem. The adaptation problem is considered as refining the existing model $min_\theta L(\theta_n)$, $\theta_n = X(\theta_{n-1}, ...\theta_{n-k})$, where L – loss function, θ – hyperparameters set, θ_0 – initial hyperparameters (initial model) that are used as a core of method, X – the iterative process of new model building, based on previous hyperparameters.

Neural Architecture Search Definition. In the neural architecture search problem we don't have the initial value of hyperparameters. It limits the capabilities of methods that rely on the quality of the initial approximation. The formal process can be described as follows: $L(\theta_n)$, $\theta_n = X(\theta_{n-1}, ...\theta_{n-k})$, $\theta_0 = \mathbf{0}$.

Distributed Hyperparameters Optimization. Since both problems that we regard in this article are large-scale hyperparameters optimization problems that typically utilize a lot of computational resources. The usage of distributed technologies and HPC is essential to carry on such type of problems in a meaningful time. Moreover, since CoDeepNEAT utilizes evolution-based techniques, it has a natural fit for parallel computations. With other methods, even which doesn't imply parallel implementation, benefits of distributed optimization can be obtained by running different tuners at the same time. The system we've chosen is NNI (Neural Network Intelligence) [6], because it provides a tunable interface that allows easily integrate bindings to different HPC schedulers in rather broad cluster configurations. Some notes about SLURM integration to NNI were presented in [13].

3   Techniques for Tuning Hyperparameters

CoDeepNEAT. The CoDeepNEAT (CoEvolution DeepNEAT) [7] is a rather popular NAS method based on utilizing ideas of evolution methods to the NAS problems. In general, CoDeepNEAT employs the concept of cooperative evolution of modules and the blueprints and use the idea of representing and encoding a group of layers as a subject for evolution, proposed in the DeepNEAT [7]. In general, CoDeepNEAT operates two populations: the modules population that encodes the set of layers or parts of the network (like LSTM cells, GRU cells, etc.), and the population of blueprints, which describes how modules of each should be connected to form a fully-functional network. Of course, blueprints don't encode the particular blocks, but the type-identification (evolution level) of the block. So, the blueprint is a network graph where the vertices correspond to modules and edges to connections between them. But due to the mutations modules on each side of the edge may have different dimensions, CoDeepNEAT handles it in a semi-automatic manner and allows the user to either use general upsampling/downsampling strategies or provides custom once. During the fitness step of the evolution, the ANN built from modules according to the particular blueprint. Then it performs training on the provided dataset. Still, with a small number of epochs, the fitness function's value is distributed in the population of modules and templates as an average among all networks containing this module or constructed using this blueprint. Since evolution-based techniques are respectively widely used for general optimization problems and have possibilities of parallel implementations, the performance analysis of CoDeepNEAT implementation and its comparison to other NAS methods of different types were made in [12]. It proves a high degree of parallelism and beneficial usage of NVLink technologies when the large NAS-tuning tasks like data-labelling with LSTM, building RNN blocks from scratch and impact of different types of interconnecting GPU-GPU utilization multi-GPU clusters.

The CoDeepNEAT evolution scheme is demonstrated in Fig. 1. CoDeepNEAT proves its convergence rate and applicability compared to its predecessors since this method has more possibilities for mutations. The most negligible mutations

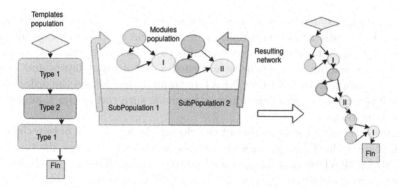

Fig. 1. Evolution scheme of CoDeepNEAT [7]

among the population of templates or modules lead to a significant change in final networks.

4   NAS Search Space Optimization

Rather different approaches can be used for optimizing the efficiency of evolutionary algorithms, like using different types of mutations per each set, using egalitism policies (transferring best items to the next generations). In generic NAS trainers like CoDeepNEAT, one of the main points of the optimization is the search space and its limitations (e.g. it's not the best variant to use many GRU parts before the feature extraction CNN parts even in reinforcement learning tasks). So one of the root causes is to use the information of the previous tasks launches. Such optimizations part considered as the crucial part of the system described in [13]. Since we've observed the difference in performance between launches in adaptation mode and NAS mode, we've performed tests in this article separately; however, we can't reuse the observations that correspond to the different problem kind (Adaptation or FullNAS).

4.1   "Mini-Benchmarking" Approach

The key idea of the "mini-benchmarking" approach is to create some divided clusters of networks where some pre-optimised (either with MorphNET or with CDN-tuned) ANN topologies, where the block constraints are obtained as the blocks used in the l recent generations. The k different classes corresponding to the other problem types are tuned with CDN/MoprhNET, and topologies are stored in the off-line section. In the initial trial, where the model is optimised, the corresponding class is picked with the Random Forest method. Classification is performed by analysing the input model as a graph of blocks and particular features. As the base of such benchmarks set, we decided to use as base two most popular and up-to-date benchmarks in NAS: NAS-HPO-BENCH [15] and NAS-BENCH-201 [14] and add its semi-class tasks from [13] like HRM prediction and TinyImageNET.

How to Apply Information in Fine-Tuning Adaptation. The key idea of our method is to use a similar encoding as in DeepNEAT [7]. We encode the input model as the graph with nodes corresponds to a block of layers with some pre-defined max folding size. Then we use such a set of input layers and use the similarity approach from CoDeepNEAT to compare blocks and the order of such folded layers to the original encoding and provide such certain block information to the later phases.

After determining the number of the closest classes, we can obtain the initial distributions of both blueprints and modules. With such encoding, it's possible to use CoDeepNEAT decomposing procedure to set up both initial populations and perform a co-evolution step from the closest first approximation. The limitations of the possible modules can be defined as follows:

- if we peek class t we peek all l initial distributions as the first steps with the initial model.
- All footprints from the last t have been picked from.
- If the $l * generation\_size > current\_trialgenerationsize$, the first selection is performed in the bipartite tournament manner.

If the number of classes is much larger than the t, the possible search space can be decreased on module steps up to $1 - \frac{Numclasses}{t}$.

How to Apply Information in NAS. In the NAS tasks, where the user doesn't provide the particular input model, the user can peek at the mix of the already presented classes to obtain a similar speedup as in fine-tuning adaptation.

Building the "Benchmarking" Databases. A lot of tools that provide different levels of NAS benchmarking approaches have been established recently. Of course, different tools and benchmarks have different purposes. In this paper, we are taking into consideration only a few of them that have the following properties:

- Has general applicability and has capability of testing modern NAS methods with modern ANN-based datasets.
- Has ability to reflects certain difference of hyperparameters tuning specific of methods.
- Has wide acceptance in NAS community and have ability of automatic integration.

To fit these criteria, we've picked two major benchmarking datasets: NAS-HPO-BENCH [15] and NAS-BENCH-201 [14]. In NAS-HPO-BENCH authors proposed an approach for building a small benchmarking suite that can be performed in a relatively small amount of time. It consists of 4 suites (Protein, Naval, Slice and Parkinson) and about 150 tasks correspondingly. However, this suite only covers a limited amount of ANNs' areas of applicability and mainly focuses on the precision of hyperparameters optimization with limited discrete areas of certain hyperparameters. The authors used the fANOVA method [16] to analyze the importance of specific hyperparameters across the whole models in different parts of the benchmarks suite. After all, the two problems of this benchmark are narrow to the particular range of the tasks (medical image recognition). Another approach is described in [14]. The authors provided a quite different approach for building a dataset. They took only three novel tasks from the image-recognition area: CIFAR-10, CIFAR-100, ImageNet-16-120. After all considerations, we have decided to use both approaches. We have built our benchmarking suite on top of the NAS-HPO-BENCH [15] with adding more info from NAS-BENCH-201 [14] and custom tasks for RNNs, including LSTM/GRUs and complex tasks as HRM data prediction.

Adding New Classes to the Benchmark DB. With our approach adding new benchmarks requires running the new set of experiments and obtaining the slice of the last l generations of certain tasks. Then new reclassification to get the new classification to be performed. It means that the peeking classifier method should be scalable for reclassification. However, since the number l and the number of classes is usually small, like in NAS-HPO-BENCH (144 classes), it shouldn't be considered as a serious problem.

5   Automatic System Architecture

The brief architecture of the NAS system that supports execution of tuning problems using HPC cluster was described in [13]. The following changes were applied to support this new approach in our system of hyperparameters tuning:

1. The new entity that is used as storage for modules and corresponding classes in each part of the "benchmarking suite".
2. Classifier that obtains certain set of available modules for the trials.

So now, the NAS or adaptation can be run in two different modes: utilizing the previous information from storage or producing new benchmarking data for it. Before NAS, we run our classifier and then pick the limited set of the available modules. So the classifier runs after the tuners and cluster configuration choose but before the actual optimization problem starts. Post-processing is unaffected for the tuners selection. Also, we supported additional workflow for integrating such data for model-dependent post-tuners. Such integration was described in [13].

6   Experiments

6.1   Experimental Setup and Configuration

Clusters Configuration. The following clusters and their configurations were used for the experimental study of the proposed approach (Fig. 2).

- 4 × nodes of Polus cluster with 2 × IBM POWER8 processors with up to 160 threads, 256 GB RAM and 2 × Nvidia Tesla P100 on each node [9].
- 33 nodes of Lomonosov-2 cluster with Intel Xeon E5-2697 v3 2.60 GHz with up to 28 threads, 64 GB RAM and Tesla K40s on each node [10].

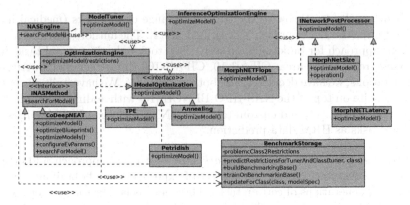

Fig. 2. Modules UML class diagram, that briefly describe system's architecture with Tuners [6]

Setting Up the Custom "Benchmarking DB" and It's Configuration. We've decided to build two sets of benchmarks to analyze scalability and further performance improvements of suggested Mini-benchmarking for limiting search space of HPO tuners. The first one is the modified versions of NAS-BENCH-HPO and NAS-BENCH-201. In both cases, we've added three different problems to cover RNNs, and semi CNN-RNN approaches with canonical solutions as well. As new problems, we've added:

- HRM data prediction on UBFC-RPPG [13]
- Tiny ImageNET
- minified CoLa dataset (sampled 10%).

Two modified datasets were divided into the two groups of "benchmarks":

- Small dataset, where the all resulted networks are CNN without recurrent layers (Fashion-MNIST, Tiny ImageNET, and CIFAR-100, minified CoLa).
- Large dataset where hybrid structures of ANN provide some benefits to convergence like: UBFC-RPPG, Protein, ImageNET-16-120, Parkinson.

Baseline Results. As baseline results we run only NAS problem on both large and small groups. Accuracy on each is presented in Table 1. Speedup of NAS task can be observed in Fig. 3. Of course, in some datasets (like CoLa and Protein, ImageNet-16-120), the provided accuracy is far from perfect but comparable to some simple implementations which can be analytically obtained like simple approaches from [15]. For some others like UBFC-RPPG and MNIST-like task, the provided accuracy is comparable to the well-known implementations [13].

The Parallel efficiency highly depends on the number of modules available for NAS and tuning correspondingly, such effect was also shown in [13], and it means the less number of different types of modules we use in problem is the more benefits from the parallel implementation we can obtain. It means we should either minimize extra-types of nodes for each problem with better

Table 1. CoDeepNEAT accuracy on different parts of the composed benchmarking data

Protein	UBFC-RPPG	Fashion-MNIST	Tiny ImageNET	CIFAR-100	Imagenet-16-120	CoLa
0.643	0.702	0.83	0.672	0.738	0.651	0.682

classification or decrease the difference between modules increasing the folding factor for analysis.

Convergence and Speedup in Small and Large Groups of "Benchmarks". For evaluation, we tried to analyze the difference between the convergence and speedup of using the "benchmarking" approach in the different groups and among the whole set of datasets to analyze which parts are more crucial or essential dependencies or blocks variations among each type of the problems.

Folding Factor Analysis. To analyze benefits, we vary folding factor between 1 and 10, and performed tests on data in a small group. The impact of such variation can be observed in Fig. 4. It's shown that folding factor 3 is optimal in many cases for the "small part" of our "benchmarking" data; increasing the folding factor to more than 7 leads to loss of accuracy in many parts of benchmarks like UBFC-RPPG and Protein. The importance of the folding factor is related to the particular classifier and how particularly thus encoding represents similarities for each node. For CoDeepNEAT, it means we can utilize the same encoding that we use in modules population [7] and such layout can be reformulated with the same folding factor for a group of layers or even connected noes of the modules population or not.

Convergence Analysis. We analysed average accuracy and loss per generation in NAS and HPO-tuning tasks. Graphs can be found in Fig. 5. In each of the experiments, we also close two or more class tasks to measure how accurate the generalised method can found networks from the unknown tasks. Accuracy on this validation dataset is presented in Fig. 6, except for Tiny ImageNET/ImageNET-16-120 because of similarities in group encodings. So as we can see, in general, CoDeepNEAT, even in such unknown tasks, can rely on the similarities that he can observe in data. So if the tasks are pretty unknown (like UBFC-RPPG or Protein), it can recreate carefully only partial networks with worse accuracy. The average population accuracy among first 50 epochs is presented in Fig. 7.

Parallel Efficiency. Parallel experiments have been performed on 32 nodes of the Lomonosov cluster for the Large dataset and on 4 nodes of Polus in Small datasets. Graphs for parallel efficiency (the ratio between observed speedup and the ideal one) after experimenting in both parts are presented in Fig. 8. Increasing of parallel efficiency during the NAS in both configurations demonstrates the how beneficial of decreasing search-space dimensions for large-scalable tasks can be done with such approach and it means that it's possible to reduce the required computational power for NAS and cluster utilization if you already have set of tasks that you've optimized before.

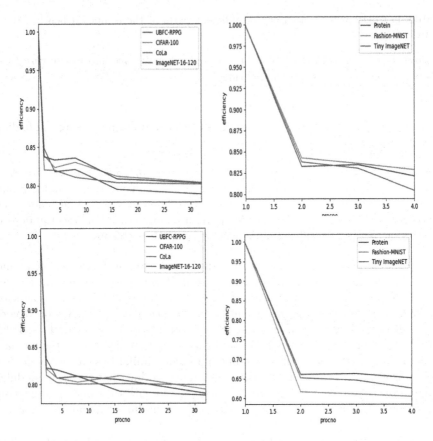

Fig. 3. Parallel efficiency of CoDeepNEAT on "large" and "small" parts of "benchmarking" data

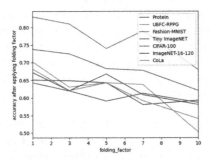

Fig. 4. Impact of folding factor to the accuracy of resulting networks and speedup in Adaptation and NAS

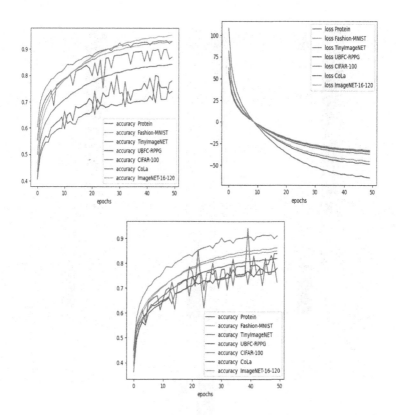

Fig. 5. Accuracy and loss of NAS and adaptation problems

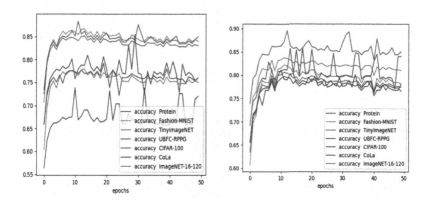

Fig. 6. Accuracy on validation in NAS (left) and adaptation parts

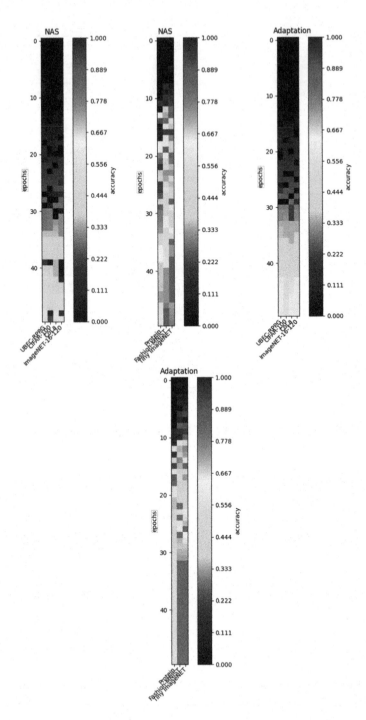

Fig. 7. Average accuracy of first 50 epochs in NAS and adaptation modes

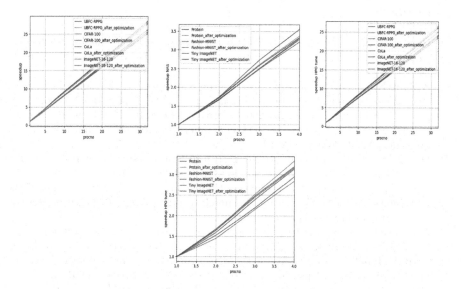

Fig. 8. Comparison of benefits on each speedup.

7   Conclusion

The approach of NAS methods optimization with the "mini-benchmarking" approach was tested in distributed clusters environment and integrated to the Automatic NAS-tuning system described in [13]. To analyze the approach, we built a
custom benchmarking dataset that incorporates existing data from NAS-HPO-
BENCH and NAS-BENCH-201. The boost of accuracy can be observed in both
modes of hyperparameters tuning in all problem scales of benchmarking data.
The amount of computational power reduced up to 7%. During NAS tasks, the
observable changes may have a various impact, including the improving average
accuracy and speedup on each part of the benchmarking dataset. The average
speedup among each part is about 5% in NAS tasks and about 3.5% in adaptation tasks. The accuracy boost in NAS tasks and Adaptation tasks can reach
even 10%, if the training problems that used for classifying complements each of
the data, also in general, it's observed that in adaptation tasks, the difference in
accuracy boost from the classification is up to 1.05 more than in NAS problems.
It enables more efficient cluster utilization when similar NAS/adaptation tasks
are processed, that demonstrated in Fig. 8. Also, It seems possible that using
such an approach allows creating more sophisticated device-dependant tuners
using collected information about the last generation.

Acknowledgements. Reported study was funded by RFBR according to research
project №20-07-01053. The research is carried out using the equipment of the shared
research facilities of HPC computing resources at Lomonosov Moscow State University.

References

1. Bergstra, J.S., et al.: Algorithms for hyper-parameter optimization. In: Advances in Neural Information Processing Systems (2011). https://doi.org/10.5555/2986459. 2986743
2. Amado, N., Gama, J., Silva, F.: Parallel implementation of decision tree learning algorithms. In: Brazdil, P., Jorge, A. (eds.) EPIA 2001. LNCS (LNAI), vol. 2258, pp. 6–13. Springer, Heidelberg (2001). https://doi.org/10.1007/3-540-45329-6_4
3. Liu, H., Simonyan, K., Yang, Y.: DARTS: differentiable architecture search. arXiv preprint arXiv:1806.09055 (2018)
4. Devlin, J., et al.: BERT: pre-training of deep bidirectional transformers for language understanding. arXiv preprint arXiv:1810.04805 (2018)
5. Real, E., et al.: Large-scale evolution of image classifiers. In: Proceedings of the 34th International Conference on Machine Learning-Volume 70. JMLR.org (2017). https://doi.org/10.5555/3305890.3305981
6. Neural Network Intelligence, April 2020. https://github.com/microsoft/nni
7. Miikkulainen, R., Liang, J., Meyerson, E., et al.: Evolving deep neural networks. In: Artificial Intelligence in the Age of Neural Networks and Brain Computing. Elseiver, pp. 293–312 (2019). https://doi.org/10.1016/B978-0-12-815480-9.00015-3
8. CoDeepNEAT implementation base, April 2020. https://github.com/sash-a/CoDeepNEAT
9. Polus cluster specifications, April 2020. http://hpc.cs.msu.su/polus
10. Voevodin, Vl., et al.: Supercomputer Lomonosov-2: large scale, deep monitoring and fine analytics for the user community. J. Supercomput. Front. Innov. 6(2), 4–11 (2019). https://doi.org/10.14529/jsfi190201
11. Bobbia, S., Macwan, R., Benezeth, Y., Mansouri, A., Dubois, J.: Unsupervised skin tissue segmentation for remote photoplethysmography. Pattern Recogn. Lett. (2017). https://doi.org/10.1016/j.patrec.2017.10.017
12. Khamitov, K., Popova, N.: Research of measurements of ANN hyperparameters tuning on HPC clusters with POWER8. In: Russian Supercomputing Days 2019: Proceedings of International Conference, Moscow, 23–24 September 2019, pp. 176–184 (2019)
13. Khamitov, K., Popova, N., Konkov, Y., Castillo, T.: Tuning ANNs hyperparameters and neural architecture search using HPC. Supercomputing, 536–548 (2020). https://doi.org/10.1007/978-3-030-64616-5_46
14. Dong, X., Yang, Y.: NAS-bench-201: extending the scope of reproducible neural architecture search. arXiv preprint arXiv:2001.00326 (2020)
15. Klein, A., Hutter, F.: Tabular benchmarks for joint architecture and hyperparameter optimization. arXiv preprint arXiv:1905.04970 (2019)
16. Hutter, F., Hoos, H., Leyton-Brown, K.: An efficient approach for assessing hyperparameter importance. In: International Conference on Machine Learning. PMLR (2014)

On the Prospects of Quantum Computing in Models of Social Behavior

Yuri Ozhigov[1,2(✉)]

[1] Faculty of Computational Mathematics and Cybernetics, Moscow State University of M.V. Lomonosov, Vorobievi Gori, GSP-2, 2 Hum. Building, SQI, Moscow 119992, Russia
ozhigov@cs.msu.su

[2] Institute of Physics and Technology RAS of K.A. Valiev, Nakhimovski prosp. 32-a, Moscow, Russia

Abstract. The development of supercomputer technologies naturally leads to the use of the quantum language not only at the level of the element base, as in existing computers, but also in the logic of the computations themselves. It is shown how the transition to a quantum language in Computer Science will allow the use of a single mathematical apparatus and computational methods in such different fields as chemistry and social behavior. The importance of the quantum approach to sociology is justified in the concept of the Khrennikov "social laser". This paper provides a precise justification for the "crowd effect" - the peak-like nature of the excitement of large social groups, based on the Tavis-Cummings-Hubbard model.

Keywords: Quantum computer · Quantum computing · Computer modeling · Decoherence · Social laser · Quantum politics

PACS: 03.65 · 87.10

1 Introduction

The development of computer technologies in the 21st century has reached a fundamental milestone: the need for predictive modeling of complex processes. This task is new, it has not been solved in the past. The traditional mathematical apparatus, based on the analysis of infinitesimals, is sharpened for simple processes, the dynamics of which are somehow reduced to separate particles that do not interact with each other. A typical example: solid state physics, the main model of which is a chain of interacting harmonic oscillators. Formally, such oscillators, when moving to a quantum description, will be in an entangled state throughout the entire evolution. However, the application of the so-called canonical transformation, which in this case takes the form of the Fourier transform on the coordinates of the oscillators, completely reduces this state, so that the dynamics of this system becomes simple (see [1]). The canonical transformation means the transition to the so-called quasiparticles, which for a solid body

© Springer Nature Switzerland AG 2021
V. Voevodin and S. Sobolev (Eds.): RuSCDays 2021, CCIS 1510, pp. 365–375, 2021.
https://doi.org/10.1007/978-3-030-92864-3_28

are called phonons. A similar technique in electrodynamics gives quanta of the electromagnetic field - photons.

Thus, in the past, exact natural science was concerned with simple systems, although at first glance they seemed very complex. For these systems, there was always some canonical transformation that radically reduced their complexity, making it possible to directly use computers. This opportunity is very valuable. To understand the need for a fundamental reduction of the complexity of the system under study before using computers, it is enough to compare the limits of the capabilities of modern supercomputers that can operate with vector spaces of dimension no more than 10^{10} with the number of particles in a real macroscopic system - a mole of matter - the Avogadro number, of the order of 10^{23}.

Mathematical and computer modeling is always understood as the ability to predict the behavior of the system under consideration. For a simple system, classical physics is sufficient: here an elementary time interval can be taken not too small, so that the characteristic action dS on it will far exceed the Planck constant $\hbar \approx 3 \cdot 10^{27}~erg \cdot sec$. In complex systems, the points of unstable equilibrium are so often located that the elementary time interval must be many orders of magnitude smaller, so that the elementary action is equal in order of magnitude to Planck's constant; here classical mechanics loses its power and must be replaced by quantum mechanics.

So, in complex systems, predictive modeling is only possible on a quantum basis. Models of chemistry and even some biological processes based on classical representations do not have predictive power; they only illustrate graphically what is obtained in experiments.

However, the transition to a quantum representation of the process dramatically exacerbates the problem of complexity. The dimension of the Hilbert space of quantum states increases as an exponent of the number of elements in the system under consideration. Physics of the 20th century coped with this difficulty only when studying simple processes; here, on the basis of the canonical transformation, it was often possible to find an analytical solution to the problem, and to do without computers at all. This is how the results described in standard textbooks on quantum theory were made. Such tasks, in general, have already been solved. They gave us modern computer technology, on which all IT technologies are based; all this is the fruit of quantum mechanics. The next frontier: the path from chemistry to biology, requires a radical revision of the old methods. This milestone lies very close: there is still no predictive computer model of chemical reactions. Not to mention the much-needed model of the living.

In nuclear physics, we also move in the dark. This science is mainly experimental, which leads to certain failures in the use of the energy of the atomic nucleus.

The recognition of this situation led physicists to the idea of a quantum computer. For the first time, the problem was clearly formulated by Richard Feynman, who proposed to build this device on the basis of gates - quantum devices capable of performing elementary operations on 1–3 quantum bits (qubits), so that the dynamics of a rather complex real system can be modeled on the qubit system at the quantum level (see [2]).

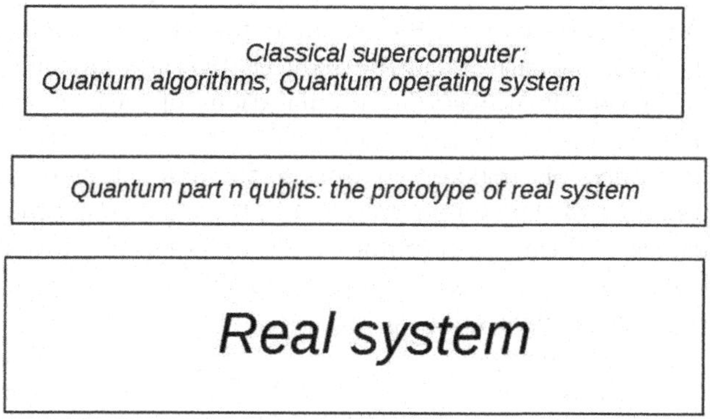

Fig. 1. Complex systems modeling scheme

Thus, the traditional scheme of computer modeling, consisting of a classical computer applied directly to the simulation of a real system, is supplemented with a new element - the quantum part of the computer, consisting of several tens or even hundreds of qubits. This part, being, on the one hand, a simplified prototype of a real system, on the other hand, is completely available to our control, since we create it (unlike a natural object that we do not create). The scheme of quantum modeling is shown in the Fig. 1.

The quantum operating system and all modeling programs are loaded into the memory of a classical computer, which uses classical signals to control the dynamics of the quantum part, so that at the end of the simulation we can observe its state, and get information about the assumed behavior of the real system. This is quantum computing.

Note that we can use quantum computing methods at the level of a quantum operating system, even without having a physical implementation of the quantum part in the Fig. 1, or having a limited version of it (for example, a source of biphoton signals embedded in a classical distributed computing system, as in [3]). In this case, we will not have a full-fledged quantum computer, but we will be able to implement the quantum ideology of modeling reality, and even get the so-called quantum superiority for some types of tasks.

The development of quantum computing in the last 20 years has shown one problem and three possibilities.

The problem is called decoherence. Spontaneous destruction of the quantum state as a result of the influence of the environment. The proposed methods of decoherence suppression in the form of quantum correction codes [4] have not yielded results and remain mostly theoretical exercises. Apparently, decoherence can not be likened to the force of friction, it has a more fundamental nature. The very apparatus of Hilbert state spaces has limitations in complexity when applied to real systems. This complexity-accuracy constraint has the character of a well - known coordinate-momentum or time-energy uncertainty relation.

We define the complexity $C(\Psi)$ of a quantum state $|\Psi\rangle$ as the maximal number of entangled qubits in its representation, which is minimized on all possible permutations of the basis vectors. For example, for GHZ state $|00...0\rangle + |11...1\rangle$ the complexity is 1, because it can be reduced by the sequential CNOTs to the product of one qubit states. The permutations of basis states is the well known canonic transformation; the sample of it is the above mentioned Fourier transform that reduces entangled oscillators to the non entangled phonons.

The measurement of the system prepared in the state $|\Psi\rangle$ is the only way to find its amplitudes, and thus the accuracy $C(\Psi)$ of its representation is the total number of the samples of the system prepared in this state that can be available for us and ready for the measurement.

We thus obtain the relation

$$A(\Psi)C(\Psi) \leq Q \tag{1}$$

for some dimensionless constant Q, which finding is the main goal of experiments in quantum computing. For any two level system $C(\Psi) = 1$ so we can determine it with the highest accuracy. The opposite side of (1) is the system with the extremely large complexity, for which the application of quantum theory is under question at all. We try to elusidate the question about the possibility to apply QC to system with tremendous complexity: the social behavior of the humans; however, here the complexity is not the maximum, because we do not touch the human actions as in the political process, only states of individual excitations that is the subject of sociology.

2   Finite-Dimensional Quantum Models

The quantum representation of the state of the system differs from the classical one in that if in the classical representation the system can be in the states $|0\rangle, |1\rangle, ..., |N - 1\rangle$, then in the quantum state $|\Psi\rangle = \sum_{j=0}^{N-1} \lambda_j |j\rangle$ it is in all these states *simultaneously* - in each with its own complex amplitude λ_j, so that the probability of its detection in the state $|j\rangle$ is $p_j = |\lambda_j|^2$. That is, the microcosm is in principle probabilistic in nature, but if the probability theory itself examines only the properties of the distribution p_j that has already arisen, then quantum mechanics allows us to predict the *dynamics* of changes in this distribution over time.

The fundamental property of quantum theory is its linearity. Its mathematical apparatus is Hilbert spaces and operators in them - Hermitian and unitary. The abstraction of infinities here is only a tribute to history and the possibility of justifying analytical techniques; computational models will always be finite-dimensional. The most difficult thing to include in such models is the electromagnetic field, the most computationally expensive element of any system.

This problem was solved in the 60s of the last century by Jaynes and Cummings [5]; its physical prototype is the Fabry-Perot interferometer, consisting of two mirrors that limit the cavity in which a photon of a certain mode can live long enough, up to a few milliseconds. Several atoms of the same type [6] are placed in the cavity, in each of which the ground and excited states are distinguished - the eigenstates of the atomic energy operator, denoted by $|0\rangle$ and $|1\rangle$, respectively, so that the energy difference of these states $\delta E = E_1 - E_0 = \hbar\omega$ coincides with the energy of the photon held in the cavity[1].

This allows a detailed mathematical and numerical study of the interaction of charged particles with the field - the main "motor" of the real evolution of a complex system. The cavities can be connected by optical fiber waveguides, which allows photons to move from cavity to cavity. This allows us to simulate the environment into which a real photon can fly or fly from it to the system of atoms in question in a certain cavity - see Fig. 2. This is the physical prototype of the Tavis-Cummings-Hubbard model.

The basic state of the TCH model has the form $|C_1, C_2, ..., C_k\rangle$, where the state of the i th cavity $|C_i\rangle$ has the form $|n_i\rangle_{ph}|atom_1^i, atom_2^i, ..., atom_{m_i}^i\rangle$ where the first component is the number of photons in the cavity mode, the rest are the states of the atoms in it.

The time evolution of such a system looks like the application of the unitary operator $U_t = exp(-\frac{i}{\hbar}Ht)$ to initial state: $|\Psi(t)\rangle = U_t|\Psi(0)\rangle$, where the Hamiltonian has the form

$$
\begin{aligned}
H_{TCH} &= \sum_{i=1}^{k} H_i + \sum_{i<i'} v_{i,i'}(a_i^+ a_i + a_i^+ a_{i'}), \\
H_i &= \hbar\omega a_i^+ a_i + \sum_j \hbar\omega \sigma_{ij}^+ \sigma_{ij} + (a_i^+ + a_i)\sum_j g_{ij}(\sigma_{ij}^+ + \sigma_{ij})
\end{aligned}
\tag{2}
$$

- the first term in H_{TCH} is the sum of the energies of the cavities, the second is the energy of the transition of the photon from the cavity to the cavity, and the energy operator of the cavity i has the form H_i, where the field operators in the cavity i are the creation and annihilation of the photon a_i^+, a_i, and the atomic operator of excitation and relaxation of the jth atom in the cavity i σ_{ij}^+, σ_{ij}. The action of field operators on the basis states of the field and atomic operators on the basis states of atoms has the form:

$$
\begin{aligned}
a|n\rangle &= \sqrt{n}|n-1\rangle, a^+|n\rangle = \sqrt{n+1}|n+1\rangle, \\
\sigma^+|0\rangle &= |1\rangle, \sigma^+|1\rangle = 0, \sigma|0\rangle = 0, \sigma|1\rangle = |0\rangle.
\end{aligned}
\tag{3}
$$

The TCH model is difficult to compute, since the interaction of the field with the atom contains terms $a\sigma$ and $a^+\sigma^+$ that do not store energy separately; however, for weak interactions, when $g \ll \hbar\omega$, you can omit these terms by writing the interaction energy as $g(a\sigma^+ + a^+\sigma)$, which makes natural sense: the atom is excited by absorbing a photon, and the atom relaxes by emitting

---

[1] Half of the wavelength of the photon $\lambda/2$ should coincide with the distance between the mirrors, then the interference of the field inside the cavity will be the most constructive and the lifetime of the photon inside it will be the maximum.

a photon. This kind of Hamiltonian H_{TCH}^{RWA} is called the RWA approximation. This sense of interaction makes it possible to apply this model to a wide class of phenomena, even beyond the scope of physics, for example, to the social behavior of human society.

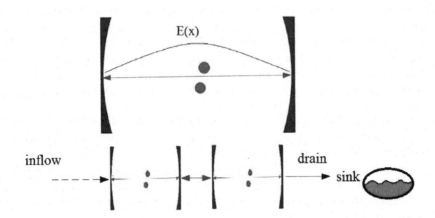

Fig. 2. Physical prototype of the Tavis-Cummings-Hubbard model

It is important that the Tavis-Cummings-Hubbard Hamiltonian in the RWA approximation is convenient for computer calculations: the state space in it decays into a direct sum of subspaces of finite dimension that are invariant with respect to H_{TCH}^{RWA}, which makes it possible to parallelize the evolution operator U_t numerically. Thus, we can use standard linear algebra packages to model rather complex processes, for example, the interaction of ensembles of several hundred two-level atoms with fields inside a system of optical cavities. This model can also be modified for chemical interactions. Let's look at some applications of this model in the community behavior.

3   The Simplest Model of Community Behavior

The first example of the application of quantum concepts to the human community was given by A. Y. Khrennikov in the book [7], where a community of individuals, called social atoms, which interact with the field of excitation of social energy, consisting of bosons, is considered. An example of bosons is just the electromagnetic field, whose operators obey the relations (3).

We will consider the Khrennikov social laser in the framework of the TCH model, and find out the nature of the exchange of excitation between two equally large groups of social atoms.

Society in the simplest model is represented as an ensemble of individuals, each of which is declared a social atom. In the simplest case, this is a two-level atom; in a more detailed analysis, it is necessary to introduce other levels:

$0, 1, 2, ..., d$ and consider different types of transitions between them. For two-level atoms, the transition from the excited $|1\rangle$ level to the main $|0\rangle$ level is accompanied by the emission of additional energy.

This energy manifests in different ways depending on the context. In a street crowd, it can be shouts, calls; in social networks - comments, links, drawings, etc. - to build a mathematical model, it is necessary to abstract from the specific type of actions that accompany the release of the social energy of the atom. This abstraction is unusual for sociology, it is purely mathematical. The transition from concrete actions to the abstraction of social energy reveals the general quality of such actions, which manifests itself despite their heterogeneity: the state of the individual does not depend on how he "relaxed" or, on the contrary, "aroused" - all this is the result of either the emission of social energy or its absorption from the outside.

Since social energy is emitted and absorbed by the atoms, which have only two levels: the main and the excited, we must assume that this energy is distributed in portions, that is, quantized. The general "energy field" of society is characterized by a state with a certain number of quanta of social energy, that is, the number $n = 0, 1, 2, ...$ - the greater this number, the more excited the field of social energy.

In the field of social energy, individual quanta are indistinguishable - its state is characterized only by their total number n; we cannot determine which particular quantum of social energy caused the excitation of a particular atom. In a real situation, this may raise questions: an individual can often say that it "overstayed his patience" and led to action - but this is just a common illusion. In everyday life, we do not have terms that denote energy: we operate only with the actions of people, their visible actions. So, we can say that this atom emitted a quantum of energy, but we can not identify the quantum itself, but only the individual. Any individuals here are distinguishable, only the quanta of social energy are indistinguishable.

Moreover, energy quanta behave in a strange way. The more excited the field is, the easier it is for a single quantum to attach to it. Conversely, it is more easily removed from the field, the more it is excited. This strange situation in quantum physics has a very specific name: this field consists of bosons. Such is, for example, the electromagnetic field. The strange behavior of quanta of social energy is actually observed in the behavior of a society, which is more easily excited (and the faster it "cools down") the more it is already excited; this feature of behavior is clearly visible in the examples given in the book [7].

The mathematical model of the social arousal field is exactly the single-mode electromagnetic field described in the previous section. The specific type of operators a^+ and a in the formula (3) it expresses the dependence of the rate of excitation and relaxation of the field depending on its current state. And these formulas follow precisely from quantum electrodynamics, from the quantization of Maxwell's equations!

We come to the surprising conclusion that the mathematical apparatus born of quantum physics reflects social reality, even in the very simple form of two-level social atoms. The Jaynes-Cummings model with a single atom in the optical cavity serves as a rough approximation of the social behavior of an individual atom that is in communication with "itself", that is, with the field of its own social excitation. A simple calculation for the H_i Hamiltonian from (2), taken in the singular, gives the so - called Rabi oscillations - sequential transitions of the form $|n + 1\rangle_{ph}|0\rangle \leftrightarrow |n\rangle_{ph}|1\rangle$ - the absorption and emission of a quantum of energy by a social atom, the period of which is $\pi\hbar/g\sqrt{n}$, from which it can be seen that the more excited the field is, the more often the ground and excited states of the atom will alternate.

It is important that the law of change of the state of the atom and the field has the form of a sinusoid

$$|\Psi(t)\rangle = cos(tg\sqrt{n}/\hbar)|n + 1\rangle_{ph}|0\rangle_{at} + sin(tg\sqrt{n}/\hbar)|n\rangle_{ph}|1\rangle_{at} \qquad (4)$$

The collective of social atoms within the sphere of action of a single field will then be described by the Tavis-Cumings model. The prototype of such a model is a crowd in a square, or an Internet platform, etc. Here it is important that the field of social excitement is shared. The fulfillment of this condition is not trivial. For example, if we allow the spatial separation of individuals without the possibility of instantaneous communication (Internet), the field of excitation will not be shared. In this case, we will not be able to consider the Tavis-Cummings model with a single cavity as adequate, and we must apply the more complex Tavis-Cummings-Hubbard model.

Now, using the Tavis-Cummings model, we calculate the dynamics of the state of an ensemble of n atoms and a single-mode field. We will assume that the force of interaction of all atoms with the field is the same, and the initial state has the form of complete relaxation of the atomic ensemble with a certain field energy inside the cavity: $|\Psi_{in}\rangle = |m\rangle_{ph}|00...0\rangle_{at}$.

Then, in the course of evolution, we will get only the so-called uniform states, all the basic components of which have the same Hamming weight. Let $B = \{1, 2, ..., n\}$ be the set of all atoms, $J(B)$ is the set of classical binary states of atoms from the set B. We define the uniform state of the atoms from the set B as

$$\{k_B \succ = \frac{1}{\sqrt{C_n^k}} \sum_{j \in J(B) \ 1(j)=k} |j\rangle, \qquad (5)$$

where $1(j)$ is the Hamming weight of the binary tuple j, that is, the number of units in it. Note that the uniform states are mutually orthogonal due to the fact that they have no common basic components. For the characters $\{, \}, \succ, \prec$, we assume Dirac rules similar to the rules for handling the characters $|, >, <$.

Let L_{eq}^B be a uniform subspace, that is, a linear shell of states of the form $|p\rangle\{k_B \succ$ for all $k = 0.1, ..., |B|$; $p = 0.1, ...$, where $|p\rangle$ is the Fock state of photons. Consider the restriction of the Hamiltonian H_{TC} to L_{eq}^B, which we denote by $\tilde{H}_{TC}^B$. Then we can write this Hamiltonian in a new basis consisting of uniform states. This matrix will have the form

$$(\tilde{H}^B_{i_p,i_B;j_p,j_B}) = (\prec i_B\}\langle i_p|H_{TC}|j_p\rangle\{j_B \succ),$$

where i_p, i_B is the initial number of photons and atomic excitations, j_p, j_B is the final number. To calculate its elements, we first note that the nonzero terms of the matrix must satisfy the equalities

$$i_p - j_p = i_B - j_B = \pm 1,$$

the first of which is the law of conservation of energy, and the second follows from the form of the Hamiltonian H_{TC}. The non-zero elements of the matrix are conveniently expressed in terms of numbers

$$p = min\{i_p, j_p\}, \; b = min\{i_B, j_B\}.$$

We then have

$$\tilde{H}^B_{i_p,i_B;j_p,j_B} = \begin{cases} \hbar\omega(p+b), & \text{if } i_B = j_B, \; i_p = j_p, \\ g(n-b)\sqrt{\frac{p+1}{C_n^b C_n^{b+1}}}, & \text{otherwise}, \end{cases} \tag{6}$$

The first equality is for diagonal elements, there is simply the energy of a given state. The second is obtained as follows. The coefficient g is the force of the interaction of atoms with the field, $\sqrt{p+1}$ is the effect of the identity of photons (in the creation-annihilation operators), the product of the binomial coefficients in the denominator is taken from the normalizing constants in the definition of uniform states (5), the multiplier $(n-b)$ is the number of summands equal to the number of possible atoms whose excitation is removed when a photon is emitted in the process under consideration.

Using the n - atomic system, you can get an artificial "atom" with $n+1$ levels: $\{0 \succ, \{1 \succ, \{2 \succ,..., \{n \succ$, so that the energy gaps between two adjacent levels are the same: $E_k - E_{k-1} = \hbar\omega$, $k = 1, 2, ..., n$.

This artificial "atom" is a mathematical image of a homogeneous society interacting with the field of social excitement generated by the society itself. Individuals absorb the social energy that they themselves have released in the course of relaxation. It is interesting to find out the dynamics of such a system.

For uniform states, there is an analog of Rabi oscillations - collective oscillations. Let $n = 2k$ be even. We divide the atoms into two groups, and we will denote the first group by the subscript 1, and the second by the subscript 2. Consider two basic states: $|\psi_1\rangle = |0\rangle_{ph}|00...0\rangle_1|11...1\rangle_2$ and $|\psi_2\rangle = |0\rangle_{ph}|11...1\rangle_1|00...0\rangle_2$. In these states, there are no free photons; in the first, the first group of atoms is in the ground state, and the second is in the excited state, and in the second, vice versa. If you start the evolution with one of these states, for example, with $|\psi_1\rangle$, it will immediately turn into a superposition, the atomic part of each member of which is a uniform state of atoms, and all uniform states will be present here. However, after a certain period of time, the entire amplitude will concentrate on the second state - on $|\psi_2\rangle$, then everything will repeat, etc., that is, we will get a collective analog of the Rabi oscillations.

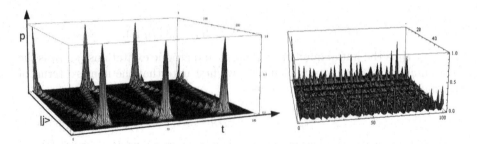

Fig. 3. Collective oscillations of the state of society and the field of excitation. The probability peaks correspond to the excitation states of all the atoms of the first and second groups, respectively

However, the nature of collective oscillations will be different from Rabi for a single atom. The amplitude peaks at our two states will become more and more sharp as n increases, and the nature of the oscillations will thus be far from the sinusoidal form of monatomic oscillations (see Fig. 3). The oscillations will have a similar character, even if two groups of atoms are located in different cavities connected by an optical fiber (the Tavis-Cummings-Hubbard model).

The stability of states of the type $|\psi_{1,2}\rangle$ suggests that two groups of atoms can mutually and qualitatively maintain the same dynamic scenario, even if they are distant from each other. The reason for this behavior is the interference of amplitudes; it is the interference involving photons that makes such support possible at a distance. Remote support for dynamic scenarios, in which photons emitted by one group "find" another group ready to receive them, occurs due to the fact that for all other states, the amplitude is distributed over a large number of them, which dramatically reduces the probability of finding a system of atoms in these "extraneous" states.

So, numerical simulations have given us a special, comb-like picture of the exchange of social energy between two groups of atoms. This is exactly the picture observed in the social process. A large group of people can very quickly - and unexpectedly - become aroused to a very high degree, after which relaxation occurs just as quickly. This quality of mass is observed at crucial moments in history, which explains many amazing phenomena.

An example is the revolutions that take place, at first glance, on an "empty place". Historians traditionally interpret such phenomena as the manifestation of the activities of hidden groups of revolutionaries, but this is a superficial assessment! The ultra-rapid nature of the excitability of a large group of social atoms, unlike the behavior of an individual, is a completely natural phenomenon, independent of any hidden malicious actions. Lenin in 1917 did not limit the overthrow of the autocracy in Russia, the February revolution was, to a certain extent, a surprise for him. His success was due to a quick awareness of the events that were happening, but not to their precise planning. The events themselves are related to the natural patterns of behavior of complex systems that can give quantum representations.

Knowledge of these patterns allows a small group of individuals to successfully manipulate the behavior of a huge number of individuals who behave like social atoms, which is the subject of so-called "quantum politics". This knowledge is also useful for ensuring sustainable development and a certain stabilization of society; it can be obtained by improving quantum models like the one given.

4 Conclusion

We partially justified the thesis about the possibility of applying quantum computing methods in the humanitarian sphere - social models of behavior of large groups of people. These two directions are actually connected by a common mathematical apparatus - quantum models. The use of these models allows us to accurately calculate the behavior of a simple ensemble of social atoms, and to scale this calculation to ensembles consisting of more complex objects with greater individuality.

Acknowledgements. The paper was prepared in the Moscow Center for Fundamental and Applied Mathematics.

References

1. Mattuk, F.: Feynman Diagrams in the Problem of Many Bodies. Mir, Moscow (1974)
2. Feynman, R.P.: Simulating physics with computers. Int. J. Theor. Phys. **21**(6/7), 467–488 (1982)
3. Ozhigov, Y.I.: Distributed synthesis of chains with one-way biphotonic control. Quantum Inf. Comput. **18**(7–8), 0592–0598 (2019)
4. Shor, P.W.: Scheme for reducing decoherence in quantum computer memory. Phys. Rev. A **52**, R2493(R) (1995)
5. Jaynes, E.T., Cummings, F.W.: Comparison of quantum and semiclassical radiation theories with application to the beam maser. Proc. IEEE **51**(1), 89–109 (1963). https://doi.org/10.1109/PROC.1963.1664
6. Tavis, M.T.: A Study of an N Molecule Quantized (2017). https://arxiv.org/abs/1206.0078
7. Khrennikov, A.: Social Laser: Application of Quantum Information and Field Theories to Modeling of Social Processes. Jenny Stanford Publishing (2020). 280 pages, ISBN-10 981480083X, ISBN-13 978–9814800839

Qualitative and Quantitative Study of Modern GPU Synchronization Approaches

Ilya Pershin[✉], Vadim Levchenko, and Anastasia Perepelkina

Keldysh Institute of Applied Mathematics, Moscow, Russia

Abstract. Parallel processing of data is the foundation of the computing power of all contemporary computers. High degree of parallelism (from 10^2 on desktop CPU to 10^8 on supercomputers) is a real challenge for scientists and programmers who are craving for efficient use of the available resources. The facts that modern computers are hierarchical systems and that the parallelism on each level has its own hardware specifics further complicates the problem. In this paper we study the level of Nvidia GPU SM communication, since it is the fundamental level of GPU parallelism. We discuss the three approaches to SM synchronization starting from the most simple and moving onto the most complex one. The sample codes snippets for the CUDA toolkit are included and commented on in detail. A new 'tau-model' is developed for the comparative analysis of the latency of different synchronization methods in parallel systems. The model is applied to the benchmark stencil code and the quantitative estimates of the latency are obtained. The pairwise synchronization with the use of manually coded semaphores is more efficient than the barrier synchronization present in the CUDA library.

Keywords: CUDA · Cooperative groups · Roofline model · Domain decomposition · Latency hiding

1 Introduction

Parallelism is very important in modern computing. Even smartphones often have 6–8 cores. The desktop processor Ryzen 9 5950X has 16 cores, and each core can run 2 threads processing one vector operation on 256-bit registers (8 single-precision floating-point numbers) per clock cycle with AVX2 vectorization. Thus, three levels of parallelism are already present. Their sizes are 16, 2, and 8 correspondingly and the total degree of parallelism is 256. Similarly, the degree of parallelism in the Intel Core i9-10980XE processor is $18 \cdot 2 \cdot 16 = 576$. The numbers for GPU are even higher. One GeForce RTX 3090 has 82 streaming multiprocessors (SMs) (Fig. 1), each containing four processing blocks, and each processing block can perform 16 floating point operations per cycle in two datapaths. Thus, the total degree of parallelism is $82 \cdot 4 \cdot 2 \cdot 16 = 10496$.

© Springer Nature Switzerland AG 2021
V. Voevodin and S. Sobolev (Eds.): RuSCDays 2021, CCIS 1510, pp. 376–390, 2021.
https://doi.org/10.1007/978-3-030-92864-3_29

The degree of parallelism in supercomputers [4] is up to 10^8 which is provided by an even more complex hierarchy of levels of parallelism.

A high degree of parallelism leads to a higher theoretical FLOPs number, as well as to more complexity in efficient code implementation. Here, efficiency is the ratio of the software performance to the peak performance of specific hardware. One fundamental efficiency limitation is Amdahl's law. Here we stress two more hardware issues that prevent obtaining high performance. Note that Amdahl's law is stated for an ideal parallel computer, and does not take into account the existence of shared resources in the computers.

The first issue is the memory wall [12]. The performance of a large class of problems, which are called memory bound, is limited by the memory bandwidth, and the real performance is no more than a few percent of the peak performance. The Roofline Model [19] serves as an excellent illustration for this issue. One solution to the issue is to promote the memory-bound problems closer to the compute-bound domain [10].

The second issue is the load balancing. If there are plenty of parallel processors, such as cores, which perform independently, this issue is irrelevant. However, this is rare. It is often necessary to perform many data exchanges between cores during the execution, so synchronization of data pipelines is required. The synchronization leads to delays, however, if the synchronization latency is low compared with the computing time costs, the influence of load balancing on the total performance is small.

There are a few extensions to the Roofline Model that take latency [6,11] or even power consumption [8] into account. However, when pre-specified microarchitectural parameters [6] or hardware counters [8] are used to obtain latency boundings, this makes it difficult or impossible to use such models on other architectures, e.g. Nvidia.

In this work, we propose a model similar to the Roofline Model, which illustrates the shift of the codes from latency-bound to compute-bound, which we call 'tau-model' (Sect. 4). In contrast, tau-model does not use any additional architecture specifications or built-in profilers, but requires some source code patching for the sake of performance measurements. Specifically, we study the problem of load balancing between SMs in an Nvidia GPU and aim to minimize the latency of their synchronization.

The peak performance of GPU is at least an order of magnitude higher than the top CPU performance, but its efficient use requires a similar increase in the GDDR memory bandwidth in comparison to the DDR bandwidth. These numbers are obtained by increasing the access latency. Thus, the issue of load balancing is very relevant for GPU.

2   Hardware and Software Parallelism in CUDA

Compute Unified Device Architecture (CUDA) [3] is a toolkit for development of general purpose programs which run on Nvidia GPU. The code is written in an extension of C++, and the program abstractions are built specifically for Nvidia

GPU hardware. The latter allows precise low-level control over the GPU, and the flip side is the porting restrictions to other hardware.

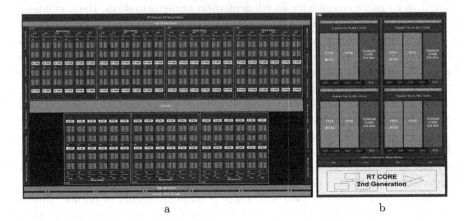

Fig. 1. GA102 Full GPU with 84 SMs (a) and ampere streaming multiprocessor (b)

The basis of the device hierarchy is the Graphics Processing Clusters (GPC) level. The number of GPC depends on the specific GPU chip (Fig. 1a). GPCs share the global memory and the L2 cache, but otherwise they are separate GPUs, each of which contains a Raster Engine[1] and several Texture Processing Clusters (TPC). Each TPC contains PolyMorph Engine[2], as well as two Streaming Multiprocessors (SM). Each SM has its own RayTracing Core[3], L1 data cache/shared memory subsystem, and two processing blocks. Each has a 64 KB register file, an L0 instruction cache and 16 FP32 & 16 INT32 Cuda Cores[4] or 16 FP32 & 16 FP32/INT32 CUDA Cores[5] (Fig. 1b). 16 CUDA cores execute 16 vector operations on FP32 or INT32 type data each clock cycle.

CUDA parallelism software model is based on the 'Single Instruction, Multiple Threads' (SIMT) paradigm. Multiple threads (more than the hardware degree of parallelism) are created, and the processor can switch context between threads to cover the latency of data I/O operations. The threads on one SM are grouped into blocks. The threads in one block use fast L1 data cache/shared memory subsystem. The number of threads in a block is often in the 256–1024 range. The slower global memory and its L2 cache are used to coordinate different blocks. Inside one block, the barrier synchronization is available to a programmer as a __syncthreads command which synchronizes all threads, and the Cooperative Groups tools allow to synchronize only a part of them.

---

[1] Transforms geometric primitives into raster images.
[2] Enables tesselation, i.e. a dynamic detalization of objects.
[3] Turing, Ampere architectures.
[4] Turing architecture.
[5] Ampere architecture.

While one SM can process up to 2048 threads in 1–8 blocks, these blocks are independent, and may be synchronized only through the global memory. During execution, the threads of one block are divided into warps (groups of 32 threads), and, inside the warp, warp shuffle operations are available for synchronization.

The blocks of threads are collected in a grid. Two options are available for block distribution in a grid.

Traditionally, blocks are distributed between SMs *asynchronously*. It is possible to create any number[6] of blocks. When computing kernel is run, each SM takes 1–8 blocks, executes all required operations, and takes the next blocks after that. This continues until all blocks are processed. Unlike it was described for the threads in a block, the context switch for blocks in a grid is not performed. It is impossible to run a 'heavy' operation with global memory in the first block and continue with a next block while the first one is not finished. Data dependencies between blocks of one grid may lead to undefined behavior, i.e. deadlocks or race conditions.

A grid is queued for execution with a CUDA kernel call. It performs initialization and synchronization with the global memory. Often, in an asynchronous mode, many kernels are run one after another, or one kernel is called in a loop. Each data exchange should be accompanied with such synchronization, and this allows to hide the latency of the 'boundary'[7] loads and stores in a kernel run.

In some algorithms, frequent (in comparison to other operations) data exchange between blocks is required. If the block which uses many registers and shared memory is run asynchronously, its state is dumped to the global memory and loaded again many times, and this decreases the computing efficiency.

The number of SMs per GPU grew with each new architecture, so since CUDA 9 a *synchronous* SM execution mode is introduced, which utilizes Cooperative Groups. In it, the number of blocks is limited by a number of available SMs in the GPU. Each SM takes 1–8 blocks and works with them until the whole cooperative kernel is finished. In this mode, the data may be exchanged through the global memory and L2 cache, while everything else stays in the register file and the shared memory. To execute such kernels a special syntax is used, but the blocks remain the same, with an additional ability to read and write to the same memory cells. Such operations still require synchronization. A barrier synchronization command `this_grid().sync()` is available. However, in stencil code implementation we have encountered performance limitations caused by the latency of barrier synchronization. Thus, we developed a pair-wise synchronization method for this mode (Sect. 3.3) to increase the efficiency of the synchronous mode.

3 Problem Statement and Implementation

The Lattice Boltzmann Method (LBM) [17] stencil scheme is used for the benchmark implementation. It is an explicit two-stage scheme which simulates fluid

---

[6] Up to 2^{63} when 3D indexing is used [3].

[7] The kernels are often consist of data load, computation and data save in that order.

dynamics on a rectangular grid. As a stencil method, its efficient implementation is a relevant research topic [21].

In LBM, in each cell the fluid flow is a combination of microscopic flows f_i with constant velocities $\vec{c}_i$, where $i = 1 \ldots Q$. The macroscopic parameters of the flow are expressed through these flows: density is $\rho = \sum_i f_i$, current density is $\rho \vec{u} = \sum_i f_i \vec{c}_i$, etc.

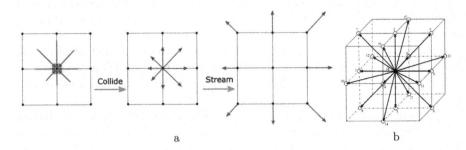

a   b

Fig. 2. Two stages of LBM (a) and the D3Q19 LBM stencil (b)

The *collision* stage is local and it 'mixes' the microscopic flows in each cell (Fig. 2a).

$$f_i^*(\vec{x}, t) = \Omega(f_1(\vec{x}, t), \ldots, f_Q(\vec{x}, t))$$

The *streaming* stage moves the numerical values of the flows into the adjacent cells according to the $\vec{c}_i$ vector:

$$f_i(\vec{x} + \vec{c}_i, t + 1) = f_i^*(\vec{x}, t)$$

Here we take $Q = 19$ (Fig. 2b) and the collision operator Ω in the BGK form [5].

The Recursive Domain Decomposition (RDD) method [16] is used for the implementation. It implements multilevel geometric parallelism with the storage of data (f_i) in the SM register file during the whole simulation in the *synchronous* GPU mode. The 3D mesh is decomposed into rectangular blocks (Fig. 3), and each level corresponds to a level of parallelism. For the data exchange in warps, warp shuffle operations are used; for the data exchange in blocks, the shared memory is used; for the data exchange in a grid, the global memory is used, however, everything is contained in the L2 cache. The RDD blocks are as large as can be contained in the register file and the shared memory correspondingly. Since the stencil takes only one cell in every direction, the majority of the data persist in the higher and faster storage levels. Only the boundary cells of the RDD block are accessed in every exchange, and if the block is large its surface to volume ratio is rather small.

The method description in the following does not rely on the numerical scheme specifics, since we focus on the SM synchronization modes. Thus, let us take an abstract problem of uniform processing of a `data` array according to some rule for many iterations.

Fig. 3. Three levels of Recursive Domain Decomposition. The data in white blocks are stored in the register file. The data exchanges across the red boundaries are performed with warp shuffles, across the blue boundary the exchanges are performed through the shared memory, and across the green boundary the exchanges are through the L2 cache. (Color figure online)

3.1 Asynchronous Implementation

The asynchronous code is relatively simple (Fig. 4). In the `main` function, the `init_data` procedure fills the global memory with initial data, `step_kernel` is the computational kernel run in a loop, `utilize_data` is the post-processing of data. The number of CUDA blocks is generally much higher than the number of SMs and scales with the simulation data size. The intermediate diagnostics of the `data_g` array in the loop is possible, however, here we consider only the case when it is required only at the finish of computation.

In the `step_kernel`, the `read_global` procedure load a small portion of data from the global memory into the local memory of the thread `data_l`. The size of the data depends on a numerical scheme. The amount of data required for one stencil application is enough. The `compute` is a local processing procedure. In it, the threads of one block can exchange data through the shared memory. It is important that the threads of different blocks run independently. After the processing, the data are saved to the global memory in `write_global`. In LBM, the `compute` is the collision stage, and the streaming stage is performed with the read/write operations into the global memory.

The computing kernel should be finished after each iteration since the `read_global` in one thread may use the data written by another thread in a previous step of the algorithm. In the asynchronous mode, it is the only way to ensure the correctness of such exchanges.

```
__global__ void step_kernel(float *data_g) {
    float data_l[/**/];
    read_global(data_g, data_l);
    compute(data_l);
    write_global(data_g, data_l);
}

int main (){
    init_data(data_g);

    int threads = 512; //or 256 or 1024
    int blocks = /**/
    for(int it = 0; it < iterations; ++it) {
        step_kernel<<<blocks, threads>>>(data_g);
    }

    utilize_data(data_g);
    return 0;
}
```

Fig. 4. The asynchronous code

```
const int threads = 512; //or 256 or 1024
const int blocks = /**/; //SM number or 2*SM or 3*SM or 4*SM

__device__ volatile float block_data_g[blocks][/**/];

__global__ void step_kernel(float *data_g, int iterations) {

    extern __shared__ float block_data_s[];

    float data_l[/**/];
    read_global(data_g, data_l);

    for(int it = 0; it < iterations; ++it) {
        compute(data_l);

        intra_block_write(data_l, block_data_s);
        __syncthreads();
        inter_block_write(data_l, block_data_g);

        auto grid = cooperative_groups::this_grid();
        grid.sync();

        inter_block_read(data_l, block_data_g);
        __syncthreads();
        intra_block_read(data_l, block_data_s);
    }

    write_global(data_g, data_l);
}

int main (){
    init_data(data_g);
    assert(blocks == max_coop_blocks(threads, step_kernel));

    std::array<const void*, 2> args = {&data_g, &iterations};
    size_t shmem = /**/;
    cudaLaunchCooperativeKernel(reinterpret_cast<void*>(step_kernel),
        blocks, threads, const_cast<void**>(args.data()), shmem);

    utilize_data(data_g);
    return 0;
}
```

Fig. 5. The code for the cooperative mode

3.2   Synchronous Implementation with Cooperative Groups

The first synchronous implementation (Fig. 5), in the `main` function the following procedures are called:

- `init_data` fills global memory with the initial data values;
- `max_coop_blocks` uses `cudaOccupancyMaxActiveBlocksPerMultiprocessor` to perform runtime block number assertion;
- creation of the argument array an kernel launch are performed in `cudaLaunchCooperativeKernel`;
- post-processing with `utilize_data`.

`cudaLaunchCooperativeKernel` is mandatory for cooperative mode. The `shmem` is the precomputed size of the required shared memory, and its value depends on the numerical scheme (35.8 KB for RDD LBM D3Q19).

The number of threads and blocks are defined with constants. The number of blocks should be divisible by the number of SMs, so that each SM take 1 (2, 3, 4) blocks for execution. It allows synchronous exchange of the data on the boundaries of the RDD blocks, and the rest stays in the registers throughout all iterations. In contrast, in the asynchronous mode, all data are required to be dumped to the global memory after each iteration.

The possible simulation size is limited by the global storage in the asynchronous mode and by the total register file size in the synchronous mode. Both limitations may be mitigated by the used of algorithms with space-time wavefront [9,20] with the use of special data structures [14].

In the `step_kernel`, the data is loaded from the global memory to the local memory of the thread `data_l`, and saved back after the execution. For the efficient use of the GPU resources, it is preferable to fill the register file as densely as possible. At the same time, register spills should be avoided.[8]

The `launch_bounds` allows additional control over the number of block in an SM.

Between read and write commands the main computation takes place. Unlike the asynchronous mode, an arbitrary number of iterations may be performed in the loop In an iteration, the scheme update is performed, and the data exchange in a block `intra_block` and between blocks `inter_block` takes place. For this purpose, the two arrays `block_data_g` and `block_data_s` are declared in the shared and the global memory correspondingly.

Their configuration and size depend on the numerical scheme and the exchange topology (983 KB and 35.8 KB for RDD LBM D3Q19). However, the size of these arrays is relatively small since the major portion of the data remains in the registers. In RDD for stencil problems, these arrays contain the data of the cells on the surface of the 3D rectangular data blocks.

The `block_data_g` array is declared as **volatile**. This is mandatory whenever data in global memory is shared in the synchronous codes. According to the

---

[8] The compile option `-Xptxas="-v"` may be used to output the number of registers per thread (up to 256) and check for register spills.

CUDA documentation [2], the CUDA compiler can store the global and shared memory accesses in the L1 cache. Since both the L1 cache and the register file are local for a block, this behavior can interfere with the correct inter-block data exchange through this array, that is, these caches are not coherent. The volatile qualifier ensures that each global memory access is translated into an uncached read or write instruction. Note that L2 may be used even if volatile is set since it is shared for the whole GPU device.

The data exchange code must be accompanied by corresponding synchronization commands. Otherwise, data race is inevitable. For the synchronization inside a block, the built-in __syncthreads command is used. For the synchronization of all blocks (i.e. of a grid), the this_grid().sync() method is used. Currently (as of CUDA 11) this is the only official grid synchronization method in a cooperative execution. A lack of the correct synchronization before or after the exchange operations leads to difficulties in debugging, thus, it is advised to be particularly careful in writing the synchronization procedure.

The described code is still not optimal. The Cooperative Groups method provides a barrier synchronization for the whole grid at once. That is, every block waits for all other blocks before it continues. It was experimentally verified [16] that this procedure has a noticeable latency, which decreases the performance of the simulation code. If the synchronization command is simply erased here, the code speeds up significantly. This simple test shows that the block synchronization may be optimized further.

There is one more detail that allows decreasing the number of synchronization events by half. If in the exchanges between blocks the data processed with the compute command is written in the same space from which it was read before, the synchronization between these operations is not required. This way these operations 'merge' into one local (in regards to other blocks) operation read-compute-write. The synchronization after write and before read remains necessary, since the block reads the new data from a different place in the memory, which are written there by a different block. In pairwise block exchanges it is convenient to assign a buffer to each block, and to perform the read-compute-write operation alternately on one buffer or the other. In this method, the 'odd' and 'even' loop iterations are introduced, and the blocks refer to their own buffers or the buffers of the neighbor blocks interchangeably. This is a general approach recommended for the implementation of synchronous codes with data exchange, not limited to GPU codes.

3.3   Synchronous Implementation with Semaphores

Let us consider the exchange topology, that is, a graph structure in which the nodes are CUDA blocks. The nodes are linked if there is a data exchange between the blocks. The links may be bilateral or unilateral in the unsymmetrical case. In stencil simulation with RDD, this graph is constant in time, homogeneous (excluding the boundary), its links are bilateral, and the degree of the nodes is low. With such topology the this_grid().sync() command is superfluous. The block has to only wait for the signal of its adjacent blocks.

To take advantage of this detail, the barrier synchronization is replaced with pairwise semaphore communication [7,15]. An array of flags (Fig. 6) is created. The size of the array is defined by the number of links in the graph. In D3Q19 LBM, each node has 18 links, so 18 semaphores per block are defined. Each semaphore is represented with an integer. The **volatile** qualifier is required here just as it was for the block_data_g array since the semaphore array is the shared data. A better performance was obtained in the implementation where not just 4 bytes, but at least one memory transaction sector (32 bytes) is allocated per semaphore. Thus the Aligned<int> class which aligns its data (val) to 32 bytes is used.

```
template <typename T>
struct __align__(32) Aligned
{
    T val;
};

__device__ volatile Aligned<int> parities[/**/][6];
```

Fig. 6. Implementation of semaphores

A local read-compute-write was defined above, which separates odd and even data access operations. Accordingly, the parities semaphore arrays stores a value (0 or 1) that shows if the block is odd or even. The size of the array is the product of the number of blocks and the degree of the graph nodes.

The main loop in Fig. 5 is replaced (Fig. 7).

```
for(int it = 0; it < iterations; ++it) {
    compute(data_l);

    intra_block_write(data_l, block_data_s);
    __syncthreads();
    inter_block_write(data_l, block_data_g);

    __syncthreads();
    if(/**/) {{
        __threadfence();
        parities[/**/][/**/].val = parity;
    }}

    parity = !parity;

    while(parities[/**/][/**/].val != parity);

    inter_block_read(data_l, block_data_g);
    __syncthreads();
    intra_block_read(data_l, block_data_s);
}
```

Fig. 7. Implementation of semaphore synchronization in the compute loop

After the write operation, inside the **if** block, the semaphores are updated in the current or the neighbor block according to the parity.

If there are 18 exchanges per block, 18 semaphore switches are required. Since this is much less than the number of threads in a block, the `if(/**/)` condition chooses the threads that perform the write. The choice depends on the implementation. The semaphore switch signals that the data are updated and can be read if the block parity is appropriate. There is an additional `__syncthreads` before the condition. It ensures that the previous write operation is finished in all threads of the block before the semaphores are switched. A `__threadfence` command before `parities` update is required for a correct order of global memory access. This is due to the fact that the CUDA compiler can arbitrarily change the write accesses to the global memory. Without `__threadfence`, some write instructions in `inter_block_write` may be performed after the update in `parities`, so that the semaphore is switched earlier than it should.

The `while` block implements the wait for the appropriate parity of the data in the current or the neighboring CUDA-block. It is assumed that all threads in the block perform the read, so the `if(/**/)` filter is omitted. As soon as the data that are to be read are ready and the corresponding semaphore is switched by a neighboring block, the threads of the current block pass the `while` line and perform the read operations.

4   Benchmarks and Tau Model

The performance of the implementation of the synchronous mode with Cooperative Groups and with semaphores was tested on RTX 2070 (Turing) and RTX 3090 (Ampere). The stencil problems are traditionally memory-bound, however, by plotting the performance results over the Roofline Model [19] it is observed that, with RDD, D3Q19 LBM has a significantly higher arithmetic intensity and the performance is close to the ridge point for both devices (Fig. 8) Near the ridge point, both memory bandwidth and peak performance limitations are relevant, thus the RoofLine Model in insufficient. Moreover, the points are far from the RoofLine. Thus, other limitations take place. For a better comparison of the two implementations, a new *tau-model* is developed.

Let us take an abstract computer ("black box") that processes some data. It may be either a CPU or a GPU. Let us assume that the computer can perform N update iterations, where each iteration has M operations of *local processing (computing)* and K *synchronization operations* of data. Denote the total computation time by $T(N, M, K)$. Then the *iteration time* is defined as

$$\tau(M, K) = \lim_{N \to \infty} \frac{T(N, M, K)}{NM}$$

In the 'usual' RDD D3Q19 LBM code (Sect. 3), $M = 1$ and $K = 1$. The variation of M and K is needed to study the computational dependencies of the code. The `compute` is directly repeated M times in succession, and the instructions which implement data exchanges are repeated K times. This is done to make either the computational part or the synchronization part heavier. This way, the

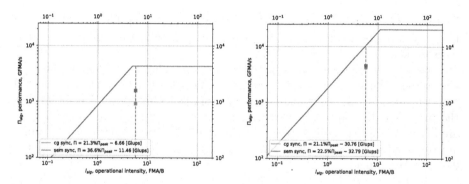

Fig. 8. Roofline model: RTX 2070 & RTX 3090. The inclined line is the memory bandwidth limit (memory-bound), the horizontal line it the peak performance limit (compute-bound). 1 Glups is one billion of LBM cell updates per second.

influence of such an increase on a total performance can be observed, and only one code is enough to study a wide range of possible problems.

Let us define *computation time* as $\tau_l = \lim\limits_{\substack{M \to \infty \\ K = const}} \tau(M, K)$, that is, the process-

ing time when the delays for synchronization are negligible, i.e. the number of computations in each iteration is sufficiently high. Let us define *synchronization latency* as $\lambda_s = \lim\limits_{\substack{K \to \infty \\ M = const}} [\tau(M, K+1) - \tau(M, K)]$, that is, the processing when the synchronization overshadows the computation. Finally, let us denote an abstract *arithmetic intensity* as $\iota = \frac{M}{K}$ and plot the $\tau(\iota) = \tau(M, K)$ dependency for the code described in Sect. 3 (Fig. 9).

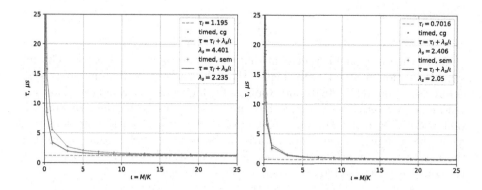

Fig. 9. Tau model: RTX 2070 & RTX 3090

The time τ depends not only on the M to K ratio but also on their absolute values. This contribution is not large in comparison to the dependency on ι. Thus, only the points with either $K = 1$ or $M = 1$ are plotted. This way, the whole range of ι is covered.

Before the measurement, the GPU device is warmed up for several minutes to equalize the temperature and frequency and minimize their influence on the measurement.

The points in Fig. 9 are on a curve that tends to a horizontal line on the right and to the vertical line on the left. With nonlinear least squares fit implemented with the use of `scipy` [18], `pandas` [13] and `ampule` [1] libraries it was found that the curve is indeed approximated with $y = a + \frac{b}{x}$, and the a and b coefficients are τ_l and λ_s correspondingly, according to their definition. The τ_l and λ_s values are obtained in fitting (shown on the graph), and latency values are in the $2.05 - 4.4\,\mu s$ range.

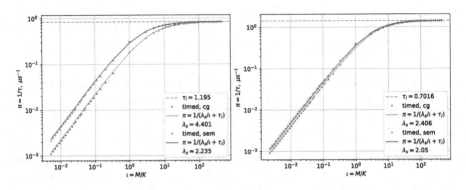

Fig. 10. Tau-model in the inverse units and logarithmic scale. RTX 2070 & RTX 3090

Further, the tau-model is plotted in the inverse units of *performance* in a log-log plot (Fig. 10):

$$\pi \equiv \frac{1}{\tau} = \frac{1}{\frac{\lambda_s}{\iota} + \tau_l}$$

With the tau-model it is evident that the latency of the Cooperative Groups synchronization is about twice higher than the latency of the semaphore synchronization on RTX 2070, and about 20% higher on RTX 3090. Thus, the tau-model demonstrates a noticeable improvement in the barrier synchronization of the grid in the Ampere architecture in comparison with a previous one, while the semaphores perform similarly on both devices. Note that λ_s are not the universal constants of the chosen synchronization method, but depend on the code since they include the time for data exchange.

Now, some useful qualitative relations can be obtained. Let us introduce the *synchronization time* $\tau_s = \frac{\lambda_s}{\iota}$ and *synchronization performance* $\pi_s = \frac{1}{\tau_s}$, and state the three laws which follow from the tau-model.

- $\tau = \tau_s + \tau_l$ – the time for one iteration is a sum of the synchronization time and the computation time;
- $\frac{1}{\pi} = \frac{1}{\pi_s} + \frac{1}{\pi_l}$ – the inverse performance of an update is the harmonic sum of the synchronization performance and the peak computing performance;

– $\tau_s = \frac{\lambda_s}{\iota}$ – the synchronization time is a ratio of the synchronization latency and the arithmetic intensity. This is in an agreement with Little's law.

The simplicity of these statements leads to believe that they may be sufficiently universal, and the tau-model may be as widely applied as the RoofLine Model. It is important the wide range in ι was necessary to verify the hyperbola, but for the application purposes only several points on the graph are enough to find τ_l and λ_s and use the model for any ι.

5   Conclusion

In this work, we presented a detailed discussion of the capabilities and issues of the asynchronous and synchronous (cooperative) Nvidia GPU parallelism. The RDD algorithm for the D3Q19 LBM is proposed, and it has two synchronization options: a barrier synchronization in the Cooperative Groups framework, and manual synchronization with semaphores. With the use of semaphore synchronization on the GPU with the Turing architecture or the use of either of them on the GPU with the Ampere architecture, the obtained LBM D3Q19 performance surpassed the best LRnLA implementation [21].

For the analysis of the results, a new *tau-model* is developed. With it, we found how the algorithm performance depends on the performance of pure computation, synchronization latency, and arithmetic intensity. This model not only provides quantitative and qualitative estimates of the performance limits of an LBM scheme but also exposes the improvement of the barrier grid synchronization in the Ampere GPU in comparison to the earlier Nvidia GPU architectures.

In conclusion, the relatively new synchronous mode of GPU computing seems promising for the HPC area since it allows linking the hierarchy of parallelism and the hierarchy of memory. The arithmetic intensity which is unobtainable in the asynchronous mode together with a sufficiently good implementation of synchronization makes the locality wall issue surmountable.

References

1. Ampule: minimalistic tool designed for repeated non-interactive processing and plotting of tabular data. https://github.com/Toucandy/ampule. Accessed 15 Apr 2021
2. CUDA C++ programming guide v11.2.2. https://docs.nvidia.com/cuda/cuda-c-programming-guide/index.html. Accessed 15 Apr 2021
3. CUDA toolkit documentation v11.2.2. https://docs.nvidia.com/cuda/. Accessed 15 Apr 2021
4. Top500 supercomputer list. https://top500.org/lists/top500/2020/11/. Accessed 15 Apr 2021
5. Bhatnagar, P.L., Gross, E.P., Krook, M.: A model for collision processes in gases. I. Small amplitude processes in charged and neutral one-component systems. Phys. Rev. **94**(3), 511 (1954)

6. Cabezas, V.C., Püschel, M.: Extending the roofline model: bottleneck analysis with microarchitectural constraints. In: 2014 IEEE International Symposium on Workload Characterization (IISWC), pp. 222–231. IEEE (2014)

7. Dijkstra, E.W.: Cooperating sequential processes. In: The Origin of Concurrent Programming, pp. 65–138. Springer, New York (1968). https://doi.org/10.1007/978-1-4614-5468-7_18

8. Ilic, A., Pratas, F., Sousa, L.: Beyond the roofline: cache-aware power and energy-efficiency modeling for multi-cores. IEEE Trans. Comput. **66**(1), 52–58 (2016)

9. Levchenko, V., Zakirov, A., Perepelkina, A.: GPU implementation of ConeTorre algorithm for fluid dynamics simulation. In: Malyshkin, V. (ed.) PaCT 2019. LNCS, vol. 11657, pp. 199–213. Springer, Cham (2019). https://doi.org/10.1007/978-3-030-25636-4_16

10. Levchenko, V., Perepelkina, A.: Locally recursive non-locally asynchronous algorithms for stencil computation. Lobachevskii J. Math. **39**(4), 552–561 (2018)

11. Lorenzo, O.G., Pena, T.F., Cabaleiro, J.C., Pichel, J.C., Rivera, F.F.: 3DYRM: a dynamic roofline model including memory latency information. J. Supercomput. **70**(2), 696–708 (2014)

12. McKee, S.A.: Reflections on the memory wall. In: Proceedings of the 1st conference on Computing frontiers, p. 162 (2004)

13. McKinney, W., et al.: Pandas: a foundational python library for data analysis and statistics. Python High Perform. Sci. Comput. **14**(9), 1–9 (2011)

14. Perepelkina, A., Levchenko, V., Zakirov, A.: Extending the problem data size for GPU simulation beyond the GPU memory storage with LRnLA algorithms. J. Phys: Conf. Ser. **1740**, 012054 (2021)

15. Pershin, I., Levchenko, V., Perepelkina, A.: GPU implementation of a stencil code with more than 90% of the peak theoretical performance. In: Voevodin, V., Sobolev, S. (eds.) RuSCDays 2019. CCIS, vol. 1129, pp. 51–63. Springer, Cham (2019). https://doi.org/10.1007/978-3-030-36592-9_5

16. Pershin, I.S., Levchenko, V.D., Perepelkina, A.Y.: Performance limits study of stencil codes on modern GPGPUs. Supercomput. Front. Innov. **6**(2), 86–101 (2019)

17. Succi, S.: The Lattice Boltzmann Equation: For Complex States of Flowing Matter. Oxford University Press, Oxford (2018)

18. Virtanen, P., et al.: SciPy 1.0: fundamental algorithms for scientific computing in python. Nat. Methods **17**(3), 261–272 (2020)

19. Williams, S., Waterman, A., Patterson, D.: Roofline: an insightful visual performance model for multicore architectures. Commun. ACM **52**(4), 65–76 (2009)

20. Yount, C., Duran, A.: Effective use of large high-bandwidth memory caches in HPC stencil computation via temporal wave-front tiling. In: 2016 7th International Workshop on Performance Modeling, Benchmarking and Simulation of High Performance Computer Systems (PMBS), pp. 65–75. IEEE, Salt Lake (2016). http://ieeexplore.ieee.org/document/7836415/

21. Zakirov, A., Perepelkina, A., Levchenko, V., Khilkov, S.: Streaming techniques: revealing the natural concurrency of the lattice Boltzmann method. J. Supercomput., 1–19 (2021)

Rust Language for Supercomputing Applications

Andrey Bychkov[1] and Vsevolod Nikolskiy[1,2(✉)] ⓘ

[1] National Research University Higher School of Economics,
Moscow, Russian Federation
{abychkov,v.nikolskiy}@hse.ru
[2] Joint Institute for High Temperatures of RAS, Moscow, Russia

Abstract. Rust is a promising compiled programming language that has gained in popularity in recent years, as well as support from corporations. It allows one to create efficient code, but it also provides a higher level of security and predictability. In this paper, we study how Rust is currently ready for building supercomputing applications. Performance testing when creating new code, using math libraries, and using multithreading shows that the language is capable of delivering C++-level performance without any special effort. MPI benchmarking on the cluster shows that the technology does work without the overhead.

Keywords: Rust language · MPI · Rayon · Shared-memory parallelism · BLAS

1 Introduction

Most scientific and supercomputer software is written in C, C++, and Fortran. These languages have long and rightfully taken their place since they have many advantages. Their popularity is an advantage itself: these languages are familiar to most developers and there is a wealth of educational and reference material available to learn them. They have support in all supercomputing distributions, including build tools, debugging tools, profiling tools, and a wide variety of IDEs. They support various parallelization technologies including MPI and OpenMP, and GPU technologies. These languages allow one to create very fast code and provides a large set of ready-made highly optimized libraries.

On the other hand, the disadvantages of these languages are significantly manifested in the development of scientific software. The development of scientific software is often carried out by scientists and researchers who have specialized education in their subject area and only use technologies to solve their problems, but they do not have the same high qualifications in software development. In addition, a large amount of code is created to solve specific problems in the framework of research projects without expectations of further support and is not accompanied by sufficient documentation and testing. In such conditions, the highest flexibility of the C/C++ languages and countless ways to cause a

V. Voevodin and S. Sobolev (Eds.): RuSCDays 2021, CCIS 1510, pp. 391–403, 2021.
https://doi.org/10.1007/978-3-030-92864-3_30

hard-to-localize error can be an obstacle to the growth of projects and the cooperation of the developers. It is characteristic that in some projects, additional conventions and restrictions on the use of the language are introduced to provide more predictability of the code.

The Rust language looks like an interesting option for developing supercomputer applications. It was introduced in 2009 to Mozilla Research as a replacement for C++ with a focus on safety and efficiency in concurrent application development. Moreover, it is a binary compiled language that works without a garbage collector or runtime environment. Rust keeps access to the lowest level - sometimes it is even positioned as a system language, and the use of Rust in the Linux kernel is discussed. As it stands, the language compiler uses the LLVM backend and provides a high level of optimization and performance. At the same time, the language offers higher guarantees of safety and reliability by the ownership and borrowing system and the powerful type system.

Initially, there was skepticism about the language (there are quite a few initiatives of this kind, most of which will forever remain only small academic projects) but over the years, the language has developed significantly and today continues to rapidly gain popularity. It not only won community love [1], but also received the support of the corporations. In 2021, the autonomous non-profit organization Rust Foundation [2] was founded by AWS, Huawei, Google, Microsoft, and Mozilla, all of which use the language for their own purposes.

Apparently, Rust may soon appear in Linux distributions. In this study, we want to answer the question of whether Rust is currently ready for use in new supercomputing projects and what difficulties may arise. We ran a series of experiments to answers the questions that will be presented in the following chapters: 1) literature review; 2) comparing Rust with C++ when writing simple code from scratch and using existing math libraries; 3) the use of multithreading in systems with shared memory, e.g. within a single node; 4) the use of MPI for programming clusters and creating massively parallel codes.

2   Related Work

In the systematic mapping study [3] the authors analyzed 420 articles from relevant digital libraries to characterize the main paradigms and properties of programming languages used in high-performance computing. The expert sample and the literature sample of the study both demonstrate the dominance of C/C++. The expert sample also confirms the importance of such technologies as MPI, OpenMP, and CUDA. Nevertheless, Rust language is not mentioned in the study, even though some more exotic technologies are presented.

In [4] the authors present programmability studies undertaken by Sun Microsystems in its participation in the DARPA High Productivity Computing Systems (HPCS) program. It is suggested that existing languages including Fortran meet the requirements, and the main difficulties in HPC come from sources other than languages. On the other hand, the scale of software projects is important in this matter, and the transition to larger projects increases the role of expressiveness and reliability of languages.

The survey [5] aims to characterize the MPI usage in HPC applications. It confirms the previous conclusions that C++ is the dominant language in MPI programs. The authors noticed that about 2/3 of the programs use a mixture of MPI and some multithreading models like OpenMP. This shows that safe multithreading capabilities in Rust are very relevant in the supercomputing industry. Also, it is worth noting that most programs (42%) rely only on MPI 1.0 functions. This means that full coverage of the original functionality of modern MPI implementations is not required to achieve the applicability of MPI libraries in an emerging programming language.

The paper [6] discusses the Rmpi library and tools. The library provides access to the MPI functions in Rust and aims to stay very close to the original C interface. The paper presents a set of MPI latency and delay benchmarks that show that Rust is compatible with C. However, at the moment Rmpi only includes a subset of the original interface.

Technical report for the Los Alamos National Laboratory [7] discusses the use of Rust in HPC. The presentation considers MPI, shared memory parallelism, matrix management, vectorization, and GPU acceleration. The author of the presentation is also the contributor to the RSMPI library, which is used in this study. The report refers to 2018 and since then, many of the covered topics have been developed.

In [8] the authors used the LLVM backend to generate GPU kernels directly from Rust. They used very low-level features but Rust was used to build higher-level abstractions. Since that time, there have been many changes in both Rust and GPU programming, but the article demonstrates the technical capabilities and high expressiveness of the language Unfortunately, there is currently no established way to program GPUs in Rust.

The first empirical study on real-world Rust usage [9] sheds light on the real issues and difficulties in using Rust, while most of the related literature focuses on the benefits of Rust. The authors found plenty of blocking and non-blocking concurrency bugs. They propose solutions to the identified classes of problems by the amplification of the Rust bug detectors.

Already in 2015, Rust-bio [10] was published. It is an open-source library for bioinformatics. This is an example of a successful application of Rust in computational biology and is still active and has many contributors. In [11] Rust was used for astrophysics. The researchers compared the performance of Rust, Fortran, C, and Go on a simple benchmark problem, and Rust initially showed the best performance. The authors describe positive experiences of using the language in their field.

3   Simple Code and Mathematics Libraries

The C, C++, and Fortran ecosystem often uses GNU compilers or architecture-specific compilers such as the Intel compiler in high-performance computing. Rust, on the other hand, uses LLVM as its backend, which can be a source of speed drawbacks compared to some of the compilers in the above languages.

In this section, we will first compare the speed of the code generated by the C++ and Rust compilers with examples from linear algebra. Next, we will measure the overhead when using wrappers around foreign libraries in Rust using the LAPACK library as an example.

3.1   Benchmarks

For this and further sections we will use a laptop for numerical experiments with the following parameters:

- Intel(R) Core(TM) i7-8750H CPU. The upper frequency limit in turbo boost mode is at 4.10 GHz. Despite dynamic CPU frequency is widely used in modern HPC [12], but it can significantly complicate the correct interpretation of the microbenchmarks. In this regard, we fix the frequency of our CPU to 3.90 GHz.
- Ubuntu 20.04 operating system via WSL2 on Windows 10.
- We compile C++ and Rust by g++ 10.2, clang++ 10.0 and rustc 1.54.0-nightly compilers.

For C++ benchmarks we use Google-benchmark framework. Each function is repeated at least 1000 times, and the number of repetitions is increased for small matrices. To remove artifacts, we run the tests 10 times and calculate the average.

For Rust benchmarks use Criterion framework. The setup is similar to C++ benchmarks. Wet also set warm-up time explicitly to at least 3 s, confidence level to 95%, and minimal execution time to 10 min by using additional Criterion features.

3.2   Matrix Multiplication

We start exploring possibilities of Rust compiler with a common linear algebra problem - matrix multiplication. A naive solution gave us almost the same performance for all compilers that is presented in Fig. 1. It also shows that it is possible to get much more performant results. Implementing a cache-aware version of the algorithm has drastically changed the results. Figure 2 illustrates that the performance of the Rust code has not improved as much as the C++ code. By using analyzers such as LLVM-MCA, we found that loop unrolling is not used as much for Rust code as it is for C++. Also, analysis shows that memory dependence prediction has performed poorly for Rust code. In order to overcome these challenges, we tried unsafe disabling bounding checks and forced loops unrolling by using unroll crate [13]. Unfortunately, these methods have not changed the performance. However, rewriting code *a Rust way* by using iterators and high-level functions increased the performance by ∼30%. It was easier to force the compiler to optimize the C++ code and use vector operations. Despite our efforts, common middle-end optimization results does not achieve expected level of performance in Rust. As it has been shown in [14] optimization in Rust

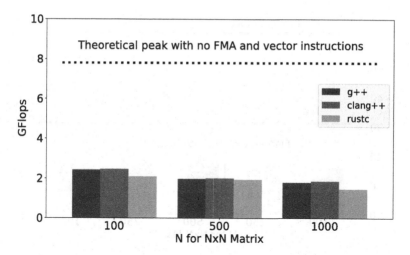

Fig. 1. Performance comparison of naive matrix multiplication for pure Rust and pure C++. Performance is measured in GFlops and is calculated as the number of operations $2N^3$ divided by the consumed time and higher performance is better.

can require specific skills and deep understanding of type system and compiler. However, the example of highly optimized libraries in Rust shows that you can get closer to peak performance. One of such libraries is considered in Sect. 3.3.

3.3   Linear Algebra Libraries

State-of-the-art libraries in HPC are often efficient solutions to many problems both in performance and in programming time. Thus the ability to use foreign language libraries in Rust appears to be important. In order to measure possible side effects, we evaluate benchmarks for the Rust wrapper of BLAS/LAPACK implemented in OpenBLAS [15].

Figure 3 shows the difference between linear algebra library written in pure Rust *nalgebra*, its optimized version coupled with BLAS *nalgebra-lapack*, and BLAS wrappers for C++ and Rust. As we can observe, the difference between libraries using BLAS is negligible, while pure Rust library has a significant loss of speed. When comparing, it was noticeable that the performance drawdown was largely due to the difference in the algorithmic component.

Figure 4 illustrates that the Rust wrapper for BLAS does not introduce any performance leaks. We also compare BLAS results with matmultiply crate [16] written in pure Rust. It appears that matmultiply is approximately two times slower than BLAS which is still a good result. It also proves that matrix multiplication, as well as other functions, can be effectively written in Rust. The authors

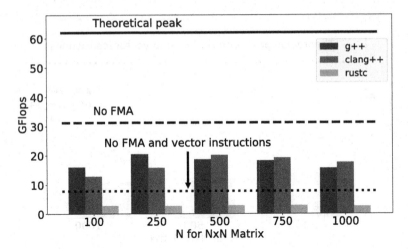

Fig. 2. Performance comparison of cache-aware matrix multiplication for pure Rust and pure C++. Performance is measured in GFlops and is calculated as the number of operations $2N^3$ divided by the consumed time.

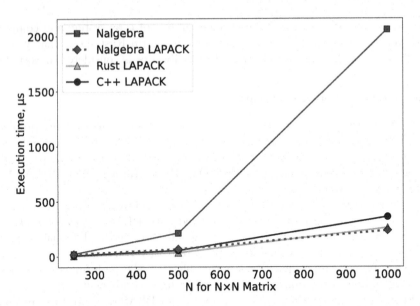

Fig. 3. Performance comparison of SVD operation for pure Rust library and various BLAS/LAPCK wrappers.

of matmultiply achieved this by explicitly using SIMD, FMA, and modern algorithms, which is in good agreement with our hypothesis of the performance drawdown in Sect. 3.2.

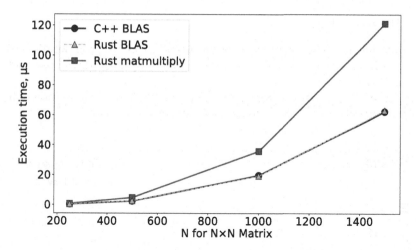

Fig. 4. Performance comparison of matrix multiplication operation for Rust and C++ BLAS wrappers accompanied with pure Rust matrix multiplication crate.

4   Shared-Memory Parallelism

Shared memory parallelism is an interprocess communication technique in which memory may be simultaneously accessed by multiple threads. Libraries that provide an interface for working with shared memory are usually coupled together with the task scheduler: an algorithm that distributes tasks among processes. The common approach for working with shared memory in C, C++, and Fortran is the OpenMP library. OpenMP was initially aimed at effectively structured parallelism, e.g. `omp for` utilizes the *work sharing* scheduling approach where each work item is scheduled onto a processor when it is spawned. The later OpenMP versions add the task-based programming model [17]. However, it is difficult to combine structured and unstructured parallelism [18]. On the contrary, Rust libraries typically use the *work stealing* approach [19]. In a work-stealing scheduler, each processor has a queue of initially distributed work items. During the execution of a program, any work item can spawn another one and put it in the queue. When a processor empties its queue, it can "steal" a work item from others processes. Thus, the use of work-stealing simplifies the design of parallel programs, allowing one to effectively create and utilize new work items, as well as adjust the initial distribution of works for a specific task. However, in scientific computing, shared memory parallelism often requires only to parallelize a loop with a predictable execution time of work items. Thus, the benefits of work-stealing may not be used and become sources of overhead. In the course of our work, we will compare the OpenMP library in C++ and the Rayon library [20] in Rust.

4.1 Benchmarks

The experiment was performed by using benchmarks. All computation times are given in microseconds and were obtained on a laptop with the parameters, presented in Sect. 3.1.

Figure 5 shows the benchmark results for trapezoidal rule integration of function $\tan^3(\text{erf}(x))$ for $x \in [0, 1]$ divided into 10^7 intervals.

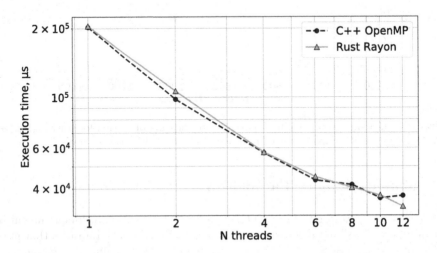

Fig. 5. Performance comparison between C++ OpenMP and Rust Rayon in numerical integration benchmark

5   MPI

MPI is the standard choice for building massively parallel applications for computer clusters with low-latency interconnect. Moreover, with the shared memory extension added in MPI-3, it is able to replace OpenMP [21], which is considered in Sect. 4.

Despite the high level of abstraction and usability that MPI provides, there are still many errors that a system written in C or C++ cannot recover from at runtime. For instance, there are numerous memory-related errors such as segmentation faults, use-after-free, and dereferencing null-pointer. There are also issues with accessing memory in a parallel system, such as data races, deadlock, etc.

Rust-mpi library aims to solve some of the problems mentioned above by using features of Rust itself. It provides a higher-level interface to mpi.h with the following guarantees:

1. Memory safety;
2. Absence of data race;
3. Absence of undefined behavior;
4. Incorporating verbosity into types.

The following is a detailed description of the described guarantees.

5.1 Memory Safety

Rust guarantees that certain memory-related errors will not appear in safe code:

1. Use-after-free;
2. Double free;
3. Dereferencing null-pointer;
4. Buffer overflow;
5. Uninitialized variables.

Rust also guarantees that there are no memory leaks in safe code. This is achieved with the help of ownership and borrowing techniques [2]. The only memory error we have managed to find is an error in logic when interacting with buffers. For example, when one gathers data into a buffer with not enough capacity, a runtime error is inevitable.

5.2 Absence of Data Races

Data races are impossible in pure Rust: either there exists only one mutable reference to the memory slice or multiple read-only references. In the case of MPI, one cannot have a buffer where data is written and sent at the same time. In case if you have to reuse the buffer, you either have to use an immutable copy of the buffer or provide a code that can guarantee for every slice of the buffer that there can not be a data race there.

5.3 Absence of Undefined Behavior

There is no undefined behavior (UB) in pure Rust. For the unsafe code, Rust strongly suggests using wrappers of every external function and every unsafe Rust function with possible UB. According to this paradigm, rust-mpi introduces a distinct mpi-sys library, that wraps functions in mpi.h and handles errors.

5.4   Incorporating Verbosity into Types

Rust can hide context information inside of its types, which is utilized by rust-mpi. Thus, one does not have to specify the sizes of buffers and their types when using rust-mpi. For example, *Gather* operation in C++

```
MPI_Gather(sendbuf, send_len, MPI_INT32_T,
           rbuffer, rbuffer_len, MPI_INT32_T,
           root_rank, MPI_COMM_WORLD);
```

is converted into Rust like

```
root_process.gather_into_root(&sendbuf[..], &mut rbuffer[..]);
```

5.5   Benchmarks

Of course, all of these guarantees require certain overhead costs. However, most of this overhead should be eliminated at compile time according to the *zero-cost-abstraction* concept of Rust. In this section, we compare the rust-mpi library with pure mpi. Our experiments are a series of benchmarks of the main MPI operations. The benchmarks were evaluated by HSE HPC cluster cHARISMa [22,23] by using 16 MPI threads in various node configurations. The cluster consists of 26 computing nodes, each node includes two Intel Xeon Gold 6152 (22×3.70 GHz), the nodes are connected by InfiniBand EDR (2×100 Gbit/s).

Figure 6 describe All-Reduce and Reduce operations for various node configurations. Each subfigure has a label in form $N - T$, where N is the number of nodes and T is the number of MPI processes for each node. Subfigure 6 on the top-left corner describes a benchmark that runs on 16 distinct nodes with a single MPI thread on each one. This benchmark mostly measures internode communication speed and we have not observed any distinct difference between rust-mpi and pure mpi for any MPI operation. Subfigure 6 on the center-right describes results for the run with 4 distinct nodes with 4 MPI threads on each one. This benchmark as well as benchmarks for the other MPI operations shows that Rust compares favorably to pure mpi, which is an unexpected outcome. Further research has shown that benchmarks on a single node reach a similar performance. Thus, we hypothesize that in a highly loaded cluster, the comparison of a small number of nodes is unreliable (but still consistent in our experiments). To verify our results, we will launch benchmarks when the cluster is mostly unloaded.

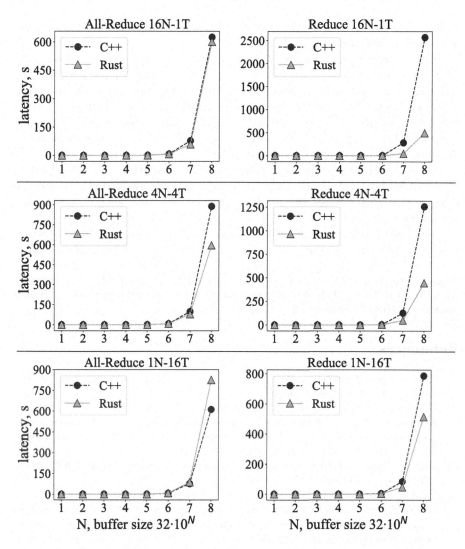

Fig. 6. Comparison of All-Reduce and Reduce operations for various architectures. The y-axis is latency in seconds and the x-axis is the buffer size, described as $32 \cdot 10^{N}$

6   Conclusion

In this article, we have provided an overview of Rust and a performance comparison between C/C++ and Rust. The code generated by the Rust language ecosystem has been shown to be competitive compared to C++. It was also shown that the parallelization tools do not lose their effectiveness in the transition from C++ to Rust while receiving guarantees of Rust. During the development of benchmarks, it became clear that the restrictions on the code imposed by Rust radically change the programming paradigm compared to C++, pushing us to higher-level abstractions.

In our experiment, we found that the first naive implementation of matrix multiplication algorithms in both languages shows very similar performance. However, it is far from the peak performance of the processor. On the other hand, an example of state-of-the-art implementation of matrix multiplication shows that on Rust one can get much closer to this value. The optimization process in Rust requires specific skills. It seems that further improvements to the optimizer could make this process easier.

We discovered the unexpected difference between Rust and C++ performance in MPI latency benchmarks. It is important to revalidate the results by using unload cluster since the results shown in the graph were obtained on a partially loaded system.

As it has been shown in [8], Rust is capable of GPU programming. In further work, we would study modern Rust GPU tools and measure their performance.

Acknowledgment. This work is supported by the Russian Science Foundation under grant № 20-71-10127. This research was supported in part through computational resources of HPC facilities at NRU HSE.

References

1. Stack overflow developer survey. https://insights.stackoverflow.com/survey/2020# most-loved-dreaded-and-wanted
2. Rust foundation. https://foundation.rust-lang.org/
3. Amaral, V., et al.: Programming languages for data-intensive HPC applications: a systematic mapping study. Parallel Comput. **91**, 102584 (2020). https://www.sciencedirect.com/science/article/pii/S0167819119301759
4. Loh, E.: The ideal HPC programming language. Commun. ACM **53**(7), 42–47 (2010). https://doi.org/10.1145/1785414.1785433
5. Laguna, I., Marshall, R., Mohror, K., Ruefenacht, M., Skjellum, A., Sultana, N.: A large-scale study of MPI usage in open-source HPC applications. In: Proceedings of the International Conference for High Performance Computing, Networking, Storage and Analysis, SC 2019. Association for Computing Machinery, New York (2019). https://doi.org/10.1145/3295500.3356176
6. Kübrich, M.: Integration and Test of RUST Tool Support for MPI. Bachelorarbeit, Technische Universität München, Munich (2020)
7. Gaspar, A.J.: Rust in HPC. Los Alamos National Laboratory technical report, December 2018
8. Holk, E., Pathirage, M., Chauhan, A., Lumsdaine, A., Matsakis, N.D.: GPU programming in Rust: implementing high-level abstractions in a systems-level language. In: 2013 IEEE International Symposium on Parallel Distributed Processing, Workshops and Phd Forum, pp. 315–324 (2013)
9. Qin, B., Chen, Y., Yu, Z., Song, L., Zhang, Y.: Understanding memory and thread safety practices and issues in real-world Rust programs. In: Proceedings of the 41st ACM SIGPLAN Conference on Programming Language Design and Implementation, PLDI 2020, pp. 763–779. Association for Computing Machinery, New York (2020). https://doi.org/10.1145/3385412.3386036

10. Köster, J.: Rust-Bio: a fast and safe bioinformatics library. Bioinformatics **32**(3), 444–446 (2015). https://doi.org/10.1093/bioinformatics/btv573

11. Blanco-Cuaresma, S., Bolmont, E.: What can the programming language Rust do for astrophysics? Proc. Int. Astron. Union **12**(S325), 341–344 (2016)

12. Calore, E., Gabbana, A., Schifano, S.F., Tripiccione, R.: Evaluation of DVFS techniques on modern HPC processors and accelerators for energy-aware applications. Concurr. Comput. Pract. Exp. **29**(12), e4143 (2017). https://onlinelibrary.wiley.com/doi/abs/10.1002/cpe.4143

13. Larionov, E.: Crate unroll. https://docs.rs/unroll/0.1.5/unroll/

14. Lindgren, M.: Comparing parallel Rust and C++. https://parallel-rust-cpp.github.io/introduction.html

15. Ukhov, I., Teramura, T.: openblas-src: the rust package provides a source of BLAS and LAPACK via OpenBLAS. https://github.com/blas-lapack-rs/openblas-src

16. Crate matmultiply. https://github.com/bluss/matrixmultiply

17. Duran, A., Teruel, X., Ferrer, R., Martorell, X., Ayguade, E.: Barcelona OpenMP tasks suite: a set of benchmarks targeting the exploitation of task parallelism in OpenMP. In: 2009 International Conference on Parallel Processing, pp. 124–131 (2009)

18. Maroñas, M., Sala, K., Mateo, S., Ayguadé, E., Beltran, V.: Worksharing tasks: an efficient way to exploit irregular and fine-grained loop parallelism. In: 2019 IEEE 26th International Conference on High Performance Computing, Data, and Analytics (HiPC), pp. 383–394 (2019)

19. Matsakis, N.: Rayon: data parallelism in Rust. https://smallcultfollowing.com/babysteps/blog/2015/12/18/rayon-data-parallelism-in-rust/

20. Matsakis, N., Stone, J.: Rayon - a data parallelism library for Rust. https://github.com/rayon-rs/rayon

21. Szustak, L., Wyrzykowski, R., Halbiniak, K., Bratek, P.: Toward heterogeneous MPI+MPI programming: comparison of OpenMP and MPI shared memory models. In: Schwardmann, U., et al. (eds.) Euro-Par 2019. LNCS, vol. 11997, pp. 270–281. Springer, Cham (2020). https://doi.org/10.1007/978-3-030-48340-1_21

22. Kondratyuk, N., et al.: Performance and scalability of materials science and machine learning codes on the state-of-art hybrid supercomputer architecture. In: Voevodin, V., Sobolev, S. (eds.) RuSCDays 2019. CCIS, vol. 1129, pp. 597–609. Springer, Cham (2019). https://doi.org/10.1007/978-3-030-36592-9_49

23. Kostenetskiy, P., Chulkevich, R., Kozyrev, V.: HPC resources of the higher school of economics. In: Journal of Physics: Conference Series, vol. 1740, p. 012050 (2021)

Study of the Algorithms Information Structure as the Basis of a Training Workshop

Alexander Antonov[1,2(✉)] [iD] and Nikita Volkov[1,3]

[1] Lomonosov Moscow State University, Moscow, Russian Federation
[2] Moscow Center of Fundamental and Applied Mathematics,
Moscow, Russian Federation
[3] "TESIS" Company, Moscow, Russian Federation

Abstract. The study of the algorithms parallel structure is becoming increasingly important for any specialists dealing with high-performance computing. Theoretical information on this topic is included in various training courses of many higher educational institutions. However, the usual form of practical training is only the execution of tasks for the parallel implementation of specific algorithms. In the course "Supercomputing Simulation and Technologies" at the Faculty of Computational Mathematics and Cybernetics at Lomonosov Moscow State University, we have proposed a new type of practical task related to the study, description and visualization of the algorithms parallel structure. Using the AlgoView visualization system developed by the authors, the study of the information structure can be carried out without access to high-performance computing systems. The same approach is planned to be used in the AlgoWiki Open encyclopedia of parallel algorithmic features.

Keywords: Algorithms information structure · High-performance computing education · Supercomputing simulation and technologies · Parallel programming · Supercomputers · Algolang · AlgoView · AlgoWiki

1 Introduction

Parallel computing is used everywhere today. In any modern supercomputer there is a huge potential for parallelism, the effective use of which allows one to reach the maximum level of performance. But in order to use the existing hardware parallelism, it is necessary to unleash the parallelism potential of applications running on a given supercomputer. This is a daunting task that is being addressed by many research groups around the world.

In some cases, the compiler or even some hardware circuits can cope with solving the problem of detecting parallelism. But in the general case, these approaches are not applicable or ineffective. There are some tools available to find the parallelism of sequential programs, but their applicability is also very limited.

© Springer Nature Switzerland AG 2021
V. Voevodin and S. Sobolev (Eds.): RuSCDays 2021, CCIS 1510, pp. 404–414, 2021.
https://doi.org/10.1007/978-3-030-92864-3_31

Within the framework of various training courses, theoretical approaches to solving this problem are considered. It is generally accepted that the study of the theory in this case must necessarily be accompanied by the solution of practical problems, allowing one to better assimilate and consolidate the studied material. Most often, students are asked to parallelize some algorithms and check the efficiency of the resulting parallel implementation on some of the available high-performance computing systems [1–3].

This paper describes another type of parallel application analysis workshop that does not involve the use of supercomputers. In this approach, the algorithm parallel structure is described in a special language called Algolang, after which it is visualized and explored using the AlgoView algorithms information structure visualization system. This workshop was tested in 2020 as part of the training course "Supercomputing Simulation and Technologies" at the Faculty of Computational Mathematics and Cybernetics at Lomonosov Moscow State University.

The technologies used in this workshop are also actively used in the Algo-Wiki Open Encyclopedia of Parallel Algorithmic Features [4,5]. The algorithm description in AlgoWiki consists of two parts [6]. The first describes the machine-independent properties of the algorithms themselves. The core of the description of parallel properties of algorithms is the analysis of their information structure. Its visualization and study of properties become possible when using the Algo-View algorithms information structure visualization system. The second part of the algorithm description in AlgoWiki contains the properties of specific software implementations [7], complemented by the results of running these implementations on various high-performance computing platforms [8].

2   Practical Assignment 2020

The practical assignments in the course "Supercomputing Simulation and Technologies" took various forms [9]:

- Practical Assignments on the Study and Description of the Structure and Properties of Algorithms (2016);
- Practical Assignments on Scalability Study (2017–2019);
- Practical Assignments on the Information Structure of Algorithms and Programs (2019).

The main feature of the practical assignment variant in 2020 was the use of a special language for describing the algorithms information structure called Algolang and the AlgoView algorithms information structure visualization system. Previously, this system was not available for mass use, but now a web interface has been prepared within the developed Algoload system, which allowed more than 200 students to independently use the capabilities of the AlgoView system.

The idea of this practical assignment was to give every student a piece of C code, ask him/her to write its information graph description in a proposed language and analyze the resulting visualization, defining the following information graph properties:

- Vertex count;
- Edge count;
- Critical route length;
- Maximum parallel form width;
- Edge types count;
- Presence of parametric edges (those are edges with length defined by exact values of external parameters present in information graph description);
- Regular subregions count (a regular subregion is a set of vertices that all have outgoing edges of the same type).

3   Algolang Language

3.1   General Approach

The main goal of this research is developing a language for information structure description. This language is supposed to be somewhere in between algorithm implementation source code and direct description of algorithm information graph through a list of vertices and edges. Our work began with specifying language requirements, some of which are conceptual, while others are purely technical and refer to making the use of language more convenient. Thus, we came up with the initial list of requirements:

- An algorithm information graph is described, not the algorithm itself;
- Computational blocks of the initial algorithm are retained by its information graph description;
- Description contains enough information for automated build of graph 3D-models;
- A widespread file format should be used for storing descriptions.

Overall, the proposed language is not a programming language, even though the descriptions are supposed to be automatically visualized later on. It was decided to implement visualization environment through further development of our previously created AlgoView visualization system described in [10] and [11]. The difference in concept is only the language used for graph description. Technical differences are, however, more fundamental and will be spoken of later in this paper.

3.2   Language Description

Algolang is a markup language for algorithm information graphs. It's designed for compact yet meaningful description of a graph that can be used as a base for building its visualization in a form of 3D-model. Algolang implicitly describes graph vertices and edges through logical expressions that define their existence. In case a description is made based on algorithm implementation program, these logical expressions, as a rule, refer to logical expressions seen in the program's source code.

Algolang is applicable to program fragments that belong to an extended linear class. The concept of linear class is known from [12]. We're then extending it by allowing logical expressions that define variable values, loop borders and control switches to be nonlinear. The typical structure of a graph description provided in Algolang is as follows:

1. The entire graph is described as a set of pivot polyhedrons [12]. Every polyhedron is described once regardless of how many assignment operators refer to it.
2. Every pivot polyhedron description consists of two parts. Firstly, ranges for every parameter defining its pivot cycle [12] are given. Then, a separate linear iterations space [12] and a set of data dependencies is described for every assignment operator referring to the given polyhedron.
3. Every linear iterations space is described as a set of operation blocks each containing a function that returns a Boolean value for each integer point P within a pivot polyhedron. This value for a given point determines whether the vertex exists. Every operation block also has a set of dependency blocks in it; each of those refers to an integer point Q in some pivot polyhedron. The edge (P,Q) is existent when and only when both Boolean function returns true for P and Q is known to be an existent integer point.

Below the Extended Backus-Naur form (EBNF) [13] for basic Algolang syntax is given:

```
<Algorithm> ::== <algo><Parameters> { <Block> } </algo>
<Parameters> ::== <params>{ <Parameter> } </params>
<Parameter> ::== <param name = "<Name>" type = "<Type>[value =
"<Number>"]></param>
<Type> ::== int |float
<Block> ::== <block[id = "<Number>"] dims = "<Number>">{Argument}
{Vertex}</block>
<Argument> ::== <arg name = "<Name>" val = "<RegExp>..<RegExp>">
</arg>
<Vertex> ::== <vertex condition = "<RegExp>" type = "<Number>">
{Source}</vertex>
<Source> ::== <in [bsrc = "<Number>"] src = "<RegExp>{,<RegExp>}">
</in>
```

Here, <Number> is any integer value, <Name> is any ASCII string. <RegExp> is, in theory, any regular expression, but our own software that works with Algolang relies on an Exprtk open-source library when it comes to <RegExp> evaluations and it's thus recommended to follow their rules for writing <RegExp>. Name fields of <Argument> and <Parameter> can be used as variables in <RegExp>. In Fig. 1, an example of information algorithm description in Algolang is given.

```
<?xml version="1.0" encoding="UTF-8"?>
<algo>
  <params>
    <param name = "N" type = "int" value = "10"></param>
  </params>
  <block id = "0" dims = "2">
    <arg name = "i" val = "1..N"></arg>
    <arg name = "j" val = "1..N"></arg>
    <vertex condition = "(2 * i + j) <= (N + 1)" type = "1">
    </vertex>
    <vertex condition = "((2 * i + j) > (N + 1)) and ((i + j) <= N)" type = "1">
      <in src = "i - 1, j + 2 * (N + 1 - i - j)"></in>
    </vertex>
    <vertex condition = "((i + j) > N) and ((2 * i + j) <= (2 * N))" type = "1">
      <in src = "i, j - 1 - 2 * ((i + j) - N - 1)"></in>
    </vertex>
    <vertex condition = "((2 * i + j) > (2 * N)) and ((i + j) <= (2 * N - 1))" type = "1">
      <in src = "i - 1 * (2 * i + j - 2 * N), 1"></in>
    </vertex>
    <vertex condition = "((i + j) > (2 * N - 1))" type = "1">
    </vertex>
  </block>
</algo>
```

Fig. 1. An example of information algorithm description in Algolang

4   Algoload System

The entire system is deployed on Docker containers [14] started within a Kubernetes cluster [15]. The cluster itself runs on hardware that is part of MSU SRCC service network. Two versions of the system were tested. The first one consisted of two Docker containers, one designed to run instances of a new 3D-model generator within it, while the other was intended to handle end user interactions. However, further tests showed that for internal use this architecture was an overcomplicated solution and a single container was dealing with the load well enough.

Inner container environment is based on python:3.6-alpine, backed up with a Flask framework [16], which is used to implement web system "business logic", and Gunicorn web server [17], used to deploy the system. All visualization system components are placed within a root folder of the web system /usr/home/websystem and file interactions never touch files outside the environment. This folder's hierarchy strictly follows the web system's hierarchy and is thus needed to be listed here. The folder contains four primary elements:

– User data database file;
– Folder that contains an executable graph builder;
– Folder that contains a web service;
– Folder that contains user work directories.

This web service is definitely the biggest innovation but the detailed investigation of its implementation outside user interaction context does not lie within the subject of this paper.

5   AlgoView Visualization System

Creation of a new language specified for descripting of information graphs structure arose a set of new demands. Firstly, it was necessary to rebuild the core of the previously developed AlgoView visualization system [10]. Moreover, the server component mentioned in [11] is now the one and only supported interface; the end user no longer needs to install client applications on his system.

Still, some of the system's components have gone through certain changes besides redesign of the graph architect for use of newly developed information graph description language. The largest among these changes if the architect's capability of building not only the graph 3D-model itself, but also its basic characteristics, such as maximum depth of cycle nests, parallel form height and width, amount of regular subregions and so on. Viewer module now can, as shown in Fig. 2, display these characteristics within the visualization window. Another small yet important change is the possibility of building graph 3D-models for specific values of external parameters embedded in graph description.

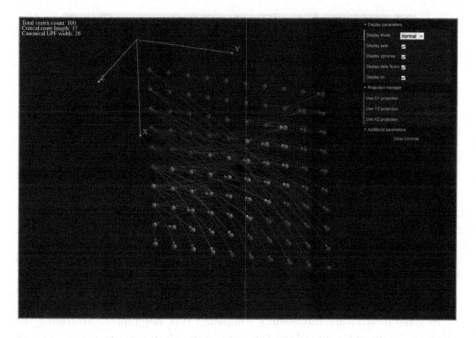

Fig. 2. AlgoView system using

6   Practical Assignment Results

The specific assignment variant of each student was determined by the following parametric fragment of the C program:

```
for(i = 2; i <= n+1; ++i)
   C[i] = C[i+p1] * e;
for(i = 2; i <= n+1; ++i)
   for(j = 2; j <= m+1; ++j)
      B[i][j] = B[i+p2][j+p3] + p4*C[i];
for(i = 2; i <= n+1; ++i){
   A[i][1][1]=(1-p4)*C[i]+B[i][m];
   for(j = 2; j <= m+1; ++j){
      for(k = 1; k <= n-1; ++k)
         A[i][j][k] = A[i][j][k] + p5*A[i-p6][j-(1-p6)][1] +
                                   (1-p5)*A[i-(1-p6)][j-p6][k];
}
```

After the substitution of specific values of the parameters p1..p6, a version of the program was obtained for visualizing and studying its information structure. An example of the resulting variant is shown in Fig. 3.

```
1    for(i = 2; i <= n+1; ++i)
2        C[i] = C[i-2] * e;
3    for(i = 2; i <= n+1; ++i)
4        for(j = 2; j <= m+1; ++j)
5           B[i][j] = B[i-1][j-1] + C[i];
6    for(i = 2; i <= n+1; ++i){
7        A[i][1][1]=B[i][m];
8        for(j = 2; j <= m+1; ++j)
9           for(k = 1; k <= n-1; ++k)
10              A[i][j][k] = A[i][j][k] + A[i][j-1][k];
11   }
```

Fig. 3. A source code variant

Figure 4 shows the description of the fragment from Fig. 3 in the Algolang language, and Fig. 5—a variant of its visualization in the AlgoViev system, obtained in one of the student's works.

This assignment was carried out by 173 students, the results are shown in Table 1.

In general, students successfully completed this assignment. Mastering the Algolang language for describing the algorithms information structure was not a very difficult task, and the active use of the AlgoView visualization system helped to get rid of a number of existing shortcomings, as well as add a number of new useful features.

```xml
<?xml version = "1.0" encoding = "UTF-8"?>
<algo>
    <params>
        <param name = "N" type = "int" value = "5"></param>
        <param name = "M" type = "int" value = "4"></param>
    </params>
    <block id = "0" dims = "1">
        <arg name = "i" val = "2..N+1"></arg>
        <vertex condition = "" type = "1">
            <in src = "i - 2"></in>
        </vertex>
    </block>
    <block id = "1" dims = "2">
        <arg name = "i" val = "2..N+1"></arg>
        <arg name = "j" val = "2..M+1"></arg>
        <vertex condition = "" type = "1">
            <in src = "i - 1, j - 1"></in>
            <in bsrc = "0" src = "i"></in>
        </vertex>
    </block>
    <block id = "2" dims = "3">
        <arg name = "i" val = "2..N+1"></arg>
        <arg name = "j" val = "1..M+1"></arg>
        <arg name = "k" val = "1..N-1"></arg>
        <vertex condition = "(j == 1) and (k == 1)" type = "1">
            <in bsrc = "1" src = "i, M"></in>
        </vertex>
        <vertex condition = "(j > 1) or (k > 1)" type = "1">
            <in src = "i, j - 1, k"></in>
        </vertex>
    </block>
</algo>
```

Fig. 4. Algolang description of the variant

Table 1. Final assessments (2020)

Year	2020
Students	173
5 (Excellent)	136 (78.6%)
4 (Good)	32 (18.5%)
3 (Satisfactory)	2 (1.2%)
2 (Unsatisfactory)	3 (1.7%)
Average mark	4.74

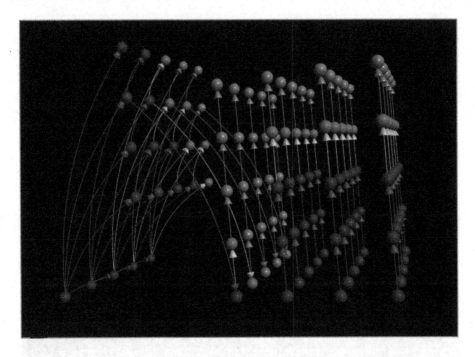

Fig. 5. Visualization of the variant

7   Conclusions

The variant of the practical assignment described in the paper can be used in various training courses, including the topic of parallel computing. In this case, the parallel properties of the algorithm can be investigated without going to a real high-performance computing platform. A workshop held in 2020 as part of the training course "Supercomputing Simulation and Technologies" at the Faculty of Computational Mathematics and Cybernetics at Lomonosov Moscow State University showed the applicability of this approach and the high quality of assimilation of the material by students.

To implement this approach we have developed a Algolang language that allows building 3D-models of an information graph with the help of its description. We have also updated our AlgoView visualization system so it's, firstly, capable of automatically building given models in a form of a list of edges and vertices put on a regular grid in 3D Cartesian space and, secondly, is fully available through our web service. The developed systems were tested with the help of our students, who provided a lot of useful feedback on small bugs and inconveniences that have been worked on. However, two big goals still remain. The first one is a more strict definition of algorithm families the developed language is applicable to, hence the best definition we currently have is all algorithms of extended linear class. The second is direct connection of information graph description to algorithm implementations (source code).

The technologies used to conduct the workshop within the training course "Supercomputing Simulation and Technologies" are also used to study and visualize the algorithms information structure within the AlgoWiki Open encyclopedia of parallel algorithmic features development project.

Acknowledgements. The work on the creation of the Algolang language and the AlgoView visualization system is supported by the Russian Foundation for Basic Research (grant N. 19-07-01030). The work on the development of the functionality of the AlgoWiki system is carried out at Lomonosov Moscow State University with the financial support of the Russian Science Foundation, agreement No. 20-11-20194. The work on the creation and verification of the content formation model in the AlgoWiki system is supported by Russian Ministry of Science and Higher Education, agreement No. 075-15-2019-1621. The research is carried out using the equipment of the shared research facilities of HPC computing resources at Lomonosov Moscow State University [18].

References

1. Meyerov, I., Bastrakov, S., Barkalov, K., Sysoyev, A., Gergel, V.: Parallel numerical methods course for future scientists and engineers. Commun. Comput. Inf. Sci. **793**, 3–13 (2017). https://doi.org/10.1007/978-3-319-71255-0_1

2. Qasem, A.: Modules for teaching parallel performance concepts. In: . Prasad, S.K., Gupta, A., Rosenberg, A., Sussman, A., Weems, C. (eds.) Topics in Parallel and Distributed Computing. Enhancing the Undergraduate Curriculum: Performance, Concurrency, and Programming on Modern Platforms, pp. 59–78. Springer (2018). https://doi.org/10.1007/978-3-319-93109-8

3. Antonov, A.S., Voevodin, Vl.V., Popova, N.N.: Parallel structure of algorithms and training computational technology specialists. J. Phys. Conf. Ser. **1202** (2019). https://doi.org/10.1088/1742-6596/1202/1/012021

4. Open Encyclopedia of Parallel Algorithmic Features. http://algowiki-project.org

5. Voevodin, V., Antonov, A., Dongarra, J.: AlgoWiki: an open Encyclopedia of parallel algorithmic features. Supercomput Front. Innov. **1**(2), 4–18 (2015). https://doi.org/10.14529/jsfi150101

6. Voevodin, V.: An open AlgoWiki encyclopedia of algorithmic features: from mobile to extreme scale. Num. Methods Program. **16**(1), 99–111 (2015). https://doi.org/10.26089/NumMet.v16r111

7. Antonov, A., Voevodin, V., Voevodin, Vl., Teplov, A.: A study of the dynamic characteristics of software implementation as an essential part for a universal description of algorithm properties. In: 24th Euromicro International Conference on Parallel, Distributed, and Network-Based Processing Proceedings, 17th–19th February, pp. 359–363 (2016). https://doi.org/10.1109/PDP.2016.24

8. Antonov, A., Nikitenko, D., Voevodin, Vl.: Algo500 – a new approach to the Joint Analysis of Algorithms and Computers. Lobachevskii J. Math. **8**(41), Special issue "Supercomputing Applications, Algorithms and Software Tools" (2020). https://doi.org/10.1134/S1995080220080041

9. Antonov, A., Voevodin, V.: The algorithms properties and structure study as a mandatory element of modern IT education. Commun. Comput. Inf. Sci. **1331**, 524–535 (2020). https://doi.org/10.1007/978-3-030-64616-5_45

10. Antonov, A.S., Volkov, N.I.: An AlgoView web-visualization system for the Algo-Wiki project. Commun. Comput. Inf. Sci. **753**, 3–13 (2017). https://doi.org/10.1007/978-3-319-67035-5_1

11. Antonov, A., Volkov, N.: Interactive 3D representation as a method of investigating information graph features. Russian supercomputing days. In: Proceedings of the International Conference 24–25 September 2018, Moscow, Russia. Moscow State University, pp. 262–273 (2018). https://doi.org/10.1007/978-3-030-05807-4_50

12. Voevodin, V., Voevodin, Vl.: Parallel Computing. BHV-Petersburg, St. Petersburg. 608 p. (2002)

13. ISO/IEC 14977 : 1996(E). https://www.cl.cam.ac.uk/~mgk25/iso-14977.pdf

14. Merkel, D.: Docker: lightweight Linux containers for consistent development and deployment. Linux J. **239**(2) (2014)

15. Production-Grade Container Orchestration. https://kubernetes.io/

16. Copperwaite, M., Leifer, C.: Learning Flask Framework. Build dynamic, Data Driven Websites and Modern web Applications with Flask. 250 p, Packt Publishing. Birmingham (2015)

17. Gunicorn – Python WSGI HTTP Server for UNIX. https://gunicorn.org/

18. Voevodin, V., et al.: Supercomputer Lomonosov-2: large scale, deep monitoring and fine analytics for the user community. Supercomput. Front. Innov. **6**(2), 4–11 (2019). https://doi.org/10.14529/jsfi190201

The Impact of Compiler Level Optimization on the Performance of Iterative Poisson Solver for Numerical Modeling of Protostellar Disks

Igor Chernykh[1]([✉])[iD], Eduard Vorobyev[2], Vardan Elbakyan[3], and Igor Kulikov[1]

[1] Institute of Computational Mathematics and Mathematical Geophysics SB RAS,
Novosibirsk, Russia
{chernykh,kulikov}@ssd.sscc.ru
[2] University of Vienna, Vienna, Austria
eduard.vorobiev@univie.ac.at
[3] South Federal University, Rostov-on-Don, Russia

Abstract. In this paper, we describe a new version of the Poisson solver for numerical simulation of astrophysical problems. The main novelty consists in the motion of the grid. It is very useful for studying the properties of protostellar disks in both single and double/multiple systems at the early stages of protostellar disk evolution. Our early developed code used special intrinsics for activating AVX-512 features of Intel Xeon Scalable processors. It gives us perfect performance but we can't use this code on other platforms. The last version of code was written without intrinsics, but with special techniques for simplifying auto-vectorization and auto parallelization compilers functions. With these techniques, we achieved more than 100-time acceleration of our code on the 2nd generation of Intel Xeon Scalable processors. In this paper, we present the performance results of new code with and without auto-vectorization/auto parallelization compilers features.

Keywords: Massively parallel supercomputers · Astrophysics · Code optimization · Performance analysis

1 Introduction

For the past decade, the most of research papers in high-performance computing and numerical simulation of different problems using supercomputers are dedicated to parallel algorithms, parallel programming techniques, performance analysis, and tests. Last years we can see the very fast growth of different CPU and GPU architectures. Every two years we get new series of Intel and AMD CPUs as well as NVIDIA and AMD GPUs. ARM CPUs show very high potential

© Springer Nature Switzerland AG 2021
V. Voevodin and S. Sobolev (Eds.): RuSCDays 2021, CCIS 1510, pp. 415–426, 2021.
https://doi.org/10.1007/978-3-030-92864-3_32

for high-performance computing. No. 1 system in November 2020 TOP500 list is based on ARM architecture. The situation with hardware for high-performance computing reminds the mobile device market. The peak performance of CPUs and GPUs growing very fast, but the growth of performance of real applications looks not so optimistic. One of the main problems, from our point of view, is the efficient use of hardware. In our recent papers [1–6], we show that we can speed up our codes using low level CPU intrinsics. But the problem of this approach in the mapping to the processor architecture. The best way to create an efficient program is to write code with constructions that the compiler understands and knows how to autovectorize [7–9] and make it parallel. In our paper, we will show how to create effective auto vectorized and autoparallelized code on the example of a Poisson solver for numerical simulation of astrophysical problems.

2   Mathematical Model and Numerical Simulation

In this section we present the results of solving the Poisson equation for three different initial mass distributions in the computational zone: sphere, ellipsoid, and triaxial ellipsoid. We use 3D cartesian grid with 100^3 grid zones. The size of computational grid is equal to 2. The boundary values of gravitational potential are found by using the multipole expansion method described in [10].

In Fig. 1 we show (in log scale) the 2D slice of gravitational potential (top left) and the gradient of the potential (bottom left) calculated for a homogeneous sphere with density $\rho = 1.25 \times 10^5$ and radius $R = 0.7$. The relative divergence (in log scale) of numerical values from the analytical ones is presented in the right column of the figure and is calculated as

$$\Phi_{\text{div}} = \frac{\Phi_{\text{an}} - \Phi_{\text{num}}}{\min(\Phi_{\text{an}}, \Phi_{\text{num}})}, \tag{1}$$

where Φ_{an} and Φ_{num} are, respectively, the analytical and numerical values of potential or its gradient. The analytical values of gravitational potential and its gradient for all three configurations considered in this section are taken from [11] (Eqs. 91–103) and can be presented as

For a homogeneous sphere with radius R and density ρ

$$\Phi(r) = \begin{cases} 2\pi G\rho(R^2 - r^2/3), & \text{if } r \leq R \\ (4/3)\pi G\rho R^3/r, & \text{if } r > R \end{cases}, \tag{2}$$

$$\nabla\Phi(r) = \begin{cases} -(4/3)\pi G\rho r, & \text{if } r \leq R \\ -(4/3)\pi G\rho R^3/r^2, & \text{if } r > R \end{cases}. \tag{3}$$

For a homogeneous ellipsoid with density ρ and semimajor axes a_1, a_2, and a_3 $(a_1 = a_2 > a_3)$

$$\Phi(r,z) = \begin{cases} \pi G\rho(a_1^2 A_1 + a_2^2 A_2 + a_3^2 A_3 - r^2 A_1 - z^2 A_1), & \text{if } \frac{r^2}{a_1^2} + \frac{z^2}{a_3^2} \leq 1 \\ \pi G\rho a_1^2 a_3 \left[\left(1 + \frac{r^2}{2(a_3^2 - a_1^2)} - \frac{z^2}{a_3^2 - a_1^2} \right) I_1 - \right. \\ \left. r^2 \frac{\sqrt{a_3^2 + \lambda}}{(a_3^2 - a_1^2)(a_1^2 + \lambda)} - z^2 \left(\frac{2}{(a_1^2 + \lambda)\sqrt{a_3^2 + \lambda}} - \frac{2\sqrt{a_3^2 + \lambda}}{(a_3^2 - a_1^2)(a_1^2 + \lambda)} \right) \right], & \text{if } \frac{r^2}{a_1^2} + \frac{z^2}{a_3^2} > 1 \end{cases} \tag{4}$$

$$\nabla\Phi(r,z) = \begin{cases} 2\pi G\rho\sqrt{r^2 A_1^2 + z^2 A_3^2}, & \text{if } \frac{r^2}{a_1^2} + \frac{z^2}{a_3^2} \leq 1 \\ 2\pi G\rho a_1^2 a_3 \left[\left(\frac{r I_1}{2(a_3^2 - a_1^2)} - \frac{r\sqrt{a_3^2 + \lambda}}{(a_3^2 - a_1^2)(a_1^2 + \lambda)} \right)^2 + \right. \\ \left. \left(\frac{z I_1}{a_3^2 - a_1^2} + z \left(\frac{2}{(a_1^2 + \lambda)\sqrt{a_3^2 + \lambda}} - \frac{2\sqrt{a_3^2 + \lambda}}{(a_3^2 - a_1^2)(a_1^2 + \lambda)} \right) \right)^2 \right]^{1/2}, & \text{if } \frac{r^2}{a_1^2} + \frac{z^2}{a_3^2} > 1 \end{cases} \tag{5}$$

where

$$A_1 = A_2 = [\sqrt{1 - e^2}/e^3]\arcsine - (1 - e^2)/e^2, \tag{6}$$

$$A_3 = 2e^{-2} - 2[\sqrt{1 - e^2}/e^3]\arcsine, \tag{7}$$

$$e = \sqrt{1 - (a_3/a_1)^2}, \tag{8}$$

$$I_1 = \frac{\pi}{\sqrt{a_1^2 - a_3^2}} - \frac{2}{\sqrt{a_1^2 - a_3^2}}\arctan\sqrt{\frac{a_3^2 + \lambda}{a_1^2 - a_3^2}}, \tag{9}$$

$$\lambda = \left[(r^2 + z^2 - a_1^2 - a_3^2) + \sqrt{(a_1^2 + a_3^2 - r^2 - z^2)^2 - 4(a_1^2 a_3^2 - r^2 a_3^2 - z^2 a_1^2)} \right]/2, \tag{10}$$

For a homogeneous triaxial ellipsoid with density ρ and semimajor axes a_1, a_2, and a_3

$$\Phi(r,z) = \begin{cases} \pi G\rho(a_1^2 A_1 + a_1^2 A_1 + a_3^2 A_3 - x^2 A_1 - y^2 A_1 - z^2 A_3), & \text{if } \frac{x^2}{a_1^2} + \frac{y^2}{a_2^2} + \frac{z^2}{a_3^2} \leq 1 \\ 2\pi G\rho\frac{a_1 a_2 a_3}{\sqrt{A_{13}}} \left[K_1 E + K_2 F + K_3 \sqrt{\frac{A_{13}}{(a_1^2 + \lambda)(a_2^2 + \lambda)(a_3^2 + \lambda)}} \right], & \text{if } \frac{x^2}{a_1^2} + \frac{y^2}{a_2^2} + \frac{z^2}{a_3^2} > 1 \end{cases} \tag{11}$$

where

$$K_1 = 1 - \frac{x^2}{A_{12}} + \frac{y^2}{A_{12}}, \tag{12}$$

$$K_2 = \frac{x^2}{A_{12}} - A_{13}\frac{y^2}{A_{12}A_{23}} + \frac{z^2}{A_{23}}, \tag{13}$$

$$K_3 = \frac{(a_3^2 + \lambda)y^2}{A_{23}} - \frac{(a_2^2 + \lambda)z^2}{A_{23}}, \tag{14}$$

$$A_{12} = a_1^2 - a_2^2, \quad A_{13} = a_1^2 - a_3^2, \quad A_{23} = a_2^2 - a_3^2, \tag{15}$$

$$\lambda = \max(x_1, x_2, x_3), \tag{16}$$

where x_1, x_2, and x_3 are solutions of cubic equation $x^3 + bx^2 + cx + d = 0$ with

$$b = a_1^2 + a_2^2 + a_3^2 - x^2 - y^2 - z^2, \tag{17}$$

$$c = a_3^2 a_2^2 + a_3^2 a_1^2 + a_2^2 a_1^2 - x^2(a_2^2 + a_3^2) - y^2(a_1^2 + a_3^2) - z^2(a_1^2 + a_2^2), \tag{18}$$

$$d = a_1^2 a_2^2 a_3^2 - x^2 a_2^2 a_3^2 - y^2 a_1^2 a_3^2 - z^2 a_1^2 a_2^2, \tag{19}$$

and $E(m, \theta)$, $F(m, \theta)$ are respectively complete and incomplete elliptic integrals with modulus $m = \sqrt{A_{12}/A_{13}}$ and angle (in degrees) $\theta = (180/\pi)\arcsin(\sqrt{A_{13}/(a_1^2 + \lambda)})$.

The relative divergence for the potential is maximal at the edge of the sphere and is about 0.2%, while for the gradient of the potential the divergence reaches about 1%.

The main idea for vectorization of Poisson solver was taken from [13]. Following these recommendations, our main loop in Poisson solver looks like on Fig. 2. It implements the conjugate gradient method for solving the Poisson equation using 27-point discretization of the Laplace operator.

In Fig. 1 we present the results for the gravitation potential of the triaxial ellipsoid configuration, shown from two different perpendicular 2D slices. The triaxial ellipsoid has homogeneous density $\rho = 1.25 \times 10^5$ and semimajor axes equal to 0.8, 0.4, and 0.1. The relative divergence inside the triaxial-ellipsoid is not calculated since for the best of our knowledge there are no analytical solutions for the gravitational potential inside the triaxial ellipsoid. The relative divergence outside of the triaxial ellipsoid are about a few percents. Due to the code optimizations, it became possible to compute this standard astrophysical test for Poisson solver on one node with two AVX-512 compatible CPUs.

3   Performance Analysis

In our research, we used NKS-1P high-performance system from the Siberian Supercomputer Center. This system consists of nodes with Intel Xeon E5-2697Av4 (Broadwell architecture), Intel Xeon Platinum 8268 (Intel Xeon Scalable 1st generation architecture), Intel Xeon Gold 6248R (Intel Xeon Scalable 2nd generation architecture) processors. Each node has two CPUs and 128–192 GB DRAM. We used Intel Parallel Studio XE 2019 [12] for compilation, building, and performance analysis of our code. Intel Fortran Compiler was used for building our Poisson solver. We used the next three compiler's directives for our tests:

1. Building solver without optimization.

$$ifort - o < output - name > -g < file_name >$$

2. Building solver with autovectorization (AVX2/AVX512).

$$ifort - o < output - name > -axCORE - AVX512$$

$$-g - O3 - qopt - report = 5$$

$$-qopt - report - phase = vec < file_name >$$

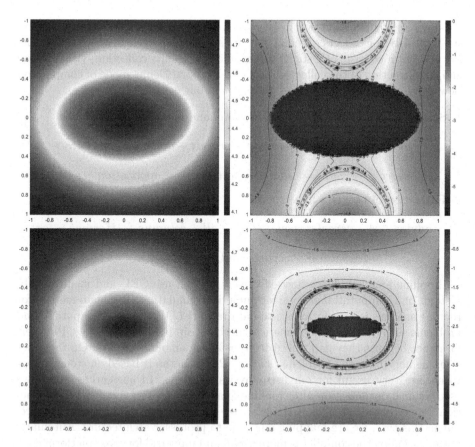

Fig. 1. 2D slices of the gravitational potential for the triaxial ellipsoid (left column) and the relative divergences (right column) from the analytics. The triaxial ellipsoid has homogeneous density $\rho = 1.25 \times 10^5$ and semimajor axes equal to 0.8, 0.4, and 0.1.

3. Building solver with autovectorization (AVX2/AVX512) and autoparallelisation.

$$ifort - o < output - name > -axCORE - AVX512$$

$$-g - O3 - qopt - report = 5$$

$$-qopt - report - phase = vec - parallel < file_name >$$

We used $-g$ compiler's option in all cases for Intel Advisor's performance analysis. Intel Advisor collects different statistics from each cycle of the code. Statistics collection consists of 2 steps: survey and trip counts collection, visualization and/or extraction of the collected data into a report. Debug mode of compilation slow down the program, but less than 20% in our case.

1. Survey collection and trip count by command line with advisor:

$$advixe - cl - collectroofline - project - dir < project - dir >$$

$$-search - dirall :=< source - path > -- < application - path >$$

2. Extraction of the data in a report:

$$advixe - cl - reportsurvey - show - all - columns -- format = text$$

$$-- report - outputreport.txt$$

Roofline analysis shows how effectively we can use CPU and memory subsystems of a computational node for numerical simulation. The main metrics for roofline analysis is a performance-to-data ratio (FLOPS/byte). Compute bound problems such as stochastic numerical methods are bounded only by CPUs performance because they don't need to transfer big amounts of data. On the other side, memory bounded problems, such as PDEs methods based on stencils approach, are very useful for our astrophysics problems. In our earlier works, we used manual optimization after roofline analysis with using direct CPU instruction for vectorization. This is the best way for achieving the best performance, but in this case, we are mapping our code to processor architecture. Automatic optimization by the compiler is more useful and universal for cross-platform code development, but we need to help the compiler with an understanding of safe optimization, such as the dependence of data between different loops and so on. In our work, we developed and realized an algorithm that can be effectively optimized by a compiler. There are many talks about effectiveness of vectorization in modern CPUs.

Some developers think, that it is enough simple SIMD instructions and CPUs should have as much common cores as it's possible [14]. On the other side people, who needs to process big amounts of arithmetical data. But there is a fact, if you want to achieve the best performance on Intel Xeon Scalable processors, you should use vectorization.

```
do while(Residual > EPS .and. NumIter < 1000)
  psn_q = 0.d0                              ! q = Az

  forall(i = 2:N+1, k = 2:N+1, l = 2:N+1)
    psn_q(i,k,l) = -38.d0/9.d0 * psn_z(i,k,l) +
      4.d0/9.d0  * ( psn_z(i+1,k,l) + psn_z(i-1,k,l) +
                     psn_z(i,k+1,l) + psn_z(i,k-1,l) +
                     psn_z(i,k,l+1) + psn_z(i,k,l-1) ) +
      1.d0/9.d0  * ( psn_z(i,k+1,l+1) + psn_z(i,k-1,l+1) +
                     psn_z(i,k+1,l-1) + psn_z(i,k-1,l-1) +
                     psn_z(i+1,k,l+1) + psn_z(i-1,k,l+1) +
                     psn_z(i+1,k,l-1) + psn_z(i-1,k,l-1) +
                     psn_z(i+1,k+1,l) + psn_z(i-1,k+1,l) +
                     psn_z(i+1,k-1,l) + psn_z(i-1,k-1,l) ) +
      1.d0/36.d0 * ( psn_z(i+1,k+1,l+1) + psn_z(i-1,k+1,l+1) +
                     psn_z(i+1,k+1,l-1) + psn_z(i-1,k+1,l-1) +
                     psn_z(i+1,k-1,l+1) + psn_z(i-1,k-1,l+1) +
                     psn_z(i+1,k-1,l-1) + psn_z(i-1,k-1,l-1) )
  end forall

  alphazn = sum(psn_q * psn_z)             ! alzn = (q,z)
  alpha = alphach/alphazn                  ! al = alch/alzn
  psn_x = psn_x + alpha * psn_z            ! x = x + al * z
  psn_r = psn_r - alpha * psn_q            ! r = r - al * q
  psn_q = psn_r                            ! q = r
  betach = sum(psn_q * psn_r)              ! btch = (q,r)
  betazn = alphach                         ! btzn = alch
  alphach = betach                         ! alch = betach
  beta = betach/betazn                     ! bt = btch/btzn
  psn_z = psn_q + beta * psn_z             ! z = q + bt * z
  NormR = dsqrt(sum(psn_r * psn_r))        ! |r|

  Residual = NormR/NormRight
  NumIter = NumIter + 1
  print *,NumIter,Residual

enddo
```

Fig. 2. Main loop of Poisson solver.

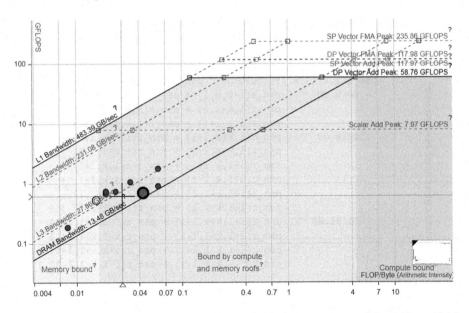

Fig. 3. Roofline chart for unoptimized Poisson solver on one core of Intel Xeon Gold 6248R. (Color figure online)

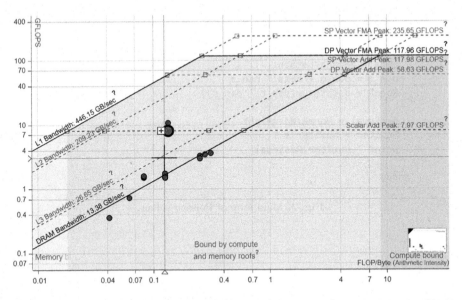

Fig. 4. Roofline chart for autovectorized (AVX512) Poisson solver on one core of Intel Xeon Gold 6248R. (Color figure online)

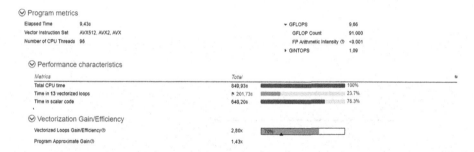

Fig. 5. Roofline chart for autoparallelised and autovectorized (AVX512) Poisson solver on 2xIntel Xeon Gold 6248R.

Figure 3 and Fig. 4 show that we achieved performance growth from 0.61GFLOPS to 3.08GFLOPS with auto-vectorization for one core of Intel Xeon Gold 6248R CPU. We also added −*parallel* key for compilation, and we can see the results in Fig. 5. We achieved 80.22GFLOPS for 2 Intel Xeon Gold 6248R CPUs with auto parallelization and auto-vectorization directives of Intel Fortran Compiler from the Intel Parallel Studio XE 2019. The red dot on the figures shows the FLOPS/byte value of the main loop in our program which is shown in Fig. 2.

How to maximize the performance? The first of all, you should follow next simple rules of successful autovectorization [15]:

- The loop count can't change once the loop starts by the code inside the loop.
- Control flow shouldn't be changed by special statements.
- There shouldn't be data dependencies with other indexes of the loop due to the memory conflict problem.
- Conditionals sentences (if/else) can be used if they don't change the control flow, and are only used to conditionally load A or B values into a C variable. In fact, the best performance can be achieved only without conditional sentences inside loop.

Typical Poisson solvers are based on Fourier spectral methods. But, in the case of astrophysical problems, one of the best approximation schemes is the 27-points scheme [16]. The Poisson's equation transforming into a large number of algebraic systems of linear equations which forms a block tri-diagonal matrix. This approximation gives the lowest absolute error in our case. Figure 2 shows that we don't change control flow, loop count in code, and not using conditional sentences. It is also very important to use the forall loop in case of Fortran code for best auto-vectorization and auto parallelization.

The other side of optimization is to help the compiler in understanding your data.

Figure 6 shows the hierarchy of AVX registers from 128 to 512 bits. XMM registers are used for AVX instructions, YMM registers are used for AVX2 instructions, and ZMM registers are used with AVX-512 CPU instructions. AVX and

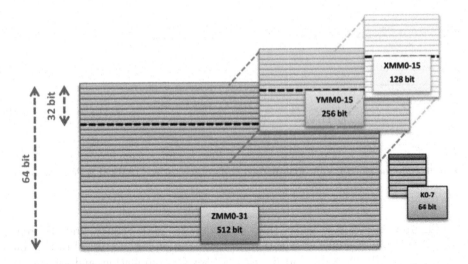

Fig. 6. AVX registers of Intel Xeon Scalable processors (Optimizing Intel Compiler 2019 presentation).

AVX2 instructions are also supported by the latest AMD processors. This is why is very important to create universal CPU code. Our previously works [5,6,17,18] are based on using of AVX-512 intrinsics, because internal autovectorization optimization of compilers can't help us with performance. Latest Intel C++/Fortran compiler became better with autovectorization. Latest Intel C++ and Fortran compilers are good with aligning data for vectorization, but they are conservative with the usage of registers. Intel Advisor sometimes during the Roofline analysis process suggests using ZMM registers. You can use compiler option -qopt-zmm-usage=high with your code to force the usage of AVX-512 registers. But this suggestion will take effect in performance only with enough data to process. In case of our Poisson solver, we have 10% slow down of code performance for $192 \times 192 \times 192$ test grid size. But for the real problems, with a grid size of more than $512 \times 512 \times 512$, the AVX-512 registers became more effective.

Autoparallelized and auto vectorized Poisson solver works faster more than 100 times than code without optimizations, and auto parallelization gives more than 20 times speedup in comparison with the only auto-vectorization. We think, that in the case of real problems the speedup will be more impressive because of 27 points template and code quality which gives us more compute-bound performance analysis results than the memory bounded.

Finally, for better performance, it can be recommended to help the compiler with better vectorization predictions, the better decision of functions to inline and ordering, improving cache behavior. Sometimes compiler can calculate and replace some loops with the static data during the compilation and linking procedure. In our case, replacing conditionals sentences with simple arithmetic operations gave us more operations but better performance, because FMA and AVX instructions can add and multiply at once with 8 double-precision numbers

Table 1. Performance of the new Poisson solver. Compiled by Intel Fortran Compiler from Intel Parallel Studio XE 2019 with and without autovectorization and auto parallelisation

Architecture	No optimization, GFLOPS	AVX autovectorization (AVX2—AVX512), GFLOPS	Auto parallelisation, GFLOPS
Intel Xeon E5-2697A v4, 2.6 GHz	0.51	2.7	–
Intel Xeon Platinum 8268, 2.9 GHz	0.62	3.46	–
Intel Xeon Gold 6248R, 3 GHz	0.61	3.08	80.22

per CPU cycle. Enforcing the use of ZMM registers (AVX-512) should be tested in any case. Fortunately, this is very easy.

4 Conclusion

We developed new astrophysical code which helps modern compilers to autovectorize and makes it parallel. We used standard FORTRAN constructions without any low-level instructions. We achieved up to 3 times code speedup with autovectorization and more than 100 times speedup with auto-vectorization and auto parallelization due to Intel's vectorization loops tutorial. Table 1 shows the performance comparison. We propose a more accurate code for solving the Poisson equation. An example of the slowest loop can be found in this paper. The structure of this loop helps the compiler with understanding how to vectorize code: the loop count didn't change once the loop starts, control flow didn't change by special statements, there are no external and internal data dependencies, there are no conditionals sentences. We presented the results of solving the Poisson equation for three different initial mass distributions in the triaxial ellipsoid computational zone as a test. The relative divergence for the potential is maximal at the edge of the sphere and is about 0.2%, while for the gradient of the potential the divergence reaches about 1%. This standard test for Poisson solver can be computed on one standard computational node with two AVX-512 compatible CPUs because of 100x code speedup.

Acknowledgments. The reported study was funded by RFBR and FWF according to the research project 19-51-14002 (RFBR) and I4311 (FWF). Authors would like to thank Siberian Supercomputer Center for supercomputing facilities.

References

1. Kulikov, I., Chernykh, I., Glinsky, B.: Numerical simulations of astrophysical problems on massively parallel supercomputers. In: AIP Conference Proceedings, vol. 1776, p. 090006 (2016)

2. Kulikov, I., Glinsky, B., Chernykh, I., Nenashev, V., Shmelev, A.: Numerical simulations of astrophysical problems on massively parallel supercomputer. In: Proceedings of the 2016 11th International Forum on Strategic Technology, IFOST 2016, pp. 320–323, 090006 (2017)
3. Glinsky, B., Kulikov, I., Snytnikov, A., Chernykh, I., Weins, D.: A multilevel approach to algorithm and software design for exaflops supercomputers. In: CEUR Workshop Proceedings, vol. 1482, pp. 4–16 (2015)
4. Kulikov, I.M., Chernykh, I.G., Snytnikov, A.V., Glinskiy, B.M., Tutukov, A.V.: AstroPhi: a code for complex simulation of dynamics of astrophysical objects using hybrid supercomputers. Comput. Phys. Commun. **186**, 71–80 (2015)
5. Kulikov, I.M., Chernykh, I.G., Glinskiy, B.M., Protasov, V.A.: An efficient optimization of HLL method for the second generation of Intel Xeon Phi processor. Lobachevskii J. Math. **39**(4), 543–551 (2018). https://doi.org/10.1134/S1995080218040091
6. Kulikov, I.M., Chernykh, I.G., Tutukov, A.V.: A new parallel Intel Xeon Phi hydrodynamics code for massively parallel supercomputers. Lobachevskii J. Math. **39**(9), 1207–1216 (2018). https://doi.org/10.1134/S1995080218090135
7. Siso, S., Armour, W., Thiyagalingam, J.: Evaluating auto-vectorizing compilers through objective withdrawal of useful information. ACM Trans. **16**(4), 1–23 (2019). Article: A40
8. Stevens, N., et al.: The ARM scalable vector extension. IEEE Micro **37**(2), 26–39 (2017). Article: 7924233
9. Amiri, H., Shahbahrami, A., Pohl, A., Juurlink, B.: Performance evaluation of implicit and explicit SIMDization. Microprocess. Microsyst. **63**, 158–168 (2018)
10. Kulikov, I., Vorobyov, E.: Using the PPML approach for constructing a low-dissipation, operator-splitting scheme for numerical simulations of hydrodynamic flows. J. Comput. Phys. **317**, 318–346 (2016)
11. Stone, J.M., Norman, M.L.: ZEUS-2D: a radiation magnetohydrodynamics code for astrophysical flows in two space dimensions. I. The hydrodynamic algorithms and tests. Astrophys. J. Suppl. **80**, 753 (1992)
12. Intel Parallel Studio XE. https://software.intel.com/content/www/us/en/develop/tools/oneapi/commercial-base-hpc.html
13. Intel vectorization and loops. https://software.intel.com/content/www/us/en/develop/documentation/cpp-compiler-developer-guide-and-reference/top/optimization-and-programming-guide/vectorization/automatic-vectorization/vectorization-and-loops.html
14. I Hope AVX512 Dies A Painful Death. https://www.phoronix.com/scan.php?page=news_item&px=Linus-Torvalds-On-AVX-512
15. Automatic vectorization. https://www.codingame.com/playgrounds/283/sse-avx-vectorization/autovectorization
16. Shiferaw, A., Mittal, R.C.: An efficient direct method to solve the three dimensional Poisson's equation. Am. J. Comput. Math. **1**, 285–293 (2011)
17. Kulikov, I., Chernykh, I., Snytnikov, A., et al.: Numerical modelling of astrophysical flow on hybrid architecture supercomputers. In: Parallel Programming: Practical Aspects, Models and Current Limitations, pp. 71–116 (2014)
18. Kulikov, I., Chernykh, I., Tutukov, A.: A new hydrodynamic model for numerical simulation of interacting galaxies on Intel Xeon Phi supercomputers. In: Journal of Physics: Conference Series, vol. 719(1), p. 12006 (2016)

Universal Assessment System for Analyzing the Quality of Supercomputer Resources Usage

Vadim Voevodin[✉] and Sergey Zhumatiy

Lomonosov Moscow State University, Moscow 119991, Russia
{vadim,serg}@parallel.ru

Abstract. With the increasing complexity of modern supercomputer systems, it becomes more difficult to assess the quality of their usage, since the number of factors that can have an impact on it increases significantly. However, it is very important to study this problem, since the potential of many modern supercomputers is far from being fully utilized. At the moment, to assess the quality of the supercomputer usage, simple indicators (like CPU user load or simply the ratio of compute nodes occupied by running jobs) are most often used, each considering only one specific aspect or being too coarse. Such indicators, although they do help to draw some conclusions on the supercomputer functioning, do not allow to quickly get a general idea of how efficiently certain resources are utilized.

To obtain more insightful and accurate information about the usage quality of certain types of computational resources like memory or communication network, in this work, a system of assessments is proposed that allows performing a comparative performance analysis of applications, users or projects. Based on these assessments, ranking can be carried out, which allows, in particular, to single out the cases of the most or least efficient resource utilization.

Keywords: High-performance computing · Supercomputer · Performance analysis · Workload analysis · Resource utilization · Monitoring data

1 Introduction

The general question of supercomputer usage efficiency has been of interest almost from the very moment of the appearance of the high-performance computing field [1]. The reason is straightforward—supercomputers have always provided enormous computing power, but they have also always been very complex, so creating a parallel program that will efficiently use all the capabilities of a supercomputer is an extremely difficult task. At the same time, the complexity of supercomputers is constantly and rapidly increasing over time, so the issue of analyzing the efficiency of using their resources becomes more and more urgent.

© Springer Nature Switzerland AG 2021
V. Voevodin and S. Sobolev (Eds.): RuSCDays 2021, CCIS 1510, pp. 427–442, 2021.
https://doi.org/10.1007/978-3-030-92864-3_33

To date, a huge variety of different approaches have been proposed as well as a lot of software tools have been implemented that allow exploring and solving this issue from different sides. So, languages and libraries for developing parallel programs are constantly being improved, which makes it easier to create more efficient HPC programs. Also, a lot of performance analysis tools (profilers, debugging tools, tools for collecting and analyzing traces of parallel programs, etc.) have been implemented and successfully used in practice.

In addition, a lot of research has been carried out affecting another important, albeit less studied area—the quality of supercomputer functioning in general. Within this area, the object of consideration is not one separate job, but the components of the entire supercomputer—for example, supercomputer job flow or major components of supercomputer infrastructure. Such studies are needed so that the management and system administrators of supercomputer centers can assess as fully and quickly as possible different aspects of the supercomputer center work that are of interest to them—the utilization of available supercomputer resources, the optimality of system software and hardware equipment configuration, the adequacy of the selected policies and quotas, and many others.

At the moment, a set of fairly simple metrics is usually used in practice to assess the utilization of supercomputer resources. So, to assess the load of compute nodes, the processor load, the intensity of reading/writing to memory, and sometimes just the percentage of nodes occupied by running jobs are most often estimated; to assess the I/O work, the volume of read/written bytes or the frequency of opening/closing files are considered; etc. These metrics are usually pretty easy to collect and can really help in getting a general idea of how intensively supercomputer applications are using a particular computational resource. However, it would often be much more insightful to move from considering a set of independent narrowly specified metrics to a more unified assessment, which makes it possible to assess the quality of work with a certain type of supercomputer resources as a whole. For example, one is more interested in evaluating not the frequency of L1 cache misses but the general efficiency of using memory subsystem. Moreover, by analyzing the existing standard metrics, we can usually roughly estimate only the intensity of resource usage, but we cannot in any way determine whether the provided computational resource is being used efficiently enough, or it is a bottleneck that slow down the application. For example, in the absolute majority of cases, a frequency of reading from files obtained for a certain job does not allow us to understand whether it is possible to work with the file system more efficiently, i.e. to run this job faster.

Our research is aimed at solving this issue. In this paper, we describe a system of more "intellectual" assessments of the quality of the supercomputer resources usage, which helps to assess how efficiently the work with the selected computational resource is organized in user applications.

The main contribution of this paper is the proposal of such an assessment system which helps to automatically evaluate the quality of supercomputer resource usage like memory subsystem or CPU, for all jobs running on the supercomputer.

This system allows analyzing, comparing and ranking the utilization quality of individual jobs, users or software packages by using only one assessment for each resource type. It doesn't depend on any specific job features and is suitable for applying on other computing systems, which makes it universal.

The rest of the paper is organized as follows. Section 2 presents the current state-of-the-art and our background in this area. Section 3 describes the general idea behind the proposed solution, as well as dives into details of how assessments are designed. Technical details on assessment implementation are touched upon in Sect. 4, and some examples of using proposed assessments in practice are shown in Sect. 5. Section 6 concludes the research described in this paper.

2   Background and Related Work

The question of the workload and efficiency analysis of supercomputer centers is touched upon in different studies. There are a number of papers like [2–4] presenting holistic reports on the operation of specific HPC systems. In these papers, a variety of aspects of supercomputer functioning are considered—properties of the jobs being launched, such as the duration, the number of processes used, or the software libraries used; job efficiency in terms of CPU or GPU load, intensity of communication network usage; distribution of job, node-hours or efficiency characteristics between partitions or subject areas; and many others. There are also works that study in more detail the efficiency of individual aspects of supercomputer behavior. For example, authors of [5] discusses in detail how the job properties and trends in resource consumption have changed over several years of operation of two large supercomputers, Intrepid and Mira. Another article [6] discusses the causes of low I/O throughput and provides a dedicated software solution to detect them. There are quite a lot of related works in general, but they are, in our opinion, are either not portable, or consider in detail one specific aspect of supercomputer operation, as well as sometimes require significant efforts to apply them on other systems. In our case, we want to provide a set of universal and easy-to-understand assessments that will help easily and quickly obtaining a first glance of resource usage.

On the other hand, there are studies and tools that are aimed at carefully assessing the quality of the computing resources usage by single applications. First of all, a lot of analysis software is developed, e.g. profiling and trace analysis tools like Scalasca, HPCToolkit, mpiP, Vampir, Paraver or Valgrind, debugging software like Arm Forge or Totalview, etc. All such software are surely helpful, when you want to dive into details and understand features, bottlenecks and behavior of one selected application.

There are also several studies aimed at developing a set of universal metrics for initial evaluating of efficiency characteristics of a single program, which are more related to the scope of our paper. For example, a hierarchy of metrics is proposed by the PoP project [7], which are intended to evaluate parallel programs and provide a quantitative way of measuring relative impact of the different factors inherent in parallelization. There are metrics that assess, for example, load balance efficiency across processes or parallel efficiency that shows inefficiency in splitting computation over processes and then communicating data between processes. This approach was originally intended for a detailed analysis of one selected application, and it is difficult to apply it to study the supercomputer job flow as a whole (which is of interest in our work), since it requires profiling applications causing a noticeable overhead. There are also approaches like Top-down [8,9], within which the load of certain resources is analyzed. This approach is very well suited for analyzing the utilization of different hardware components and thus detecting bottlenecks that prevent higher performance, but it is also initially intended for analyzing a single program, since it requires collecting a significant amount of profiling data. Moreover, this approach is low-level and requires noticeable effort in order to figure out how to correctly interpret the results. However, it should be noted that the ideas proposed in these approaches formed the basis of the solution proposed in this paper.

In our Research computing center in Lomonosov Moscow State University, we have previously developed a TASC software suite [10], which automatically detects performance issues in all user jobs running on the supercomputer, as well as helps system administrators and supercomputer center management to evaluate the performance and utilization of various software and hardware components of the entire supercomputer using a specialized flexible web-based report system [11]. The automatic detection of job performance issues is implemented using a set of predefined rules, each of which is intended to detect one particular issue. A set of 30 rules is implemented, allowing to notify users about low utilization of computational resources, problems with inefficient MPI usage, incorrect job launches, etc. These rules can be viewed as an intermediate step from the analysis of simple low-level performance characteristics (like CPU load or number of bytes received via network per second), which is commonly performed in practice, towards general assessments of usage quality, the development of which is the purpose of this work. These ideas are further used while developing some of the assessments proposed in this paper, as shown in the next section.

3   Description of the Assessment System

3.1   General Approach

The purpose of this work is to develop an assessment system that will allow evaluating and comparing the usage quality of certain types of supercomputer resources in HPC applications. For each resource type, it is supposed to set one metric, which will allow you to quickly and at the most general level analyze individual supercomputer jobs, users or projects. We consider the following types of resources: 1) processor (CPU), 2) memory subsystem, 3) MPI network, 4) file system (I/O), 5) graphics processor (GPU).

Now let's describe the general approach to assessing the quality of resource usage. The most basic object that we want to evaluate is one job launch. At first, it is necessary to answer the following question—what the user wants most when analyzing the efficiency of his program? From our point of view, he is most interested in understanding whether the job can work faster due to more efficient work with different computational resources, and what kind of acceleration (and how) can be obtained. He may also be interested, but to a lesser extent, in comparing the efficiency of his jobs with other users running similar jobs, for example, users of the same library or package like GROMACS, NAMD or VASP, which can indirectly make it clear whether a more efficient implementation is possible. The same questions are also of interest for system administrator, with more focus on overall statistics and comparison between different jobs, users and projects.

In order to answer these questions, it is necessary to determine what "efficient" means in our case. In other words, what does it mean that a job is "inefficiently" or "poorly" using the given computational resource. In our opinion, two reasonable answers can be given:

1. A job underutilizes the given type of resource (CPU, memory, I/O, etc.).
2. Working with this type of resource interferes with useful computations (which can be performed by CPU or GPU). This means that a processor is idle, waiting for the execution of operations with the resource.

The first variant is a more common one, and in this case we evaluate the job performance by analyzing the intensity of using a computation resource. CPU load, load average, number of MPI bytes received per second, frequency of LLC (last-level cache) misses—all these characteristics refer to the variant 1. But the variant 2 seem to be more insightful and useful, since it helps, unlike the variant 1, to answer the aforementioned questions about what prevents the program from running more efficiently. Indeed, high CPU load by itself does not necessary means that a lot of useful work is being performed, as it can be caused by processor waiting for data from memory or a lot of branch mispredictions. High frequency of cache misses as well may not be a sign of poor performance: if data accesses are performed in parallel with useful computations, the performance is not reduced, although the interaction with memory subsystem is inefficient. And this is true for most common characteristics that refer to the variant 1.

That's why it was decided to develop an assessment system that helps to get answers according to the second, more insightful variant. However, we note that since two answers touch upon slightly different aspects of resource utilization, it is sometimes worth using both assessment types for a more detailed and holistic analysis, which are more likely to complement rather than replace each other.

It should also be noted that we understand that low quality of resource usage can't be optimized in some cases, for example, due to the properties of the algorithm being implemented in a user job. But our goal is to assess the quality in general; understanding the root causes of that is a next, very complex task which can be performed using, for example, performance analysis tools.

3.2   Proposed Assessments

After a thorough study of possible new and existing options, the following set of assessments was selected, short description of which is given in the Table 1.

For each assessment, it is specified what existing evaluates it is based on as well as the origin of these evaluates, and a short comment explaining its meaning is given. Assessments for a particular resource type will be further referred as score$_{type}$, where type can be "cpu", "mem", "mpi", "io" or "gpu".

Table 1. A brief description of the proposed assessments

Resource type	Assessment based on (origin)	Comment
CPU	Retired (top-down)	Estimates the fraction of the CPU time when it was fully utilized performing useful computations
Memory	Memory bound (top-down)	Estimates the fraction of time that the processor was somehow idle, waiting for data from memory
MPI network	CommE (PoP)	Evaluates how much of the job execution time is occupied by data exchange and not computations
	MPI rules triggering (our research)	Generally the same, only by our means and by indirect indicators
I/O	I/O rules triggering (our research)	Evaluates by indirect indicators if the noticeable part of job execution time is occupied by I/O operations (using I/O network), and not computations
GPU	Retiring and memory bound (top-down/our research)	GPU analogues of retiring and memory bound

CPU is a resource which performs useful computations, so it is necessary to assess how fully it is utilized performing useful actions. An IPC characteristic is often used in this case, which shows the average number of retiring (useful and successfully executed) Instructions Per Cycle. This is quite a meaningful metric in general—in modern processors maximum IPC value is usually 4, making it quite easy to get a rough universal estimation of CPU usage quality. For example, it is considered that an IPC value equal to 1 or more is considered acceptable for HPC applications [12]. But this value for real-life applications is highly dependent on type of operations, which makes it not so useful for our purpose. There is a more accurate and understandable version of this characteristic—**Retiring** metric (see [9]) from Top-down approach developed by Intel. This metric represents a fraction of CPU time (in term of pipeline slots) utilized by useful work. It is measured as a percentage, making it easy to analyze and use, while representing exactly what we need—how fully the CPU is utilized by useful computations. This metric is calculated using hardware counters, see Sect. 4.

The main goal of *memory subsystem* is to bring data as quickly as possible to the processor. It doesn't perform useful computations by itself, so this means that the quality of memory usage in our case is determined by how often the processor has been idle while waiting for data from memory. Common characteristics like amount of load/store operations per second or frequency of cache misses can't help in this case, since they evaluate memory usage intensity disregarding the CPU being idle or not. But there is one more Top-down metric that assesses exactly what we need—**Memory Bound** (see [9]). It measures the fraction of time (in term of slots) when the CPU could be stalled waiting for data from memory. As for Retiring, this metric is calculated using hardware counters.

In case of *MPI network* usage, two possible options should be described. The first metric is called **CommE** and is proposed by the PoP project [7]. As in case of Top-down assessments, this metric captures exactly what we need— it roughly measures that fraction of time spent in performing MPI operations and not useful computations. But to calculate this metric, it is necessary to collect data on the execution time of MPI operations for all jobs running on the supercomputer. There are existing tools that claim to be capable of that while showing low overheads [13,14]. But the problem is that: 1) these tools need to be properly applied, configured and verified; 2) some overheads will appear in any case while using these tools, leading to user jobs running slower; 3) usage of these tools will disable by default usage of MPI profilers and trace analyzers.

That's why it is proposed at this point to use another assessment based on a set of rules intended to detect performance issues in previously developed TASC software. As mentioned before, each rule captures one specific issue concerning job performance. There are several rules related to the MPI usage which aim at detecting the following issues:

- Working with MPI takes too much system resources (in terms of CPU system load).
- Highly intensive usage of MPI network probably caused low activity of the usage of all other computational resources.
- The average size of MPI packets is too small while MPI network being actively used, which usually leads to significant data transfer overhead.
- The job actively uses MPI network, but network locality is too low (i.e. allocated nodes located far from each other), leading to bigger data transfer latency.

Each rule is also provided with two features—confidence and criticalness. The former one represents our confidence that the specified performance issue can be accurately detected by the suggested criterion. It takes a value from 1 (not sure at all) to 5 (completely sure). The latter one indicates how critical the detected performance issue is. It takes a value from 1 (the performance issue is unimportant or no issues were found) to 5 (incorrect job behavior, we can automatically cancel it).

Based on these rules and their features, the assessment of MPI network usage (**score_mpi**) can be calculated according to the formula (1).

$$score_{mpi} = \sum_{i:triggered\ mpi\ rules} conf_i \times crit_i \times 100/maxscore_{mpi} \qquad (1)$$

where $maxscore_{mpi}$ is a maximum available $score_{mpi}$ (in case all rules triggered). In this case $score_{mpi}$ is a percentage of maximum score, the more the value—the worse MPI usage is.

Two notes should be made. First, we plan to add more rules for detecting issues related to the MPI efficiency, which will help to make $score_{mpi}$ more precise. Second, if in future it is found technically possible to calculate the CommE PoP metric without significant overheads, we plan to switch to it, since it seems to provide a more insightful and accurate assessment.

At the moment no precise metrics have been found to evaluate the quality of *I/O* usage. But since the vast majority of modern supercomputers do not have local disks, and therefore all work with the file system is performed over the network, it is possible, as in the case of MPI, to monitor network traffic caused by I/O operations. In this case, the similar list of rules as described for MPI (except for the last one, since no I/O traffic appear between nodes) can be applied in the I/O case. The only thing needed is to differentiate the MPI and I/O network traffic. The assessment ($score_{io}$) is typically the same, only applied for I/O rules. We also plan to improve this assessment by introducing more rules, since it doesn't capture, for example, any issues concerning number of files used.

The *graphics accelerator*, as the CPU, is also a resource that perform useful computations. And since it also have on-board memory subsystem, the same considerations as in case of CPU and its memory subsystem apply here. Therefore, **GPU Retiring** and **GPU Memory Bound** assessments, being analogues of aforementioned Top-down metrics, are proposed to assess the quality of using these types of resources.

3.3   Possible Benefits of Using the Proposed System

Let us illustrate how such a solution could be useful in practice, in our opinion. This assessment system is primarily intended for supercomputer administrators, and with its help, following useful actions can be performed:

- Search for jobs (as well as users, projects, or used software libraries) with the worst assessments for the selected resource type. This will allow administrators to quickly find the most inefficient jobs and pay more attention to them, in particular, draw users' attention to these problems or help them with the elimination of their root causes (especially if the reason for their occurrence is not in the job itself, but the supercomputer software or hardware environment).
- Track the dynamics of assessments changing (and their distribution across users and projects) over time. This will allow understanding if the overall situation with the supercomputer job performance is getting worse or not, as well as detecting possible seasonal fluctuations that are often present in the job flow and are associated, for example, with the grant reporting periods, seasonal activity of different users, or simply with the time of day.

- Detect correlations between low assessments in jobs and properties of the hardware and software environment where these jobs are launched. This can help identify: 1) incorrectly or improperly configured nodes; 2) poorly built or configured packages or system software; 3) unusual patterns of job behavior that poorly map to the architecture of the target supercomputer.
- Detect jobs that should be more efficient, according to the similar jobs launched previously. To solve this task, methods are needed to find similar jobs. Such research is being carried out at the Research Computing Center of Moscow State University [15], within which two methods (static and dynamic) have already been developed, determining similar jobs based on comparing function names from the executable and analyzing performance data from system monitoring during job runtime, respectively.

Such methods can also be useful for the supercomputer users. For example, applying these methods will help to alert users about their currently running jobs with assessments being too low, as well as abnormally low indicators in general during some time period. Also, when integrated with search methods for similar jobs (mentioned above), it will be possible to notify users that a previously launched similar job was noticeably more efficient, assuming that there is a performance issue with the current job launch that should be investigated.

4 Details on the Implementation of the Assessments

In this section we touch upon the technical aspects on collecting necessary input data and calculating the proposed assessments. We also share our progress in performing this in practice on our Lomonosov-2 supercomputer [16].

The Top-down-based metrics, Retiring and Memory bound (for assessing quality of CPU and memory subsystem usage), are calculated using hardware counters. Several versions of formulas were found to calculate these metrics. The first, simpler one, was proposed in the initial article describing Top-down approach [8]. The rest were found in the source code of two performance analysis tools (they use the same formulas)—Intel VTune Amplifier 2019 installed on the Lomonosov-2 supercomputer (the latest VTune version is described in [17]) and pmu-tools [18]. There are three formula versions in the analysis tools due to different profiling modes being used as well as depending on Simultaneous Multithreading (SMT) being enabled or not.

Since the formulas from the analysis tools are used in practice and refine the one from the initial paper, they seem to be more precise and therefore more insightful. On the Lomonosov-2 supercomputer, we have SMT enabled, so we took the corresponding VTune formula for the Retiring metric. The same can't be done in our case for Memory bound, since its formula requires collecting too many hardware counters, which causes significant overheads when being collected for all jobs running on the supercomputer. So, we took the simpler formula described in the initial paper. The exact formulas are stated in (2)–(3). Capitalized names correspond to specific hardware sensor names.

$$\text{score}_{\textbf{cpu}} = Retiring = UOPS\_RETIRED.RETIRE\_SLOTS/ \\ (2 * CPU\_CLK\_UNHALTED.THREAD\_ANY) \tag{2}$$

$$\text{score}_{\textbf{mem}} = Memory\ bound = (CYCLE\_ACTIVITY.STALLS\_LDM\_PENDING + \\ RESOURCE\_STALLS.SB)/CPU\_CLK\_UNHALTED.THREAD \tag{3}$$

We use DiMMon monitoring system [19] also developed in our Research computing center for collecting data from hardware counters, but any other suitable monitoring system can be used as well. DiMMon has a module for collecting hardware counters using PAPI [20]; exact PAPI analogues for all sensors were used. This enables us to collect selected performance characteristics for all job running on the supercomputer. In order to verify the values from the counters we collect using DiMMon, we have compared them to the values obtained using *perf* utility, which acted as a reference in our case, while profiling a series of different benchmarks. We have used simple benchmarks implementing stencil computations, graph algorithms like Page rank, matrix multiplication and matrix transpose, etc. The results showing the accuracy of the implemented assessments are shown in Sect. 5.

It should be noted that a more advanced and presumably more precise formula is available for the Retiring metric, but it was discovered in practice that PAPI isn't capable to precisely collect all the necessary counters we need in this case. It needs to work in multiplexing mode (since the number of required hardware counters to collect is bigger than the one that can be collected in parallel), and in this case the values for some counters noticeably differ; this is mostly related to the CPU_CLK_UNHALTED.ONE_THREAD_ACTIVE counter. The reason for such PAPI behavior is currently unclear. Probably the reason is that we have to use quite old PAPI 5.6 due to technical issues (e.g. due to the old 3.10 version of the Linux kernel used on Lomonosov-2 compute nodes).

The collection of other assessments is the following. As mentioned in the previous section, formula (1) is used for MPI and I/O resource types, with the difference in exact rules used in it. The implementation of rules was previously executed within the TASC software and evaluated on the Lomonosov-2, therefore the only thing needed in order to calculate corresponding assessments is to implement the stated formula. The triggering of all rules of interest is stored in TASC database for every job running on the supercomputer, so this information is easily collectible in our case.

The GPU case is currently the least studied, so no exact formulas are available at the moment. But the Retiring and Memory bound metric analogues should be possible to collect using, for example, nvprof utility [21]. This is planned to be studied in the near future.

5   Evaluation of the Developed Assessment System

In this section, first results obtained in practice using our assessments are shown. Two groups of assessments are considered: Top-down based $score_{cpu}$ and $score_{mem}$, as well as $score_{mpi}$ and $score_{io}$ based on job performance issues detected using TASC.

5.1   Assessing CPU and Memory Usage

Proposed $score_{cpu}$ and $score_{mem}$ assessments are based on metrics from widely used Top-down approach, so there is no need to verify if these metrics correctly reflect the program properties in general. However, it is necessary to check if we properly collect these metrics. For this purpose, we conducted experiments on several tests that implement well-known computational kernels, and compared our assessments with the values obtained using Intel VTune Amplifier 2019 for these tests. The following tests were used:

- matrix_transp—naive matrix transpose implementation with sequential writing to the output array and indirect addressing of the input array;
- random_access—test for benchmarking random memory accesses, implement sequential store into large output array using random elements from small input array;
- triada—copy one large array into another one using indirect index array (b[j] = a[ind[j]]);
- stencil_1D—processing two linear arrays (input and output) in the following way: each element with index i of the output array is calculated as a sum of $2 * R + 1$ elements of the input array with indices from $i - 1$ to $i + 1$;
- matrix_mult—naive implementation of classic matrix multiplication (without blocking);
- page_rank—graph algorithm for measuring "importance" of graph vertices;
- n_body—solving N-Body problem.

Test execution times ranged from seconds to minutes (all experiments were conducted on one node of Lomonosov-2 supercomputer). Within all tests, number of threads equal to the number of physical cores were used; parallelization were implemented using OpenMP. Experiments with other number of threads were also conducted, and the ratio of values between our assessments and Top-down metrics were the very similar.

The results are shown in Table 2 (sorted by the $score_{cpu}$ value). For each test, we present the values of our assessment and the corresponding Top-down metric, as well as the difference between them. Each experiment for collecting our assessments were conducted 5 times, average values are presented. The spread of values is very small—for every test the difference between the biggest and smallest values are less than 1%, both for $score_{cpu}$ and $score_{mem}$. The same is true for Intel Vtune, only 3 experiments were carried out for each test. All metrics are calculated as a percentage and therefore take values from 0 to 100.

Table 2. Comparison of values obtained using our assessments and Intel VTune

Benchmark	CPU usage			Memory usage		
	$score_{cpu}$	Retiring	diff.	$score_{mem}$	Memory bound	diff.
matrix_transp	3,38	3,50	−0,12	95,86	92,10	3,76
random_access	10,14	10,20	−0,06	81,66	75,00	6,66
triada	11,25	11,50	−0,25	84,30	76,00	8,30
stencil_1D	11,65	11,80	−0,15	83,67	78,70	4,97
matrix_mult	19,75	19,80	−0,05	72,37	62,40	9,97
page_rank	25,73	26,00	−0,27	60,41	48,10	12,31
n_body	52,14	53,30	−1,16	19,72	10,40	9,32

According to the results provided, we calculate $score_{cpu}$ very accurately—it differs from Retiring by slightly more than 1% only in case of n_body test, in all other cases the difference is less than 0.25%. The accuracy of memory usage assessment is not so high—Memory Bound and $score_{mem}$ values differ by more than 10% for page_rank, in other cases less than 10%. The problem here is that the formula used for $score_{mem}$ is too simple and does not capture all the peculiarities of using the memory subsystem. But, as it was stated before, more complex and precise formulas are unavailable in our case. Nevertheless, we consider that the resulting values are accurate enough for initial assessment of memory usage quality (which is the goal of our assessment system), e.g. the ranking of tests based on Memory Bound and $score_{mem}$ differs only in case of triada and stencil_1D test, which are similar according to Memory Bound values.

5.2 Assessing Network Usage

The latest versions of rules needed for calculating $score_{mpi}$ and $score_{io}$ according to formula (1) were implemented and used on a daily basis starting from June 1 in 2021 (the latest rule refinement were made specifically for the purpose of this project). We have collected and analyzed the statistics on these assessments for different users and software packages. Some interesting conclusions that can be drawn from these assessments are given below.

At first, the overall statistics for all users that have been running their jobs on the Lomonosov-2 supercomputer within the chosen time period was studied. The top 8 users sorted by $score_{io}$ are shown in Fig. 1. Each row corresponds to a particular user login, showing his assessments as well as node-hours consumed (nodeh), number of job launches (count), average number of nodes used (num_nodes) and average values of most interesting performance characteristics—user CPU load, amount of bytes received via MPI network per second (MPI_recv/s) as well as read and written via I/O network per second (FS_recv/s and FS_send/s).

score_mpi	score_io	nodeh	count	num_nodes	CPU load	MPI_recv/s	FS_recv/s	FS_send/s
12.77	21.95	3,374	2	30	11 %	891.2KB	49.7MB	745.9B
5.03	17.55	28,056	66	26	34 %	775.0B	10.9MB	6.7MB
7.49	17.18	12,741	23	22	15 %	657.0KB	19.5MB	61.4KB
1.82	15.05	26,512	35	27	59 %	382.3B	6.3MB	2.1MB
8.51	14.63	249	3	4	46 %	1.0MB	82.0MB	4.3MB
5.38	13.86	3	19	14	24 %	350.4KB	218.9MB	756.1B
4.26	13.66	36,654	45	25	50 %	142.9B	7.2MB	2.0MB
5.47	12.54	13,554	7	16	51 %	1.7KB	12.5MB	3.5MB

Fig. 1. List of Lomonosov-2 users with highest score$_{io}$ values during June–August 2021

It was discovered that the #1 and #3 logins belong to one particular user (working in two scientific projects), showing that in general this user works with I/O inefficiently. Looking in more detail at his jobs, we found out that in most of his jobs a rule about too small I/O packets was triggered, while I/O usage intensity is quite high—e.g. read speed for #1 login is 49.7 MB/s, which is a high value for an average, being #6 read speed between all users during this period. In this case, overheads on transferring I/O packets supposedly are noticeable, degrading the overall job performance. Moreover, some of these jobs had another rule triggered, showing overall low job activity with high I/O intensity, which strengthens our assumptions about noticeable overheads. It should be also noticed that #1 user login also shows the highest score$_{mpi}$ value of 12.77, making this user the most inefficient both in using MPI and I/O networks, according to our assessments. In this case it is definitely worth contacting this user in order to understand the reasons for such behavior—is it caused by inefficient software implementation (usually can be fixed) or properties of the algorithm being implemented (usually can't be changed).

Proposed assessments can help not only with overall ranking, but with comparing particular package usage as well. Figure 2 shows top LAMMPS package users with highest score$_{mpi}$ during the same time period. As seen, the value for the top user is drastically higher than values for other users—24.48, which is a quarter of maximum score of 100%, versus only 3.93 for the second highest value. The detailed study of this user jobs revealed that in 54 out of 77 jobs too small MPI packets were detected. This seems to be not so crucial in this case, since average MPI usage intensity is 3.1 MB/s, which is actually quite low. But there were also 50 jobs where the rule, which says that working with the MPI network takes up too many system resources, was triggered. This rule means that MPI usage intensity is noticeable but not very high, and wherein CPU system load is too high. This can mean that MPI data transfer is organized inefficiently, and too small MPI packets is one of the most likely reasons for that.

score_mpi	score_io	nodeh	count	num_nodes	CPU load	MPI_recv/s	FS_recv/s	FS_send/s
24.48	0.00	3,297	77	2	40 %	3.1MB	12.5B	39.3KB
3.93	0.30	3,853	146	10	77 %	17.9MB	918.1B	54.0KB
0.64	0.00	5,658	30	12	41 %	575.0KB	1.5KB	53.3KB
0.51	0.38	11,154	116	13	54 %	35.4MB	3.9KB	64.9KB
0.26	1.54	2,709	100	14	44 %	16.3MB	12.9KB	228.3KB

Fig. 2. List of top Lomonosov-2 users of LAMMPS package with the highest score$_{mpi}$ values during June–August 2021

Usage of proposed assessments doesn't help to understand the root causes of low quality of resource usage, but this was originally supposed to be performed using other analysis tools like TASC [10] or job performance analysis tools. The goal of the assessment system is to help in performing initial overall analysis, which allows detecting potential performance issues worth studying in more detail.

6   Conclusions and Future Work

In this paper, we have proposed an approach for assessing the quality of supercomputer resources usage using a developed assessment system. These assessments can be calculated automatically for all jobs running on a supercomputer, allowing quickly analyzing and comparing the utilization quality of individual jobs, users or software packages. This system is partially based on the existing metrics from the Top-down approach and the means for identifying performance issues proposed in the TASC system, but the proposed idea of their application for the specified goals is new. This assessment system is universal, since it allows automatically evaluating any jobs, regardless of their properties or launch parameters, and can be quite easily implemented on other computing systems.

In the future, we plan to complete the implementation of the assessment system in the GPU part, as well as improve the accuracy of the scores for MPI and I/O by expanding the set of rules for identifying performance issues. We also plan to make a distribution package of this assessment system suitable for installation on other systems.

Acknowledgments. The results described in this paper were achieved at Lomonosov Moscow State University with the financial support of the Russian Science Foundation (agreement No. 21-71-30003). The research is carried out using the equipment of shared research facilities of HPC computing resources at Lomonosov Moscow State University.

References

1. Cantrell, H.N., Ellison, A.L.: Multiprogramming system performance measurement and analysis. In: Proceedings of the Spring Joint Computer Conference, 30 April–2 May 1968, pp. 213–221 (1968)

2. Jones, M.D., et al.: Workload analysis of blue waters (2017). http://arxiv.org/abs/1703.00924
3. Simakov, N.A., et al.: A workload analysis of NSF's innovative HPC resources using XDMoD, p. 93. arXiv preprint arXiv:1801.04306 (2018)
4. Hart, D.L.: Measuring TeraGrid: workload characterization for a high-performance computing federation. Int. J. High Perform. Comput. Appl. **25**(4), 451–465 (2011). https://doi.org/10.1177/1094342010394382
5. Patel, T., Liu, Z., Kettimuthu, R., Rich, P., Allcock, W., Tiwari, D.: Job characteristics on large-scale systems: long-term analysis, quantification and implications. In: 2020 SC20: International Conference for High Performance Computing, Networking, Storage and Analysis (SC), pp. 1186–1202. IEEE Computer Society (2020)
6. Isakov, M., et al.: HPC I/O throughput bottleneck analysis with explainable local models. In: 2020 SC20: International Conference for High Performance Computing, Networking, Storage and Analysis (SC), pp. 455–467. IEEE Computer Society (2020)
7. POP Standard Metrics for Parallel Performance Analysis: Performance Optimisation and Productivity. https://pop-coe.eu/node/69
8. Yasin, A.: A top-down method for performance analysis and counters architecture. In: ISPASS 2014 - IEEE International Symposium on Performance Analysis of Systems and Software, pp. 35–44. IEEE Computer Society (2014). https://doi.org/10.1109/ISPASS.2014.6844459
9. Top-Down Microarchitecture Analysis Method Using VTune. https://software.intel.com/en-us/vtune-cookbook-top-down-microarchitecture-analysis-method
10. Shvets, P., Voevodin, V., Nikitenko, D.: Approach to workload analysis of large HPC centers. In: Sokolinsky, L., Zymbler, M. (eds.) PCT 2020. CCIS, vol. 1263, pp. 16–30. Springer, Cham (2020). https://doi.org/10.1007/978-3-030-55326-5_2
11. Shvets, P.A., Voevodin, V.V.: "Endless" workload analysis of large-scale supercomputers. Lobachevskii J. Math. **42**(1), 184–194 (2021). https://doi.org/10.1134/S1995080221010236
12. Meaning of IPC. https://software.intel.com/content/www/us/en/develop/documentation/vtune-help/top/reference/cpu-metrics-reference/ipc.html
13. Schulz, M., De Supinski, B.R.: PN MPI tools: a whole lot greater than the sum of their parts. In: Proceedings of the 2007 ACM/IEEE Conference on Supercomputing, pp. 1–10 (2007). https://doi.org/10.1145/1362622.1362663
14. Elis, B., Yang, D., Pearce, O., Mohror, K., Schulz, M.: QMPI: a next generation MPI profiling interface for modern HPC platforms. Parallel Comput. **96**, 102635 (2020). https://doi.org/10.1016/j.parco.2020.102635
15. Shaikhislamov, D., Voevodin, V.: Solving the problem of detecting similar supercomputer applications using machine learning methods. In: Sokolinsky, L., Zymbler, M. (eds.) PCT 2020. CCIS, vol. 1263, pp. 46–57. Springer, Cham (2020). https://doi.org/10.1007/978-3-030-55326-5_4
16. Voevodin, V.V., et al.: Supercomputer Lomonosov-2: large scale, deep monitoring and fine analytics for the user community. Supercomput. Front. Innov. **6**(2), 4–11 (2019). https://doi.org/10.14529/jsfi190201
17. Intel VTune Profiler. https://software.intel.com/content/www/us/en/develop/tools/oneapi/components/vtune-profiler.html
18. Intel PMU profiling tools. https://github.com/andikleen/pmu-tools

19. Stefanov, K., Voevodin, V., Zhumatiy, S., Voevodin, V.: Dynamically reconfigurable distributed modular monitoring system for supercomputers (DiMMon). Procedia Comput. Sci. **66**, 625–634 (2015). https://doi.org/10.1016/j.procs.2015.11.071

20. Terpstra, D., Jagode, H., You, H., Dongarra, J.: Collecting performance data with PAPI-C. In: Müller, M., Resch, M., Schulz, A., Nagel, W. (eds.) Tools for High Performance Computing 2009, pp. 157–173. Springer, Heidelberg (2010). https://doi.org/10.1007/978-3-642-11261-4_11

21. nvprof profiling tool guide. https://docs.nvidia.com/cuda/profiler-users-guide/index.html#nvprof-overview

Distributed and Cloud Computing

Desktop Grid and Cloud Computing: Short Survey

Evgeny Ivashko[1,2](✉)

[1] Institute of Applied Mathematical Research, Karelian Research Centre of RAS,
Petrozavodsk, Russia
ivashko@krc.karelia.ru
[2] Petrozavodsk State University, Petrozavodsk, Russia

Abstract. In this paper a short survey on Desktop Grid and Cloud computing paradigms combination is presented. There are four approaches are considered: (1) extension of a Cloud by Desktop Grid's nodes; (2) extension of a Desktop Grid by a Cloud nodes; (3) implementation of Cloud services on top of Desktop Grid's nodes; and (4) implementation of a Desktop Grid as a Service.

Keywords: Desktop Grid · BOINC · Volunteer computing · Cloud computing

1   Introduction: Desktop Grid and Cloud Computing

Recent years, Cloud computing concept is receiving keen interest and is being widely adopted. It offers clients specialized applications, data bases, various computing resources, and different information technology management functions as a service through the Internet or a dedicated network. Several converging and complementary factors have led to cloud computing's emergence as a popular computing service-delivery model that appeals to all stakeholders. Cloud computing had become a radical new computing services delivery and business model, and a paradigm change in information technology; users can have cloud services when and where they need them and in the quantity that they need, and pay for only the resources they use. The concept also offers huge computing power, flexibility, reliability, on-demand scalability, and utility-like availability at low cost.

According to the National Institute of Standards and Technology (abbr. NIST, USA), *Cloud computing* is a model for enabling convenient, on-demand network access to a shared pool of configurable computing resources (e.g., networks, servers, storage, applications, and services) that can be rapidly provisioned and released with minimal management effort or service provider interaction[1].

---

[1] https://www.nist.gov/programs-projects/nist-cloud-computing-program-nccp.

© Springer Nature Switzerland AG 2021
V. Voevodin and S. Sobolev (Eds.): RuSCDays 2021, CCIS 1510, pp. 445–456, 2021.
https://doi.org/10.1007/978-3-030-92864-3_34

Cloud computing has the following inherent properties:

- On-demand self-service: computing capabilities (e.g. server time and network storage) can be unilaterally automatically provisioned as needed).
- Broad network access: capabilities are accessible through heterogeneous thin or thick client platforms (e.g., mobile phones, tablets, laptops, and workstations).
- Resource pooling: computing resources (e.g. storage, processing, memory, and bandwidth) are pooled to serve multiple consumers, and are dynamically assigned and reassigned according to demand.
- Rapid elasticity: capabilities can be elastically provisioned and released commensurate with demand. Available capabilities often appear to be unlimited.
- Measured service: resource use is automatically controlled and optimized through metering capabilities, appropriate to type of service (e.g., storage, processing, bandwidth, and active user accounts).
- Multitenancy: cloud computing is a shared resource that draws on resource pooling as an important feature. It implies use of same resources by multiple consumers, called tenants.

There are three main services provided by Cloud computing:

1. Software as a service (SaaS): use of applications that run on the cloud.
2. Platform as a service (PaaS): deployment of applications on the cloud infrastructure; may use supported programming languages, libraries, services, and tools.
3. Infrastructure as a service (IaaS): provisioning of processing, storage, networks, etc.; may deploy and run operating systems, applications, etc.

One of the key attractive points of cloud services is use of Service Level Agreements (abbr. SLA). Service Level Agreement is the key document between the cloud service provider and consumer which binds them for a certain time period with the commitment of defined services. SLA guarantees Quality of Service (abbr. QoS), which is one of the SLA's key parameters of a trusted relationship. QoS parameters e.g. trust, security, privacy, resource management, risk management etc. get together to result in forming a viable SLA between service provider and consumer. QoS repository and assessment framework as well as a committed provider for a consumer reserving its resources whether the consumer uses it or not leads to a trusted relationship in cloud.

Meanwhile, with the growth of computing power of personal computers and speeding up regular Internet connection, a Desktop Grid computing concept more and more raises its potential.

Desktop Grid is a distributed high-throughput computing system which uses idle resources of non-dedicated geographically distributed computing nodes connected over regular network. In common case the nodes of a Desktop Grid are either desktop and laptop computers of volunteers connected over the Internet (Volunteer computing) or an organization desktop computers connected over local area network (Enterprise Desktop Grid).

Desktop Grid computing can provide large computing capacity at low cost, but presents challenges due to high device heterogeneity, low reliability, etc. There is a number of middleware systems to implement a Desktop Grid: BOINC, Condor, XtremWeb, and others (see [1]). The most popular and standard de-facto for Volunteer computing is BOINC, which is an open-source middleware system originally developed to support the SETI@home project. The potential capacity of Volunteer computing is on the order of hundreds of ExaFLOPS [2].

Desktop Grid advantages are the following:

- ease of deployment and support,
- low cost,
- high scalability,
- significant potential peak performance,
- ease of software development,
- etc.,

and disadvantages:

- slow connection between the server and computing nodes,
- limited computational capacity of separate nodes,
- high heterogeneity of software, hardware, or both,
- lack of availability information,
- low reliability of computing nodes,
- lack of trust to computing nodes.

Comparing to computing clusters (supercomputers) Desktop Grids are limited by "bag-of-tasks" problems with independent parallelism and low data/compute ratio, such as Monte-Carlo simulations, parameter sweep opti-mization, combinatorics, etc. Therefore Desktop Grids are less widespread com-paring to computing clusters and Computational Grids.

The researchers also paid attention to comparing Desktop Grid and Cloud computing paradigms. In (outdated but systematic analysis) paper [3] authors address the following questions:

- What are the performance tradeoffs in using one platform over the other?
- What are the specific resource requirements and monetary costs of creating and deploying applications on each platform?
- In light of those monetary and performance cost-benefits, how do these plat-forms compare?
- Can cloud computing platforms be used in combination with desktop grids to improve cost-effectiveness even further?

The authors examine those questions using performance measurements and mon-etary expenses of real Desktop Grids and the Amazon Elastic Compute Cloud (abbr. EC2).

In result, the authors determined the cost-benefits of Cloud computing versus Volunteer computing applications; calculated Volunteer computing overheads for platform construction, application deployment, compute rates, and completion times.

- the ratio of volunteer nodes needed to achieve the compute power of a small Amazon EC2 instance is about 2.83 active volunteer hosts to 1,
- monthly Volunteer computing project costs range between 5K–12K, and startup costs range from 4K to 43K,
- if cloud computing systems are to replace Volunteer computing platforms, pay-per-use costs would have to decrease by at least an order of magnitude,
- cost of a 1000-node cloud will exceed that of Volunteer computing system after three days,
- 4 months on EC2 with 1000 nodes can support over a year of SETI@home,
- with 12K per month, SETI could purchase a maximum of 2 TeraFLOPS sustained over a month with HighCPU instances,
- use of hybrid approaches where a Volunteer computing server is hosted on a cloud to lower the start-up and monthly costs could save ranges between 40–95% depending on resource usage. In general, if bandwidth needs do not exceed 100 Mbit and storage needs are less than 10 TB's, hosting a server on a cloud is likely cheaper than conducting a project on one's own,
- server bandwidth on cloud is particularly expensive.

Concluding, the research [3] shows that Cloud computing is much more beneficial than Volunteer computing in terms of costs and computing performance; meanwhile, hosting the server of a Volunteer computing project in a cloud is the best way to reduce costs.

Years later research [2] shows different results. D. Anderson highlights that the monetary cost of Volunteer computing is divided between volunteers and scientists: volunteers pay for buying and maintaining computing devices, for the electricity to power these devices, and for Internet connectivity; scientists pay for a server and for the staff (system administrators, programmers and web developers needed to operate the Volunteer computing project). The author estimates operating costs of a typical Volunteer computing project on the order of $100 K per year (this involves a few Linux server computers and a part-time system administrator). Several BOINC projects (Einstein@Home, Rosetta@home, SETI@home) are of this scale, and they average about 2 PetaFLOPS throughput each, while use of compute-intensive Amazon EC2 instances have total cost of $43.52 M per year for 2 PetaFlops – 435 times the cost of using Volunteer computing; the cost is lower for "spot" instances – about $8.21 M/year. Thus, Volunteer computing is potentially much cheaper than EC2; the numbers are similar for other cloud providers.

As both paradigms – Cloud computing and Desktop Grid computing – have their own advantages, there is a number of works related to integration of these approaches. The common idea is to get flexibility, reliability and user-friendliness of a Cloud service, and cheap and powerful computing resources of a Desktop Grid.

The paper is devoted to analysis of different ways used to integrate Desktop Grid and Cloud computing paradigms.

2   Survey

In this paper we consider the following different ways of Desktop Grid and Cloud computing paradigms combination:

1. extension of a Desktop Grid using a Cloud;
2. extension of a Cloud using a Desktop Grid resources;
3. implementation of a Cloud basing on a Desktop Grid resources;
4. providing Desktop Grid as a cloud service;
5. other ways.

2.1   Extension of a Desktop Grid Using a Cloud

The idea behind of extension of a Desktop Grid using a cloud is the following. The computing nodes of a Desktop Grid are unreliable, they could leave the computing network without any notification. This is a big problem, especially in case of "tail" completion (completion of the last tasks of a computing experiment, see [4,5]). Use of cloud resources allows to significantly improve reliability, speedup the computations and even provide good SLA keeping low costs.

One of the first such works is described in paper [6], where Aneka – a platform for developing scalable applications on the Cloud – is presented. It enhancing Desktop Grid infrastructures with Cloud resources, with offering QoS to users, motivating the adoption of Desktop Grids as a viable platform for application execution. The paper highlights the key concepts and features of Aneka that support the integration between Desktop Grids and Clouds and presents an experiment showing the performance of this integration.

Another pioneer approach was presented as a part of EDGeS project. The aim of the EDGeS project was to create an integrated infrastructure that combines the advantages of service and Desktop Grid concepts. In paper [7], the authors first focus on bridging from BOINC-based desktop grids towards EGEE-like service grids[2], i.e., making desktop grids able to utilize free service grid resources. The solution is based on a generic grid-to-grid bridge, called 3G Bridge. In the second part of the paper the authors show how the 3G Bridge and EDGeS Bridge services can be used to implement the reverse direction interconnection of BOINC and EGEE grids. The paper [5] details the results of the EU FP7 EDGI project focusing on the cloud developments and usability improvements. It details how clouds have been utilized to shorten completion time on the EDGeS@home volunteer Desktop Grid and to boost the performance of the supported gLite VO. It also describes how this service can be exploited by the gLite user communities of European Grid Initiative all over Europe.

Finally, paper [8] introduces connectivity and interoperability issues of Clouds, Grids and computing clusters, and provides solutions to overcome these issues. The authors propose several possible ways to pool Cloud resources for executing bag of tasks type jobs and present two implementations based on BOINC

---

[2] Enabling Grids for E-sciencE, abbr. EGEE; the project officially finished in 2010.

and Condor. The paper details performance measurement results obtained by executing parameter study type applications using the two implementations.

The more recent example of extension of a Desktop Grid using a Cloud is BOINC@TACC [9]. It uses virtual machines for running BOINC jobs in a Cloud.

2.2   Extension of a Cloud Using a Desktop Grid Resources

As it was mentioned above, Cloud resources are much more expensive than Desktop Grid resources. So, use of computing nodes of a Desktop Grid to provide cloud services promises to improve economics of the services keeping high level of SLA. This reasoning lays behind the papers [10–12].

Everest is a web-based distributed computing platform that uses service-oriented approach and cloud computing models to overcome complexity of distributed computing infrastructures. Paper [10] discusses the possible approaches for integration of Everest and BOINC-based Desktop Grids and presents the prototype implementation. This implementation enables Everest users to seamlessly access computing resources of Desktop Grids and build generic or domain-specific web services for submission and automation of computations in Desktop Grids.

Interesting results earned authors of [11]. The paper investigates how a mixture of dedicated (and so highly available, i.e. cloud) hosts and non-dedicated (and so highly volatile, i.e. Desktop Grid) hosts can be used to provision a processing tier of a large-scale web service. The authors discuss an operational model which guarantees long-term availability despite of host churn, and study multiple aspects necessary to implement it, including: ranking of non-dedicated hosts according to their long-term availability behavior, short-term availability modeling of these hosts, and simulation of migration and group availability levels using real-world availability data from a number of non-dedicated hosts. The authors also study the tradeoff between a larger share of dedicated hosts vs. higher migration rate in terms of costs and SLA objectives. This yields an optimization approach where a service provider can find a suitable balance between costs and service quality.

In [12] authors propose a cloud infrastructure that combines on-demand allocation of resources with opportunistic provisioning of cycles from idle cloud nodes to other processes by deploying backfill virtual machines (VMs). Nimbus cloud computing toolkit is used to implement an experimental testbed, which is able to deploy backfill VMs on idle cloud nodes for processing an high-throughput computing workload. The experiments show an increase in IaaS cloud utilization from 37.5% to 100% during a portion of the evaluation trace but only 6.39% overhead cost for processing the high-throughput computing workload. So, the paper shows that a shared infrastructure between IaaS cloud providers and an high-throughput computing job management system can be highly beneficial to both the IaaS cloud provider and users by increasing the utilization of the cloud infrastructure (thereby decreasing the overall cost) and contributing cycles that would otherwise be idle to processing high-throughput computing jobs.

2.3   Implementation of a Cloud Basing on Resources of a Desktop Grid

One of the most attractive ideas which is the direct evolution of the Desktop Grid concept is implementation of a Cloud basing on non-dedicated computing resources. Desktop cloud platforms run clusters of virtual machines taking advantage of idle resources on desktop computers. These platforms execute virtual machines along with the applications started by the users in those desktops. This require adaptation of internal Cloud architecture (brokers, billing, etc.) to unreliable and dynamic structure of computing nodes network. The most advanced and known systems are UnaCloud [13–17] and Cloud@Home[3] [18–21] which will be considered in more details below. Another emerging system is cuCloud presented in [22] which is basing on virtual machines. One more example presents Volunteer Computing as a Service (VCaaS) based Edge Computing infrastructure [23]. In the paper the authors proposed and discussed a three layer Volunteer Computing as a Service based Edge Computing infrastructure. The proposed volunteer Edge computing architecture is a blend of Volunteer Computing, Mobile Computing, IoT, and Cloud Computing. The next example is a concept of "Desktop Clouds": gathering non-dedicated and idle resources in order to provide Cloud services [24].

UnaCloud

Paper [25] presents UnaCloud, which is an opportunistic cloud computing Infrastructure as a Service (IaaS) model implementation. UnaCloud is aimed at providing computing resources (i.e. processing, storage and networking) to run arbitrary software (including operating systems and applications) at low costs. The IaaS model is provided through the opportunistic use of idle computing resources available in a university campus. For that, UnaCloud has to deal with the problems associated to use commodity, non-dedicated, distributed, and heterogeneous computing resources that are part of different administrative domains. The authors developed an IaaS architecture based on two strategies: an opportunistic strategy that allows the use of idle computing resources in a non-intrusive manner, and a virtualization strategy to allow the on-demand deployment of customized execution environments. The proposed solution shows high efficiency in the deployment of virtual machines for academic and scientific projects.

One of the big problems limiting scalability of UnaCloud is large transmission times. To launch a virtual computing site, the platform first determines which computers can run the virtual machines and copies the corresponding images to these computers. Use of TCP-based protocol to copy those images results in large transmission times and frequent reaching a timeout. Paper [14] reports the efforts to scale the deployment in UnaCloud to support computing sites with a large number of nodes. The authors have implemented and evaluated multiple protocols for transferring virtual machine images; using BitTorrent, a P2P file transfer protocol, and other protocols, UnaCloud can deploy up to 100 virtual machines, one per desktop, in less than 10 min. Although this time is twice the

---

[3] Seems to be nondeveloping.

offered by Amazon EC2, it is better than the exhibited by dedicated private clouds using software such as OpenStack and VMWare vCloud.

The next paper [13] shows and analyzes the execution of a MPI-based application (Gromacs, molecular dynamic application) over a UnaCloud infrastructure supported by desktop computers. The main objective is to find a solution to support Gromacs-MPI on UnaCloud. Although the computing results were finally obtained, the handle of resource discovery and failure recovery on the opportunistic infrastructure were performed manually, restricting the application scope of the solution. To eliminate these restrictions, a mechanism to automate the process execution on UnaCloud was identified and proposed.

The work [16] describes the main characteristics and settings of UnaCloud. The platform is improved custom virtual machine settings, which allow MPI applications to tolerate the loss of a computing node without having to restart the whole simulation (through checkpointing). The authors also describe the new focus on a self-service paradigm, which consists of offering the user the possibility of managing his own virtual machines and software.

Several cloud technologies such as Tensorflow or Hadoop that rely on master-worker architectures are sensitive to failures in specific nodes. To support these types of applications, it is important to understand which failures may interrupt the execution of these clusters, what faults may cause some errors and which strategies can be used to mitigate or tolerate them. Using the UnaCloud platform as a case study, paper [26] presents an analysis of the failures that may occur in desktop clouds and the mitigation strategies available to improve dependability.

Cloud@Home

The main goal of Cloud@Home is to implement a volunteer-Cloud paradigm which allows to aggregate Cloud infrastructure providers. Cloud@Home proposes to incorporate some elements of Volunteer computing into the Cloud paradigm involving into the mix nodes and devices provided by potentially any owners or administrators, disclosing high computational resources to contributors and also allowing to maximize their utilization. Papers [18–21, 27] present and discuss the main characteristics of the platform: providing quality of service and service level agreement facilities on top of unreliable, intermittent Cloud providers. The solution is based on a logical organization of all the resources into a hierarchical cluster, implementing autonomic, distributed and self-adapting algorithms to manage the hierarchical infrastructure according to the resource availability variations. Some of the main issues and challenges of Cloud@Home, such as the monitoring, management and brokering of resources according to service level requirements are addressed through the design of a framework core architecture. All the tasks committed to the architecture's modules and components, as well as the most relevant component interactions, are identified and discussed from both the structural and the behavioural viewpoints. In result, Cloud@Home paradigm aims at merging the benefits of cloud computing-service-oriented interfaces, dynamic service provisioning, and guaranteed QoS-with those of Volunteer computing-capitalized idle resources and reduced operational costs. The authors specifically focus on SLA-QoS aspects, describing how to provide SLA based QoS guarantees through Cloud@Home on top of non-QoS oriented Cloud Providers.

2.4 Desktop Grid as a Service

Finally, the most natural way of Desktop Grid and Cloud computing paradigms combination is to provide high-throughput computations as a cloud service.

In paper [28] the authors propose the ideas how to make Desktop Grid and particularly Volunteer computing more attractive for scientists. These ideas are the following:

- The extension of service grids with support of inexpensive BOINC resources will turn the attention of service grid users towards BOINC systems.
- The access of BOINC systems via workflow-oriented science gateways will enlarge the number of user communities that can use BOINC systems in their daily work.
- Providing QoS requirements in BOINC systems by extending them with on-demand cloud resources will attract user communities whose applications have got some time constraints.

In paper [29] the authors draw conclusions on more than a decade for running grand challenge applications basing on BOINC. The authors show those technologies, and particularly virtualization and cloud solutions, that make BOINC Desktop Grids more generic and speed up the execution of existing grid-enabled parameter sweep applications without porting them to BOINC and eliminate the tail problem of volunteer BOINC systems. They also show a technology by which institutional and public desktop grids can be created in a few minutes in clouds and used without any BOINC knowledge.

The paper [30] completes the work started in the EU FP7 EDGI project for extending service grids with volunteer (global) and institutional (local) Desktop Grids. The Generic BOINC Application Client (GBAC) concept described in the paper enables the transparent and automatic forwarding of parameter sweep application jobs from service grid Virtual Organizations into connected desktop grids. GBAC that introduces virtualization for the volunteer BOINC is also considered as a first step towards establishing volunteer cloud systems.

2.5 Other Ideas

There are also other ideas related to Desktop Grid and Cloud computing combination. Among them is of interest an idea of mobile clouds. Since smartphones and other mobile devices have drastically improved their computing performance and data storage/transfer capabilities, one is able to extend Desktop Grids to mobile devices. It also could be implemented basing on Cloud computing principles.

The paper [31] review current research effort towards Mobile Computing. The authors present several challenges for the design of Mobile Cloud Computing service and propose a concept model to analyze related research work.

The paper also provides survey on Mobile Cloud Computing architecture, application partition & offloading, and context-aware service.

The paper [32] presents one of the first mobile cloud computing paradigm that delivers applications to mobile devices by using cloud computing. Among others, the paper [33] develops this approach. A mobile cloud computing model, in which platforms of volunteer devices provide part of the resources of the cloud, inspired by both Volunteer computing and mobile edge computing paradigms. These platforms may be hierarchical, based on the capabilities of the volunteer devices and the requirements of the services provided by the clouds. The cloud itself is based on the resources of nearby mobile devices. In the focus is the orchestration between the volunteer platform and the public, private or hybrid clouds. This new model can be an inexpensive solution to different application scenarios, highlighting its benefits in cost savings, elasticity, scalability, load balancing, and efficiency.

3   Conclusion

Both Cloud computing and Desktop Grid concepts are attractive for the users. Their combination gives additional benefits. In such a way, extension of a Cloud by Desktop Grid's nodes promises lower costs; extension of a Desktop Grid by a Cloud nodes promises higher reliability; implementation of a Desktop Grid as a Service gives more convenient access; finally, implementation of a Cloud services on top of a Desktop Grid's computing nodes promises low costs and big value of available resources.

References

1. Rahmany, M., Sundararajan, A., Zin, A.: A review of desktop grid computing middlewares on non-dedicated resources. J. Theor. Appl. Inf. Technol. **98**(10), 1654–1663 (2020)
2. Anderson, D.: BOINC: a platform for volunteer computing. J. Grid Comput. **18**, 99–122 (2020)
3. Kondo, D., Javadi, B., Malecot, P., Cappello, F., Anderson, D.: Cost-benefit analysis of cloud computing versus desktop grids. In: IPDPS, pp. 1–12, June 2009
4. Ivashko, E., Nikitina, N.: Replication of "Tail" computations in a desktop grid project. In: Voevodin, V., Sobolev, S. (eds.) RuSCDays 2020. CCIS, vol. 1331, pp. 611–621. Springer, Cham (2020). https://doi.org/10.1007/978-3-030-64616-5_52
5. Kovács, J., Marosi, A., Visegradi, A., Farkas, Z., Kacsuk, P., Lovas, R.: Boosting gLite with cloud augmented volunteer computing. Futur. Gener. Comput. Syst. **43**, 12–23 (2015)
6. Calheiros, R., Vecchiola, C., Karunamoorthy, D., Buyya, R.: The Aneka platform and QoS-driven resource provisioning for elastic applications on hybrid clouds. Futur. Gener. Comput. Syst. **28**, 861–870 (2012)
7. Farkas, Z., Kacsuk, P., Balaton, Z., Gombás, G.: Interoperability of BOINC and EGEE. Futur. Gener. Comput. Syst. **26**, 1092–1103 (2010)

8. Marosi, A.C., Kacsuk, P.: Workers in the clouds. In: 2011 19th International Euromicro Conference on Parallel, Distributed and Network-Based Processing, pp. 519–526 (2011)

9. Arora, R., Redondo, C., Joshua, G.: Scalable software infrastructure for integrating supercomputing with volunteer computing and cloud computing. In: Majumdar, A., Arora, R. (eds.) SCEC 2018. CCIS, vol. 964, pp. 105–119. Springer, Singapore (2019). https://doi.org/10.1007/978-981-13-7729-7_8

10. Sukhoroslov, O.: Integration of Everest platform with BOINC-based desktop grids. In: CEUR Workshop Proceedings of the Conference BOINC:FAST 2017, pp. 102–107, August 2017

11. Andrzejak, A., Kondo, D., Anderson, D.: Exploiting non-dedicated resources for cloud computing. In: 2010 IEEE Network Operations and Management Symposium - NOMS 2010, pp. 341–348, May 2010

12. Marshall, P., Keahey, K., Freeman, T.: Improving utilization of infrastructure clouds. In: 2011 11th IEEE/ACM International Symposium on Cluster, Cloud and Grid Computing, pp. 205–214 (2011)

13. Garcés, N., Castro, H., Delgado, P., Gonz'lez, A., Jaramillo, C.A., Peñaranda, N., Delgado, M.d.P.: Analysis of Gromacs MPI using the opportunistic cloud infrastructure UnaCloud. In: 2012 Sixth International Conference on Complex, Intelligent, and Software Intensive Systems, pp. 1001–1006 (2012)

14. Chavarriaga, J., Forero, C., Padilla Agudelo, J., Muñoz, A., Cáliz-Ospino, R., Castro, H.: Scaling the Deployment of Virtual Machines in UnaCloud, pp. 399–413, January 2018

15. Osorio, J.D., Castro, H., Brasileiro, F.: Perspectives of UnaCloud: an opportunistic cloud computing solution for facilitating research. In: 2012 12th IEEE/ACM International Symposium on Cluster, Cloud and Grid Computing (CCGrid 2012), pp. 717–718 (2012)

16. Ortiz, N., Garcés, N., Sotelo, G., Méndez, D., Castillo-Coy, F., Castro, H.: Multiple services hosted on the opportunistic infrastructure UnaCloud. In: Proceedings of the Joint GISELA-CHAIN Conference (2012)

17. Plazas Montañez, L.F., et al.: Opportunistic IaaS platform based on containers. B.S. thesis, Uniandes (2019)

18. Cunsolo, V.D., Distefano, S., Puliafito, A., Scarpa, M.: Volunteer computing and desktop cloud: the cloud@home paradigm. In: 2009 Eighth IEEE International Symposium on Network Computing and Applications, pp. 134–139 (2009)

19. Distefano, S., Puliafito, A.: Cloud@home: toward a volunteer cloud. IT Profess. 14, 27–31 (2012)

20. Cuomo, A., Di Modica, G., Distefano, S., Rak, M., Vecchio, A.: The cloud@home architecture - building a cloud infrastructure from volunteered resources, pp. 424–430, January 2011

21. Distefano, S., et al.: QoS management in cloud@home infrastructures, pp. 190–197, October 2011

22. Mengistu, T.M., Alahmadi, A.M., Alsenani, Y., Albuali, A., Che, D.: cuCloud: volunteer computing as a service (VCaaS) system. In: Luo, M., Zhang, L.-J. (eds.) CLOUD 2018. LNCS, vol. 10967, pp. 251–264. Springer, Cham (2018). https://doi.org/10.1007/978-3-319-94295-7_17

23. Mengistu, T.M., Albuali, A., Alahmadi, A., Che, D.: Volunteer cloud as an edge computing enabler. In: Zhang, T., Wei, J., Zhang, L.-J. (eds.) EDGE 2019. LNCS, vol. 11520, pp. 76–84. Springer, Cham (2019). https://doi.org/10.1007/978-3-030-23374-7_6

24. Alwabel, A., Walters, R.J., Wills, G.B.: A resource allocation model for desktop clouds. In: Web Services, pp. 258–279. IGI Global (2019). https://doi.org/10.4018/978-1-5225-7501-6.ch016

25. Rosales, E., Castro, H., Villamizar, M.: UnaCloud: opportunistic cloud computing infrastructure as a service. In: CLOUD COMPUTING 2011 the Second International Conference on Cloud Computing GRIDs and Virtualization, pp. 187–194 (2011)

26. Gómez, C.E., Chavarriaga, J., Castro, H.E.: Fault characterization and mitigation strategies in desktop cloud systems. In: Meneses, E., Castro, H., Barrios Hernández, C.J., Ramos-Pollan, R. (eds.) CARLA 2018. CCIS, vol. 979, pp. 322–335. Springer, Cham (2019). https://doi.org/10.1007/978-3-030-16205-4_24

27. Cuomo, A., et al.: An SLA-based broker for cloud infrastructures. J. Grid Comput. **11**, 1–25 (2012)

28. Kacsuk, P.: How to make BOINC-based desktop grids even more popular? In: IEEE International Symposium on Parallel and Distributed Processing Workshops and PHD Forum, pp. 1871–1877, June 2011

29. Kacsuk, P., et al.: Desktop grid in the era of cloud computing, pp. 187–206, January 2015

30. Marosi, A., Kovács, J., Kacsuk, P.: Towards a volunteer cloud system. Futur. Gener. Comput. Syst. **29**, 1442–1451 (2013)

31. Noor, T.H., Zeadally, S., Alfazi, A., Sheng, Q.Z.: Mobile cloud computing: challenges and future research directions. J. Netw. Comput. Appl. **115**, 70–85 (2018). https://www.sciencedirect.com/science/article/pii/S1084804518301504

32. Huerta-Canepa, G., Lee, D.: A virtual cloud computing provider for mobile devices. In: Proceedings of the 1st ACM Workshop on Mobile Cloud Computing & Services: Social Networks and Beyond, MCS 2010, vol. 6, January 2010

33. Alonso Monsalve, S., Garcia-Carballeira, F., Calderón, A.: A heterogeneous mobile cloud computing model for hybrid clouds. Futur. Gener. Comput. Syst. **87**, 651–666 (2018)

Multi-cloud Privacy-Preserving Logistic Regression

Jorge M. Cortés-Mendoza[1] , Andrei Tchernykh[1,2,3(✉)] ,
Mikhail Babenko[4] , Bernardo Pulido-Gaytán[2] ,
and Gleb Radchenko[1]

[1] South Ural State University, Chelyabinsk, Russia
{kortesmendosak, gleb. radchenko}@susu. ru
[2] CICESE Research Center, Ensenada, BC, Mexico
{chernykh, lpulido}@cicese. edu. mx
[3] Ivannikov Institute for System Programming, Moscow, Russia
[4] North-Caucasus Federal University, Stavropol, Russia
mgbabenko@ncfu. ru

Abstract. Clouds can significantly reduce the cost and time of business solutions. However, cloud services introduce significant security and privacy challenges when they process sensitive information. For instance, a dataset for machine learning could contain delicate information that traditional encryption approaches cannot protect during data analysis. Homomorphic Encryption (HE) schemes and secure Multi-Party Computation (MPC) are considered solutions for privacy protection in third-party infrastructures. In this paper, we propose a Multi-Cloud Logistic Regression based on Residue Number System (MC-LR-RNS) that provides security, parallel processing, and scalability. To validate the efficiency and practicability of the solution, we provide its analysis with different configurations, datasets, and cloud service providers. We use six available datasets from medicine (diabetes, cancer, drugs, etc.) and genomics. The analysis shows that MC-LR-RNS provides the same levels of quality as non-HE solutions and improved performance due to multi-cloud parallel computations.

Keywords: Cloud security · Homomorphic encryption · Secure multi-party computation · Residue number system · Privacy-preserving logistic regression

1 Introduction

The increasing use of cloud computing to store, retrieve, and process data motivates Cloud Service Providers (CSPs) to find more secure and efficient manners to offer services. One limitation in the massive adoption of cloud services focuses on security and privacy issues. Users want to delegate the data control to a CSP (third-party entity) in a secure way.

CSPs provide data protection from theft, leakage, deletion, integrity, etc., at different levels. However, techniques based on firewalls, penetration testing, obfuscation, tokenization, Virtual Private Networks (VPN) cannot protect the information during its

© Springer Nature Switzerland AG 2021
V. Voevodin and S. Sobolev (Eds.): RuSCDays 2021, CCIS 1510, pp. 457–471, 2021.
https://doi.org/10.1007/978-3-030-92864-3_35

processing. Conventional data encryption does not avoid this security problem. For example, a dataset with delicate information must be decrypted to be processed with a Machine Learning (ML) model. The ML technique needs full access to the raw data to apply statistical analysis, also known as model training. Decrypting the data involves significant risk when the ML model is executed on a cloud service.

Homomorphic Encryption (HE) and secure Multi-Party Computation (MPC) have become alternatives to solve data processing vulnerabilities. Both approaches aim to guarantee that the remote untrusted party does not learn anything about the computation input or output. They can provide secure processing in cloud computing environments (in general, for any third-party infrastructure).

On one side, HE cryptosystems can perform certain mathematical operations directly on the ciphertext, so the data can be processed even if it is encrypted. Unfortunately, these systems suffer from complicated designs, low computational efficiency, and high computing complexity [1].

On the other side, MPC systems can compute functions by the collaboration between several entities, where each entity keeps individual input private. Regrettably, they suffer from the online requirement, multiple communication rounds, and overhead in storage and computations [2]. Even with their downsides, we can apply both approaches to certain kinds of domains, like ML.

In recent years, the Residue Number System (RNS) is used to accelerate HE cryptosystems processing [3] and cloud storage [4]. Furthermore, it can be seen as a Secret Sharing scheme (SS) and a variant of HE [4]. This widely-known number theory system codes the original numbers as tuples of residues that can be processed in parallel. Additionally to its inherent parallelism, the advantages of RNS include security, scalability, error detection, and correction [5]. These systems exhibit limitations for operations related to the magnitude of numbers, but they have been applied efficiently for solving several problems.

A system based on HE and MPC can provide adequate security levels. Moreover, its RNS implementation can pursue the system all the advantages of RNS. To enrich the ML as a Service (MLaaS) paradigm, we propose the Multi-Cloud Logistic Regression based on Residue Number System (MC-LR-RNS) algorithm, which processes confidential information securely using several cloud environments. Our contribution is multifold:

- We propose a logistic regression algorithm with homomorphic encryption and secure multi-cloud computing based on a residue number system.
- We perform the training and testing processes of the logistical regression model homomorphically, that is, over encrypted data and without secret keys.
- Our approach inherits the residue number system's advantages, such as parallelism and scalability.
- We analyze the algorithm performance with six available datasets of different medicine domains (diabetes, cancer, drugs, etc.) and genomics.

The paper is structured as follows. The next Section describes the foundations of logistic regression and gradient descent. Section 3 discusses related works in the domain of HE schemes, secure MPC and RNS systems. Section 4 presents the multi-cloud logistic regression algorithm. Section 5 analyzes the performance of the proposed algorithm. Finally, we conclude and discuss future work in Sect. 6.

2 Logistic Regression and Gradient Descent

Logistic Regression (LR) is a statistical method for analyzing and predicting a binary (or dichotomous) outcome (success/failure, yes/no, etc.). The inference model depends on the characteristics of the elements in the dataset.

A dataset X defines N elements of dimension d, and Y establishes their binary labels. Formally, each element is determined by $x^{(i)} \in \mathbb{R}^d$ and its corresponding label $y^{(i)} \in \{0, 1\}$ for $i = 1, 2, \ldots, N$.

The logistic/sigmoid function is the basis in the LR inference, the LR hypotheses is $h_\theta(x^{(i)}) = g(\theta^T x^{(i)})$, for the sigmoid function $g(z) = \frac{1}{1+e^{-z}}$, a parameter $\theta^T = [\theta_0, \theta_1, \ldots, \theta_d]^T$, and the characteristics of the input element $x^{(i)} = [1, x^{(i)}_1, x^{(i)}_2, \ldots, x^{(i)}_d]^T$, where $\theta^T x^{(i)}$ defines a linear combination of multiple explanatory variables.

The model's efficiency depends on θ because it describes a likelihood function used to make the inference. A simplification of this function for the whole data by logarithmic function is

$$
J(\theta) = -\frac{1}{N} \sum_{i=1}^{N} y^{(i)} \log\left(h_\theta\left(x^{(i)}\right)\right) + \left(1 - y^{(i)}\right) \log\left(1 - h_\theta\left(x^{(i)}\right)\right) \tag{1}
$$

The training phase in LR focuses on finding θ^*, the value that minimizes $J(\theta)$ and maximizes the correct classification of elements in X. Moreover, θ^* can be used to estimate the binary classification of new data. For example, it is possible to guess the binary label $y' \in \{0, 1\}$ for a given data $x' = [1, x'_1, x'_2, \ldots, x'_d] \in \mathbb{R}^{d+1}$ by setting:

$$
y' = \begin{cases} 1 \text{ if } h_{\theta^*}(x') \geq \tau \\ 0 \text{ if } h_{\theta^*}(x') < \tau \end{cases} \tag{2}
$$

where the threshold τ is defined in the range $0 < \tau < 1$ with a typical value equal to 0.5.

Several techniques are used to minimize $J(\theta)$. However, the Gradient Descent (GD) algorithm is the standard option. It is a first-order optimization algorithm to minimize values of derivative functions. At each iteration, GD updates the parameter θ in the opposite direction of the slope concerning the partial derivative of $J(\theta)$, defined by $\nabla_\theta J(\theta)$.

A significant parameter in GD is the learning rate α. It determines the change of the model in response to the estimated error at each iteration. Defining α is a fundamental optimization problem because it is involved in the updates of θ. High values of α can converge to a suboptimal solution or provoke an unstable training. Meanwhile, low values of α cause a slow convergence or impact the search process.

Batch Gradient Descent (BGD), Stochastic Gradient Descent (SGD), Momentum Gradient Descent (MGD), and Nesterov Accelerated Gradient (NAG) are the main variants of the original GD commonly used in the literature [6]. They find θ^* by considering different data amounts and rules to update θ.

BGD, also known as vanilla gradient descend, is the straightforward version of GD. The algorithm uses all the elements in the dataset to update θ. Simplicity and convergence to a global minimum for non-convex surfaces are the significant advantages of this algorithm. Unfortunately, the slow convergence time, limited memory problems, and access speed make BGD unfit for big datasets.

Algorithm 1 shows the standard implementation of BGD where the value of θ is updated according to α and $\nabla_\theta J(\theta)$. In each iteration, all elements in the training set are processed to update the values of θ. Algorithm 2 presents the GD procedure to compute $\nabla_\theta J(X, Y, \theta)$, it uses the logistic function defined by $g()$.

Algorithm 1. Batch Gradient Descent
Input: $X, Y, \theta, \alpha, and\ nIter$.
Output: θ.
1   For $i \leftarrow 1$ to $nIter$
2      $\theta \leftarrow \theta - \alpha \times \nabla_\theta J(X, Y, \theta)$

Algorithm 2. Gradient Descent
Input: $X, Y, and\ \theta$.
Output: gd
1   For $i \leftarrow 1$ to $len(X)$
2      $pCost \leftarrow g(\theta \times x^{(i)}) - y^{(i)}$
3   For $j \leftarrow 1$ to $len(x^{(i)})$
4         $gd_j \leftarrow gd_j + pCost \times x^{(i)}_j$
5   For $i \leftarrow 1$ to $len(gd)$
6      $gd_i \leftarrow gd_i / len(X)$

3   Related Work

Homomorphic Encryption (HE) and secure Multi-Party Computation (MPC) are active research fields and have a long list of approaches and improvements [7–10]. Multiple types of HE schemes are developed using different techniques. They are grouped based on the number and type of supported operations: Fully (FHE), Somewhat (SHE), and Partially (PHE) Homomorphic Encryption schemes [11].

For instance, additively HE scheme produces ciphertext $c_+ = c_1 \ddot{+} c_2$, where c_1 and c_2 content the encrypted messages m_1 and m_2, respectively, and $\ddot{+}$ defines the homomorphic versions of $+$, the decryption of c_+ produces $m_1 + m_2$.

Similarly, a multiplicatively HE scheme generates $c_\times = c_1 \ddot{\times} c_2$ with $\ddot{\times}$ as the homomorphic version of $\times$ and the description of $c_\times$ is equal to $m_1 \times m_2$. Moreover, we can define a homomorphic function $\ddot{f}$ as a function that only contains homomorphic operations, i.e., $\ddot{\times}$ and $\ddot{+}$.

Yao proposed the first secure MPC solution [23]. The author described the problem with a situation where two millionaires want to compare/analyze their riches without disclosing their assets, i.e., in a privacy-preserving manner.

A secure two-party HE scheme computation considers a Holder party (Hp) and External party (Ep). Hp sends its encrypted input data c_{Hp} to Ep, which can compute any polynomial function $\ddot{f}(c_{Hp})$ over the ciphertext space. Then Ep returns the encrypted result of $\ddot{f}(c_{Hp})$ to Hp for decryption. This idea can be generalized to a multi-party's approach where all the external parties collaborate to process $\ddot{f}(c_{Hp})$. Multi-key-HE (Mk-HE) [12] and Threshold-HE (Th-HE) [13] are examples of Multi-Party HE techniques.

Secret Sharing (SS) techniques define another approach to MPC. They focus on distributing shares between different parties to compute functions. The decryption is performed only when enough parties are gathered.

We present the last advances with respect to LR with HE schemes and secure MPC. Also, relevant related works in the domain of RNS as HE scheme and secure MPC.

Yang et al. [2] provide a review of existing outsourcing schemes using several secure computation methods. The authors describe the related works of four techniques: secure MPC, pseudorandom functions, software guard extensions, and perturbation approaches. Additionally, they show theories and evolution of HE schemes and their applications, from basic operations to application-specific tasks.

Cheon et al. [14] propose the Ensemble GD (EGD) algorithm to compute LR models based on subsets of the dataset. In EGD, standard GD processes each partial dataset and then averages all the fractional results. The dataset division improves the execution time of LR by reducing the number of iterations to train the model.

Jiang et al. [15] propose a Secure LR (SecureLR) for training and testing without compromising data security on public cloud servers. SecureLR builds upon HE methodologies with hardware-based security reinforcement through Software Guard Extensions (SGX). The hybrid cryptographic solution provides data security and efficiency in storing and processing biomedical information in public clouds.

Han et al. [16] provide a hybrid approach of a privacy-preserving LR with MPC and HE for training and inference. The scalable solution minimizes the need for key management and computation complexity in an encrypted state. The authors use a two-party additive SS scheme to control noises of expensive HE operations such as bootstrapping.

Cortés-Mendoza et al. [17] develop and analyze the performance of homomorphic versions of BGD, SGD, MGD, and NAG based on RNS. The authors compare their performance with the non-homomorphic versions and two state-of-the-art HE algorithms. The results show that proposed solutions have similar accuracy with non-homomorphic algorithms, increased classification performance, and decreased training time compared with the HE algorithms.

Miranda-López et al. [5] propose a two-level scheme based on a Redundant RNS with backpropagation (2Lbp-RRNS) for increasing reliability of a configurable and secure multi-cloud data storage. 2Lbp-RRNS can identify and recover from errors under various scenarios. Additionally, the authors evaluate encoding/decoding speeds with three algorithms under seven cloud storage providers.

Our work focuses on proposing a multi-cloud LR algorithm with RNS as a variation of HE. Similar to [5], we use RNS to design HE and MPC functions for multi-cloud computing environments to provide security, parallel processing, and scalability.

4 Multi-cloud Logistic Regression with Residue Number System

4.1 Residue Number System

A Residue Number System (RNS) is a numerical system widely studied and used in cryptography and computation with large integers. This variation of the finite ring isomorphism system represents integer numbers as residues over a moduli set. The RNS representation provides several advantages over the traditional Weighted Number System (WNS), like decimal and binary number systems.

The main advantages of RNS include operations with the absence of carries within the position of each residue, positional independence between residues (the magnitude is not related with the position of the residues), and the same speed to operate with long and short numbers. A standard operation with long words is slower due to the carry propagation. RNS dials with smaller numbers (residues). RNS has gained considerable interest in HE schemes due to these characteristics [3, 18, 19].

A moduli set $CPN = \{p_1, p_2, \ldots, p_n\}$ of n pairwise co-prime numbers defines the representation of the values in the range of $P = \prod_1^n p_i$. An integer number $a \in [0, P-1)$ is defined in RNS as $\bar{a} = (a_1, a_2, \ldots, a_n)$ where $a_i = |a|_{p_i}$ represents the remainder of the division of a by p_i.

The arithmetic operations in RNS exhibit valuable properties. For instance, given $\bar{a} = (a_1, a_2, \ldots, a_n)$ and $\bar{b} = (b_1, b_2, \ldots, b_n)$ as the representation in RNS of two integer's numbers a and b, then:

$$\bar{a} \otimes \bar{b} = (a_1, a_2, \ldots, a_n) \otimes (b_1, b_2, \ldots, b_n)$$

$$= \left(|a_1 \otimes b_1|_{p_1}, |a_2 \otimes b_2|_{p_2}, \ldots, |a_n \otimes b_n|_{p_n} \right) = (c_1, c_2, \ldots, c_n) = \bar{c} \tag{3}$$

where $c_i = |c|_{p_i}$ for $i = 1, 2, \ldots, n$ and $\otimes$ denotes one operation: addition, multiplication, or subtraction.

According to (3), the RNS can be defined as a variant of HE [2], i.e., it performs mathematic operations over numbers encrypted using RNS. Additionally, this representation of numbers can be seen as coding and SS scheme, and then we can use it for secure data processing and storage. Every integer $a \in [0, P-1)$ represented with a n-tuple can be recovered using the Chinese Remainder Theorem (CRT)

$$a = \left(\sum_{i=1}^n a_i P_i r_i \right) \bmod P, \forall i = 1, \ldots, n \tag{4}$$

where $P_i = P/p_i$ and r_i is the multiplicative inverse of $P_i \bmod p_i$.

The representation of real values in RNS is a relevant theme. We use a scaling factor to represent real values in the integer domain. For any real value $a_R \in \mathbb{R}$, $a = \lfloor 2^{powerInt} a_R \rfloor$. A disadvantage of RNS focuses on the complex operations requiring the magnitude of a number, e.g., comparison, division, sign, overflow detection, etc.

The latest advances in the RNS field focus on efficient division algorithms and the comparison of numbers [20, 21].

4.2 Logistic Regression with Residue Number System

In [17], we developed the BGD algorithm with RNS (BGD-RNS) to provide security in the training and inference phases of the LR model. It allows computing LR in a two-party infrastructure without worrying about data leaking.

Algorithms 3 and 4 present the procedures of BGD-RNS and GD-RNS that process data using ciphertexts. The basic HE operations for RNS values are defines by $\ddot{+}, \ddot{-}$, and $\ddot{\times}$ for addition, subtraction, and multiplication (see Eq. 3), respectively.

The HE functions $rns()$, $\ddot{g}_1()$, and $\ddot{s}()$ provide RNS coding of real values, polynomial approximation of sigmoid function (see Sect. 4.4), and reduction of scaling factor. The unencrypted information in the algorithms is only the number of iterations $nIter$.

Algorithm 3. RNS Batch Gradient Descent
Input: $\bar{X}, \bar{Y}, \bar{\theta}, \bar{a},$ and $nIter.$
Output: $\bar{\theta}.$
1   $\overline{av} \leftarrow rns(1/leng(\bar{X}))$
2   **For** $i \leftarrow 1$ **to** $nIter$
3     $\bar{\theta} \leftarrow \bar{\theta} \ddot{-} \ddot{s}(\bar{a} \ddot{\times} \nabla_{\theta} J(\bar{X}, \bar{Y}, \bar{\theta}, \overline{av}))$

Algorithm 4. RNS Gradient Descent
Input: $\bar{X}, \bar{Y}, \bar{\theta},$ and $\overline{av}.$
Output: $\overline{gd}$
1   **For** $i \leftarrow 1$ **to** $len(\bar{X})$
2     $\overline{pCost} \leftarrow \ddot{g}_1(\bar{\theta} \ddot{\times} \overline{x^{(i)}}) \ddot{-} \overline{y^{(i)}}$
3   **For** $j \leftarrow 1$ **to** $len(x^{(i)})$
4       $\overline{gd}_j \leftarrow \overline{gd}_j \ddot{+} \overline{pCost} \ddot{\times} \overline{x^{(i)}}_j$
5   **For** $i \leftarrow 1$ **to** $len(\overline{gd}_j)$
6     $\overline{gd}_j \leftarrow \overline{gd}_j \ddot{\times} \overline{av}$

The function $\ddot{s}()$ eliminates the scaling factor of θ at each iteration. The HE multiplication $\ddot{\times}$ increases the accumulated scaling factor in the result of the operation. So, we use the CRT to unencrypt the information (see Eq. 3), then remove the scaling factor in the value and encrypt the data again. In this sense, this function imposes a strong restriction to run Algorithm 3 in a secure third-party because it must access the elements in *CPN*. Even with this restriction, the only risk of information loss is partial computing of θ.

Additionally, Algorithm 4 can be executed in a distributed manner because RNS values are independent arithmetic units, where the maximum number of entities depends on the size of *CPN*. Each entity can receive information of all values $\bar{X}, \bar{Y}, \bar{\theta},$ and $\overline{av}$ based on one element in *CPN*, so the entities have limited or partial access to the sensitive information. We use this idea to propose a multi-cloud version of LR with RNS.

4.3 Multi-cloud Logistic Regression

The Multi-Cloud Logistic Regression based on Residue Number System (MC-LR-RNS) protects a dataset's information by codifying the data using an RNS and providing partial information to each processing entity (party) based on a co-prime number. We use the term cloud to define a specific party because it provides the necessary resources for storing and processing data.

The preprocessing of the algorithm stores the $i - th$ residue of $\overline{X}, \overline{Y}$, and $\overline{av}$ in the $i - th$ cloud. For example, with a *CPN* of n values and the element $\overline{x^{(k)}} \in \overline{X}$ then

$$\overline{x^{(k)}} = \left[\overline{1}, \overline{x^{(k)}}_1, \overline{x^{(k)}}_2, \ldots, \overline{x^{(k)}}_d\right]^T$$

$$= \left[(x_{0,1}^{(k)}, \ldots, x_{0,n}^{(k)}), (x_{1,1}^{(k)}, \ldots, x_{1,n}^{(k)}), \ldots, (x_{d,1}^{(k)}, \ldots, x_{d,n}^{(k)})\right]^T$$

where $\overline{1} = (x^{(k)}_{0,1}, \ldots, x^{(k)}_{0,n})$ and $\overline{x^{(k)}}_j = (x^{(k)}_{j,1}, \ldots, x^{(k)}_{j,n})$, see Eq. (2).

$\overline{x^{(k)}}$ can be stored and processed with n clouds in a distributed environment as:

$$\widetilde{x^{(k)}}_1 = \left(x_{0,1}^{(k)}, x_{1,1}^{(k)}, x_{2,1}^{(k)}, \ldots, x_{d,1}^{(k)}\right) \text{ in } cloud_1,$$

$$\widetilde{x^{(k)}}_i = \left(x_{0,i}^{(k)}, x_{1,i}^{(k)}, x_{2,i}^{(k)}, \ldots, x_{d,i}^{(k)}\right) \text{ in } cloud_i,$$

$$\cdots$$

$$\widetilde{x^{(k)}}_n = \left(x_{0,n}^{(k)}, x_{1,n}^{(k)}, x_{2,n}^{(k)}, \ldots, x_{d,n}^{(k)}\right) \text{ in } cloud_n,$$

where $x^{(k)}_{j,i}$ defines the element k in the dataset X, with respect to the feature j and the residue i ($\left.x^{(k)}_j\right|_{p_i}$).

From the previous description, we can define $\tilde{X}_i = (\widetilde{x^{(1)}}_i, \widetilde{x^{(2)}}_i, \ldots, \widetilde{x^{(n)}}_i)$ as the information of all elements in the dataset X for $p_i \in CPN$ that have to be processed in $cloud_i$. Similarly, we can generate $\tilde{Y}_i$ and $\tilde{av}_i$. In general, the $cloud_i$ can compute Algorithm 4 using $\tilde{X}_i, \tilde{Y}_i, \tilde{av}_i$, and p_i instead to $\overline{X}, \overline{Y}$, and $\overline{av}$; note that all of them are only sent one time.

Algorithm 3 execution can be done in a local machine or cloud environment. At each iteration i, this resource sends $\tilde{\theta}_i$ to each $cloud_i$, respectively, and waits to receive $\tilde{gd}_i$ from all $cloud_i$. Later, it decrypts $\overline{\theta}$ in order to remove the scaling factor and updates the value of $\overline{\theta}$. Finally, it repeats the procedure *nIter* times and provides $\overline{\theta}^*$ by sending or storing the information. We define $\tilde{\theta}_i = (\theta_{0,i}, \theta_{1,i}, \theta_{2,i}, \ldots, \theta_{d,i}), \forall i = 1, \ldots, n$, by

$$\overline{\theta} = \left[\overline{\theta}_0, \overline{\theta}_1, \ldots, \overline{\theta}_i, \ldots, \overline{\theta}_d\right]^T$$

$$= \left[(\theta_{0,1}, \ldots, \theta_{0,i}, \ldots, \theta_{0,n}), \ldots, (\theta_{1,1}, \ldots, \theta_{1,i}, \ldots, \theta_{1,n}), \ldots, (\theta_{d,1}, \ldots, \theta_{d,i}, \ldots, \theta_{d,n})\right]^T$$

If we group the values with respect to *CPN*, then

$$\rightarrow \left[(\theta_{0,1}, \theta_{1,1}, \ldots, \theta_{d,1}), \ldots, (\theta_{0,i}, \theta_{1,i}, \ldots, \theta_{d,i}), \ldots, (\theta_{0,n}, \theta_{1,n}, \ldots, \theta_{d,n})\right]^T$$

$$= \left[\tilde{\theta}_1, \ldots, \tilde{\theta}_i, \ldots, \tilde{\theta}_n\right]^T$$

Figure 1 presents the MC-LR-RNS. The information is distributed amount several clouds, which allows the parallel processing of the data. At the end of the execution, the result can be recovered from the partial results of all of the clouds. Moreover, RNS allows recovering the result even if some clouds do not provide their results. Figure 2 shows an example of the MC-LR-RNS with four clouds. The local machine has access to CPN and $\bar{\theta}$ but never to the information in the dataset, and clouds only have partial access to the dataset.

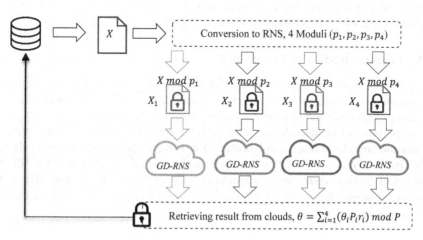

Fig. 1. Multi-cloud logistic regression based on RNS.

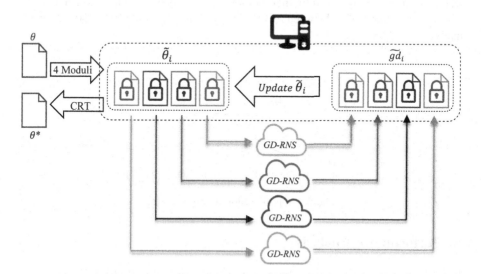

Fig. 2. Four-cloud logistic regression training.

At the beginning of the procedure, the *Hp* computes and sends $\tilde{\theta}_i$ to *cloud$_i$*. In each iteration, the *cloud$_i$* receives $\tilde{\theta}_i$ and executes GD-RNS for the residue p_i with the previously stored information $\tilde{X}_i$, $\tilde{Y}_i$, and $\tilde{av}_i$. Then, all of the clouds send $\tilde{gd}_i$ back to *Hp* in order to update $\overline{\theta}$. The process stops after *nIter* iterations, and *Hp* uses CRT to get θ^*. The evaluation process can be done similarly to the training process in MC-LR-RNS,

One important topic related to the implementation of MC-LR-RNS focuses on the sigmoid or logistic function. It is a fundamental part of GD algorithm that cannot be directly implemented in homomorphic systems. Usually, the logistic function is approximated using polynomials of different degrees.

4.4 Logistic Function Approximation

The approximation of logistic or sigmoid function is widely studied in the implementation of a homomorphic LR with GD. Several functions to find a balance between the error of estimate and time of evaluation are proposed [22].

A polynomial of high–degree offers a better approximation, but it increases the evaluation time. In contrast, a polynomial of low degree provides a shorter evaluation time, but it increases the error with respect to the original function. Additionally, the number of multiplications in a ciphertext is bounded in the HE domain. Hence, the polynomial degree is limited. Our approximate polynomial to $g(x) = \frac{1}{1+e^{-x}}$ of degree one is defined as follows:

$$g_1(x) = 0.5 + (0.25 \times x) \tag{5}$$

where $+$ and $\times$ are replaced by their homomorphic version $\ddot{+}$ and $\ddot{\times}$ to generate $\ddot{g}_1$.

The maximum error between $g(x)$ and $g_1(x)$ is approximately 1.50033 in the interval $[-4, 4]$, see Fig. 3.

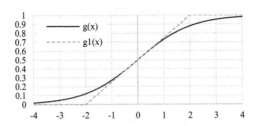

Fig. 3. Approximation function of $g(z)$.

5   Performance Analysis

In this section, we describe the estimated execution time of the MC-LR-RNS and define several relevant configuration parameters that impact performance. We use the execution time provided by BGD-RNS (see Algorithms 3 and 4) as a basis for MC-LR-RNS.

BGD-RNS was implemented using JDK 1.8.0_221 64-bit. All timings were obtained running on a computer with Windows 10 of 64-bit OS and an Intel (R) Core (TM) i5-8400 CPU 2.8 GHz with 8 GB of memory, and 1 TB of HDD.

Our analysis considers six standard datasets in the literature [17]; see Table 1. The continuous input variables of each element are normalized in the range of [0, 1]. We use the simple min-max normalization method $x' = \frac{x - \min(x)}{\max(x) - \min(x)}$ where x is the original value and x' the normalized value.

We use the 5-fold Cross-Validation (5CV) technique to define the size of training and testing sets. It divides the dataset randomly into five subsets: four are used to train the model, and one set is used to validate it. Table 1 summarizes all datasets' characteristics with the size of training and testing sets according to 5CV.

Table 1. Datasets characteristics and size of sets.

Dataset	Name	N	Features	N-Training	N-Testing
Lbw	Low Birth Weight study	189	9	151	38
Mi	Myocardial Infarction	1,253	9	1,002	251
Nhanes3	National Health & Nutrition Examination	15,649	15	12,519	3,130
Pcs	Prostate Cancer Study	379	9	303	76
Pima	Indian's diabetes	728	8	582	146
Uis	Umaru Impact Study	575	8	460	115

We perform a series of experiments to analyze the performance of the MC-LR-RNS with several moduli sets. We consider a scaling factor of 16-bits to represent real values with integer values. The moduli sets are formed with the seven pairwise co-primes described in Table 2. The four configurations for CPN are $CPN_4 = \{p_1, \ldots, p_4\}$, $CPN_5 = \{p_1, \ldots, p_5\}$, $CPN_6 = \{p_1, \ldots, p_6\}$, and $CPN_7 = \{p_1, \ldots, p_7\}$.

Table 2. Pairwise co-primes numbers.

i	p_i	i	p_i
1	18446744073709551629	5	18446744073709551709
2	18446744073709551653	6	18446744073709551757
3	18446744073709551667	7	18446744073709551923
4	18446744073709551697		

Table 3 presents the encoding time for the four CPN configurations in milliseconds (ms). All elements in the dataset are encoded and stored. Table 4 shows the size of encoded elements for the four CPN in kilobytes (KB), the two-parties describe the size of $\overline{X}$ and n-parties the size of $\tilde{X}_i$ for $i = 1, \ldots, n$. CPN_i defines the amount of information that each cloud receives for the execution of the MC-LR-RNS algorithm. The encoding increases the size of the dataset for each cloud between 51% and 127% with respect to the original file.

Table 3. Encoding time for the datasets (ms).

Name	Lbw	Mi	Nhanes3	Pcs	Pima	Uis
CPN_4	1.6598	4.5582	115.2573	2.9012	5.1091	3.6586
CPN_5	1.7345	5.0794	130.3134	2.9601	5.5510	3.8535
CPN_6	1.7731	5.4239	142.6047	3.1949	5.9270	4.3861
CPN_7	1.8927	5.9176	158.3269	3.3365	6.1721	4.9097

Table 4. Size of encoding dataset for RNS models (KB).

Type	Name	Lbw	Mi	Nhanes3	Pcs	Pima	Uis
–	Original	3.22	18.5	583	6.95	16.5	8.56
Two-parties	CPN_4	23.3	122	3,400	53.4	111	76.9
	CPN_5	29.1	152	4,250	66.7	138	96
	CPN_6	34.9	183	5,100	80.0	166	115
	CPN_7	40.7	213	5,950	93.0	193	134
n-parties	CPN_i	5.94	31.3	882	13.5	28.1	19.5

Table 5 displays the timing for several operations, where each value represents the average of 30 executions in ms. CPN_i defines the time that each cloud needs to process an operation, only with the information about residue p_i. $\tilde{s}$ can be computed when all of the $\tilde{gd_i}$ are in the same party.

Table 5. Timing for several RNS operations (ms).

Type	Name	$\ddot{+}$	$\ddot{\times}$	$\ddot{g}_1$	$\ddot{s}$
Two-party	CPN_4	0.00183	0.00126	0.00247	0.04113
	CPN_5	0.00223	0.00169	0.00322	0.04471
	CPN_6	0.00251	0.00185	0.00373	0.04648
	CPN_7	0.00267	0.00231	0.00419	0.04924
n-parties	CPN_i	0.00078	0.00049	0.00091	–

Table 6 shows the execution time per iteration of GD-RNS for the four CPN in ms. We can see the reduction in the processing time given the high parallelism, it is possible because there is no dependence between residues.

Table 6. Execution time per iteration of the RNS Gradient Descent algorithm (ms).

Type	Name	Lbw	Mi	Nhanes3	Pcs	Pima	Uis
Two-party	CPN_4	5.5352	25.6278	397.2103	10.4362	19.6756	15.5063
	CPN_5	6.3970	28.3116	462.6057	12.6245	23.3749	16.6354
	CPN_6	7.0138	31.3182	541.5101	14.8078	27.5683	17.6031
	CPN_7	7.6259	33.5338	622.0440	15.8415	31.1588	18.6651
n-parties	CPN_i	1.6320	5.4066	88.8803	2.7888	4.7461	3.1503

We can estimate the transmission time to the cloud concerning several CSPs. Table 7 presents the average access speeds of seven CSPs and the estimation time to send/receive a file of 1 KB size. The time to send $\tilde{\theta}_i$ and receive $\tilde{gd}_i$ from $cloud_i$ depends on the slower cloud in the process; Egnyte, OneDrive, Salesforce, and Sharefile for the four models.

In general, we see that the send/receive times are higher than encoding and processing times, so communication represents the algorithm's major time consumer. This situation is different for dataset Nhanes3, where the communication represents between 9.2% and 29.7% with respect to the processing time and the providers Egnyte and Sharefile.

Table 7. Estimation time to send/receive 1 KB of information for seven clouds [5].

#	Cloud	Average speed (MB/s)		Time (ms)	
		Upload	Download	Send	Receive
1	Google Drive	2.98	3.06	2.685	2.614
2	Dropbox	2.93	3.25	2.730	2.462
3	Box	2.55	2.62	3.137	3.053
4	Egnyte	1.70	2.30	4.706	3.478
5	OneDrive	1.46	2.18	5.480	3.670
6	Salesforce	0.64	0.71	12.500	11.268
7	Sharefile	0.51	0.75	15.686	10.667

The parallel processing reduces the processing time between 76.5% and 23.1% for different configurations of CPN. Additionally, GD-RNS and MC-GD-RNS show high parallelism. Communication in MC-GD-RNS is a significant limit, even with the bit of information sent and received. Moreover, it depends on the iteration number in the training of the ML model. So, using an efficient LR algorithm can reduce the training time and improve its efficiency.

MC-LR-RNS provides the same levels of quality solution as BGD-LR-RNS because they both have the same basis. Their difference is the number of clouds involved in the training of the model.

6   Conclusion

In this paper, we propose a privacy-preserving logistic regression algorithm for multi-cloud with secure-multi party and homomorphic encryption based on a residue number system.

We provide an analysis of its performance with several configurations and datasets of different medicine domains (diabetes, cancer, drugs, etc.) and genomics. The multi-cloud logistic regression algorithm can perform the training, testing, and prediction processes with ciphertexts. We show that it can provide security, parallel processing, and scalability with minor time increases in the training process.

However, further study is required to assess its actual efficiency and effectiveness in real systems. This will be the subject of future work in the real cloud environment.

Acknowledgment. The research was funded by RFBR and Chelyabinsk Region, project number 20-47-740005.

References

1. Acar, A., Aksu, H., Selcuk Uluagac, A., Aksu, H., Uluagac, A.S.: A survey on homomorphic encryption schemes: theory and implementation. ACM Comput. Survey. **51**(4), 1–35 (2018)
2. Yang, Y., et al.: A comprehensive survey on secure outsourced computation and its applications. IEEE Access **7**, 159426–159465 (2019)
3. Bajard, J.C., Eynard, J., Hasan, M.A., Zucca, V.: A full RNS variant of FV like somewhat homomorphic encryption schemes. In: International Conference on Selected Areas in Cryptography pp. 423–442 (2016)
4. Chervyakov, N., Babenko, M., Tchernykh, A., Kucherov, N., Miranda-López, V., Cortés-Mendoza, J.M.: AR-RRNS: Configurable reliable distributed data storage systems for Internet of Things to ensure security. Futur. Gener. Comput. Syst. **92**, 1080–1092 (2019)
5. Miranda-López, V., et al.: 2Lbp-RRNS: Two-levels RRNS with backpropagation for increased reliability and privacy-preserving of secure multi-clouds data storage. IEEE Access **8**, 199424–199439 (2020)
6. Ruder, S.: An overview of gradient descent optimization algorithms. arXiv preprint arXiv: 1609.04747 (2016)
7. PALISADE. https://palisade-crypto.org/community. Accessed 7 Apr. 2021
8. HElib. https://github.com/homenc/HElib. Accessed 7 Apr. 2021
9. HEANN. https://github.com/snucrypto/HEAAN. Accessed 7 Apr. 2021
10. Micrsoft SEAL. https://github.com/Microsoft/SEAL. Accessed 7 Apr. 2021
11. Pulido-Gaytan, B., et al.: Privacy-preserving neural networks with Homomorphic encryption: challenges and opportunities. Peer-to-Peer Netw. Appl. **14**(3), 1666–1691 (2021)
12. Chen, H., Dai, W., Kim, M., Song, Y.: Efficient multi-key homomorphic encryption with packed ciphertexts with application to oblivious neural network inference. In: Proc. 2019 ACM SIGSAC Conf. on Computer and Communications Security, pp. 395–412 (2019)
13. Mouchet, C., Troncoso-Pastoriza, J.R., Hubaux, J.P.: Multiparty homomorphic encryption: from theory to practice. IACR Cryptol. ePrint Arch., 304 (2020)
14. Cheon, J.H., Kim, D., Kim, Y., Song, Y.: Ensemble method for privacy-preserving logistic regression based on homomorphic encryption. IEEE Access. **6**, 46938–46948 (2018)

15. Jiang, Y., et al.: SecureLR: secure logistic regression model via a hybrid cryptographic protocol. IEEE/ACM Trans. Comput. Biol. Bioinf. **16**(1), 113–123 (2019)
16. Han, K., Jeong, J., Sohn, J.H., Son, Y.: Efficient privacy preserving logistic regression inference and training. IACR Cryptol. ePrint Arch., 1396 (2020)
17. Cortés-Mendoza, J.M., et al.: LR-GD-RNS: enhanced privacy-preserving logistic regression algorithms for secure deployment in untrusted environments. In: SIoTEC 2021 - 2nd Workshop on Secure IoT, Edge, and Cloud systems (2021)
18. Tchernykh, A., et al.: Towards mitigating un-certainty of data security breaches and collusion in cloud computing. In: 2017 28th Int. Workshop on Database and Expert Systems Applications (DEXA). pp. 137–141 (2017)
19. Tchernykh, A., et al.: Performance evaluation of secret sharing schemes with data recovery in secured and reliable heterogeneous multi-cloud storage. Clust. Comput. **22**(4), 1173–1185 (2019)
20. Babenko, M., et al.: Unfairness correction in P2P grids based on residue number system of a special form. In: 2017 28th International Workshop on Database and Expert Systems Applications (DEXA). pp. 147–151 (2017)
21. Babenko, M., et al.: Positional characteristics for efficient number com-parison over the homomorphic encryption. Program. Comput. Softw. **45**, 532–543 (2019)
22. Pulido-Gaytan, B., et al.: Privacy-preserving toward fast and accurate polynomial approximations for practical homomorphic evaluation of neural network activation functions. In: SPCLOUD 2020 - International Workshop on Security, Privacy, and Performance of Cloud Computing (2021)
23. Yao, A.C.: Protocols for secure computations. In: 23rd Annual Symposium on Foundations Of Computer Science, pp. 160–164 (1982)

National Research Computer Network of Russia: Development Plans, Role and Facilities in Ensuring the Functioning of the National Supercomputer Infrastructure

Alexey Abramov[1,2]([📧]) [iD], Anton Evseev[1] [iD], Andrey Gonchar[3] [iD],
and Boris Shabanov[3] [iD]

[1] St. Petersburg Branch of Joint Supercomputer Center of the Russian Academy
of Sciences, Saint Petersburg 199034, Russia
{abramov, evseev}@runnet.ru
[2] Peter the Great St. Petersburg Polytechnic University,
Saint Petersburg 195251, Russia
[3] Joint Supercomputer Center of the Russian Academy of Sciences,
Moscow 119334, Russia
{andrey.gonchar, shabanov}@jscc.ru

Abstract. The paper is devoted to the discussion of issues of ensuring the current functioning and development plans of the new generation National Research Computer Network (NIKS). The goals, main functions and tasks of NIKS as a national research and education network of Russia are denoted. The current state of NIKS is considered – telecommunications infrastructure within the country and abroad, service portfolio and user base. The key areas of work and activities to ensure the accelerated development of the NIKS infrastructure and service platform for the period 2021–2024 within the framework of the National Project "Science and Universities" are presented. The proposed criteria and principles for selecting of research organizations and higher education institutions of Russia for connecting to NIKS are discussed. Special attention is paid to the role of NIKS as a high-speed telecommunications infrastructure to connect supercomputer centers of the National Supercomputer Infrastructure.

Keywords: National Research Computer Network of Russia · National research and education network · Telecommunications infrastructure · Leading research and educational organizations · Supercomputer centers · National supercomputer infrastructure

1 Introduction

The accumulated world experience in the creation and development of global telecommunication networks emphasizes the special role of research and education (R&E) networks in these processes. In most countries of the world, at different periods of time, special industry networks were created and systematically improved, which have an accepted name – National Research and Education Network (NREN) [1–4].

© Springer Nature Switzerland AG 2021
V. Voevodin and S. Sobolev (Eds.): RuSCDays 2021, CCIS 1510, pp. 472–486, 2021.
https://doi.org/10.1007/978-3-030-92864-3_36

The general principles of NREN's operation have historically been developed through years of collaboration of such networks, including in supranational and continental consortia of R&E networks.

NREN is generally defined as an information and telecommunication network with characteristics superior to those of public networks; a high-level infrastructure at the national level, which operates for the benefit of science and education fields, ensures network connectivity of target users and inter-networking with foreign NRENs and consortia with high quality requirements, access of users to global information and communications technologies (ICT) space as well as central to the development and implementation of services aimed at the R&E community [1, 4–7].

Today, NRENs operate as integral parts of national ICT infrastructures in more than 150 countries around the world, are mainly coordinated by the state educational and scientific authorities, and provide infrastructure and service opportunities for leading domestic R&E organizations including for participation in international research projects, in the implementation of which up-to-date telecommunications, advanced network technologies and services are intensively used (for example, LHC, ITER, XFEL, FAIR, LIGO, DUNE, Belle II, SKA, EUMETSAT).

In Russia, the main functions of NREN are performed by the new generation National Research Computer Network (in Russian transcription – NIKS, https://niks.su) created in 2019 on the assignment of the Ministry of Science and Higher Education of the Russian Federation (further – the Ministry) by Joint Supercomputer Center of the Russian Academy of Sciences (JSCC RAS) by the integration of Federal university computer network RUNNet [5, 8] and network of the Russian Academy of Sciences RASNet both were operated for 25 years.

The Ministry has designated JSCC RAS as administrator and operator of NIKS. JSCC RAS has the necessary organizational and technological capabilities, the substantive experience and human resources, acting as a telecom operator on the basis of licenses for the provision of relevant services that ensure compliance with the requirements of the legislation of the Russian Federation in the field of ICT [5, 9–11].

Achievement of individual goals of the updated National Project "Science and Universities" for 2021–2030 (further – the National Project) and related federal projects assume, among others, solving problems of creating an advanced infrastructure for research and development, innovation, including the creation and development of network of scientific facilities of the MegaScience class (NICA, SKIF, SSRS-4, PIK, XCELS, etc.), world-class research centers, world-class R&E centers, competence centers of the National Technology Initiative, engineering centers.

The range of tasks of the National Project includes the development of infrastructure and support for the functioning of a distributed network of centers for collective use of scientific and technological equipment, support for the creation and development of potentially demanded unique scientific facilities for various purposes, providing access for research groups to national and foreign information resources, big data arrays and services, participation of Russian scientists and research groups in international projects that offer access to new competencies and resources.

It seems quite obvious that a specialized network of the R&E sphere corresponding to the up-to-date level of industry achievements should act as one of the strategic components of the country's ICT infrastructure, contributing to solving problems, achieving results and key indicators of national projects and programs.

One of the goals of the Federal Project "Development of infrastructure for scientific research and training" (as part of the National Project) is the development of NIKS in the interests of R&E organizations of Russia, including with the aim of offering access to advanced scientific infrastructure of collective use (supercomputer centers, centers for collective use, unique scientific facilities, digital collections, data banks) by increasing the capacity of the network backbone, territorial accessibility and a set of services.

As the characteristics of the result of the Federal Project, it has been determined that NIKS will provide R&E organizations of the country with opportunities to carry out research and development in priority areas of scientific and technological development, to participate in large local and international research projects based on the use of a sustainable and up-to-date sectoral information and telecommunications network, integrated into the infrastructure of world NRENs.

At the end of 2020, JSCC RAS developed the concept and the roadmap for the functioning and development of NIKS for 2021–2024 [12], approved by the line Ministry, which carries out the administrative functions of project management. During the working-out of the concept, goals, objectives and priorities identified in documents of strategic planning in the field of R&E, the main trends in the use of ICT in science and education, the substantive international experience of NRENs functioning were taken into account.

In the same year, with the direct participation of JSCC RAS the concept for the creation and ensuring of the functioning of the National Supercomputer Infrastructure (NSI) [13] was developed and also approved by the Ministry. The main goals of the creation of NSI are declared to furnish the research, educational and industrial organizations of Russia with ample opportunities for performing cutting-edge scientific research, the development of new technologies, competitive knowledge-intensive industrial products and training of personnel using high-performance computing (HPC) systems of various classes and the formation of a professional community of researchers and consumers of supercomputer resources to ensure the country's scientific and technological leadership in the global digital economy.

In the assignment of the President of the Russian Federation (Pr-647 dated 04/10/2020), the task has been set to enhance the power of computing resources of Russian supercomputer centers (SCC), taking into account the needs of R&E organizations located throughout the country, in carrying out HPC, establishing the order of interaction of SCCs among themselves and with sectoral organizations on the base of NIKS, increasing its network bandwidth and territorial accessibility.

In these conditions, one of the key tasks of NIKS is to build a target high-speed telecommunications infrastructure for linking SCCs in the sphere of R&E of the country, providing researches with remote access to supercomputer centers located in the leading sectoral organizations in a secure environment, by contributing to increase the level of accessibility and workload of SCCs.

The present paper contains the description of the current state of the infrastructure platform of NIKS, gives general characteristics of the user base, criteria and principles developed for selecting R&E organizations to connect to NIKS, discusses the main planned directions for the progressive growth of the telecommunications infrastructure of the network for 2021–2024, its role and facilities in ensuring the functioning of NSI.

2   NIKS'2021: Telecommunications Infrastructure, Network Connectivity and User Base

2.1   An Overview of the Telecommunications Infrastructure of NIKS

The functioning of NIKS is based on the operation and development of a global heterogeneous data transmission network that provides direct network interaction of target users, network actors and external generators of big data [5, 8, 10–12]. As part of the telecommunications infrastructure, as well as other networks of similar in scope and functions, the backbone network infrastructure, regional infrastructure and access infrastructure are distinguished. The High-level design of the NIKS architecture as of the beginning of 2021 is shown in Fig. 1.

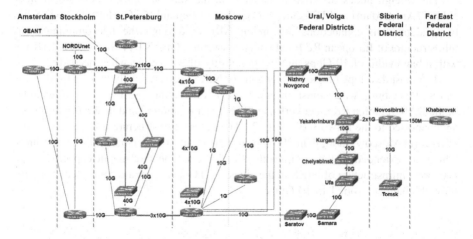

Fig. 1. High-level design of the NIKS architecture (at the beginning of 2021).

The geographically distributed network is now provided by 14 routers, over 90 communication nodes performing different functions and built on different types of telecommunications equipment. The NIKS backbone infrastructure connects its nodes (federal and regional nodes in Russia and foreign ones), communication channels between them which together form the global network from Amsterdam to Khabarovsk.

The federal-level backbone communication nodes are located in Moscow and St. Petersburg, they are connected in the cities by high-speed channels with full redundancy. The nodes between cities are connected by four channels (4 × 10 Gbps), organized on the basis of physically independent links. The federal nodes are connected by backbone channels with regional backbone nodes and access nodes, with regional

R&E networks of the country, with foreign NRENs, and also have direct connectivity with networks of some leading commercial telecommunications operators for access to public networks and Internet.

The regional nodes located in several major cities of the country (Yekaterinburg, Kurgan, Nizhny Novgorod, Novosibirsk, Perm, Samara, Saratov, Tomsk, Ufa, Chelyabinsk, Khabarovsk) are backbone nodes with telecommunications equipment used to connect to NIKS of R&E organizations from the corresponding regions. Typical throughput capacity of communication channels within Russia is today 1...10 Gbps. The segment of the backbone infrastructure of NIKS in the European part, connecting Moscow, Nizhny Novgorod, Perm, Yekaterinburg, Kurgan, Chelyabinsk, Ufa, Samara and Saratov, is a transport ring with a bandwidth of 10 Gbps.

The operation of the NIKS backbone infrastructure abroad is based on an established cooperation with the R&E network of Nordic countries, NORDUnet [3] (for access to the resources of foreign NRENs) and interconnection with several Tier-1 operators (for access to Internet and interconnection with individual NRENs outside Europe).

The foreign nodes of NIKS are located at the sites of NORDUnet (Stockholm), Nikhef (Amsterdam) and IT Center for Science of Finland (CSC, Helsinki). NIKS has two independent connections to foreign NRENs through the telecommunications infrastructure of European R&E networks consortium GÉANT [4, 14] and NORDUnet with a bandwidth of 10 Gbps and the possibility of expanding when needed.

The most developed regional segments of NIKS are historically located in Moscow and St. Petersburg, where most of higher education institutions, numerous of institutes of the RAS, regional R&E networks, and a number of cultural and health organizations are connected to the network (see Fig. 2). The access infrastructure is based on the use of own (in Moscow, more than 300 km) or leased (in St. Petersburg) fiber-optic lines, which are extended to the equipment of end users. The throughput capacity of the backbone infrastructure of NIKS in the cities is 10 Gbps; users are connected, as a rule, through channels from 1 to 10 Gbps.

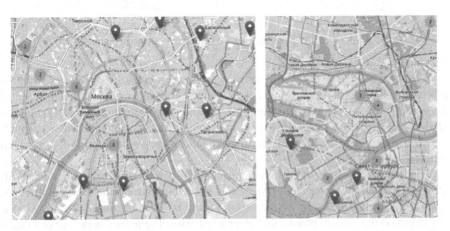

Fig. 2. User map of NIKS for 2021: Moscow (left) and Saint Petersburg (right), fragments.

In other cities with the backbone nodes of NIKS "last miles" are commonly leased by organizations themselves. In cities where there are no such nodes, the last miles, as a rule, are leased or provided by commercial operators, from which channels are ordered between nodes of operators and telecommunications sites of organizations. Network switches with 1/10 Gbps ports are used as access equipment at the regional nodes of NIKS.

Type and speed of connection, as well as a set of services provided to each user, are formed individually, taking into account the technical possibility and financial conditions, on the basis of the existing requirements for a guaranteed bandwidth in the data transmission network when interacting with other users of NIKS and external R&E networks.

NIKS has implemented interconnections with the networks of the leading Russian research centers in the field of high energy physics: members of NRC "Kurchatov Institute" and Joint Institute for Nuclear Research with 10 Gbps capacity each.

The network participates in inter-network traffic exchange at several IX nodes (AMS-IX, MSK-IX, SPB-IX, NSK-IX, DATA-IX, PITER-IX, etc.), has non-commercial peer-to-peer connections with most large Russian and a number of foreign telecommunications operators (more than 30 connections, more than 200 Gbps in total). NIKS is ranked as the Top10 in Russia by the level of network connectivity (together with commercial Internet service providers – Rostelecom, Transtelecom, Vimpelcom, RASCOM, MegaFon, MTS, et al.) and occupies at the moment the 67th place in the world according to well-known and recognized CAIDA's ranking (AS3267, see https://asrank.caida.org).

2.2   General Characteristics of the User Base of NIKS

Over the course of 25 years of operation of the RUNNet and RASNet networks, stable groups of target users have formed who actively engage the infrastructure and services of the networks in their R&E activities.

At the beginning of 2021, NIKS, which inherits two sectoral networks, had points of presence in all the Federal Districts, in 37 regions and 40 cities of the country, directly providing telecommunications services to more than 150 state higher education institutions, scientific and research organizations [5, 9–12].

Such a representative geography of users has been formed mainly by higher education institutions – users of Federal university network RUNNet. Institutes of the RAS outside Moscow and St. Petersburg have connections either to commercial telecommunications operators or to regional sectoral networks, often without access to NIKS and foreign NRENs resources and services.

The target user base of NIKS is formed now by R&E organizations of 15 federal executive authorities, while 80% of them are subordinated to the Ministry of Science and Higher Education of the Russian Federation. The number of higher education institutions among the latter is 79, scientific and research organizations – 63 (including 48 institutes of the RAS).

Among NIKS users today are Lomonosov Moscow State University, Saint Petersburg State University, a number of federal and national research universities, large scientific and research centers and institutes of the RAS. 21 of 31 of the most powerful supercomputer systems of Russia hosted by R&E organizations (from the actual Top50 list, http://top50.supercomputers.ru) are connected to NIKS (as part of respective SCCs).

It should be noted here that more than two-thirds of NIKS users are situated in Moscow, Moscow area and St. Petersburg. A picture of the real number of users in "non-capital" regions cannot be considered reliable, since in many of them regional R&E networks are historically functioning. The operators of such networks are usually sectoral organizations of the region's most developed in ICT and connected to NIKS. Behind such organizations, in some cases, dozens of local research, educational and other organizations may be "hidden".

Among regional networks are the following: RSSI (Moscow), ROKSON (St. Petersburg), PERSONA (Perm Territory), IRNOC (Irkutsk region), KUBANnet (Krasnodar Territory), SENet (Republic of Tatarstan), networks of the Far Eastern, Siberian, Ural branches of the RAS, etc. [10]. In accordance with the designated position of the Ministry, it is not planned to bring separate federal funding to such networks in the future, which may result in a complete cessation of activities with consequences for users. As a reasonable alternative, it is advisable to consider the integration of the remaining networks with their technological and user components into a single infrastructure of NIKS.

3 Directions for the Development of the Infrastructure and Service Platform of NIKS

3.1 Criteria and Principles for Selecting Organizations to Connect to NIKS

As part of a comprehensive project development plan, it is clearly necessary to work out and approve objective criteria and principles for selecting organizations to connect to NIKS with the provision of appropriate infrastructure and service capabilities.

JSCC RAS has developed a new procedure for connecting organizations to NIKS, criteria and principles of selection, taking into account aims, first, those set for 2021–2024 by the National Project. In addition, other documents of strategic planning in the field of R&E, digital development, as well as current methods and results of assessing the activities of organizations were taken into account.

At this stage, within the framework of the activities of the National Project, it is planned to ensure connection to NIKS of the leading research organizations and higher education institutions, belonging to one of the following categories:

- higher education institutions, which, in accordance with the Federal Law "On Education in the Russian Federation" dated December 29, 2012 No. 273-FZ, are authorized to develop and approve independently educational standards for all the levels of higher education;
- research organizations and higher education institutions of the 1st category determined in accordance with the Decree of the Government of the Russian Federation dated April 8, 2009 No. 312 "On the assessment and monitoring of the performance

of research organizations carrying out research, experimental design and techno-logical work for civil purposes";

- national research universities;
- federal research centers;
- universities under the jurisdiction of the Government of the Russian Federation.

The total number of organizations that meet the listed criteria, calculated on the basis of information sources available on the Internet (official websites of the Ministry, Rosstat, regulatory and methodological documents from https://sciencemon.ru, etc.) as of the beginning of 2021 is 347 from 50 regions of Russia.

The set of criteria and, as a consequence, the list of organizations connected to NIKS can be adjusted in agreement with the Ministry, making changes to the National Project and existing strategic planning documents for the sphere of R&E and technologies.

3.2 Main Directions of Development of the Telecommunications Infrastructure

It should be admitted that at the moment, in terms of the level of development of the network infrastructure, NIKS is noticeably inferior to the world's leading NRENs. Thus, the bandwidth of the backbone infrastructure of the most developed European NRENs is 100 Gbps and higher (including Germany, Italy, Great Britain, Ireland, the Netherlands, Switzerland, Sweden, Finland, Norway, Czech Republic, Slovakia, Poland, Romania), two of the largest sectoral national-level computer networks of the USA (multipurpose research and education network Internet2 [15], and problem-oriented scientific "energy" network ESnet [16]) – 400 Gbps. NRENs of China, Brazil, the Republic of Korea, Australia, Canada and a number of other countries have a typical network capacity of 100 Gbps. The widespread use of DWDM technology makes it possible to increase the bandwidth of networks, practically, unlimitedly.

In accordance with the concept and the roadmap for the functioning and devel-opment of NIKS for 2021–2024 the backbone infrastructure upgrade will be carried out with an increase in the bandwidth in its main directions up to 100 Gbps, an expansion of the geography of the location of network access nodes and a portfolio of services for R&E community.

The key goal of the NIKS development project is to create a world-class NREN infrastructure to ensure high-speed access to research results, to objects of scientific infrastructure of collective use, the application of advanced ICT to increase the effi-ciency and effectiveness of research, technical and educational activities.

The concept and the roadmap for the development of the network infrastructure and services of NIKS cover implementation of the following main activities [10, 11]:

- expanding the territorial accessibility of NIKS;
- increase in network bandwidth of NIKS;
- connection to NIKS of leading research organizations and higher education insti-tutions of Russia (in accordance with the annually approved lists);
- connection to NIKS of leading SCCs for collective use in the sphere of R&E of Russia (for more details, see the next section);

- connection to NIKS of centers for collective use and unique scientific facilities, which have the ability to perform research in remote access mode and located in the leading research organizations and higher education institutions (in accordance with the list to be formed and approved);
- provision of high-speed network connectivity and user access to data centers of unique scientific facilities of the MegaScience class network;
- development and modernization of NREN-level services of NIKS for education, science and technology (as part of the following service groups – infrastructure services, basic network services and telematics services, infrastructure monitoring and management services, information technology services and specialized services for R&E) [17].

The solution to the problem of expanding the territorial accessibility of NIKS involves the creation of backbone communication nodes in the Southern, Siberian and Far Eastern Federal Districts (in cities with the largest presence of the leading R&E organizations), as well as the formation of new ring and linear segments of the NIKS backbone infrastructure in certain regions of the country. The increase in network bandwidth will be achieved through a phased upgrade of the existing nodes and communication channels of the backbone network.

The leading research organizations and higher education institutions will be connected to NIKS through the previously considered criteria and principles at a speed of at least 1 Gbps; in some cases, if there are special requirements, an increase can be considered. The choice of organizations and the order of their connection to NIKS in the planning periods will be made based on the existing interest of the organizations, the availability of technical capabilities determined at the stage of the pre-project survey, economic expediency, as well as the level of demand for high-speed R&E connectivity.

The performance indicators determined that by 2024 90% of the leading research organizations and higher education institutions, 100% of large SCCs in the sphere of R&E.

Key expected results from the implementation of the work plan for the development of NIKS include [10, 11]:

- expanded territorial coverage, ensured the presence of NIKS in all federal districts, in more than 50 regions of the Russian Federation;
- ensured the capacity of network segments corresponding to the growing needs; improved domestic telecommunications connectivity in the interests of key participants in scientific and scientific-technical interaction;
- increased availability and level of utilization of objects of research infrastructure for collective use (first – high performance SCCs);
- ensured stable interconnection of leading Russian organizations in the field of R&E with advanced foreign NRENs and research projects;
- conditions created for the full participation of Russian scientists in global research projects based on the use of ICT tools; contributed to an increase in the number of completed projects within the framework of domestic and international cooperation of scientific and scientific-technological collaborations;

- developed and implemented into operation on the basis of NIKS demanded R&E services in the interests of target groups of users, increased number of users of service solutions.

3.3 NIKS as the Telecommunications Infrastructure for High-Speed Connectivity of SCCs of NSI

The dramatic increase in the number of virtual research communities in the first decades of the 21st century, the implementation of a number of large-scale international research projects led to systemic changes in research methods and technologies, organization of computations, processing large amounts of experimental and numerical modeling data, and analysis of the results [4, 17]. It is impossible not to mention here the intensively conducted research and development in the field of machine learning and artificial intelligence, intelligent information systems.

There is an exponential growth in the volumes of generated and stored scientific data, the performance of supercomputer systems, and at the same time, the requirements for the telecommunications infrastructure from individual projects that rely on distributed data processing by participants in sustainable research collaborations are increasing. In most cases, the requirements cannot be satisfied by commercial operators of public networks, and the corresponding tasks historical assigned and solved at the level of the local NRENs or within the framework of integrated infrastructure of world NRENs [1, 4].

In this regard, it is sufficient to mention international research projects of the MegaScience class in the field of high-energy physics at CERN based on the Large Hadron Collider (LHC), using the world-wide LHC Computing Grid (WLCG) infrastructure, the project to create an experimental thermonuclear reactor ITER, and the project to create the world's largest radio telescope SKA (Square Kilometer Array) [17]. According to CERN estimates, during the Run 4 experiment session at the modernized LHC (planned for 2028–2030), the volume of "filtered" data requiring processing will exceed 400 PB per year. It is expected that after SKA reaches full capacity (in 2024), it will be necessary to store and process in a distributed mode about 10 PB of compressed data per day.

The implementation of such global projects by leading research centers involves the use of specially designed dedicated data transmission networks isolated from the public Internet with special characteristics, readiness for peak loads, ensuring QoS for transmission operations critical to the quality of the provided service and distributed processing of expensive and high-value data generated on the basis of unique scientific facilities in the advanced SCCs of PFLOPS and, in the long term, exascale levels.

The projects and programs PRACE (Europe), INCITE and XSEDE (USA), HPCI (Japan) are well-known among specialists examples of projects currently being implemented by the leading countries of the industry aimed at integrating supercomputer resources based on high-speed telecommunication networks [9, 13].

PRACE (Partnership for Advanced Computing in Europe) project [18] is aimed at providing access to computing resources and data management services for large-scale scientific and engineering applications based on the infrastructure of the European R&E networks GÉANT.

The platform is based on the Multidomain Virtual Private Network (MD-VPN) service developed by GÉANT, which is delivered by seamless transport infrastructure that is able to transport L3VPN and point-to-point L2VPN over several network providers [9, 19]. The MD-VPN service offers an end-to-end international network service that enables European researchers to collaborate via a common private network infrastructure. The service delivers the security and reassurance of a VPN, with logical isolation of data services from internet traffic and a seamless environment that minimizes the effect of firewalls, ensuring high-throughput performance.

INCITE (Innovative and Novel Computational Impact on Theory and Experiment) – the US Department of Energy (DOE) program to accelerate scientific discoveries and technological innovations by awarding, on a competitive basis, time on supercomputers to researchers with computationally intensive projects [20]. The program provides a portfolio of national HPC facilities housing some of the world's most advanced supercomputers and open to researchers from academia, government laboratories and industry.

The key objective of the project XSEDE (Extreme Science and Engineering Discovery Environment) is substantially enhancing the productivity of a growing community of scholars, researchers, and engineers through access to advanced digital services that support open research, coordinate and add significant value to the leading supercomputers, high-end visualization and data analysis resources funded by the NSF and other agencies of the USA [21].

It is quite obvious that the implementation of such large-scale projects would not have been possible without the availability and systematic use of the infrastructure and service capabilities of the developed NRENs of the USA – Internet2 and ESnet.

HPCI (High-Performance Computing Infrastructure) is a shared computational environment that connects the major supercomputers as well as data storages of universities and research institutions in Japan via high-speed infrastructure of NREN (SINET) [22]. The mission of HPCI is to realize the scientific and technological computing environment where a wide range of users in Japan can access national HPC resources efficiently and efficiently.

It should be noted that the EU CEF-2 (The Connecting Europe Facility) [23] program, launched in 2021, aimed at stimulating investment in digital communication infrastructure, including the improvement of trans-European telecommunication networks, provides for the organization of high-speed sustainable network connectivity between SCCs of European countries with a phased expanding the capacity of the backbone infrastructure to several Tbit/s (by 2027). At the first stage of the project, SCCs will be connected to the backbone with 100 Gbps channels, and at the second phase – with multi 100 Gbps and terabit channels.

Briefly addressing the situation with the HPC industry in Russia, one should state its critical lag behind the leading countries of the world. In the current world TOP500 list (https://top500.org) of the most powerful supercomputers in the world (November 2020), Russia is represented by only two systems and is in 17th place in the ranking of countries in terms of the total peak performance of HPC systems. For comparison: China has delegated 214 of its computing systems to the list, the USA – 113, Japan – 34, France –18, Germany – 17. Our country falls behind China in terms of total peak performance by 90 times, and from the USA – by almost 70 times. Above Russia, in particular, are located such countries as Brazil, Australia, Saudi Arabia, Taiwan, Ireland, etc. In terms of specific indicators of the provision of researchers with computing resources, Russia lags an order of magnitude behind the EU and even more significantly – from three world leaders: China, the USA and Japan.

Within the framework of target programs of the EU (EuroHPC), the USA (CORAL), Japan and China, it is planned to equip their territories by the mid-2020s with world-class supercomputer infrastructure, while the total planned peak performance of HPC systems will be (in EFLOPS): in the USA and China – 5, EU – 3, Japan – 2 [13].

In order to overcome the current gap in the level of equipment with HPC resources in Russia and the leading countries of the world, the concept for the creation and ensuring of the functioning of NSI suggested a view on the basic principles and directions of development of supercomputer resources and technologies in the country, a set of measures to create and ensure the functioning of NSI taking into account modern global trends and internal needs. As part of the implementation of activities, it is planned to create in Russia by 2025 a national network of 20–25 SCCs, data storage and processing centers, including 3 world-class centers equipped with exascale HPC systems.

The existing HPC centers in Russia are isolated objects that are not interconnected within the framework of a single infrastructure. High-quality access to SCCs from the campuses of individual R&E organizations is implemented at an insufficient level.

In the course of the realization of the step-by-step action plan indicated in the NSI concept in relation to the use of the NIKS infrastructure and service platform to be improved, it is assumed [13]:

- creation of a high-speed telecommunications infrastructure for linking of SCCs on the base of NIKS and the formation of requirements for it (2020–2021);
- development of telecommunications infrastructure with special requirements (automated resource management, end-to-end monitoring, federated authentication and authorization, etc.) within NIKS for the purposes of NSI (2022–2023);
- implementation of special requirements of NSI for telecommunications infrastructure of NIKS and linking of all SCCs of NSI with the provision of backbone connectivity of 40–100 Gbps (including with international R&E networks) and connection of SCCs to the backbone at speeds of at least 10 Gbps (2024–2025).

After the fulfillment of the above tasks it will be possible to implement high-performance data exchange between SCCs and data processing centers, which is necessary for organizing computations, and will allow the use of specialized NIKS services, including seamless and secure access of users from R&E organizations of the country to HPC and information resources.

The concept and the roadmap for the functioning and development of NIKS for 2021–2024 [12], responding to the conditions of the NSI concept, involves solving the problem of linking the SCCs in the sphere of R&E of Russia using high-speed communication channels with special requirements. The connection to NIKS of the most powerful SCCs is supposed to be carried out at a speed of at least 10 Gbps.

The criterion and principle for the selection of SCCs for the connection to NIKS is the simultaneous fulfillment of the following requirements:

- functioning of SCC as a center for collective use;
- the total peak performance of SCC as of the beginning of 2021 is at least 100 TFLOPS (the specified limit will be clarified during the project).

It can be noted that at the moment only 10 SCCs satisfy the declared requirements.

A separate and very important task on the path of development and effective use of NSI is the creation of an environment for unified interaction of SCCs on the base of NIKS. The solution of this problem involves the establishment of a procedure for interaction of SCCs with each other, with R&E organizations and the provision on its ground of single unified access for users to the resources of SCCs (based on the national identity federation and SSO technologies). Any detailed discussion of this issue is beyond the scope of the paper, those of interest are recommended to refer to the works [24–30] and the references therein.

4 Conclusion

Mutually agreed and successful implementation of the concept of the functioning and development of the new generation National Research Computer Network and the concept for the creation and ensuring of the functioning of the National Supercomputer Infrastructure apparently will enhance the effects from solving the stated problems and the achievement of the required targets.

NIKS and NSI as complementary infrastructure and services digital platforms are essential components for leading edge research and development in end-to-end digital technologies.

The issues discussed in the paper and the accumulated world experience emphasize the essential role of NIKS in ensuring the functioning of NSI, without the accelerated improvement of the telecommunications infrastructure of the network it would be difficult to fulfill some challenges facing the NSI project.

Acknowledgment. The publication was carried out within the framework of the state assignment of the SRISA RAS "Conducting fundamental scientific research (47 GP)" on topic No. FNEF-2021-0014. 0580-2021-0014" (Reg. No. 121031300097-1).

References

1. Allocchio, C., Balint, L., Berkhout, V., Bersee, J., Izhvanov, Y., et al.: A History of International Research Networking: The People who made it Happen. Wiley-VCH, New York (2010)
2. Ryan, J.: A History of the Internet and the Digital Future. Breaktion Books Ltd., London (2015)
3. Lehtisalo, K.: The History of NORDUnet: Twenty-five years of networking cooperation in the Nordic countries. http://www.nordu.net/history/book.html. Accessed 15 Apr 2021
4. GÉANT Compendium of National Research and Education Networks in Europe – 2020 Edition. https://compendium.geant.org. Accessed 15 Apr 2021

5. Abramov, A.G., Evseev, A.V.: Conceptual aspects of creating a new generation national research computer network in the Russian Federation. Inf. Technol. **25**(2), 724–733 (2019). https://doi.org/10.17587/it.25.724-733

6. Vasenin, V.A.: Russian Academic Networks and Internet (Status, Problems, Solutions). REFIA, Moscow (1997)

7. Izhvanov, Y.L.: Research and education computer networks. Past, present and development trends. Educ. Resour. Technol. **2**, 17–25 (2017)

8. Abramov, A.G., Evseev, A.V.: RUNNet: infrastructural and service basis of the national research and education network of the Russian Federation. In: Proceedings VIII International Conference "Distributed Computing and Grid-Technologies in Science and Education" (GRID 2018). CEUR Workshop Proceedings, vol. 2267, pp. 52–57 (2018). http://ceur-ws.org/Vol-2267/52-57-paper-8.pdf

9. Savin, G.I., Shabanov, B.M., Baranov, A.V., Ovsyannikov, A.P., Gonchar, A.A.: On the use of federal research telecommunication infrastructure for high performance computing. Bull. South Ural State Univ. Ser. Comput. Math. Softw. Eng. **9**(1), 20–35 (2020). https://doi.org/10.14529/cmse200102

10. Abramov, A.G., Gonchar, A.A., Evseev, A.V., Shabanov, B.M.: The new generation National research computer network: current state and concept of development. Inf. Technol. **27**(3), 115–124 (2021). https://doi.org/10.17587/it.27.115-124

11. Abramov, A.G., Evseev, A.V., Gonchar, A.A., Telegin, P.N., Shabanov, B.M.: National Research Computer Network of Russia: regulatory status and plans for the development of regional telecommunications infrastructure in 2021–2024. CEUR Workshop Proceedings, vol. 2930, pp. 29–37 (2021). http://ceur-ws.org/Vol-2930/paper3.pdf

12. The concept of the functioning and development of the new generation National Research Computer Network for 2021–2024. Minobrnauki of Russia, Moscow (2021)

13. The concept for the creation and ensuring of the functioning of the National Supercomputer Infrastructure. Minobrnauki of Russia, Moscow (2020)

14. GÉANT – the official website. https://www.geant.org. Accessed 15 Apr 2021

15. Internet2 – the official website. https://internet2.edu. Accessed 15 Apr 2021

16. ESnet – The Energy Sciences Network. https://www.es.net. Accessed 15 Apr 2021

17. Abramov, A.G.: Service platform of a new generation national research computer network in the context of development prospects. Informatization of Educ. Sci. **48**(4), 47–65 (2020)

18. PRACE – Partnership for Advanced Computing in Europe. https://prace-ri.eu. Accessed 15 Apr 2021

19. GÉANT VPN services. https://www.geant.org/Services/Connectivity_and_network/Pages/VPN_Services.aspx. Accessed 15 Apr 2021

20. INCITE – The Innovative and Novel Computational Impact on Theory and Experiment. https://doeleadershipcomputing.org. Accessed 15 Apr 2021

21. Towns, J., Cockerill, T., Dahan, M., et al.: XSEDE: accelerating scientific discovery. Comput. Sci. Eng. **16**(5), 62–74 (2014)

22. HPCI – High-Performance Computing Infrastructure. https://www.hpci-office.jp. Accessed 15 Apr 2021

23. CEF-2 – The Connecting Europe Facility Digital Program. https://consilium.europa.eu/media/38507/st07207-re01-en19.pdf. Accessed 15 Apr 2021

24. Fortov, V.E., Savin, G.I., Levin, V.K., Zabrodin, A.V., Shabanov, B.M.: Creation and application of a high-performance computing system based on high-speed network technologies. J. Inf. Technol. Comput. **1**, 3–10 (2002)

25. Shabanov, B., Ovsiannikov, A., Baranov, A., Leshchev, S., Dolgov, B., Derbyshev, D.: The distributed network of the supercomputer centers for collaborative research. Program Syst. Theor. Appl. **8**(4), 245–262 (2017)

26. Broeder, D., Jones, B., Kelsey, D., et al.: Federated Identity Management for Research Collaborations. https://cdsweb.cern.ch/record/1442597. Accessed 15 Apr 2021

27. Basney, J., Fleury, T., Gaynor, J.: CILogon: a federated X.509 certification authority for cyberinfrastructure logon. Concurrency Comput. Pract. Exp. **26**(13), 2225–2239 (2014)

28. Baranov, A.V., Shabanov, B.M., Ovsyannikov, A.P.: Federative identity for the distributed infrastructure of the supercomputer centers. Proc. Sci. Res. Inst. Syst. Anal. Russ. Acad. Sci. **8**(6), 79–83 (2018). https://doi.org/10.25682/NIISI.2018.6.0011

29. Abramov, A.G., Vasilyev, I.V., Porhachev, V.A.: Development of the authentication and authorization infrastructure for the identity federation within the eduGAIN and eduroam projects based on the RUNNet network. ITNOU Inf. Technol. Sci. Educ. Manag. **4**, 56–64 (2017)

30. Abramov, A.G., Vasilyev, I.V., Porhachev, V.A.: Principles of functioning and management of the identity federation RUNNetAAI in the framework of interfederal interaction with the eduGAIN project. Informatization Educ. Sci. **47**(2), 40–47 (2019)

Project Progress Forecasting
in a Desktop Grid

Evgeny Ivashko[1,2,3(✉)] and Valentina Litovchenko[3]

[1] Institute of Applied Mathematical Research, Karelian Research Centre of RAS,
Petrozavodsk, Russia
`ivashko@krc.karelia.ru`
[2] Petrozavodsk State University, Petrozavodsk, Russia
[3] Laboratory for Digital Technologies in Regional Development, KRC of RAS,
Petrozavodsk, Russia

Abstract. Desktop Grid is a widely-used high-throughput concept to perform scientific computing. A common Desktop Grid project consists of a large number of tasks which are to be distributed to computing nodes. By its nature a Desktop Grid deals with a number of uncertainties which affect on a project runtime estimation. In this paper we present a linear regression-based statistical model for project progress forecasting. We present an algorithm and experiments results.

Keywords: Desktop grid · BOINC · Runtime estimation · Completion time · Point prediction · Confidence interval · Linear regression

1 Introduction

High-performance computing plays increasing role in the modern science and technology. It is used to develop new materials, medicine, types of industrial products, etc. The main high-performance computing tools are computing clusters and Computational Grids. But with the growth of computing power of personal computers and speeding up regular Internet connection, a Desktop Grid computing concept more and more raises its value.

Desktop Grid is a distributed high-throughput computing system which uses idle resources of non-dedicated geographically distributed computing nodes connected over regular network. In common case the nodes of a Desktop Grid are either desktop and laptop computers of volunteers connected over the Internet (Volunteer computing) or an organization desktop computers connected over local area network (Enterprise Desktop Grid). A computing system's nature dictates its inherent properties, i.e. advantages:

- ease of deployment and support,
- low cost,
- high scalability,

V. Voevodin and S. Sobolev (Eds.): RuSCDays 2021, CCIS 1510, pp. 487–497, 2021.
https://doi.org/10.1007/978-3-030-92864-3_37

- significant potential peak performance,
- ease of software development,
- etc.,

and disadvantages:

- slow connection between the server and computing nodes,
- limited computational capacity of separate nodes,
- high heterogeneity of software, hardware, or both,
- lack of availability information,
- low reliability of computing nodes,
- lack of trust to computing nodes.

Having in mind the number of consumer desktop and laptop computers in the world and their average performance, one could estimate potential capacity of Desktop Grids in the order of hundreds of Exaflops [1]. However, comparing to computing clusters Desktop Grids are limited by "bag-of-tasks" problems with independent parallelism and low data/compute ratio, such as Monte-Carlo simulations, parameter sweep optimization, etc. Therefore these systems are less widespread comparing to computing clusters and Computational Grids. That is why not so much attention is paid by researchers to study inherent properties of Desktop Grids.

One of such inherent properties is a problem of a computing project runtime estimation – forecasting the time when a specific subset of tasks are going to be finished. In the common case a Desktop Grid has a dynamic structure and non-stationary computing performance (uncertainties affecting runtime estimation are discussed in Sect. 2). That is why this problem is hard to solve in practice. In this paper we concentrate on a weaker problem of a project progress forecasting – forecasting the time when a specific number of arbitrary tasks is going to be finished.

We present a statistical approach to this problem. Based on this approach we developed a forecasting procedure and performed numerical simulation. This work advances our previous research [2] where we implemented Holt statistical model to the same problem.

A set of tasks runtime estimation is a complicated and many-sided problem; it is often considered as a part of a more complex task scheduling problem.

The author of [3] considers a problem of campaign (or in our terms – a Desktop Grid project) completion time optimization. An important part of the optimization is a "campaign deadline" τ_c depending on the available resources R_A for the corresponding application A that runs n_A campaigns, on the remaining amount of work to be done W_c as well as on the current time stamp t:

$$\tau_c = t + \frac{W_c \cdot n_A}{R_A}.$$

The author uses point estimation of available resources which should be refreshed every time then the value changes in a significant way. This approach has clear flaws: first, the current available resources of a Desktop Grid are unknown because it is unknown how many nodes perform computations at the moment;

second, it does not take into account changes in a Desktop Grid performance; third, it assumes that the remaining amount of work to be done is known in advance. However, the proposed approach shows its advantage against non-optimized tasks distribution.

In our work we do not try to estimate a single task runtime. But it is a goal of a number of research papers. There are several reasons for a single task runtime estimation. First, it helps to prevent long-running tasks from ending up on a resource where they do not have a chance to complete. Second, it helps to set up reasonable deadlines. Third, in combination with other data it helps to provide researchers information on a set of tasks runtime.

BOINC platform itself has advanced capabilities on a task runtime estimation[1]. However, there are different approaches on tasks runtime estimation proposed by researchers.

Papers [4] and [5] deal with a novel tasks scheduling mechanism based on predicting the runtimes of parameter sweep tasks. The aim is to reduce the number of tasks prematurely interrupted due to insufficient resource availability by matching predicted resource availability windows with predicted tasks runtimes. The authors propose a parameter sweep prediction framework called GIPSy (Grid Information Prediction System). A task runtime prediction technique is developed based on a number of models such are Radial Basis functions, Kriging Models, Nearest Neighbour prediction, Neural Networks, Support Vector Machines and Polynomial approach. The authors of [6] demonstrate the advantages of relatively short workunits from the point of view of performance.

The rest of the paper is organized as follows. Section 2 highlights specifics of the Desktop Grid concept and BOINC software as the most commonly used middleware for Desktop Grids. In the Sect. 3 we describe a forecasting and statistical models used to calculate point prediction and confidence intervals. In the Sect. 4 the numerical results are presented. Finally, the Sect. 5 gives final remarks and conclusion.

2   Desktop Grid and BOINC

This section briefly describes an architecture and workflow of a BOINC-based Desktop Grid, highlights the inherent uncertainties which affect runtime estimation.

As it was stated above, a Desktop Grid uses idle resources of non-dedicated geographically distributed computing nodes connected over regular network (Internet or LAN). There is a number of middleware systems for Desktop Grid organization. Among them Open Source BOINC software platform is nowadays considered as a de facto standard for Volunteer computing and it has been a framework for many independent projects since its appearing.

In this paper we refer a Desktop Grid as a distributed computing network, consisting of a server and a number of computing nodes; a Desktop Grid project

---

[1] https://boinc.berkeley.edu/trac/wiki/RuntimeEstimation.

– as a Desktop Grid equipped with an application and a set of tasks; a BOINC project – as a Desktop Grid project running by BOINC software; a project runtime estimation problem – as a problem of forecasting the time of a certain set of tasks completion; a project progress forecasting problem – as a problem of forecasting the time of a completion time of a number (which is less than a number of tasks in a project) of arbitrary tasks. This paper is aimed at a project progress forecasting as a part of a project runtime estimation problem. We are based on a BOINC-based Desktop Grid but the work can be generalized on other Desktop Grid middleware with the same architecture.

The architecture and workflow of a BOINC-based Desktop Grid is following [1]. BOINC as the most of Desktop Grid platforms uses the client-server model. The client part is able to employ idle resources of a computer for computations within BOINC projects. The server part consists of several subsystems responsible for tasks generation and distribution, results reception and assimilation, etc.

The server holds a large number of mutually independent tasks that are pieces of a whole computationally heavy problem. Computing nodes are able to connect to the server. Being in the idle state, a computing node makes a request and receives one or more tasks from the server, then process them independently from other clients. When a node finishes the processing, it reports results back to the server.

New computing nodes join a volunteer computing project using publicly available server address. The nodes are also free to leave a project without any notification to the server. An individual deadline is set for each task instance to limit its completion time. If the server does not get a result before the deadline, the task instance is considered lost. It is not easy to determine the optimal deadline value: the lower value lead to more frequent deadline violations due to specific clients availability periods or insufficient computing power; the higher deadline value leads to higher time wasted when a task instance is lost.

The client part is able to work at an arbitrary number of computers with various hardware and software characteristics (from mobile devices to supercomputers). Sometimes high software and hardware heterogeneity causes errors in tasks processing or producing a wrong answer. For this reason the computing model employed in BOINC implies that each computational task can exist in multiple instances (replicas). All replicas are computed separately and their results are compared. The BOINC settings allow creating and distributing more task replicas dynamically as needed. The quorum concept is used to define the minimal number of successful results to obtain for one computational task. This also provides protection against so called sabotage – intended wrong answer report aimed to harm the project or to cheat project credits (credits is a form of volunteers motivation, some kind of a volunteer usefullness rating which depends on contributed computing power).

The replication mechanism as a form of redundant computing can serve a number of purposes, first of all, the reliability, by increasing the chance to obtain the correct answer in time even if some nodes switch off without having finished the task. This helps, in its turn, to improve efficiency, provided that nodes are unreliable in general, by decreasing average time of waiting for an answer.

By its nature, a Desktop Grid deals with a number of uncertainties which affect runtime estimation. These uncertainties can be classified into three groups: *Desktop Grid* level, *Node* level and *Task* level.

The listed above uncertainties make any intuitive runtime estimation too rough in the most cases. It should be mentioned that uncertainties on the node level in the common case make impossible runtime estimation of a specific set of tasks or even a specific task. In particular, distribution of a client availability and unavailability intervals raises a problem of large variance in a task completion time [7] or even in multiple deadline violation [3].

3   Mathematical Model

Here we provide the formal problem statement and assumptions used in the model.

We consider a Desktop Grid consisting of a number of computing nodes; the Desktop Grid meets the following assumptions:

1. the number of nodes does not change drastically in time;
2. there is no periodicity behind the Desktop Grid activity;
3. there is no any task complexity pattern behind the tasks or all the tasks have the same complexity.

This section presents a statistical approach to the problem of a set of tasks runtime estimation. We describe a forecasting and statistical models, the latter is based on a linear regression model. We also propose a scaling method used to perform long-term forecasting and parameters adjustment procedure needed for better prognosis. Finally, we describe several tricks used to reduce resources consumption during runtime estimation.

3.1   Forecasting Model

As it was stated above, we consider a time series made by retrieved results. To make a forecast one should determine a functional dependence reflecting to time series. This functional dependence is called a forecasting model. The model should minimize squared difference between forecasted and observed values on a specified horizon (look-ahead period). Basing on the forecasting model, one should find out forecasted values and confidence interval.

We consider a cumulative process of results retrieving in a Desktop Grid. This process can be described by a time series

$$z(t) = [z(t_1), z(t_2), \ldots, z(t_k)]. \tag{1}$$

The values of this process are observed at discrete time points $t = t_1 < t_2 < \cdots < t_k$ with non-uniform intervals between them. Note, that the process itself is steadily increasing, so $z(t_i) < z(t_j) \; \forall j > i$. At the forecasting point t_k one should estimate a time point t_p, at which observed value $z(t_p)$ will exceed a specified value A.

For convenience, turn to considering a transformed process

$$y_i = z^{-1}(t_i), i = 1, \ldots, k, \tag{2}$$

which describes time points of i-th result retrieving. Then at step k (forecast point) one should estimate the value of process y_i at step A $(A > k; \; p = A - k$ is a look-ahead period).

With a view to forecast, take the following assumptions. First, assume that there is a functional dependence between time and values of the process:

$$y(t_i) = F(t_i, b) + \varepsilon_t, \tag{3}$$

here ε_t – is a random error with a normal law of distribution and b is a constant shift. Second, this dependence is piecewise linear with up trend.

From the point of view of Desktop Grids these assumptions mean the following. The observed process describes time points of new results retrieving. So, it is strictly increasing (two results can not be retrieved at the same moment and results can not be cancelled later). An angle of the trend line describes performance of a Desktop Grid (the less the angle to x axis, the more performance has the computing system). The performance can vary, changing the trend appropriately. We assume that change in performance is linear because non-linear changes usually relate to non-stationary behavior of a BOINC-project: start, computing competitions and so on. Such non-linear effects are limited to a transition period and subside quickly.

3.2   Statistical Model

The model is based on assumption that the value y_i has linear dependence on time t_i. This is a linear regression model, which is described by the following formula:

$$\widehat{y}_i = a \cdot t_i + b + \varepsilon_i, \tag{4}$$

here a, b – coefficients of the regression, ε_i – white noise, $i > 1$. The coefficients of the regression can be found using the least-squares deviation method (see for example [8]).

The least-squares deviation method minimizes sum of errors squared magnitudes of observed and estimated values using the following formula:

$$S = \sqrt{\frac{\sum_{i=1}^{k}(y_i - \widehat{y}_i)^2}{k}},$$

where y_i – observed values, $\widehat{y}_i$ – estimated values, and k – number of values.

The estimated values are defined by a regression equation (4). The general assumption is that the less the difference between observed and estimated values, the better the prognosis is.

The optimal coefficients a and b are defined by the following formulae [9]:

$$a = \frac{2(2k+1)}{k(k-1)} \sum_{i=1}^{k} y_i - \frac{6}{k(k-1)} \sum_{i=1}^{k} i \cdot y_i, \tag{5}$$

$$b = -\frac{6}{k(k-1)} \sum_{i=1}^{k} y_i + \frac{12}{k(k^2-1)} \sum_{i=1}^{k} i \cdot y_i. \tag{6}$$

The difference between estimated value and point prediction could appear due the following reasons:

1. inaccuracy of parameters estimation;
2. error caused by white noise ε_t.

These errors can be covered by a prognosis confidence interval. The confidence interval relates to uncertainty of the trend value; it is defined by the following formula [8]:

$$\widehat{y}_{k+p} \pm t_\gamma \cdot S_y \cdot \sqrt{\frac{k+1}{2} + \frac{(k+p-\bar{t})^2}{\sum_{t=1}^{k}(t-\bar{t})^2}}, \tag{7}$$

where

- y_{k+p} – point prediction at the moment $k+p$, here k is the number of observed values and p – prediction period;
- t_γ – value of Student t-statistic;
- S_y – square root of difference between estimated and observed values;
- $t = 1, 2, \ldots, k$ – counting number of an observed value;
- $\bar{t} = \frac{k+1}{2}$ – mean counting number.

Square root of difference between estimated and observed values is defined by the following formula:

$$S_y = \sqrt{\frac{\sum_{i=1}^{k}(y_i - \widehat{y}_i)^2}{k-1}}, \tag{8}$$

here y_i – observed values, $\widehat{y}_i$ – estimated values, and k – number of observed values.

Hence, confidence interval width depends on confidence level of t-statistic, prediction period length, square root of difference between estimated and observed values, and the number of observed values.

Finally, confidence interval calculation is performed by formula (7), using point prediction (4) with the coefficients, defined by formulae (5) and (6), and square root of difference between estimated and observed values calculation formula (8).

4   Numerical Experiments

The developed statistical model was verified using available statistics of volunteer computing project RakeSearch [10]. The available data of the project contains information on workunit/result/host ids, results create/sent/received times, outcome, elapsed/cpu times. The summary on the number of records and time periods covering by input data are given in Table 1; the data set is depicted on Fig. 1.

Table 1. Input data characterization.

	RakeSearch
Time period	06/09/2017–14/11/2017
Number of records	117 579
Number of nodes	1081

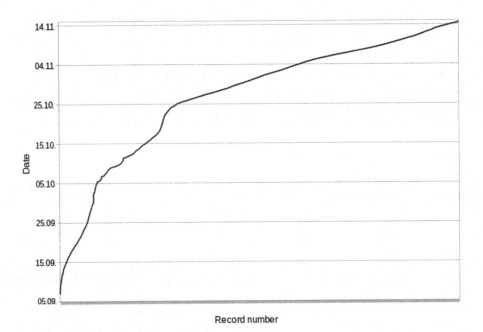

Fig. 1. Historical results receiving times of RakeSearch project.

As one can see, the project data could be approximated by a piecewise linear function (see Fig. 2; one can use automatic approximation basing, for example, on cumulated error).

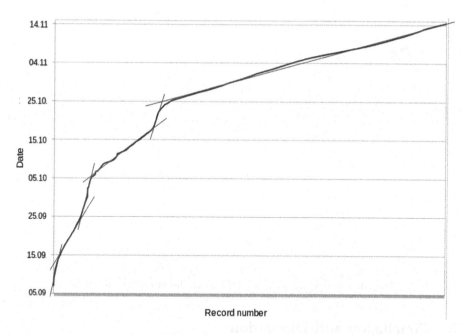

Fig. 2. Piecewise linear approximation of historical results receiving times of Rake-Search project.

To make a project progress forecast we considered sequences of tasks with random length (from 100 to 1000 tasks) with random look-ahead periods (from 10 to 200 tasks). The experiments showed good covering of real data by confidence intervals. Prosperous verification motivated us to implement prognosis module into RakeSearch administrative interface, where it is used now in ongoing work. Below are presented the examples of prognosis interface, verification experiments and real-life prognosis.

An example of a project progress forecasting (based on newer results of Rake-Search project) is given in Fig. 3. In the figure the blue line shows results receiving time, solid line is an approximation according to statistical model, arrow is the point forecast and the red line at the arrow is a confidence interval.

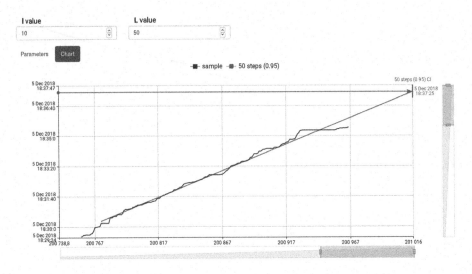

Fig. 3. Forecasting with $p = 50$ and confidence interval 0.95.

5   Conclusion and Discussion

The paper presents a statistical approach to a project progress forecasting in a Desktop Grid. The initial problem is hard due to stochastic nature of the processes lying behind it.

In the paper we present a mathematical model of a project progress forecasting. We use a statistical model of a point prediction basing on linear regression model. Our experiments on available data of volunteer computing projects show good agreement of real and predicted values. It works even despite of a number of uncertainties, such are high heterogeneity of tasks and big number of in practice a confidence interval is more useful than a point prediction. So, we provide confidence intervals estimation as well.

Basing on the described mathematical and statistical models, we develop an algorithm and a BOINC-module. The module could be integrated into a volunteer computing project to provide a real-time set of tasks runtime estimation.

However, the approach is worth only if the initial assumptions are hold (as they hold for the most of the Desktop Grid projects). They are: the number of nodes does not change drastically, computationally diverse tasks are mixed, there is no periodicity. In other cases other approaches should be used.

References

1. Anderson, D.P.: BOINC: a platform for volunteer computing. J. Grid Comput. **18**, 99–122 (2019). https://doi.org/10.1007/s10723-019-09497-9
2. Ivashko, E., Litovchenko, V.: Batch of tasks completion time estimation in a desktop grid. In: Voevodin, V., Sobolev, S. (eds.) RuSCDays 2018. CCIS, vol. 965, pp. 500–510. Springer, Cham (2019). https://doi.org/10.1007/978-3-030-05807-4_42

3. van Amstel, D.: Scheduling for volunteer computing on the BOINC server infrastructure. MA thesis, Ecole (2012)
4. Hellinckx, P., Verboven, S., Arickx, F., Broeckhove, J.: Predicting parameter sweep jobs: from simulation to grid implementation. In: 2009 International Conference on Complex, Intelligent and Software Intensive Systems, pp. 402–408, March 2009
5. Verboven, S., Hellinckx, P., Arickx, F., Broeckhove, J.: Runtime prediction based grid scheduling of parameter sweep jobs. In: 2008 IEEE Asia-Pacific Services Computing Conference, pp. 33–38, December 2008
6. Bazinet, A.L., Cummings, M.P.: Subdividing long-running, variable-length analyses into short, fixed-length BOINC workunits. J. Grid Comput. **14**(3), 429–441 (2016), https://doi.org/10.1007/s10723-015-9348-5
7. Javadi, B., Kondo, D., Vincent, J.M., Anderson, D.: Discovering statistical models of availability in large distributed systems: an empirical study of seti@home. Parall. Distrib. Syst. IEEE Trans. **22**, 1896–1903 (2011)
8. Brink, D.: Essentials of Statistics. Bookboon, London (2010). https://books.google.ru/books?id=PeRirk_hxycC
9. Chetyrkin, E.: Statistical Forecasting Methods, vol. 200. Statistics (1977)
10. Manzyuk, M., Nikitina, N., Vatutin, E.: Employment of distributed computing to search and explore orthogonal diagonal Latin squares of rank 9. In: Proceedings of the XI All-Russian Research and Practice Conference "Digital Technologies in Education, Science, Society" (2017)

Searching for Orthogonal Latin Squares via Cells Mapping and BOINC-Based Cube-and-Conquer

Eduard Vatutin[1] ⓘ, Oleg Zaikin[2](✉) ⓘ, Maxim Manzyuk[3] ⓘ,
and Natalia Nikitina[4] ⓘ

[1] Southwest State University, Kursk, Russia
`evatutin@rambler.ru`
[2] Swansea University, Swansea, UK
`o.s.zaikin@swansea.ac.uk`
[3] Internet portal BOINC.ru, Moscow, Russia
`hoarfrost@rambler.ru`
[4] Institute of Applied Mathematical Research, Karelian Research Centre of RAS,
Petrozavodsk, Russia
`nikitina@krc.karelia.ru`

Abstract. This study focuses on searching for pairs of orthogonal diagonal Latin squares of order 10. Consider a cells mapping in accordance to which one diagonal Latin square is mapped to another one. Given a certain cells mapping schema, the problem is to find a pair of orthogonal diagonal Latin squares of order 10 such that they match the schema (or to prove that such a pair does not exist). The problem is reduced to the Boolean satisfiability problem (SAT). Three mapping schemes are considered, and for each of them a SAT instance is constructed. If a satisfying assignment is found for an instance, the corresponding pair of orthogonal Latin squares can be easily extracted from it. The Cube-and-Conquer approach is used to solve the instances. The cubing phase is performed on a sequential look-ahead SAT solver, while on the conquer phase an experiment in a BOINC-based volunteer computing project is launched. In the experiment, for two out of three schemes orthogonal pairs are found.

Keywords: Volunteer computing · BOINC · Latin square · MOLS · SAT · Cube-and-Conquer

1 Introduction

Volunteer computing [1] is a type of distributed computing that uses resources owned by private persons. Alternatively, volunteer computing can be considered as a type of desktop grid computing [2]. Volunteer computing is a quite cheap and natural approach to solving computationally hard problems that can be decomposed into independent subproblems. Such problems appear, for example, in astronomy, medicine, cryptography, and combinatorics. During the last two

V. Voevodin and S. Sobolev (Eds.): RuSCDays 2021, CCIS 1510, pp. 498–512, 2021.
https://doi.org/10.1007/978-3-030-92864-3_38

decades, a number of important and challenging problems from these areas were successfully solved in volunteer computing projects. Most of such projects are based on BOINC (Berkeley Open Infrastructure for Network Computing [3]). Note, that BOINC is quite flexible and can be also used to create enterprise desktop grids (see e.g. [4]). Though launching and maintaining a BOINC-based volunteer computing project is not an easy task, if its team cope with that and also take into account volunteers' feedback, the project can attract significant computational resources [5].

Latin square is a very simple yet important combinatorial design [6]. One of the most well-studied property between two Latin squares is orthogonality. Many theoretical and practical problems (e.g. from cryptography and coding theory) can be reduced to finding systems of orthogonal Latin squares. One of the most well-known open mathematical problem is to determine the existence of a triple of mutually orthogonal Latin squares of order 10.

Though as a rule "pure" combinatorial algorithms are applied for finding systems of orthogonal Latin squares (see e.g. [7,8]), it is also possible to reduce these problems to the Boolean satisfiability problem (SAT [9]). Despite significant recent progress in complete SAT solving algorithms [10,11], even the best SAT solvers can (sometimes) show competitive results only if there are few to no solutions in the considered problem related to orthogonal Latin squares. It means that the corresponding SAT instance has only few satisfying assignments or it is unsatisfiable, respectively. Note that even in this case such SAT instances in practice are very hard, that is why distributed algorithms are crucial to deal with them. Recently, Cube-and-Conquer has showed itself as a very powerful distributed SAT solving algorithm [12]. In this study, a BOINC-based Cube-and-Conquer SAT solver is implemented and applied to finding orthogonal diagonal Latin squares.

A brief outline of the paper is as follows. In Sect. 2, preliminary information regarding orthogonal diagonal Latin squares is given. Section 3 describes how cells mapping can be used to find orthogonal (diagonal) Latin squares. In Sect. 4 the cells mapping approach is reduced to SAT, and several cells mapping schemes are investigated via the BOINC-based Cube-and-Conquer SAT solver. Finally, related works are discussed and conclusions are drawn.

2   Orthogonal Diagonal Latin Squares

A *Latin square* of order N is a square table $N \times N$ filled with N different symbols (e.g. $0, \ldots, N-1$) in such a way, that all symbols within a single row or single column are distinct [6]. A *diagonal Latin square* is a Latin square in which all symbols in both main diagonal and anti-diagonal are distinct. A *transversal* of a Latin square of order N is a set of N entries, one selected from each row and each column such that no two entries contain the same symbol.

All Latin squares can be divided into *isotopy classes* such that any Latin square from an isotopy class can be produced from any other Latin square from the same class by permuting rows, columns, or symbols names. *Isotopism* is an equivalence relation. Another equivalence relation on the set of Latin squares is *main class isotopism.* The corresponding classes are called *main classes.* Each such class contains up to six isotopy classes. Latin square that is a lexicographically minimal representative of a main class is called a *canonical form.*

Two Latin squares $A = (a_{ij}), B = (b_{ij})$ of order N are *orthogonal* if all ordered pairs $(a_{ij}, b_{ij}), 0 \leq i, j \leq N-1$ are distinct. A set of Latin squares of the same order, all pairs of which are orthogonal, is called a set of *mutually orthogonal Latin squares* (MOLS). For diagonal Latin squares, *MODLS* is defined similarly. MODLS are quite rare compared to MOLS. The first pair of MODLS of order 10 was presented in [13].

As a rule, searching for an orthogonal mate for a given Latin square A of order N is performed via the Euler-Parker method (see e.g. [14]). According to this method, the orthogonal mate can be easily constructed from a set of N disjoint transversals of A, so the goal is to find such a set. It should be noted, that searching for disjoint transversals is the most time-consuming part of the Euler-Parker method. In [15] the problem of searching for a set of N disjoint diagonal transversals (required for finding MODLS) was reduced to the exact cover problem that in turn was solved by DLX, an implementation of the Algorithm X [16].

Self-orthogonal Latin square (SOLS) denotes a Latin square that is orthogonal to its transpose (see e.g. [17]). It gives another approach for finding MOLS. For diagonal Latin squares, SODLS is defined similarly. *Enhanced self-orthogonal diagonal Latin square* (ESODLS) denotes a diagonal Latin square that is orthogonal to some diagonal Latin square from the same main class [18]. It is clear that ESODLS is a generalisation of SODLS and can be also used to find MODLS without dealing with transversals.

It is also possible to reduce finding MOLS or MODLS to Integer Programming [19,20], Constraint Programming [19,20], or SAT [9,21]. The resulted instances are solved via solvers from the corresponding areas, and then the solution of the original problem is constructed. In the present paper, the SAT approach is employed for finding new pairs of MODLS of order 10.

3   Finding Orthogonal Latin Squares via Cells Mapping Schemes

In this section, cells mapping schemes for Latin squares are proposed, then such schemes for ESODLS are described, and finally a search for ESODLS cells mapping schemes of order 10 is discussed.

3.1   Cells Mapping Schema

Consider two Latin squares A and B of order N. Assume that in both squares cells are numerated from 0 to $N^2 - 1$ (left-to-right, top-to-bottom), and $A[i]$ denotes value of i-th cell, $0 \leq i \leq N^2 - 1$ (similarly for B). A *cells mapping schema* (CMS) for an ordered pair of squares (A, B) is a permutation p of N^2 integer numbers $0, \ldots, N^2 - 1$ such that $p[i] = j, 0 \leq i, j \leq N^2 - 1$ iff $A[i] = B[j]$. Therefore p shows how cells of A can be mapped onto cells of B. This fact is denoted as $p(A) = B$. Note, that any CMS for order N can be naturally represented not only as a permutation of size N^2, but also as a $N \times N$ table. A pair of Latin squares A and B *matches* a CMS (or, interchangeably, CMS *matches* the pair of Latin squares) if A can be mapped onto B via the CMS.

Example 1. CMS

$$(0, 5, 10, 15, 4, 1, 14, 11, 8, 13, 2, 7, 12, 9, 6, 3).$$

is equal to

$$\begin{pmatrix} 0 & 5 & 10 & 15 \\ 4 & 1 & 14 & 11 \\ 8 & 13 & 2 & 7 \\ 12 & 9 & 6 & 3 \end{pmatrix}.$$

The following pair of Latin squares matches the CMS:

$$A = \begin{pmatrix} 0\,2\,3\,1 \\ 3\,1\,0\,2 \\ 1\,3\,2\,0 \\ 2\,0\,1\,3 \end{pmatrix}, B = \begin{pmatrix} 0\,1\,2\,3 \\ 3\,2\,1\,0 \\ 1\,0\,3\,2 \\ 2\,3\,0\,1 \end{pmatrix}$$

It should be noted that for some CMS enormous number of pairs of Latin squares can be matched, while for others no such pairs can be matched at all. In the above example two Latin squares are orthogonal. An example of the CMS with no matched MOLS is a *trivial* CMS, i.e. such a CMS p that $p[i] = i, 0 \leq i \leq N^2 - 1$. For $N > 1$, a trivial CMS does not give an orthogonal mate since it maps a Latin square to itself (if $N = 1$, the single existing Latin square is orthogonal to itself).

It is clear that there are $(N^2)!$ different CMS for order N. A *fixed point* in a CMS p is such a number i that $p[i] = i$ (see e.g. [22]). Note, that for order N a trivial CMS has N^2 fixed points. It can be shown that if a CMS matches some pair of MOLS, then the CMS has at most N fixed points. It follows from the fact that for order N there are only N different variants of fixed points: $(0, 0), (1, 1), \ldots, (N - 1, N - 1)$. Therefore if there are more than N fixed points, then at least one of these pairs of symbols will occur more than once, thus violating the orthogonality condition.

Given an arbitrary pair of MOLS A and B, a CMS p can be extracted from it. For this purpose it is required to find such cells with numbers i_1 and i_2, for which $A[i_1] = v_1, B[i_1] = v_2, A[i_2] = v_2, B[i_2] = v_1, p[i_1] = i_2, p[i_2] = i_1$. Such CMS are the simplest ones that match some MOLS; in each such CMS there are N 1-cycles and $N^2 - N$ 2-cycles. These CMS are called *canonical*. It can be shown that if two Latin squares A and B are orthogonal, and a canonical CMS maps A onto B, then the CMS also maps B onto A. This fact is denoted by $p(A) = B, p(B) = A$.

3.2 ESODLS CMS

CMS can be naturally connected with SODLS (see Sect. 2).

Example 2. Consider a SODLS of order 4 with cells numerated as follows:

$$\begin{pmatrix} 0 & 1 & 2 & 3 \\ 4 & 5 & 6 & 7 \\ 8 & 9 & 10 & 11 \\ 12 & 13 & 14 & 15 \end{pmatrix}.$$

The corresponding CMS in the form of a 4×4 table is

$$\begin{pmatrix} 0 & 4 & 8 & 12 \\ 1 & 5 & 9 & 13 \\ 2 & 6 & 10 & 14 \\ 3 & 7 & 11 & 15 \end{pmatrix}$$

The same CMS in the form of a permutation is

$$(0, 4, 8, 12, 1, 5, 9, 13, 2, 6, 10, 14, 3, 7, 11, 15).$$

CMS can also be connected with ESODLS (see Sect. 2). By applying to a trivial CMS all possible equivalent transformations, which are used to construct a main class of diagonal Latin squares given any its representative [23], a set of CMS is obtained that is called a set of *ESODLS CMS*. The number of ESODLS CMS for order N is equal to the maximal size of main classes of diagonal Latin squares of order N with the fixed first row, see sequence A299784[1] in the online encyclopedia of integer sequences (OEIS) [24]. For order 10, there are 15 360 ESODLS CMS.

   Orthogonality cycle of length k is such a set of Latin squares $\{L_1, \ldots, L_k\}$ that L_i is orthogonal to L_{i+1} for $1 \le i \le k - 1$, and finally L_k is orthogonal to L_1. It is clear that a canonical CMS gives an orthogonal cycle of length 2. At the present moment, only orthogonal cycles of length 2 and 4 are known for diagonal Latin squares of order 10 [25].

   Some ESODLS CMS are not canonical, but they also can have matching pairs of MODLS. For example, during the search for MODLS of order 10 in neighbourhoods of generalised symmetries, 2 orthogonal cycles of length 4 were found [26]. In each of these orthogonal cycles diagonal Latin squares are obtained from each other by applying one of two ESODLS CMS: one direction for one CMS. Figure 1 shows these orthogonal cycles. Each ESODLS CMS from the figure has 25 4-cycles, so they are not canonical. It can be shown that a consequent applying of a CMS forms an orthogonal cycle of length equal to least common multiple of cycles lengths in the CMS. Theoretically, for order 10 from some ESODLS CMS (e.g. with 10 1-cycles and 30 3-cycles) it would be possible to obtain an orthogonal cycle of length 3, i.e. a triple of MODLS of order 10.

---

[1] https://oeis.org/A299784.

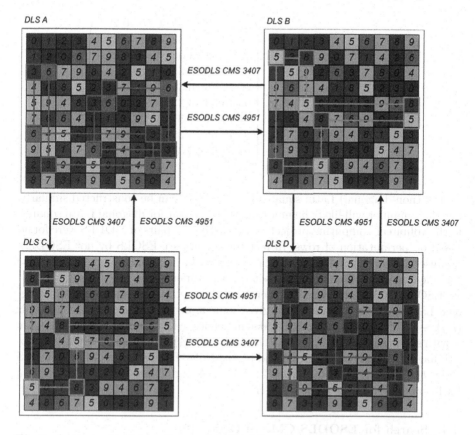

Fig. 1. An example of an orthogonal cycle of four diagonal Latin squares (DLS) and two CMS. DLS stands for diagonal Latin square.

Two CMS from the figure are as follows:

$$CMS_{3407} = \begin{pmatrix} 9 & 69 & 19 & 59 & 29 & 79 & 49 & 89 & 39 & 99 \\ 3 & 63 & 13 & 53 & 23 & 73 & 43 & 83 & 33 & 93 \\ 8 & 68 & 18 & 58 & 28 & 78 & 48 & 88 & 38 & 98 \\ 4 & 64 & 14 & 54 & 24 & 74 & 44 & 84 & 34 & 94 \\ 7 & 67 & 17 & 57 & 27 & 77 & 47 & 87 & 37 & 97 \\ 2 & 62 & 12 & 52 & 22 & 72 & 42 & 82 & 32 & 92 \\ 5 & 65 & 15 & 55 & 25 & 75 & 45 & 85 & 35 & 95 \\ 1 & 61 & 11 & 51 & 21 & 71 & 41 & 81 & 31 & 91 \\ 6 & 66 & 16 & 56 & 26 & 76 & 46 & 86 & 36 & 96 \\ 0 & 60 & 10 & 50 & 20 & 70 & 40 & 80 & 30 & 90 \end{pmatrix},$$

$$CMS_{4951} = CMS_{3407}^{-1} = \begin{pmatrix} 90\ 70\ 50\ 10\ 30\ 60\ 80\ 40\ 20\ 0 \\ 92\ 72\ 52\ 12\ 32\ 62\ 82\ 42\ 22\ 2 \\ 94\ 74\ 54\ 14\ 34\ 64\ 84\ 44\ 24\ 4 \\ 98\ 78\ 58\ 18\ 38\ 68\ 88\ 48\ 28\ 8 \\ 96\ 76\ 56\ 16\ 36\ 66\ 86\ 46\ 26\ 6 \\ 93\ 73\ 53\ 13\ 33\ 63\ 83\ 43\ 23\ 3 \\ 91\ 71\ 51\ 11\ 31\ 61\ 81\ 41\ 21\ 1 \\ 95\ 75\ 55\ 15\ 35\ 65\ 85\ 45\ 25\ 5 \\ 97\ 77\ 57\ 17\ 37\ 67\ 87\ 47\ 27\ 7 \\ 99\ 79\ 59\ 19\ 39\ 69\ 89\ 49\ 29\ 9 \end{pmatrix}.$$

For (non-diagonal) Latin squares ESOLS CMS can be constructed similarly, but their number will likely be much higher than that for diagonal Latin squares. In the volunteer computing project RakeSearch [27], pairs of MODLS were found based on permutation of rows. In fact these pairs are ESOLS by not ESODLS, because the corresponding canonical forms of Latin squares coincide, but the canonical forms of diagonal Latin squares can differ.

ESODLS CMS are close to generalised symmetries/automorphisms of diagonal Latin squares. Each of them gives some transformation F that maps cells $(i, j) \to (i', j')$. In case of generalised symmetries, cells of a diagonal Latin square A with symmetry are mapped onto themselves: $f(A) = A$ (case 1), while orthogonal diagonal Latin squares are found by the Euler-Parker method. For ESODLS CMS $f(A) = B, f(B) = A$ (case 2), where A and B are orthogonal diagonal Latin squares from the same main class.

3.3   Search for ESODLS CMS of Order 10

Given a CMS, it is possible to construct all matching pairs of MOLS by the depth-first search. Note, that transversals are not required in this case. For some CMS all matching pairs of MOLS can be found in few seconds, yet for other ones the search can take days. The runtime can be significantly reduced via the usage of a dedicated implementation with bit arithmetic and nested loops (see e.g. [28]). One more further step is a GPU-implementation. For ESODLS CMS the runtime (and the number of matching orthogonal pairs) is usually several orders of magnitude higher than that for an arbitrary CMS. Note that a CMS can be obtained randomly or from known pairs of MOLS.

For about four thousand ESODLS CMS (out of 15 360) of order 10, all matching pairs of MODLS of order 10 can be found quite fast on a computer via the depth-first search. To find all pairs of MODLS for other ESODLS CMS, in the volunteer computing project Gerasim@Home [29] a computational experiment was launched. For each CMS, workunits (computational tasks in a volunteer computing project) were formed as follows: values of two cells of the first diagonal Latin square were chosen randomly such that they did not violate the constraints. As a result, values of two corresponding cells (set by the CMS) of the second diagonal Latin square were assigned automatically. Then on a volunteer computer values of other CMS cells (98 out of 100) were filled via the depth-first search algorithm mentioned above. It turned out, that some workunits can be processed very fast, but for others the runtime can be extremely high. That is why a time limit of 10 h was set for workunits. When the time limit was reached, all pairs of MODLS found so far (if any) were saved and returned to the server. It turned out, that for none of the studied CMS all workunits could be processed within the time limit. In the future it might be possible to reduce the search spaces without decreasing the number of solutions. As a result of the experiment, 33 240 canonical forms of ESODLS of order 10 were found. This allowed setting a new lower bound $a(10) \geq 33\ 240$ in OEIS sequence A309210[2].

4   Finding MODLS via CMS, Cube-and-Conquer, and BOINC

This section studies three ESODLS CMS of order 10, for which no pairs of MODLS were found in the experiment described in Subsect. 3.3. In particular, CMS_{3407} and CMS_{4951} from Subsect. 3.2 were taken, and also the following CMS:

$$CMS_{1234} = \begin{pmatrix} 27\ 26\ 21\ 25\ 29\ 20\ 24\ 28\ 23\ 22 \\ 37\ 36\ 31\ 35\ 39\ 30\ 34\ 38\ 33\ 32 \\ 87\ 86\ 81\ 85\ 89\ 80\ 84\ 88\ 83\ 82 \\ 47\ 46\ 41\ 45\ 49\ 40\ 44\ 48\ 43\ 42 \\ 7\ \ 6\ \ 1\ \ 5\ \ 9\ \ 0\ \ 4\ \ 8\ \ 3\ \ 2 \\ 97\ 96\ 91\ 95\ 99\ 90\ 94\ 98\ 93\ 92 \\ 57\ 56\ 51\ 55\ 59\ 50\ 54\ 58\ 53\ 52 \\ 17\ 16\ 11\ 15\ 19\ 10\ 14\ 18\ 13\ 12 \\ 67\ 66\ 61\ 65\ 69\ 60\ 64\ 68\ 63\ 62 \\ 77\ 76\ 71\ 75\ 79\ 70\ 74\ 78\ 73\ 72 \end{pmatrix}.$$

The problems of finding pairs of MODLS of order 10 that match these ESODLS CMS were reduced to SAT. In its decision version SAT is formulated as follows: for an arbitrary Boolean formula to determine if it is satisfiable or not [9]. SAT is historically the first NP-complete problem, thus it is possible to effectively reduce plenty of known problems to it. In the last three decades, SAT solvers have become very effective, that is why nowadays both practical and theoretical problems from various ares are reduced to SAT and solved by SAT solvers. In practice a Boolean formula is usually represented in Conjunctive Normal Form (CNF) that is a conjunction of disjunctions (clauses). If a SAT instance is way too hard for a sequential solver, then parallel (multithreaded) or distributed solvers can be applied to it [30].

In the remaining of the section, a SAT encoding for the considered problems is discussed, then the experimental results obtained via a Cube-and-Conquer SAT solver in a volunteer computing project are presented.

---

[2] https://oeis.org/A309210.

4.1 SAT Encoding

Consider the following problem: given a CMS of order N to find a pair of MODLS of order N that matches this CMS, or to prove that no such pair exists. First, the SAT encoding for finding a pair of MODLS from [31] was taken for this purpose. Briefly, the encoding is as follows: each of two diagonal Latin square of order N is represented as an $N \times N \times N$ incidence cube where dimensions are identified with the rows, columns, and the symbols. A cell with coordinates $(i, j, k), 0 \leq i, j, k \leq N - 1$ contains 1 iff the cell (i, j) of the Latin square contains k, 0 otherwise. It is clear that if any two coordinates in the incidence cube are fixed, then the remaining "line" contains exactly one 1. Every cube cell is naturally encoded by one Boolean variable, so each diagonal Latin square of order N is encoded by N^3 Boolean variables. A similar approach can be found e.g. in [32].

Two groups of clauses are added to the CNF: the first one reflects the diagonal Latin square conditions, while the second one reflects the orthogonality conditions. Clauses from the first group contain only variables of the corresponding square, while clauses of the second group contain variables from both squares. The so-called *naive* encoding of the orthogonality condition was used, for details see [31]. For order 10 the corresponding CNF consists of 2 000 variables and 434 440 clauses. Recall that this CNF encodes the problem of finding a pair of MODLS of order 10.

The described base CNF can be quite naturally used for constructing a CNF that encodes finding pairs of MODLS of order 10, which match a given CMS. Assume that due to CMS (see Subsect. 3.1) some cell of the first square must be equal to a certain cell of the second square. Recall that each square cell is encoded by N Boolean variables, so it is needed to encode the fact that two corresponding Boolean arrays of size N are equal. Since the equality of two Boolean variables x, y is encoded by two clauses $(x \vee \neg y) \wedge (\neg x \vee y)$, $2N$ clauses are needed to encode equality of two Boolean arrays of size N. Since CMS has N^2 entries, $2N^3$ clauses are required in total to reflect the CMS conditions. Taking this into account, three CNFs were constructed by adding to the base CNF 2 000 2-literal clauses, which correspond to three considered CMS. It means that each of three CNF consisted of 2 000 variables and 436 440 clauses.

It is known that the first row in the first diagonal Latin square can be fixed in ascending order $0, \ldots, N - 1$ without reducing the amount of the corresponding pairs of MODLS. This was reflected by adding 10 one-literal clauses, so finally each of three CNF consisted of 2 000 variables and 436 450 clauses.

4.2 Solving in RakeSearch via Cube-and-Conquer

All three constructed CNFs turned out to be too hard for sequential SAT solvers, that is why Cube-and-Conquer [12] was applied to them. Its parallelisation strategy is a variant of Divide-and-Conquer. According to Cube-and-Conquer, on the *cubing* phase a look-ahead SAT solver [11] is launched on a CNF and splits the problem into *cubes*. On the *conquer* phase a simplified subproblem is constructed based on each cube, then these subproblems are solved via a Conflict-driven clause learning (CDCL) SAT solver [10]. Since cubes can be processed independently, the conquer phase can be easily parallelised.

It is usually crucial to minimise a CNF before launching a look-ahead solver. All three CNFs were minimised via the CADICAL CDCL solver [33] of version 1.3.0. In particular, this solver was launched in the minimisation mode for 1 min on a personal computer on each CNF. The minimised CNFs (which encode exactly the same problems) had the same number of variables, but much less clauses—about 152–155 thousand instead of 436 thousand.

On the first stage, the MARCH_CU look-ahead solver [34] was launched on the minimised CNFs on a computer. The splitting parameter n was equal to 580, that value was chosen in accordance with preliminary experiments. As a result, 5 506 614, 5 507 514, and 4 144 254 cubes were generated for CMS_{3407}, CMS_{4951}, and CMS_{1234}, respectively. To exclude simple cubes, the KISSAT [33] CDCL solver of version sc2020 was launched on them with the time limit of 5 s. This experiment was held on a supercomputer. It turned out, that 2 265 747, 2 660 949, and 2 359 952 cubes were not processed within the time limit, respectively. To process these 7 286 648 cubes, a BOINC-based volunteer computing project RakeSearch [27] was used as an umbrella project, i.e. as a project that can solve problems posted by various scientific teams, see e.g. [35]. 7 286 648 cubes were divided into 364 334 workunits (at most 20 cubes in each).

As a computing application, a modification of the MINISAT [36] CDCL solver of version 2.2 was used. This solver had already been used earlier as a base of a similar computing application [29], so it was quite easy to implement a new computing application on top of it. Four versions of the computing application were implemented: Windows x86, Windows x64, Linux x86, and Linux x64. For each cube the limit of 5000 MINISAT restarts was set, that roughly corresponds to about 3 min runtime on one core of a modern desktop CPU.

The experiment started on 20 July 2020 and ended on 9 September 2020. In total, 1 611 computers of 625 volunteers took part in it. Finally, all 364 334 workunits were processed successfully. Processing of almost all cubes was interrupted due to the restart limit, but on 29 of them satisfying assignments were found. As a result, 18 pairs of MODLS of order 10 were found for CMS_{3407} and 11 ones for CMS_{4951}. The first found pair for CMS_{3407} is:

$$
\begin{pmatrix}
0\,1\,2\,3\,4\,5\,6\,7\,8\,9 \\
5\,6\,7\,9\,2\,0\,4\,8\,3\,1 \\
9\,8\,1\,7\,5\,6\,0\,2\,4\,3 \\
6\,3\,5\,2\,0\,9\,1\,4\,7\,8 \\
1\,0\,6\,4\,8\,7\,3\,9\,2\,5 \\
2\,4\,8\,5\,6\,3\,9\,0\,1\,7 \\
4\,2\,9\,0\,3\,8\,7\,1\,5\,6 \\
3\,9\,4\,8\,7\,1\,2\,5\,6\,0 \\
7\,5\,0\,6\,1\,4\,8\,3\,9\,2 \\
8\,7\,3\,1\,9\,2\,5\,6\,0\,4
\end{pmatrix}
\begin{pmatrix}
8\,3\,2\,5\,6\,4\,7\,1\,9\,0 \\
3\,4\,8\,7\,5\,9\,0\,6\,1\,2 \\
9\,7\,6\,2\,0\,3\,1\,8\,5\,4 \\
0\,6\,1\,3\,7\,5\,9\,2\,4\,8 \\
5\,2\,9\,4\,1\,7\,8\,3\,0\,6 \\
1\,8\,5\,9\,2\,0\,6\,4\,7\,3 \\
7\,9\,4\,6\,3\,2\,5\,0\,8\,1 \\
2\,1\,3\,0\,9\,8\,4\,7\,6\,5 \\
6\,5\,0\,8\,4\,1\,3\,9\,2\,7 \\
4\,0\,7\,1\,8\,6\,2\,5\,3\,9
\end{pmatrix} .
$$

The first pair for CMS_{4951} is:

$$
\begin{pmatrix}
0\ 1\ 2\ 3\ 4\ 5\ 6\ 7\ 8\ 9 \\
3\ 6\ 9\ 5\ 7\ 2\ 1\ 0\ 4\ 8 \\
5\ 0\ 8\ 6\ 3\ 9\ 2\ 1\ 7\ 4 \\
6\ 2\ 4\ 1\ 5\ 3\ 8\ 9\ 0\ 7 \\
9\ 4\ 5\ 8\ 2\ 7\ 0\ 6\ 3\ 1 \\
1\ 9\ 7\ 2\ 6\ 4\ 3\ 8\ 5\ 0 \\
4\ 3\ 6\ 0\ 9\ 8\ 7\ 2\ 1\ 5 \\
7\ 8\ 3\ 4\ 1\ 0\ 9\ 5\ 2\ 6 \\
8\ 5\ 1\ 7\ 0\ 6\ 4\ 3\ 9\ 2 \\
2\ 7\ 0\ 9\ 8\ 1\ 5\ 4\ 6\ 3
\end{pmatrix}
\begin{pmatrix}
9\ 5\ 8\ 0\ 4\ 6\ 1\ 2\ 7\ 3 \\
3\ 0\ 5\ 2\ 6\ 4\ 8\ 7\ 1\ 9 \\
8\ 1\ 4\ 5\ 7\ 2\ 3\ 9\ 0\ 6 \\
4\ 9\ 7\ 6\ 3\ 1\ 2\ 0\ 5\ 8 \\
7\ 2\ 0\ 8\ 1\ 5\ 6\ 3\ 9\ 4 \\
2\ 6\ 9\ 7\ 8\ 3\ 5\ 1\ 4\ 0 \\
5\ 8\ 2\ 4\ 9\ 0\ 7\ 6\ 3\ 1 \\
1\ 3\ 6\ 9\ 0\ 8\ 4\ 5\ 2\ 7 \\
6\ 7\ 1\ 3\ 2\ 9\ 0\ 4\ 8\ 5 \\
0\ 4\ 3\ 1\ 5\ 7\ 9\ 8\ 6\ 2
\end{pmatrix}.
$$

As for CMS_{1234}, processing of all corresponding cubes was interrupted due to the restart limit, so at the moment it is still unclear whether any pair of MODLS matches this CMS.

It turned out that all found pairs are isomorphic to known pairs that were found earlier in the neighborhoods for generalized symmetries (see [26]). Nevertheless, the results show that Cube-and-Conquer is able to cope with the considered combinatorial problem. All found pairs, corresponding CNFs, as well as sources of the CNF generator, workunit generator, and computing application can be found online[3].

5   Related Works

A number of distributed Cube-and-Conquer solvers are known: aimed at BOINC-based enterprise desktop grid computing [37]; aimed at cluster and cloud computing [38]. Recently, Cube-and-Conquer was used for solving various combinatorial problems, e.g. the Boolean Pythagorean triples problem [39] and Lam's problem [40].

A parallel tree search was implemented in the volunteer computing project yoyo@home [41]. In [42] the Branch-and-Bound method was implemented in an enterprise BOINC-based desktop grid.

In the volunteer computing project SAT@home [29], pairs of MODLS of order 10 were found by a Divide-and-Conquer SAT solver. In opposite to Cube-and-Conquer, in this solver cubes are generated by a black-box optimization algorithm that employs the Monte Carlo method [43]. In some experiments, SAT@home was used in combination with computing clusters [44].

The volunteer computing project Gerasim@Home [29] was used to enumerate diagonal Latin squares of order 9 [45]. At the present moment, this project searches for canonical forms of diagonal Latin squares or order 10 [25]. In the volunteer computing project RakeSearch, an ensemble of orthogonality graphs for the set of all diagonal Latin squares of order 9 was constructed [27]. This ensemble was based on pairs of MODLS of order 9, found via row permuting techniques.

---

[3] https://github.com/Nauchnik/SAT-at-home/tree/master/src_boinc_satcmsdls.

6   Conclusions

The present paper proposes a new approach for finding pairs of orthogonal Latin squares. It also describes the first distributed Cube-and-Conquer SAT solver aimed at volunteer computing. The solver was applied to hard SAT instances, which encode the problem of finding pairs of orthogonal diagonal Latin squares of order 10 via the proposed approach. A computational experiment in a BOINC-based volunteer computing project made it possible to find the sought pairs.

In the future we are planning to try other look-ahead SAT solvers in the cubing phase and modern CDCL SAT solvers in the conquer phase. Also we are planning to perform more detailed comparison of the SAT solver with combinatorial algorithms on the considered problems.

Acknowledgements. Authors thank all RakeSearch and Gerasim@home volunteers, whose computers took part in the experiments. Oleg Zaikin was supported by EPSRC grant EP/S015523/1. Eduard Vatutin was supported by intra-university grant for SWSU development program (Priority 2030) No. PR2030/2021.

References

1. Anderson, D.P., Fedak, G.: The computational and storage potential of volunteer computing. In: Sixth IEEE International Symposium on Cluster Computing and the Grid (CCGrid 2006), Singapore, 16–19 May 2006, pp. 73–80. IEEE Computer Society (2006)
2. Cerin, C., Fedak, G.: Desktop Grid Computing, 1st edn. Chapman & Hall/CRC, Boca Raton (2012)
3. Anderson, D.P.: BOINC: a platform for volunteer computing. J. Grid Comput. **18**(1), 99–122 (2020). https://doi.org/10.1007/s10723-019-09497-9
4. Ivashko, E., Chernov, I., Nikitina, N.: A survey of desktop grid scheduling. IEEE Trans. Parallel Distrib. Syst. **29**(12), 2882–2895 (2018)
5. Yakimets, V., Kurochkin, I.: Roadmap for improving volunteer distributed computing project performance. In: Voevodin, V., Sobolev, S. (eds.) RuSCDays 2019. CCIS, vol. 1129, pp. 690–700. Springer, Cham (2019). https://doi.org/10.1007/978-3-030-36592-9_56
6. Colbourn, C., et al.: Latin squares. In: Handbook of Combinatorial Designs. Discrete Mathematics and Its Applications, 2nd edn, pp. 224–265. Chapman and Hall/CRC (2006)
7. McKay, B.D., Meynert, A., Myrvold, W.: Small Latin squares, quasigroups, and loops. J. Comb. Des. **15**(2), 98–119 (2007)
8. Egan, J., Wanless, I.M.: Enumeration of MOLS of small order. Math. Comput. **85**(298), 799–824 (2016)
9. Zhang, H.: Combinatorial designs by SAT solvers. In: Biere, A., Heule, M., van Maaren, H., Walsh, T. (eds.) Handbook of Satisfiability, Frontiers in Artificial Intelligence and Applications, vol. 185, pp. 533–568. IOS Press (2009)
10. Marques-Silva, J.P., Lynce, I., Malik, S.: Conflict-driven clause learning SAT solvers. In: Biere, A., Heule, M., van Maaren, H., Walsh, T. (eds.) Handbook of Satisfiability, Frontiers in Artificial Intelligence and Applications, vol. 185, pp. 131–153. IOS Press (2009)

11. Heule, M., van Maaren, H.: Look-ahead based SAT solvers. In: Biere, A., Heule, M., van Maaren, H., Walsh, T. (eds.) Handbook of Satisfiability, Frontiers in Artificial Intelligence and Applications, vol. 185, pp. 155–184. IOS Press (2009)
12. Heule, M.J.H., Kullmann, O., Biere, A.: Cube-and-Conquer for satisfiability. In: Hamadi, Y., Sais, L. (eds.) Handbook of Parallel Constraint Reasoning, pp. 31–59. Springer, Cham (2018). https://doi.org/10.1007/978-3-319-63516-3_2
13. Brown, J., Cherry, F., Most, L., Parker, E., Wallis, W.: Completion of the spectrum of orthogonal diagonal Latin squares. In: Lecture Notes in Pure and Applied Mathematics, vol. 139, pp. 43–49 (1992)
14. Knuth, D.E.: The Art of Computer Programming, Volume 4A: Combinatorial Algorithms. Addison-Wesley Professional (2013)
15. Vatutin, E., Nikitina, N., Belyshev, A., Manzyuk, M.: On polynomial reduction of problems based on diagonal Latin squares to the exact cover problem. In: Bychkov, I.V., Tchernykh, A., Feoktistov, A.G. (eds.) Proceedings of the 2nd International Workshop on Information, Computation, and Control Systems for Distributed Environments (ICCS-DE 2020). CEUR Workshop Proceedings, vol. 2638, pp. 289–297 (2020)
16. Knuth, D.E.: Dancing links. In: Millenial Perspectives in Computer Science, pp. 187–214 (2000)
17. Brayton, R., Coppersmith, D., Hoffman, A.: Self-orthogonal Latin squares of all orders $n \neq 2, 3, 6$. Bull. Am. Math. Soc. **80**, 116–118 (1974)
18. Vatutin, E., Belyshev, A.: Enumerating the orthogonal diagonal Latin squares of small order for different types of orthogonality. In: Voevodin, V., Sobolev, S. (eds.) RuSCDays 2020. CCIS, vol. 1331, pp. 586–597. Springer, Cham (2020). https://doi.org/10.1007/978-3-030-64616-5_50
19. Appa, G., Mourtos, I., Magos, D.: Integrating constraint and integer programming for the orthogonal Latin squares problem. In: Van Hentenryck, P. (ed.) CP 2002. LNCS, vol. 2470, pp. 17–32. Springer, Heidelberg (2002). https://doi.org/10.1007/3-540-46135-3_2
20. Rubin, N., Bright, C., Cheung, K.K.H., Stevens, B.: Integer and constraint programming revisited for mutually orthogonal Latin squares. CoRR arXiv:2103.11018 (2021)
21. Bright, C., Gerhard, J., Kotsireas, I., Ganesh, V.: Effective problem solving using SAT solvers. In: Gerhard, J., Kotsireas, I. (eds.) MC 2019. CCIS, vol. 1125, pp. 205–219. Springer, Cham (2020). https://doi.org/10.1007/978-3-030-41258-6_15
22. Bogart, K.P.: Introductory Combinatorics, 2nd edn. Harcourt Brace Jovanovich, San Diego (1990)
23. Vatutin, E., Belyshev, A., Kochemazov, S., Zaikin, O., Nikitina, N.: Enumeration of isotopy classes of diagonal Latin squares of small order using volunteer computing. In: Voevodin, V., Sobolev, S. (eds.) RuSCDays 2018. CCIS, vol. 965, pp. 578–586. Springer, Cham (2019). https://doi.org/10.1007/978-3-030-05807-4_49
24. Sloane, N.J.A.: An on-line version of the encyclopedia of integer sequences. Electr. J. Comb. **1**, 1–5 (1994)
25. Vatutin, E., Titov, V., Zaikin, O., Kochemazov, S., Manzuk, M., Nikitina, N.: Orthogonality-based classification of diagonal Latin squares of order 10. In: Proceedings of the VIII International Conference on Distributed Computing and Grid-Technologies in Science and Education (GRID 2018). CEUR Workshop Proceedings, vol. 2267, pp. 282–287 (2018)
26. Vatutin, E., Belyshev, A., Zaikin, O., Nikitina, N., Manzyuk, M.: Investigating properties of generalized symmetries in diagonal Latin squares using volunteer computing. High-Perform. Comput. Syst. Technol. **3**(2), 39–51 (2019). (in Russian)

27. Manzyuk, M., Nikitina, N., Vatutin, E.: Start-up and the results of the volunteer computing project RakeSearch. In: Voevodin, V., Sobolev, S. (eds.) RuSCDays 2019. CCIS, vol. 1129, pp. 725–734. Springer, Cham (2019). https://doi.org/10.1007/978-3-030-36592-9_59

28. Kochemazov, S., Zaikin, O., Vatutin, E., Belyshev, A.: Enumerating diagonal Latin squares of order up to 9. J. Integer Sequences **23**(1), 1–21 (2020). Article 20.1.2

29. Vatutin, E., Zaikin, O., Kochemazov, S., Valyaev, S.: Using volunteer computing to study some features of diagonal Latin squares. Open Eng. **7**, 453–460 (2017)

30. Balyo, T., Sinz, C.: Parallel satisfiability. In: Hamadi, Y., Sais, L. (eds.) Handbook of Parallel Constraint Reasoning, pp. 3–29. Springer, Cham (2018). https://doi.org/10.1007/978-3-319-63516-3_1

31. Kochemazov, S., Zaikin, O., Semenov, A.: The comparison of different SAT encodings for the problem of search for systems of orthogonal Latin squares. In: International Conference Mathematical and Information Technologies - MIT 2016. CEUR Workshop Proceedings, vol. 1839, pp. 155–165 (2017)

32. Lynce, I., Ouaknine, J.: Sudoku as a SAT problem. In: International Symposium on Artificial Intelligence and Mathematics, ISAIM 2006, Fort Lauderdale, Florida, USA, 4–6 January 2006 (2006)

33. Biere, A., Fazekas, K., Fleury, M., Heisinger, M.: CaDiCaL, Kissat, Paracooba, Plingeling and Treengeling entering the SAT competition 2020. In: Balyo, T., Froleyks, N., Heule, M., Iser, M., Järvisalo, M., Suda, M. (eds.) Proceedings of SAT Competition 2020 - Solver and Benchmark Descriptions. Department of Computer Science Report Series B, vol. B-2020-1, pp. 51–53. University of Helsinki (2020)

34. Heule, M., Dufour, M., van Zwieten, J., van Maaren, H.: March_eq: implementing additional reasoning into an efficient look-ahead SAT solver. In: Hoos, H.H., Mitchell, D.G. (eds.) SAT 2004. LNCS, vol. 3542, pp. 345–359. Springer, Heidelberg (2005). https://doi.org/10.1007/11527695_26

35. Kurochkin, I.: The umbrella project of volunteer distributed computing Optima@home. In: Ivahsko, E., Rumyantsev, A. (eds.) Proceedings of the Third International Conference BOINC-Based High Performance Computing: Fundamental Research and Development (BOINC:FAST 2017). CEUR Workshop Proceedings, vol. 1973, pp. 35–42 (2017)

36. Eén, N., Sörensson, N.: An extensible SAT-solver. In: Giunchiglia, E., Tacchella, A. (eds.) SAT 2003. LNCS, vol. 2919, pp. 502–518. Springer, Heidelberg (2004). https://doi.org/10.1007/978-3-540-24605-3_37

37. Biró, C., Kovásznai, G., Biere, A., Kusper, G., Geda, G.: Cube-and-Conquer approach for SAT solving on grids. Ann. Math. Inform. **42**, 9–21 (2013)

38. Heisinger, M., Fleury, M., Biere, A.: Distributed cube and conquer with Paracooba. In: Pulina, L., Seidl, M. (eds.) SAT 2020. LNCS, vol. 12178, pp. 114–122. Springer, Cham (2020). https://doi.org/10.1007/978-3-030-51825-7_9

39. Heule, M.J.H., Kullmann, O., Marek, V.W.: Solving and verifying the Boolean Pythagorean triples problem via cube-and-conquer. In: Creignou, N., Le Berre, D. (eds.) SAT 2016. LNCS, vol. 9710, pp. 228–245. Springer, Cham (2016). https://doi.org/10.1007/978-3-319-40970-2_15

40. Bright, C., Cheung, K.K.H., Stevens, B., Kotsireas, I.S., Ganesh, V.: A SAT-based resolution of Lam's problem. In: Thirty-Fifth AAAI Conference on Artificial Intelligence, AAAI 2021, pp. 3669–3676. AAAI Press (2021)

41. Fang, W., Beckert, U.: Parallel tree search in volunteer computing: a case study. J. Grid Comput. **16**(4), 647–662 (2018). https://doi.org/10.1007/s10723-017-9411-5

42. Ignatov, A., Posypkin, M.: BOINC-based branch-and-bound. In: Voevodin, V., Sobolev, S. (eds.) RuSCDays 2018. CCIS, vol. 965, pp. 511–522. Springer, Cham (2019). https://doi.org/10.1007/978-3-030-05807-4_43

43. Semenov, A., Zaikin, O., Kochemazov, S.: Finding effective SAT Partitionings via black-box optimization. In: Pardalos, P.M., Rasskazova, V., Vrahatis, M.N. (eds.) Black Box Optimization, Machine Learning, and No-Free Lunch Theorems. SOIA, vol. 170, pp. 319–355. Springer, Cham (2021). https://doi.org/10.1007/978-3-030-66515-9_11

44. Afanasiev, A.P., Bychkov, I.V., Zaikin, O.S., Manzyuk, M.O., Posypkin, M.A., Semenov, A.A.: Concept of a multitask grid system with a flexible allocation of idle computational resources of supercomputers. J. Comput. Syst. Sci. Int. **56**(4), 701–707 (2017). https://doi.org/10.1134/S1064230717040025

45. Vatutin, E.I., Kochemazov, S.E., Zaikin, O.S.: Applying volunteer and parallel computing for enumerating diagonal Latin squares of order 9. In: Sokolinsky, L., Zymbler, M. (eds.) PCT 2017. CCIS, vol. 753, pp. 114–129. Springer, Cham (2017). https://doi.org/10.1007/978-3-319-67035-5_9

Toward Crowdsourced Drug Discovery: Start-Up of the Volunteer Computing Project SiDock@home

Natalia Nikitina[1]([✉])[iD], Maxim Manzyuk[2][iD], Marko Jukić[3,4][iD],
Črtomir Podlipnik[5][iD], Ilya Kurochkin[6][iD], and Alexander Albertian[6][iD]

[1] Institute of Applied Mathematical Research, Karelian Research Center
of the Russian Academy of Sciences, Petrozavodsk, Russia
nikitina@krc.karelia.ru
[2] Internet portal BOINC.ru, Moscow, Russia
hoarfrost@rambler.ru
[3] Faculty of Chemistry and Chemical Engineering, University of Maribor,
Maribor, Slovenia
[4] Faculty of Mathematics, Natural Sciences and Information Technologies,
University of Primorska, Koper, Slovenia
[5] Faculty of Chemistry and Chemical Technology, University of Ljubljana,
Ljubljana, Slovenia
[6] Federal Research Center "Computer Science and Control" of the Russian Academy
of Sciences, Moscow, Russia
assa@isa.ru

Abstract. In this paper, we describe the experience of setting up a
computational infrastructure based on BOINC middleware and running
a volunteer computing project on its basis. We characterize the first series
of computational experiments and review the project's development in
its first six months. The gathered experience shows that BOINC-based
Desktop Grids allow to efficiently aid drug discovery at its early stages.

Keywords: Desktop Grid · Distributed computing · Volunteer
computing · BOINC · Virtual drug screening · Molecular docking ·
SARS-CoV-2

1 Introduction

Among the variety of high-performance computing (HPC) systems, Desktop
Grids hold a special place due to their enormous potential and, at the same
time, high availability. Desktop Grids combine non-dedicated geographically distributed computing resources (typically, desktop computers) connected to the
central server by the Internet or a local access network. The nodes perform
computations for the Desktop Grid in their idle time. The resources are usually
provided either by the volunteer community or by individuals and organizations
related to the performed research. Such a computational infrastructure allows

© Springer Nature Switzerland AG 2021
V. Voevodin and S. Sobolev (Eds.): RuSCDays 2021, CCIS 1510, pp. 513–524, 2021.
https://doi.org/10.1007/978-3-030-92864-3_39

to efficiently solve computationally intensive scientific problems in the areas of mathematics [1], physics [2], astronomy [3] and others.

Upon the onset of COVID-19 pandemic in 2020, bio-medicine computational problems received a particular attention of scientists all over the world. At the same time, the public interest to such problems considerably raised, allowing the scientists to gather unprecedented amounts of computational resources.

In particular, a volunteer computing project Folding@home gathered the resources of 2.4 exaflops in early 2020, becoming the first world's exascale system, more powerful than the Top500 supercomputers altogether [4]. The overall potential of Desktop Grids is estimated as hundreds of exaflops [5], much more than the total power of all existing supercomputers.

Folding@home is a prominent example of a world-wide volunteer computing project, one of the many run by the world's leading research institutions. Computational capacities provided by the volunteer community allow such projects to perform large-scale computational experiments and process large amounts of data for solving urgent problems of social importance and wide public interest. This is the case of the fight against novel coronavirus disease since the beginning of 2020 [6–10].

In contrast, an organization may employ its own idle computational resources within an enterprise-level Desktop Grid. Such approach is particularly useful at the very early stages of research when computational experiments are irregular or subject to significant changes. Enterprise Desktop Grids support the research of a localized importance such as studying rare or neglected diseases [11].

To organise and manage Desktop Grid-based distributed computations, a number of software platforms are used. The most popular platform among them is BOINC (Berkeley Open Infrastructure for Desktop Computing) [5]. Among the 157 active largest projects on volunteer computing, 89 are based on BOINC [12]; that is, BOINC can be considered a *de-facto* standard for the operation of volunteer computing projects. The BOINC platform is an actively developing Open Source software and provides rich functionality for running projects both at the global and at the enterprise level.

This paper addresses the start-up of a BOINC-based volunteer computing project SiDock@home aimed at drug discovery. The main computationally intensive problem to solve in the process of drug discovery is the virtual screening, an *in silico* alternative to high-throughput screening. We describe the problem of the virtual screening and a series of computational experiments held within SiDock@home at its first mission: the fight against SARS-CoV-2.

2   Preliminaries

2.1   Virtual Drug Screening

HPC tools assist drug discovery at its first stages [13,14] which is natural considering the complex nature of biochemical processes, enormous sizes of the libraries of existing and synthesizable chemical compounds and fragments.

In this work, we consider structure-based virtual screening, a computational technique based on molecular docking of a library of small compounds against a specified therapeutic target. Molecular docking is a problem of continuous optimisation and, as a consequence, belongs to the bag-of-tasks class of problems efficiently solved using Desktop Grids. It is a complex and computationally demanding procedure [15] performed using a variety of software tools (see, e.g., [16] for a detailed review). As this is a computer-aided simulation of a biochemical process, there are yet a number of aspects to improve, and new approaches are being developed and implemented.

In the presented project, we employ a developing molecular docking software CmDock [17] which started in 2020 as a fork of an open-source software RxDock [18], aimed at optimisation, implementation of new features and utilisation of modern hardware, namely GPU computational resources.

2.2   BOINC-Based Volunteer Computing

The detailed description of BOINC architecture, functions and mechanisms is provided in [5]. In brief, the computational process may be described as follows. BOINC middleware has a server-client architecture. The server generates a large number of tasks that are mutually independent parts of a computationally-intensive problem such as virtual screening. The clients are the computers of any supported architecture voluntarily provided by the community.

When a client computer is idle, it requests work from the server, receives tasks, and processes them independently. In SiDock@home, a single task performs molecular docking of 2 000 ligands against a specified target and pre-filters the obtained results according to the specified HTVS protocol. Another replica of the same task is sent to another computer of another user to facilitate the check of results. Such a replication mechanism provided by BOINC allows one to balance between speed and accuracy of computations. Although task replication is known to be most efficient in the end phase of a computational experiment [19], it also allows to reduce the time of an initial phase when the application is subject to implementation errors.

Upon finishing, the client reports results back to the server. The results are checked for correctness and validity, and stored for further usage such as post-filtering. In SiDock@home, we consider a result *correct* if it reports a positive number of ligands successfully docked. The results of two replicas of the same task are considered *valid* if they report the same set of ligands successfully docked. Such checks allow to automate the processing of the most common types of errors and to speed up the computational process.

Mechanisms implemented in BOINC middleware allow efficient scaling of the project as new clients join a project. At the same time, increase of the number of clients causes increase of the Desktop Grid throughput, and, consequently, necessitates scaling of the server resources to process all the workflow.

Unlike computational clusters and supercomputers, Desktop Grids are devoid of high-speed interconnection between computational nodes, homogeneity, reliability, and a scheduled availability of the nodes. These disadvantages restrict the class of the computational problems solved on Desktop Grids and impose difficulties when organizing the computational process.

However, the practice of many BOINC projects has proven the high efficiency of the Desktop Grids built with help of the community. Essential features of the Desktop Grid technology are their affordability, adaptability and a high potential in the quick attraction of a large number of voluntarily provided computing resources.

BOINC maintains the record of the performed work in the form of credit [20] which, in the most common case, is calculated as follows. Each host $h \in H$ is assigned a value a_h, a peak performance of its CPU flops, estimated with an internal BOINC benchmark. When a task τ has been executed on host h, BOINC registers the elapsed time $T_{h\tau}$. The amount of credit the host would get for the task is $C_{h\tau} = T_{h\tau} \cdot a_h \cdot CS$. If the result passes a validity check on the server and the quorum has been met, the host is awarded $C_{h\tau}$ (or an appropriately adjusted value if quorum exceeds 1).

Here, $CS = \frac{200}{86\,400} \times 10^9$ (a Cobblestone) is a constant unifying the effective work of heterogeneous computers with a reference one that would do one gigaflop/s based on the Whetstone benchmark and receive 200 credits a day.

BOINC credit system and leader boards serve for unifying the contributions made by the geographically distributed, highly heterogeneous computing nodes.

2.3   The Project SiDock@home

SiDock@home [21] stems from a citizen science project "*Citizen science and the fight against the coronavirus*" (COVID.SI) [22] which originally performed virtual screening of a library of ten million of small molecules against multiple potential therapeutic targets, and based on an original middleware platform. For the purposes of the project popularization and scaling, SiDock@home was started as a BOINC-based extension of COVID.SI.

Following the course of research of COVID.SI, we considered a set of 59 targets to screen first of all (see Table 1). We use 3D structural models of targets generated by the D-I-TASSER/C-I-TASSER pipeline [23] as well as PDB database and a uniquely designed chemical library of a billion of compounds.

In [24], we overview the drug discovery problem being solved and the project's place among other BOINC-based projects fighting against SARS-CoV-2. In [25], we provide the performance dynamics of the project's Desktop Grid during the first six months of its work.

Figure 1 presents the capacity dynamics and illustrates the growth of available computational resources. The maximal theoretical capacity of all registered computers is depicted by the dashed line filled with light gray. Due to the principles of the Desktop Grid operation, a maximum of a computer's resources is unlikely to be available to a BOINC project. The solid line filled with dark gray represents the capacity actually available to BOINC tasks, considering the limitations imposed by the clients.

To summarize, the project's Desktop Grid has reached the scale of a modern supercomputer in the first six months and keeps growing as the community's interest to the project rises.

Table 1. Targets for the first set of computational experiments in SiDock@home.

Target ID	The protein	Organism	Source of structure	PDB code
1-21	3CL Pro	SARS-2	Snapshots from MD trajectory	
26-34	Spike protein	SARS/ MERS/ SARS-2	Crystalographic structures	2AJF,2DD8, 3SCL, 5X58,6ACK,6LZG, 6M0J,6M17,6VW1
35-37	DHODH	Human	Crystalographic structures	4IGH,4JTU,4OQV
41-48	PL Pro	SARS/ MERS/ SARS-2	Crystalographic structures	2FE8,3MP2,4OW0, 6W9C,6WRH,6WUU, 6WX4,6WZU
49-50	FURIN	Human	Crystalographic structures	5JXH, 5MIM
51-54	Methyl transferase	SARS-2	Crystalographic structures	6W4H,6W61, 7C2I,7C2J
55-56	E Protein	SARS/ SARS-2	NMR/ Homology model	5X29 (SARS) 5X29 Homology (SARS-2)
58-59	PL Pro	SARS-2	Homology models	Based on 3E9S, 5E6J, 6W9C

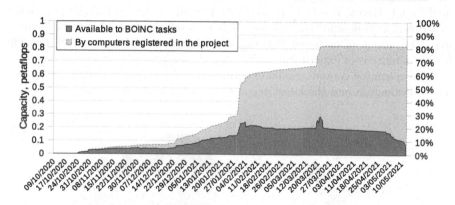

Fig. 1. Capacity dynamics of the project's Desktop Grid in 6 months.

3   Computational Experiments

In this section, we describe the setup of the initial series of computational experiments performed in SiDock@home.

The first mission of SiDock@home is aimed at several targets playing important roles in the life cycle of SARS-CoV-2. Virtual screening for each target defines an independent computational experiment, which is a batch of BOINC tasks to complete. Each BOINC task consists of molecular docking of an independent compound (or a subset of compounds) against the target.

For the molecular docking, we have employed native applications RxDock [18] and CmDock [17] using the BOINC wrapper program [26]. The resulting applications `rxdock-boinc`, `cmdock-boinc` and `cmdock-boinc-zip` have been implemented, so far, for Linux 64-bit, Windows 64-bit and Mac OS 64-bit but ARM binaries of CmDock are available for the future.

In each application, input files for a BOINC task include a package of small compound models (ligands), a target model and a description of the screening protocol. In the third application, `cmdock-boinc-zip`, packages of ligands are transferred in a compressed form to save disc space on the server.

The sizes of the input packages of ligands were selected so as to comply with conventional principles of BOINC projects where a task takes on average 1–2 hours to complete on an average desktop computer. However, the runtime may depend also on other factors such as the size of the supposed binding site.

Figure 2 and Fig. 3 illustrate the difference between sizes of binding sites of targets 3CL^{pro} (1st computational experiment) and Eprot (5th computational experiment). Task runtimes are directly correlated to cavity volumes and the numbers of grid points.

In order to minimize the waste of computational resources, checkpoints mechanism was implemented in the BOINC application.

At the moment of preparing this paper, the full library of ligands had been screened against the targets 3CL^{pro}, PL^{pro} (in two variants) and RdRp. The fifth target, Eprot, is still in process. As the first result of the computational experiments, 30 prospective compounds have been sent to a laboratory for testing. The process of exchange between dry-lab and wet-lab is iterative and will involve hundreds of experiments.

The upcoming computational experiments will be created basing on the biological evaluation and the latest scientific knowledge about the targets.

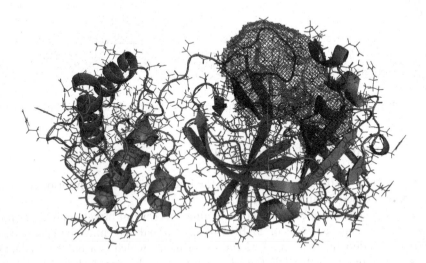

Fig. 2. The protease 3CL^{pro}, the target of the first computational experiment, with a ligand docked at the binding site of volume $3106.25 A^3$ (24 850 points).

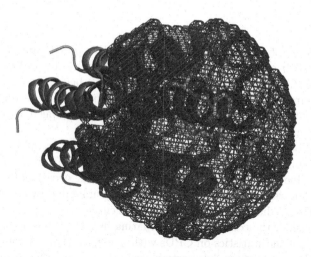

Fig. 3. The envelope protein (E) pentamer, the target of the fifth computational experiment, with a ligand docked at the binding site of volume $5068.25 A^3$ (40 546 points).

3.1   Server

In Table 2, we summarize the information on the servers used in SiDock@home. Initially, the project's server part was deployed in an Ubuntu 18.04 LTS-based machine referred to as **Cloud**. In six months of operation, two hardware servers were installed: **Humpback** (Russia) and **Gray** (Slovenia).

Table 2. Servers of the project SiDock@home as of May 2021.

Server	Functions	Characteristics
Cloud	BOINC server (6 months); development; storage and processing of I/O files (rxdock-boinc, cmdock-boinc)	Cloud virtual machine at 4 virtual cores of Xeon 6140, 8 Gb RAM, 32 Gb SSD, 512 Gb HDD
Humpback	BOINC server; storage and processing of I/O files (cmdock-boinc-zip)	HP DL 380 Gen8; 2x Intel(R) Xeon(R) CPU E5-2620 v2 @ 2.10 GHz (12 cores, 24 threads), 32 Gb RAM, 2x HDD 4Tb SAS, RAID 1.
Gray	Auxilary server; storage of the library; archivation; computations	2x Intel(R) Xeon(R) CPU E5-2680 v4 @ 2.40 GHz (14 cores, 28 threads), 64 Gb RAM, 2×10 Tb HDD, RAID 1.

3.2   Clients

As of the middle of May 2021, the number of active participants is about 2 000 with about 8 000 computers. These numbers are subject to dynamic changes due to a BOINC community competition held in the beginning of May. After its ending, the number of active participants and computers is expected to decrease. At the longer time range, however, these numbers are expected to grow as the project develops.

Since the beginning of the project, the total gained credit has approached 753 463 286 Cobblestones calculated by users, 752 484 194 by computers. The difference is due to the fact that some participants occasionally delete their computers from the project; however, the data accumulated by computers allows to evaluate the credit dynamics with a high accuracy.

Let us consider the computers participating in SiDock@home in more detail. Table 3 provides the statistics on CPUs with non-zero credit. As of the middle of May 2021, CPUs of 1 293 models participate in the project. One observes a parity between Intel® and AMD vendors; the total credit is of the same order. The number of AMD-based computers is almost two times less than Intel®-based ones, but the number of cores and the recent average credit are higher.

Overall, the presented data testify that, despite of the fact that AMD takes about 20% of the world market, BOINC volunteer community (which highly appreciates the CPU performance) rates AMD high (about 29% of contributions) and tends to purchase the latest CPU models.

Table 3. CPUs participating in SiDock@home.

Vendor	Number of computers	Number of cores	Total credit	Recent average credit
<not detected>	69	552	1 969 693	24 214
ARM	49	268	335 590	17 117
AMD	3 627	118 303	362 273 292	6 508 317
CentaurHauls	1	2	664	0
Intel®	9069	111 263	388 131 880	6 267 857

Apart from the total computational performance, a project's scale may be characterized by the number of active participants and the relative distribution of their contributions. In Fig. 4 and 5, we graphically depict the leader board of participants by the total credit of the projects SiDock@home and RakeSearch [27] of a different size. The diagrams illustrate the heterogeneity of the contributions.

But what is more important, one observes the difference in the roles that individual contributions play. The top users are definitely making significant contributions, but their aggregated fraction becomes less with the community's growth, even despite the fact that the large "group users" (accounts that combine multiple computers, for example, belonging to the same organization) join the

SiDock@home, credit of tens of users

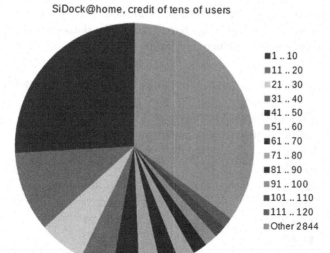

Fig. 4. User credit statistics in the project SiDock@home (2 964 participants).

RakeSearch, credit by tens of users

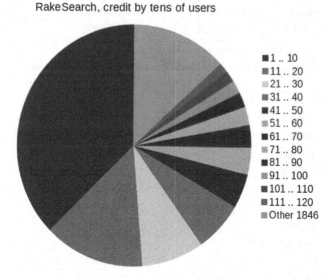

Fig. 5. User credit statistics in the project RakeSearch (1 966 participants).

project and actively participate. The project of a larger scale (SiDock@home) bases mostly on a large number of relatively small contributions, while in the project of a smaller scale (RakeSearch), large contributions dominate.

Finally, in Table 4, we provide the distributions of individual contributions in comparison with a project's top participant. The data show that individual contributions have more variance in a larger-scale project.

Table 4. Distribution of the total credit among participants of two BOINC projects.

RakeSearch, small-scale project		
Credit, % of the leader	# of participants with larger credit	% of participants with larger credit
0,00%	2964	98,37%
10,00%	23	0,76%
20,00%	11	0,37%
30,00%	5	0,17%
40,00%	2	0,07%
50,00%	2	0,07%
60,00%	2	0,07%
70,00%	1	0,03%
80,00%	1	0,03%
90,00%	1	0,03%
100,00%	1	0,03%
SiDock@home, medium-scale project		
Credit, % of the leader	# of participants with larger credit	% of participants with larger credit
0,00%	3905	97,82%
10,00%	38	0,95%
20,00%	18	0,45%
30,00%	9	0,23%
40,00%	7	0,18%
50,00%	5	0,13%
60,00%	3	0,08%
70,00%	3	0,08%
80,00%	2	0,05%
90,00%	1	0,03%
100,00%	1	0,03%

4   Conclusion

Drug discovery is a time-demanding and resource-demanding process that typically lasts for 10–12 years. At its first stage, virtual screening may assist in selection of prospective compounds *in silico* and reduce the consumption of time and money. In this paper, we describe the start-up of the drug discovery project SiDock@home and a series of computational experiments on performing virtual screening in the fight against SARS-CoV-2. Furthermore the project is evolving towards other areas of medicinal chemistry where active compounds for the study of Ebola, Malaria and targets relevant to oncology will be examined.

Citizen science initiatives and, in particular, BOINC projects on bio-medicine have always attracted many volunteers due to their socially important subjects. With the onset of a pandemic of COVID-19, the community's interest raised up to an unprecedented level.

We believe that BOINC community is able to provide the scientists with even more computational resources so as to support the research at all scales.

Acknowledgements. The first initial library (one billion of compounds) was prepared with the generous help of Microsoft that donated computational resources in the Azure cloud platform [28]. We all from COVID.SI are grateful and looking forward to future collaborations.

We would like to thank all volunteers who provide their computers to the project. Discussions and advice on the project forum are greatly appreciated.

Funding. This work was partly supported by the Scholarship of the President of the Russian Federation for young scientists and graduate students (project "Game-theoretical mathematical models and algorithms for scheduling in high-performance heterogeneous computational systems"), the Slovenian Ministry of Science and Education infrastructure, project grant HPC-RIVR, and by the Slovenian Research Agency (ARRS), programme P2-0046 and J1-2471, the Physical Chemistry programme grant P1-0201; Slovenian Ministry of Education, Science and Sports programme grant OP20.04342.

References

1. Gerasim@home main page. https://gerasim.boinc.ru/. Accessed 12 May 2021
2. LHC@home. https://lhcathome.web.cern.ch. Accessed 12 May 2021
3. Einstein@Home. https://einsteinathome.org. Accessed 12 May 2021
4. Folding@home - fighting disease with a world wide distributed super computer (2020). https://foldingathome.org. Accessed 12 May 2021
5. Anderson, D.P.: BOINC: a platform for volunteer computing. J. Grid Comput. **18**, 99–122 (2020)
6. Together We Are Powerful - Folding@home. https://foldingathome.org. Accessed 12 May 2021
7. Rosetta@home. https://boinc.bakerlab.org. Accessed 12 May 2021
8. World Community Grid - home. https://www.worldcommunitygrid.org/. Accessed 12 May 2021
9. TN-Grid. http://gene.disi.unitn.it/test/. Accessed 12 May 2021
10. IberCIVIS. https://boinc.ibercivis.es/. Accessed 12 May 2021
11. Ivashko, E., Nikitina, N., Möller, S.: High-performance virtual screening in a BOINC-based enterprise desktop grid. Vestnik Yuzhno-Ural'skogo Gosudarstvennogo Universiteta. Seriya "Vychislitelnaya Matematika i Informatika" **4**(1), 57–63 (2015). (in Russian)

12. Distributed Computing - Computing Platforms. http://distributedcomputing. info/platforms.html. Accessed 12 May 2021

13. Puertas-Martín, S., et al.: Is high performance computing a requirement for novel drug discovery and how will this impact academic efforts? Expert Opin. Drug Discov. **15**(9), 981–985 (2020). PMID: 32345062

14. Sarvagalla, S., Kondapuram, S.K., Devi, R.V., Coumar, M.S.: Resources for docking-based virtual screening. In: Coumar, M.S. (ed.) Molecular Docking for Computer-Aided Drug Design, pp. 179–203. Academic Press, Cambridge (2021)

15. Shoichet, B.K., McGovern, S.L., Wei, B., Irwin, J.J.: Lead discovery using molecular docking. Curr. Opin. Chem. Biol. **6**(4), 439–446 (2002)

16. Pagadala, N.S., Syed, K., Tuszynski, J.: Software for molecular docking: a review. Biophys. Rev. **9**(2), 91–102 (2017). https://doi.org/10.1007/s12551-016-0247-1

17. CmDock. https://gitlab.com/Jukic/cmdock. Accessed 12 May 2021

18. Ruiz-Carmona, S., et al.: rDock: a fast, versatile and open source program for docking ligands to proteins and nucleic acids. PLoS Comput. Biol. **10**(4), e1003571 (2014)

19. Ghare, G.D., Leutenegger, S.T.: Improving speedup and response times by replicating parallel programs on a SNOW. In: Feitelson, D.G., Rudolph, L., Schwiegelshohn, U. (eds.) JSSPP 2004. LNCS, vol. 3277, pp. 264–287. Springer, Heidelberg (2005). https://doi.org/10.1007/11407522_15

20. CreditNew - BOINC. https://boinc.berkeley.edu/trac/wiki/CreditNew. Accessed 12 May 2021

21. SiDock@home. https://sidock.si/sidock. Accessed 12 May 2021

22. Home - COVID.SI. https://covid.si/en. Accessed 12 May 2021

23. Modeling of the SARS-CoV-2 Genome using I-TASSER. https://zhanglab.ccmb. med.umich.edu/COVID-19. Accessed 12 May 2021

24. Nikitina, N., Manzyuk, M., Podlipnik, Č., Jukić, M.: Volunteer computing project SiDock@home for virtual drug screening against SARS-CoV-2 (submitted)

25. Nikitina, N., Manzyuk, M., Podlipnik, Č., Jukić, M.: Performance estimation of a BOINC-based Desktop Grid for large-scale molecular docking (2021, submitted)

26. WrapperApp - BOINC (2020). https://boinc.berkeley.edu/trac/wiki/ WrapperApp. Accessed 12 May 2021

27. Manzyuk, M., Nikitina, N., Vatutin, E.: Start-Up and the results of the volunteer computing project RakeSearch. In: Voevodin, V., Sobolev, S. (eds.) RuSCDays 2019. CCIS, vol. 1129, pp. 725–734. Springer, Cham (2019). https://doi.org/10. 1007/978-3-030-36592-9_59

28. Cloud Computing Services — Microsoft Azure. https://azure.microsoft.com/en-us/. Accessed 12 May 2021

Using Mobile Devices in a Voluntary Distributed Computing Project to Solve Combinatorial Problems

Ilya Kurochkin[1,2](✉) ⓘ, Andrey Dolgov[2], Maxim Manzyuk[3] ⓘ,
and Eduard Vatutin[4] ⓘ

[1] Institute for Information Transmission Problems of Russian Academy
of Sciences, Moscow, Russia
[2] The National University of Science and Technology MISiS, Moscow, Russia
[3] Internet Portal BOINC.Ru, Moscow, Russia
hoarfrost@rambler.ru
[4] The Southwest State University, Kursk, Russia
evatutin@rambler.ru

Abstract. A large number of personal mobile devices and the presence of powerful computing processors on them allows one to use them as computing nodes. The idle computing power of mobile devices can be used in distributed computing systems. This paper discusses the use of personal mobile devices in the project of voluntary distributed computing. The features of computing on mobile devices are discussed. The results of computational experiments on a desktop grid system are presented. Setting up a BOINC-based desktop grid system for efficient use of mobile devices as computing nodes is discussed.

Keywords: Desktop grid · BOINC · Mobile device · Voluntary distributed computing project · Orthogonal diagonal Latin squares

1 Introduction

In recent years, the use of mobile devices has increased significantly worldwide. According to Digital Trends, the number of smartphone users in the world in 2020 reached 6.1 billion and it continues to increase. The current capabilities of these devices have also significantly increased. Thanks to the latest advances in low-power processors, mobile devices can perform resource-intensive operations, which allow ones to consider these devices as computing platforms.

Using the advantages of smartphones and tablets, over the past decade, some research projects have investigated the problem of including mobile devices in distributed computing systems. The inclusion of mobile devices in the network and computing infrastructure has led to the emergence of new categories of networks. One of these new categories is a mobile network, which has been defined as a network that includes at least one mobile device. Users can connect their mobile devices to the network (smartphones, tablets and etc.) mainly for two purposes: to gain access to network resources and/or to make the resources of their mobile devices available to

© Springer Nature Switzerland AG 2021
V. Voevodin and S. Sobolev (Eds.): RuSCDays 2021, CCIS 1510, pp. 525–537, 2021.
https://doi.org/10.1007/978-3-030-92864-3_40

network users. A computing network consisting exclusively of mobile phones with the participation of millions of individual devices distributed around the world can reach the level of performance of a supercomputer.

The current work focuses on the use of mobile devices as providers of computing resources. The main idea of the work is to use idle computing resources of mobile devices for calculations, without compromising the use for their intended purpose. It is necessary to conduct various computational experiments to study the behavior of a grid system consisting of heterogeneous devices of different processor architectures and different operating systems, with subsequent adjustment of various project parameters. Correctly selected parameters of the distributed computing project can both increase the level of utilization of nodes in the grid system, and significantly reduce the calculation time of the entire experiment. As a result of the study, the parameters of a BOINC-based desktop grid are recommended, which effectively works with various types of processor architectures and OS of personal devices. This can be useful for large computational experiments, which last several months in a desktop grid.

2 BOINC Software

The use of idle resources of personal computers became popular in the late 1990s, when access to the global Internet became available to the average user [1]. The first public desktop grid systems appeared – projects of voluntary distributed computing: SETI@home [2], Folding@home, GIMPS. These first projects of voluntary distributed computing used the power of ordinary users' computers connected to the Internet to solve research problems that require large computing capacities [3].

The project of voluntary distributed computing is a deployed public grid system of personal devices that solves one or more computing tasks. A public grid system uses the computing resources of volunteers who provide the resources of their computing devices. The project can be deployed in the interests of one research group (SETI@home), several research groups using a common set of applications (Climateprediction.net, nanoHUB@home) or several independent groups of scientists (World Community Grid, BOINC@TACC).

There are platforms for organizing distributed computing, for example, BOINC, HTCondor, Askalon, Grid engine, Globus toolkit. One of the most common is BOINC. SETI@home, LHC@home, World Community Grid and several dozen other distributed computing projects use the BOINC platform.

BOINC consists of a server and a client part. The BOINC server part consists of many separate services (daemons) that share a common MySQL database. These services include a work generator, a scheduler, a feeder, a transition, a validator, an assimilator, a file deletion tool, and a database purger.

The client part of BOINC consists of three programs: the main client manages the execution of tasks and file transfer, the graphical interface (BOINC manager) allows volunteers to monitor and track calculations, an additional screensaver shows the graphics of the application for performing tasks in standby mode.

Third-party developers have implemented alternative graphical interfaces; for example, BoincTasks is a graphical interface for Windows that can manage multiple clients. For hosts without a display, BOINC provides a command-line program that provides the same functions as the manager.

The BOINC platform is used by many voluntary distributed computing projects. Some of them are based in universities and research laboratories, others are managed by private groups or individuals. As an example of public projects [4] that support computing on Android devices, we can cite: Asteroids@home, Einstein@home, LHC@home, Moo! Wrapper, Rosetta@home, Universe@Home, World Community Grid.

3   Integration of Mobile Devices into the Desktop Grid

Initially, mobile devices were integrated with networks as a user interface for managing and monitoring network resources [5]. Since the earliest mobile devices with wireless network capabilities had very limited resources, they could not share their resources with the network, and even if they could, their contribution would not be significant enough to justify the effort required to integrate them into the network. In addition, wireless networks were not as advanced, reliable and fast as they are today. However, mobile devices have been successfully integrated to effectively provide access to the grid network via a wireless network for management and monitoring [6, 7]. For this kind of integration, connectivity and energy efficiency are not important problems, because if the mobile device is disconnected from the network, there will be no reduction in resources. On the other hand, using mobile devices as a grid system user interface allows users to extract grid system resources from any place where there is a wireless connection. In addition, access to network resources from a mobile device allows you to perform computing tasks that are otherwise impossible to perform on a mobile device due to its lack of resources.

Over time, the capabilities of mobile devices have been improved at exponential rates. In addition, wireless networks have become faster, more reliable and more affordable. For example, 4G allows you to stay connected to the Internet most of the time, moving over large areas, such as cities or highways. In addition, many public places, such as airports, hotels and restaurants, have their own Wi-Fi networks, which are cheaper and faster than 4G networks. These facts allow you to connect mobile devices to the grid system. Even more, since modern mobile devices have a large number of available resources, they can share resources such as a processor, memory, video processor or storage space [7]. Public mobile grids (MoGrid, MORE, Mobile OGSI.NET and other) began to appear [7], which used mobile devices as full-fledged computing nodes [8].

However, mobile devices have not only connection restrictions, but also the limited power of their batteries. Due to the limited power supply, mobile devices are less reliable in the grid network than stationary ones. In addition, the traditional network idea that a particular device will always be connected from the same place is no longer true. As a result, technological solutions that work for stationary devices [9] may not work for mobile devices [10–12]. Summing up, we can say that the main problems of integrating mobile devices with the grid are [13]:

- power consumption: each operation performed by the processor or each byte transmitted requires the consumption of a device battery, the charge of which remains limited;
- availability: since the devices are connected via wireless networks and due to their mobile nature, it is very likely that the time available on the grid system will not be constant.

These features can have a negative impact mainly on the timing of the work sent, and in the best case they will not be completed. If the device's battery is low or the user disconnects (voluntarily or unintentionally), the tasks are not completed. Therefore, it is important that mobile grids take into account these limitations and disadvantages and act in such a way as to ensure the reliability of the completion time.

That is why BOINC was chosen as the platform for the deployment of the mobile grid. The BOINC platform meets the following requirements:

- the ability to perform tasks written in C++;
- performing tasks on mobile devices;
- the availability of the platform's source code for making changes and the quality of the platform's technical documentation.

However, BOINC requires the expansion of certain functionality specific to the mobile grid by fine-tuning the server part, as well as the implementation of a computing application for Android OS. The choice of Android platform at this stage of the study is due to a large percentage of devices with such a platform and its openness (GNU GPL 2.0). Mobile devices running on iOS can also be integrated into a grid system, which is confirmed by ongoing researches [14, 15].

4   Computational Application

4.1   Algorithm

Combinatorial problems related to the research of DLS properties [16] have already been solved in several grid systems: SAT@home [17], RakeSearch, Gerasim@home [16].

The algorithm of the computational application [16, 18] works according to a general scheme, which can be represented as:

- generating a random diagonal Latin squares (DLS) [19];
- the selected numerical characteristic is calculated for it;
- the actions are repeated in a cycle, the extreme (minimum and maximum) values of the selected numerical characteristic and the corresponding Latin squares are remembered.

The first M elements of the matrix, together with the main and side diagonals, are filled in recursively. Next, the DLS is filled in according to the principle of the minimum of possibilities $|S| \rightarrow min$, i.e. the cell a_{ij} is selected for filling, in which you can put a minimum of values. This principle makes it possible to reduce the arity of nodes in the combinatorial search tree, thereby significantly increasing its pace. Each next

i,j-th element is filled with a value from the allowed set of values S_{ij} [20], which can be defined as:

$$S_{ij} = U \backslash \bigcup_{k=1}^{N} \{a_{ik}\} \backslash \bigcup_{k=1}^{N} \{a_{kj}\} \backslash \bigcup_{k=1}^{N} \{a_{kk}\} \backslash \bigcup_{k=1}^{N} \{a_{k,N-k}\},$$

where $U = \{0, 1, 2, \ldots, N-1\}$ – the set of available values of the elements of the square, determined by its order N, a_{ij} is the value of the i,j-th element of the square.

The intermediate set of used values will be stored together with the generated DLS and changed simultaneously with the change of its elements.

The allowed set of S_{ij} values at each new iteration is estimated using the selected WRS heuristics:

$$f_{WRS}\left(s_{ij}^{l}\right) = g_{ij}^{\left(s_{ij}^{l}\right)} \cdot (1 + 2d(r_k - 0, 5)) \rightarrow \max, l = \overline{1, M\left(S_{ij}\right)}$$

Where function $g_{ij}^{\left(s_{ij}^{l}\right)}$ calculates the weight of possible values, and the final element is selected according to the maximum value of the function $f_{WRS}\left(s_{ij}^{l}\right)$ with some pseudo-randomness r_k.

The resulting value is entered both in the DLS matrix and in the arrays of used values. If it is impossible to select an element at the i,j-th step, i.e. $\left|S_{ij}\right| = 0$ the algorithm performs a combinatorial return, moving to the previous step based on the path traveled, where the elements are re-evaluated taking into account the values used. The process of generating all new DLS is considered complete when the entire possible subset of DLS has been generated from the original incomplete DLS, i.e. the first cell of the path has no valid elements to choose from. The generation stops, the algorithm proceeds to record the results.

Each new received DLS is sent to estimate the number of partial and full cycles. The algorithm selects all possible pairs of numbers from the first row and counts the number of formed cycles in the composition of this DLS, i.e. it alternately finds the second number from the selected pair in a row or column. An example of one of the found cycles can be seen in Fig. 1.

```
# Max cycles = 123
{
0 1 2 3 4 5 6 7 8 9
3 2 0 1 6 8 4 9 7 5
2 3 1 7 8 0 9 6 5 4
5 7 9 4 0 1 8 3 2 6
6 8 5 9 3 4 7 0 1 2
7 9 4 8 5 6 0 2 3 1
8 6 7 2 1 9 5 4 0 3
9 5 3 6 2 7 1 8 4 0
4 0 6 5 7 2 3 1 9 8
1 4 8 0 9 3 2 5 6 7
}
```

Fig. 1. One of the circles for pair 0–2

This operation is performed for all possible pairs of the set $U = \{0, 1, 2, \ldots, N - 1\}$. The minimum and maximum values found are stored in variables for subsequent entries in the results.

4.2 Development

The computational application of the project for calculating the characteristics of the DLS is developed in the C++ language. This programming language was chosen for several reasons:

- BOINC mainly supports the C++ language, since the BOINC API is a set of C++ functions;
- the implemented algorithm implies complex and resource-intensive mathematical calculations;
- it is necessary that the application has versions for several different platforms (Windows, Linux, Android);
- it is necessary to minimize conflict situations when building the application, and ensure ease of debugging the source code.

Thus, the computing application will run on all major operating systems supported by BOINC. This, in turn, allows you to increase the number of potential computing nodes involved in the project.

5 Setup Project Parameters

The main configuration of the BOINC project is controlled by a file named cofig.xml. This file is created when executing the make project script, with the ability to edit and configure various parameters for the project tasks.

The option of one result per host (one_result_per_host_per_wu) sends no more than one result of this working unit to this host. This is useful if most of the hosts of a certain class belong to a single user and you need to reduce the impact of faulty hosts on validation.

The limit parameter for sending tasks to the user (one_result_per_user_per_wu) allows you to send no more than one instance of a given task to the current user. This increases the efficiency of replication-based validation, because it becomes more difficult to get all the instances of a given task to a single user.

The maximum number of working units (max_wus_in_progress, N) (max_wus_in_progress_gpu, M) are parameters that limit the number of tasks performed on this host and, thus, limit the average task execution time. The BOINC client reports the resources used by the running jobs; in this case, the maximum number of running jobs on the CPU is $N * NCPUS$.

The parameter (max_wus_to_send, L) responsible for the maximum number of tasks returned to the scheduler request, which is calculated according to $L * (NCPUS + GM * NGPUS)$.

The node's confidence coefficient (*daily_result_quota, MRD*). Each host has an *MRD* field in the interval [1... *daily_result_quota*]. Initially, the coefficient is equal to the value of *daily_result_quota* and is adjusted when the host sends good or bad results. The maximum number of tasks sent to this host for a 24-h period is *MRD * (NCPUS + GM * NGPUS)*.

It should be used in order to limit the impact of faulty hosts.

The configuration of work units (workunits) is carried out at the stage of their creation by the job generator (work generator). The characteristics of the working unit are set as properties of the DB_WORKUNIT class, with the subsequent transfer of the object to the task creation function in the create_work database using the BOINC API functionality.

The minimum quorum size (min_quorum) is designed so that when the number of successful results of the set value is reached, the validator runs a check for matching the values of the working unit. If the strict majority agrees, this result is considered correct and is entered into the project database.

The replication parameter (target_nresults) means the number of work units created at the job generation stage. The set value must not be lower than the value of the minimum quorum size.

The delay_bound option is the upper limit of the time (in seconds) between sending the result to the client and receiving the response. The scheduler will not return a result if the estimated completion time exceeds this value. If the client does not respond within this interval, the server "refuses" the result and generates a new result that will be assigned to another client.

The complexity of the working unit (rsc_fpops_est) is an estimate of the number of floating-point operations required to complete the task. It is used to estimate how long a task will take on a given host.

The maximum allowable complexity of the working unit (rsc_fpops_bound). The upper limit of the number of floating-point operations required to complete the task. If this limit is exceeded, the task will be aborted.

The computational complexity parameters (rsc_fpops_est, rsc_fpops_bound) are expressed in terms of the number of floating-point operations. For example, suppose that the task takes 1 h to complete on a machine with a reference performance of 1 GFLOPS; then the "size" of the j-th working unit is $3.6 * 10^{12}$ FLOP.

To get estimates of the size of the working units averaged over the last tasks, you can use the link to the statistics of the number of flops in the administrative web interface of the project.

Table 1 shows the values of the configurable parameters during the four experiments.

Table 1. Server parameter values in various experiments.

Server parameter	Experiment 1	Experiment 2	Experiment 3	Experiment 4
one_result_per_host_per_wu	FALSE	FALSE	TRUE	TRUE
one_result_per_user_per_wu	FALSE	FALSE	TRUE	TRUE
max_wus_in_progress	1	1	10	10
max_wus_in_progress_gpu	1	1	1	1
gpu_multiplier	default	default	0	0
max_wus_to_send	1	1	50	50
daily_result_quota	1	1	8	8
min_quorum	3	3	2	2
target_nresults	3	3	3	2
delay_bound	172800	259200	432000	432000
rsc_fpops_est	1.00E + 15	1.00E + 14	1.00E + 13	1.00E + 13
rsc_fpops_bound	1.00E + 16	1.00E + 16	1.00E + 16	1.00E + 16

Based on the results of the experiments, the average time spent by the connected devices on problems of the same order of complexity was calculated.

The average time for working units of complexity 10^{15} FLOP was 9 h. For the complexity of 10^{14} FLOP, the average time spent was 3.5 h. For 10^{13} FLOP, the average time decreased to 0.9 h.

6   Results

To assess the state of the deployed desktop grid, as well as to study the operation of mobile devices and tablets as computing nodes together with personal computers and laptops, a number of computational experiments were launched using the implemented application for generating and calculating the characteristics of DLS. During the experiments, the parameters of the server part of the project were configured.

For the tests carried out, a set of tasks was defined in the amount of 1000 input text files, on the basis of which the working units of the project were generated in an amount equal to the replication parameter (target_nresults).

At the initial stage, the computing application was tested for compatibility with various OS and node processor architectures, during which all new hosts were gradually connected. In the end, the number of devices that took part in the calculation of tasks was 14 pieces. Of these, 1 desktop computer (Linux ×64), 2 laptops (Windows ×64), 10 mobile devices (Android arm, arm64), as well as 1 tablet (Android arm).

The first experiment (experiment 1) was conducted with the default parameters of the BOINC server. One working unit was calculated at each node. Based on the estimates obtained at the first stage, the computational complexity of the problem (rsc_fpops_est) averaged 1015 FLOP. The average number of results obtained for the presented period was 22 units. The maximum time to complete one task was 27 h. The average time spent by the device on the task was about 9 h. Summing up the results of the first experiment, it was concluded that the complexity of the initial task is too great not only for mobile devices, but also for PCs. It was decided to reduce the computational complexity of the tasks and reduce the number of combinations specified in the input files.

In the second experiment (experiment 2), the number of tasks sent to the nodes did not change, however, the complexity of the task was reduced by an order of magnitude and amounted to 1014 FLOP. This approach provided an average execution time of one working unit of 3.5 h and raised the average number of results obtained to 49 pieces. According to the results of the second experiment, it can be concluded that the time required for the node to calculate the working unit has decreased at least three times.

An acceptable rate of the obtained results was found in the course of experiment 3. The computational complexity of the problem was 1013 FLOP, which led to 0.9 h of average time spent. This allowed the server to process an average of 721 results per day.

The diagrams (Fig. 2) show the distribution of the average daily number of completed tasks of some computing nodes during the third experiment.

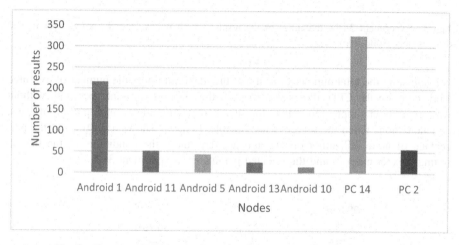

Fig. 2. Experiment 3, the number of results obtained on average per day.

The analysis of the dynamics of the results obtained by the server over a 48-h period of time is carried out. The beginning of measurements on 27.04.2021 21:03 and 30.05.2021 22:31, the end of 29.04.2021 21:05 and 01.06.2021 22:43 for experiments 2 and 3, respectively. As can be seen from the graphs in Fig. 3, in the intervals between 01:00 and 03:00, the server does not receive any results, which is explained by the unavailability of the server at this time due to a reboot. This situation should be taken into account in the process of computational experiments, preloading the nodes with additional tasks in order to prevent idle hosts waiting for new working units from the server. From the graphs presented, it can be seen that the number of results increases after 03:00 at night, since each node tends to send calculated tasks when the server starts responding to client requests. In Fig. 3, in addition to the dynamics for all computing nodes, the dynamics of the results obtained for 48 h is shown only for Android devices.

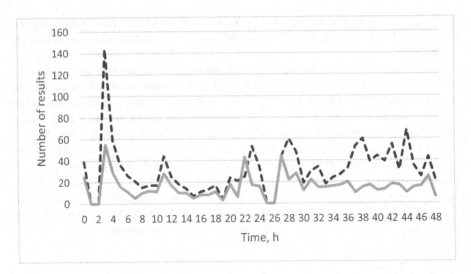

Fig. 3. Experiment 3, the dynamics of the results for all nodes (dotted line) and for mobile devices only (solid line)

Adjusting the total number of sent and the maximum possible number of executed work units on the CPU allows you to keep the node in constant operation, without wasting time on simple: requests to the server, receiving a new small portion of tasks, no calculations when the server is unavailable. Figure 4 shows a diagram of the percentage of node utilization on average per day under the conditions of the default settings (experiment 2) and the selected parameters (experiment 3).

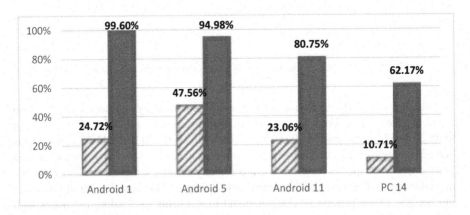

Fig. 4. Experiment 2 and 3, average percentage of device utilization per day

The parameters max_wus_in_progress, max_wus_in_progress_gpu, max_wus_to_send were equal to 1, which allowed limiting the number of tasks on the nodes. This approach, in turn, is not effective, since the volume of tasks on the hosts is very limited, which leads to idle computing power after the completion of the received working units, time is spent on frequent requests of the device to the server, and in the case of a reboot or problems on a remote server, computing work is completely stopped until the connection is restored.

Subsequently, the parameters *max_wus_in_progress* and *max_wus_to_send* were changed to the values 10 and 50, respectively, which allowed to increase the number of stored working units to 10 * *NCPU*, and the number of tasks sent to 50.

Based on the estimates obtained in the diagram (Fig. 3), it can be noted that the selected parameters led to almost constant (more than 90%) loading of Android 1 and Android 5 devices, which were connected to the network all the time, and were used only for calculations. The percentage of PC 14 downloads increased almost 6 times when using the computer for other purposes.

Delay_bound is an important parameter of the project, since overdue tasks are recreated by the scheduler on the server, thereby losing intermediate results and increasing the total time of the experiment. Given the specifics of using Android devices in grid systems, it is necessary to set this parameter with a margin of several days. Figure 5 shows the ratio of overdue results to successful ones (experiments 1, 2 and 3).

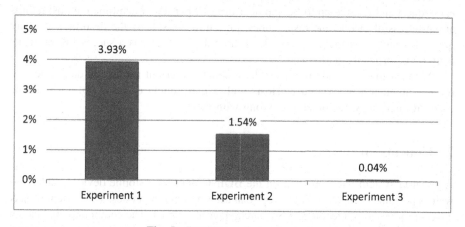

Fig. 5. Percentage of overdue tasks

Initially, the *delay_bound* parameter was 48 h, which led to the loss of almost 4% of the results and was a strict restriction, provided that the average computational complexity of the working unit was 1015 FLOP, and the average calculation time reached 9 h. At these values, the device should work only on one task, without disconnecting from the power supply.

In experiment 2, *delay_bound* increased to 72 h, while the complexity of the working unit decreased by an order of magnitude. In total, the percentage of lost tasks was 1.54%.

By the experiment 3, there were no working units that did not have time to be completed, with the exception of 1 task that was intentionally stopped. The *delay_ bound* parameter, set to 5 days, is well suited for conducting further experiments.

Given the mechanics of task replication in the BOINC project, it is important to remember that it is unacceptable for one device to receive all copies of one task, because in case of a malfunction or incorrect operation of the application, situations arise when the same, but incorrect result of all replicas from the device is returned to the server, after which it successfully passes validation and is entered into the database. All these nuances were taken into account in the process of 3 experiments. In order to minimize the number of incorrect results, it is necessary to prohibit the issuance of replicas of the same task to one user or host by activating the options *one_result_ per_host_per_wu*, *one_result_per_user_per_wu*. The *daily_result_quota* parameter was also adjusted and reduced. Sometimes there are hosts in the project that "make mistakes" in all the working units that are sent to them. Often these machines are incorrectly configured or have some other operating system or a problem with the installation of BOINC that needs to be fixed. To reduce the impact of these devices on the project, we use *daily_result_quota* so that these hosts do not destroy hundreds or thousands of tasks per day.

The *daily_result_quota* parameter is usually 8 tasks per processor core. The host can request and receive up to this number of tasks per day. Each time the host returns an unsuccessful or overdue result (does not return a result by the deadline), its daily quota of results is reduced by one. Each time the host returns a successful result, its daily quota of results is doubled.

Provided that the node returns at least some successful results, its daily quota of results should remain around 8. Hosts with a daily quota of results of 1 should be checked: there may be something wrong with them.

7   Conclusion

A test grid system was deployed on the BOINC platform. Mobile devices, tablets, as well as personal computers and laptops can act as computing nodes. The current project covers processor architectures: ×86, aarch64, arm, ×86-64. The computing application is available for several operating systems, including Android. Several computational experiments were conducted with various parameters on a test grid system from personal devices in order to configure the project parameters. The parameters of the voluntary distributed computing project were configured, the configuration made it possible to reduce the time of conducting computational experiments, increase the percentage of device utilization and reduce the percentage of overdue tasks.

Acknowledgements. This work was by RFBR according to the research projects № 18-29-03264 and № 19-07-00802.

References

1. Foster, I., Kesselman, C.: The Grid: Blueprint for a New Computing Infrastructure. Morgan Kaufmann Publishers, Burlington (1998)
2. Anderson, D.P.: BOINC: a platform for volunteer computing. J. Grid Comput. **18**(1), 99–122 (2019). https://doi.org/10.1007/s10723-019-09497-9
3. BOINC projects: List BOINC projects, 20 March 2021. https://boinc.berkeley.edu/projects.php
4. Zeng, W., Zhao, Y., Song, W., Wang, W.: Wireless grid and storage system design. In: 2008 International Conference on Intelligent Information Hiding and Multimedia Signal Processing (2008)
5. Rings, T., et al.: Grid and cloud computing: opportunities for integration with the next generation network. J. Grid Comput. **7**, 375–393 (2009)
6. Black, M., Edgar, W.: Exploring mobile devices as Grid resources: using an ×86 virtual machine to run BOINC on an iPhone. In: 2009 10th IEEE/ACM International Conference on Grid Computing. pp. 9–16. IEEE (2009)
7. Kumar, M.P., Bhat, R.R., Alavandar, S.R., Ananthanarayana, V.S.: Distributed public computing and storage using mobile devices. In: 2018 IEEE Distributed Computing, VLSI, Electrical Circuits and Robotics (DISCOVER), pp. 82–87. IEEE (2018)
8. Curiel, M., Calle, D.F., Santamaría, A.S., Suarez, D.F., Flórez, L.: Parallel processing of images in mobile devices using BOINC. Open Eng. **8**(1), 87–101 (2018)
9. Mazalov, V.V., Nikitina, N.N., Ivashko, E.E.: Task scheduling in a desktop grid to minimize the server load. In: Malyshkin, V. (ed.) PaCT 2015. LNCS, vol. 9251, pp. 273–278. Springer, Cham (2015). https://doi.org/10.1007/978-3-319-21909-7_27
10. Curiel, M.J., Payares, A.G.: Scheduling strategies for mobile devices in BOINC. Revista Eletrônica Argentina-Brasil de Tecnologias da Informação e da Comunicação **1**(13) (2021). https://doi.org/10.5281/zenodo.4445243
11. Wang, S.-D., Hsu, I.-T., Huang, Z.-Y.: Dynamic scheduling methods for computational grid environments. In: International Conference on Parallel and Distributed Systems, vol. 1 (2005)
12. Freund, R.F., et al.: Scheduling resources in multiuser, heterogeneous. In: Presented at the 7th IEEE Heterogeneous Computing Workshop (1998)
13. Du, L., Yu, Z.: Scheduling algorithm with respect to resource intermittence in mobile grid. In: 2010 6th International Conference on Wireless Communications Networking and Mobile Computing (WiCOM) (2010)
14. Black, M., Edgar, W.: Exploring mobile devices as grid resources: using an ×86 virtual machine to run BOINC on an iPhone. In: 2009 10th IEEE/ACM International Conference on Grid Computing, pp. 9–16. IEEE (2009)
15. Shah, S.C.: Recent advances in mobile grid and cloud computing. Intell. Autom. Soft Comput. **2017**, 1–13 (2017)
16. Vatutin, E., Zaikin, O., Kochemazov, S., Valyaev, S.: Using volunteer computing to study some features of diagonal Latin squares. Open Eng. **7**(1), 453–460 (2017)
17. Zaikin, O., Kochemazov, S.: The search for systems of diagonal Latin squares using the SAT@ home project. Int. J. Open Inf. Technol. **3**(11), 4–9 (2015)
18. Colbourn, C.J., Dinitz, J.H.: Handbook of Combinatorial Designs, 2nd edn. Chapman & Hall/CRC, Boca Raton (2006)
19. Shao, J., Wei, W.: A formula for the number of latin squares. Discrete Math. Semant. Scholar **110**(1–3), 293–296 (2021). https://doi.org/10.1016/0012-365X(92)90722-R
20. Vatutin, E., Belyshev, A., Nikitina, N., Manzuk, M.: Evaluation of efficiency of using simple transformations when searching for orthogonal diagonal Latin squares of order 10. In: Jordan, V., Filimonov, N., Tarasov, I., Faerman, V. (eds.) HPCST 2020. CCIS, vol. 1304, pp. 127–146. Springer, Cham (2020). https://doi.org/10.1007/978-3-030-66895-2_9

Author Index